The Old Rose Advisor, Volume I

No. 3 in The Old Rose Researcher Series

The Old Rose Advisor, Volume I

Updated, Enlarged, and Revised Second Edition

Brent C. Dickerson

Authors Choice Press
San Jose New York Lincoln Shanghai

The Old Rose Advisor, Volume I
Updated, Enlarged, and Revised Second Edition

Authors Choice Press
an imprint of iUniverse.com, Inc.

For information address:
iUniverse.com, Inc.
5220 S 16th, Ste. 200
Lincoln, NE 68512
www.iuniverse.com

ISBN: 0-595-17293-8

Printed in the United States of America

"These roses sing, 'I have kept the faith, I have fought a good fight.'" [ARA40]

Contents to Volume I

Preface to Volume I

"On appearing before the tribunal of public opinion, every author who has not cherished an unreasonable estimate of his own qualifications, must necessarily be impressed with considerable anxiety respecting the probable reception of his work…The present work is the first of its kind that has ever been attempted…Owing to the indispensable nature of this work, it makes no positive claim to the character of an original composition, in the strict acceptation of that term." [D]

So began the first edition of *The Old Rose Advisor*. The "considerable anxiety" has at length been replaced by authorial gratitude to discerning Readers and perceptive reviewers alike who have been able to scout out the usefulness of having at their fingertips a compendium of comments and descriptions of roses ranging from the first articles—written with "considerable anxiety" often by the breeders themselves—announcing to a skeptical world their precious new introductions, to reflective paragraphs pondering classic, beloved roses with which experts had collectively had fifty or a hundred years of experience. The necessity of going back to "the thing itself," and not piling on theory after theory based on supposition and misinformation, has, I think, been demonstrated such that the sophisticated rosarian will cast a baleful eye on those who try to fly the various tattered old banners once saluted but now eyed warily if not completely discredited—false banners such as "'La France' was the first Hybrid Tea" or "the first Polyanthas were a cross of Chinas and Multifloras" and the like. When the Truth is so rich, as it is in Rosedom, we need not resort to Legend!

This is not a mere reprinting of the First Edition. Every word has literally had at least a cursory re-examination—the book was retyped from scratch. Changes have been made. Continuing research has focused or updated many dates, attributions, names, parentages, and classifications. New sources of information have been consulted and have been tapped to enrich many entries. Some "modern" descriptions have been deleted owing to suspicion that they possibly described a misidentified rose. More "extant or important" varieties have been added as their existence or importance has become manifest; in particular, an effort has been made to include the chronological first several cultivars in each category, even when they fell into obscurity immediately upon introduction long long ago. The supplemental listings in each chapter have been assimilated into the main listings such that each chapter is one continuous alphabetical listing rather than two. The first edition's illustrations have been omitted!—out of consideration for the pocket-books of, in particular, those buyers of the first edition whose investment still bows their bookshelves; these loyal Readers should not have to pay twice for the same pictures, beautiful though they be. The length of the book has made it necessary to divide it into two volumes. To accommodate the split, we have included the *Key to Citations* in the first volume as well as in the second.

As before, we have received the anxious and ready assistance of a number of rosarians and non-rosarians the world over, without whose friendly cooperation this effort would have turned out very differently indeed. The great rosariums of L'Haÿ and Sangerhausen were particularly generous in their help, for which we can only give my inadequate but warmest thanks. Among libraries, special mention must go to the Libraries of the University of California at Berkeley and the Library of the U.S. Department of Agriculture, as well as to the Bibliothèque Nationale in Paris, and the collections of the Société d'Horticulture d'Angers et du Département de Maine-et-Loire and the Société Nationale d'Horticulture of France. The Tuna Club in enchanting Avalon, California, provided unique assistance, as did Les Amis de Vieux l'Haÿ in France. Mrs. Paul Gardner and Mr. George C. Thomas IV were most gracious and helpful with our researches on Capt. Thomas. Dr. E. Charles Nelson provided valuable information on several Irish and English cultivars for this second edition. The Conard-Pyle Co., at the forefront of American rose commerce for lo! these many years, provided with the greatest generosity research material of the highest importance in clarifying the American side of more modern rosedom. Special assistance in various particulars pertaining to the second edition was provided by Paul Barden, Philippe Gautreau, Henry Kuska, William Grant, Sandy Brown, Robert B. Martin Jr., Karl King, John Starnes Jr., Ingrid Verdegem, Jill Perry, Daniel Lemonnier, Donna Stewart, and Barbara Tchertoff, as well as by others whose names are mentioned in the course of the text. The ever-helpful and efficient staff members of the Inter-Library Loan department at the Library at California State University, Long Beach—Cathrine Lewis-Ida and Sharlene Laforge, two of the most long-suffering individuals in this whole process—obtained for the author whole shoals of books imagined unobtainable; the length of the "Works Consulted" listing is, to a great degree, a monument to their efforts. The able and important overseas assistance we received from Mme. Christiane Delacour and, particularly, the indefatigable Monsieur Georges Massiot—a true *débrouillard*—in negotiating Gallic intricacies as well as in helping me to obtain copies of valuable, rich, rare material is not only deeply appreciated by the author, but is also yet another example of the generosity and spirit shown by the French throughout these pages. It will be one of the greater rewards of our work if the good will which we have received so abundantly from so many is adequately reflected in the information and pleasure which this book provides.

We must continue to acknowledge the kind assistance rendered by those who contact the author, correcting some error or misreading committed when weary eyelids dropped *too* low, apprising us of the veritable existence of a cultivar thought extinct, or informing us of remarkable characteristics hitherto unrecorded—relaying as well the source of the information. There will always be mysterious names to be explained, obscure genealogies to be supplied or unraveled, and reclusive facts to be coaxed from their dark hermitages. Biographical information is always difficult to come by for these modest breeders and nurserymen; more would be welcomed. A work of this nature is built on the cooperative vigilance of all; it is by running such efforts through the mill of disseminated information and human experience that we may grind it into something more perfect and more useful.

The debt which the author, and we all, owe to Guerrapain, Vibert, Laffay, Prévost fils, Sisley, Rivers, Buist, William Paul, Lacharme, Ellwanger, Singer, Van Fleet, Capt. Thomas—indeed, to all contributors to rose literature and rose progress who are listed or unlisted—is unpayable, just as the real camaraderie we have felt working with these our *silent* partners is undeniable. If some readers are moved to take a closer look at *their* work—their writings, their roses, their thoughts—perhaps then some of this debt will have been repaid, and one of our goals met.

"The number of varieties has become so considerable that it is difficult if not impossible for the amateur to deal with the interminable list of names that breeders old or new have given their introductions. It became necessary to have a guide, a special work which contained, methodically arranged, all the necessary information…This work…gives a true-to-life presentation of the most popular roses…[I]t is not necessary to demonstrate the utility of this *Dictionnaire*: It is incontestable…the *Dictionnaire des Roses* may, in a word, be considered as the Rosarian's complete library. In presenting the description of six thousand roses [*The Old Rose Advisor*, with its 2,514 entries, together with *The Old Rose Adventurer*, with its 2,510 (including the four added in the new *Advisor's* Appendix 10), yield 5,024 entries; and many additional old roses will be found described in *The Old Rose Informant*], will I be able to satisfy everyone? No! In giving my readers a *précis* of everything that appeared in the rose world…, will I have a complete work? No! In making known each book published till now, will I satisfy my readers? No! Critics, hear me: I have listened to the comments of able men, I have followed the counsels of capable persons— and I laugh at those who nit-pick or complain simply for the pleasure of nit-picking or complaining. I publish this book with the wish of providing a needed service. Will I bring it off? I hope so!" [S]

List of Abbreviations
and Key to Citations

Textual Abbreviations

aff.	affiliated with, affiliation
att.	attributed, attributed to, attributes, attribution
B	Bourbon
Br.	Breeder
c	circa
cert.	certainly
cl.	climber
Cl.	Climbing
class.	classification
conf.	confused
dat.	date, dated, dates, dates it
desc.	descendant of, descended (possibly remotely) from
dev.	developed
DP	Damask Perpetual
ev.	evidently
gen.	generation
Gig	Gigantea
HB	Hybrid Bourbon
HCh	Hybrid China
HN	Hybrid Noisette
hort.	horticultural
HP	Hybrid Perpetual

HT	Hybrid Tea
N	Noisette
orig.	originally, originated in
Pol	Polyantha
poss.	possibly
pres.	presumably
prob.	probably
sdlg.	seedling, seedling of
spt.	sport, sport of
supp.	supposedly, supposes
syn.	synonym, synonyms, synonymy, synonymous, synonym of, synonymous with
T	Tea
trans.	translation
unc.	uncertain
unk.	unknown
var.	variety, variety of, variation
w/	with
-[year]	the year specified, or before
?	questionable, unsubstantiated
???	otherwise unknown

Key to Citations

Full bibliographical listings for these works will be found in the Bibliography at the end of Volume II.

A: *Roses, or A Monograph...*, by Henry Andrews, 1805 and 1828.

AbR: *Cours Complet d'Agriculture...*, by Abbé Rozier, 1793.

AC: *La Rose*, by A. de Chesnel, 1838.

ADE: Departmental Archives of Essonne at Corbeil, France.

Adk: *Catalogue*, by Alexander Dickson, year as indicated.

ADVDM: Departmental Archives of Val-de-Marne at Creteil, France.

ADY: Departmental Archives of Yvelines at Versailles, France.

AHB: *The Tree Rose*, by A[rthur] H[enry] B[osanquet], 1845.

An: *Annales de Flore et de Pomone*, 1832-1848.

AnM-L: *Annales du Comice Horticole de Maine-et-Loire*, 1859.

ARA: *American Rose Annual*, year as indicated. Quoted by kind permission of the American Rose Society.

Au: *The Australasian Rose Book*, by R.G. Elliott, ca. 1925.

AxD: *Rose Catalogue*, Alex. Dickson & Sons, Ltd., Newtownards, Ireland, year as indicated.

BBF: *The Flower-Garden, or Breck's Book of Flowers*, by Joseph Breck, 1851.

BBF66: *New Book of Flowers*, by Joseph Breck, 1866.

BCD: Interpolated material by Brent C. Dickerson.

BJ: *Le Bon Jardinier*, 1865 edition.

BJ06: *Le Bon Jardinier*, 1806 edition.

BJ09: *Le Bon Jardinier*, 1809 edition.

BJ09s: *Supplément à...Bon Jardinier*, 1809.

BJ17: *Le Bon Jardinier*, 1817 edition.

BJ24: *Le Bon Jardinier*, 1824 edition.

BJ30: *Le Bon Jardinier*, 1830 edition.

BJ40: *Le Bon Jardinier*, 1840 edition.

BJ53: *Le Bon Jardinier*, 1853 edition.

BJ58: *Le Bon Jardinier*, 1858 edition.

BJ63: *Le Bon Jardinier*, 1863 edition.

BJ70: *Le Bon Jardinier*, 1870 edition.

BJ77: *Le Bon Jardinier*, 1877 edition.

Bk: *Roses and How to Grow Them*, by Edwin Beckett, 1918.

Br: *A Year in a Lancashire Garden*, by Henry Bright, 1879.

BSA: *The Garden Book of California*, by Belle Sumner Angier, 1906.

Bu: *The Rose Manual*, by Robert Buist, 1844.

B&V: *List of Roses Now in Cultivation at Château Eléonore, Cannes...*, by Henry Charles Brougham, 3rd Baron Brougham & Vaux, 1898.

C: *Beauties of the Rose*, by Henry Curtis, 1850-1853. Facsimile reprint, 1980, by Sweetbriar Press; additional material by Leonie Bell.

CA: *Descriptive Catalogue*, California Nursery Company, 1888 *et sequitur*, year as indicated.

Cal: *Catalogue* of Calvert & Company, 1820.

Capt27: Article "Tea Roses for Southern Clmates," by Capt. Goerge C. Thomas, in ARA27.

Capt28: Article "Climbing Roses for Southern Climates," by Capt. George C. Thomas, in ARA28.

CaRoI (*et seq.*): *The California Rosarian*, published by the California Rose Society, 1930-1932.

Cat12: *Official Catalogue of Roses*, by the [British] National Rose Society, 1912 edition.

CC: *Catalogue* for the Wasamequia Nurseries, New Bedford, MA, by Henry H. Crapo, 1848. In ARA26.

CdF: *La Culture des Fleurs*, anonymous, 1712.

C'H: *Dictionnaire Universel des Plantes...*, by Pierre-Joseph Buc'hoz, 1770.

C&Jf: *Fall Catalog*, The Conard & Jones Co., yearly 1897-1924, as specified. Quoted by kind permission of the Conard-Pyle Co.

C&Js: *Spring Catalog*, The Conard & Jones Co., yearly 1897-1924, as specified. Quoted by kind permission of the Conard-Pyle Co.

Ck: *Catalogue, Marie Henriette Chotek Rosenschulen*, by Marie Henriette Chotek, 1926.

CM: *Histoire des Roses*, by Charles Malo, 1821.

C-Pf: *Fall Catalog*, The Conard-Pyle Co., yearly 1925-1934, as specified. Quoted by kind permission of the Conard-Pyle Co.

C-Ps: *Spring Catalog*, The Conard-Pyle Co., yearly 1925-1934, as specified. Quoted by kind permission of the Conard-Pyle Co.

Cr: *Catalogue* of Cranston's Nurseries, various years as noted.

C-T: *Almanach des Roses*, by Claude-Thomas Guerrapain, 1811.

Cw: *La Rose Historique*, by Edm. Van Cauwenberghe, 1927.

Cx: *Les Plus Belles Roses au Début de Iième Siècle*, by the Société Nationale d'Horticulture de France, 1912.

Cy: *The French Revolution. A History*, by Thomas Carlyle, 1837.

Cy2: *Oliver Cromwell's Letters and Speeches*, 3rd edition, by Thomas Carlyle, 1849.

Cy3: *The History of Friedrich II of Prussia, Called Frederick the Great*, by Thomas Carlyle, 1865.

D: *A General History and Collection of Voyages and Travels*, by Robert Kerr, 1824.

D&C12: *Catalog*, Dingee & Conard Co., 1912.

DH: *Journal d'Horticulture Pratique et de Jardinage*, 1844-1847, edited by Martin-Victor Paquet.

DO: *Roses for Amateurs*, by Rev. H. Honywood D'Ombrain.

DP: *Sommaire d'une Monographie du Genre Rosier...*, by de Pronville, 1822.

DP: Article "My Favorites…," by D. Bruce Phillips, in *Pacific Horticulture*, vol. 43, no. 3, 1982. Quoted by kind permission of *Pacific Horticulture*.

Dr: *Everblooming Roses*, by Georgia Torrey Drennan, 1912.

DuC: *The Flowers and Gardens of Madeira*, by Florence duCane, 1909.

E: *Gardens of England*, by E.T. Cook, 1911.

ECS: City Archives of Soisy-sous-Etioles, France.

Ed: *The Amateur's Rosarium*, by R. Wodrow Thomson, 1862.

EER: Article "A Short History of theTea Rose," by E.E. Robinson, in *The Rose*, vol. 17, no. 3, 1969.

EER2: Article "The Early Hybrid Perpetuals," by E.E. Robinson, in *The Rose*, vol. 13, no. 3, 1965.

EJW: *California Garden-Flowers*, by E.J. Wickson, 1915.

EL: *The Rose*, by Henry B. Ellwanger, 1882.

ElC: Article "Old Roses and New Roses," by Henry B. Ellwanger, in *Century Magazine*, vo. 4, 1883.

ET: Article "Help Wanted in Texas?", by Edward Teas, from ARA28.

ExRé: *Guide pour servir à la visite de notre Exposition Rétrospective de la Rose*, from Roseraie de l'Haÿ, 1910.

F: *Les Roses*, by Louis Fumierre, 1910.

Fa: *In a Yorkshire Garden*, by Reginald Farrer, 1909.

FeR: *La France en Russie*, by Eugène Delaire, 1900.

Fl: *The Florist*, vol. 1, 1848.

FlCa: *Floricultural Cabinet*, date as specified.

F-M: *The Book of the Rose*, 4th edition, by Andrew Foster-Melliar, 1910.

F-M2: *The Bookd of the Rose*, 2nd edition, by Andrew Foster-Melliar, 1902.

F-M3: *The Book of the Rose*, 1st edition, by Andrew Foster-Melliar, 1894.

F-M4: *The Book of the Rose*, 3rd edition, by Andrew Foster-Melliar, 1905.

FP: *The Book of Roses*, by Francis Parkman, 1871.

Fr: *Dictionnaire du Jardinier Français*, by Monsieur Fillassier, 1791.

FRB: *Tea Roses*, by F.R. Burnside, 1893.

GAS: *Climbing Roses*, by G.A. Stevens, 1933. Quoted by kind permission of the copyright holder, the McFarland Co.

G&B: *Roses*, by Gemen & Bourg, ca. 1908.

GeH: *The Rose Encyclopædia*, be Geoffrey W. Henslowe, 1934.

Gf: *Catalogue*, J.-B. Guillot fils, 1856.

GG: *In a Gloucestershire Garden*, by Henry N. Ellacombe, 1896.

GJB: *Vägledning genom Linnés park 1836*, manuscript by G.J. Billberg, 1836.

Gl: *The Culture of Flowers and Plants*, by George Glenny, 1861.

Go: *The Rose Fancier's Manual*, by Mrs. Gore, 1838.

God: *Catalogue des Rosiers*, by Godefroy, 1831.

Gp: *Catalogue*, by J.-B. Guillot père, 1844/1845.

Gp&f: *Catalogue*, J.-B. Guillot père & fils, 1852.

Gx: *"La Malmaison" Les Roses de l'Impératrice Joséphine*, by Jules Gravereaux, 1912.

H: *A Book About Roses*, by S. Reynolds Hole, 1906 printing.

Hd: *The Amateur's Rose Book*, by Shirley Hibberd, 1874.

HDk: *Catalogue*, year as indicated, by High Dickson.

Hj: Unpublished correspondence with Thomasville Nurseries, Inc. Quoted by kind permission of Thomasville Nurseries, Inc.

HmC: *My Roses and How I Grew Them*, by Helen (Crofton) Milman, 1899.

Hn: *The Amateur Gardener's Rose Book*, by Julius Hoffmann, English language edition, 1905.

HoBoIV: *The Horticultural Review and Botanical Magazine*, 1854.

HRH: *A Gardener's Year*, by H. Rider Haggard, 1905.

HstI (*et sequitur*): *The Horticulturist*, 1846-1875.

Ht: *Le Livre d'Or des Roses*, by Paul Hariot, 1904.

HuD: *Catalogue* from the Royal Nurseries of Hugh Dickson, Belfast, Ireland, year as indicated.

Hÿ: *Les Roses Cultivées à l'Haÿ en 1902,* from Roseraie de l'Haÿ, 1902.

J: *Roses for English Gardens,* by Gertrude Jekyll, 1902.

J-A: *Le Jardinier-Amateur,* edited by Eugène Pirolle, 1826.

J-As: *Premier Supplément, le Jardinier-Amateur,* edited by Eugène Pirolle, 1827.

JC: *Cultural Directions for the Rose,* 6th edition, by John Cranston, 1877.

JDR: *Journal des Roses,* year as indicated, edited by Jean Cherpin, published 1854-1859 in Lyon.

JF: *Les Roses,* by Hippolyte Jamain & Eugène Forney, 1873.

Jg: *Rosenlexikon,* by Auguste Jäger, pub. 1970, data collected in the 1920s and 1930s.

JHP: *Journal d'Horticulture Pratique,* 1850.

JP: *Roses: Their History, Development, and Cultivation,* by Rev. Joseph H. Pemberton, 1920.

JPV: *Réponse à…Pirolle,* by Jean-Pierre Vibert, 1827.

JR: *Journal des Roses,* year as indicated, edited by Cochet & Bernardin, published 1877-1914 in Melun.

Jwa: *Warren's Descriptive Catalogue,* by J.L.L.F. Warren, 1844.

K: *The Rose Manual,* by J.H. Nicolas, 1938. Quoted by kind permission of the publishers, Doubleday & Co., Inc.

K1: *Eversley Gardens and Others,* by Rose G. Kingley, 1907.

K2: *Roses and Rose-Growing,* by Rose G. Kingley, 1908.

Kr: *The Complete Book of Roses,* by Gerd Krüssman, 1981. Quoted by kind permission of the publisher, Timber Press.

L: *Gardening in California,* 3rd revised edition, by William S. Lyon, 1904.

LADR: *Les Amis des Roses,* issues 1946-1962, as indicated.

Lam: *Encyclopédie Méthodique…,* section on roses by Lamarck, 1804.

Lam/Poir: *Encyclopédie Méthodique. Botanique. Supplément,* by J.L.M. Poiret, 1816.

LaQ: *Instruction pour les Jardins Fruitiers et Potagiers...*, by Jean de la Quintinye, 1695.

Lc: *Les Rosiers*, by Jean Lachaume, revised by Georges Bellair, ca. 1921.

L-D: *La Rose...*, by Jean Louis Augustin Loiseleur-Deslongchamps, 1844.

LeB: *Traité des Jardins...*, by Abbé le Berriays, 1789.

LeR: *Histoire Généalogique des Rosiers*, by Antoine LeRouge, unpublished manuscript dated 1819, with additional material from 1820.

LF: *Prix Courant des Espèces et Variétés de Roses*, by Jean Laffay, 1841.

LF1: Death Certificate of Jean Laffay, town records of the Municipality of Cannes, France, 1878.

L'H: *l'Horticulteur Français*, 1851-1872, year as indicated.

LR: *La Rose*, by J. Bel, 1892.

LS: *Nomenclature de Tous les Noms de Roses*, 2nd edition, by Léon Simon, 1906.

Lu: *Luther Burbank. His Methods and Discoveries*, vol. 9, by Luther Burbank, 1914.

M: *Gardening in California*, by Sidney B. Mitchell, 1923. Quoted by kind permission of the publishers, Doubleday & Co., Inc.

MaCo: *Manuel Complet de l'Amateur des Roses*, by Boitard, 1836.

MaRu: *La Nouvelle Maison Rustique...*, by J.-F. Bastien, 1798.

MCN: *Minutier Central des Notaires* at the French National Archives in Paris.

Mdv: *The Virgin Unmask'd*, by Bernard Mandeville, 1709.

MH: *The Magazine of Horticulture*, edited by C.M. Hovey, Boston & New York, various years as indicated.

M'I: *The Book of the Garden*, by Charles M'Intosh, 1855.

M-L: *Travaux du Comice Horticole de Maine-et-Loire*, various years as indicated.

MLS: Article "Roses in Kansas City," by Minnie Long Sloan, in ARA28.

MonL/deP: *Monographie de Genre Rosier*, translation of Lindley by de Pronville, with an added appendix by de Pronville, 1824.

M-P: *The Culture of Perennials*, by Dorothy M.-P. Cloud, 1925. Quoted by kind permission of the publishers, Dodd, Mead & Co., Inc.

M-R: *Catalogue*, by Moreau-Robert, year as indicated.

MR8: *Modern Roses 8*, published by The McFarland Company, 1980. Quoted by kind permission of The American Rose Society and The McFarland Company.

M-V: *l'Instructeur-Jardinier*, 1848-1851, edited by Martin-Victor Paquet.

Mz: *Catalogue*, by Miellez of Esquermes, various years as indicated.

N: *Die Rose*, by Thomas Nietner, 1880.

No: *Manuel Complet du Jardinier*, by Louis Noisette, 1825.

No26: *Manuel Complet du Jardinier*, by Louis Noisette, 1826 edition.

No28: *Manuel Complet du Jardinier, Supplément No. I*, by Louis Noisette, 1828.

No35: *Manuel Complet du Jardinier, Supplément No. II*, by Louis Noisette, 1835.

NRS: *Rose Annual*, year as indicated, issued by the [British] National Rose Society. Quoted by kind permission of the Royal National Rose Society.

OB: *Oekonomisch-Botanische Beschreibung*, by Rössig, 1799.

OM: *The Rose Boo*, by H.H. Thomas, 1916.

P: *The Rose Garden*, 1st edition, by William Paul, 1848.

P1: *The Rose Garden*, 10th edition, by William Paul, 1903.

P2: *Contributions to Horticultural Literature, 1843-1892*, by William Paul, 1892.

PaSo: *Paradisi in Sole: Paradisus Terrestris*, by John Parkinson, 1629.

Pd: *Le Bilan d'un Siècle*, by Alfred Picard, tome 3, 1906.

Pf: *Catalogue Descriptif...du Genre Rosa*, by Prévost fils, 1829.

Pfs: *Supplément au Catalogue des Roses...*, by Prévost fils, 1830.

PH: *Henderson's Handbook of Plants and General Horticulture*, "New Edition" (*i.e.*, 2nd), by Peter Henderson, 1889.

PlB: *Choix des Plus Belles Roses*, by Martin-Victor Paquet *et al.*, 1845-1854.

PP28: Article "Proof of the Pudding" in ARA28.

Pq: *Le Jardinier Pratique*, by Jacquin & Rousselon, 1852.

PS: Article "Roses in Brazil," by Mrs. Paul C. Schilling, in ARA28.

R1(through 7): *The Garden*, vols. 1-7, "founded and conducted by William Robinson," 1872-1875.

R8: *The Rose-Amateur's Guide*, 8th edition, by Thomas Rivers, 1863.

R9: *The Rose-Amateur's Guide*, 4th edition, by Thomas Rivers, 1846.

RATS: Article "Roses Across the Sea" in ARA28.

Rea: *Flora: seu De Florum Cultura*, 1665.

RG: *Rosetum Gallicum*, by Desportes, 1828.

R-H: *Revue-Horticole*, year as indicated, issues 1829-1877. Quoted by kind permission of the publishers.

R-HC: *Revue-Horticole*, centenary number, 1929. Quoted by kind permission of the publishers.

Riv: *Roses et Rosiers*, by Rivoire père & fils, with Marcel Ebel, 1933.

RJC: *Revue des Jardins et des Champs*, year as indicated, 1860-1871, edited by Jean Cherpin.

R&M: *Catalogue*, by Robert & Moreau, year as indicated.

Ro: *The English Flower-Garden*, 8th edition, by William Robinson, 1903.

RP: Article "Roses—The Ophelia Strain and Kindred Spirits," by Reginald Parker, in *The Rose*, vol. 13, no. 3, 1965.

RR: Article "Check List of Red Tea Roses," by R. Robinson, in *The Rose*, vol. 13, no. 1, 1964.

Rsg: *Die Rosen/Les Roses*. Rössig's *Die Rosen*, with parallel French version by de Lahitte, 1802-1820.

RZ: *Rosen-Zeitung*, vol. 1, 1886.

S: *Dictionnaire des Roses*, by Max Singer, 1885.

SAP: *Journal de la Société d'Agronomie Pratique*, 1829.

SBP: *Parsons on the Rose*, by Samuel B. Parsons, 1888.

SDH: *Newry Roses*, catalogs by T. Smith of Daisy Hill Nursery, 1903-1929.

SHj: Article "Old Roses for the South," 1949, and address "Tea Roses for Florida," 1951, by Samuel J. Hjort. Quoted by kind permission of Sarah L. Hjort of Thomasville Nurseries, Inc.

SHP: *Annales de la Société d'Horticulture de Paris*, year as indicated.

Sn: *Rosenverzeichnis*, 3rd edition, Rosarium Sangerhausen, 1976.

SNH: *Journal de la Société Nationale d'Horticulture*, year as indicated.

SRh: *Société d'Horticulture Pratique du Rhône*, year as indicated.

S-V: *Catalogue des Plantes...*, by J. Sisley-Vandael, 1835-1836.

S-Vs: *Supplément...*, by J. Sisley-Vandael, 1839.

Sx: *The American Rose Culturist*, by C.M. Saxton, 1860.

T1: *The Old Shrub Roses*, by Graham S. Thomas, 1956. Quoted by kind permission of the author and of the publishers J.M. Dent & Sons, Ltd.

T1H: Writings of Dr. Hurst in *The Old Shrub Roses* by Graham S. Thomas.

T2: *Climbing Roses Old and New*, by Graham S. Thomas, 1983. Quoted by kind permission of the author and of the publishers J.M. Dent & Sons, Ltd.

T3: *Shrub Roses of Today*, by Graham S. Thomas, 1980. Quoted by kind permission of the author and of the publishers J.M. Dent & Sons, Ltd.

T4: *The Graham Stuart Thomas Rose Book*, by Graham Stuart Thomas, 1994. Quoted by kind permission of the publishers, Sagapress and Timber Press.

Th: *The Practical Book of Outdoor Rose Growing*, by Capt. George C. Thomas, 1920. Quoted by very kind permission of the Thomas family.

Th2: *Roses for All American Climates*, by Capt. George C. Thomas, 1924. Quoted by very kind permission of the Thomas family.

ThGl: *The Gladiolus*, by Matthew Crawford, 1911.

T&R: *Les Roses*, by Claude-Antoine Thory and Pierre-Joseph Redouté, 1817-1824.

TS: Article "Roses of Australia," by T.A. Stewart, in ARA28.

TW: *Cultivated Roses*, by T.W. Sanders, 1899.

URZ: *Ungarische Rosenzeitung*, edited by Ernst Kaufmann, date as indicated. Basic translation kindly supplied by Mr. Erich Unmuth.

V1: *Observations sur la Nomenclature et le Classement des Roses*, by Jean-Pierre Vibert, 1820.

V2: *Essai sur les Roses*, by Jean-Pierre Vibert, 1824-1830.

V3: *Catalogue*, by Jean-Pierre Vibert, 1826.

V4: *Catalogue*, by Jean-Pierre Vibert, 1836.

V5: Page from town records of Montfort-l'Amaury containing *l'Acte de décès* concerning the death of Jean-Pierre Vibert, 1866.

V6: *Le Mouvement Horticole*, 1866.

V7: Minutes of the February 8, 1866, meeting of the *conseil d'administration de la Société Nationale d'Horticulture.*

V8: *Catalogue*, by Jean-Pierre Vibert, 1844.

V9: *Catalogue*, by Jean-Pierre Vibert, 1831.

VD: Article "Roses on the Mexican Coast," by V.E. Dillon, in ARA28.

V-H: *Flore des Serres et des Jardins de l'Europe*, by Louis Van Houtte, 1845-1880.

VPt: *Almanach Horticole*, 1844-1848, year as indicated, edited by Martin-Victor Paquet.

Vrp: *Réponse à…Pirolle*, by Jean-Pierre Vibert, 1827.

W: *Climbing Roses*, by Helen Van Pelt Wilson, 1955. Quoted by kind permission of Helen V.P. Wilson.

War: *Warren's Descriptive Catalogue*, by J.L.L.F. Warren, 1844.

Way45: *Catalog*, by Wayside Gardens, 1945.

WD: *Roses and Their Culture*, 3rd edition, by W.D. Prior, 1892.

W/Hn: Interpolations by translator John Weathers in *The AmateurGardener's Rose Book*, by Julius Hoffmann, 1905.

Who: *The Western Horticultural Review*, vols. As indicated, 1850-1853.

Wr: *Roses and Rose Gardens*, by Walter P. Wright, 1911.

WRP: *Manual of Roses*, by William R. Prince, 1846.

Ÿ: *Inventaire de la Collection*, from Roseraie de l'Haÿ, 1984. Quoted by kind permission of the *Service des Espaces Verts du Conseil Général du Val de Marne*.

Zla: *La Rose et l'Industrie de l'Essence de Roses en Bulgarie*, by Dr. As. Zlataroff, 1926.

Chapter One

Preliminary

Prefatory

"How shall I dare to tread upon the territory of the Rosarian? For nothing so exasperates the specialist as when the mere amateur comes along and blithers bright nonsense about his own particular pet subject on which he has accumulated the wisdom of years. Therefore go I very daintily, for fear of the pruning knives of the National Rose Society banded unanimously against me." [Fa] "When it is considered, that almost everybody of note, engaged in the propagation and sale of the Rose, has, more or less, written upon the subject of its culture, and that amateurs of some experience have added their share to the Rose literature of the age, it cannot be anticipated

1

that much can be offered that has not, in some form or other, [already] been given to the public." [Gl]

Taking these thoughts to heart, we have gathered in this work the comments and observations of those who have written on the Rose, concentrating on material written between 1790 and 1920. As valuable as the notes of any individual author are, it has always seemed to the author that what was required was the broader view. Because one critic cries, "Horrible…horrible," when confronted with a variety which has somehow managed to provoke his particular ire, and his book is the one a gardener happens to read, that gardener may become alienated from a rose which is perfectly suited to his climate or taste. One purpose of this book, then, is to give the Reader a wider perspective on these cultivars, a perspective taking advantage of the many years that they have been in cultivation, so that he may choose wisely for his own garden having been able to compare the various opinions of a century and more of experts and fanciers. "For comparisons are not odious. It is only those who have good reason for dreading them who forged the silly lie that they are; comparisons are the very sole basis of all judgement, of all moral and religious ideas that the world has ever conceived, or ever will, or ever could." [Fa] Like the cultivars themselves, these "old" opinions are valuable and should not be neglected in the mistaken notion that "new" is intrinsically good. They were expressed by focused people who had day-to-day familiarity with the good and the bad of these old roses; modern rosarians—even the most widely experienced of them—have only a selective, skewed knowledge of these sorts, based for the most part on what has survived, and ultimately grounded in something so misleading as how they compare with modern roses. We have concentrated upon the opinions offered between 1790 and 1920, then, because that is when fresh eyes and minds expert in the niceties of these old classes combined to present them relative to their contemporaries, because works of this period are more difficult for most gardeners to obtain and consult, and because—the newer ones are still under copyright! Even these newer and newest books, however modern, scholarly, pretty, dignified, likable, self-confident, or valuable they may be—and most are indeed all of the above—do not cover all of the available material. Nowhere could one find a *complete* list of the extant varieties for any of the classes. It has been our goal to list all of the cultivars which still exist, along with others which, though extinct, have some distinctive quality, whether physically, or more abstractly in the history of rose progress. These latter seemingly extinct varieties will be found listed in square brackets; we may all hope that they too will eventually be found in living condition, reports of their extinction having been "greatly exaggerated." Many existing cultivars which are very desirable indeed will be found not in commerce, but rather clinging to existence in rosaria perhaps public perhaps private, or in botanical gardens, or in great collections such as France's Roseraie de l'Haÿ or Germany's Sangerhausen. Can we bring these again into commerce? Express your interest in them to nurserymen and vendors; beat the drum for them; let their beauties once again be expanded to a world never more in need of them than now! For these cultivars—all of them—have their value in the horticultural world on both the æsthetic and breeding levels. The Hybrid Perpetuals, Damask Perpetuals, and Hybrid Chinas help solve the "what roses for my cold-winter conditions?" problem, while the Teas, Chinas, and Noisettes deserve to reclaim ground from the Hibiscuses, Oleanders, and Bougainvilleas in the subtropical regions. Furthermore, complicated as they are, the rather purer genetic backgrounds of the older roses make them more desirable breeding material than are the infinitely more miscellaneous and complex modern hybrids. These lines of breeding deserve further attention and work; their possibilities have by no means been exhausted.

The genealogies of some of these roses, particularly those developed in the earliest years, were often the product of after-the-fact guesswork by the breeders or introducers—not that these were simply pulled out of thin air, as the number of sorts good for breeding was limited, and the characteristics of each were well known by the hybridists. These genealogies, then, should be regarded in many cases as earnest attempts and educated guesses rather than as received doctrine. Even as careful a worker as Lambert was evidently undecided as to whether his famous Hybrid Tea 'Kaiserin Auguste Viktoria' was derived from 'Perle des Jardins' × 'Belle Lyonnaise' or to 'Coquette de Lyon' × 'Lady Mary Fitzwilliam'. Both were quoted in periodicals which he read; and, though he was given to correcting the Press's errors, he never wrote in to correct either attribution. Either seems likely; in such cases, we give both.

The quotations in the entries have been pared down to a minimum to make room for the greatest amount of diversity with the least amount of *needless* repetition; some repetition is necessary to represent the predominance of one opinion or another. The Reader will be intrigued by the varying and often opposing observations and opinions! Such is the world of Roses, a pluralistic world of varying conditions and subjective perceptions, perhaps giving us an insight into the larger world. Modern writers have sometimes made comments which we have not been able to resist including; we have made sparing use of these with the much appreciated permission of the writer and/or publisher. The key to the citations, both modern and "old," is located both in the abbreviations section of Volume I, and in the Bibliography in Volume II.

The order followed in each entry varies with the nature of the remarks available. One wishes that one had had for every cultivar the resources we had for 'Gloire de Dijon'! There is no attempt to follow a chronological order. Rarely are the opinions expressed in rosedom developmental; most often, they are spontaneous, personal, usually based—refreshingly—on the gardener's own experience with the variety in question, the thing itself, not on worked-over and indeed overworked exegesis and elaborations of foregoing theories. Time is an empty distinction is this connection, as in so many others. We are not overly fond of the word "old" as applied to these roses; it suggests an arcanum which unfortunately alienates as many people as it attracts. The author has known people to wrinkle up their noses and say, "Old rose? Who would want an *old* rose?", as if we were discussing an aged sheep or yesterday's sandwich. These roses are not old in that way, decrepit, decaying. They were simply *developed* "of old"; and specimens now on the market are as young and vigorous as the specimens of last year's All-America selection at the local nursery. The breeding which produced them could have taken place in 1990 as easily as in 1890—but the eye which selected them as being desirable material was an eye trained in the æsthetics of another time. This, however, should be no barrier to appreciation. Ramifications of the same æsthetic are still admired today when we listen to Offenbach or Puccini, and read Dickens or Conan Doyle—or most particularly when we appreciate the visual artists of the era—the designers, the architects, the *artists*—because Horticulture and plant-breeding are also popular *Arts*, much as novels, clothes-design, gastronomy, and theater-arts were and remain. Those who appreciate the finer things are still delighted today by the beautiful in Horticulture just as they cherish man's productions in any of the other arts. The special cachet of Vibert or Lacharme stamps their work no less than the spirit of Renoir, Atget, or Nijinsky infuses *theirs*. Yes, these are "old" roses, but as we do not distinguish other works of the time as "old," the distinction seems rather forced, rather unfair. Nothing should be dismissed because of the historical accident of its having been developed at one particular time or another; everything bears its special quality as a gift to us, and forever. We need only make the effort to reach out and accept the gift.

Research holds many rewards; so it was always with the greatest pleasure that the author would find himself on some crisp, wintry morning turning the pages of the *Journal des Roses*, the *American Rose Annual*, or any of the other hundred and more materials which stand behind this work. Though the romance of our tale seems to diminish—as romance will—as we approach the present, the research nevertheless has held very exotic, very exciting episodes even as it has also much of the homey—and even more of the very human! More than once, armies—Napoleonic, Prussian, Allied—have marched over the rosefields before our eyes; we take the cure at Vichy with Monsieur Lévêque; stand, eagle-eyed, with

Mme. Beluze at the maison Beluze window; attend Monsieur Desprez at his death-bed as he calls, one last time, for the rose that bears his name; look with young Mr. Rivers one fine morning in June over his first bed of seedlings; join Rev. Foster-Melliar gazing in quiet appreciation at the beauty of a row of white roses "just as the dusk of a July evening comes on"; even find a memorable apotheosis for an ill-starred stray cat. The author hopes that he has been able to communicate to the Reader some of the excitement, pleasure, and life experienced in preparing these pages; and that, by the time he turns the last page, he will have a fuller understanding not only of the roses, but also of their world.

"The little work which follows took much time and effort. Perhaps it could be said that one's leisure time could be better employed by writing more useful things: the questions of nomenclature and of horticultural history are only of moderate interest to the present generation of amateur growers! One may respond to those of this inclination [*presumably with a shrug*] that, very well, such is their opinion; but, as for me, in wishing to learn about these things myself, I like to hope all the while that a historical outline such as this would be interesting and useful to others as well. Last, I cannot hide a hope that, apart from the pure chimeras which seem to have guided these researches, perhaps the admonishing spirits—the professional rose-breeders—who know to read between the lines, will find there something of profit." [JR31/128]

Poetical

"Of all the flowers with which Nature has embellished our gardens, the Rose is that which unites the brilliance of the most beautiful blossoms with the most agreeable fragrance. In the farthest ages, in the homes of the ancients as well as the moderns, it always occupied the premier place. Is that so strange? This amiable flower appeals to and at the same time charms all the senses; it is attractive to all ages: the young girl, the fortunate lover—the happy couple seek it out and gather it eagerly; it becomes for them the troth of their amours. And when finally life's Winter deadens all our senses, it is the sweet perfume of a rose that brings them back again for a moment." [V1] "And then, in the cyclones of snow and ice, begins the spring...And on the dead rose-bushes hang a thousand buds, like withered moths, dark amid the whirling snowflakes. The Japanese cherish their gift of condensing a whole aspect of nature or emotion into one tiny phrase: listen:

> *Furu-dera ya;*
> *Kane-mono iwazu*
> *Sakura chiru.*

For here is the crystallized loneliness of spirit:

> *Ancient temple;*
> *Voiceless bells;*
> *Falling cherry petals.*

What could be more delicately and more completely pictorial? And, like all pungent and memorable portraits of human emotion, direct and simple and naked. But if we of the West desire...to condense into a phrase the blackest and lowest hour of winter, I, at least, cannot better express it to myself than by that picture of all the little blackened wasted rose-buds, standing stiff on their dead boughs in a snowstorm.—Bah, let them quickly be pruned away—hideous reminders of bygone beauty." [Fa]

Historical

"The culture of the Rose, handed down from antiquity, has never ceased in Europe; but it was the Moors in Spain who were the first, among modern peoples, to give particular attention to their culture. The fine plains of Valencia, the gardens of Cordova and of Granada were the true rose-beds—which are not to be found today." [JF]

"The Rose was, for quite some time, neglected, unlike certain other flowers: Anemones, Hyacinths, Carnations, and Tulips, which were the object of extreme enthusiasm in the 18th and 19th Centuries, sometimes beyond all reason. Because of their brightness—as well as their suckers— some specimens of a small number of species and varieties persisted in cultivation, among which were the Gallicas, the Damasks, and the Centifolias—the most popular. But if indeed someone were to plant many roses, it would only be for the various usages of pharmacists or perfumers. The Dutch were the first to propagate Roses by seed. They particularly favored the Gallicas. It wasn't long before they had cornered the Rose market. At that time, France didn't have the specialized rose-breeding of the establishments of Dupont and Vilmorin, of Paris; Godefroy, of Ville-d'Avray; Descemet, of St.-Denis; and Vibert, of Chennevières-sur-Marne." [F]

"Among those in our country [*France*] who have increased our pleasures, Monsieur Descemet without a doubt takes a place of honor. Because of his numerous seedlings developed over more than a dozen years, produced methodically, his wonderful results, his acute observations, as well as the more than two hundred interesting varieties due to him, he merits such a place. Fanciers and others who set great value on Rose progress will always regret those events of 1814 and 1815 which forced him to take his knowledge and efforts elsewhere [*Russia*]. I [*Vibert*] was fortunate enough to be able to save his large and interesting collection from being dispersed. His breeding material, his plants being studied, and more than ten thousand seedlings of all ages passed into my hands. Monsieur Descemet had amassed a great many notes on his seedlings; the origins of a part of his seedlings were contained in those notes. This precious work, which gave us valuable notions concerning the tricks of Nature and about which varieties are the best to sow, was destroyed as a consequence of that war; a small part which was fortunately preserved makes me regret all the more the lost remainder, which would have spared me much time and effort." [V1]

"The most well-known collection was that of Malmaison, formed for the Empress Joséphine by Dupont; and those of the Luxembourg, under the direction of Hardy. About three hundred varieties could be named, mostly Gallicas, before they were added to, rather later, by Hardy, Prévost of Rouen, Vibert, Laffay, etc. Along with the Gallicas, the classes of Centifolias, Mosses, Damasks, and Portlands were being formed...Meanwhile, the China and Tea-Scented Roses were brought onto the scene between 1798 and 1810, along with Noisettes and Bourbons a few years later. Of these early varieties, however, few other than the Common China are still with us. The seedlings increased; and, in 1828, the number of old varieties quintupled, over and above the nearly 300 varieties of Chinas, Bourbons, Teas, and Noisettes...Jacques, gardener at the Neuilly estate of the Duc d'Orléans (who became King Louis-Philippe I), developed the Sempervirens class, in which is 'Félicité et Perpétue'; then Vibert, Laffay, Beluze, Hardy, and other breeders gave us, up through the middle of the 19th Century, such varieties as the following: 'Aimée Vibert', 'Lamarque', 'Mme. Hardy', 'Mrs. Bosanquet', 'Cramoisi Supérieur', 'Persian Yellow', 'Safrano', 'Hermosa', 'Triomphe du Luxembourg', 'Ophirie', 'Céline Forestier', 'Chromatella', 'Solfatare', 'Souvenir de la Malmaison', 'Niphetos', 'Souvenir d'un Ami', '[Mlle. de] Sombreuil'. Meanwhile, the race of Hybrid Perpetuals was being developed with: 'Duchesse de Sutherland', 'Baronne Prévost', 'Ernestine de Barante', 'Géant des Batailles', 'Lion des Combats', 'La Reine'—enough! The others are well known. The appearance of these beautiful remontant varieties, which are much the greater part of our modern collections, brought about the neglect of the old sorts, the Gallicas, Damasks, Centifolias, etc.; their decline and fall came quickly." [F]

"The trade of cultivating Roses in France is in the hands of many individuals; and to visit that country with the view of forming a collection is (I speak from experience) a laborious undertaking. As far as my powers of observation serve me, I should think the establishments where they are grown for sale, in the neighborhood of Paris, vary in extent from one to five acres; and there are others, situate in various parts of France, nearly all of like extent. It is thus that English amateurs, who may chance to visit any of them, are usually disappointed, owing to the contrast of their Rose Gardens to those of England, which are much more extensive. The most splendid collection in France [*as of 1848, that is*] is that in the Jardin du Luxembourg in Paris, which is under the supervision of Monsieur Hardy. Most of the plants there are of some age, and flower most profusely in the season. It is true that they look rather drawn; but when we consider their proximity to the heart of the city, it is surprising that they flourish so well." [P]

With the appearance of the Hybrid Perpetuals came, at length, the development and proliferation of the Rose Show, a factor of great, though largely untold, significance; their rise signals the decline of the rose as a garden plant considered as such, making way for the rose considered as a blossom with its plant as mere appendage. These rose shows, first notably organized in 1865, "to whom much of the success of the Exhibition is due" [R-H65], did Rosedom the great favor of stimulating the imaginations and efforts of the hybridists of the day. Rose shows have also played their part in standardizing—for better or worse—our ideas of what a rose should look like; the "bigger is better" mystique was, and still is, bolstered by the nature of competition in such exhibitions; and this, in turn, underlies the common notions of how a rose plant should be pruned. Bernardin's "special rose exposition" at Brie-Comte-Robert in 1865 was, in its way, the quiet revolution making modern rosedom what it is today.

"I sometimes fear that the passion for large, well-formed blossoms, and the desire for novelty, will make some of the dear old Roses of our child-hood pass into entire neglect." [Br]

Practical

"Cultivate none but the best, and cultivate them thoroughly." [FP]

"It is suggested that roses in the different classes should be grown where they are best adapted to the various climates." [Th2] "At all times of the year roses need constant and watchful care; and the amateur—especially if a woman, hampered with tiresome petticoats—must have space in which to move, in order to pick off caterpillars, cut the flowers whether alive or dead, and see to all the various needs of the plants, such as weeding, watering, manuring and pruning." [K2]

"The object in pruning a Rose is to give it suitable form, and to rejuvenate the branches as much as possible for the best flowering. It is difficult to be specific, but pruning ought to be done according to the vigor of the variety, the exposure, and particular culture followed. The general rules one might state are: For varieties of feeble growth which are very floriferous, prune to 2 or 3 eyes; for those of varying growth, 4 or 5 eyes; for strong-growing or climbing, 6-15 eyes. Roses are pruned during the first days of March. Pruning consists of cutting out the dead or weak branches, eliminating competition between branches so that they do not cross, and in rejuvenating the plant as much as possible by cutting out the secondary branches." [LR]

"*Do not* choose the varieties for your garden from exhibits at shows. The blossoms there I know are fine, and the temptation is great to have some of the novelties sent on to you. Do not yield to it. The exhibition specimen may be the special effort of a variety which for garden decoration may be practically worthless." [Bk]

"Unfortunately, descriptions are sometimes rather fantastic, but everyone will allow how extremely difficult it is to describe any rose…[T]he beauties of the rose are difficult to translate [*from sight to words*]; entire pages must be devoted to the description of each variety if one would give an exact picture of the rose described." [G&B]

Explanatory

The roses are listed by the names under which they were originally introduced—when determinable—or, where there is any doubt as to synonymy, under the name with which they enjoyed the widest distribution. The ritual of "release to commerce" being the deciding factor, the names introducers provided are preferred to those bestowed prospectively by the breeder. Let us heed the "earnest desire" of one breeder/introducer, however, and prefer 'Panachée d'Angers' to the earlier name 'Commandant

Beaurepaire', particularly as the latter was a name intended for a non-remontant form. As in all contracts, there must be a "meeting of the minds" to put the contract into force! The date given for a cultivar is ideally that of the year in which it was released to commerce—not the year in which it was bred, or in which it first bloomed; a rose originally announced in late 1885 as being for the "1885-1886 season" would be listed as an 1885 rose. A date with a hyphen preceding, as-1885, indicates that the rose was released *in that year or before*.

Main entries in square brackets [ ] refer to those roses which are, or seem to be, extinct, but which are nevertheless important or interesting enough that to leave them out of this account would be a disservice. The next element in an entry is the name of the breeder and/or introducer, followed by the date of introduction. In the item "Laxton/G. Paul, 1876," Laxton is the breeder and G. Paul the introducer, which will be the order followed throughout. A solitary name indicates the introducer, who *may* also be the breeder. In very rare cases, some further figure will have played an important part as a "middleman" in some way, as for instance in the case of 'Cramoisi Supérieur', which has the attribution "Coquereau/Audiot/Vibert"; in this case, Coquereau bred the rose and presented it to Monsieur Audiot, who, recognizing its merit, interested Vibert in releasing it to the world in his catalog. Then the synonyms, if any, are listed. It is worth remembering that a "synonym," in this connection, is not a word or name of equal merit to be used interchangeably with the "original" name; it is an appellation which is "incorrect" for some reason, which has however been used at some point, and which should be kept in mind should it pop up in research material, or on a label at a rosarium...Next would come the parentage, if it is known. We most usually do not know the parents of these old roses! And the parentages given, as discussed above, are always open to question, and yet are never to be regarded as intentional or sinister mis-statements by those from whom I have culled the information. The *fact* in many cases being unascertainable, the *conjecture* of an expert—usually the raiser—surely weighs in as important evidence. Following the parentages are the quotations, arranged in whatever order their content suggested, but generally beginning with remarks on color and other characteristics of the blossom, continuing with characteristics of the leaves and plant in general, and ending with such cultural and/or historical data as is available and relevant. To lazily list the quotes chronologically would present a mish-mash, as, overwhelmingly, the descriptions constitute an observer's first-hand reaction to a rose, rather than a point of development in a chronological continuum of ideas. Rarely do we see ideas developing in this discipline!—but where they do, the development is presented; otherwise, they are simply grouped in whatever way seems most telling, chronology be damned. Each quotation is followed by a code designation in square brackets, which designation specifies the work from which it came; the designation-code is "translated" in the reference key located after the list of abbreviations in Volume I, and in the Bibliography in Volume II.

The guiding principle in choosing the format and arrangement of this book has been primarily to serve the needs of the "rank and file" gardener, who is the backbone of all horticulture, and then, secondarily, to provide for the special needs of the enthusiast and the researcher. Because of this, we have avoided the more chaotic flights of botanical and taxonomic fancy—most of which the world finds toggling back and forth as the years pass on!—in favor of the traditional conventions of horticulture, which are clearer, more stable, and more familiar to the majority of those using this book. "We will not list [*the roses*] in the scholarly style, as Lindley, de Pronville, Prévost, and others, have done, but will instead use the commercial nomenclature, indeed the best to use with nurserymen." [Pq] Otherwise—"Is human Writing, then, the art of burying Heroisms and highest Facts in chaos; so that no man shall henceforth contemplate them without horror and aversion...? What does [*the writer*] consider that he was born for; that paper and ink were made for?" [Cy2]

What indeed!

Chapter Two

Damask Perpetuals

"What is the rose called 'des Quatre Saisons'? Where did it originate? No one can say!…Is a person able to establish common characteristics to form a more or less homogeneous group? No! One finds here many roses classified as 'Portlands' which are very different from the Type—for example, 'Rose du Roi', 'Julie [de] Krudner', 'Célina Dubos'—varieties which, by their bearing and growth, have little in common with the 'Quatre Saisons' rose with which they are classed." [JR9/56-57]

Ah, the mysterious Damask Perpetuals! Profuse in synonyms—'Quatre Saisons', 'Monthly Roses', 'Tous-les-Mois', 'Perpetuals'—but rare in cultivation now, and obscure in their origins even 'way back when! Nevertheless, they are always delightful inhabitants of the choicest gardens, bridging the gap in rose-progress between the old once-blooming European roses and the newer rebloomers springing from the Chinas and Teas. What is their history? Which one was the first? Vague supposed mentions of "twice-blooming" roses have been cited in the poetry of ancient Rome; here is Virgil in the fourth of his *Georgics*:

> And I myself, were I not even now
> Furling my sails, and, nigh the journey's end,
> Eager to turn my vessel's prow to shore,
> Perchance would sing what careful husbandry
> Makes the trim garden smile; of Pæstum, too,
> Whose roses bloom and fade and bloom again;
> How endives glory in the streams they drink,
> And green banks in their parsley, and how the gourd
> Twists through the grass [...]

—how much credit can we allow to these remarks, especially when we find that a literal reading of the Latin original refers not to *twice-bearing roses* but rather to *twice-bearing Pæstum*? Is the poet being fanciful? Is he referring to "forced" roses—a reasonable possibility, as the Romans had their sort of greenhouses, heated by hot water in pipes. Most likely, it is simply a poetical expression for the often-mentioned natural bounteousness of Pæstum and Campania in general; the latter is indeed referred to in a classical *Flora* as "twice-blooming Campania" without reference to roses. Rosarians have long credited the rose called 'Bifera' with being an ancient rose, more by recent tradition than on any firmer basis, as the rose we know under that name seems to have been unknown—at least, to the rosarians of France, England, Holland, and Germany—until sometime around 1806 and certainly by 1820. Montaigne mentions, as seeing in Ferrara in 1580, a rose which was said to bloom every month of the year; but we have no way of knowing if this was perhaps a chance importation of a China Rose, or was indeed the debut of the Damask Perpetuals. It could well have been the 'Monthly Rose', which had appeared on the horticultural stage by 1633 in

Italy, being known in both England and Holland by 1669, and in France by 1695 as the 'Tous-les-Mois'; it was apparently what Rivers has in mind when differentiating "our very old Damask Rose, the Red Monthly," from "the comparatively new rose, 'Rose à Quatre Saisons' of the French." [R8] To continue with seemings, this "old Damask Rose, the Red Monthly," seems to be the cultivar referred to when we learn that "there was, some time ago, a new type of Perpetuals going by the name of 'Trianon' because the Red Damask was particularly noted in that area." [JDR54/30] "I was at Rouen in September 1829, at the home of an English plantsman [*probably London-based Calvert, who had premises in Rouen as well*] whose garden had been left to itself for awhile, and noticed there, among the seedlings, a semi-double rose blooming, which, aside from its remontant qualities, showed characteristics I hadn't seen in other sorts. Some cuttings of this rose were given to me, and, as the place had the name 'Trianon', that is what I named the rose. Having sown the seed of this rose for 8 or 9 years without having gotten more than one good variety, I sowed instead the seed of some flesh-colored semi-doubles with foliage which was different; after having repeated this for three or four years, I was able to raise a white, and the seeds of *this* were what I subsequently sowed, for the most part. The greater part of my seed-bearers are in their 5th or 6th generation; and it is really quite extraordinary to see such diversity among plants springing from the same Type…The number of such Roses descending from my Perpetual 'Trianon', doubles and semi-doubles, has surpassed 40, and I am sure to add many to the number of doubles before too many years have passed. Many of these roses bloom in clusters of 50 to 60 blossoms; their diameter varies from 3-8 cm [ca. 1-3 inches]; most waft an elegant perfume. From purest white to light purple, all shades are found; but, above all, it is in the details of their appearance that Nature has exercised freedom: wood, leaves, thorns, manner of growth—all vary…Such, then, are the reasons I have set up a new division of Perpetuals…Let me add an important observation: Within this set of roses are plants which bloom the first year from seed, which does not ordinarily happen with Chinas, Noisettes, or Bourbons;

last year, 10 or 12 young plants bloomed in July. All of these Roses coming from this 'Trianon' seem to me to be very receptive to pollination from other varieties—or perhaps it is because of their own inherent qualities that they show so much variation, which seems to me to be the more likely explanation [*signed*: Vibert, Angers, June 28, 1846]." [dH47/282]

"The Musk Rose lives on in the 'Trianons' and 'Portlands' under the names 'Sapho', 'Blanche-Vibert', 'Delphine Gay', 'La Candeur', etc." [JDR54/42] But, after 'Bifera' and the race of Monthly Roses, how do the Portlands fit into this? In 1775, Weston lists the 'Portland Crimson Monthly Rose', already "to be readily found," separately from the Monthly Rose group (which latter now had developed into several varieties); by 1785, as we learn from Buc'hoz, it had entered France, though evidently not making much of a splash, as Fillassier does not mention it in 1791. In 1805, Andrews reports that it is "said" that the rose was named "in compliment to the late Duchess"—second Duchess of Portland, who died in 1785. But, as to its origin, the nearest we come is second-hand information recorded in 1882 by a writer who *seems* to have a first-hand account at his elbow as he writes: "At the end of the last century or the beginning of this one…was found at Portland, England, a rosebush quite dis-similar to *R. damascena bifera*, from which came the seed, a seed which was in most probability a hybrid with *R. gallica* because the new acquisition showed certain resemblances to both species. It had semi-double flowers, scarlet-purple, successively until frost. It was called the 'Portland Damask'…Some years later, perhaps about 1820, Godefroy, nurseryman at Ville d'Avray (Seine-et-Oise), developed a sub-variety of Portland dissimilar enough to its progenitor to begin a new race by the name of Perpetual Rose. Its foliage was light green, its flowers pink, semi-double, in clusters, and remontant until November." [JR6/153]

"In 1815, remontant roses were still rare; one can only find two in the Portland series, the biferas 'Palmyre' and 'Venusta'. In the month of August in that same year, 'Rose du Roi' was developed from seedlings grown in 1814…[*at*] Sèvres, near St.-Cloud…" [JF] (but see under 'Rose du Roi'). As we shall see, these Damask Perpetual roses were to lead to further rose progress, giving rise to a new race which would at length eclipse their parents: "Jacques, the King's gardener at Neuilly, developed from the Portland the hybrid 'Athalin', a variety which, like 'Malton', is an excellent seed-bearer. 'Athalin', crossed with 'Rose du Roi', would later give remontant roses having the Portland character—a short and stiff flower-stem, with the blossom nestling among the leaves—which distinguished the first descendants of 'Athalin', varieties of feeble growth and weak remontancy. Rosarians gave these Portland-derived varieties the name Hybrid Portlands to distinguish them from other remontant hybrids." [JF] Truth to tell, the name given was one rather more familiar to us: Hybrid Perpetuals. "[In the *Hybrid* Perpetuals,] the leaves are completely glabrous, and smooth in youth; however, in age, they thicken a little, becoming stiff and slightly rugose; it is this which distinguishes these *hybrids* from *true Portlands*, which have soft, slender, downy leaves." [l'H51/121]

But let us return to the true Damask Perpetuals. "As the culture of this class of roses is at present but imperfectly understood, I shall give the result of my experience as to their cultivation, with suggestions to be acted upon according to circumstances. One peculiar feature they nearly all possess—a reluctance to root when layered; consequently, Perpetual Roses, on their own roots, will always be scarce: when procurable, they will be found to succeed much better on poor dry soils than the budded plants, which require a rich soil. Perpetual Roses, as a general rule however, require a superabundant quantity of food: it is therefore perfectly ridiculous to plant them on arid lawns, and to suffer the grass to grow close up to their stems, without giving them a particle of manure for years. Under these circumstances, the best varieties, even the 'Rose du Roi', will scarcely ever give a second series of flowers. To remedy the inimical nature of arid soils to this class of roses, an annual application of manure on the surface of the earth is quite necessary...I have said that this treatment is applicable to dry poor soils; but even in good rose soils it is almost indispensable; as it imparts such increased vigor, and such a prolongation of the flowering season, as to amply repay the labor bestowed. If the soil is prepared as directed, the plants will twice in the year require pruning: in November, when the beds are dressed, and again a short time before the first flowering in June. At the November pruning, cut off from every shoot of the preceding summer's growth about two-thirds; if the shoots are crowded, remove some of the entirely. If this autumnal pruning is attended to, there will be at the end of May, or early in June, the following summer, a vast number of luxuriant shoots, each crowned with a cluster of buds. Now, as June roses are always abundant a little sacrifice must be made to insure a fine autumnal bloom; therefore, leave only half the number of shoots to bring forth their summer flowers, and shorten the remainder to about half their length. Each short-ened branch will soon put forth buds; and in August and September the plants will again be covered with flowers. In cultivating Perpetual Roses, the faded flowers ought immediately to be removed; for in autumn the petals do not fall off readily, but lose their colour and remain on the plant, to the injury of forthcoming buds." [WRP]

"This nearly extinct class of roses should find in the heart of the rosar-ian a warm corner, because of their splendour when planted in masses, for they are in truth genuine bedding roses, and bloom superbly from July to October; their colours rich, their odour spicy and refreshing." [Hd] "The neglect of them is a patent instance of good things lost sight of from the caprice of fashion, or want of knowledge by the moderns of their existence." [WD]

À Fleur Double Listed as 'La Moderne'.

[**Adèle Mauzé**] (Vibert, 1847) syn. 'Rose de Trianon Double'
"Flowers rose, large and full; curious foliage." [P] "Flower 6-7 cm [ca. 2½ inches], double, pink. Wood and foliage unique." [M-L46/271] "Flower medium-sized, full; color, light pink; growth vigorous." [S]

[**Amanda Patenotte**] (Vibert, 1845) syn. 'Amande Patenotte'
"Pale rose color, very double, protuberant fine globose form, large, splendid." [WRP] "7 cm [ca. 2 ¾ inches], full, deep pink, globular, very fragrant."

[VPt47/127] "Blossom medium-sized, full, plump, of a bright purple pink. Elegant foliage." [An46-47/209] "Bright rose-coloured flowers, globular, and very double: this has the above mentioned fragrance [*"briar or Dog Rose"*] remarkably powerful." [R9] "Dark rose, large and full; form, globular. Habit, erect; growth, moderate." [P] "Canes hardly thorny at all; foliage medium, of a light green; flower nestling within the foliage (peduncle about a centimeter long [ca. 3/8 inch]), ovary smooth, glabrous; calycinate divisions medium-sized; corolla a very bright cerise red." [dH47/253] "(By some ranked as a Hybrid Perpetual, and perhaps justly so)…one of the very finest of this class; it is a most admirable flower…it is new, and in great request even in France at 15 to 20 francs each plant. I last year paid 22 francs, and was deemed favored." [WRP]

Amandine (Vibert, 1846)
"Pale rose, large and full." [P] "7-8 centimeters, full, delicate pink." [VPt47/126] "Flower large, full; color, light pink." [S] "*Rivers*—Blush—with centre deep rose—large—fine. *Paul*—Delicate rose—large and full. *Wood*—Deep blush—globular and very double. *Curtis*—Outer petals light blush with deeper centre—beautiful. 'Amandine' was raised by Monsieur Vibert, the well known Nurseryman, and rose cultivator of Angers, in 1844, and is a very distinct and superb blush variety, of good habit and great fragrance; we figure it as the best of his Trianon group, or division or perpetuals, which we have long desired to notice. Mr. Rivers has favored us with his remarks on the subject, which so exactly coincide with our own opinion, that we cannot do better than transcribe his words. 'Some four or five years since, Monsieur Vibert, of Angers, having raised seedlings from a very old autumnal blooming variety, called 'Belle de Trianon', founded a new group, which contained thirty or more varieties, some of these passably good, and which obtained favour with one or two rose growers; but with the exception of 'Sidonie' and the subject of our present notice, 'Amandine', nearly all have deservedly gone out of culture; but these, however, although placed amongst the 'Belle de Trianon' roses,

belong more properly to our well known Hybrid perpetuals, having departed largely from their type. 'Amandine' is really a very fine and distinct rose, a free grower, and free autumnal bloomer. Our frequent making divisions, or groups of roses, with but slight distinctive characters, cannot be too much discouraged!'..." [C]

Arthur de Sansal
Listed as a Hybrid Perpetual.

Autumn Damask
Listed as 'Bifera'.

[**Belle de Trianon**] (Prévost,-1826) trans., "Trianon Beauty"
"Pale pink." [LS] "A semi-double rose with the exact scent of the wild briar or Dog Rose." [R9] See also 'Adèle Mauzé'.

[**Belle Fabert**] (Fabert,-1826) syn. 'Grand Perpetual'
"Deep pink." [V4] "Full, flat, very large, beautiful." [LF] "Bright rosy crimson, sometimes tinted with purple, very large and full; form, globular. Very sweet." [P] "Brilliant." [HstI:308] "Handsome carmine-pink, often tinted with maroon." [S] "Large, deep pink, full d'ble, convex." [WRP] "Very large, very double, attaining 5 in[ches] in diameter [ca. 1.25 dm], pink, not very regular." [Go] "Very sweet-scented." [M'I] "A true perpetual Rose of great excellence, requiring a rich soil and good culture to bloom in perfection. It has one great fault,—the flowers produced in July are so large that they almost invariably burst; but its autumnal flowers are much more symmetrical." [R9]

Bernard (Breeder unknown, 1836) syn. 'Mme. Ferray', 'Perpetual Pompon'
Sport or seedling of 'Rose du Roi'.
"Pink." [V4] "Delicate pink, full, flat, medium-sized, superb." [LF] "Bright salmon-pink, flowers double, small, and beautiful, quite a gem, habit dwarf." [JC] "Flowers salmon, of medium size, full; form, cupped. A beautiful little Rose." [P] "Very fragrant. This rose will flourish better on

the Boursault stock than on the Dog Rose." [R9] "A most beautiful new rose, with rather small flowers, but they are very double and finely shaped, of a delicate carmine color: this is a true Perpetual, and a most desirable rose." [WRP] Has been attributed to Rivers, on what grounds we know not; Vibert seems very familiar with its origin, referring to it at one point as one of several varieties which was introduced as a seedling, but which investigation rather proved to be a sport. Bernard, stage name of the French actor/comedian Wolf, fl. 1830s.

Bifera (Persoon,-1807) syn. 'Autumn Damask', 'Quatre Saisons', *R. damascena bifera*, *R. damascena semperflorens*, 'Rose of Castile', 'Rose of Pæstum' Possibly *R. gallica* × *R moschata*.
"Growth very vigorous; canes fairly strong, branching; bark light green, with numerous brown thorns which are very sharp and nearly straight. Foliage ample, handsome green, slightly rugose, 5-7 oval, rounded, finely dentate leaflets; petiole strong, thick, armed with 4-5 little prickles. Flower to 3 inches [ca. 8 cm] or so, nearly full, cupped, solitary on the branchlets, more often in clusters in which the number of blossoms varies according to the vigor of the cane; color, delicate pink, brighter in the center, petal edges paler; peduncle short, glandular. Calyx tubular; sepals leaf-like. The 'Quatre-Saisons' rose is the most fragrant of all roses, and is much besought for its perfume; but its name is unjustified, as it is not very remontant; pretty hardy, it nevertheless suffers in the coldest winters." [JF] "When the plant is left to itself, it blooms but little, often only once, and indeed perhaps not at all...Plant the specimen in a pot and prune all the canes short enough to produce shoots which terminate in a blossom. After the bloom, it is necessary to withhold water from the plants in such a way as to stop growth and make them shed their leaves; then prune them and water them again. The new shoots don't wait to grow, and, in their turn, produce their blossoms. If this travail is repeated in just the right way, one is able, in a year, to get four bloom periods, justifying the 'Quatre Saisons' appellation...The 'Rosier des Quatre-Saisons', after having been

cultivated on the grand scale—in pots for the flower markets, as well as for industrial uses, and perfume production, is on the point of disappearing…It will rejoin its many kinsmen, 'Gloire des Perpétuelles', 'Lodoïska', 'Antinoüs', 'La Magnanime', 'Palmyre', 'Mme. Ferray', 'Joséphine Antoinette', which are said to belong to the same clan, and for which one today may similarly search in vain." [R-H85]

Bifera Italica
See 'Henriette' and 'Quatre Saisons d'Italie'.

Blanche-Vibert (Vibert, 1847) syn. 'Blanc de Vibert'
"White, tinged with flesh, large, very full, flat form; often comes with a green center." [EL] "Flowers yellowish when first opening, changing to white, of medium size, full." [P] "One of the purest whites." [HstXXX:45] "Flower 6-7 cm [ca. 3 inches], full, matte white, yellowish when opening, crested at the center. Flower very beautiful and quite unique in its genre." [M-L46/271] "Blooms well in the autumn." [FP] "Light green foliage." [G] "Vigorous, branches upright and short." [S]
We add something on Vibert himself: "Monsieur Vibert…has devoted all of his attentions since 1810 to growing Roses." [L-D] "Monsieur J.-P. Vibert, member of the Horticultural Society of St.-Denis (Seine)…Winter of 1833-34. For more than twenty years, Monsieur Vibert has devoted himself exclusively to raising roses, and has done so with passion and discernment. His establishment serves as a model to the others which have sprung up since; and though his success continues and grows, Monsieur Vibert announces in this catalog which is to be published that he will quit business in 1835, and sell at that time all his roses, greenhouses, frames, and acreage together or separately, depending upon the wishes of the buyers. It is distressing that Monsieur Vibert is retiring! However, the fruit of his long experience will not be forgotten; he has published many highly regarded papers, and it seems that there will be no shortage of people requesting such information." [R-H33] Many of the rose-breeders with whom we are concerned have left us as earthly biography little more than

their mute living proxies, their roses. While a person can with relative ease garner rough sketches of the lives of some of the better-known *rosiéristes*, the lives of the two most influential fathers of modern rose-breeding—Vibert and Laffay—have remained until now quite as mysterious as those of the least significant. It has been only with the very greatest difficulty that any researcher has been able to come up with even the given name of either of the two; and, as to such basic biographical information as birth-dates and death-dates—! The importance of these two men to rose-advancement mandates interest in them as human beings. We thus take great pleasure in offering to the reader the following on Vibert (and, later, some words on Laffay), the most important facts of which were gathered through the assistance of my colleague, the indefatigable Monsieur Massiot:

Jean-Pierre Vibert was born on January 31, 1777, in Paris, to Robert Vibert and Aimée Françoise (Leiris) Vibert. [V5] His parents, who had in all five children [ADE], were of the "small businessman" class in society. His father was a hosier, and indeed other relations were haberdashers or hosiery makers. To grow up in Paris as the decay of aristocracy—and of the monarchy itself!—began to fill the nostrils of the French; to be age 12 when the Bastille fell; to have a king guillotined ten days before his 16th birthday, war declared on England a few days later; to see a "Reign of Terror" surround his 17th birthday; to see Napoléon, a few months later, restore a sort of order by main force; blood, battle, death on all sides; *this* was the youth of our Vibert. His grandson tells us (in *The Century* magazine, vol. 51, p. 79) *not* of a quiet, shy horticulturist in the making, shunning violence, finding inner peace in rustic solitude; *au contraire*, he tells of "Jean-Pierre Vibert, a soldier of the First Republic and of Napoleon, who, compelled by his many wounds to leave the army, became a gardener because he loved flowers." He was indeed a sergeant in the elite corps which became *les Voltigeurs* in Napoléon's First Army of the Republic, and suffered his serious wounds during the Italian campaign at the siege of Naples in 1799 [V2]. We do not know how much he was incapacitated by these "many wounds," but in due course he began to work as a hardware salesman at a store located at 178 rue du Four in Paris [MCN, ECS], between the Seine and the Luxembourg Palace in the St.-Germain quarter of Paris, where we find him on July 20, 1804, taking out a ten-year loan [MCN] in the amount of 28,000 francs (in present terms, about $100,000) at a rate of 5.1%, the lender being one Mme. Pezé, herself the widow of a hardware dealer—perhaps his former boss—and the collateral being the mortgage on a house which his father and mother owned at 38 rue des Moulins on the other side of the Seine in Paris. With this loan, he bought a hardware store of his own at 30 rue du Four—a long street, and a good one for business—near the church St. Germain des Prés. By 1805, we find him married to the former Adélaïde Charlotte Heu.

As a hardware store owner, he would have sold gardening tools in particular, because there were still at that time numerous gardens in Paris, particularly in the southern quarters where the Revolution had dispossessed numerous religious houses. Thus it was that a few hundred yards from Vibert's store could be found, in the rue St.-Jacques, the garden of Monsieur Dupont, a great rose fancier, collector, and breeder patronized by the Empress Joséphine; in his *jardin de Ste.-Marie*, he had brought together all of the roses then known to Europeans, making it a demonstration garden—a veritable "school of roses." [SHP36/140-141, L-D] Perhaps through professional relations, or perhaps only out of initial curiosity, Vibert began a friendship with Monsieur Dupont, which developed his taste for roses and their culture. Vibert had himself put together a small collection of roses in 1810 in a Parisian garden near the then limits of the city, on the Boulevard Montparnasse [SHP36], an area then rather out in the countryside. Thus began his career as a *rosiériste*.

Though the term of his loan was ten years, falling due in 1815, Vibert had reserved the right to make occasional payments against the debt, a provision which he made use of, repaying 8,000 francs November 5, 1808, and another 10,000 the 5th of March in 1812, all of which would seem to indicate that he was prospering. But, about 1811 or 1812, he sold his hardware store and left Paris with his wife and three children Théodore, Aimée, and Adélaïde, for the village of Soisy-sous-Etioles, along the Seine, about 18 and a half miles from Paris. [MCN] This town was the cradle of his mother's family. [ECS; "mother," not "wife" as one sees elsewhere.] His father, now retired from business, was the town's mayor; and two of his own sisters lived there. [MCN, ECS] Vibert seems to have stayed only a short time in Soisy. Having doubtless found better ground for his roses, in 1813 he went north to Chennevières-sur-Marne, where he would stay until 1827. The third and final payment on the loan was made on the due date in 1815, the mortgage on the collateral being released on the 18th of August. That same year, the respected Jean Descemet, who had bred roses since about the year 1800 in St. Denis, near Paris [V1], and was in 1815 indeed mayor of the city, was obliged to flee the country in the aftermath of the allied English, Prussian, and Russian invasion following Napoléon's loss at Waterloo June 18. Descemet's nursery was evidently sacked by the invading armies; and requests for indemnification from the French government went unheeded. [Go] Vibert thereupon purchased from a no-doubt anxious Descemet his nursery stock and, it appears, other "movables" at the site, in particular those of Descemet's breeding notes which were not destroyed in the invasion, as well as ten thousand rose seedling of all ages, comprising the progeny of perhaps 250 individual species and varieties. During a season unfavorable for such an undertaking, on August 3, 1815, Vibert moved all of these young plants to his nursery at Chennevières. Nearly all the stock survived and bloomed in the following years, providing more than a hundred new varieties "which later proved of consequence in the culture of this plant [*i.e., the Rose*]." [SHP29/146] He was becoming known; the very first Hybrid China, introduced that year, was named after him.

"*What luck!*" one would be tempted to exclaim on learning of all of this; "*These must have been happy, prosperous years for Vibert and his family!*" But Fate would have it otherwise. Just a month later came the death of his five-year-old daughter Adélaïde, on September 4, 1815, at the house of her grandparents at Soisy [ECS], staying there no doubt while Jean-Pierre and Adèle were trying to accommodate Descemet's material at what must now have been a very crowded nursery. [SHP29/146, L-D] A few months later, on February 17, 1816, occurred the sad death of his young wife (age 30) [ADVM, ADY], leaving him to raise his two remaining children Théodore and Aimée alone. Later that year, in the pages of Vibert's first commercial catalog [SHP29/150], could be found a new Gallica rose—'Adèle Heu'.

Oddly enough, in that busy year of 1815 he had requested and obtained the post of tax-collector at Chennevières for that community and for two others nearby—doubtless to supplement his income. This sort of job, however, was not very time-consuming, and did not affect his horticultural work nor the publication of his catalogs. He retained this office for some twelve years. [ADY, ADVM, ADE, SHP29] In 1820, his useful and interesting essay *Observations sur la Nomenclature et le Classement des Roses* was published, followed in 1826 by the first *cahier* of his equally meritorious *Essai sur les Roses*. Meanwhile, in 1825, he began selling the important 'Gloire des Rosomanes', one of the most influential roses of all. Enlarged by several purchases over the years, his nursery had by now attained the size of about 4 hectares, almost entirely devoted to roses, though he also grew fruit-trees as something of a fancier. [SHP29/147] Also in 1825, he introduced into France the new yellow Tea ('Parks' Yellow Tea-Scented China', as it came to be called; he called it 'Thé Jaunâtre'—"yellowish Tea") from England [SHP29/149], a plant which was at length to be of the greatest importance to French—and general—rose progress. He also introduced into France at this time the yellow Banksia and the Roxburghii (Microphylla). [SHP29/149] Plagued by insects (cockchafers) and their depredations at Chennevières, he moved operations to Descemet's old community of St. Denis in January of 1827, choosing the site with care, though the acreage was slightly smaller than that which he had at Chennevières. [SHP29/147, SHP36/142] It was also in this year that he became a founding member of the Société d'Horticulture de Paris, the first of its sort in France. [SHP27]

Wide travel, to find new roses to offer and breed with, was part of his regular business practice. In 1829, he happened to be visiting the somewhat abandoned garden of an Englishman in Rouen when he found there a valuable Damask Perpetual, parent of his special 'Trianon' line of DPs which was to be developed by him and his successors for some 50 years [dH47/282], plants not only important in the beauty they brought—and bring—to gardens, but also of immense importance in their position as parents, with the Bourbons, Hybrid Chinas, etc., of the original Hybrid Perpetuals, which were in turn to be a parent of the predominant rose of the Twentieth Century, the Hybrid Tea.

In January, 1835, evidently intending to retire, as we gather from the above excerpt from *Revue-Horticole*—he was now 58 years old—he sold his property at St. Denis and moved to Longjumeau, just south of Paris, taking with him not only his roses but also 267 fruit trees and numerous grape vines. [SHP36/143] Soon, however, his plans of retirement changed. In 1836, he wrote, "My firm, which I founded in 1815 and where only roses are cultivated for sale, is the first of its sort which has existed in France. Thirty years of practice in this specialty, numerous and repeated experiments with all adjuncts of rose culture, and longstanding habits of scrutiny, study, and comparison of the products of this beautiful family—such at least are the claims which I have on the public's confidence. I quite know that the long and sustained welcome which Science, Fanciers, and Commerce have been so kind as to honor me with imposes obligations on me, and thus it is that I have decided to respond to these marks of favor by putting off retirement. "To cover the costs of my garden, and, above all, to husband my time—these are my goals. Without seeking to extend my [*commercial*] relations, I will with pleasure accept orders from those people who understand what it costs these days in time, care, and money to obtain truly distinct novelties...I will always continue with my seedlings—I will never abandon them; I will propagate them, and the greater part of my material will be from them. Forced to accommodate the demands the business, I have deleted from my stock, over several years, many roses which are in small demand…My goal is to grow, for sale, only the most interesting roses of each group—those in which the characteristics are the most distinct. Thus it is that, wanting to break up the uniformity of color—sometimes too frequent in our single-colored roses—I have for a long time devoted myself to marbled roses, striped roses, spotted roses, and the like. If, with such Roses so worthy of interest, I have any success, it would perhaps only be the due of my long perseverance…This year's catalog, though it contains about 150 thoroughly new, undistributed, good roses, is far from showing all those which I grow. I have seen, for several years, so many grave errors committed by those who hurry to propagate [*unknown roses*] from untrue descriptions or faulty observations that I can hardly believe my eyes. A propagator who buys [*new material*] too cheaply and too quickly is the failing of the day; making a sale is the prime interest of certain people who don't even know the names of the roses they send out!…My 'school' [*demonstration garden*], which encompasses more than 1,300 specimens, nearly all own-root, will always be kept up with great care in a manner which will leave no doubt as to the true identity of the species or varieties which make it up. These specimens, which will not be sold, are just the thing to help fanciers make their choice. No other such school…exists in Paris or anywhere thereabouts." [V4]

Vibert's old enemies the cockchafer grubs proved daunting at Longjumeau, and after a mere three years there, he left in 1839 and went to Angers, far from his long-accustomed Parisian environs, and much to the distress of Parisian rose-fanciers: "The largest and most complete rose nursery—that of Monsieur Vibert—is being moved from Longjumeau to Angers. Fanciers regret this move…but hope that, in imitating this Dean of Rosarians, they are able to come up with worthy successors who have not only his knowledge but also his integrity." [R-H39] He had long since entered into good commercial relations with the horticulturists in the region of Angers, France, a region which boasted rosarians both numerous and qualified. He knew as well that the Angevin sun seemed less favorable to the growth and spread of vermin. [V8] Another reason could have been that agriculture there in the valley of the Loire, and the proverbial mild conditions of the region. Vibert, always of course interested in roses, was interested not only in fruit trees but also in grape vines. At St. Denis as well as at Longjumeau he had grown grape vines for the production of raisins; but the Parisian region was not sunny enough, and the raisin, if it ripened at all, did not usually have a high enough sugar content.

In Angers, he seems to have kept up his industriousness and his contacts, indeed visiting England at some point [L-D], no doubt calling on the then-young William Paul and Thomas Rivers, the latter of whom had himself been raising roses since about 1820. Vibert indeed received Rivers at his own premises one day: "In the month of July, 1842, I [*Rivers*] was at Angers, and looking over the gardens of Monsieur Vibert, when his foreman brought me a bouquet of yellow Roses, some in bud and some about half expanded. I had never in my life-time seen anything so beautiful [*as the soon-to-be-released 'Chromatella'*]." [C] From the end of 1843, he added to each of his rose catalogs a catalog of raisin vines, and at the same time mingled articles on the Vine with those on the Rose. Always full of energy, in 1845, at the age of 68, he once again moved to enlarge his premises, staying however in the conurbation of Angers.

But another sadness came into his life. His son, Théodore, an artist, died in 1850. We do not know if this loss prompted the elder Vibert's actions, but, in 1851, he sold the Angers business to his gardener Monsieur Robert—probably the aforementioned foreman with the yellow roses—and retired to the countryside back in the environs of Paris at Montfort l'Amaury, a calm, picturesque area surrounded by forests. Here, at his ease, finally able to have his time to himself, he wrote occasional articles an letters for various publications, and no doubt tended his personal collection of roses, keeping up these activities for some fifteen years. Around the end of 1865, at age 88, he wrote an article on anomalies in roses the for journal of the Société Nationale d'Horticulture, which had grown out of the organization he helped found nearly forty years before (the Société d'Horticulture de Paris), "and more recently wrote the Société several letters with some interesting facts." [V7] "Some days before his death," reports his grandson Jehan-Georges Vibert, the son of Théodore, "while arranging his daily bouquet in a vase, he said to his grandson: 'See, my child, a man knows truly what he has loved best on earth only when in his last days he finds it still in his heart. Like the rest of the world, I have thought that I adored and detested many men and many things. In reality I have loved only Napoleon and roses. Today, after nearly a century of rebellion against all the unjust things I have seen and all the evils from which I have suffered, there remain to me only two objects of profound hatred: the English, who overthrew my idol, and the white worms that have destroyed my roses.'" (The previous is from the pages of vol. 51 of *The Century* magazine, for which Jehan Georges Vibert wrote articles, in English; a recent foreign author has reported a varying, later, version of this which is at odds with other known facts about Jean-Pierre Vibert's opinions; the above is the original version as presented to *The Century* magazine by J. G. Vibert.) Soon after, on January 27, 1866, four days before his 89th birthday, he died "about two in the morning in his home" [V5], "without suffering" [V7].

Of miscellaneous information, we have the following. "Monsieur Vibert is not only an excellent horticulturist; he is also an enlightened writer." [SNP29/149] And indeed, in addition to the works mentioned above, he also provided many detailed and professional articles on various aspects of horticulture, such as on the artificial cross-breeding of roses in the 1831 *Annales de la Société d'Horticulture de Paris* (pp. 68-71), on the acclimation of plants [SHP37/129-134], on grape vines (in the 1850 edition of *Mémoires de la Société Centrale d'Agriculture*), two on his nemesis the cockchafer grub (1827 and 1863), various articles on the physiological effects of grafting and budding roses or grape vines (1846, 1851, two in 1865), and, in 1827, a long a masterly counter-attack to certain hazy assertions made by Monsieur Pirolle, another horticulturist of the day. His spirited grandson Jehan Georges Vibert, of Paris, the very successful "*artiste-peintre*" who lived from September 30, 1840 to July 28, 1902), was a witness at the recording of J.-P. Vibert's death, which was also witnessed by Charles E. Souhaité, "age 34, friend of the deceased." [V5] In 1867, Moreau-Robert, successor to his old firm back in Angers, dedicated a Mossy Remontant to him, 'Souvenir de Pierre Vibert', a rose which is still extant. Napoleonic soldier, tireless experimenter in rose breeding, traveler, writer—indeed, controversialist—perhaps he was inspired by the meaning of his name; "Vibert," one finds, is a form of "Guibert" or "Gilbert," which is a Teutonic name meaning "War-Bright," or (more prosaically) "he who is illustrious in combat." Thus it was with Jean-Pierre Vibert. "We should wreathe his tomb with our homage and our respect." [V6]

Buffon (Breeder unknown,-1821) syn. 'Joséphine'
"Pale rose." [Cal] "Having large, plump [*pommées*] blossoms, like the Centifolia; very double; flesh." [BJ30] "*Flowers*, middle-sized, very full, pale pink." [Go] Comte Georges Louis Leclerc de Buffon, influential French naturalist and theorist, lived 1707-1788.

Capitaine Rénard (Breeder unknown,-1843) syn. 'Capitaine Raynard', 'Rose du Roi Strié', 'Striped Crimson Perpetual'
"A very fickle flower, is usually pale flesh color, striped with crimson, but some flowers lose the stripe entirely." [WRP] "Blossom large, very full; color, white." [S]

Casimir Delavigne (Vibert, 1848)
"Blossom large, full, nuanced lilac." [S] "Flowers full, from 8-9 cm across [ca. 3 ¼ inches], violet-red and crimson; globular form." [M-V49/233]

Celina Dubos (Dubos, 1849) syn. 'Céline Dubois', 'Rose du Roi à Fleurs Blanches'
Sport of 'Rose du Roi' (DP)
"We are unable to resist the pleasure of noting…a new variety which is both perpetual and very remontant, called 'Célina Dubos'." [R-H49]

"White or nearly white…worthy of attention both from its origin and quality…its flowers are well shaped, very durable, and highly fragrant." [R8] "Medium-sized, full, lightly blushed white." [BJ] "Grayish white." [S] "The new white Damask Perpetual 'Célina Dubos', with very pale blush center, though believed to be a sport from 'Rose du Roi', is very constant, and is the nearest approach to white amongst the Perpetuals." [HstX:398]

Céline Bourdier (Robert, 1852)
"6-7 cm [ca. 2 ½ inches], full, bright red." [R&M62] "Vigorous bush; canes upright, very thorny; flower medium-sized, full; petals folded, giving it the form of a rose-window; color, red shaded with lilac." [S]

Céline Dubois
Listed as 'Celina Dubos'.

Césonie (Vibert,-1836)
"Flowers dark rose, large and full; form, compact." [P]

Charlemagne
Listed as 'Président Dutailly'.

Christophe Colombe (Robert, 1854)
"Blossom from 11 to 15 cm [ca. 4 ¼-6 inches], very full, flat, amaranth purple, darker at the center." [l'H55/51] "From 11-13 cm [ca. 4 ¼-5 inches], full, flat, amaranth." [R&M62] "Blossom very large, full, flat; color, grenadine, with a deep ruby center." [S] Christophe Colombe, alias Christopher Columbus, alias Cristoforo Colombo, discovered a New World, or at least a world new to southern Europeans.

Comte de Chambord (Robert & Moreau, ca. 1860)
"Feeble growth; branches with bumps, dingy green, somewhat spiny; flower of moderate size, somewhat full; color, pale flesh." [S] I have been unable to find other published remarks contemporary with the release of this variety. There is suspicion that what is sold in modern times as

'Comte de Chambord' is perhaps actually 'Mme. Boll'; here are comments about what is at present in commerce as 'Comte de Chambord: "Bright pink fading to lilac-mauve...a plump plant...fragrant." [G] "Vigorous erect bush...very fragrant pinkish lilac, full, flat flowers...continuously. Outstanding...3×3 [ft; ca 1×1 m]." [B]

D'Italie
Listed as 'Quatre Saisons d'Italie'.

D'Italie Rose
Listed as 'Quatre Saisons d'Italie'.

Damas d'Italie
Listed as 'Quatre Saisons d'Italie'.

Delambre (Robert & Moreau, 1863)
"Carmine." [LS] "Double, deep reddish pink flowers freely produced on a compact plant with good foliage...3×2 [ft; ca. 9×6 dm]." [B]

Desdémona (Vibert, 1841)
"Medium-sized, double, carmine-red." [V8] "Of a carmine-red hue, delightfully fragrant, but sometimes fails to bloom well in autumn." [WRP] "For its delicate colour, and exquisite fragrance, is worthy of culture, though its tendency to autumnal blooming merely, is discouraging." [Bu] Desdemona, victim of Othello's jealousy in Shakespeare's tragedy.

Dombrowski
Listed as a Hybrid Bourbon.

Double
Listed as 'La Moderne'.

Duchess of Portland
Listed as 'Portlandica'.

[**Duchesse de Montmorency**] (R. Lévêque, 1844)
"Flower, double, large, globular, and of a fine bright satiny rose color."
[MH45/28]. "Blossom large, very full, cupped; color, delicate pink, shaded lilac; much to be recommended for its late bloom." [S]

Duchesse de Rohan (R. Lévêque, 1847)
"Lilac pink." [LS] "Growth very vigorous; leaves dark green, often touched black; flower large, full, opening with difficulty; more to be recommended for its buds than for its blossom; color, bright pink bordered very delicate pink." [S] "Canes large and vigorous, with small, numerous, recurved, yellowish-brown thorns; leaves comprised of 5 medium-sized leaflets, fairly frequently bullate, regularly and finely dentate, fresh green, borne on an upright, strong stalk; blooms in a bouquet of 3 or 5, ovary medium-sized, nearly turbinate, without constriction [*at the neck*]; sepals longly foliaceous. Flowers 8-10 cm across [to 4 inches], very full, plump, beautiful bright red nuanced dark violet. The first rows of petals are a paler pink, making it look like one of our beautiful Gallicas." [An47/19]

[**Ebène**] (Boyau, 1844) trans., "Ebony"
"Medium-sized, full, changeable violet purple." [BJ53] "Medium-sized, double, violety purple, the darkest of the sort." [V8] "Weak-growing plant; blossom medium-sized, full; color, violet purple." [S] "Although not so black as ebony, yet very dark. I have seen it, in fine sunny dry weather, of that beautiful dark velvety colour peculiar to the Tuscany Rose; and this is its character in France. In moist weather, however, it becomes stained with a dingy brown, and it is then really any thing but pretty: it blooms freely in autumn, and gives very double and well-shaped flowers." [R9]

Félicité Hardy (Hardy, ca. 1831) syn. 'Mme. Hardy'
This is the rose much better known in modern times as 'Mme. Hardy', and as a Damask. We remember it here, under its release name, with an early description, due to its being a Damask Perpetual hybrid, as we see:
"Hybrid of Portland and Damask...dedicated to Mme. Hardy. A very

vigorous bush with long, erect canes which are light green and armed with numerous unequal thorns, long and straight for the most part; the leaves are large and smooth, nearly all with 7 leaflets which are regularly dentate, a handsome green above and slightly pubescent beneath. One notes that here, as with many other roses, the lower leaves have oval-rounded leaflets, while the higher leaves are oval-elliptical. The leafstalk is hispid and slightly prickly. The blossoms are a very pure white, full, flat above, 3 ¾ inches across [ca. 8 cm], centifolia perfume, in corymbs on long and strong thorny stems; bud large, round, pink outside; ovary oval, hispid; some sepals become foliaceous at the top and pinnatifid on the sides. This rose is one of the best introductions in a long time." [R-H32] We give further remarks on this rose in our book *The Old Rose Adventurer.*

Grand Perpetual
Listed as 'Belle Fabert'.

Gros Fruit
Listed as 'La Moderne'.

[Henriette] (Italy,-1811) syn. 'Bifera Italica'
"Wood strong and vigorous, not very many thorns. Leaves very beautiful, deeply cut, gay green. Calyx big, elongate, glabrous, top constricted. Bud pointed, beautiful shape, overtopped by its sepals, seven or eight on the same stem. The blossom is large, not very double, but well formed, a beautiful delicate pink, very fragrant, blooming from June 10 to 15. A single stem, with its leaves and half-open buds, makes a nice bouquet." [C-T] "This variety of the Damask Rose came to us from Italy; wood strong, vigorous, clothed with few thorns; its leaves are a light gay green; calyx fat, elongate, and glabrous. Buds pointed and well covered by the extension of the calyx, seven or eight on the same peduncle; flower large, and not very double, well formed, of a delicate color of pink, very fragrant. One lone branch, accompanied by its leaves, buds, and blossoms, can make a perfect

bouquet of the nicest appearance. Opens from the 10th to the 19th [*of June*]." [LeR] There is probable synonymy between 'Henriette', 'Henriette Boulogne', and 'Quatre Saisons d'Italie', with which lattermost 'Henriette' already shares its synonym 'Bifera Italica'.

Henriette Boulogne (Breeder unknown,-1839)
"Flesh." [TCN, where listed as "less freely remontant."] "Pink, large, full, cupped." [LF] "A good rose, but rather an inconstant autumnal bloomer." [WRP] Probably synonymous with 'Henriette' and 'Quatre Saisons d'Italie', *qqv*. If we accept this synonymy, the "Boulogne" part of the name of this cultivar is possibly owing to the arrival of this cultivar from Italy via the much-respected rosarium of the botanist Dumont de Courset, located in Boulogne, France.

Indigo (Laffay,-1845) syn. 'Perpétuelle Indigo'
"Bluish violet, velvety, quite novel in tint." [MH45/Aug.Ad.3] "Blossom large, full, flat; color, deep grenadine." [S] "Medium-sized, double, slaty deep violet, flat." [R&M62] "Flowers medium size, very double, flat, and of a very dark purple. This is one of the Portland or old perpetuals [*as opposed to the "new" Hybrid Perpetuals*]." [MH45/28] "'Indigo', like ['*Ebène*'], a new rose, is equally extravagantly named: this was raised from seed by Monseiur Laffay. I have been quite at a loss to conceive how he could by any fair means imagine the colour of this rose to be indigo; he might certainly, with equal justice, have named it ultramarine, for it is as much like one as the other: in colour it is of a deep slaty purple; flowers, rather flat and not fully double." [R9]

Iolande
Listed as 'Yolande d'Aragon'.

Jacques Amyot (Varangot, 1844)
"Lilac-pink." [LS] "Deep rose, fine." [FP] "Short canes." [JDR54/45] "Vigorous, climbing, practically thornless." [S] "Canes reddish at first, later changing to dark green, with occasional small thorns, canes very

noticeable due to the young buds, which are violet or reddish. Leaves composed of 5 leaflets, sometimes 7, oval-pointed, beautiful dark green, finely and regularly dentate; stem big and thick, long, reddish, covered with glandular bristles which are close-set; sepals elongate and foliaceous. Flower very full, from 7-9 cm across [to ca. 4 inches], beautiful purplish red, double; the central petals are for the most part split in bud [*fendus en bouton*]. This flower resembles a beautiful purple Ranunculus." [dH45/279] "Seed-bearing by this new variety is almost out of the question. The blossom looks ordinary enough, but all the stamens have become petaloid; the pistil, for its part, has developed a sort of pink crater at its tip, where may be found scaly petaloids as well as nectar from each of the young ovules." [R-H51] Jacques Amyot, Bishop of Auxerre and translator, lived 1513-1593. The situation with 'Jacques Amyot' continues very confused; there are persistent reports of a Noisette 'Jacques Amyot', with attribution "Varangot, 1850"—though we have been unable to track down positive evidence of it. If the two are to be separated, then, the DP is red-purple, and the Noisette is deep rose or lilac-pink.

Jacques Cartier (Moreau-Robert, 1868)

There is confusion between this variety and the shorter 'Marquise Boccella', which also see. "Vigorous; light pink, center darker; flower large, full." [S] "About 100 mm across [ca. 4 inches]...clear rich pink...fading to paler pink...quartered, have button eyes...fragrant." [G] "Full, flat...clear pink. Recurrent...a strong scent...4×3 [ft; ca. 1.25 m×9 dm]." [B] Though poorly represented in the old literature, this is one of the great varieties among old roses. The bush grows thick and tall, to perhaps 6 ft (ca. 2 m) when established and happy, making a deep green, healthy plant (only slight touches of mildew); contrariwise, 'Marquise Boccella' barely reaches up to 3 ft high. 'Jacques Cartier' blooms heavily in the first flush of bloom, then off and on for the rest of the growing season; bloom on 'Marquise Boccella' is sparse throughout the growing season. Aside from height and floriferousness, the two varieties appear identical.

[Jeanne Hachette] (Vibert,-1836)
"Flowers lilac rose, large and double; form, globular." [P] "Bush with short canes; leaves a pale green; calyx-tube very fat, often being an inch long [ca. 2.5 cm] and ten *lignes* around [ca. 1¼ inch/3 cm]; flowers full, very large, a very light pink at the center, and paler yet along the edges." [MaCo] Boitard allots the obtention of this variety to Coquerel, possibly correctly (possibly not); one wonders if there is confusion with a pre-1829 Damask—or if the pre-1829 Damask was really a Damask Perpetual—and Vibert's Gallica 'Jeanne Hachette' is no doubt contributing to the confusion.

Jeune Henry (Descemet,-1815) trans., "Young Henry"
"Velvety red." [LS] "Red, medium size, full, tall." [Sn] "*Branches*, tinged with purple. *Flowers*, full, purplish, of a deep vivid red." [Go] Not to be confused with Vibert's Centifolia of the same name, which was bright pink.

Joasine Hanet (Vibert, 1846) syn., 'Johasine Hanet'
"Flower 5-6 cm across [ca. 2 ¼ inches], full, purple-red." [M-L46/274] "6 cm [ca. 2.3 inches], full, purple red, corymbiferous, in a rosette." [VPt47/126] "Vigorous; flower medium-sized, full, growing in clusters, very floriferous; color, bright grenadine." [S] The foundling rose making the rounds under several names such as 'Portland from Glendora' appears to us to be this rose.

Johasine Hanet
Listed as 'Joasine Hanet'.

Joséphine
Listed as 'Buffon'.

Jules Lesourd (Robert & Moreau, 1863)
"Light red." [Jg] "7-8 cm [ca. 3 inches], full, globular, very bright red." [M-R65]

Julie de Krudner (Laffay, 1847)
"Pale flesh; form, compact." [P] "Remontant." [JR20/149] "Growth very vigorous; flower medium-sized, full; flesh pink." [S]

La Moderne (Breeder unknown,-1820) syn. 'À Fleur Double', 'Double', 'Gros Fruit'; trans., "The Modern One"
"Blush." [Cal] "*Shrub*, with feeble thorns. *Flowers*, large, semi-double, of a pale purplish pink." [Go]

[**La Volumineuse**] (Breeder unknown,-1835) trans., "The Massy One"
"Flesh-pink." [S-V] "Intense flesh." [TCN] "Rosy blush, worthless." [P] "A magnificent rose, very large and finely shaped; but, though it often blooms finely in autumn, it must not be depended upon as a true perpetual." [R9] Not to be confused with the Agathe 'Volumineuse'.

Laurent Heister (Robert & Moreau, 1859)
"Slaty carmine." [LS] "Blazing carmine." [Ÿ] "Very remontant." [AnM-L59/36] "Vigorous bush, blossom from 7-9 cm across [ca. 2.75-3.5 inches], full, light lilac pink, perfect form. In form, this plant resembles the Gallica 'Comte [Boula] de Nanteuil'." [AnM-L59/212]

Le Prince de Galles (Breeder unknown,-1826)
"Deep pink." [V3] "Deep pink." [BJ40] "Bush with purplish, unarmed canes; leaflets smooth, large, dark green, sharply dentate; calyx-tube narrow and extremely long; sepals terminating in a very long point; blossom large, full; light red, or deep bright pink." [S] Not to be confused with the ca. 1845 Hybrid Perpetual, which was cerise, lighter at the edges.

Lee's Crimson Perpetual
Listed as 'Rose du Roi'.

Lelieur
Listed as 'Rose du Roi'.

Lesueur (Robert, 1853)
"7-9 cm [ca. 2¾-3½ inches], full, violety red pink, cupped, in a rosette, in clusters." [R&M62] "Flowers large, full, violet red-pink, cupped, well-formed, in a rosette; in a corymb; wood and foliage dark green." [l'H54/12] "Very vigorous bush; flower large, full, formed of very muddled petals, and growing in corymbs; color, reddish violet." [S]

[Louis-Philippe I] (C. Duval, 1832)
Seedling of 'Rose du Roi'.
Purplish red." [TCN] "Carmine." [LS] "Crimson, shaded with dark purple; form, expanded; colours rich and fine. A good seed-bearer." [P] "Very large, full flowers, deep violet, elegant fragrance." [An32/312] "Bush vigorous, with young canes knobbly; thorn very numerous, fine, unequal and slightly curved,; leaves large, composed of seven oval leaflets which are evenly dentate, and which have several prickles under the rachis; calyx-tube pear-shaped; flowers very large, full, a beautiful deep violet, grouped in threes to fives." [MaCo] "Its immense size, under proper cultivation, and its dark purple colour, make it even yet desirable: it is also a true perpetual." [R9]

Marbrée (Robert & Moreau, 1858) trans. "Marbled"
"Very large, full; bright rose-pink, marbled white." [S] "A many petalled, sizable rose of clear, rose pink, marbled white. Little or no fragrance...4×2 [ft.; ca. 1.25×.6 m]." [B] In what I have seen in commerce, the flower is neither "full" nor "many petalled," but aggressively semi-double, opening flat. A very good variety to use for breeding purposes, passing on its marbled appearance.

Marie de St.-Jean (Damaizin, 1869)
"Growth pretty vigorous; canes medium-sized, slightly thin, upright; bark light green, with numerous dark gray, fine, straight, unequal thorns. Leaves, glaucous green, strongly nerved, divided into 3 or 5 oval-rounded, finely dentate leaflets; leafstalk slender, armed with some small prickles.

Flowers about 2 ¼ inches across [ca. 6 cm], very full, plump, nearly always solitary; color, pure white; outer petals fairly large, center petals smaller and muddled; pretty bud, white shaded carmine; flower stalk short and glandulose. Calyx tubular; sepals leaf-like. This variety has the look of 'Rose du Roi', and is very remontant and very fragrant; hardy." [JF]

Marie Robert (Robert, ca. 1850)

"Frosty pink." [LS] "Lilac pink." [Ÿ] Not to be confused with the Noisette of the same name.

Marquise Boccella (Desprez/Cochet, 1840)

"Rich rosy blush, distinct, perfect." [WRP] "Pink, large." [HoBoIV/319] "Medium-sized, full, flesh with darker center." [Pq] "Delicate flesh, a decided acquisition among a class of Roses the prevailing colours of which are purple and crimson." [P2] "Light pink; a stout and short grower; the petals are singularly reflexed." [MH51] "Circumference almost blush, large and full; form compact. Habit, erect; growth, robust. A beautiful Rose, and very sweet; the petals small in comparison with others of the group, but more numerous." [P] "Very fragrant; very pretty exhibition rose; handsome light green foliage." [S] "The most abundant bloomer." [HstXI:224] "Very pale flesh; habit dwarf—more so than any of the preceding [*a group including, in part, 'Baronne Prévost' (HP), 'Duchesse de Sutherland' (HP), and 'La Reine' (HP)*], and very compact." [MH49] "In habit it is dwarf, and yet very robust; its flower-stems are very stiff and erect; colour pale blush; flowers large, very double, and fragrant." [R9] "This rose was raised at Yèbles...by Monsieur Desprez, one of the great hybridists of our time...[It] is one of the remontant hybrids of unknown provenance, or Portlands, under the same heading as 'Rose du Roi'. One can reproach such varieties for hiding their light under a bushel basket, as it were, by bearing their flowers down in the foliage...It is trying that we cannot obtain Portlands which are perfectly remontant and of a color other than a more or less dark pink...It has been available to the public since 1840, and up till now has not been surpassed; what is more, it doesn't even have any serious rivals...Leafy branches furnished with numerous prickles or short harmless bristles; stipules with narrow 'wings,' smooth, ciliate, attached to the petiole at nearly a right angle, an arrangement forming two auricles or acute 'teeth' at the base of the leaf; flower stalks very short, bristling with red bristles; ovary glabrous, elongate; sepals foliaceous, rugose; blossom surrounded by foliage, ordinarily opening one or two buds." [PlB] There has been modern confusion between this variety and 'Jacques Cartier'; the primary difference between the two appears to be height—'Marquise Boccella', as we have seen, is "stout and short," and "habit dwarf...and very compact"; contrariwise, the plant in modern commerce as 'Jacques Cartier' easily reaches to six feet (2 m) in a season, whether grafted or own-root.

Mathilde Jesse (Laffay, 1847)
"Fiery red." [Jg] "Flame pink." [LS]

Miranda (de Sansal, 1869)
"Flower large, full; color, delicate pink." [S] "3.2 inches across [ca. 8 cm], semi-double, fragrant, recurrent; growth upright, medium." [Kr] A beautiful and "different" Damask Perpetual, the flowers informal and graceful. Not to be confused with the white China nor the purple-red Gallica, both of the same name. Miranda, the charming and modest daughter of Prospero in Shakespeare's *The Tempest*.

Mme. Boll
Listed as a Hybrid Perpetual.

Mme. Ferray
Listed as 'Bernard'.

Mme. Knorr
Listed as a Hybrid Perpetual.

Mme. Souveton (Pernet père, 1874)
"Medium growth; bloom abundant and continuous; flower medium-sized, fairly full, cupped, delicate pink touched with white." [S]

Mogador (Varangot, 1844) syn. 'Rose du Roi à Fleurs Pourpres'
Sport of 'Rose du Roi'.
"Brilliant crimson, often shaded with rich purple, large and full; form, cupped. Habit, branching; growth, moderate. A superb kind." [P] "Flowers medium-sized." [S] "Cupped and elegant: its flowers are, perhaps, a little more double than are those of its parent; and its habit is more robust." [R8] "Evidently a more constant bloomer at Monsieur Varangot's [*than 'Rose du Roi'*] but reverts to the type in many areas." [R-H46] "Branches with red bristles; thorns very small; foliage light green with a yellow tint; flower to 4 inches [ca. 1 dm], full; center petals recurved, dark red, often violet-purple." [R-H44] "Thorns...thick, closely-set. Foliage...5-7 leaflets of medium size, pointed, regularly dentate; flower stem strong, upright, reddish, also bristling with thick bristles, as is the ovary, which is long and covered with glandular hairs; calyx very long, slightly leaf-like [*sepals*]." [dH45/278] "'Rose du Roi à Fleurs Pourpres' is its legitimate appellation. A cultivator in France, *un peu de charlatan*, named it 'Mogador', soon after the French victory over the Moors; and, to give it a name pronounceable by English florists, the principal rose growers have agreed to call it, the 'Superb Crimson Perpetual'. It was last summer, 1845, indeed a most superb rose: colour, brilliant crimson, slightly shaded with purple; shape, cupped and elegant: its flowers were, perhaps, a little more double than those of its parent; and its habit is more robust." [R9] Despite Rivers' comment, it appears that the name 'Mogador' was the one under which this rose was introduced.

[Monthly Rose] (Breeder unknown,-1633) syn. 'Quatre Saisons', 'Tous-les-Mois', 'Year-Round Rose'
"A sort of red Musk Rose bearing its flowers in clusters." [LaQ] "It doesn't grow more than 3 ft high [ca. 1 m]; its name [*'Tous-les-Mois'*] comes from its characteristic of blooming nearly all year when one encourages new growth by pruning after each bloom. Its blossom, a beautiful red, though double is less so than the Centifolia's—but the perfume is more intense. It has three

varieties: flesh-colored, white-flowered, and very pale pink. All make numerous clusters of flowers." [Fr] *"Red Tous-Mois of Gardeners.* The ordinary red 'Tous Mois', grown by all gardeners, has wood a little less prickly [*than that of the Common Damask*], and does not grow as vigorously. Usually, it bears six to ten blossoms on the same petiole. [C-T] The 'Monthly Rose'/'Red Tous-Mois', "grown by all gardeners," was evidently one of the parents of the Bourbon race. For a study of the 'Monthly Rose' and its earliest descendants, please see our book *The Old Rose Informant.*

[**Palmyre**] (Vibert, 1817)
"Flesh." [TCN] "Lilac nuanced pink, full, flat, medium sized, beautiful." [LF] "Blush, with rosy pink centre, of medium size, full; form, compact." [P] "Canes long and vertical; flower medium-sized, double, regular; pale pink becoming flesh." [MaCo] "Following, except in point of colour, the 'Rose du Roi'." [P2] "[Resembles 'Marquise Boccella'.]" [VPt46/83]

Panachée de Lyon (Dubreuil, 1895) trans., "Lyon's Striped One"
Sport of 'Rose du Roi'.
"Very pretty and regular striping of the flowers. The ground color is a uniform China pink with regular brilliant purple-red flames. The form and perfume are those of 'Rose du Roi'." [JR19/148] "Pink striped red." [LS] "Rose, purple, red; vigorous." [TW]

Papa Vibert (Dickerson/Sequoia, 2001)
Seedling of 'Marbrée' (DP).
"Deep pink to Rose, spotted white. The bud is an intense ruby red. This is a much improved version of 'Marbrée', of which it is a seedling, having a more robust plant with better and thicker foliage on bristly, absolutely erect canes growing to three feet [ca. 1 m] or so in height. The blossoms are even more of an improvement over those of 'Marbrée', being more distinctly spotted, fuller, more fragrant, longer lasting, and better shaped, beginning in a globular form; then, as the flower matures, the petals begin to reflex beautifully. The spotting is usually most pronounced in the

Spring. The variety shares its parent's preference for cooler weather, blooming best in the Spring and then again with the return of cooler weather in the Fall, and similarly having a tendency to defoliate at the height of Summer, though not as badly as with 'Marbrée'. The plant is healthy and good in the garden, modestly claiming its own bit of space and not encroaching on or growing over neighboring plants. Can also be used as either a pollen parent or a pod parent by those interested in breeding new Damask Perpetuals. The first blossom on the original plant appeared on Easter Day about the year 1994. This is the first new Damask Perpetual to be released in more than a century, and the first of the new millenium. Named after the great rose-breeder Jean-Pierre Vibert (1777-1866), who delighted in spotted roses." [BCD]

Pergolèse (Robert & Moreau, 1860)
"Amaranth." [LS] "Medium-sized, full, crimson." [S] "Carmine, medium-sized, full." [N] Much like 'Rose de Rescht', but deeper in color, blossoms a bit larger and more regularly formed, and usually coming singly on the stems—a very good color to enrich and deepen the rosarium's palette. Giovanni Battista Pergolesi, Italian composer, lived 1710-1736.

Perpetual Pompon
Listed as 'Bernard'.

Perpetual White Moss
Listed as 'Quatre Saisons Blanc Mousseux'.

Portland Blanc (Vibert, 1836) trans., "White Portland"
"Very pure white." [V4] "Flower medium-sized, double, white, with some flesh before opening." [S] "Biferous, pure white, full, flat, large, superb." [LF] "Medium-sized, full, white, not always opening well." [V8] "Nearly white, a rose of large size, perfect in form, quite fragrant, and a good grower; it is yet scarce, but a few seasons will make it nearly as plentiful as any other variety." [Bu] "A white rose of great beauty; it however rarely opens in our moist climate; a true perpetual rose like it would be invaluable." [R9]

Portland Pourpre (Prévost, ca. 1830) trans., "Purple Portland"
"Deep bright crimson, semi-double." [WRP] "Semi-double, medium, deep purple." [V8] "Bush with weak thorns; flower large, semi-double, light purplish pink." [S]

Portlandica (Breeder unknown,-1775) syn., 'Duchess of Portland', 'Portland Rose'
"Flowers deep rose, tinted with purple, large and semi-double; form, cupped. A pretty colour, and most abundant summer bloomer." [P] "Flowers semi-double, sparkling maroon." [No] "One of the most striking by the brightness of its color, and its precious quality of blooming from Spring to Fall. The leaves are ovate. The thorns which cover the wood are both long and short, all mixed together, and hooked, flesh-color on the young wood. The flower buds are pointed and crowned with lacinated leaflets formed by the elongated sepals. This rose, which is only semi-double, is very flashy; its color is a handsome red which makes it distinct and noticeable among all other sorts, especially in the Fall, when no others of that color are to be found. This rose, grafted on the Briar, forms a good head, and is easily contained by pruning." [C-T]

Président Dutailly (Dubreuil, 1888) syn., 'Charlemagne'
"It sprang from seeds culled from a group of Gallica roses which had not been artificially pollinated. These seeds were sown in 1882. The original plant bloomed for the first time in 1885. The size of its blossoms, its penetrating scent, and its perfect form all attracted the attention of fanciers from the beginning. But when joined with its happy faculty of reblooming, of flowering in the Fall, like the HPs...I could not wait to propagate it, and classed it in a new category, that of Reblooming Gallicas, which, I hope, will be enriched later with other varieties of different colors. Here is its description: Vigorous, with strong canes, erect, covered with numerous small thorns mixed with stiff bristles. Foliage ample, luxuriant, matte green above, glaucescent beneath. Flowers upright, borne on stiff stems which carry 3 or 4 blossoms at the end of the cane; perfectly cupped; buds

globular; petals numerous, gracefully arranged; beautiful crimson red with carmine reflections towards the center, velvety maroon amaranth towards the outside. Elegant and penetrating scent." [JR12/169-170]

Préval (Préval, ca. 1821)
"Flesh." [TCN] "Delicate blush, large and full; form, expanded." [P] "Flowers very double, large, and of a pale pink." [AC] "A fine large flower, of a pale roseate hue, perfect compact form, and fragrant; a free bloomer." [WRP] "Raised, around 1821, by Monsieur Préval, at Eturqueray, between Bourg-Achard and Pont-Audemer, département of Eure. *Ovary*, obconical, glabrous and smooth at the summit, often rayed green on a pale ground. *Flower*, large, full or very multiple, pale pink. This rose is freely biferous, and ordinarily gives more beautiful flowers at the second bloom. Grafted, it is rare that it keeps good growth after the first year." [Pf]

Quatre Saisons
See 'Monthly Rose'.

Quatre Saisons Blanc Mousseux (Laffay, 1835) syn. 'Perpetual White Moss' Sport from 'Bifera'.
"White, buds handsome and well mossed, flowers good size and tolerably double, blooming in clusters." [JC] "White, of medium size, double; form, expanded, blooming in large trusses, very mossy, but produced sparingly in the autumn." [P] "Still an excellent variety; its white blossoms, in tight clusters, make it perhaps the most interesting of the group." [R-H63] May be classed as a Mossy Remontant.

Quatre Saisons d'Italie (Florence/Dupont,-1812) syn. 'Bifera Italica', 'D'Italie', 'D'Italie Rose', 'Damas d'Italie', 'Rosier de la Malmaison'. (See also below.)
"Delicate pink." [RG] "Vermilion, sometimes striped." [Ÿ] "Flowers medium-sized, fairly double, flesh, well-formed as well as plenteous." [J-A] "Bush with diffuse canes; leaflets oval-lanceolate, acute, with teeth which are pointed, villose, and non-glandulose; peduncles glandulose;

tube of calyx obconical, glabrous at the tip; flowers medium-sized, semi-double, fragrant, a light pink or bright flesh in the middle, pale at the edges." [MaCo] "Open *bush* about 0.6 m high [ca. 2 ft]; *prickles* very numerous, small, short, unequal, almost straight. *Leaflets* 5 or 7, large, ovate, bright green, simply serrate, glabrous above, paler and slightly hairy beneath and on margins; petioles villose, with small, yellowish prickles; stipules fairly broad, acute, gland-edged. *Flowers* in threes at the cane-tips; bracts subtending the lateral pedicels elongate, acute; pedicels and *receptacles* glandular-hispid; *sepals* overtop the bud, 3 pinnatifid, 2 simple; *petals* in 4-5 ranks, large, delicate pink, paler towards the base, cordately notched. *Hips* elongate-ovoid, red. This rose stands out among the Damasks by way of its large flowers, often over 7.5 cm across [ca. 3 inches]—but only when on its own roots, as the size is noticeably smaller on grafted specimens. Dupont received it from Florence twenty years ago [*ca. 1805?*] and distributed it. It has little scent, but compensates for this by its grace and elegance. Although long known, it remains rare, but can be seen grafted in Catel's fine collection. On its own roots, it is tender and needs full sun." [T&R] Evidently re-introduced by Victor Verdier in 1865. There was also a white version. Alongside the above-listed synonyms, there are other very probable ones: Vibert lists, in 1820, a non-remontant Quatre-Saisons 'Rose d'Italie', and W. Paul, in 1848, a deep rose 'Belle Italienne'. All of these should be compared with two Damask Perpetuals which we also list, 'Henriette' and 'Henriette Boulogne'; it should be noted that 'Quatre Saisons d'Italic' at least shares its synonym 'Bifera Italica'—if not indeed its very identity—with 'Henriette'.

Rembrandt (Moreau-Robert, 1883)
"Growth very vigorous, very floriferous; flower very large, full; color, vermilion red shaded carmine, sometimes striped white; flower stalk long and strong." [S] "Blooms continuously over a long season. Good foliage well retained. Flowers of cutting value." [Capt28] Rembrandt van Rijn, Dutch artist, lived 1606-1669.

Robert Perpétuel (Robert, 1856) trans., "Perpetual Robert"
"Violet pink, medium size, full, medium height." [Sn]

Rose de Rescht (Breeder unknown, date uncertain)
"Fragrant bright fuchsia-red long blooming…very double…60 mm [ca. 2 inches] across." [G] "Deep rose-red, very double blooms…3×3 [ft; ca. 1×1 m]." [HRG] "Pompom-like. Scented. Abundant foliage. Remontant." [B] "Shrub upright, compact; leaves large, particularly for the size of the plant, dark green, attractive, not much affected by mildew. Blossoms can fade rather quickly to a slaty shade, and do not last long; the fallen petals reveal a bright white nub. Fragrance delicious. Vigorous, but dwarf. One of the most delightful roses." [BCD] Rescht, a provincial capital in Persia. Is it a traditional Persian rose, previously unknown to the West; or is it an old Western rose, brought to Persia probably some time in the 1800s, perhaps during the French rapprochement circa 1807? Research continues.

[Rose de Trianon] (Vibert, ca. 1830)
"Semi-double…pink." [V4] "Bright pink, blooming in large clusters; the plant is of dwarf habit." [WRP] "Flowers rose, of medium size, double; form, cupped." [P] "Full; color, flesh pink; vigorous." [S] 'Adèle Mauzé' which we also list, was also known as 'Rose de Trianon Double'. *Cf.* Prévost fils' 'Belle de Trianon' above.

Rose de Trianon Double
Listed as 'Adèle Mauzé'.

Rose du Roi (Écoffay/Souchet/Lelieur, 1819) syn. 'Lee's Crimson Perpetual', 'Lelieur'; trans., "Rose of the King"
"Bright red, of perfect form, with the fragrance of the old Damask rose, and is a new constant and profuse bloomer." [WRP] "Bright crimson, large, double, very fragrant; occasionally blooms in autumn." [EL] "Flowers, middle-sized, bright red, often more vivid at the second flowering than in the spring. Remarkable from its calyx, which has often six sepals." [Go] "Outer petals large, obovate, the others smaller and smaller

as they approach the center; flower stem short, with numerous glandular hairs. Calyx tubular, slightly constricted at the top, having (like the flower stem) numerous glandular hairs; sepals leaf-like." [JF] "Seeds abundantly...the seedlings will bloom in three years." [Bu] "Very vigorous; branches of medium size and upright; bark light green; reddish where the sun strikes, bristling with very numerous little prickles, unequal and very sharp; foliage light green, slightly bullate, of 5-7 oblong finely-toothed leaflets; leafstalk slender and elongated, pubescent and lacking prickles; flower, about 2.5 inches across [ca. 6 cm], well held, upright, open, usually solitary; color, a handsome bright carmine red with violet reflections. Much recommended, very remontant, and very fragrant." [S]

"One of the most beautiful and remontant and remontant varieties. It is the first to appear in our markets, and the last to give a blossom in our gardens. From the beginning of Spring until frost, the 'Rose du Roi' is, for all intents and purposes, constantly bearing graceful, ravishing flowers, from which escape an agreeable aroma which gladdens the mind and calms our perturbed senses. It was discovered not by Comte Le Lieur [*sic*], former director of the Royal Gardens, as is generally believed; rather, it was Monsieur Écoffay, old gardener of the florist of Sèvres [*Monsieur Souchet*], who raised it is 1819 from seedlings he had sprouted in 1816. Its appearance was greeted with enthusiasm because, at that time, perpetual or quatre-saisons roses were uncommon. To raise so perfect a rose was a veritable triumph; one can see why Comte Le Lieur...or the florist of Sèvres would pose as the father of 'Rose du Roi'." [PlB] "Struck by the plant's constant bloom, Souchet took it to Comte Lelieur...and the mother-plant, carefully tended, flowered beautifully in 1816. It bore at first the name 'Comte Le Lieur', then afterwards took on the name 'Rose du Roi' because of Louis XVIII's regard for it. It is perfectly remontant, and its merit cannot be denied." [JF] "This fine rose was raised from seed, in 1812, in the gardens of the palace of Saint Cloud, then under the direction of Le Comte Lelieur, and named by him 'Rose du Roi'; owing, I suppose, to Louis the Eighteenth soon after that time being restored, and presenting an opportunity for the Comte to show his loyalty: it is not recorded that he changed its name during the hundred days to 'Rose de l'Empereur'! It is asserted that it was raised from the Rosa Portlandica, a semi-double bright-coloured rose...Every gentleman's garden ought to have a large bed of ['Rose du Roi'], to furnish bouquets during August, September, and October: their fragrance is so delightful, their colour so rich, and their form so perfect." [R9] "Evokes the memory of all of a tragic past: 1812—the Russian campaign, the decline of the Empire; many French hearts beating for the return of the Bourbons; and it was this hope which was entrusted to a beautiful rose of an intense red—the color of the blood shed since 1789." [JR31/92] "It is about thirty years since this famous rose was grown from seed in the gardens of one of the royal palaces near Paris, remaining comparatively obscure, and was considered a rare article in England in 1831, where I first saw it growing, carefully surrounded by rods to keep its admirers at a distance. In 1832 or 3 I imported it as the gem of the day, and it is still admitted to be the king of Perpetuals, blooming profusely and perfectly from June until Christmas; the colour is bright red (not crimson,) a perfectly formed flower, with all the fragrance of a Damask Rose, and without any extra pruning never fails to bloom the whole season—richly deserving a place in every garden." [Bu] "I have met with a remark of Monsieur Desprez', the celebrated rose amateur at Yèbles, that he has sown thousands of seeds of 'du Roi'..., and never yet obtained a Perpetual rose. In all, the characters of *Rosa gallica* are visible. But we must remember this variety partakes largely of the nature of the Gallica." [P] "The boundary between Gallica and Portland is not as easy to draw as one might think." [JR12/170] One hears speculation that it was being grown and listed by 1810; but we suspect that there is perhaps confusion with some other rose being called 'Rose du Roi'.

Rose du Roi à Fleurs Pourpres
Listed as 'Mogador'.

Rose du Roi Strié
Listed as 'Capitaine Rénard'.

Rose of Castile
Listed as 'Bifera'.

Rose of Pæstum
Listed as 'Bifera'.

Rosier de la Malmaison
Listed as 'Quatre Saisons d'Italie'.

[Sapho] (Vibert, 1847)
"Flower 5 cm [ca. 2 inches], a lightly fleshed white, full." [M-L46/271] "Flower of medium size, full; color, white, shaded flesh pink." [S] "Blooms in corymbs, blossoms medium to large, double, white." [JR9/88] Announced in 1846. Not to be confused with 'Thé Sapho', a synonym for 'Mrs. Bosanquet' (a Bourbon), nor with the circa 1846 Setigera 'Sappho', nor with the 1889 Tea. Sappho, Greek poetess, fl. 600 B.C.; wrote of roses, but not as their being the Queen of Flowers, it seems.

Sidonie
Listed as 'Sydonie'.

Striped Crimson Perpetual
Listed as 'Capitaine Rénard'.

Sydonie (Vibert, 1847) syn. 'Sidonie'
"Rosy blush, very delicate, and very sweet." [HstVIII:381] "Large flowers of a rose or bright salmon...blooms profusely." [FP] "Soft pink." [JR2/60] "Flesh." [LS] "8 cm [ca. 3 inches], full, pink, superb flower." [M-L47/361] "Blooms four times a year." [JR6/43] "Rose color, medium size, very full, quartered form, very free blooming, very hardy; five to seven leaflets, red thorns. Its poor shape destroys its usefulness." [EL] "Habit, erect." [P] "Blooms in a cluster having 4-10 blossoms, depending upon the plant's

vigor. One notes as well the delicious Damask fragrance. Its flowers, big to very big, a little flat when fully open, have a slightly muddled center. The color is a brilliant soft pink, well-held, remontant until heavy frost, vigorous bush, quite hardy, and very floriferous." [JR6/153-154]

Tous-les-Mois
See 'Monthly Rose'.

[Venusta] (Descemet,-1814) trans., "Charming"
"A new French variety, yet very rare; the flower is of a delicate rosy hue, and very double." [WRP] "Flower medium-sized, full; delicate pink." [S] "*Calyx*, having frequently six sepals. *Flowers*, middle-sized, full, of a very light pink." [Go]

Year-Round Rose
See 'Monthly Rose'.

Yolande d'Aragon (Vibert, 1843) syn. 'Iolande'
"Flowers deep pink, their margin lilac blush, large and full; form, cupped. Habit, erect; growth, robust. The flowers of this variety are produced in immense clusters in summer." [P] "Of a rosy blush color, full double and beautiful." [WRP] "Deep-pink flowers, and is an abundant autumn bloomer." [FP] 'Lilac-rose, flat form, straggling habit, worthless." [EL] "Sumptuous flowers of over 75 mm, [ca. 3 inches]...very double and very fragrant...bright pink towards the centre...tall to about 1.5 metres [ca. 5 ft]...luxuriant light green foliage." [G] "Globular flowers of considerable size. Bright, rich pink in colour. Scented. Growth upright...4×3 [ft; ca. 1.25×1 m]." [B] Yolande d'Aragon, wife of Louis II of Anjou and the Two Sicilies.

Chapter Three

Chinas

"*Rosa chinensis*, Jacq.... Introduced in 1768. Brought from China to England by Captain Ekeberg, who visited Canton in 1766 and 1767...*Rosa semperflorens*, Curt.... Introduced in 1789. Introduced in England in 1789 by William Kerr, then by Slater, and in France in 1798 by Barbier, surgeon from Val-de-Grâce. Blooms constantly, and propagates and hybridizes with ease." [ExRé] "This charming race of Roses was discovered in China by Gustave Ekeberg, Swedish Captain of the Admiralty, in one of his many trips to the Celestial Empire, whence he furthermore brought a Tea tree [*Thea sinensis*], which he introduced into his Scandinavian homeland in 1763. The original of this wonderful class...was described and named by Jacquin in his *Obervationes Botanicæ*,

Vienna, 1764-1771. Ph. Miller, in his *Dictionnaire des Jardiniers...*Paris, 1785, also gives a description of this rose, taken from plants growing in England. One goes on to read that live specimens of the typical form were re-introduced into England ten or fewer years later. According to Lindley, the original plant was a little bush of delicate growth and constitution, with semi-double flowers which were crimson, and which it bore only once a year. The *Botanical History of Roses*, London, 1820, tells us that English gardens of the time already had many magnificent semi-double crimson varieties of *R. chinensis*, but that we, the French, evidently had some much more beautiful which, at that time, were not in the roseries of our cross-channel neighbors. These varieties just mentioned were mainly cultivated at the Trianon by Monsieur Barrier, a distinguished fancier and caretaker of that château; and it was in the city of Rennes where they first saw the light of day, though the name of their fortunate breeder has been forgotten." [JR7/119]

"At the name of a rose so interesting that all its qualities are cherished, which already is responsible for such a great number of varieties, and which, moreover, is so rich in promise, there is a natural curiosity as to who first introduced it to Europe. One finds—not without surprise—that the name of such a man is nearly unknown here [*France*] as well as in England; and that all of my enquiries on the subject seemed to have proven fruitless, when Mr. Sabine, secretary of the London Horticultural Society...let me know the name of the gentleman in question. He bore the name 'Ker,' and took this rose from Canton in China to the garden of the King [*Kew, presumably*] around 1780. It seems that, about the same time, another gentleman by the name of Slater introduced a second variety of dark color, which I alas do not otherwise know.... The Chinas...have alone received from Nature the ability to bloom without interruption; cold, certainly, stops their growth in Winter; but, in their homeland, growth is *not* suspended; and the example of specimens grown here under glass leaves no doubt in that regard. They differ from those roses which we designate 'Perpetuals' [*i.e., Damask Perpetuals*] in that their branches, without exception, are fully floriferous, while with these others they are only partially so. This advantage, so invaluable and unique, does not seem to have excited the same admiration upon introduction to France that it does nowadays…Returning to the origin of its cultivation in France, we find that the first specimen was given to the Jardin des Plantes around 1800, probably by an Englishman—but by whom in particular it is impossible to say. Dr. Cartier, a distinguished fancier, was the second to cultivate it, and it was he who obtaining from sowings in 1804 the full-flowered variety [*'Bengale Centfeuilles'*]. The introduction of the China to France, and, later, that of the Noisette, have had the very greatest influence on the Rose, an influence well worth noting…'Sanguinea', the 'Pompon d'Automne', 'Atro-Purpurea', and, one might say, the greater portion, have, by all pertinent reports, a resemblance in the particulars of their growth to the Common China; a number of them, however, diverge singularly, it is reported, in their ovary and in their internal structure. Let us moreover note that the fruits of 'Sanguinea' as well as those of all the maroon-colored ones very much resemble those of the Gallica…Up to the present [*1826*], white was pretty much the only color not to be found in the Chinas—but that difficulty has now, for the most part, been overcome. I have among my seedlings a very beautiful variety of which all the branches bear blossoms of the purest white, without any tinge of pink or flesh; this rose, somewhat green at the center, is quite double (70-75 petals on grafted specimens); unfortunately, it doesn't set seed. If perhaps this rose can't be classified with the Chinas, it is at least a variety intermediate between them and the Noisettes." [V2] "That which bears the name 'China Rose' and is hawked about the streets as such was raised in the Museum's temperate house; and it was only in 1804 that commerce brought it into the amateur's greenhouse, where it was raised as something marvelous…It was a distinguished Parisian doctor, a great rose fancier, who—the first in France—procured for himself the common China; he presented it to the venerable A. Thouïn, who had only expected to see a Centifolia with the look of a China. Dr. Cartier made numerous sowings of this rose, and, in 1818, obtained the Common China which is so well known in our gardens." [JF]

"We cannot recommend *too* highly to flower-lovers the roses called 'Chinas'; they bloom continuously in our climate, they are richly colored, the plants are hardy, and the perfume is elegant." [JR34/171] "From the first days of Spring until the frosts of Autumn, these charming bushes are covered in flowers…The varieties belonging to this section are quite numerous, and, over many years of seed-sowing, some very curious colors have been obtained. However, in spite of such meritorious novelties, one should not neglect such great old varieties as 'Cramoisi Supérieur', 'Ducher', 'Impératrice Eugénie', 'Sanglant', 'Prince Eugène de Beauharnais', 'Ordinaire' [*i.e., 'Parsons' Pink China*], 'Louis-Philippe', etc., which are always in demand." [JR23/24-25] "So many factors contribute to vary the colors of Roses that it is impossible to satisfactorily classify them in this way…Everyone knows that most of the white Chinas some- times pink, and 'Le Vésuve', 'Le Camélia', and the full-flowered China, though ordinarily pink, are often maroon…The Chinas are very much more variable, by report, than are the other species." [V2] "The China Rose, and all the short-jointed, smooth-barked kinds that are like them in habit, will strike [*root*], bud, graft, grow, and bloom, in any month of the year." [Gl] "They are all fairly hardy, and bloom very freely during summer and autumn when grown in beds or borders of rich, well-drained soil, and in a sunny position. They are not suitable for heavy cold soils or sunless positions. China roses always produce the best effect when grown by themselves." [TW]

The Chinas may conveniently be divided into three sections: (1) Those affiliated with 'Parsons' Pink China', usually having "gay green foliage, plain green on top, ashy green beneath, and little or no purple on the fully-developed [leaflet-] tips." [JR23/104] (2) Those affiliated with 'Slater's Crimson China', usually having "mutable foliage, leaflets sometimes short, sometimes longly oval-lanceolate, sometimes indeed acuminate, depend- ing upon the branch; [leaflets] dark green bordered purple brown within, and around the edges dark green more or less washed purple. Wood slender or fairly slender, nearly upright, making small thick bushes." [JR23/104] (3) "Another group, completely different from the preceding...was obtained by crossing 'Rival de Pæstum' [*a China × Tea hybrid which we list with the Teas*] with 'Mme. Falcot' (T), making a special sort which, crossed again with Falcot gave this series extra floriferousness and attractiveness; and we define it as follows: vigorous, bushy, numerous smooth stems of an upright nature; sparsely thorned, with slightly recurved thorns of a medium size; flexuous, fairly long flower stem; round calyx surmounted by long sepals; foliage dark purplish green; leaflets pretty large, lanceolate, dentate, with sharp prickles beneath the leafstalk; flower medium to large, double, lightly perfumed; color varies from China rose to Indian pink, more or less dark; the most characteristic varieties are: 'Mme. Laurette Messimy', 'Aurore', 'Irène Watts', 'Mme. Eugène Résal', 'Souvenir de J.-B. Guillot', and 'Comtesse du Caÿla'; less characteristic...[is] 'Souvenir de Catherine Guillot'." [JR33/137-139] And so we see that China × Tea hybrids, and Teas with characteristics making them more of the "decorative" class than of the "exhibition" class (less double, less well-formed, smaller blossoms, blooming in clusters) tend to be apportioned to the China group. In many classes, "classness" is a concept rooted in *appearance* and/or *behavior*—entirely appropriate in such a pragmatic art as Horticulture.

"Well! Ker and Gilbert Slater have endowed Europe with our most beautiful Oriental Roses; and yet no one has given a thought to remembering them by bestowing either one or the other's name on any of these most beautiful roses." [PlB]

À Fleurs Blanches
Listed as 'De Cels'.

Agrippina
Listed as 'Cramoisi Supérieur'.

Alba
Listed as 'De Cels'.

Alice Hamilton (Nabonnand, 1903)
From 'Bengale Nabonnand' (Ch) × 'Parsons' Pink China' (Ch)
"Flower very large, semi-full, well formed, large petals, light and sweet perfume; color, brilliant velvety crimson red, madder reflections; pretty, long bud, nearly always solitary; very beautiful, compact, dark green foliage; very vigorous, very floriferous." [JR27/164]

Alice Hoffmann (Hoffmann, 1897)
"Pink, touched cherry." [LS] Alice Hoffmann, daughter of Albert Hoffmann, first rosarian of the Sangerhausen Rosarium.

Animating (China/England,-1817) syn., 'Bengale Animée'
"Crimson." [Ÿ] "Purplish pink." [LS] "Flower small, full; color, pale lilac." [S] "Pale rose." [Cal] "Deep pink." [RG] "Pinkish red China, with a tea scent..., newly imported by the English in 1817...Its wood is vigorous, with leaf and flower like those of the Common China, less delicate than its sisters [*i.e., the adjoining entries in LeRouge's manuscript, the roses 'Belle Cythérée'—alias 'Hume's Blush Tea-Scented China'—and 'La Spécieuse'*], it is a true riddle we have handed the botanist who finds it in commerce as, as with those fair others, there aren't any fanciers who can make it bloom all year." [LeR] "*Canes*, often elongate, and then bearing several leaves with 7 leaflets. *Peduncle* hispid-glandulose. *Ovary* glabrous, oval or ovoid-pyriform, often narrow, swollen at the base and extenuating to the tip into a narrow collar. *Flower* medium-sized, full, fragrant, purplish pink or pale lilac, often poorly formed." [Pf] "0.6 m high [ca. 2 ft] or more if kept in a temperate house; *branches* diffuse, branching; *prickles* sparse, unequal, hooked. *Leaflets* 5 (-7), acute, or ovate, serrulate, green and glossy above, paler beneath; petioles slightly tomentose, with small prickles extending up the midribs of the leaflets; stipules narrow, denticulate, acute. *Flowers* scented, clustered at the branch tips on branching, glabrous peduncles;

pedicels glandular hispid; *receptacles* globose, glabrous; *sepals* entire or pin-natifid, glandular outside; *petals* many-seriate, deep pink, notched, never expanding well. *Hips* pale red. This rose comes from England…and was introduced [*into France*] by Boursault some years ago. The perfume recalls that of *R. indica fragrans* [*that is, the Tea Rose*]. It only flourishes and develops its forking peduncles well under the protection of a temperate house, with free root-run, and is consequently rarely seen outdoors. It is easily propagated by cuttings." [T&R]

[Antoinette Cuillerat] (Buatois, 1897)

"Flower semi-double, electric white on a bright coppery sulphur yellow ground, petals' edges lightly colored violet carmine; vigorous bush forming a compact plant constantly covered with bloom." [JR21/147] "Beautifully formed flowers." [C&Js99]

Archduke Charles

Listed as 'Archiduc Charles'.

Archiduc Charles (Laffay, ca. 1825) syn./trans. 'Archduke Charles'

Affiliated with 'Parsons' Pink China' (Ch).

"Pink, changing to crimson, full, flat, superb." [LF] "Deep red, double and well formed." [Dr] "Rose…margin almost white when newly expanded, gradually changing to rich crimson, from which peculiarity the plant bears flowers of various tints at the same time; very large and full; form expanded." [P1] "Sometimes one-half of the flower is white, the other crimson red." [HstXXX:142] "A noble variety…; the points of the petals are frequently tipped with bright red." [Bu] "I have seen them in France nearly black." [R8] "Very fine show flower." [HstIV:478] "I find it fascinating and delightful, the opening blossoms often being extremely well formed, and laden with a subtle musty banana scent; 2 to 4 inches across [to ca. 1 dm]; often in clusters; profuse; sometimes nodding when fully expanded. Plant compact and leafy with good foliage, large and handsome on the strongest shoots, rich green, some mildew (easily controlled); very decorative with numerous chalky pink, rich pink, glowing rose, and deep crimson blossoms studding the bush. Sets seed rarely, usually in the Fall, though all floral parts appear well and functional throughout the year; ovary oval, characteristic of the Chinas. Most charming and rewarding." [BCD] "Bush of ordinary growth, with upright branches which are smooth, armed with a small number of reddish, curved thorns which are enlarged at the base. Leaves composed of three and more often five slightly lanceolate leaflets of a dark green with regular reddish serrations. Flowers numerous, double, of medium size, in a cluster, regular in form, like a cup. The petals are very intense, brilliant pink. The ovary is glabrous, while the peduncle has small glandular bristles. This charming China…blooms a lot a has a very charming appearance." [An35/373] "We believe it was introduced into England about ten years since [*making 1840*]…this and several of the Indicas we do not recommend to be grown on their own roots, their habit being, when thus grown, to throw up unwieldy suckers, greatly to the detriment of the rest of the plant." [C] "A profuse bloomer, moderate grower. One of the best changeable Roses. Unique." [HstVI:368] "4×3 [ft; ca. 1.25×.9 m]." [HRG] Archduke Charles of Austria, 1771-1847.

Arethusa (W. Paul, 1903)
"Clear yellow, apricot shading. Foliage very good. Growth fair." [Th2] "Flower medium-sized, full, light yellow tinted apricot yellow. Of the 'Queen Mab' sort." [JR30/186] "Creamy yellow tinted orange and shaded with pink on a 3×3 [ft; ca. 1×1 m] plant." [HRG] "Rather ragged petals…[blooms] in clusters. Foliage shiny but somewhat sparse." [B1] "Very floriferous; vigorous." [Cx] Arethusa, a celebrated spring or fountain near Syracuse, Sicily, as well as its naiad.

Aurore (Widow Schwartz, 1897)
Seedling of 'Mme. Laurette Messimy' (Ch).
"Vigorous, delicate foliage tinted purple; flower large, full, ground color golden yellow fading to cream tinted dawn gold and carmine pink. Very beautiful variety." [JR21/148]

[**Beau Carmin**] (Descemet,-1810) trans., "Beautiful Carmine"
"Carmine nuanced with purple-black." [TCN] "Purple maroon, shaded very fine." [JWa] "Flower medium-sized, full; color, velvety carmine red." [S] "A rich dark crimson-shaded rose, raised in the Luxembourg Gardens, and a fine and distinct variety." [R9] Though attributed as above, I have found no listings for it antedating 1835; indeed, as we see, Rivers allots its creation not to Descemet but rather to the Luxembourg Palace gardens, Hardy being implicated thereby; but perhaps the pre-1820 'Beau Carmin du Luxembourg' was indeed another variety; *or* perhaps the Luxembourg obtained it from Descemet; perhaps the addition of "du Luxembourg" to the name of the pre-1820 variety indicates a need to differentiate it from another 'Beau Carmine' China also existing in pre-1820. There is never any shortage of things to ponder in Old Roses.

Beauty of Glenhurst (Morley/Nottle, 1985)
Seedling of 'Parsons' Pink China' (Ch).
Single, pink. The introducer of this cultivar, Trevor Nottle, tells us (in unpublished correspondence): "The rose 'Beauty of Glenhurst' was named by me and raised and grown by June & Brian Morley. I introduced it in the one year I was a rose wholesaler! It would have been 1985 so it would have been raised from seed June gathered in 1979 and grown in 1980. It is a very vigorous bush to about 3.5 meters (about 10 feet) and the same across. It flowers in huge corymbs and while the flowers are not large (about 5-7 cm [ca. 2-3 inches]), they are so dense that the impact overall is that of a mass of pink color."

Beauty of Rosemawr (Van Fleet/Conard & Jones, 1903)
"Carmine, with bright red in depths of the rose. Incessant bloomer." [Dr] "Carmine and crimson." [LS] "Fairly dense, upright-growing...fragrant, loosely formed, soft carmine...paler veining...3×2 [ft; ca. 9×6 dm]." [B] "Rather short of foliage for my taste." [B1] "Fairly vigorous, hardy, very floriferous, giving large flowers, full, fragrant, of a handsome carmine pink veined vermilion and white. Certain catalogs class 'Beauty of Rosemawr'

as a China, others as a Tea; it is simply a hybrid of the two." [JR32/141] "We take pleasure in recommending this Grand New Rose, because we feel sure it will please all who want fine Hardy Ever-Blooming Roses. It was selected from among our choicest hybridized seedlings as combining more good qualities for general planting than almost any rose we know. It has stood for five years entirely unprotected in the open ground and never failed to bloom continuously every season. We are so confident of its value that we have named it after our place—'Beauty of Rosemawr'...It is a healthy, vigorous grower, making a strong, handsome bush, entirely hardy, needs no protection, begins to bloom very quickly and continues blooming the whole season until stopped by hard frost. The flowers are large and perfectly double, with fine overlapping petals and raised centre. The color is a lovely shade of rich carmine rose, exquisitely veined with fine crimson and white markings, exceedingly beautiful and delightfully fragrant." [C&Js03]

Bébé Fleuri (Dubreuil, 1906)
"Medium growth, dark foliage, very floriferous. Blooms in clusters of three to five flowers, China pink varying to currant red, sometimes striped white. Very dwarf, but vigorous." [JR30/150]

Belle de Monza (Villoresi/L. Noisette and Vibert, 1819) trans., "Monza Beauty"
"Maroon-violet." [LS] "Pale cherry, produced in elegant clusters, of medium size, semi-double; form cupped. A showy rose." [P1] "*Branches*, erect. *Tube of calyx*, smooth, oval-turbinated. *Flowers*, almost full, middle-sized; of a very pale purple, often marbled with a deeper shade. *Petals*, those of the centre, narrow and wrinkled. This beautiful rose is one of more than twenty varieties of the Bengal or China rose created by Signor Villaresi [*sic*], superintendent of the Archducal gardens at Monza, in the Milanese." [Go] Ev. re-introduced by Vibert in 1840.

Belle Hébé (Laffay,-1834) syn. 'Hébé'
"Pink." [LS] "Blossoms double, medium-sized, bright pink around the edges, flesh in the middle." [MaCo] Hebe, cup-bearer (along with Ganymede) to the Olympian gods.

Bengale Centfeuilles (Cartier, 1804) trans., "Centifolia China"
Seedling of 'Parsons' Pink China'
"Pink bordered deep wine." [LS] "Intense pink, middle-sized, full." [N] "Middle-sized, hemispherical, almost full; varying from lilac-pink to light claret." [Go] "Dr. Cartier, who holds a distinguished place among our fanciers, was the second to grow [*'Parsons' Pink China'*]. In 1804, he grew the double variety [*'Bengale Centfeuilles'; 'Parsons' Pink China' was considered to be a semi-double*] from seed… The first seeds [*from 'Parsons' Pink China'*] were sown by Monsieur Cartier; and with the three which came to bloom, one with double flowers was found…we didn't have any further varieties [*of China roses other than this new double one—to be called 'Bengale Centfeuilles'—and 'Parsons' Pink China'*]." [V2] Boitard, in his editorship of the 1824 *Bon Jardinier*, mentions a very double China "with flowers like those of the Centifolia rose," and records it as being at Monsieur Louis Noisette's famous nursery as originally coming from Florence; but Vibert, upon doing some investigation of the matter, found that Noisette had no idea of what Boitard was talking about; and so the attribution of 'Bengale Centfeuilles' to Noisette, which has formerly prevailed, appears to be incorrect, and based on Boitard's error. Jamain and Forney also possibly err in the story reported in the head-note to this chapter; it appears that they have confused 'Bengale Centfeuilles' with the 'Common China'—or perhaps what we assume is the 'Common China' is not what they or their source assumed. We can understand Thouïn's expectations of seeing a Centifolia if the rose being brought to him was named 'Bengale Centfeuilles' (i.e., "China-Centifolia"); listen: "It was a distinguished Parisian doctor, a great rose fancier, who—the first in France—procured for himself the Common China; he presented it to the venerable A.

Thouïn, who had only expected to see a Centifolia with the look of a China." [JF] Straightening out the story, the likely truth is that, as we have already seen, Dr. Cartier indeed did procure for himself the 'Common China'—that is, 'Parsons' Pink China'—and then, also as we have seen above, he obtained seed from the plant, raised 'Bengale Centfeuilles' from that seed, and then presented *that* to "the venerable A. Thouïn."

Bengale d'Automne (Cartier,-1820) trans., "Autumn China"
"Variable red." [Ÿ]

[Bengale Nabonnand] (Nabonnand, 1886)
"Of exceptional vigor; flower large, full, imbricated, erect; large foliage, glossy dark green; very dark velvety purplish red, coppery, shaded yellow. The most beautiful China, and one of the most profuse. Unique." [JR10/170] A parent of 'Alice Hamilton' (Ch).

Bengale Pompon (Vibert,-1820)
This name refers to a strain encompassing different cultivars, rather than to a clone. "Growth of moderate vigor; branches slender and twiggy, divergent; bark smooth, green, and reddish on the young growths; thorns the same color, slender, long, slightly hooked, very sharp; leaves small, dark green; leafstalks slender, dark green, slightly reddish beneath; flower small, to perhaps an inch across [ca. 2.5 cm], nearly full, usually cupped; solitary, or in clusters on the vigorous branches; color, light pink or red, depending upon the variety." [S] "*Shrub*, from one to two feet high [ca. 3-6 dm]. *Leaflets*...never tinged with purple. *Tube of calyx*, oval, smooth. *Flowers*, semi-double, light pink." [Go]

Bengale Sanguinaire (Desprez, 1838) trans., "Blood-Red China"
"Flowers crimson, small and very double." [P] "Growth weak, sprawling; branches, leaves, and flower stalks very purple; blossom medium size, slightly globular, very double; velvety, very bright crimson purple; petals concave, having a white nub; twenty to thirty-five styles." [S]

[**Bichonne**] (Gaucher, 1809) trans., "Pet"
"Monsieur Gauché, gardener and garden-decorator, has been so kind as to give me a specimen of this rose. Its flowers, of a quite bright color with paler touches, have some crinkled petals and a pretty look..." [BJ09] "A variety of the crimson China [*referring to 'Slater's Crimson China'*] exists under the name 'Bichonne', having the same characteristics; it differs only by the vigor of its shoots and the petals in its blossoms—they are often edged and mixed with white, and are crinkled and frilled, giving it the name 'Bichonne'. Several fanciers also call it 'Bengale Panaché'. This rose can grow three to four feet high [ca. 1-1.3 m], making a sort of pyramid which is very effective by way of the quantity of flowers it gives; they are the most fragrant of those of this sort. It appears that we owe this rose to the efforts of Madame Gaucher of Paris; she grew it carefully for several years, and successfully—she's the one who has distributed it in commerce." [C-T] Andrews had it under his eye "for the last eight years, and always considered it as an abortive rose that would return to a more perfect state: but finding the irregular, incurved and unequal expansion of its petals still remain unaltered, no further doubt remains of its being a permanent character...It is to be met with in almost every collection." [A]

Blanc
Listed as 'De Cels'.

Blue Rose (China/Milford, ca. 1810) syn. 'Pourpre'
"[N]umerous purple flowers...The purple variety is said to have been first imported from China about the year 1810, to the gardens of Lord Milford, under the appellation of the Blue Rose; and as such many of them were sold at a guinea each, although the plant had not then flowered: such is the fascinating force of novelty, which even in embryo has the power to charm. This rose of expectation, when its blooms unfolded, no heavenly blue disclosed, but a red purple, which as it faded off became much paler, less brilliant, but of a bluer or colder purple, which gives to the fresh opened blossoms a very different appearance contrasted with

those retiring; and although the blue's celestial tint is wanting, it is nevertheless a graceful and very abundant flowering rose." [A] "Moderate growth; flower medium sized, deep purple." [S] "*Canes*, slender. *Ovary*, glabrous, obconical, sometimes having a circular expansion at the base. *Bud*, globular. *Flower*, medium-size, full, bluish purple. *Styles*, 70-90." [Pf] "*Tube of calyx*, long and narrow in the throat. *Sepals*, simple. *Flowers*, small or middle-sized, single; of a purple-crimson. *Petals*, spatulated. *Styles*, six to fifteen." [Go] "Dwarf." [Sn]

Cels Multiflora
Listed as a Tea.

Comtesse du Caÿla (P. Guillot, 1902)
From crossing a seedling (of 'Rival de Pæstum' and 'Mme. Falcot') with 'Mme. Falcot'.
"Orange-red...salmon-pink with age...loose...fragrant." [Hk] "Flower large, full, fragrant, varying from carmine nasturtium red, tinted orange on the reverse of the petals, to coppery orange yellow, shaded carmine; very pretty." [JR26/131] "Flower large, fairly full, cupped; very floriferous; vigorous." [Cx] "It does not bloom freely enough to warrant its being planted for effect in the garden." [OM] "Very free flowering...3×3 [ft; ca. 1×1 m]." [B] "Small, semi-double, flat, fragrant;...Continuous bloom. Compact growth; 2-3 [ft; ca. 6 dm-1 m]." [Lg] "Highly scented." [B1] "Tea and sweet-pea scent." [T3] "Beautiful plant with fine canes and small foliage and the coppery orange flowers which are different." [ARA29/50] "Rather sparse, bronzy-green foliage...harmonizes very well with its flowers...of a very branching and straggling habit of growth...flowers freely and with wonderful persistency...we may at times find all mixtures of red, pink, and orange, in varying proportions and inextricably mixed, but the colour is always striking and attractive. Unlike most of the Chinas, which are not particularly fragrant, 'Comtesse du Caÿla' is decidedly sweet-scented, with the perfume of the Tea Rose...without full sunshine it does not seem nearly so floriferous...on the whole very free from mildew and other diseases." [NRS/12] "Personal preference for best China." [Th]

[**Charlotte Klemm**] (Türke, 1905) syn., 'Sirena'
From 'Alfred Colomb' (HP) × 'Cramoisi Supérieur' (Ch)
"Fiery red.—Moderately vigorous.—Garden.—A fine China." [Cat12]
"Growth dwarf; flower large, full, flat, sparkling scarlet red." [JR30/25]
NRS12/70 indicates that 'Charlotte Klemm' is less compact and less erect
than is 'Fabvier' (Ch), being on the other hand more "showy in the
autumn garden." "For those who wish a bed of Roses something after this
colour [*that of 'Gruss an Teplitz' (B)*] I should be inclined to recommend
either 'Petrus Donzel' [*'Monsieur Petrus Donzel', China, A. Schwartz,
1903*], very like a dwarfer 'Gruss an Teplitz', or better still, 'Charlotte
Klemm'." [NRS12/95] Charlotte Klemm, probably daughter or wife of
the Klemm of Hoyer & Klemm, "rose-growers of Dresden." [JR37/10]

Cramoisi Supérieur (Coquereau/Audiot/Vibert, 1835) syn., 'Agrippina',
'Queen's Scarlet'; trans., "Superior Crimson"
Supp. seedling of 'Slater's Crimson China'
"The following letter, addressed to Monsieur Scipion Cochet, came our
way: *July 24, 1883. Mon Cher Monsieur S. Cochet, The rose 'Cramoisi
Supérieur' was raised in 1832 by Monsieur Coquereau, a fancier at la Maître
École, near Angers (Dept. Maine-et-Loire), who presented it to another fancier
of that area, Monsieur Audiot. This latter took it to Monsieur Vibert, then at
Longjumeau, who released it to commerce in 1835. Sincerely yours, Petrus
Rosina.*" [JR7/120] "Unequalled crimson." [Ed] "Velvety crimson."
[HoBoIV/320] "Flowers are so finely formed, and its crimson tints so
rich." [R8] "Intense maroon; flower medium-sized; cupped; very floriferous; vigorous." [Cx] "Bright carmine." [R-H35] "Blood-red. Rich velvety
texture. Free and constant." [Dr] "Though an old rose, this is still one of
the best and most popular of its class…it is cupped, beautifully formed,
and of a rich, brilliant crimson, with a delicate white stripe in the center of
each petal. It is one of the most hardy and desirable of the old China
Roses." [SBP] "Perhaps no rose gives so great a succession of
flowers…which are of the richest scarlet crimson, very glowing. The rose

being pendulous, the edges reflex most gracefully, to exhibit more fully as it were the extreme richness and velvety scarlet of their inner sides...Nothing can exceed the richness and beauty of a large head of 'Cramoisi Supérieur' on a low stem covered with its graceful flowers in constant succession." [C] "Perfect globular shape." [HstXI:225] "Semi-double, cupped...only slightly scented...3×3 [ft; ca. 1×1 m]." [B] "Continuous supply of flowers." [L] "Universally admired for its brilliant crimson cup formed flowers, perfectly double; it is a strong grower, and should be in every collection." [Bu] "Growth moderate." [P1] "Good foliage. Medium growth. The climbing sport is better." [Th2] "Thin stems...small leaves." [Hk] "Weak and straggling growth." [K2] "Sturdy and free-blooming, free from disease and insect attacks." [UB28] "A good bedding variety." [EL] "Fairly vigorous; branches slender and nodding; bark light reddish green; prickles red, narrow, elongated, straightish, and quite sharp; leaves smooth, dark green, shiny, somewhat reddish, 5-7 oval leaflets, pointed, red-tinted along the fine serration; leafstalks narrow, armed with numerous prickles; flower about 2 in across [ca. 5 cm], globular, a little quilled, solitary on the branchlets, or in clusters on the more vigorous branches; color, bright crimson; flower stalk, fairly large, but thin and bending under the weight of the blossom; pretty buds." [S] "Calyx glabrous and rounded." [JF] "Especially valued for its fine buds...the best of the [*China*] class." [EL] "Perfect." [JWa]

[**Cruenta**] (China/T. Evans/Colville, ca. 1810)
"Blood red." [RG] "Bright crimson." [Cal] "Beautiful color, which varies." [MonL/DeP] "Would seem to be the Type of many others of the same sort. It is fairly delicate, its growth only rising indeed to a foot and a half [ca. 6 dm]; grafted, it is more robust and can [*some words illegible, probably to the effect of "overtop"*] the growth of our hybrids a little when palisaded out in the open. Its leaves are narrow, and its flower—velvety crimson, with ten petals of an inch and a half in diameter [ca. 4 cm]. It does much better grafted at two and a half feet [ca. 7.5 dm], and makes a bush which

is always in bloom." [LeR] "Bloomed in England for the first time in Colville's Nursery about 1810. This most beautiful of the purple Chinas blooms in the orangery or a very sheltered frame in early Spring, the flowers being outstanding for their volume and perfection of form. It can be successfully grafted on *canina* or the Common China; but in this case the blossoms will be smaller and appear only at the end of June." [T&R]

Darius (Laffay, 1827)
"Violet-lilac." [TCN] "Lilac-purple, full, flat, large, beautiful." [LF] "Calyx tube conical, oblong, often slightly gibbose on one side at the base; flower large or medium large, very double, light violet or lilac, sometimes slightly fragrant." [MaCo] "Tall." [Sn] Darius the Great, King of Persia, lived ca. 558-486 B.C.

[De Cels] (Cels, 1804) syn., 'À Fleurs Blanches', 'Alba', 'Blanc', 'Subalba'
Almost certainly a seedling from 'Parsons' Pink China'.
"The white-flowered variety differs from [*'Parsons' Pink China'*] by way of its buds, which are less covered by the calyx-membranes, and its wood, which is less vigorous. It is, so to speak, very playful, the same specimen giving some pink flowers, others flesh-colored, others veined pink and white, and finally some very white ones. It enjoys the advantage of producing more branchlets that does [*'Parsons' Pink China'*, etc.], and, consequently, more flowers; but, on the other hand, it is not so easy to propagate. Grafted onto the Briar, it is more easily pruned, formed, and shaped than is the pink one; often one lone bud, which in the latter variety gives only one shoot or branch, grows six or eight, all bearing flowers. This is a variety which merits being cared for and grown." [C-T] "Mediocre, being inconstant." [MonL/deP]

[Douglas] (V. Verdier, 1848)
"Deep, rich cherry red; large full flowers; very sweet, constant and profuse bloomer." [C&Js02] "Very vigorous bush; branches short, bright green, not very thorny; beautiful bright dark green foliage; flower large, full, globular; color, delicate pink. Much to be recommended for borders and bedding." [S]

Ducher (Ducher, 1869)

"Mid-sized double blooms of creamy-white…constant bloom, vigorous to 4 [ft; ca. 1.25 m]." [HRG] "Pure white, of medium size and fine form, full. Promising as a free and continuous white bedding Rose." [P1] "Double but flat. Good white decorative…Foliage, good to very good." [Th] "One is tempted to guess that 'Ducher' has Tea heritage…vigorous, with slender branches, sometimes large, divergent; smooth bark of light green, furnished with reddish, long thorns which are somewhat numerous. The foliage is glossy, light green, and divided into 3-5 narrow leaflets, elongated and pointed. The flowers, which reach about 4 inches across [ca. 1 dm], are full, well-formed, and either solitary or, on vigorous branches, in clusters. The outer petals are large, the inner ones petite and folded. The bud is quite pretty. This variety is very remontant. It is the only really vigorous white China." [JR8/89] "Of moderate vigor; blooms in panicles; flower medium-sized, full, fragrant, in a reflexing cup; pure white; very floriferous." [S] "[The thorns are] long, reddish, substantial, slightly hooked, and very sharp…flower-stem slender and slightly nodding. Calyx ovoid." [JF] "Dislikes frost." [S] Born at Lyon in 1820, "Claude Ducher died the 24th of this month [January, 1874]…Claude Ducher was 54 years old. He was a devoted rosarian, honest, intelligent, and hard-working, esteemed by all his colleagues. He developed quite a number of good Roses which shine in our collections, particularly in the Tea class." [R-H74]

Duchesse de Kent (Laffay,-1835) syn./trans., "Duchess of Kent"

"Incarnate rose color." [JWa] "Pink." [TCN] "Creamy white, sometimes beautifully edged with rose, then very pretty and distinct, small and full; form, cupped." [P] "Medium-sized, full, light pink." [V8] "Large, full, well-formed, light pink." [R-H42] "A neat pale rose, of a dwarf habit, and rather small sized flower." [Bu] "Quite a gem: so perfect is the shape of its very double and delicately coloured flowers, that it must and will become a favourite." [R9] "Has given way to new and superior varieties." [WRP]

Duke of York (W. Paul, 1894)
"Rosy-pink and white. Distinct." [H] "Variable between rosy-red and white, sometimes pale with deep red centres, sometimes white edged and tipped with carmine in the way of 'Homère'." [P1] "Deep pink, shading to white, bordered and touched pink; flower large, full, quartered; floriferous; vigorous." [Cx] "Semi-double blooms on a bushy plant to 3 [ft; ca. 1 m]." [HRG] "Branching habit...3×2 [ft; ca. 1 m × 6 dm]." [B] "Dark shiny foliage." [B1] "A good and very floriferous variety." [JR19/53]

Elise Flory (Guillot père, 1852) syn., 'Elyse Fleury'
"Fine rose, large and full." [FP] "Bright pink." [S] "Pink, shaded." [LS] "Ordinary pink at the center, paling along the edges, resembling the Bourbon 'Triomphe de la Duchère'." [l'H52/148] "Growth vigorous; flowers medium or large, full, nuanced pink; strong stem." [l'H56/198]

Eugène de Beauharnais (Hardy, 1837)
"Amaranth, the buds beautiful when first unfolding, sometimes dying off blackish crimson, large and very double; form cupped." [P1] "Beautiful bright lake, a free bloomer through the summer and autumn...free grower...A charming variety." [HstVI:368] "Of moderate growth." [S] "Bush of ordinary growth, with upright branches; [*thorns*] equal, reddish; leaflets of a glaucous green, purplish at the edges; flowers numerous, medium-sized, in a cluster, full, well-formed, with petals of a beautiful violet-red. One of the most beautiful Bengals [*i.e., Chinas*] existing." [An37/25] "By way of preamble to my botanical description, let me say that I don't want you to conclude that the China 'Eugène Beauharnais' is quite without spines or thorns; *au contraire*, it is part of a group of heavily thorned varieties. But the thorns are quite rare in the vicinity of the flowers...so rare indeed that one can ordinarily cut a blossom with a branch several decimeters long without having a single thorn on the cutting. I must concede that, beneath the leafstalk, there are two or three small, sharp, recurved prickles. As for the bush, it is very vigorous, with shiny wood, slightly brown, very glabrous, and, as previously stated, having

occasional thorns which are flat or flared and rusty brown. The leaves are small, with five oval leaflets, very much elongated, somber green beneath...they are regularly and finely dentate like a saw, and have a purplish edge of the shade found on the underside of the leaves, the glow of which seems to have penetrated the dentation. The stipules are short; the young shoots of this rose are an intense purple...The flowers are borne on a stem 1 ½-2 [ca. 3-5 cm], which is not strong enough to hold the flower upright; it nods like Zeus with a grace and imposing majesty, even (I would say) with respect. The ovary is short, glabrous, green; the five sepals are entire, sometimes green, most often as purplish as the leaves, always bordered with a short whitish down which is not readily apparent. The corolla is a perfect miniature: its diameter is about 2 inches [ca. 5 cm], sometimes 2 ¾ inches [ca. 7 cm]. The very numerous petals are cupped in the middle of the flower, and in a rosette towards the perimeter; they are imbricated in the most perfect manner towards the center, where they are very small, and leave a little gap which nevertheless does not allow the stamens to spoil the picture. The line of the outward petals is slightly reflexed. This gives the blossom a graceful convexity, above all when seen from the side. The color—oh, the color is the sparklingest brightest that we have ever seen in a red rose. The outer petals are intense carmine; those of the center are browner, one might say of maroon velvet. The scent is very elegant and sweet." [PlB] "'Prince Eugène' is a very rich crimson rose, being in colour between 'Cramoisi Supérieur', and 'Roi des Cramoisis' [*see below for a note on this latter cultivar*]; perfectly double and hardy...[*Now turning to another rose for comparison,*] 'Roi des Cramoisis' was brought by me, in 1839, from Paris, where I saw the original plant, around which there was a regularly beaten path made by its admirers, of which I was one, never before having seen a dark rich crimson rose with so much odour; the flowers too were large, fully double, and cup formed; the plant three or four feet high [ca. 1 m], and fully loaded with its gorgeous blossoms. It has since appeared in several collections, having been imported under the name of [*that other China rose,*] 'Eugène Beauharnais'...it grows freely, and is well worth cultivating." [Bu] 'Roi des Cramoisis' (Breeder unknown,-1839) may thus be mixed up with 'Eugène de Beauharnais' in collections and commerce; but, back to 'Eugène de Beauharnais' itself: "A good sort, but inferior to 'Agrippina' [*i.e., 'Cramoisi Supérieur'*]." [EL] This China is not to be confused with the similarly-named cupped HP from Moreau-Robert of 1865. Prince Eugène de Beauharnais, Duke of Leuchtenberg and Prince of Eichstädt; Empress Joséphine's son; lived 1781-1824. The interesting cactus *Leuchtenbergia principis* is also named after Eugène de Beauharnais.

Fabvier (Laffay, 1832) syn. 'Général Fabvier'
"Dazzling crimson with white stripe." [H] "Bright red." [TCN] "Scarlet, semi-double." [HoBoIV/320] "Rosy-crimson." [EL] "Bright reddish purple." [JWa] "Crimson scarlet, of medium size, semi-double; form expanded. One of the most brilliant of Roses, very showy." [P1] "Deep crimson…here and there a petal streaked with white, the glorious colour heightened by the golden stamens of the expanded blooms, is most charming…'Fabvier' is always gay, no matter how wet the weather." [JP] "Fiery crimson; velvety." [Go] "Sparkling bright red." [Pq] "The bright red flowers are poised on strong, erect stems, and make a first-rate display." [OM] "Small dark green foliage and an erect yet compact habit of growth…The flowers are of medium or rather small size for a China, and of excellent colour—light crimson to crimson scarlet, with a well marked white eye. They have little beauty of form, but produce a good effect in the bed, though the petals are rather thin…a sweet and clean little perfume…quite free from disease…inclined to resent too hard pruning…He [*Mr. Easlea*] considers that, next to the old Pink China [*'Parsons' Pink China'*], 'Fabvier' is the very best of the tribe." [NRS/12] "Placed in a bed with other Chinas, 'Général Fabvier' can be picked out at a great distance. Slender habit, vigorous branches, very productive flower clusters, and magnificent appearance are its principal obvious characteristics, to which we will add the following: Bark green, smooth, furnished with very long

thorns which are quite slender, hooked, and sharp, and of a light purple. Leaves somber green, of 5-7 leaflets, with the leafstalk and main vein of the leaflets furnished with prickles and glandular hairs which are more or less strong depending upon where they are. The leaflets are sometimes heart-shaped, but most often a pointed a very long oval, always finely and elegantly toothed; the stipules, ciliated with notable finesse and symmetry, are glabrous, narrow, long, drawn up above the petiole, and terminating in two long points. The tip of the young growth is a very delicate purple. Flowers of a very dark poppy red, sometimes a bright carmine, large to about 2 ½ inches across [ca. 6 cm], somewhat full, carried on still, upright stems, holding the blossom perfectly. This rose was raised by Monsieur Laffay at Bellevue…who dedicated it to one of our most distinguished generals. This was the brave general who had the courage, in the bosom of our House of Peers…to protest against the many extortions made by the public administration as well as against the importunate entreaties which, all too often, took advantage of the members of the two Houses of the French parliament." [PlB]

Fellemberg
Listed as a Noisette.

Fimbriata à Pétales Frangés (Jacques, 1831) syn., 'Œillet de St.-Arquey', 'Rose de St.-Arquey', 'Rose-Œillet de St.-Arquey', 'Serratipetala'
"Bright red." [HoBoIV:318] "Serrated…like a damaged carnation." [G] "Mean with its blooms, gaunt in growth." [Hk] "Somewhat vigorous; branches weak; flower medium-sized, full, flat; color, bright red, exterior petals crinkled." [S] "Monsieur Vilfroy, chief gardener [*of the Abby St. Nicholas-au-Bois*], made, in 1911, some cuttings of a horticultural form of Jacquin's *R. chinensis*; the slips were placed in a cold frame also containing slips of carnations. Mme. Faure, manageress of the château, and Monsieur Vilfroy both noted with stupefaction in 1912 that, by a strange coincidence, many of the rose cuttings bore flowers which could easily be mistaken for carnations!! The cuttings were carefully tended. Mme. Faure did

us the honor of asking our opinion of the value of the rose; and we must deem it the most curious rose to be developed in a long time...The 'Rose de St.-Arquey', propagated through our efforts, will be released to commerce probably in the fall of 1915, to the joy of fanciers of new roses and of plant oddities. Nothing similar to this exists; it is a true novelty." [JR37/182-183] "This curious rose which saw the light of day in 1911 at the Abby St. Nicholas-au-Bois, in the Département de l'Aisne, is certainly one of the most interesting novelties to come along in quite some time...[It] resembles a carnation to such a degree that, placed on the stem of a carnation plant which has blossoms of the same shade, it can't be distinguished from them...As for the rest of the plant, the branches and foliage are typical *R. chinensis*, whence it came. We presented the 'Rose de St.-Arquey' at a meeting of the French National Horticultural Society last August 28th [*1913*] in the name of his happy discoverer Mme. Faure; it excited the curiosity of both amateur and professional." [JR38/21] "The rose may be...'Fimbriata'...raised by Monsieur Jacques in 1831...For unknown reasons, the rose had degenerated and lost its carnation type, which, however, being innate, became again apparent in the frame." [K]

Général Fabvier
Listed as 'Fabvier'.

Général Labutère (Breeder unk.,-1906)
"Bright pink." [LS] "Varying cerise, double, globular, lighter on backs of petals. Leaves dark green. Plant healthy, vigorous, open." [BCD]

Gloire des Rosomanes
Listed as a Bourbon.

Granate (Dot, 1948)
"Crimson red." [Ÿ]

Hébé
Listed as 'Belle Hébé'.

Henry's Crimson China (A. Henry, 1885) syn., *R. chinensis spontanea*
"Four to twenty feet in height [ca. 1.25-6 m]…crimson, pink, or white."
[Hk]

Hermosa
Listed as a Bourbon.

Hume's Blush Tea-Scented China
Listed as a Tea

Institutrice Moulins (Charreton, 1893) trans., "Governess Moulins"
"Carmine pink." [Ÿ]

Irène Watts (P. Guillot, 1895)
Seedling of 'Mme. Laurette Messimy' (Ch)
"Salmon; flower very large, full, quartered; very floriferous." [Cx] "White
tinted pale pink…2×2 [ft; ca. 6×6 dm]." [B] "Salmon-white in bud,
changing to salmon-rose; long buds, very free and good." [P1] "Dark
green foliage margined with purple." [B1] "Vigorous, very floriferous,
with numerous branches, bushy; leaves purplish green; bud elongate,
salmon-white; flower large, full, well-formed, varying from pinkish
salmon-white to a very delicate China pink." [JR19/147] "A neat compact
grower, and continuous bloomer all summer and fall." [C&Js99]

Jean Bach Sisley (Dubreuil, 1898)
"Opening delicate silvery-rose, outer petals salmon-rose lined and veined
with carmine, large for its class, and very sweet; a beautiful and distinct
variety." [P1] "Pale pink and white, blushing deep rose…4×3 [ft; ca.
1.25×1 m]." [HRG] "Bright foliage; floriferous. Flowers solitary, or in
threes at the end of vigorous branches; of notable form in
opening…Flower well-held, erect on its stem." [JR22/163]

L'Ouche (Buatois, 1901)
"Light pink shaded yellow." [LS] "Pale rosy flesh reflexed with yellow;
large, full, fine conical buds; growth vigorous." [P1] "Double pink flowers

of old fashion form on bushy plant." [HRG] "Fairly dark, thick foliage."
[B1] "Vigorous, with strong-growing wood, well-branched. Foliage
ample, bronze-green. Flower large, full; bud conical and of a pretty flesh
pink, yellow at the nub." [JR26/3]

[**La Spécieuse**] (China,-1819) trans., "The Misleading One"
"This one is said to have just arrived from China [i.e., *Tonquin*]. It is,
without contradiction, the most beautiful and the most perfect of the
Chinas. At up to five *louis* a cutting, it hardly sells. It is not for young
Misses, who neither have it nor want it. It is the sister of 'Belle Cythérée'
[*i.e., 'Hume's Blush Tea-Scented China'*]. It is worth every sacrifice for lovers
to offer this one to their beloveds! This beautiful rose has the thorns and
leaves of the Chinas, of medium size; it is fairly vigorous though its
branches be slender and difficult to graft. Its flowers, which are continuous without a moment of rest, are superb, large, and as full as the
Centifolia, of which it has the form and grace. Its color is the most beautiful poppy of the most ravishing sparkle. At first sight, one would believe it
to be an offspring of this family's velvety semi-double [*i.e., 'Slater's
Crimson China'*], to which it has a partial resemblance before bloom. It is
propagated by buds, cuttings, and grafting, though it requires the temperate house, or to be kept close inside some days. I'm certain that it can't be
left out in the open air unless you protect it with straw. This flower is a
precious acquisition, blooming all year." [LeR]

[**Laffay**] (Laffay, ca. 1825)
"Lilac-y red." [TCN] "Flower medium-sized, full, bright cerise red."
[MaCo] Concerning Monsieur Laffay himself: "*Catalog of Roses cultivated
by Monsieur Laffai* [sic], *rue Rousselet-Saint-Germain, P No. 17, Paris.*
Monsieur Laffai having been especially devoted to the culture of Roses,
and loving them warmly, it is natural that his collection is the most complete in having both the most and the newest. Let it be stated of him that
his trips to England, Belgium, and Holland as well as his correspondents
in Italy have not let him miss a single beautiful rose nor fail to make any

sacrifice to obtain it. He furthermore has often bred his own varieties from seed, and his industry has been such that it would be difficult to find a good rose that was *not* stocked on his premises on rue Rousselet." [R-H36] "Since I [*Laffay*] began cultivating roses, I have devoted myself to growing seedlings of this beautiful family: In the beginning, the pretty varieties which I thus obtained encouraged me to renew those first attempts which were so lucky; but Nature is occasionally capricious! As we know few of her secrets, the several years which followed didn't always produce the results which I had obtained in my first tries. My perseverance, however, in continuing made me certain that with new combinations she would reward me with her treasures. And so, over a number of years, I have developed some wonderful roses in that precious group of *hybrids with constant bloom*, and am occupied, at the present time, with propagating them so that I can offer them to the fanciers who are looking for them as soon as possible; thus they will be able to enjoy varieties of elegant fragrance, rich color, and (above all) hardiness—like those they are already used to, but over the *whole* season. Despite the preference which I seem to give to this new sort of roses, I am nevertheless always involved with other sorts. I must, however, admit that the Noisettes, Chinas, and Teas are occasionally neglected in budding because I have decided to grow only the most meritorious, and those only as potted plants [*i.e., as 'own-root' plants in pots, not as budded 'standards' (tree-roses) or budded 'dwarfs' (bush-roses)*]. These varieties, exotic by nature, are too risky to attract those nurserymen who otherwise would grow them." [LF] "M. Laffay wrote to me [*W. Paul*] last autumn [*1847*]…: 'It is my intention to cease cultivating the Rose, in a commercial sense. My project was to do so this autumn, and to install myself in the south of France, in the land of oranges and palm-trees; but my father, who is very aged, wished that we should not quit Paris this winter. This rather alters our plans of emigration, although they are only retarded. But it is very possible that I may yet offer you some good roses, especially of the Hybrid Moss, for I intend to make a sowing of several thousands of seeds of these varieties. Thus I presume that my seed-plot will be worth visiting for some years to come. I am persuaded that in future we shall see many beautiful Roses, which will efface all those that we admire now. The Mosses will soon play a grand part in Horticulture.'" [P] "My first recollection of Roses is of the occasion when I [*George Paul*] went as a lad to Paris with my father to see the first great French Exhibition in 1855, and visited Mr. Laffay, who had retired to a house and garden amidst the woods of the Paris suburb of Belleville [*sic*], taking with him his seedlings Roses." [NRS17/101]

One tries, with meager results, to put together a time-line for Jean Laffay, who is—like Vibert—curiously obscure for being a leader in his field acknowledged as such in his own lifetime, and who, what is more, was known for "his good and generous nature" [R-H63/295]. *Sic transit gloria mundi!* After the very greatest efforts, we may offer the following: Born at Paris on August 17, 1794, to Jean Laffay (who himself died at about 90 on July 14, 1852) and his wife Jeanne (Fagotay) [LF1], by 1825 he has set up for himself at Auteuil, having formerly been "head gardener" to the nurseryman Ternaux of that community, with whom, no doubt, he released his first introductions around 1815—perhaps as early as 1810 [LS, JG]; is still there in 1829 [R-H29]—an important year in his life, as his marriage contract is dated February 28 of that year; Mme. Laffay's name was Apollonie (Fournier). In 1835, he imported from England the remontant Pimpinellifolia 'Stanwell Perpetual' [SHP35/125]. By 1836, we see him in Paris at 17 rue Rousselet-St. Germain [R-H36]; by 1837, he is established at Bellevue-Meudon [An40], where, rather well-to-do, he remains—at first in business, and then retired—until at least 1855 [NRS17/101] or so, during which period he achieved his great pioneering triumphs in the development of the Hybrid Perpetual. The area of Bellevue was the quondam home of the Marquise de Pompadour, mistress of Louis XV, who bought it for her in 1757; sold as "national goods" at the Revolution, the château and grounds were preserved intact up to 1819, when there were bought by one Guillaume, who demolished the château and sold the grounds bit by bit in large parcels. The Laffays bought at least two of these plots, in February and August of 1837, thereafter reselling at least four smaller portions of this land. It is possible that they had purchased the property by way of speculation, as this desirable location overlooking one part of Paris could have been expected to rapidly appreciate in value. At length, Laffay put into effect his 1847 plans to remove to the South—*but* with a difference. The Bellevue-Meudon voting lists for 1857 bear a small notation next to his crossed-out name: *Parti en Afrique*—"Left for Africa"! The year 1859 found him at Kouba in Algeria, a community above Algiers where one has a good panorama of the city and its harbor, and which is known for its good air and few frosts. At length, however, in 1877, we find him back in France, an honorary member of the Société Nationale d'Horticulture—he had been, like Vibert, a founding member in 1827 of its predecessor the Société d'Horticulture de Paris—living at his Villa Apollonie at Cros Vieil, Cannes, where he died April 15, 1878 [LF1]; he and his wife are buried along the "Allée du Silence" in the Cannes cemetery. We find no indication of offspring. "The Société Centrale d'Horticulture de France lost, in 1878,...Laffay, the celebrated rose-breeder who has given our gardens so many magnificent varieties." [SNH/24] "Report to the Council of Administration, in the name of the Floricultural Committee, on How to Use the Gift of Mme. Laffay. By Monsieur Eugène Delamarre, Secretary of the Committee. Sirs, You have charged the Committee of Floriculture to find the best way of using the sum donated by Mme. Laffay in memory of Monsieur Laffay, her husband, the late member of the Society, who was one of the devotees of *methodical* breeding of the Rose, and who developed many good varieties of Roses, among which I will mention only 'La Reine', which everybody knows, and which will for a long time stand at the head of the remontant hybrids. A special Commission composed of Messrs. Margottin père, Jamain, C. Verdier, Lévêque fils, Millet fils, Hérivaux, Bergman, Leprieur, Dutitre, Bachoux, and Delamarre, named by the Committee, after having considered the remarks of Monsieur Eugène Verdier, who represented Mme. Laffay, herewith renders you the following proposals, which the

Committee has approved: The Commission believes it is just and equitable to convert Mme. Laffay's generous gift into medals which will be awarded to the Lyonnais specialists who are the flower of French breeders and who have truly brought rosiculture forward as a result of their great number of very good varieties. These able Lyonnais horticulturists don't have the same opportunity as the Parisians to get the rewards which they so justly merit. The Commission thus believes it appropriate to recommend to you that Mme. Laffay's gift be used to strike three medals, two in gold for Messrs. Lacharme and Guillot fils, and one of silver gilt for Widow Ducher [*representing both herself and the late Monsieur Ducher*], all three Lyonnais horticulturists, for their outstanding obtentions, in particular 'Captain Christy'; La France', and 'Mlle. Marie Van Houtte' [*sic*]." [SNH/272-273].

Laffay is the name of the region of Lyon and le Massif Central (Clermont-Ferrand), Written also "Lafay," it means *hêtraie* or *Beech Grove*, and is perhaps more familiar in its diminutive form, "Lafayette." Always in the forefront of breeding, whether with the "new" Noisettes, Teas, and Chinas in 1820, the "new" Hybrid Perpetuals in the middle of his career, or the "new" Hybrid Mosses and who knows what in Africa at the end, Jean Laffay has as his lasting monument the great and distinguished influence which his work has had on rose progress.

[Laure de Broglie] (Dubreuil, 1910)

From 'Baronne Piston de St.-Cyr' (Ch; Dubreuil, 1901, light incarnate; parentage unknown) × 'G. Nabonnand' (T).

"Bush of good growth, shrubby, branching, robust, blooming in large clusters on the strongest canes or solitarily on others, long stems. Bud very long on strong peduncle, blush ivory-white. Flowers large, full, perfect form, white shaded bright incarnadine. Very fetching and novel coloration. Extremely decorative, blooms without pause from May to November. Just the thing for bedding and pot-culture." [JR34/168]

Le Vésuve (Laffay, 1825) trans., "Vesuvius"

"Intense carmine shading to pink; many colors on the same specimen; flower very large, very full; very vigorous; very floriferous." [Cx] "Flower medium-sized, full, shining red tinted pink." [LR] "Handsome, intense red." [No] "Bears some flowers rich crimson and some rosy pink." [K2] "Wine red with buff center." [Capt28] "...[D]ouble, large; pink, turning to flame-colour." [Go] "...[D]ouble, large, pink passing to fiery red. Calyx tube narrow, long, claviform, narrowing imperceptibly into the peduncle." [S] The most perfectly formed rose that I have seen. It is as regularly imbricated as a Camellia; quite large, and of a lovely bright pink color." [HstXV:29] "'Flower, of medium size, not singly borne, varying from pink to crimson red.' [Pf]. All the descriptions of this variety which we have found seem to us to have been taken from Prévost's catalog, as they are completely similar. The China 'Le Vésuve' forms a pretty, bushy small shrub, vigorous, very floriferous, and having nice shiny green foliage. Bedded, or in a group, it produces a fine effect." [JR15/72-73] I do not see the carmine/crimson/red shades, nor the variability, on what is presently in commerce as 'Le Vésuve', though it is nevertheless a very beautiful rose. It appears that 'Lemesle' is *not* a synonym; at least, it appears that, originally, 'Lemesle' was another rose.

Lemesle
See under 'Le Vésuve'.

Louis-Philippe (Guérin, 1834) syn., 'Louis-Philippe d'Angers'

"Velvety crimson, full, cupped, large." [LF] "Bright crimson." [TCN] "Dark crimson, the edges of the centre petals almost white, of medium size, full; form, globular." [P1] "Fimbriated petals." [ARA40/37] "Stimulating fragrance of spices." [ARA39/48] "Of moderate vigor, giving very pretty flowers, full, globular, and deep maroon. This description is in our opinion the only one which is quite exact." [JR23/25] "Crimson; an inferior 'Agrippina' [*i.e.*, 'Cramoisi Supérieur'*]." [EL] "Small double red flowers and shiny, green foliage...a great favorite as a hedge rose." [SH]

"Has done so well in Florida that it is called the 'Florida Rose'."
[ARA25/112] "Has not an equal for growth, in good soils frequently making a shoot six feet long [ca. 1.75 m] in one season; the flowers are large, perfectly double, of a globular form; the circumference of the bloom is of a dark crimson colour, the centre a pale blush, making it altogether perfectly distinct." [Bu]

Louis XIV
Listed as a Hybrid Perpetual.

[**Lucullus**] (Guinoisseau-Flon, 1854) syn., 'Red Pet'
"Flowers medium-sized, in clusters, very full, opening well, velvety black-purple." [l'H54/34] "Very vigorous…color bright purple at first, then after fully open velvety deep purple. This China is one of the most recommendable." [S] "The Black Rose; splendid large rich crimson, extra full and fragrant, very double and a constant and profuse bloomer. Excellent for bedding and garden culture." [C&Js02] Parent of 'Pink Soupert' (Pol). Lucius Licinius Lucullus, fl. 1st century B.C.; successful Roman military man who, following the ingratitude of the Roman people, did some notable gardening in Rome.

[**Maddalena Scalarandis**] (Scalarandis, 1901)
"Both buds and flowers are extra large and exceedingly beautiful, and its productiveness is truly astonishing, the whole bed being a perfect blaze of bloom for weeks and months; color, dark rich rose on deep yellow ground elegantly flamed with scarlet and crimson." [C&Js06] "This grand and beautiful Rose attracted wide attention in our Rose Exhibit at the Saint Louis World's Fair last year, and was one of the leading varieties in group 108 for which we were awarded a Grand Prize." [C&Js05]

Marquisette (Ducher, 1872)
"Pink with some salmon." [Ÿ]

Miss Lowe's Variety (Lowe, 1887)
"Single crimson." [P1]

[Mme. Desprez] (Desprez,-1835)
"White." [TCN] "Pure white, double, cupped, large, beautiful." [LF] "Very fine white." [CC] "White tinged with lemon, large and very double; form, cupped." [P] "A fac-simile of a Double White Camellia, with the most agreeable fragrance." [Bu] "Foliage smooth; numerous clusters; flowers pretty full, large (3 inches [ca. 7.5 cm]), pure white." [R-H35]

Mme. Eugène Résal (P. Guillot, 1894)
Seedling of 'Mme. Laurette Messimy' (Ch).
"Coppery rose; vigorous." [J] "Bicolored, nankeen-yellow shaded intense pink; flower large, semi-double, cupped, fragrant; floriferous; very vigorous." [Cx] "Variable, ranging from coppery-red to bright china-rose on an orange ground, exceedingly rich and effective, large and double, with fine petals. Splendid for massing." [P1] "This rose is not one of the first flowers in Spring; but it is one of the last flowers in Fall, which makes it precious. It seems to contradict the appellation 'Monthly Rose', as it tends to bloom continuously from Spring to Fall...[F]oliage of a dark green." [JR23/41] "From seed gathered from the China 'Mme. Laurette Messimy', and down in 1887 by Monsieur Pierre Guillot...It is a vigorous bush, compact and blooming abundantly until frost. The blossoms are large, double, or full; the buds, elongate, of two colors, nasturtium-red shading to a very bright China pink, with a ground of orange–yellow changing to coppery-pink. But with its vigor, its luxuriant foliage both 'purple' and glossy, and its buds and flowers looking like big variegated Nasturtiums, I think that, when planted in groups or beds, this will prove to be one of the happiest acquisitions for such purposes." [JR19/56]

Mme. Laurette Messimy (Guillot et fils, 1887)
From crossing an un-named seedling of 'Rival de Pæstum' (T) and 'Mme. Falcot' (T) with 'Mme. Falcot' (T).
"Coppery yellow brightened by flame and shaded intense pink; flower large, full, fragrant; very floriferous; vigorous." [Cx] "Medium size, not well filled, Chinese pink, ground colour bright saffron yellow. Very free-flowering, soon over, but very effective; continuous till autumn." [Hn] "Graceful flowers...salmon-rose tints." [E] "Very vigorous; flower large or moderate, double or full, well formed, tapered bud; beautiful sparkling China pink, very bright coppery yellow at the base." [JR11/149] "Fair degree of perfection [*in cool seasons*]." [L] "Very free...vigorous for its type...4×3 [ft; ca. 1.25×1 m]." [B] "Ample glossy leaves of grayish green." [B1]

Monthly Rose
Somewhat generic for all China roses; but, where specific, indicating 'Parsons' Pink China'; also generic for the early Damask Perpetuals, as well as specific to 'Monthly Rose' (DP).

Mrs. Bosanquet
Listed as a Bourbon.

Mutabilis (Breeder unknown,-1896) syn. 'Tipo Idéale'
"Honey-yellow to orange and red." [B] "Spreading...to 8 [ft; ca. 2.5 m]...soft yellow changing to pink then crimson, excellent rebloom." [HRG] "Large single flowers." [Hk] "Beautiful clusters...stems and leaves...are red." [DP] "Of Oriental grace, with chiffoned petals poised delicately as if about to flutter away. It shares with many of the Sasanqua Camellias their sort of artless elegance." [BCD] "May be partly derived from the Tea Rose." [T3] Oddly enough, gets touches of rust (which seem to do no harm)—most unusual in either Chinas or Teas; does *not* get mildew—which Chinas and sometimes Teas will get; has small, few-

seeded hips, which set only in the Fall for me; and generally marches to the beat of a different drummer in all things. Its recorded history is very much on the scantling side; but it is said to have gone from China to Réunion (the Île-Bourbon; though Breon does not list it in his 1825 *Catalogue des Plantes* for that isle) to Italy before being generally distributed (see W.J. Bean, *Trees and Shrubs Hardy in the British Isles*, 8th ed. revised). Phillips & Rix report that one Prince Ghilberto Borromeo gave a specimen to Henri Correvon of Geneva in 1896. Researchers should not confuse it with da Costa's double Tea 'Mutabilis', and should be generally cautious, as 'Mutabilis' is a much-used name.

Napoléon (Laffay, ca. 1835)
"Blush." [M'I] "Yellow, tinted crimson." [LS] "Flower large, full, flared; pale pink touched crimson." [S] "Blush, mottled with pink, large and double; form, cupped." [P1]

Némésis (Bizard, 1838)
"Crimson, later quite dark," [N] "Flowers full or semi-full, colored deep red." [JR23/104] "Flower small, full, velvety dark crimson; petals muddled." [S] "Crimson, changing blackish, larger and more robust in habit than [*other "Fairy Roses"*]." [P] "Dainty small leaves on a dwarf twiggy bush. The flowers are double, quite small, of rich plum crimson with coppery shadings, borne in small clusters early in the summer and in great heads on the strong shoots later. Not much scent. 2 to 3 ft [ca. 6-9 dm]" [T3] We learn from *Les Amis des Roses* no. 215 (page 5), that Monsieur Bizard was Angers' advisor to the royal court, and that Monsieur Millet, first president of the Angers Horticultural Society (and, at least in the 1840s, president of the *Comice Horticole de Maine-et-Loire*), said that Bizard was to some degree responsible for the rose-growing predilections of Angers, being the first person in town to put together a collection of roses. He was to breed and release many, as well.

New Red Pet
Listed as 'Red Pet'.

Œillet de St.-Arquey
Listed as 'Fimbriata à Pétales Frangés'.

Old Blush
Listed as 'Parsons' Pink China'

Old Crimson
Listed as 'Slater's Crimson China'.

Papillon (Dubourg,-1828)
"Purple." [LS] "Rose red, medium size, full, dwarf." [Sn] Not to be confused with the climber of the same name by Nabonnand.

Parks' Yellow Tea-Scented China
Listed as a Tea.

Parsons' Pink China (China/Parsons, 1793) syn., 'Common China', 'Monthly Rose', 'Old Blush'
"Blush, profuse flowered." [JWa] The headnote to this chapter provides its recorded history—such as it is—and whether we owe it all to Peter Osbeck of Sweden in 1752, his countryman Capt. Ekeberg's 1763 introduction, to Mr. Ker, or Keer, or Kerr, "around 1780," to a misreading by Vibert of Sabine's handwriting, making "Ker" out of "Kew," or to anything and everything else, is problematical. "I [*Loiseleur-Deslongchamps*] saw in 1798, in the greenhouses of Monsieur Barbier, chief surgeon of Val-de-Grâce and distinguished amateur botanist, the first China Rose which he had gotten from England, where it had been received from China via India in 1789— say some—in 1780 or indeed 1771 say others." [L-D] The likelihood is that the original pale pink China was "introduced" a number of times from China by all and sundry, and that the person originally responsible is quite indiscernible in the crowd by now. Jamain & Forney refer to Dr. Cartier's "full-flowered" China seedling—'Bengale Centfeuilles'—as the common

China "which is so well known in our gardens." Clearly, the early introductions were not single; extant dried botanical specimens from then indicate some degree of doubleness. Just as clearly, 'Parsons' Pink China', as known today, is not what we or anyone would describe as "full-flowered," being rather on the semi-double side. In his catalog of 1820, Vibert distinguished the common China from both the "single pink" and the "full flowered," indicating that the common China of his catalog was semi-double—as 'Parsons' Pink China' is today. Considering this, it appears that Jamain & Forney's 1873 statement about Dr. Cartier's "well-known" variety is derived from a misreading of Vibert's *Essai sur les Roses*, which seems to have been at Jamain & Forney's respective elbows as they wrote.

At any rate, it would seem that 'Parsons' Pink China' has met all comers for more than two hundred years, and has prevailed. Here is why: "One of the oldest China Roses, but one of the very best. There can be nothing more perfect than its half-expanded bud, of a light crimson, inclining to blush. It commences blooming among the earliest, and, if the old seed-vessels are picked off, will continue to bloom abundantly through the summer and autumn, even after severe frosts. It is one of the hardiest of the class." [SBP] "The flower is a dark blush or rose colour, and about three inches in diameter [ca. 7.5 cm]; it grows very strong, frequently making shoots five feet long [ca. 1.5 m] in one season in rich sandy soil." [Bu] "Pretty clear pink colouring...dainty scent and neat foliage...compact, low." [J] "Blush pink aging darker pink...twiggy...to 3 [ft; ca. 9 dm]." [HRG] "Perpetual silvery pink with a crimson flush. Upright...5×4 [ft; ca. 1.5×1.25 m]." [B] "Small, semi-double, and freely produced." [Hk] "Constant and free bloomer." [ARA31/31] "Of vigorous habit, and there are in some gardens bushy plants eight feet high [ca. 2.25 m]...[*the blossoms are*] showy from their profusion, and appear well when in bud." [WRP] "The wood is stout, of a glaucous green, bearing brown hooked prickles...vigorous in growth, flowering successively, and the fruit is ovate in form, and scarlet." [JP] "This pretty bush has only been known a short while; but already it is no longer rare, as it deserves being grown due to its merit of always being in leaf and in bloom. Its leaves, arranged like those of other roses, vary in the number of leaflets (3 or 5), which are pointed and of a delicate green lightly edged with pink. This bush, which is of a very elegant look, grows to about 3 or 4 feet. From each of its axils comes a branch bearing at its tip between one and four long buds which subsequently become lightly fragrant blossoms of great freshness, of a shade of pink nearly as intense as that of the Centifolia from Bordeaux [*'Rosier des Dames'*], though less double. To have flowers all year long, all you need to do is to cut them as they fade; they then regrow, even in Winter." [BJ06]

Pink Pet
Listed as a Polyantha.

Pompon de Paris (Breeder unknown,-1880)
Like 'Némésis', above, a Fairy Rose or Lawrenciana, which group we examine more closely in *The Old Rose Adventurer*. The name 'Pompon de Paris' is unattested in the usual literature during the period in which Lawrencianas were in vogue; this is perhaps a market-name rather than a horticultural name per se. "Flower small, pretty full; pink." [JR4/21] "1×1 [ft; ca. 3×3 dm]." [B1]

Pourpre
Listed as 'Blue Rose'.

Président d'Olbecque (Guérin, 1834)
"Cerise, often changing to crimson; pretty and distinct." [JC] "Cherry red; form, cupped." [P] Though often given as a synonym of 'Louis Philippe', was originally at least a distinct cultivar.

Primrose Queen (Lippiatt,-1918)
Sport of 'Arethusa' (Ch).
"Light yellow, medium size, full, moderate height." [Sn] "Primrose yellow. Vigorous. Winter flowerer." [Au]

Princesse de Sagan (Dubreuil, 1887)
Affiliated with 'Souvenir de David d'Angers' (T).
"Deep cherry-red, shaded maroon." [H] "Velvety crimson shaded with blackish purple and reflexed with amaranth; of medium size, full, growth vigorous." [P1] "A dark red, rather single, rose. Very small, but numberless blooms. I have often done the whole dinner-table with this rose. Useful for cutting." [HmC] "Of moderate dimensions in growth, but vigorous and robust; branches armed with many very strong and hooked thorns; leaves of 5 bright leaflets, beautiful green above, paler beneath. Buds very long in the Spring, shorter in Summer, longer than the sepals, which are long and foliaceous, whereas the ovary is short and squat. Flowers solitary, medium-sized, with long stems, upright at the ends of the branches; widely cupped, with many petals perfectly imbricated in the outer rows, somewhat concave, and slightly wavy." [JR11/183] Jeanne-Alexandrine-Marguerite Seillière, Princesse de Sagan; died 1905.

Pumila (Colville, ca. 1806)
"Flower medium sized, nearly full; virginal white." [S] "Small, double, almost star-like flowers usually borne singly on a short, slightly spreading, miniature plant with long (for size of plant) thin mid-green leaves...1×1 [ft; ca. 3×3 dm]." [B1]

Purpurea (Chenault, 1930)
"Rich, glowing, purplish crimson colour...18 inches [ca. 4.5 dm]." [T3] Not to be confused with 'Pourpre', that is, the 'Blue Rose'.

Queen Mab (W. Paul, 1896)
"Apricot, reddish suffusion, dwarf, compact habit." [Wr] "Peach, center orange." [LS] "Soft rosy apricot, centre of flower shaded with orange and the outside tinted with rose and violet. It blooms with wonderful freedom, and is one of our best roses for garden decoration, especially in the late summer and autumn, when the beautiful colours of the flowers are intensified by the lengthening nights." [P1] "Very delicate and beautiful, with

HT form. Small grower." [Th] "Flower large, semi-double, moderate vigor." [Cx] "Coppery young foliage, wiry growth to over a metre [ca. 1 yard]...very double, flat..., quartered and 60 mm [ca. 2 ¼ inches]...soft apricot which deepens." [G] "This variety is quite different from its forebears, and is superior to them by reason of the vigor of its growth, and the texture of its petals, the quality of which permits the blossom to last a long time, cupped at one point, certainly longer than other roses we know." [JR20/67] "This variety is a good example of those of the boutonnière class, like 'Ma Capucine' [T] and 'Mme. Laurette Messimy' [Ch]. Nevertheless, it differs from these two roses as well as all others by the strength and regularity of its growth, as well as by the substance of its petals, which are very strong, allowing it to last a long time as a cut flower—longer, indeed, than any other rose known." [JR20/164] See also 'Morning Glow' in the chapter on Teas.

Queen's Scarlet
Listed as 'Cramoisi Supérieur'.

[**Red Pet**] (Parker/G. Paul, 1888) syn., 'New Red Pet'
"A very pretty miniature Rose, low bushy growth, constant and profuse bloomer, small, round, very double flowers, color deep rich red, blooms all the time; fine for borders and edging, also for pot culture." [C&Js98] The "old" Red Pet would be 'Lucullus'.

[**Reine de la Lombardie**] (Breeder unk.,-1835) trans., "Queen of Lombardy" "Deep cerise." [S-V] "Large, very multiplex or full, red padding to purple." [Gp] "Blush, changing to rosy crimson, large and full; form, expanded." [P] "Medium-sized, double, purple." [R&M62] "Blossom large, full, flat; color, pale pink, passing to crimson." [S] "Of a brilliant and beautiful cherry color, of globular form and full double; the plant is of rapid growth, very hardy and blooms profusely." [WRP] A parent of Geschwind's Roxburghii 'Premier Essai'.

Rival de Pæstum
Listed as a Tea.

Rosa chinensis spontanea
Listed as 'Henry's Crimson China'.

Rosada (Dot, 1950)
From 'Perla de Alcañada' (Min Ch; parentage: 'Perle des Rouges' [Pol] ×
'Rouletii' [Min Ch]) × 'Rouletii' (Min Ch)
"Peach pink." [Ÿ]

Rose de Bengale (Breeder unk.,-1844) syn., 'Sanguinea'; trans., "Bengal
Rose"
"Bright deep crimsoned, anemone flowered." [JWa] "Bright red single
deepening with age to crimson. Twiggy, angular growth...4×3 [ft; ca.
1.25×1 m]." [B] "Interesting quilled petals." [Hk] "Continually in
flower...about a metre [ca. 3 ft]." [G] "Stouter wood and larger, darker
flowers than 'Miss Lowe'." [T3]

Rose de l'Inde (Jacquin, date unc.) trans., "Rose of India"
"Dark pink." [Ÿ]

Rose-Œillet de St.-Arquey
Listed as 'Fimbriata à Pétales Frangés'.

Rouletii (Breeder unk., 1815)
"Almost evergreen, the tiny shrub is bushy and well endowed with small
thorns. Fully double, clear pink flowers, borne in upright clusters...6×6
inches [ca. 1.5×1.5 dm]." [B1] Like 'Némésis' and 'Pompon de Paris',
another Lawrenciana.

Sanglant (Cherpin/Liabaud, 1873)
"Flower full, variable light red." [JR23/104] "Growth vigorous; flower
varying from light pink to dark pink depending upon the sun." [S]

Sanguinea
Listed as 'Rose de Bengale'.

Semperflorens
Listed as 'Slater's Crimson China'.

Serratipetala
Listed as 'Fimbriata à Pétales Frangés'.

Sirena
Listed as 'Charlotte Klemm'.

Slater's Crimson China (China/Slater, 1790) syn., 'Old Crimson', 'Semperflorens'
"A rather velvety crimson red, double rose, 2.5 to 3 inches [ca. 6.5-7.5 cm], growing in a thin stem singly and in clusters; it is truly everblooming...branching, almost twiggy, as the branches are wiry, of 3 to 4-foot height [ca. 1-1.25 m], with foliage of a deep lustrous green, showing purple or deep red in the young leaflets." [ARA33/70] "A constant daily bloomer. The bright red roses are small and nearly single, the bush dwarf and spindling, with nothing to indicate its well-known strength and longevity." [Gr] "Perfectly double, cup shaped, of a rich crimson colour...though of humble growth gives a profusion of bloom throughout the entire season." [Bu] "Brilliantly coloured flowers, and is quite one of the showiest roses; it makes quick progress when planted against a south wall...freer flowering [*than 'Cramoisi Supérieur'*]." [OM] "There is also [*along with 'Parsons' Pink China'*] a variety with blossoms of a deep and velvety crimson, quite like the other, except that the leaves are edged with brown, the blossom is less double, and the bush is generally lower, a disadvantage for which it compensates by the rich color of its flowers." [BJ06] "Its branches are slender; wood dark green; leaves shiny, tinted more or less with purple; growth short and bushy; flowers, produced singly, of a deep crimson, and the fruit is quite round." [JP] "The crimson or purple China is more delicate and not as tall as the pink-flowered ones.

Its branches are pendant, and branch out; its leaves are smaller and more delicate, and are edge and touched with an icy brown-pink. The flower is semi-double, and of a superb velvety crimson. It should enchant fanciers with the richness of its color, one always looked for in every sort of flower. Its propagation is not easy, particularly on the Briar, because of the delicacy of its wood and shoots." [C-T]

Sophie's Perpetual
Listed as a Bourbon.

Souvenir d'Aimée Terrel des Chênes (Widow Schwartz, 1897)
Seedling of 'Mme. Laurette Messimy' (Ch)
"Dwarf; elegant, handsome purple tinted foliage. Bud elongate, of many shades from golden yellow to orange apricot yellow. The open blossom is small, well formed, beautiful coppery pink nuanced carmine." [JR21/148] "A handsome new bedding rose of Tulip form, large full flowers, lovely creamy white, beautifully edged and flushed with rose crimson. A strong healthy grower, producing lovely buds and flowers the whole growing season." [C&Js05]

Souvenir de Catherine Guillot (P. Guillot, 1895)
"Darkest orange-red." [ARA27/19] "Very floriferous, branches and foliage purplish, buds long, nasturtium red mixed with carmine towards the tip. Flower large, full, well-formed, varying from carmine nasturtium red on an orange yellow ground to carmine Indian yellow; very fragrant." [JR19/147] "Coppery carmine, centre shaded with orange; an exceedingly rich-coloured Rose of great excellence; growth fairly vigorous." [P1] "Decorative; hard to establish; remarkably fine color." [ARA28/104] "May be taken as the best…of several button-hole Roses issued within the last few years, which have quite small flowers, often only semi-double, but exceedingly rich in brilliant combinations of colours." [F-M2]

Souvenir de J.-B. Guillot (P. Guillot, 1897)
"Crimson, shaded bright coppery-red. A fine buttonhole variety." [H]
"Flowers are large, full and very sweet." [C&Js99] "Very floriferous; flower
large or medium-sized, varying from nasturtium-red nuanced crimson to
light nasturtium red, depending upon the temperature. Very brilliant, novel
coloration." [JR21/147] "Very rich and effective; growth vigorous." [P1]

Subalba
Listed as 'De Cels'.

The Green Rose
Listed as 'Viridiflora' (Ch).

Unermüdliche (Lambert, 1904) trans., "Indefatigable"
From 'Mlle. la Comtesse de Leusse' (T) × 'Mme. Caroline Testout' (HT).
"Maroon, center white." [LS] "Purple-red, center white, medium size,
semi-double, dwarf." [Sn]

Viridiflora (Bambridge & Harrison, 1855) syn., 'The Green Rose'
Sport of 'Parsons' Pink China' (Ch).
"Dark green; flowers medium-sized, full; very floriferous; very vigorous; a
curiosity." [Cx] "Green flowers, of no beauty whatsoever." [EL] "An
engaging monstrosity…very easy to grow." [Hk] "Flowers…light green, in
clusters of 10-20." [l'H55/54] "[Its blossom has the scent of] pepper."
[JR33/101] "This monstrous rose has parts which are identical with those
of all other roses;…each petal is transformed into a veritable leaf identical
in texture and form to one of the stem leaves, only one is not able to see
the dentation without a lens." [S] "The Green Rose was seen in all its
glory; Monsieur Eugène Verdier exhibited many specimens…Poor Green
Rose! Just a few more years, and it will cease to be! But that's all it's capable of. Inconstant as the nuns of another reign, like them loving admiration, they know that their finery is too simple to be attractive, and that it
is necessary to take on brighter, livelier colors to secure admirers. A young
botanist, Monsieur Alphonse Lavallée, showed us this year, to good effect,

blossoms strongly tinted poppy red in which the central petals had meta-morphosed into stamens and pistils. It is thought, and for good reason, that this supposed species with green flowers, originating in Japan, is nothing other than a sport which will revert to the Type after a few years of growth...The flowers shown by Monsieur Verdier were totally green." [l'H58/61-62] "4×3 [ft; ca. 1.25×1 m]." [B] "It is so ugly that it is worth nothing, except as a curiosity; and if it ceased to be a curiosity, it would be quite valueless. It is a green rose. I got a small plant from Baltimore, in America, some years ago, and I find it perfectly hardy. It blooms very freely, and all through the summer; the bud is a perfect Rose bud in appearance, but the open flower shows that the Rose is of monstrous and not natural growth; the petals are, it seems to me, no real petals at all, but an expansion of the green heart, which often appears in Roses, and which has here been so cultivated as to take the place of the natural Rose. The petals are coarse and irregular, and have serrated edges, with a very faint scent." [Br] "'I received 'Viridiflora' from Charleston, from which it was sent me...perhaps 35 years ago [*ca. 1854*]...it was from the same source [*Monsieur Andrea Gray of Charleston?*] that I also received...'Isabella Gray'...[*signed:*] Eugène Verdier fils, 1889.'...Despite further researches, we have yet to determine the exact origin of the Green Rose." [JR13/114-115] "It is a sport from ['Parsons' Pink China']...It was caught in Charleston, S.C., about 1833, and came to Baltimore through Mr. R. Halliday, from whom I obtained it, and presented two plants to my old friend Thomas Rivers in 1837.'" [Buist being quoted second-hand in Br] 'Viridiflora' was thus evidently held a number of years before being *commercially* released. Why?: "More appropriate to the collection of the celebrated Barnum than to any serious horticultural exhibition." [R-H55]

White Pet
Listed as a Polyantha.

Chapter Four

Teas

"We have…a numerous family separated from the China roses, solely by their scent, which the French, with their usual nicety of perception, have compared very appropriately to Green Tea." [C] "They bewilder the susceptible rosarian by their exquisite elegance of form, delicacy of colour, and peculiarly refreshing fragrance, which, though likened to that of a newly-opened sample of the choicest tea, is really distinct, and, we will venture to say, unlike all other odours, whether of flowers or leaves, and the most refined and blessed fragrance obtainable in the garden of the world." [Hd] "The tea-rose is the spoilt child of the family. Natives of China, they seem to keep in their heart all the wealth of which they had a glimpse there in the far East. Their colors, so rich, so warm, so pure, so true and tender, are of infinite variety. From nankeen yellow to dark yellow, pale, pure white, salmon pink, bright red and carmine, every shade that the heavens give us at the rising and setting of the sun live again in these flowers. They are highly esteemed in the gardens of the aristocracy, and dear to the brush of the artist." [G&B]

"From the earliest to the latest, nothing in the history of the rose has been of greater importance than the creation of the Tea. Its introduction to the Occident ranks with the bountiful best gifts of the nineteenth century." [Dr] Having originated—it is speculated—in natural or man-induced crosses between forms of *R. chinensis* and *R. gigantea*, "the [blush] Tea Rose was introduced directly from China to England in 1789; recommended by London to the Empress Joséphine in 1810, it entered into cultivation around 1816." [JF] "The yellow variety was obtained from China in 1824, and, even now, after so many fine varieties have been raised, is surpassed but by few in the size and beauty of its flowers, although they are but semi-double. It has only a very slight tea-like odour...Both the Chinese varieties referred to were introduced to our country [*the U.S.A.*] by the late William Prince, the father of the author, many years before any other persons made similar importations, and the first considerable importation of varieties originated from these 2 Chinese parents [*'Hume's Blush Tea-Scented China' and 'Parks' Yellow Tea-Scented China', as they have come to be called*], was made from Loddiges & Sons of London, by the author himself." [WRP] Most of the very earliest Tea roses were delicate greenhouse varieties, of which few have survived. "Nearly 300 varieties of Tea Roses have been cataloged [*by 1845*], and 40 or 50 are still cultivated." [PlB] As time went on, however, successive crops of Tea rose seedlings began to yield stronger-growing varieties fit for outdoor planting; and it is mainly representatives of this stronger race which remain with us today.

"The roses of this section are, for the most part, of refined growth; the branches are generally slender, nodding, and slightly thorny; the bark is smooth; the leaves, divided into three, five, rarely seven leaflets, are glossy, and often more elongated than with the other sorts; the flowers, though of varying color, are generally pale, more commonly whitish or yellowish, rarely red, and wafting a light tea scent; they are nearly always solitary at the ends of the branches, and supported by feeble stems which often reflex under the weight of the blossom; the tube of the calyx (ovary) is short and rounded…when the plant is vigorous, it produces very strong branches, on which the flowers, in a cluster, vary in number according to the variety and vigor of the particular specimen." [BJ] "The short-branched [*that is, non-climbing*] varieties divide into three sorts which are quite distinct from one another in their respective characters…Certainly, such normal looking varieties as 'Catherine Mermet', 'Bougère', 'Mme. Cusin', 'Maman Cochet', [*and*] 'Souvenir d'un Ami', would, after scrutiny, be classed as Hybrid or Tea Hybrids. Their reproductive organs are generally incomplete, the hips which they produce but rarely fertile; the varieties which come down to us are more or less fixed sports with the characteristics of the Type—the same growth, flower form and doubleness, but varying in color from deep pink to white, or, rarely, yellow. Those which sport fairly frequently are quite interesting, one of the above varieties, 'Catherine Mermet', producing seven sports: 'Bridesmaid', 'Mme. Joseph Laperrière', 'Maid of Honour', 'Muriel Grahame', 'The Bride', 'Waban', 'White Catherine Mermet'…Alongside those varieties are others which are particularly fecund, such as 'Alphonse Karr', 'Anna Olivier', 'Mme. Lambard', 'Marie Van Houtte', etc., which very easily produce a multitude of hips, and the offspring of which may vary according to the parent such that it is plausible to consider them Types, or at least sub-Types…The variety 'Safrano' may be considered as the primordial Type; all the varieties which one might mention are surely related to it. Two, however—'Adam' and 'Caroline'—are particularly different: in their growth and foliage, which are somewhat scanty; in the form of the 'Caroline'-type flowers, which are medium-sized; the arrangement of the petals, which are reflexed, crumpled, and incurved upon the calyx, covering the pistils—not æsthetically, nor offering the beauty found in the

'Adam' and 'Safrano' types in which the buds and the flowers are larger and more elongated, with well-developed petals—important things, of consequence to the grace of the blossom. The characteristic of the groups formed by 'Adam' and 'Caroline' is that all their varieties are pink, varying from dark to light, without a true yellow. It is of the greatest importance that we not apply these remarks to the varieties which were the first to come out. We find the typical elements necessary to form our groups only in the modern varieties…Between 1825 and 1840, we lost the old race, and thus take as the foundation of our three groups the varieties already mentioned…

"'Caroline' is a very old variety offered by Guérin in 1835. Growth moderate, somewhat diffuse; stems slightly upright, smooth; prickles moderately abundant; foliage of medium size, leaflets oval-ish, lanceolate, light green; abundant bloom, in clusters; bud short; flowers moderately full such that the petals incurve upon the pistils; stem short, weak; calyx small, widening at the top; color, intense pink with a light coppery tint at the base; fragrant. Through its descendants, it has produced three distinct sorts: 'Souvenir de David d'Angers'…, 'Comtesse de Labarthe'…, and 'Mme. Damaizin'…

"'Souvenir de David d'Angers' and most of its varieties are character-ized by growth which tends to droop, while the other two groups tend to be upright. Their characteristic color varies from intense red to dark crim-son to wine-lee red. Its best varieties are 'Belle Panachée', 'Chevalier Angelo Ferrario', 'Colonel Juffé', 'Francis Dubreuil', Général Billot', 'Princesse de Sagan' [*which we list as a China*], 'Professeur Ganiviat', [*and*] 'Souvenir de François Gaulain'.

"'Mme. Damaizin' is characterized by very ample foliage, large flowers which are very full and fragrant—not the case with the other two—a very long calyx in the form of a cone enlarged at the top at maturity; color, salmon pink with the same characteristics to be found in 'Jeanne Abel', 'J-B. Varonne', 'Mme. Angèle Jacquier', 'Mme. Joseph Godier', 'Marquise de Querhoënt', [*and*] 'Souvenir de Jeanne Cabaud'.

"'Comtesse de Labarthe' is the only one which preserves the primitive characteristics, and which passes them on to its varieties, such as 'Comtesse Riza du Parc', 'Mme. Charles Franchet', 'Mme. Joseph Schwartz', 'Souvenir du Général Charreton', etc.

"The second group takes in those varieties descended from 'Adam', offered by Adam in 1833 [*1838, we rather think*]. All rosarians have doubtless noted the differences between this group and that of 'Safrano'. The growth of these is bushy, and the canes are often slender with medium-sized thorns, which are somewhat numerous, and hooked; the wood is smooth; the foliage is slightly scanty, with oblong and denticulate leaflets, which are also leathery, slightly rugose, and with sharp prickles beneath the leafstalk; fairly long nodding flower stem; bud rounded, slightly pointed; flower large, full, fragrant; interior petals short and narrow, outer petals large; blossom quite full, cupped; color, a pretty salmon pink of a light shade; calyx round, surmounted with sepals—quite obvious, being much inflated at maturity. Its varieties maintain the form of the calyx and cupped flower, with slight variations in the growth, which is sometimes more upright with larger foliage; 'Archiduchesse Marie Immaculata', 'Catherine Mermet', 'Ernest Metz', 'Goubault', 'Devoniensis', 'Jules Finger', 'Mme. Cusin', 'Mme. de Vatry', 'Mme. de Watteville', 'Mme. Pauline Labonté', 'Mme. Pierre Guillot', 'Maréchal Bugeaud', 'Souvenir d'un Ami', '[Mlle. de] Sombreuil', etc.

"The third group is headed by 'Safrano', offered by Beauregard in 1839. Its absolutely typical characteristics make it the variety to adopt as the Type. Due to its fertility, it is the basis of a great number of varieties with individual characteristics, which it is better to list below classed in sub-groups according to such characteristics. Growth both abundant and tall, purplish foliage composed of elongated leaflets which are dentate and furnished with sharp prickles beneath; wood smooth, reddish; thorns fairly sturdy, recurved, fairly numerous; flower stem long, slightly flexuous; calyx pretty large, pyriform, much enlarged at maturity; bud very long; flower fragrant, large, full, very elegant, with large petals nicely packed in; color, a pretty saffron yellow; makes a shrub of the first order, worthy of a place in every rosarium. We find in this group the yellow for which we have previously sought in vain: 'Beauté Inconstante', 'Comtesse de Frigneuse', 'Dr. Grill', 'Étoile de Lyon', 'Jean Pernet', 'Luciole', 'Mme. Charles', 'Mme. Chédane-Guinoisseau', 'Mme. Falcot', 'Mme. Honoré Defresne', 'Mme. Margottin', 'Mlle. Jeanne Philippe', 'Perle de Lyon', 'Perle des Jardins', Reine Emma des Pays-Bas', 'Sunset', etc....

"The varieties which differ by their coloration are 'Anna Olivier', 'Dr. Félix Guyon', '[Mlle.] Franziska Krüger', 'G. Nabonnand', 'Honourable Edith Gifford', 'Innocente Pirola', 'Louis Richard', 'Mme. Édouard Helfenbein', 'Mme. Hoste', 'Mme. Jacques Charreton', 'Mme. Lambard', 'Marie Van Houtte', 'Meta', 'Peace', 'Perle de Feu', 'Souvenir de Pierre Notting', and many others it would be easy to name. While we are on this group..., there are certain varieties which, by their particular qualities, engage our attention. One of the principal ones is 'Red Safrano', offered by Oger in 1867. It is at the root of a series of hybrids with flowers of intense pink to red to a greater or lesser degree, in which the petals are, at their bases, yellow or coppery, or with yellow reflections throughout the blossoms—though less than in the Type...'Comtesse Festetics Hamilton', 'Charles de Legrady', 'Garden Robinson', 'Général Galliéni', 'Général Schablikine', 'Mrs. B.R. Cant', 'Monsieur Tillier', 'Princesse Hohenzollern' [*more properly, 'S.A.R. Madame la Princesse de Hohenzollern, Infante de Portugal'*], '[Mme. la] Princesse [de] Radziwill', 'Souvenir d'Auguste Legros', 'Souvenir de Mr. William Robinson'.

"Another similar group, doubtless mixed somewhat with the Chinas, has a complexion intermediate between that of the Chinas and that of the Teas, and a different look for that of the above varieties; their characteristics are: upright branches which are rigid and smooth; sparse but fairly strong thorns; flower-stem medium-length, rather strong; calyx ovoid, growing into a funnel shape; foliage stiffish and of a shiny dark green with large oblong leaflets; prickles evident beneath the leafstalk; flowers large, full, fairly scentless; petals large and rounded; color varying from shaded white to intense red, lit with yellow at the base of the petals: 'Duchesse of Edinburgh', 'Baronne M. de Tornaco', 'Fiametta Nabonnand', 'Isaac Demole', 'Papa Gontier', 'Professeur d'André', 'Rainbow'." [JR33/136-139] "One might note that, in general, the Teas with flowers in clusters and with which the ovary is fusiform are from various hybridization of Tea and China. 'Baronne Henriette de Loew' (Nabonnand, 1888) would be an example, as would 'Souvenir d'Espagne' (Pries, 1888), 'Souvenir de Père Lalanne', [*and*] '[Mlle.] Marie-Thérèse Molinier'." [JR24/44]

"It is curious to look back on one's childhood and recall the awe with which Tea Roses were regarded—things too delicate and precious for any place but the conservatory." [K1] "They appear to have been designed by nature to furnish the highest test of skill and patience in rose culture, and to afford constant evidence of the fact that the cultivation of roses does not consist in merely buying the plants and sticking them in the ground, and then pruning them with a knife and fork." [Hd] "The less they are pruned the better." [OM] "The confusion arising from the misleading term 'hybrid perpetual' has effectively concealed the fact that the true perpetual bloomers are the Tea Roses, so keeping the noblest of all Roses out of gardens even in the southern counties." [Ro] "Southern gardens can have no flowers of any strain as prolific, constant, hardy, beautiful, and fragrant as the Tea and kindred roses…Where sweet violets blow and honeysuckles, heliotropes, jasmines, myrtles and spicy carnations exhale perfume upon the air, the Tea rose blends and completes the bouquet." [Dr] "In the Lower South we can grow the…Teas and Noisettes so easily that we can almost flout the rules. Common sense would tell us that we cannot grow them in soil where the drainage is positively bad. Nor can we expect to starve the bushes and still gather a profusion of bloom. I recommend the Teas because they are climatically adapted to the Lower South, require less attention than other kinds, and at least a portion of them are far better cut flower varieties than is generally believed…I think that all of us appreciate vigorous and hardy shrubs that do not have to be coddled. Tea roses come in that category. Perhaps I came easily into an appreciation of what is hardy and dependable. My father loved Tea roses, and like them he was rugged, hardy, and dependable. It seemed that like Teas he could flout climatic conditions. Although the modern Danes are a highly cultured people, and he was of that stock, they are descendants of the Vikings. Whenever the weather was cold and rainy, my father liked to walk around in it, calmly smoking his pipe turned upside down. The elements could throw whatever they liked at him; he laughed at them through a life that lasted 86 years. The Teas take whatever is thrown at them by the elements or the enemies of the rose…If you follow the rules for rose culture, plant any kind of roses you please. If you aren't going to the trouble, then plant Teas, and perhaps you will have roses anyhow." [SHj]

"In California, and nearly all States south of Richmond [*Virginia, U.S.A.*], the Tea Rose requires no winter protection, and is there seen in the greatest perfection." [pH] "Perhaps it is because Tea roses may be grown in the South with so little effort that they are passed by for other roses, many of which are disappointing in Southern gardens. Here, in Georgia, Tea roses are among the loveliest and most useful of garden roses. They are unsurpassed when planted in beds. There are varieties which can be used as specimen plants, for low hedges, for pillars, or for growing on trellises or arbors. What more could be expected of roses?" [SHj]

"Many breeders have neglected the Tea Rose for a long time to devote themselves to Hybrid Teas." [JR29/135] "There is a great opportunity awaiting the man who may be successful in raising new Teas—superior Teas—which will have the welcome they deserve when they do come to us." [NRS13/41] "While the Hybrid Teas and the Pernetianas have displaced the Teas in England,…the latter are much better adapted to our Southern, Interior-Southern, and Southwestern Zones than the first two classes, for not only do they retain their foliage wonderfully, but most of them are more lasting in form and color than the majority of the other two types…Teas in the Southwestern, Interior-Southern, and Southwestern Zones grow to prodigious size, and the best do splendidly on their own roots. The faults of the Teas in our Southern Zones are that the lighter kinds discolor in rain or heavy, damp, or very hot winds; that many have weak stems for cutting..., and a few tightly rolled varieties ball and discolor in wet ocean winds...Unquestionably, Teas are the best roses for our heated sections with long growing seasons...they last exceedingly well, and the lighter-toned varieties hold their color better than the Hybrid Teas." [Th2]

"If there are Teas among the Roses the beds will be beautiful from the first break of growth in spring. It is one of the supreme joys of the Rose-grower to watch the bed break gently, almost imperceptibly, into a tender film of bronze, which presently deepens, thickens, and darkens. The first leaves are slender, shimmery, almost intangible things. They hover over the earth like a tinted cloud. The first glimmer of the shoots is like the faint radiance of a distant firmament at dawn. There is life, there is bright-ness, there is interest in the bed long before the first flower appears." [Wr] "The roses grouped under this heading may be said to represent the crème de la crème of the rose family. Exquisite in the delicacy, variety and superb loveliness of the tints of their beautiful blooms; unspeakably delicious in their fragrance; invaluable for the freedom with which they flower, and for the long duration of their flowering period, they are unquestionably the finest class of roses we have in cultivation at the present day." [TW]

[**A. Bouquet**] (Liabaud, 1873) syn., 'A. Boquet'
"White, striped." [LS] "Not very vigorous; flowers in a cluster; large, full, whitish pink." [S] "Coppery red." [CA90]

À Cinq Couleurs
Listed as 'Fortune's Five-Colored Rose'.

[**Abbé Garroute**] (Bonnaire, 1902)
"Very vigorous well-branched bush. Flower very large, very full, always opening well. Color, coppery yellow within with carmine pink, petal edges golden china pink on a yellow ground. This beautiful variety, blooming one to a stem, is extremely floriferous." [JR26/162] "Flowers very large and fragrant." [C&Js06]

Abricotée (Dupuis, 1843) trans., "Apricot-ish"
"A large rose of a bright rosy fawn color, with a deeper centre, a superb."
[WRP] "Yellow' [LS] "Apricot colour…margins flesh…large and double;
form cupped; growth moderate. A beautiful Rose." [P1] "Flower large,
full, cupped; color, coppery yellow, and at the center apricot pink with
yellow reflections. Growth vigorous; floriferous." [S] "Colour of flowers is
as near as may be to that of the fruit from which this variety is named, of
moderate size, not full, and rather untidy form, free-flowering; grows low
with branching habit. Much resembles 'Mme. Falcot'." [B&V] "Much
esteemed." [M'I]

Adam (Adam, 1838)
"Salmon and fawn, large, sweet and fine, none better, quite distinct."
[HstXXX:142-143] "Blush-rose, very sweet, very large and full." [FP]
"Lilac-pink." [EER] "Beautiful delicate pink; flower large, cupped, fra-
grant; moderate vigor." [Cx] "Rosy blush, very large and magnificent,
with beautiful Camellia-like petals, blooms freely, moderate grower, rather
tender…Very fine." [HstVI:368] "Handsome light carmine-pink."
[JR2/141] "One of the very largest roses in this family: its flowers are not
so regularly shaped…; color, rose, very fragrant, and showy." [WRP]
"One of the finest tea-scented roses. Its flowers are…of perfect form."
[SBP] "The flowers…not very abundantly produced." [P2] "Of poor
growth and small reputation. The blooms are large, globular and very
sweet, but loose and untrustworthy, and the sort is of little value as a free-
flowerer or autumnal." [F-M3] "Buds oval-elongate…This variety was
raised around 1837 by Monsieur Adam, gardener at Rheims, and is one of
the most beautiful and elegant of the Teas…has hooked, nearly purple
thorns…the flowers ordinarily reflect a coppery pink around the center.
These characteristics closely approach those of the rose 'Souvenir d'un
Ami', which is easily distinguished by its flower stalk bristling with glandular hairs." [PlB] "Pretty vigorous; branches slender and nodding; wood
smooth, light green, with flat red thorns which are hooked, enlarged at the

base, and very sharp. Leaves shiny, of a slightly yellowish green, divided into 3 or 5 pointed and finely dentate leaflets, bristling with sharp, hooked prickles of varying size. Flower 3 ¼-3 ½ inches across [ca. 8 cm], full, widely cupped, usually solitary; color, a handsome light pink, more intense in the center; petals of the circumference large, slightly concave, those of the center rumpled; flower-stem glabrous, short, fairly thick, and nodding. Ovary urn-shaped, green with a bloom; sepals leaf-like, long and narrow, green without, whitish within. This rose wafts a light tea scent; its bud is very pretty." [JF] "Flower large, expanded, magnificently held and well borne; color, bright rose; exquisite scent; bush fairly vigorous…leaf-stalk reddish, bristling with little stickers of varying size, stickers which are hooked and very sharp. Very tender." [S] "Still rare and little-known. Wood strong with purplish-green canes having large, hooked, purplish-pink thorns. Leaves large, two pairs of leaflets with the odd one, petiole purplish crimson, prickly beneath; leaflets large, oval, serrated, wavy, fresh green, glossy above, paler beneath; rachis purplish. Blossoms solitary or in twos; peduncle glabrous, large, strong, purplish green, 4-5 cm [ca. 2 inches], bearing at the base two small purplish-green bracts. Calyx round, sepals oval with a point, green bordered purple. Flower full, big, 7-8 cm [ca. 3 inches], outer petals large, round, reflexing back; center petals more muddled, reflexing inwardly; all petals delicately colored flesh, darker at the nub in the open blossom, flesh pink in the just-opening stage. A very beautiful rose." [An41/12-13] "One of the finest." [FP]

[**Adèle de Bellabre**] (Ducher fils, 1888)
"Coppery pink." [LS] "Flowers reddish peach, shaded with carmine and yellow, large and full; growth vigorous." [CA93] "Dwarf." [JR12/166]

Adèle Jougant
Listed as 'Mlle. Adèle Jougant' in Chapter 8.

Albert Hoffmann (Welter, 1904)
From 'Souvenir de Catherine Guillot' (Ch) × 'Maman Cochet' (T).
"Pretty yellow bordered pink." [LS] Albert Hoffmann was the first official rosarian at Sangerhausen.

[Albert Stopford] (Nabonnand, 1898)
From 'Général Schablikine' (T) × 'Papa Gontier' (T).
"An improved 'Bon Silène', color dark crimson rose, very vigorous and free blooming." [C&Js02] "Flower very large, full, solitary, with large sepals, very large thick petals; color, brilliant deep carmine pink, center coppery; exterior petals deep carmine, recurved elegantly; bud long; very well formed; borne on a long stem; large foliage; very strong wood and thorns; very vigorous bush; very floriferous; fragrant." [JR22/165]

Alexander Hill Gray (A. Dickson, 1911) syn. 'Yellow Maman Cochet'
"Of deep lemon-yellow colouring and perfect form. The growth is vigorous. Unfortunately, the blooms have weak stalks and therefore droop." [OM] "Soft yellow; fragrant; double." [ARA29/95] "Vigorous, erect; all the branches end in a bud which gives birth to a blossom which is very large, full, of perfect form, high-centered, very fragrant—strong Tea scent—lemon yellow upon opening. It is the best and most beautiful Tea rose known till now; a superb plant, and to be recommended...particularly fine in the autumn." [JR36/72] "Good foliage and form; growth fair; blooming qualities good." [ARA18/110] "Long-pointed bud; large, full flowers; lasts very well; tea fragrance. Splendid foliage, seldom diseased and holds well. Fine spreading growth; long stem, sometimes weak." {Th2} "A very attractive, upright bush with large, lemon-yellow blooms. A good worker throughout the season." [ARA29/88]

Alexandra
Listed as 'The Alexandra'.

[Aline Sisley] (Guillot fils, 1874)

"Color varying from red to purplish rose." [CA88] "Large double and sweet; fine violet crimson; beautiful. 15 cts. Each." [C&Jf97] "Vigorous; foliage yellowish green; flower of the first rank, first in all votes; large, full, centifolia-form; color, deep purple mixed with red and deep violet." [S] "An 1869 seedling of Guillot fils, who released it to commerce in 1874. Vigorous and climbing, as Mr. Clarke says, it can be used on a fence...this variety is very good for forcing, and should be cut back to 4 to 6 eyes. It freezes at 10°." [JR10/12]

Alix Roussel (Gamon, 1908)

Yellow with a salmon center; large, full.

Alliance Franco-Russe (Goinard, 1899) trans., "French-Russian Alliance"

"Vigorous, floriferous, and remontant, forming a bush which can attain 3-4 feet [ca. 1-1.25 m]. The young branches are upright, Russian-copper red, with slightly hooked thorns of the same color. The foliage looks rather like that of 'Perle des Jardins'. The leaves, composed of five leaflets, are large, regularly serrated, bright green, dark above, paler beneath, with a lightly colored mid-vein. The stem is strong and rigid, the same color as the young stems, and bearing...a long bud. The flower holds this form when just opening, but then becomes progressively flatter, finally reaching a diameter of about 3.5 inches [ca. 8 cm]. The outermost petals are large, and fold back; the others are muddled. The Tea-yellow shade usually grades to salmon towards the center." [JR23/33] "An elegant bedder." [C&Js03]

[Alphonse Karr] (Nabonnand, 1878)

Seedling of 'Duchess of Edinburgh' (T).

"Rosy crimson." [EL] "Vigorous, a child of 'Duchess of Edinburgh', but even more vigorous; flower large, full, well-formed, imbricated, an illuminated crimson-maroon red, lighter at the center; floriferous. A wonderful variety." [JR3/9] "A valuable and very beautiful tea rose; fine, large buds and flowers, full and double; color bright violet crimson, deeply shaded with purplish red; center brilliant carmine, strong grower and free bloomer." [CA88] "The *Journal des Roses* has lost one of its first collaborators in the person of Alphonse Karr, who died September 22 [1890]…at the age of 82. A most distinguished writer, Monsieur Karr not only provided a literary point of view, but also had a great reputation as a horticultural publicist. Born in Paris in 1808, Karr at first turned to teaching, and became a very young professor at the Lycée Bourbon. But his vocation was literature, which he was unable to resist, and before long was a great success at it. Having tried his hand, unsuccessfully, at politics, Monsieur Karr then devoted himself to horticulture, and retired to Nice around 1852, where he took the title of Gardener…Upon the annexation of Nice, Monsieur Karr went to St.-Raphaël, where he built his home 'Maison-Close,' in the garden of which he planted a rich collection of all sorts of flowers, and in the middle of which he whiled away many peaceful moments over the many years." [JR14/161] "It is to Alphonse Karr…that we owe the first tentative steps towards the commercial culture of the Rose. In 1870, he created, in his garden in Nice, the first set-up for growing and marketing the cut flowers. Since then, that branch of horticultural agriculture has undergone enormous development." [JR34/41] And let us not forget "the celebrated dog of Monsieur Alphonse Karr, 'Freschutz'." [VPt46/84]

Amazone (Ducher, 1872)
Seedling of 'Safrano' (T).
"Deep yellow, reverse of petals veined pink." [JR12/172] "Sulphur white." [JR1/7/6] "Golden yellow. Best in bud." [H] "Its color is fairly pure, while being veined, rather obviously, salmon-pink; its blossoms are very well formed." [JR10/45] "Very beautiful flower, much to be recommended, very floriferous; blooms in threes or fours at the ends of vigorous branches; very well formed; about 3.5 inches across [ca. 8 cm], full, opens well; outer petals deep yellow, bordered pink." [S] "Of rather poor slender growth, with long pointed buds of a good deep yellow, a colour which is still much

wanted in this class…very loose and wanting in centre, of no value as a free bloomer or autumnal, and can by no means be reckoned among the best." [F-M3] "A charming Tea Rose with yellow flowers; one of the most beautiful obtained by the late Monsieur Ducher of Lyon." [VH75/167]

[American Banner] (Cartwright, 1877)
Sport of 'Bon Silène' (T).
"Flower medium-sized, semi-full; whitish pink striped lilac; exquisite perfume; dwarf bush; floriferous." [S]

[American Perfection] (Breeder unknown,-1912)
"Light pink." [D&C12]

André Schwartz (Schwartz/Rolker, 1882)
"Brilliant glowing scarlet, very bright and striking." [C&Js99] "Medium-sized or large, full, well-formed, deep crimson-red fading to cherry-red, sometimes striped white. This is the brightest color among Teas." [JR6/116] "Vigorous, well-branched, branches armed with occasional reddish, hooked thorns; the wood is smooth, without glands or bristles; it grows to perhaps a yard or so high [ca. 1 m]…The leaves are numerous, remote, of 3-5 leaflets of which the upper pair is larger and the lower smaller; the leaflets are oblong or elliptical, glabrous, shiny above, pale and sometimes glaucous beneath, sharply toothed; stipules lacy, subulate; the color of the leaves and wood is reddish bronze when young, changing to a bronzy dark green in age. The flower is largish, well-formed, petals numerous, color varying from dark crimson red, striped white within, to cerise shaded carmine, the reverse of the petals being yellowish pink. As for blooming, it is very floriferous; from May until frost it is constantly in bloom." [JR10/73]

Anna Jung (Nabonnand, 1903)
From 'Marie Van Houtte' (T) × 'Général Schablikine' (T).
"Very large, semi-double, large petals, perfectly held; color, bright pink with some salmon, tinted madder; center coppery; bud long, on a strong

stem, coppery carmine…extremely vigorous, making a strong bush; very large fairly dark foliage; very floriferous; fresh scent." [JR27/164]

Anna Olivier (Ducher, 1872)
"Yellowish flesh shaded pink; flower large, full, cupped; vigorous." [Cx] "Buff, shaded with rose." [EL] "Lively creamy blush." [C&Js05] "Colour varies from terra-cotta." [F-M2] "To obtain that lovely terra-cotta shade the soil must be naturally impregnated with iron." [FRB] "Flowers large and full, fine form, creamy buff, flushed with rose; charming in bud; vigorous growth." [W/Hn] "Rosy-flesh; base of petals, dark; a large, beautifully-formed flower." [DO] "Flowers tolerably large, smooth and beautiful; habit moderate." [JC] "Reverse of petals rose." [P1] "Shapely and well perfumed…4×3 [ft; ca. 1.25×1 m]." [B] "Easily damaged by wet." [J] "Had credit for avoiding damage from rain." [Hk] "Very vigorous and variable over the season; the Autumn flowering is perfect—distinct in form and color from the Spring blossoms. The first buds are urn-shaped, and the reverse of the petals is flesh-pink passing to red. As the season advances, the flowers produced on the present year's wood are globular, and salmon." [JR12/180] "Lovely buds." [Dr] "One of the best Tea roses for garden display; it blooms very freely and continuously. The small blooms, of good form, are pale rose and buff shades. Growth is vigorous. A fine rose for all purposes." [OM] "Extreme freedom of bloom…vigor of growth, and fair amount of hardiness." [F-M2] "Somewhat dwarf and upright; foliage a nice green." [JR9/70] "Good grower with bright foliage." [F-M] "Resistant to mildew." [JR33/37] "Foliage very good and lasting. Vigorous growth in Southern Zones." [Th2] "One of the best and most distinct." [H] "Always beautiful." [NRS/13]

[Annie Cook] (J. Cook, 1888)
Seedling of 'Bon Silène' (T).
"Delicate shade of pink; a new American rose of great promise." [CA90] "Beautiful pink to white; what is more, it is a vigorous and abundant variety." [JR16/38]

[Antoine Weber] (Weber, 1899)
"Soft, rosy flesh, edge of petals bright rose, centre of flowers pale creamy yellow, sometimes tinted with salmon and fawn; large, full and double; makes strong, healthy bushes with fine foliage. An early and abundant bloomer, producing beautiful buds and large, handsome flowers through all the growing season." [C&Js02]

[Antoinette Durieu] (Godard, 1890)
Seedling of 'Mme. Caro' (T).
"Deep yellow." [LS] "Chrome yellow." [Jg]

Archiduc Joseph (Nabonnand, 1892)
Seedling of 'Mme. Lambard' (T).
"Coppery pink." [LS] "Clear shining red, with pale pink tint." [Dr] "Pale white tinted copper." [JR20/7] "Very large, very full, cupped, perfectly poised; bud conical, pure carmine, lighter towards the tip; wood brownish red; very handsome dark ashy-green foliage; thorns sharp; color, violet-pink, center bright copper, petals edges paler. Very vigorous, splendid variety, and very floriferous." [JR16/166] "Blooms abundantly, above all through Fall…The foliage of dark ashy-green gives the plant an appearance both original and unique." [JR24/56]

[Archiduchesse Marie Immaculata] (Soupert & Notting, 1886)
From 'Mme. Lambard' (T) × 'Socrate' (T).
"Vigorous bush, flower large, full, beautiful form, outer petals very large, color light brick nuanced glossy chamois; center golden vermilion; very fragrant." [JR10/148]

Archimède (Robert, 1855)
"Rosy-fawn, darker centre, large and full." [FP] "8-10 cm [to ca. 4 inches], full, chamois pink, deeper at the center, globular." [R&M62] "Flower large, full, globular; a color all its own of pink *bois* [?; *probably a verbal transcription error for "chamois"; from hints such as this, which we see scattered in his work, our impression is that Singer dictated his work to an*

amanuensis], shaded pink, colored fawn in the middle. This variety is very recommendable; it reblooms very well; the blossoms are held singly at the tips of the branches." [S] Archimède, alias Archimedes, Greek mathematician and engineer; lived 287? BC-212 BC.

Auguste Comte (Soupert & Notting, 1895)
From 'Marie Van Houtte' (T) × 'Mme. Lambard' (T).
"Very vigorous, flower large, magnificent 'Maman Cochet' form; color, madder pink, outer petals carmine red with a large darker border, center waxy flesh pink; barely open buds are extraordinarily handsome and of long duration. Very floriferous." [JR19/148] "Well branched; the beautiful dark green foliage is never attacked by mildew or the like...strong stem...As an autumnal, it is one of the best." [JR24/8] "Constant and abundant bloomer." [C&Js98]

[**Aureus**] (Ducher, 1873) trans., "Golden"
"Not very vigorous; branches upright, with irregular thorns, sometimes hooked, sometimes straight; flower medium-sized, full; coppery yellow." [S]

[**Baron de St.-Triviers**] (Nabonnand, 1882)
Seedling of 'Isabelle Nabonnand' (T).
"A delicate flesh-coloured rose shaded to copper, half-full, free-flowering and pretty." [B&V] "Soft rose, full and good shape; fragrant." [CA88] "Very vigorous, few thorns...; flower very large, semi-full, very well formed, colored delicate flesh pink; very large petals; blooms in the Winter." [JR6/186]

[**Baronne Ada**] (Soupert & Notting, 1897)
From 'Mme. Lambard' (T) × 'Rêve d'Or' (N).
"Vigorous bush, flower very large, full, globular; color, cream white, the center magnificently chrome yellow; outer petals large, inner ones narrower. The buds are enormous...Very fragrant and floriferous." [JR21/146]

Baronne Berge
Listed as 'Mme. la Baronne Berge'.

[**Baronne Henriette de Loew**] (Nabonnand, 1888) syn., 'Therese Welter'
Said to come from a Tea × China cross.
"Large, full, beautiful pale pink, shaded with golden yellow in the center, pink outside; free flowering." [Hn] "One of the best white Tea roses for cutting." [JR16/179] "Not very full...floriferous, vigorous, having extra strong thorns, good habit, and with a dark green polished foliage which is very pretty and distinct. Especially fine as a standard, making when grown on its own roots a strong stem." [B&V] "Quite vigorous, forming wonderful thickets; wood short; blossom medium-sized, in a cluster, very full, elegantly perfumed; color, delicate pink nuanced golden yellow at the center; reverse of petals brighter pink. Top of the line for bedding; very floriferous, and good for the North." [JR12/147]

Baronne Henriette de Snoy
Listed as 'Baronne Henriette Snoy'. The obtrusive "de" arises from confusion with 'Baronne Henriette de Loew', *q.v.*

Baronne Henriette Snoy (Bernaix, 1897) syn. 'Baronne Henriette de Snoy'
From 'Gloire de Dijon' (N) × 'Mme. Lambard' (T).
"Solid light peach-flesh. Globular." [Capt27] "Petals carnation inside, outside carmine pink." [K2] "Flesh pink with deeper reverse, shapely...3×3 [ft; ca. 9×9 dm]." [B] "Large double flowers on stiff stems...this variety grew as rank as 'Mme. Lambard'...but produced larger flowers in the Spring and Summer." [SHj] "Strong plant to 4 [ft; ca. 1.25 m]." [HRG] "Of good vigor, with bronzy green foliage, purple above and below in the young growth, flower very pretty, very large, and perfectly double; petals elegantly spaced, soft, sweetly rounded, and recurved towards the tip and sides. Color flesh-pink within, with a yellowish nub; carmine China pink without, making a charming combination. Lovely." [JR21/148]

[**Baronne M. de Tornaco**] (Soupert & Notting, 1896)
From 'Marie Van Houtte' (T) × 'Papa Gontier' (T).
"Bush very vigorous; beautiful glossy dark green foliage; flower large, lightly full, of good hold, beautiful long well-formed bud, the petals large and thick; color, beautiful pearly white with golden reflections, touched with very tender pink and lined with carmine, very delicate coloration. This superb variety looks much like 'Fiametta Nabonnand', which it surpasses by its great vigor and the beauty and size of its blossoms. Excellent variety for cut flowers. Very floriferous and of an exquisite perfume." [JR20/147]

Baxter Beauty (A. Clark, after 1936?)
Sport of 'Lorraine Lee'.
Apricot-yellow.

Beauté Inconstante
Listed in Chapter 8.

[**Bella**] (California Nursery Co.?, 1890)
"Yellowish white." [LS] "Pure white; good form; splendid large pointed buds." [CA90]

Belle Cythérée
Listed as 'Hume's Blush Tea-Scented China'.

[**Belle Panachée**] (Gamon, 1902)
Sport of 'Francis Dubreuil' (T).
"Velvety crimson red, plumed and striped with lilac-y pink." [JR30/15]

Beryl (A. Dickson, 1898)
"Deep golden yellow; rather small but pretty buds." [P1] "Long bud." [JR28/31]

[**Betty Berkeley**] (Bernaix fils, 1903)
"Bright red shading to crimson scarlet, buds very long, flowers medium size; robust habit of growth; distinct and beautiful." [C&Js08] "Growth robust, with moderately thick, bright somber green foliage. Buds solitary, elegantly upright on their stiff stems, ovoid, long, uniformly intense English red, with cochineal crimson and blood red. Blossom just the same color, with moderate size and fulness. Notable for the intensity and solidity of the uncommon shade." [JR27/147]

Blanche Duranthon
Listed as 'Mme. Lucien Duranthon'.

Blanche Nabonnand (Nabonnand, 1882)
"Vigorous, semi-dwarf, flower very large, full, well-formed, imbricated, pure white, continuous…good for the North." [JR6/186]

Blumenschmidt (Kiese/J.-C. Schmidt, 1905)
Sport of 'Mlle. Franziska Krüger' (T).
"Citron-yellow flowers. Very fine garden rose. Blooms constantly." [Dr]
"Large flower, full, lemon-yellow, the outer petals blushing." [JR31/105]
"The flower, of a light yellow shaded carmine at the edges of the petals, is very resistant, and blooms in the Fall." [JR29/152] "Flower very large, full, fragrant; primrose yellow to pale pink…Repeats bloom well." [Lg]
"Green pip in center, outer petals blush rose-pink." [HRG] "Low, compact, hardy; foliage plentiful, healthy; bloom plentiful, continuous." [ARA18/124] "Vigorous, very floriferous in Autumn." [JR34/24]

[**Boadicea**] (W. Paul, 1901)
"Rich creamy pink edged with rose." [C&Js03] "Very pale peach, delicately tinted pink and violet, the center being very rich pink. The ensemble of these different colors is charming and agreeable to the eye. The flower is large with a slightly high center, long; petals large and pretty thick…Very hardy, elegant deportment, very pleasant fragrance. A good exhibition variety, and at the same time a magnificent garden variety. The

growth is vigorous and it gives flowers profusely in Summer and Fall." [JR25/85] English warrior queen of the Iceni tribe; died 62 A.D.

Bon Silène (Hardy, 1835) trans., "Good Silenus"
"Cerise red." [V4] "Red marbled with crimson, full, cupped, large, superb." [LF] "Bright rose, very large and double; form expanded. The young buds of this Rose are of the most elegant form, shewing of a rich deep crimson as the sepals part. Very sweet." [P] "Superb red." [Sx] "Flower large, double, fragrant; deep pink with white streaks." [Lg] "Very free-flowering...shapely...rich rosy crimson. Scented...3×3 [ft; ca 9×9 dm]." [B] "Deep salmon-rose, illumined with carmine, medium size, semi-double, highly scented, very free-flowering. This is only desirable in the bud state." [EL] "A very beautiful tea-scented rose, cupped, very double, and fragrant. Its color is rose, shaded with crimson, and the plant is hardy and of luxuriant growth." [SBP] "Valued for its beautiful rose-coloured, fawn-shaded buds, and vigorous growth." [Dr] "Extremely large petals; though not so double as some, yet it amply compensates for this deficiency in the size of the flowers which are of a bright rose, changing to cherry red, with an agreeable fragrance." [Bu] "Flower large, full, flat; bright rose-colored, saffron at the center." [S] "Very variable in color, and often described differently under different circumstances; the plant is robust and hardy, and will grow in any situation." [WRP] "Surpassing sweetness and brilliancy of tint, with substance of petal. The color is a clear brilliant flesh colored rose, centre paler blush slightly tinged with yellow, outer petals of great substance, beautifully cupped and of a deeper color...Of all Tea roses, this is our favorite for fragrance...a sweeter and more fruit-like scent [*than has 'Devoniensis'*], peculiarly delightful." [C] "Raspberry-scented" [JR33/101] "Low-growing, spreading...foliage sufficient, healthy; bloom moderate, continuous." [ARA18/124] "Seeds freely." [Bu] "Sprang from a bird-or wind-sown seed, in a cleft at the base of a stone monument." [Dr] "Is very much admired." [FP] "Your correspondent Monsieur Schultheis is also in error as to identifying 'Goubault'

with 'Bon Silène'; there is, perhaps, some slight resemblance between the two, but the latter is a shade darker, has better form and stronger scent, and is certainly a better variety to grow. [*signed*] H.B. Ellwanger." [JR5/45] A *striped* version of 'Bon Silène', should it turn up anywhere, would be either 'American Banner' (Cartwright, 1877) or 'Flag of the Union' (Hallock & Thorpe, date uncertain). Silenus, horse-eared, horse-tailed companion of Dionysius.

[**Bougère**] (Bougère, 1832) syn., 'Clotilde'
"Flowers deep salmon colour, very large and full; form, cupped. Growth, vigorous. A superb Pot or Forcing Rose, with thick petals." [P] "Salmon and fawn, flowers very large and full; a good rose of vigorous habit." [JC] "Floriferous, pretty hardy; flower large, full, cupped, Hydrangea pink." [S] "A singular and splendid rose; the buds and flowers are very large, full double, perfectly cup shaped, of a fine roseate hue, shaded with bronze; the plant is of vigorous growth, blooms abundantly, and is one of the most hardy." [WRP]

Bridesmaid (Moore, 1893) syn., 'The Hughes'
Sport of 'Catherine Mermet' (T).
"Clear bright pink." [H] "Deep silvery pink. Mildews." [ARA27/20] "An American sport of 'Catherine Mermet', with much higher and better colour—a clear pink. This makes it a decided improvement on the original, whose one fault is weakness of colour. In all other respects it is identical, save that it seems to me that the outer petals do not reflex and open so readily as in the type." [F-M2] "Moderately vigorous." [J]

Burbank (Burbank/Burpee, 1900)
Either from 'Hermosa' (B) × a seedling of 'Bon Silène' (T); *or* from a seeding of 'Hermosa' × 'Bon Silène'.
"Light pink and crimson." [LS] "This grand Ever-blooming Rose comes from California, and has proved one of the hardiest and best everbloomers for garden planting, flowers 3 to 3.5 inches across [ca. 8-9 cm],

very double and sweet bright rose-pink shading to silver-rose. 15 cts."
[C&Js05] "Bushy growth; blooms not distinctive or attractive."
[ARA18/115] "Very superior in color to those [*flowers*] of the 'Hermosa',
and the foliage of the plants is glossy and brilliant…a merit surpassing all
the rest, is the power of resistant of the Burbank rose…to those ever-present foes…mildew and rust." [Lu] Luther Burbank, American plant-
breeder extraordinaire; lived 1849-1926.

[**Camille Roux**] (Nabonnand, 1885)
"Very vigorous bush; thorns large and occasional; very floriferous; flower
large, full, well formed, globular; color, bright red towards the center,
pinkish at the petal edges." [JR9/166] "Fine large flowers, well filled out,
very double and highly scented; color bright carmine rose, with fiery red
centre; very striking and handsome." [CA93]

[**Canadian Belle**] (Conard & Jones, 1907)
"Rich creamy-buff with deep apricot centre finely shaded with rose and
amber, delightfully perfumed." [C&Js07]

[**Canari**] (Guillot père, 1852) trans., "Canary"
"Canary yellow, beautiful little buds, delicate habit." [EL] "Clear pale yellow, beautiful only in the bud, free habit." [JC] "Full." [S] "Well doubled,
silky bright yellow; to good effect as a bud." [l'H52/148] "A yellow flimsy
thing according to modern notions." [F-M2] "Vigorous bush; flowers
medium-sized, in clusters, canary yellow; very floriferous and pretty good
as a bud." [l'H56/200]

[**Capitaine Lefort**] (Bonnaire, 1888)
From 'Socrate' (T) × 'Catherine Mermet' (T).
"Purplish rose, reverse of petals paler; very large; buds long and large."
[CA93] "Very vigorous, canes erect;…flower very large, beautiful purple
pink, petals' reverse China pink. The flower sometimes reaches 12-14 cm
across [ca. 5-5.5 inches]." [JR12/146] "Rich violet crimson, good grower
and bloomer." [C&Js98]

[**Capitaine Millet**] (Ketten Bros., 1901)
From 'Général Schablikine' (T) × 'Mme. A. Étienne' (T).
"Bright copper-red, dark carmine reverse." [RR] "Blossom light nasturtium red, deep carmine at the edges, gold ground, large, full, fragrant, bud long, opens well, stem strong. Growth vigorous, very floriferous." [JR25/146]

Captain Philip Green (Nabonnand, 1899)
From 'Marie Van Houtte' (T) × 'Devoniensis' (T).
"Cream with carmine." [LS] "Carmine pink." [Ÿ] "Large, full, erect; large petals. Color, cream of the 'Marie Van Houtte' sort; beautiful long bud, solitary, carmine straw yellow, long stem. Handsome foliage, strong wood, strong thorns. Very vigorous, very floriferous. Fragrant." [JR23/179]

[**Caroline**] (Guérin, 1829) syn. 'Caroline de Rosny'
"Light pink, center yellowish, beautiful." [LF] "Rosy-flesh, deeper towards centre; prettily formed buds." [EL] "Blossom medium sized, full, bright pink." [S] "Blush, suffused with deep pink, large and full; form, cupped. Grows and flowers freely." [P] "A pretty rose, with flowers very double, of a bright rose color, and very perfect in their shape." [WRP] "Pale rosy-pink; a very good, hardy, free growing rose." [JC] "This is a Tea, very close to the China hybrids...Wood smooth, thorns very rare, short, light red, recurved at the tip; young branches purplish; leaves a handsome green, with five or sometimes seven leaflets which are large, oval, elongate, slightly stalked, very finely dentate, and a glaucous green or at least glossy; stipules very small, glabrous, ciliate; leafstalk usually feeble, having beneath some small prickles, and above with stiff, short, glandular hairs; flower stem long, about an inch and a half [ca. 3.5 cm], purplish, with transparent epidermis having short, stiff hairs; ovary glabrous, inflated, short; sepals short, entire, shiny, slightly ciliate with unequal red hairs, sometimes with rust-colored pubescence; bud very firm, red, ovoid; flower medium-sized, intense flesh, often with a green pip in the center. This Rose is quite pretty...it resists seven or eight degrees of frost fairly well,

being one of the few somewhat hardy Teas." [PlB] "Raised at Rosny in 1829. It makes a stocky bush, sending its canes straight up and forming a good head. Its branches are jointed, and reddish in the sun, also being armed with fairly straight small prickles; foliage with leaflets which are oval-rounded, small with the lower leaflets oval-elliptical and larger than the upper leaflets, regularly dentate like a saw. Corymbs of 3-15 delicately lilac-pink blossoms, quite full, of moderate size, well formed; flower-stalk lightly hispid; ovary turbinate, short, glabrous; sepals short, lacinate. Centifolia perfume." [R-H32] We learn from *Les Amis des Roses* no. 215 (page 5) that "Caroline" was the name of a very pretty woman of Angers, France.

Catherine II (Laffay,-1827)

"Chamois." [V9] "Flesh-pink." [RG] "Blush white." [God] "Medium, full; color, flesh; very beautiful." [S] "*Leaflets*, large. *Peduncle*, arching. *Ovary*, long and thick. *Flowers*, large, full, semi-globular, flesh, sometimes with a little lilac." [Pf] Catherine II, called "the Great," empress of Russia; lived 1729-1796.

Cels Multiflore (Hardy/Cels, 1836)

"Flesh color, very free-blooming." [EL] "White, shaded with pink, and flowers very freely." [FP] "Blush, pink centre; a very profuse bloomer." [HstXI:225] "Large size." [JWa] "Flower medium-sized, charmingly colored pink with marbling; the bush blooms constantly and abundantly. These three roses [*among which is 'Cels Multiflore'*], children of the Luxembourg, are being propagated in the establishment of the Cels Bros." [An36/96] "Flesh, large, full, flat, very floriferous, superb." [LF] "Among the best of the blush roses; indeed, for profusion of bloom it has not a rival; every flower perfect, fully double, and cup shaped, growing freely in almost any soil or situation, and is an excellent variety to force into early bloom." [Bu] "Of moderate vigor." [S] "Very hardy." [P2] As for the introducers: "*Catalog...of Monsieur F. Cels, Chaussée du Maine, No. 55; at Paris, 1832...*It will soon have been a century that the name Cels has been renowned in Europe, and it occupies a distinguished place among those responsible for the development of horticultural taste in France. J.-M. Cels, the father of the present owner of the firm, was a man of much merit who, through his wide knowledge, his spirit, and his contacts, contributed strongly to the encouragement of the taste for Horticulture among the notables of his day." [R-H32] "The First Prize for the Collection Containing the most Rare and Beautiful Plants was awarded to that exhibited by Monsieur Cels, nurseryman." [R-H32]

[Chamoïs] (Ducher, 1869)

"Flower medium-sized, semi-full; color, fawn yellow sometimes changing to coppery yellow." [S] "Buds deep apricot, when fully opened nankeen colour, distinct, flowers small; habit moderate." [JC] "'Chamois'…a *Noisette* in the form of its blossom and in its coloration, and a *Tea* in branching and foliage." [JR23/166]

[Charles de Franciosi] (Soupert & Notting, 1890)

From 'La Sylphide' (T) × 'Mme. Crombez' (T).
"Vigorous; buds long, well formed, and red-orange in color. Flower large, full, rosette-form; color, chrome yellow nuanced delicate salmon yellow; outer petals lightly tinted pink. This newcomer is uni-flowered on upright canes; it is much to be recommended for forcing in Winter." [JR14/147] "Monsieur Charles de Franciosi, president of the regional Société d'Horticulture du Nord de la France." [JR13/120]

Charles de Legrady (Pernet-Ducher, 1884)

"This splendid rose is almost unexcelled for general planting; color fine chamois red, richly shaded with violet crimson; very sweet, and a constant bloomer; extra fine." [CA93] "Very vigorous, flower large, full, very well formed, of a beautiful coloration; carmine red passing to very dark China pink; the petal edges are somewhat silvery; the plant is very floriferous." [JR8/152] "Grows stout and bushy with fine foliage, and an early and constant bloomer; makes beautiful buds and large handsome flowers, very fragrant and highly valued for garden planting. Color fine chamois-red, passing to violet-crimson; a great bearer, covered with buds and bloom all through the growing season." [C&Js02] "Dedicated to Monsieur Charles de Legrady, Councilor of Royal Commerce, member of the municipality and Chamber of Commerce and Industry of Budapest." [JR11/105]

Charles Dingee
Listed as 'William R. Smith'.

[Charles Rovelli] (Pernet père, 1876)
"Large globular flowers, very full and double, delightfully fragrant; color, a lovely shade of brilliant carmine, changing to silver rose; center and base of petals clear, golden yellow; very beautiful." [CA88] "Bush straggling, nearly always late; this rose, despite its weakness…seems to be due some recognition because of its elegant buds, which are unrivalled in color; these buds are quite perfect; despite the feeble growth, one sees it produce large or perhaps medium-sized buds which are long, solitary on the stem, of the most perfect form, and most elegantly held; their color is a superb delicate pink, darkening slightly and gradually to the petal-tips; these buds become a rose which is nearly large, full, well-formed, and delicate pink with a brighter center, according to Monsieur Petit-Coq [*alias Scipion Cochet*]." [S] The Messers Rovelli, nurserymen of Pallanza, Italy.

[Château des Bergeries] (Widow Lédéchaux, 1886)
"Vigorous, with erect branches, which are reddish; thorns fairly numerous, large, slightly recurved, brown; leaves composed of 5 oval leaflets of a handsome light green, unequally and somewhat shallowly toothed; flowers large, globular, very full, pale canary yellow, darker at the center. The bud is large and well-formed." [JR10/171]

[Claudius Levet] (Levet, 1886)
"Velvety pink." [LS] "Carmine rose, salmon center; large and full." [CA90]

Clementina Carbonieri (Bonfiglioli & figlio, 1913)
From 'Kaiserin Auguste Viktoria' (HT) × 'Souvenir de Catherine Guillot' (Ch).
"Very floriferous and vigorous; of pretty form, light violet pink; long bud of a superb shining reddish-nankeen; exterior petals nuanced violet pink, with the nubs saffron yellow." [JR38/88] "Yellow, orange, pink and salmon…very lovely rose with good foliage…3×2 [ft; ca. 9×6 dm]." [B]

Clotilde
Listed as 'Bougère'.

[Colonel Juffé] (Liabaud, 1893)
"Very vigorous plant, bushy and compact, flower medium or large, full, colored purple red, passing as soon as expanded to black purple, an excellent plant to border beds." [JR17/164]

[Comte Amédé de Foras] (Gamon, 1900)
From 'Luciole' (T) × 'G. Nabonnand' (T).
"China pink shaded saffron." [JR32/139] "This is a very charming new hardy Tea Rose, never before offered in this country [*U.S.A.*]. It is a perfectly lovely hardy ever-bloomer, makes large, elegantly-formed buds and extra fine full double flowers, with broad, thick petals, very durable and lasting. Color rich peachy pink or buff rose, with orange and fawn shading, a good healthy grower and a most constant and abundant bloomer, deliciously sweet." [C&Js05]

[Comte Chandon] (Soupert & Notting, 1894)
From 'Lutea Flora' (T) × 'Coquette de Lyon' (T).
"Vigorous, hardy, flower large, full, outer petals light yellow lake, center ones shining chrome lemon yellow; one of the brightest of its class." [JR18/147]

Comte de Sembui
Listed as 'Jean Ducher'.

[Comtesse Alban de Villeneuve] (Nabonnand, 1881)
"Vigorous; flower full, very well formed, erect; petals large and thick, coppery pink, nuanced, brightened with red at the center, shaded scarlet red. Novel coloration." [JR5/148]

[Comtesse Anna Thun] (Soupert & Notting, 1887)
From 'La Sylphide' (T) × 'Mme. Camille' (T).
"Flower large, full; exterior petals large; cupped; color, golden orange yellow nuanced saffron. Very fragrant. Vigorous." [JR11/152]

[Comtesse Bardi] (Soupert & Notting, 1895)
From 'Rêve d'Or' (N) × 'Mme. Lambard' (T).
"Vigorous, flower large, full, petals large, beautiful form, light reddish coppery yellow, center coral red with golden reflections, sometimes yellow shaded reddish. Mignonette scent." [JR19/148]

Comtesse de Caserta
Listed as 'Mme. la Comtesse de Caserta'.

[Comtesse de Frigneuse] (Guillot & fils, 1885)
Seedling of 'Mme. Damaizin' (T).
"Vigorous and very floriferous; flower large, full, well-formed; color, beautiful shining canary-yellow; the elongated buds produce a beautiful effect. Of the first merit." [JR9/165] "More full than 'Mme. Chédane-Guinoisseau', and the bud is longer." [JR10/184] "Beautifully colored foliage; buds like those of 'Niphetos', long and of good form, canary yellow, more delicate within...A great rose for bedding, and blooms well in the Fall." [JR11/18]

Comtesse de Labarthe (Bernède, 1857) syn., 'Duchesse de Brabant'
Affiliated with 'Caroline' (T).
"Salmon pink, very pretty, but not full; habit free." [JC] "Shrimp-pink." [JR30/183] "Pink, shaded with carmine-rose, very pretty in the bud." [EL] "Light silvery pink. Small." [Capt 27] "Cupped blooms of pearly shell pink, pale gold coloring at base of petals, bushy." [HRG] "Clear,

bright pink, blooming in clusters…Buds exquisite, but open roses, not double." [Dr] "Peachy pink, very fragrant, a great bloomer, forces well, a choice rose and hard to beat." [HstXXX:142-143] "Soft rose pink…with long buds like tulips…confused short petals inside." [Hk] "Very double…clear pink to rose. Shapely, cupped and free flowering with a spreading habit…3×3 [ft; ca. 9×9 dm]." [B] "Growth vigorous; flower of medium size, pretty full, globular; color, delicate flesh pink." [S] "The cupped flower is nearly totally imbricated, the petals concave, quite mucronate at the tip, partly emarginate at the center—does it not recall a China, of which 'Comtesse de Labarthe' is thus a hybrid?" [JR24/42] "Continuous supply of flowers." [L] "Small growth; shy blooming qualities." [ARA18/115] "The freest bloomer in our state [*California*]. It is usually loaded with flowers nearly the entire year." [ARA19/133] "Distills the sweetest perfume." [ARA32/21] "A pink cup brimming with fragrance." [ARA18/115] "Moderately tall, compact, vigorous, hardy; foliage plentiful, healthy." [ARA18/124] "Perfect foliage." [Th2] "Makes a stocky bush with beautiful foliage that will be attacked, but not seriously, by black-spot." [ARA39/48] "This rose grows to six feet [ca. 1.75 m], and perhaps four feet across [ca. 1.25 m], and is very profuse, a bush of this size bearing 150 blossoms and buds." [JR6/43] "Needs little care, growing to ten feet [ca. 3 m]." [ARA40/31] "Very good [*in Bermuda*]." [UB28] "A well-shaped, pleasing plant." [ARA29/88] Though more widely known as 'Duchesse de Brabant', nothing in research thus far contradicts that 'Comtesse de Labarthe' was the original name assigned by Bernède.

Comtesse de Leusse
Listed as 'Mlle. la Comtesse de Leusse'.

[Comtesse de Nadaillac] (Guillot fils, 1871)
"Bush moderately vigorous, very thorny; flower full, well formed; color, very bright flesh pink on a ground of apricot-copper; globular." [S] "Of dwarf, thorny, and, unless thoroughly well treated, weakly growth and foliage; not liable to mildew, but spoiled by rain, though more tolerant of

it than some. This is a Rose which, despite its small growth and generally feeble appearance, is commonly considered second to none as a show Rose, and it is seldom that a good stand is shown without it. The habit of this variety is peculiar, though that of 'Princess of Wales' is somewhat similar. With almost all other Roses, the finest and strongest shoots give the finest blooms, but with this sort it is very difficult to tell which will do so. A bud at the end of a very small shoot may grow and swell for weeks before opening, and will then probably show a bloom that not only for beauty, but also for size, will utterly eclipse anything that can be produced from even such strong rampant growers as 'Gloire de Dijon' or 'Climbing Devoniensis'. If the bud remains hard and well shaped—a perfect smooth cone—and swells slowly even in forcing weather, while the stem thickens and stiffens in proportion, it is a good sign. On the other hand, a thick strong, tall, fleshy shoot may open its bud almost at once and produce a comparatively poor bloom. It does decidedly best in every way as a short standard, but will also yield fairly fine flowers as a dwarf. (In speaking of standards, here and elsewhere, I would strongly advise the always asking for 'half-standards.' I know of no advantage, but of much disadvantage, in standard stems being more than two feet high [ca. 6 dm].) The blooms sometimes come divided, but when good they are first-rate indeed, in petal, fulness, and shape, and wonderful in size and lasting qualities. The colour is lovely, having many shades, and, like many other Teas, is variable. Mr. Prince can show it as a yellow Rose, but this is generally when it is too much expanded and the point is gone, pink being much more predominant than yellow in my specimens. The plants are of pretty good constitution, by which I mean that they will live and not deteriorate for years if well cultivated, and they will stand close pruning, but are tender and must be well protected from frosts. Though they are so dwarf they should not be put too close together, for the habit of growth is singularly lateral, and the principal shoots of old plants will often be nearly horizontal. It is a free-flowering sort for one of such dwarf habit, but is not of much use in the late autumn unless the weather be very fine and dry. Its freedom of bloom is a nuisance to the propagator, as it is often difficult to find a sufficiency of buds which have not started." [F-M2]

Comtesse de Noghera (Nabonnand, 1902)
From 'Reine Emma des Pays-Bas' (T) × 'Paul Nabonnand' (T).
"Pink and salmon." [LS] "Delicate salmon pink." [JR32/139]

[Comtesse de Vitzthum] (Soupert & Notting, 1890)
From 'Mlle. Adèle Jougant' (cl. T) × 'Perle des Jardins' (T).
"Vigorous; flower large, full, good form, exterior petals light yellow, center bright Naples yellow; extremely floriferous; particularly to be recommended for bedding." [JR14/147]

Comtesse de Woronzoff
Listed as 'Regulus'.

[Comtesse Dusy] (Soupert & Notting, 1893)
From 'Innocente Pirola' (T) × 'Anna Olivier' (T).
"Vigorous, bushy, blossom large, full, well formed, imbricated; color, magnificent white; bud long and nicely shaped; very floriferous and long-lasting. Excellent for forcing. Fragrant." [JR17/147] "Long buds of an immaculate white." [JR23/41]

Comtesse Emmeline de Guigné (Nabonnand, 1903)
From 'Papa Gontier' (T) × 'Comtesse Festetics Hamilton' (T).
"Delicate flesh-pink." [LS] "Flower very large, full, perfect form, fragrant, large thick petals which recurve slightly, strong stem; color, brilliant carmine red tinted crimson, center coppery, warm tones; beautiful long elegant ovoid bud, coppery carmine; bushy, very vigorous, very floriferous; handsome dark green foliage." [JR27/164]

[**Comtesse Eva Starhemberg**] (Soupert & Notting, 1890)
From 'Étendard de Jeanne d'Arc' (N) × 'La Sylphide' (T).
"Vigorous; good hold; flower large, full, good form; bud long; petals large
and strong; color, cream yellow, center chrome-ochre; edge of outer petals
lightly tinted pink. Of the first merit." [JR14/147]

Comtesse Festetics Hamilton (Nabonnand, 1892)
"Flower large, full, well formed; petals flaring, nearly always solitary; bud
long, very elegant; wood reddish; leaves very large, wavy, dark green;
thorns numerous and very strong. Color, brilliant carmine red, coppery
reflections in the center; exterior petals darker, ruddy at the edge. Very vigorous, very floriferous." [JR16/166]

[**Comtesse Julie Hunyady**] (Soupert & Notting, 1888) syn., 'Comtesse
Julie Hunyadi'
From 'Mme. Lambard' (T) × 'Socrate' (T).
"Flower large, full; beautiful form and good hold; color, Naples yellow
shaded greenish canary yellow; petals' edges lake pink. This beautiful vari-
ety sometimes produces red flowers and yellow flowers on the same plant.
The blossoms obtained through forcing in a hot-house or frame, in
Winter, are always purest yellow." [JR12/147]

[**Comtesse Lily Kinsky**] (Soupert & Notting, 1895)
From 'Marie Van Houtte' (T) × 'Victor Pulliat' (T).
"Very vigorous bush; flower large, quite full, of good form; color, pearly
white with a yellowish glow, the center a light waxy yellow sometimes
nuanced flesh." [JR19/148] "Very sweet and pretty." [C&Js98]

Comtesse Riza du Parc (Schwartz, 1876)
Seedling of 'Comtesse de Labarthe' (T).
"Clear rose, salmon tinge, coppery yellow ground. Slightly cupped."
[Capt27] "Beautiful metallic rose, changing to pink, large and full, form
globular, growth vigorous." [JC] "Bronzed rose, with a carmine tint;
medium size, moderately full, highly perfumed." [EL] "Attractive flower

of distinct color and medium size." [Capt28] "Of really strong growth, with good foliage. This Rose is very faulty in form, and a good shaped one is rare indeed. It is not large, a free bloomer, or a good autumnal, and it is only noticeable for its colour, which is a charming shade of pink, with an indefinable sensation of yellow pervading it, especially at the base of the petals." [F-M3] "Persistent and vigorous, but of uneven growth." [JR9/70] "Good growth; fair foliage, well-held." [Capt28] "Very vigorous, with branches quite reddish, smooth, with prickles lightly hooked and occasional, brownish red. Foliage is ample, comprised of 5-7 oval-elliptical leaflets, serrated, handsome somber green on top, light green beneath, taking on a purple tinge as they develop. The flower stem is long, firm, and dark, and the blossoms come singly. The flower is large, full, well held, having petals both long and wide, numerous, and of a pretty China pink with carmine reflections, shaded pinkish yellow at the base, on a copper ground. [JR4/25] "Branches erect and divergent." [S] "A distinct, effective, and most floriferous variety." [P1]

[**Comtesse Sophie Torby**] (Nabonnand, 1902)
From 'Reine Emma des Pays-Bas' (T) × 'Archiduc Joseph' (T).
"Flowers rich peachy-red with orange shading, highly perfumed; a strong grower and free bloomer." [C&Js07]

[**Coquette de Lyon**] (Ducher, 1871)
"Pale yellow; medium, or small size; pretty in bud, and useful for bedding." [EL] "Canary-yellow, flowers tolerably full, buds pretty and clustering, habit moderate." [JC] "Well-formed." [JR3/28] "Growth vigorous." [CA88] "Medium growth; flower medium-sized, full; color, silky yellow." [S] "Well shaped flowers of moderate fulness, canary yellow of rather distinct a shade. A very charming and graceful rose flowering and flourishing well under glass; outside it prefers a shady location. Rather delicate, which may be the reason why it is but seldom seen in England." [B&V]

Corallina (W. Paul, 1900)
"Deep crimson pink." [JR30/15] "Deep rosy-crimson. Specially good in the bud and for autumn flowering." [H] "Crimson and deep vermilion, shaded vivid pink." [RR] "Almost single-flowered." [NRS10/55] "Deep rosy crimson, shaded with coral red; large petals, especially beautiful in the bud state. Growth vigorous…A splendid autumnal bloomer. As free as the old pink Monthly Rose." [P1] "Small growth; very little bloom." [ARA18/115]

[**Corinna**] (W. Paul, 1893)
"Beautiful flesh-color shaded with rose and tinted with coppery-gold. The flowers are of large size, excellent shape and very freely produced." [C&Js98] "Has been compared to 'Luciole' in stature and flower color, but much more hardy; forms a very floriferous, vigorous bush. The flowers, borne on an upright firm stem, are more medium-sized than large, pink mixed with coppery yellow at the base of the petals…The very long bud will be much besought for bouquets." [JR17/85]

[**Cornelia Cook**] (A. Cook, 1865)
Seedling of 'Devoniensis' (T).
"Flower white, generally tinted pale yellow; remarkably large and quite full. This blossom exhales the exquisite perfume of its mother, which is responsible for the favor it enjoys. For a great many years, this rose has been cultivated in great quantity in frames; it is only with the recent appearance of 'The Bride' that its culture under glass has diminished." [JR16/36] "Splendid long pointed buds, pure creamy-white sometimes tinged with pale rose. Excellent substance and very sweet." [C&Js02] "Medium vigor, flowers white tinted flesh, large and very full…not opening very well, but magnificent when well grown." [JR4/61] "Canes twiggy, green at the base, slightly reddish towards the tip; thorns pretty straight, red, remote; leaves of 5 or indeed 7 leaflets (but then the last pair is very small), oval-lanceolate, tinged red at the edge; petiole red; stipules large and ciliate; peduncle long, stiff; flower 8-9 cm across [nearly 4

inches], white washed yellow, globular, outer petals shell-like; sepals long and lacy at the tip; ovary green and spherical. Unfortunately, the blossom sometimes has difficulty in opening, and pulls itself apart...Prune short." [JR10/186] The sport occurred in 1855; commercial release occurred in 1865.

[David Pradel] (Pradel, 1851)
"Pale rose and lavender, mottled, a peculiar flower, often of an enormous size, habit free and tolerably hardy." [JC] "Rose, large and full." [FP] "Large, purplish, superb." [JR3/28] "Plant pretty vigorous; flowers large, full, lilac pink maculated purple. Good variety grafted and own-root." [l'H53/223] "Moderate growth; flower large, full, globular; color, light pink marbled lilac, yellow nubs." [S] "This is a grand rose for the garden and lawn and sure to give satisfaction. It is a clean, handsome grower and an early and profuse bloomer, both buds and flowers are extra large and beautiful; color rich rosy red, elegantly shaded. Very fragrant." [C&Js05] "A distinct, old, clear lilac-rose Tea of cutting value with good foliage. Unknown in this country [*U.S.A.*] and strongly recommended for southern climates." [ARA28/101]

Devoniensis (Foster, 1838) syn., 'Magnolia Rose'
From 'Parks' Yellow Tea-Scented China' (T) × 'Smith's Yellow China' (T).
"Still unrivalled; its creamy white flowers, with their delicate rose tint, are always beautiful." [R8] "Creamy-white...centres sometimes buff sometimes yellowish, very large and full; form cupped. A splendid Rose." [P1] "Creamy-white, sometimes tinged with blush, very large, almost full; one of the most delightfully scented. Either this or the climbing variety should be in every collection; though neither is very productive." [EL] "Of high quality in its line of colour—ivory-white, with a yellowish fawn centre. In shape its flower is somewhat like that of '[Souvenir de la] Malmaison', with which favorite kind it has marked affinities...We believe that it is worthy of notice that neither of these has produced seed." [WD] "A very beautiful rose, of immense size...sometimes a shy bloomer when young."

[SBP] 'Gorgeous...nearly four inches in diameter [ca. 1 dm]." [Ed] "Perfectly unique in form, in color, and in sweetness, for no other rose has the same scent." [R1/203] "Moderate in growth." [DO] "Another new rose; though at first represented as being a fine sulphur-yellow...it proves to be a creamy-white, but when just open, in cloudy weather, is of a canary colour; when well cultivated it produces flowers of immense size, and in clusters; it grows freely, with dark green foliage, possesses a delightful fragrance far surpassing the ancient Tea Rose, and is a very valuable variety." [Bu] "'Petals thick and Camellia-like, very large and powerfully scented.' On this splendid English Rose it is hardly possible to bestow too much praise...Not only is it the most powerfully scented and the largest of its family, but its petals are so thick and waxy, its foliage so magnificent (even to the thorns which are of brilliant crimson), as to render it is every respect perfect...The fortunate raiser of this Rose was the late George Foster, Esq., of Oatland, near Devonport, whose brother Edward W. Foster has kindly favored us with the following information as to its parentage...'His opinion was that it was produced from the Yellow China by an impregnation of the Yellow Noisette "Smithii" which was growing alongside it.'...Delighting in a fertile moist soil, the 'Devoniensis', perhaps more than any other rose, amply recompenses the cultivator for all the assiduity he bestows on it." [C] "Beautiful now as then [*in Rivers' time*]." [K1]

Dr. Félix Guyon (Mari/Jupeau, 1901)
"Dark yellow, center lighter." [LS] "Deep orange, centre shaded with apricot. Very large, opens well, fine buds, and very sweet. Growth vigorous." [P1] "A yellow Tea...foliage immune to mildew and flower opens...easily. Distinctly good in southern seacoast climates." [ARA28/101] "Pretty deep green foliage and large handsome buds and flowers." [C&Js04] "Vigorous, bushy, good wood, nearly thornless, handsome foliage, beautiful buds, flowers very large, opening well; exterior color deep orange, interior shaded apricot; very fragrant, very floriferous." [JR24/147]

Dr. Grandvilliers (Perny, 1891)
From 'Isabelle Nabonnand' (T) × 'Aureus' (T).
"Reddish fawn." [LS] "Vigorous with upright branches having much foliage, and thorns both numerous and hooked. The flower is medium-sized, full, of most graceful form, and of a shade of dark buff yellow; petals pretty large, sometimes tinted on the inside, with the exterior crimson. The buds, which are very long, and usually solitary, are held flirtatiously on their stems, and grow in clusters, making a most charming sight." [JR15/146] "Dr. Grandvilliers, a well-known medical man who, for reasons of health, left Paris for Nice." [JR16/120]

Dr. Grill (Bonnaire, 1886)
From 'Ophirie' (N) × 'Souvenir de Victor Hugo' (T).
"Rose with coppery shading…free." [H] "Deep, clear yellow. An extra fine rose in every respect." [Dr] "Rosy fawn." [E] "Clear rose, coppery center. Loose." [Capt27] "Large, full, regular form, erect, coppery-yellow, with bright pink lustre." [Hn] "Good growth; well-held foliage…coppery red bud; flower double; aurora with outer petals sometimes splashed carmine…usually with good stem, but usually somewhat flat." [Capt28] "Shapely." [HRG] "Not as universally cultivated as it should be. Perfect in shape, prolific in flowers of a delicious mixture of pale copper shaded with tender pink and China-rose, it is deliciously fragrant and lasts well in water." [K1] "Hay-scented." [JR33/101] "Rather moderate in growth, a button-hole Rose only valuable in the bud, small, but free-flowering and distinct and attractive in colour." [F-M3] "Sown in 1883 by Monsieur J. Bonnaire,…the seeds, which were very numerous (about 200) didn't sprout more than a small quantity (five or six or so)…only one was found to be vigorous and worthy of the attention of the breeder, who studied it several years before releasing it to commerce, not at first having found any satisfactorily large blossoms…It is a pity that 'Dr. Grill' was not propagated [*right away*], because last Summer we did not see any so pretty, so floriferous, and so vigorous, without being a climber, that we do not hesitate for

an instant to say that this is one of the best new roses…in many years. Its extreme floriferousness and great brightness of the blossoms make one overlook the flower's lack of fulness." [JR15/40-41] "Dedicated to Dr. Grill, a flower-lover." [JR34/16]

[**Dr. Pouleur**] (Ketten Bros., 1897)
From 'Lady Zoë Brougham' (T) × 'Alphonse Karr' (T).
"Carmine-aurora, and copper-red. Globular." [ARA27/19] "Flower dawn gold, center coppery red, exterior petals striped reddish pink, medium to large, full, fragrant. Vigorous bush." [JR21/135-136]

[**Duc de Magenta**] (Margottin, 1859)
Seedling of 'Goubault' (T).
"Pale flesh delicately tinted with fawn, petals large and of a fine waxy substance, flowers large, double and exquisitely formed, handsome dark foliage and good habit." [JC] "Flower medium-sized, very full and very well formed, notable because of its beautiful coloration of pink and salmon nuanced white; this variety scores highly in different polls." [S] "Rose coloured, shaded to salmon. When grown in a situation and under circumstances congenial to its taste, it nearly approaches a floral wonder. Does equally well as a bush, standard or climber, and grows to great size. I have seen a stem as big as a man's arm, and defended by enormous thorns. It produces an abundance of flowers of good size and regularity." [B&V]

[**Duchess of Edinburgh**] (Nabonnand/Veitch, 1874) syn., 'Prince Wasiltchikoff'
Seedling of 'Souvenir de David d'Angers' (T).
"Light red." [JR1/7/6] "Red carmine. This rose of moderate size flowers very abundantly, has a good effect when the flowers are half or three quarters expanded; when full after exposure to the sun, they lose colour, become limp and are distinctly vulgar." [B&V] "Flowers of good substance." [CA88] "Its flower, held erectly but not stiffly, attains the greatest size on vigorous shoots. The blossom is well-formed, imbricated, and

slightly cupped, with pretty concave petals...some rosarians find China characteristics in this variety." [JR9/55] "A Bengal with Tea blood. Crimson, turning lighter as the bud expands; of good size, moderately full." [EL] "The 'Duchess of Edinburgh' Rose, which was sent out some five or six years ago as a 'Crimson Tea.' The misleading name of 'Tea' induced hundreds of florists to attempt its growth under the same conditions as the 'Safrano' or 'Bon Silène' class, and the consequence was in every case almost complete failure. This type evidently partakes more of the Hybrid Perpetual than of the Tea class, and as they are hardy and deciduous, refuse to bloom in midwinter unless given the rest their nature demands." [pH] "Vigorous with purple branches having a bloom, and armed with dark and formidable thorns; leaves glaucous; flower cupped, well formed, very elegant, particularly before expansion; petals concave, well disposed, carmine red, whitish on the edge; enjoys much favor in England, where it is considered as being of the first merit; doubtless the foggy climate of Great Britain is more to its liking than is ours [*of sunny France*], as here it grows very little...but for that fault, it would pass as a good rose of some merit, above all because of the well-formed buds." [S] Not to be confused with the silvery pink Hybrid Perpetual by Bennett, also from 1874.

Duchesse de Brabant
Listed as 'Comtesse de Labarthe'.

[Duchesse de Bragance] (Dubreuil, 1886)
Seedling of 'Coquette de Lyon' (T).
"Much-branched bush, with upright canes bestrewn with occasional thorns. Foliage dark green with red young shoots. Calyx reddish in youth, with foliaceous sepals overtopping the bud, which is oval. Blossom very full, and opening well, with a very firm stem; beautiful canary yellow, intense at the center, paler along the edges; outer petals gracefully recurve to the tip. Very meritorious for cut flowers." [JR10/149] Plate 148 in the first edition of *The Old Rose Advisor*, mistakenly listed as referring to the

Hybrid Perpetual 'Duchesse de Bragance', actually refers to this extinct Tea of the same name.

[**Duchesse Marie Salviati**] (Soupert & Notting, 1889)
From 'Mme. Lambard' (T) × 'Mme. Maurice Kuppenheim' (T).
"Growth vigorous, flower large, full, magnificent long buds, which open well; ground color orange, shaded and touched delicate flesh pink, center peachy red. Sometimes unshaded saffron yellow blossoms are produced. Much to be prized due to its scent of violets." [JR13/147]

[**Edmond de Biauzat**] (Levet, 1885)
"Peach color, tinted with salmon; large and full." [CA93]

[**Edmond Sablayrolles**] (Bonnaire, 1888)
From 'Souvenir de Victor Hugo' (T) × 'Mme. Cusin' (T).
"Very vigorous with upright canes; pretty bronzy foliage; flower medium to large; edge of the blossom beautiful hydrangea pink, interior peach yellow with nasturtium reflections, passing to very bright carmine pink. This variety has such variable flowers that one might be inclined to think that several different varieties had been budded together on the same stock…constant bloom." [JR12/146]

[**Édouard Gautier**] (Pernet-Ducher, 1883)
Seedling of 'Devoniensis' (T).
"Vigorous, looking like 'Jean Pernet'; flower large, full, globular, very well formed, of good hold; outer petals white, slightly pink on the reverse; interior buff yellow with light pink reflections." [JR7/160]

[**Elisa Fugier**] (Bonnaire, 1890)
From an unnamed Tea × 'Niphetos' (T).
"Very vigorous, canes upright though not very erect, looking much like 'Niphetos'. The behavior of the plant itself, however, is much better, not defoliating like 'Niphetos'; its foliage is more abundant, and is always green; bud very long; flower very large, very full, pure white lightly tinted

soft yellow at the center, good for cut flowers and very hardy." [JR14/146]
"Of moderate growth, highly spoken of at first, but at present not sustain-
ing its reputation. Of nice pointed form, but not likely to prove first-
class." [F-M3]

[Elise Heymann] (Strassheim/Soupert & Notting, 1891)
From 'Mme. Lambard' (T) × 'Mont Rosa' (T).
"Vigorous, flower very large, full, petals large, of very beautiful form;
color, coppery yellow nuanced nankeen yellow, center peach-pink, reverse
of the petals chrome yellow, touched light pink." [JR15/150] "Has the
foliage, hold, doubleness, and scent of its mother 'Mme. Lambard'; it is
distinct only in its color, which is coppery yellow nuanced nankeen yellow; the center of the flower is somewhat peach-pink, while the exterior
petals are chrome yellow nuanced light pink. 'Elise Heymann' is, above all,
very good for pot culture and for cutting." [JR17/85]

Elise Sauvage (Miellez, 1838)
"Straw yellow." [LS] "Orange-yellow, medium size, full." [EL] "Pale yellow, centre orange, in dry weather very beautiful, but the most tender and
delicate of all roses." [JC] "Flowers pale yellow, their centre sometimes
inclining to buff, sometimes to orange, large and full; form, globular. One
of the most beautiful, but of a rather delicate habit." [P] "Another of that
description of colour [*i.e.*, *'creamy yellow before it is deprived of that hue by
the sun*,*' description applied by Buist to the early Tea 'Duchesse de
Mecklenbourg'*]; though very different in growth [*from 'Duchesse de
Mecklenbourg'*], which is not so strong, yet the flowers are very large, and
make a splendid appearance when forced." [Bu] "A profuse bloomer."
[CA88] "*Rivers*—'Pale yellow—orange centre—superb', *Lane*—'Fine deep
straw—splendid,' *Wood*—'Yellow—orange centre—superb'...*Curtis*—
'centre petals pale yellow—superb orange centre—globular and pendulous.' It lacks, we are well aware, that great desideratum, substance of
petal, but in the greenhouse this hardly appears a disadvantage, for with its
fine pendulous blossoms and distinct orange yellow centre, its graceful

appearance can scarcely be exceeded. It was raised, we are informed, by Monsieur Mi[e]llez, a florist at Lisle, about ten years since...We have had most success in blooming Elise on worked plants against walls; when planted in beds or borders, unless the situation be warm and well sheltered, we would advise that it be protected in winter." [C] "Branches slender, purplish green; thorns long, pointed, not much recurved, dark red; leaves comprised of three or five small, oval-pointed leaflets of a nice fresh dark green, paler beneath; rachis purplish; petiole purplish, prickly. Flower stalk glabrous, green, with two small bracts at the base. Calyx round, sepals entire, long, pointed. Flowers full, 6 cm [ca. 2 ½ inches]; petals large, rounded, ragged in the center, yellowish white, darker at the nub." [An41/15]

[Émilie Gonin] (P. Guillot, 1896)

"This is a beautiful ever-blooming rose; ivory white, delicately tinted with orange and fawn; each petal broadly edged with bright carmine red; very large and full; quite new and scarce." [C&Js99] "Vigorous bush with a very large, full, well-formed flower, white tinted orange yellow on a darker ground, each petal much bordered bright carmine. Fragrant." [JR20/147]

[Empereur Nicolas II] (Lévêque, 1903)

"Handsome foliage and splendid large buds; dark rich crimson, flamed with brilliant scarlet." [C&Js07] "Very vigorous bush; beautiful dark green foliage; flowers very large, full; very beautiful long buds; superbly colored aniline madder, very bright; always in bloom." [JR27/165] Nicholas II, last czar of Russia; lived 1868-1918.

[Empress Alexandra of Russia] (W. Paul, 1897)

"Carmine red lightly tinted a nice shade of orange and tipped fiery red. It is large, globular, has vigorous growth and looks good whether as a plant or a cut flower." [JR21/50] "The flowers are large and double with full center and broad, thick petals. The buds are dark violet red, and the open flowers rich purplish lake deepening at centre to fiery crimson, large, full, and globular; a strong, vigorous grower, early and constant bloomer, very fragrant and desirable, quite hardy." [C&Js02]

Enchantress (W. Paul, 1896)
"Cream white, fawn center; very large, globular, petals slightly folded at the edge; vigorous; abundant bloomer." [JR20/164] "For garden decoration this Rose is almost unequalled. The plant produces a continuous supply of strong growths crowned with fine trusses of lovely cream white, buff shaded blooms; large, full, and globular form. For winter blooming it stands unrivalled." [P1] "Small growth; winterkilled." [ARA18/115] "Was the product of a cross between a Tea and a China." [JR21/66] See also 'Morning Glow' (T).

[**Enfant de Lyon**] (Avoux & Crozy, 1858) trans., "Child of Lyon"
"Beautiful creamy rose, delicately shaded with rich coppery yellow, and having the delightful fragrance of sweet anise, which is truly delicious and quite remarkable. It is a very pretty Rose, a constant bloomer and much admired." [C&Js02] "Very vigorous bush, beautiful foliage, flower large, flat, full, beautiful yellow fading to straw yellow." [JDR58/37]

[**Ernest Metz**] (Guillot & fils, 1888)
"Satiny pink. Shaded rose, very sweet." [C&Js98] "Vigorous bush; flower very large, quite full, opening well, very well formed, solitary; stem firm; bud long; color, very delicate carmine pink, center brighter, reverse of petals darker." [JR12/146]

Erzherzog Franz Ferdinand (Soupert & Notting, 1892) syn., 'Louis Lévêque'; trans., "Archduke Franz Ferdinand"
From 'Mlle. Adèle Jougant' (T) x 'Adrienne Christophle' (N).
"Vigorous, flower large, full, cupped, outer petals large, peach red on a yellow ground, interior petals peony formation, beautiful dawn gold, the center being carmine lake with golden reflections; reverse often striped magenta red like 'Luciole'. Very fragrant." [JR16/139] "Fair growth and form; not a profuse bloomer." [ARA18/115] Archduke Franz Ferdinand,

1863-1914; nephew of Emperor Franz Josef I of Austria; his assassination in Sarajevo helped spark World War I.

[Esther Pradel] (Pradel, 1860)
"Bush vigorous; leaves large, dark green, shiny; flower medium-sized, full; color, chamois, nub darker, passing to salmon." [S] "Lovely pure white buds; flowers medium size, full and sweet; profuse bloomer." [CA93] "Low bushy grower." [C&Js05]

Ethel Brownlow
Listed as 'Miss Ethel Brownlow'.

Étoile de Lyon (Guillot fils, 1881) trans., "Star of Lyon"
Seedling of 'Mme. Charles' (T).
"Deep yellow." [EL] "Large, double blooms of gold." [ARA29/95] "Fine saffron yellow, brighter in centres; large, full, and of superb form and habit; requires a hot season." [P1] "Medium size, double; medium yellow, fading lighter. Repeats bloom." [Lg] "Deep lemon, very rarely exhibited, as it must have hot, dry weather." [FRB] "Quite superior in vigor and flowering, its blossoms are cupped...very bright yellow." [JR10/45] "Unites excellent flowers with great vigor; the flowers are large, globular, full, well formed, brilliant yellow with a darker center." [JR7/157] "Could be more double...well-held, vigorous, floriferous, and persistent [*of leaf*]." [JR9/70] "The largest and most sumptuous of all yellow roses is 'Étoile de Lyon', but it must be admitted that this rose is capricious, and only opens well in warm soil." [JR12/179] "A good yellow tea rose...with proper care will bloom the year around." [BSA] "Strong good growth and foliage, but is a very disappointing Rose out of doors, having been much over-praised. The blooms come generally badly, of confused and queer shapes, and require as a rule very dry warm weather...globular shape...outer petals being short, and kept well up to the bloom...Rather liable to mildew, of good lasting qualities when dry." [F-M3] "Very low, compact, not vigorous; foliage sufficient, healthy; bloom, sparse, mostly early and late."

[ARA18/125] "Long, pointed buds and elegant roses. Delicious Tea odor. Fine habit. Free flowering." [Dr] "Small growth; blooms undersized." [ARA18/115] "This variety preserves many of the principal characteristics of its mother, but detracts from 'Mme. Charles' by way of its own vigor, floriferousness, and rich coloration…a vigorous and handsome bush with upright branches, bearing superb young foliage of a dark red which passes to intense green." [JR11/122-123] "Branches…purplish-red in color. The leaf is comprised of 5 leaflets, purplish red becoming dark green. The blossoms are scented, very large, very full, and with central petals which are narrow and muddled, surrounded by five or six rows, imbricated. The color is a bright sulphur yellow, whitish-yellow on the reverse.–One of the finest yellows yet produced." [JR5/116] "Bushy plant with soft foliage." [HRG] "Fine double flower, which needs heat to mature…a fine decorative in the Pacific South-West." [Th2] "This is undoubtedly the best Pure Yellow Rose for garden planting yet introduced." [C&Js05]

[**Exadelphé**] (Nabonnand, 1885)
"Very vigorous, branching, big-wooded, very floriferous; flower very large, very full, very well formed; color, quite yellow; extremely fragrant." [JR9/166] "A good strong grower and free bloomer; large, full, well-formed flowers, quite double and fragrant; color, fine canary yellow, passing to rich creamy white, faintly tinged with pale lemon; very sweet." [CA90]

[**F.L. Segers**] (Ketten Bros., 1898)
From 'Safrano' (T) × 'Adam' (T).
"Carminy scarlet nuanced yellowish pink, creamy white around the edge, touched mauve pink; large, very full, fragrant; bud long, opening well, strong peduncle. Vigorous bush." [JR22/132] "Extra large flowers, fine cupped form, full and deep, lovely soft rosy-pink, very sweet and handsome." [C&Js02]

Fairy Queen
Listed as 'Rosalie'.

[**Fiametta Nabonnand**] (Nabonnand, 1894) syn., 'Papa Gontier à Fleurs Blanches'
From 'Papa Gontier' (T) × 'Niphetos' (T).
"This rose has the habit, vigor, and beauty of 'Papa Gontier', a rose esteemed and appreciated by all fanciers of roses. The blossoms are as large, as are the petals, which being more numerous, embellish the flower even more. This rose has a yet greater future than its mother!!! Without going too far, we can still place it on a level with the most beautiful of all because of its coloration, which is a satiny white lightly tinted very pale carminy pink at the petal edges, giving it a cachet of perfect distinction. The ground-color, which is delicately gold, pales towards the edge of the petal, which is lined with a sweet tint of carmine; the reverse is attractively pearly. The flower is borne on a strong peduncle; its calyx is decorated with large sepals; the bud is graceful, very well formed, elongate, and lightly tinted carmine. The wood and foliage are those of 'Papa Gontier'; only the shade is a bit lighter. This variety is wonderfully floriferous; it would certainly be very good for forcing, and for cut flowers out in the open air, and will be known as being as good at the professional's as well as at the fancier's in borders and beds of those roses of the first order which are indispensible to all serious collections. Its extraordinary vigor allows us to believe that it will be very good in the North. All these praises are still too weak to make you appreciate this rose at its true merit. On top of all these qualities, it also has an elegant perfume of an exquisite finesse." [JR19/5-6]

[**Flavien Budillon**] (Nabonnand, 1885)
"Broad, thick petals; delicate pale flesh; highly perfumed." [CA90] "Very vigorous, very remontant, with big wood and long thorns; flower very large, very full, globular, imbricated, cupped; color, delicate pink." [JR9/166]

[**Fortuna**] (W. Paul, 1902)

"Flower of large size; color apricot nuanced chamois, outer petals lightly tinted red." [JR26/87] "A distinguished beauty." [C&Js07] This rose's "subtitle," "The New Riviera Rose," gives a hint of its ultimate origin; see 'Morning Glow' (T).

Fortune's Five-Colored Rose (China/Fortune, 1843) syn. 'À Cinq Couleurs', 'Quinquecolor'.

"Yellowish-white, sometimes lined with bright pink." [BJ58] "Medium-sized, full, cream white, lined purple." [R&M62] "Bush vigorous; canes bright green; thorns dark green, flattened at the base; flower large, full; color, cream-white striped with pink, touched with crimson and spotted with pink and with violet." [S] "You remember—don't you, Readers?—those charlatans who would sell so-called White-and-Red Roses, Blue Dahlias, Tri-Colored Camellias, etc.? The Roubaix Correctional Facility has sent some of these to prison; and do you know why? It is because they were poor devils, uneducated, ignorant of how to announce such things as these. Here, then, is how a very serious compilation expresses itself on the subject of the rose called 'Five-Colored': 'It seems to belong'—it says—'to the China Rose group; but it shows a very beautiful and unique look. Sometimes it is uni-colored, then white or red all at the same time on the same specimen, while often being striped with all these colors. Here, it will be as hardy as other Roses,' etc. Did the poor devils who are serving out their time for their 'moment of error' (as they say when talking about prevaricating functionaries) promise anything more than that? No!—but it is necessary to put these things in quotation-marks; otherwise, one has recourse to the botheration of the Police. Be that as it may, the bush which supposedly produces these roses is in Paris in the company of two Briars, or single Dog Roses." [dH44/328-329]

"A tri-color rose! What's all this, say I; *tricolor*—it should be called *quinquecolor*, because it is indeed a rose concerned with five colors; and on this subject, here is something written to us by our estimable colleague from the arrondissement of Lille, Monsieur Miellez: 'If my memory serves me well, one of the issues of your *Journal* from last Winter spoke in something like jest of the Five-Colored China Rose from China. One of our horticultural colleagues who had, like me, bought this rose at a very high price said meantime that he was seeing flowers with only five petals. I then was about preparing to start selling this variety, already having some thirty specimens; but your article, and what my colleague said, made me change my mind. I have kept them all for myself, thinking that, if I have been fooled, it's better that I be the only one. (Good fortune makes good friends!) I came to see—*continues Monsieur Miellez*—blossoms on this rose which were, at the same time, one white with greenish nuances, the second one yellowish with scarlet crimson stripes and light pink blotches, and a third one all crimson. All these flowers, fuller than the Common China; the peduncles strong and quite upright, petal-form a bit narrow. This rose would seem to be of luxuriant growth and, in the open air, does better than the Common China. All in all, I believe that this is a good acquisition. I will be looking at it again, because it still has many buds; if you would like some cuttings, I would be at your service!' We of course leave to Monsieur Miellez the full responsibility for what he has written to us, and we publish it under the heading of 'Information.' Calling it *Rosa mutabilis* would seem the more appropriate name, because nowhere in what Monsieur Miellez has written to us are we told of a flower of several colors, but only of a plant which seems to play with the usual laws of vegetal physiology, much like many plant-sellers would—not so long ago— play with fanciers (in these times of *barbarity* and *slavery* where money and customers are concerned); but, since the proclamation of Universal Brotherhood [*the writer has political matters and writings of the revolutionary year in which he writes, 1848, in mind*], everything and everyone is turned upside-down—there's nothing astonishing in it now being Flowers that play with the Public. I remember that I dreamed last night (and, time being so limited, there's nothing odd in spending my dreams on amusing things) that the Republic was *a flower*, and the people, the true people (as they say) were a proliferating plant the name of which escapes me, but about which I remember clearly the people conserved its fruits as with cherries and prunes, the difference being *that eau-de-vie doesn't play a part.*" [M-V48-49/158-159; the writer is editor Paquct] "The time comes for the conscientious horticulturist to observe the duty and pleasure of reviewing a judgment which was hasty and, for that reason, possibly unjust. It has been remarked, with reason, that, before formulating a definitive opinion on a plant, one should wait for it to bloom several successive years. Due to my own experience, I can't emphasize it *too* strongly that this wise principle should be observed. Thus it is that, last year, struck by the great disappointment I had suffered in seeing my *Rose of 5 Colors* bloom single and without variegation, I was quite critical of it, all the while hoping that the future would give thc lie to my statements. Today, the future has spoken, and I am happy to be able to say that the *Rose of 5 Colors* is a good rose, while more *2-Colored*; and I have it under my eye in a perfect state of bloom. Presumably, next year its blossoms will come yet fuller and more vividly colored, as the specimens gain age and vigor. It's a tea rose, nearly full, with petals of a sulphur yellow, bearing—for the most part—a beautiful big stripe or indeed band of bright crimson, to beautiful effect. Its leaves are trifoliate, smooth, of a delicate green, with petioles and petiolules [*sic*] caniculate above. This is the only rose of its section (Tea) which is freely variegated; it is very floriferous, and, henceforth, knowing what's what with it, I can recommend it to the crankiest fanciers." [V-H48/381; the writer is Van Houtte; the plate accompanying shows 5-foliate leaves, in defiance of Van Houtte's trifoliate description] "We have already discussed in the *Journal d'Horticulture Pratique* that supposed *Rose of Five Colors*. The *Instructeur-Jardinier* has, since, had occasion to mention it…Nevertheless, we wouldn't have thought that the *Rose of Five Colors* would have had any chance to show its face, or that anyone would go so far as to take seriously the fived supposed colors of this Queen of Flowers. Such is not the case! We have observed several works of *art* concerning the *Rose of Five Colors*, next to which one finds a pretty lofty price for this admirable flower. And now we have received a figure of this Rose in a foreign horticultural compilation [*referring to Van Houtte's* Flore des Serres…*from Belgium*] which demonstrates much more in the way of artistic execution than in fidelity to the rose's appearance. Anyway, let us say that, while the Rose bears the name *Five Colors*, the figure only shows three—includiing the leaves. The flower doesn't have more than two. The supposed *Rose of Five Colors* is described in Latin: '*Varietas in agro sinense enata Rosisque sinensibus spectans, flore sulphureo, coccineis lineis distincto*'. This Latin is probably a subtlety of the author, who doubtless supposes that all his readers are Géronte, and like Sganarelle he enthusiastically gives us a Latin description in which those who understand it can only see the *Rose of Two Colors*. But—someone says—a Tea Rose of two colors is good enough. Doubtless, except it is necessary to warn the Public that the rose in question is nearly single, that it blooms poorly, and that it grafts poorly, because it hangs its head like a bashful young girl. The real color of this rose, it is an unpleasant dirty yellow one in which one sees here and there one red line; but, since we speak in printing terminology, it is good to remember that the virgule in question is evident on the petals of the rose to the same degree a virgule of tiny text would appear next to the big capitals of a poster!—*Note.* A year ago or nearly, Monsieur Louis Van Houtte, who publishes today a picture of this rose, criticized it severely: 'I was hasty'—says he—'to buy myself, after seeing an announcement in an English journal, a *China Rose* that its discoverer named *Rose with Five Colors*. The rose bloomed at my premises. As I had waited some time, my disappointment was fairly great—first of all, my Rose came single, and white without any stripe. ONE of the petals showed ONE pink stripe— but it was microscopic.' The abilities of our estimable colleague are well known, and we often remark on them. What, however, will be the opinion of his vast knowledge and ability, Readers, all of this falling short of Truth when, a year later, via a picture and a page of text, the able Belgian horti-culturist comes to make a *bad single white rose* into a magnificent five-col-ored rose! Let us say further that, if Monsieur Van Houtte is a very able man, he is also a very modest one. He doubts his own knowledge and talent such that, far from believing that he could make something of his rose, he announced that he would let it bloom for another year to give it the chance to demonstrate definitively what it was worth. '*Without a doubt*', he added, 'not a great deal!'. So, we must say, because we must not set aside anything marvelous in the tale of this Rose, that the first year it bloomed in the greenhouse, it came single and uni-colored. This year it bloomed out in the open, in a good soil; it grew vigorously and grew admirable stripes—which is to say that it stands on its head the usual order of things, because we know that most white Fuchsias, striped Oleanders, etc., in the greenhouse, return to their normal tint when grown outdoors." [M-V48-49/310-311]

"Do you know how the Tea Rose called 'Five-Colored'…is quinquecolored? Let me tell you. Open the *Supplement to the last catalogs* of Monsieur Miellez, norticulturist near Lille. For this *citizen* the rose in question is already transformed from a *Tea* to a 'Five-Colored China (from China)'— that's a quote—then he adds, 'Very vigorous Rose, and very hardy [*a footnote adds:* You see that soon this wonderful rose will resist, out in the open, our most severe Winters], flower pure white or yellowish, tigered or flamed with crimson, sometimes completely pink, rarely giving two flowers just the same; fuller than the Common China, borne on a *good* peduncle [*a footnote adds:* Bravo! Monsieur Miellez, you are a charming fellow; you know very well that the China Rose hangs its head as much as a Fuchsia; you also know that it is a great fault, and you are too frank to say the contrary in letting such terms as *thick, strong, upright*, etc., serve you—you use the word *good*, which says and signifies nothing at all in describing plants!].' One would do well to ask of Monsieur Miellez an explanation or translation of such an ambiguous description as he has given us. Because, finally, how can a *pure white* rose have five colors? How can it be striped? How is a Tea in Ghent a China at Esquermes? Giving somewhat serious thought to this, one asks—I am going to make a supposition—if the sellers of plants are not all, as is known, men of good, proven, faith? Why can't they be so about this rose? In the final analysis, Tea or China, the color doesn't matter—the seller could respond to a complaining buyer, 'Your rose has been unicolored, red or white? It depends on the terrain; it is effectively sometimes *all pink*, your soil is perhaps of a nature to make it open only in that color; it's unfortunate; but that's all we can do.' I well know that no one would dare do this; I prefer to believe that the Rose will attain five colors, but over several years in the following maner: The first year you sell a little stunted plant which grows several flimsy green leaves at first, then yellows immediately; voila, two colors already. Next year, the Rose is vigorous, and grows well; its foliage is a beautiful green; the bush is covered with white flowers; as these are single, the stamens which are necessarily in the middle are yellow, which makes two colors for the flower and one for the foliage—three colors in all. Add to them the two colors of the previous year, and that makes a good *five*. And so the Rose is Five-Colored!" [M-V48-49/371-372]

[**Frances E. Willard**] (Good & Reese/Conard & Jones, 1899) syn., 'President Cleveland'
From 'Marie Guillot' (T) × 'Coquette de Lyon' (T).
"Greenish-white." [Jg] "Pure white." [CA10] "Tall, almost climbing, many strong shoots; foliage plentiful, healthy; bloom free, almost continuous." [ARA18/125] "Named in honor of the noble life and work of Frances E. Willard, The Great Apostle of the W[omen's] C[hristian] T[emperance] U[nion]. The 'White Rose' being the Emblem of this Society, it seems eminently fitting that the most beautiful of all White Roses should be named in commemoration of one who has given her life for the cause she loved, and the memory of whose good works will always live in the hearts of her country women. This beautiful rose is a strong vigorous grower and true ever-bloomer, making handsome bushes. The buds and flowers are of the very largest size—pure snow white and so full and perfect they resemble a Camellia. The fragrance is delicious, and it is claimed to be by far the grandest of all Pure White Ever-Blooming Roses." [C&Js01]

[**Francis Dubreuil**] (Dubreuil, 1894)
Affiliated with 'Souvenir de David d'Angers' (T).
"Velvety purple-red, one of the darkest of the Teas; flower large, full, cupped; very floriferous; vigorous." [Cx] "Deep crimson flower of velvety texture." [Dr] "Ox-blood red. Balls in dampness." [Capt27] "Perhaps the darkest Tea; it grows vigorously with strong stems, and gives a harvest of roses for bouquets in the Fall." [JR32/34] "Beautifully formed buds." [P1] "Robust and very remontant; flower very full, of admirable form, erect on a rigid stem at the extremity of the cane; thick petals, very regularly rounded, shapely, opening with great ease; an absolutely new color in tea roses, velvety purplish crimson-red, with intense amaranthine-cerise reflections; bud long-ovoid, and of great beauty. Considering the perfection of its form and the intensity of its purple and amaranthine tones, this variety constitutes the most beautiful red Tea Rose known." [JR18/149] "A very prettily shaped flower, but...the colour was too dull a red to be really attractive, and it was retained only as a curiosity." [NRS21/115] The lightly double very Hybrid-Tea-like rose widely sold as 'Francis Dubreuil' at present does not seem to answer satisfactorily to the above descriptions.

[**Francisca Pries**] (Pries/Ketten Bros., 1888)
"Pink striped salmon." [LS] "One of the most robust growing among the Teas, not climbing, but making long, sturdy shoots. Flowers medium size, creamy white, shaded with amber; exceedingly free flowering." [CA93] "Flower blush white, center coppery saffron, outer petals washed pink; pretty large, full, cupped, fragrant. Vigorous growth; floriferous." [JR12/181]

[**Frau Geheimrat von Boch**] (Lambert, 1897) syn., 'Mme. von Boch'
From 'Princesse Alice de Monaco' (T) × 'Duchesse Marie Salviati' (T).
"Very vigorous growth, very floriferous, with very sturdy flowers; blooms from June to November. The flowers are large, strong, quite full, of beautiful form, opening well with large petals; the buds are large indeed and long, on long stems. The color is cream with carmine on the back of the exterior petals. The perfume is of the most penetrating, and most agreeable to the

nose. Equally good as a garden plant or exhibition variety, outside or in. Dedicated to the wife of a minister of commerce and the interior." [JR21/51]

Freiherr von Marschall (Lambert, 1903)
From 'Princesse de Monaco' (T) × 'Rose d'Evian' (T).
"Dark carmine; fine foliage, often tea-colored." [Th] "Purple-rose and cochineal. Varies." [Capt27] "The color of 'Red Radiance' is much superior in every way." [ARA40/31] "Bright red. Vigorous. Blooms profusely through the entire season." [Dr] "Buds long and pointed; flowers large, full and of perfect imbricated form." [C&Js09] "Growth good, but variable in hardiness. Form and color not of the best." [ARA18/115] "Growth is good, and its buds are well formed, and of good color; it blues, however, somewhat when open." [ARA29/89] "Pointed flowers of rich carmine-red. Attractive, red foliage. Vigorous...4×3 [ft; ca. 1.25×1 m]." [B]

Fürstin Infantin von Hohenzollern (Bräuer/Ketten Bros., 1898) syn., 'Fürstin Hohenzollern'
From 'Mlle. Comtesse de Leusse' (T) × 'Marie Van Houtte' (T).
"Lilac pink on an ochre yellow ground, large, full, fragrant. Vigorous, floriferous, often blooming in clusters." [JR22/133] "Exquisite lilac rose, on ochre ground; a fascinating combination seldom seen; has a delightful delicate fragrance. A vigorous grower and good bloomer." [C&Js05]

G. Nabonnand (Nabonnnand, 1888)
"Pale rose shaded with yellow; very large petals and handsome buds. Exceedingly free." [P1] "Pale flesh, shaded rose. Long-pointed flower." [H] "Perfect form...strong stem, very long branches, extraordinarily profuse." [JR31/119] "Very vigorous; wood a handsome bronze-green; handsome foliage; bud very long, well held, flesh pink, gold reflections; flower very large, full; very large petals, which are erect; color, delicate pink shaded with yellow, a very fine color; very floriferous, quite a marvel, and excellent for Winter flowers." [JR12/147] "Some say this is the best tea-rose of all, a

little like 'Gloire de Dijon', but gentler and a better colour. It is very strong, never suffers from mildew, and grows high." [HmC] "Very large flowers, light rose shaded to yellow, not very full with extra large petals, erect. The bud is elongated, big, and of a clear rose colour, very vigorous, grows to a great size and most floriferous. After 'Paul Neyron', I know of no other rose producing blooms of such magnitude, but those in question possess the additional charm of being of good shape and delicate. Magnificent, hardy, and easy to cultivate, this rose deserves a conspicuous place in every garden, but strange to say it is by no means well-known or generally grown." [B&V]

[**Garden Robinson**] (Nabonnand, 1900)
From 'David Pradel' (T) × 'Souvenir de Thérèse Levet' (T).
"Flower large, full; color, purplish carminy red, lighter center, perfect form; very beautiful solitary bud; compact bush, vigorous, very floriferous. Fragrant." [JR25/4]

[**Général Billot**] (Dubreuil, 1896)
"Bush of good vigor, medium stature, foliage of a beautiful green; flowers with large petals, the outer ones large and imbricated, the center ones smaller and numerous, both as brilliant as silk, neatly tricolored: exterior pale amaranth violet with amethyst reflection; interior, purple crimson. Variety of a strange coloration, giving the open flower the aspect of a crimson rose nestling in an amethyst violet rose." [JR21/3]

[**Général D. Mertchansky**] (Nabonnand, 1890)
"Exquisite rosy flesh; of good large size, fine full form; petals somewhat imbricated; a good grower and constant bloomer." [CA96] "Rose to a tender scarlet, with bright centre. The bud very attractive." [B&V] "Very vigorous; flower large, full erect, very elegant, perfect in hold and form. Pretty semi-long bud, which opens well. Wood reddish; medium thorns. Color, beautiful delicate flesh pink, center more intense. Superb; very floriferous." [JR14/165]

Général Galliéni (Nabonnand, 1899)

From 'Souvenir de Thérèse Levet' (T) × 'Reine Emma des Pays-Bas' (T). "Maroon shaded violet poppy-red toned salmon—strange and bizarre." [JR36/160] "Poppy red on a white ground with coppery-pink reflections; flower large, full, cupped; very floriferous; very vigorous." [Cx] "Flower...well-held...Very warm color, exterior petals poppy red tinted blood red; pretty bud; very handsome foliage; bush branched, very vigorous, very floriferous." [JR23/179] "Marvelous in foliage and flower, one of the rare dark-flowered autumnals, it is prettier at that season than during the Summer...; flower...with a golden center." [JR36/187] "Bright cerise, base of petals coppery orange, reflexed bright red. Pointed buds. A profuse bloomer." [C&Js05] "Fair growth; not a profuse bloomer." [ARA18/115] "Foliage persistent, despite snow and rime; color bizarre and handsome." [JR38/48]

[General Robert E. Lee] (Good & Reese, 1896)

"A beautiful new tea rose originated in the South; color, soft apricot yellow, delicately tinted with rose." [C&Js98] Robert Edward Lee, honorable general for the Confederacy; lived 1807-1870.

Général Schablikine (Nabonnand, 1878)

Affiliated with 'Safrano à Fleurs Rouges' (T).

"Coppery-rose. Very free, good bedder." [H] "A free-flowering variety for the garden, having salmon-red blooms, lacking in ideal form. It grows freely, and makes a good display." [OM] "Quartered." [Hk] "Vigorous, with occasional large thorns, and reddish wood; the blossoms are large, full, cupped, and of good form. The color is brilliant copper-red, with purple reverse." [JR3/9] "Double...coppery-red and cherry...compact plant...3×2 [ft; ca 9×6 dm]." [B] "Its abundant flowers...are never wanting throughout the season—I cut a handful on November 11, last Autumn—and with its good foliage made it admirable in a group." [K1] "Resistant to mildew." [JR33/37] "Weak; winterkills." [ARA18/115] "Vigorous...beautiful plum-colored shoots and elegant leaves...five feet [ca. 1.5 m] or so." [T2] "If a law was passed that one man should cultivate but one variety of rose, I should without hesitation choose 'Général Schablikine'; for general utility it is without a rival, flowering constantly from October to summer, flowers of a fine shape and wonderful evenness; a hundred blooms could be gathered off one plant, and every one exactly resembling its neighbor; the flower-stalk has a peculiar curve, which identifies it from other sorts...This of all roses serves us the most faithfully and generously." [B&V]

[**Général Tartas**] (Bernède,-1856)
"Dark rose, large and full." [FP] "Brilliant carmine, shaded with violet purple; large and fragrant." [CA88] "Bush vigorous; canes long, very flexile, bright green touched violet on the sunny side; thorns flattened, hooked; leaves deep bright yellowish green; blossom medium-sized, full, very well formed; color, bright crimson; very remontant and blooming abundantly until frost." [S]

[**Georges Farber**] (Bernaix, 1889)
"Bush medium-sized, very vigorous; beautiful bright green foliage; buds longly oval, conical, elegantly formed; flower borne on a long, strong stem; flower pretty large, with strong thick petals uniquely pointed, outer petals velvety purple, veined and reticulated with somber fiery red, center petals cochineal red passing to light carminy cerise red on the observe, paler pink on the reverse, making an agreeable contrast." [JR13/162]

[**Georges Schwartz**] (Widow Schwartz, 1899)
From 'Kaiserin Auguste Viktoria' (HT) × 'Souvenir de Mme. Levet' (T).
"Growth very vigorous; foliage deep green tinted purple; bud long, deep chrome yellow; flower large, full, perfect form, borne on a long, strong stem, keeping until fully open its magnificent deep canary yellow color. Very floriferous, scent good and penetrating, novel coloration. Much to be recommended for bedding." [JR23/178]

[**Gigantesque**] (Hardy/Sylvain-Péan, 1835) trans., "Gigantic"
Seedling of 'Parks' Yellow Tea-Scented China' (T).
"Its pale fleshy coloured flowers are very showy." [Bu] "Flowers of the largest size, but not very perfect in form, of a pale incarnate hue, and very showy." [WRP] "Very well formed." [S] "Flesh colour, shaded with rose, very large and full. Growth, vigorous. Coarse." [P] "Deep rose, sometimes mottled; often fine, but apt to come malformed or somewhat coarse." [EL] "The blossoms of this rose are very abundant, of a deep clear pink, paler at the edges." [JR6/178] "This rose, from the Yellow Tea, maintains several characteristics of its parent. It is vigorous, with branches which spread out horizontally, armed with strong but not very numerous thorns, which are equal, very much enlarged at the base, and reddish. The leaflets are a glossy green, and some are oval while others are heart-shaped. The blossom is of very large size (about five inches across [ca. 1.25 dm]), irregular in form, with the petals placed very close together; delicate pink within, and paler at the tip; they are borne on a strong, upright, glabrous stem." [An35/146] "One of the largest Tea Roses we possess, and richly deserves its name." [R9] Parent of 'Mlle. de Sombreuil' (T). Not to be confused with Odier's similarly-named HT of 1849.

Gloire de Deventer (Soupert & Notting, 1896)
From 'Devoniensis' (T) × 'Distinction' (HT).
"Very vigorous, handsome foliage, long bud; flower large, full, opens well, cupped, well held; cream white, reverse blush pink, center darker. The contrast between these colors, and the graceful poise of the blossom, gives it its own distinctive look. Very fragrant." [JR20/148]

[**Golden Gate**] (Jones/Dingee & Conard, 1892)
From 'Safrano' (T) × 'Cornelia Cook' (T).
"Cream and orange." [LS] "The flowers are extra large, very full and finely formed; the buds are long and of the most desirable form; the color is a rich creamy white, beautifully tinged with fine golden yellow." [CA93] "Most remarkable...its flowers are very large and quite double; the buds

are long and pointed, showing the magnificent 'Niphetos' form; its color is a rich creamy white with the heart and petal bases delicate golden yellow frequently tinted light pink; it blooms very freely." [JR15/89] "Of only fair growth, with habit and foliage somewhat similar to 'Niphetos'. A rose for exhibitors, capable of producing very large, finely shaped, creamy white blooms, but not vigorous or free-flowering enough for general purposes. The name, of course, is taken from the harbour of San Francisco; but English gardeners are naturally apt to expect it to be yellow: whereas it is certainly not golden, any more than it is like a gate." [F-M2] "Insufficiently known." [JR16/38] Ev. first raised ca. 1888.

[**Golden Oriole**] (Shepherd, 1905) syn., 'Shepherd's Oriole'
Sport of 'William Allen Richardson' (N).
"Deep saffron-yellow to deep cream; blooms are small but very double; in heat retains its color and keeps a high center; gives many blooms at one time; of decorative value only. Foliage perfect and well retained. Grows to 5 feet, with sturdy habit...while showing some Noisette characteristics of wood and foliage, is not a climber and blooms singly. Distinct and beautiful." [Th2]

Goubault (Goubault,-1839)
"Salmon-pink, deliciously fragrant, beautiful in the bud; habit moderate." [JC] "Large, full, light red, saffron at the center." [V8] "Bright rose, centre buff, very large and double." [FP] "Flowers bright rose, very large and double; form expanded. The young buds of this Rose are of the most elegant form, shewing of a rich deep crimson as the sepals part. Very sweet." [P] "Large, multiplex for full, light red, dawn center, fragrant." [Gp] "Large, beautiful." [LF] "A large rosy blush inclining to yellow in the centre; very double, distinct, and fragrant; it grows freely, and will occasionally produce seed, from which fine varieties will no doubt be obtained." [Bu] "Vigorous bush; flower medium-sized, nearly full, flat, very fragrant; color, light red, saffron center." [S] "This delightful variety, one of our oldest and very finest rose colored Teas[,] was raised from seed by

Monsieur Goubault, a rose grower at Angers, in Western France, more than ten years since, and (a strong proof of its excellence) still retains the position it then gained by a combination of surpassing sweetness and brilliancy of tint, with substance of petal. The color is a clear brilliant flesh colored rose, centre paler blush slightly tinged with yellow, outer petals of great substance, beautifully cupped and of a deeper color. Being much hardier than the generality of teas, it forms a fine half standard. In the greenhouse, on stems from nine to eighteen inches [ca. 1.25-2.5 dm], its large fragrant flowers though most gracefully drooping, require no artificial support. Of all tea roses, this is our favorite for fragrance, for which indeed it is so remarkable, as to entitle it to be distinguished as the '*sweetest* of the sweet roses.' Though somewhat less powerfully scented, than our first favorite 'Devoniensis'—the perfume of which we have spoken of so highly—'Goubault' has certainly a sweeter and more fruit like scent, peculiarly delightful. The lovers of perfumes can have none more delicious than the rich odour of the opening bud." [C] "A most excellent rose, as it is remarkably robust and hardy, and will probably form a fine standard." [R4] Maurice Goubault, rose fancier and amateur breeder in Angers, France.

[Grand-Duc Pierre de Russie] (Perny/S. Cochet, 1895) trans., "Grand-Duke Peter of Russia"
"Rich rose, passing to salmon shades, a strong vigorous grower and good bloomer." [C&Js98] "Enormous flowers and buds of perfect form opening well. Color, pale pink veined darker pink. Charming." [JR19/165]

Graziella (Dubreuil, 1893)
"Vigorous, plant nicely shaped, leaves large, thick, glossy. Flower very large, expands slowly, petals satiny, brilliant, cream white tinted blush, like 'Souvenir de la Malmaison'." [JR17/168]

[**Grossherzogin Mathilde von Hessen**] (Vogler, 1869) syn., 'Grand Duchess Hilda'; trans., "Grand Duchess Mathilda"
Seedling or sport of 'Bougère' (T).
"Vigorous; flower large, nearly full; very floriferous; color, greenish white, like lily green." "Moderate in growth, but vigorous enough to produce nice flowering wood; flowers have large outer petals. The color is nankeen yellow with ochre center." [CA96]

Harry Kirk (A. Dickson, 1907)
"Lemon." [LS] "Flower large, full, well-formed; petals regular, deep sulphur-yellow." [JR35/15] "Deep sulphur yellow, passing to a lighter shade at edge of petals. The flowers are large, full, of perfect form and great substance. Buds are long and elegant. A splendid free-flowering Rose and much the best of its color." [C&Js10] "Color clear; very good in growth, foliage, and hardiness; form almost perfect in bud, not so good in open flower; fairly good bloomer." [ARA18/111] "In growth this Rose more nearly approaches the Hybrid Teas than a pure Tea; its chief feature is its colour, a good deep yellow—sulphur almost in the centre of the flower, fading to white at the edges of the petals. The flowers so far have not come so large as one would like—it is free rather than vigorous in growth—has not been exhibited very much up to the present...It will require shading and high culture." [F-M]

[**Helen Good**] (Good & Reese, 1906)
Sport of 'Maman Cochet' (T).
"Soft light pink, darker shadings. Varies." [ARA27/20] "A rose that has all the good points of the Cochets. The buds are of exquisite form; color is a delicate yellow, suffused with pink, with deeper edge." [CA10] "Has good form, size, and stem, and is lasting. Foliage very good." [Th2] "Good in growth, foliage and form; color pleasing, not of the best; fair in blooming." [ARA18/11] "Moderate height, rather compact; foliage sufficient to plentiful, healthy; bloom moderate, intermittent in flower three-fourths of the time." [ARA18/125]

Helvetia (Ducher, 1873)

"Coppery salmon." [LS] "Pink, tinged with fawn." [EL] "Growth vigorous; flower large, full, globular; color, salmon pink with peach pink center." [S] "Small growth; not a bloomer." [ARA18/116] *Cf.* 'Louis Richard'.

[Henri Plantagenet, Comte d'Anjou] (Tesnier, 1892) trans., "Henry Plantagenet, Count of Anjou"

"Brilliant China rose in color, with deeper shadings. A moderately good grower, producing an abundance of nicely formed flowers." [CA95]

Henry Bennett (Levet, 1872)

"Growth moderately vigorous; flower medium-sized, full, very fragrant; color, light pink with a deep sulphur yellow center." [S] Henry Bennet, prominent English rose breeder.

[Henry M. Stanley] (Dingee & Conard, 1891)

From 'Mme. Lambard' (T) × 'Comtesse Riza du Parc' (T).

"Deep chamois rose, delicately tinged with fine apricot yellow petals, bordered with bright carmine red." [C&Js02] "Pink and apricot." [LS] "Its color is a rare shade of pink-amber of the most delicate from the middle out, shaded with apricot yellow. Very full and fragrant." [JR16/38] "Makes a beautiful contrast to 'Golden Gate'....edged and bordered with rich carmine; deliciously scented." [CA93] "Vigorous and healthy, of elegant, neat growth; flowers of good size, quite regular, quite full, and very fragrant; light pink, sometimes nuanced salmon. This is a very freely blooming rose producing magnificent buds; presumably forcing conditions will give the best results." [JR15/88] "Low growing, rather compact, reasonably hardy; foliage plentiful, healthy; bloom moderate, intermittent, in flower about one-half the time, scattered well through season." [ARA18/125] Sir Henry Morton Stanley, lived 1841-1904; orig. John Rowlands; English explorer in Africa.

[Hermance Louisa de la Rive] (Nabonnand, 1882)

"Vigorous; flower large, full, well formed, imbricated; color, beautiful flesh white, pinker towards the center, perfect form; a magnificent variety, one of the most beautiful of the genre. Blooms in Winter and continuously." [JR6/186] "Large, full and imbricated." [B&V]

Homère (Robert & Moreau, 1858)

Possibly a seedling of either 'David Pradel' (T) or 'Goubault' (T).

"Pink, center flesh shaded whitish; flower medium-sized, full, cupped, ruffled, fragrant, very floriferous; very vigorous." [Cx] "Salmon-rose, often richly mottled; a free bloomer, moderately hardy, best in the open air; the buds are very beautiful, even though of various shades. Certainly one of the most useful tea roses." [EL] "Variable, sometimes flecked with purple." [Hn] "A peculiar and beautiful rose when in bud. Its color is rose, tipped with red, and with a salmon center." [SBP] "Striped pinkish-white and purple." [JR20/6] "Gives single flowers [*in Havana*]." [JR6/44] "Vigorous, floriferous, pretty hardy; flower large, full, globular; color rose pink with flesh-white salmon center; one of the best for the open ground. In two or three seasons, the plant makes a little spreading shrub of perhaps thirty inches [ca. 9 dm] in height. The branches end in a bud, rarely two, of moderate size; the fully expanded blossom is rather globular-elongate; barely open on its firm stem, it remains thus for several days if the temperatures are not too high. Though rainy periods are unfavorable to other varieties, 'Homère' blooms prettily right through them. Its scent resembles that of *R. semperflorens* [*i.e., 'Slater's Crimson China*]." [S] "3×3 [ft; ca. 1×1 m]." [B] "Twiggy...dark foliage." [B1] "Of very strong growth, with fair foliage, but more suited for a pillar than a wall, and best as a big bush. It has a sturdy branching habit, quite distinct from the characteristic growth of the pure Teas, and is no doubt a cross of some sort, though born long before Hybrid Teas were thought of; it is perfectly hardy, very vigorous and of strong constitution, and I wonder we have had no seedlings from it. It is not liable to mildew, and but little injured by rain, does well as a dwarf, is a free bloomer and capital in the autumn, pretty in colour, with a crimpled edge, but small in size. It is hard to prove a negative, and I will not say 'Homère' never comes perfectly shaped, because I have heard of one or two though I have not seen them. Its bad manners in this respect are the more aggravating, because each bloom has the promise of a beautiful shape but marred by a malformation. As often happens, the strongest blooms are the most imperfect, and the buds should be cut small before their promise is spoiled...A capital cottage garden Rose which should not be closely pruned, doing well anywhere." [F-M] "So well known as to hardly need description." [FRB] Homère, alias Homer, author of the great epics *The Iliad* and *The Odyssey*.

[Honourable Edith Gifford] (Guillot fils, 1882)
From 'Mme. Falcot' (T) × 'Perle des Jardins' (T).
"Very perfect white, with sometimes a pale pink centre. A very free bloomer, and a rose no garden can do without. Strong habits, and bushy but not high." [HmC] "Creamy white with centre of flesh, large, full and well formed flowers, free, thoroughly reliable and considered excellent for exhibition purposes, good growth, fine foliage, rather liable to mildew, in other respects giving little trouble and thrives well." [B&V] "Vigorous, of good stature, blossoms large or very large, full, very well formed; superb long buds; color, flesh white, light yellow ground, center salmon pink fading to white; very floriferous." [S] "Of good stout stiff but not long growth, with fine foliage, liable to mildew in the autumn, and requiring protection from rain. A very good Tea Rose indeed, an unusually large proportion of the blooms coming good, of fine shape, petal, centre and size. It is thoroughly reliable, an excellent show Rose, one of the earliest, very free blooming, a good autumnal and does excellently as a dwarf. A good Rose, and a 'good doer,' giving little trouble and ample returns." [F-M3]

[**Hortensia**] (Ducher, 1870) trans., "Hydrangea"
"[*Growth*] free...Rose color, back of petals a washed-out pink; a coarse, poor sort." [EL] "Moderate growth; flower large, very full; color, pink with yellowish reflections." [S]

Hovyn de Tronchère (Puyravaud, 1899)
Seedling of 'Regulus' (T).
"Coppery red, petals' edges silvery pink, ground of golden yellow, borne on strong stem, large, full, plump, fragrant; growth vigorous, very bushy, slightly thorny, beautiful green foliage. Very floriferous...dedicated to a rose fancier from Guîtres." [JR22/133]

Hugo Roller (W. Paul, 1907)
"Light canary yellow with claret, sometimes reddish lilac shading—varies. Low growth. Very distinct in color...Foliage, very good." [Th] "A very dainty flower; lemon-yellow, tinged with rose. It is a poor grower, though possibly worth including in one's collection for the sake of a few of the very pretty blooms." [OM] "Most attractive and distinct color; very good form; low growth; not hardy." [ARA18/111] "The seeds from which it came were sown in mixture, and the cross from which it resulted is thus not recorded; but the traits of the plant would indicate that the variety owes its origin to a cross of a Tea Rose with a Hybrid Tea, or vice-versa. The color of the blossom is a rich and handsome crimson on a ground of light yellow; the contrast of these shades loses nothing of its brilliance in the heat of Summer, approaches the cool nights of Fall changing only by developing a deeper shade of red. Of a largish medium-size or so, the blossoms are of good form, held on upright stems, and abundantly produced—qualities making a variety of the first merit for garden and bedding." [JR32/168-169]

Hume's Blush Tea-Scented China (Banks/Hume/Colville, 1810) syn. 'Belle Cythérée'

"Flesh-pink, full, flat, very large, beautiful." [LF] "Flowers large, semi-double, white with a nankeen tint, elegant tea scent." [J-A] "Blush, centre rose, large and full." [FP] "Old blush; fine high fragrance." [JWa] "Creamy-white, their centre salmon-buff, large and full; form, expanded. Growth, vigorous." [P] "Flowers, large, semi-double; of a pale pink or flesh-colour, almost white. Petals, concave, of a pale yellow at the base. Styles, filiform, straight, and salient." [Go] "Carmine, fading to blush, large flowers, somewhat loose but good in the bud; one of the most fragrant. The larger number of the Teas are descendants of this sort." [EL] "Few or none of the family possess the peculiar fragrance of this delightful rose; its large rosy blush flower buds will ever be admired; when full blown it is not so attractive as others, but will always be desirable for its agreeable odour, though perhaps one of the most difficult of the family to grow well. A liberal portion of leaf mould and sand appears to suit it." [Bu] "Strong green luxuriant shoots, with flowers varying in color from pure white to crimson." [WRP] "[I]ts peduncles are uni-floral and slightly lanate, as are its leaves, on which the odd leaflet is larger than the others. It only blooms two times a year if it is not in a suitable soil or in a good exposure. This rose is delicate; it, as well as its varieties, should spend the Winter in the orangery. However, now variety 165 [*i.e., 'Hume's Blush Tea-Scented China'*] is being grafted successfully; it gives one of the first of the beautiful flowers, flesh-coloured, very large, semi-double, and fragrant." [dP18] "Semi-double variety, of ever-blooming habit, discovered by an agent of the British East India Company, who obtained plants in 1808 from the Fan Tee Nurseries at Canton, and dispatched them to Sir Abraham Hume, of Wortlebury, who received them in 1810, and bestowed on them the name 'Hume's Blush', in honour of his wife, the Lady Amelia Hume...pale pink flowers, on half evergreen foliage consisting of five or 7 foliate leaves, borne on long sarmentose branches, armed with scattered, hooked prickles. The leaflets were responsible for the perfume after which the Teas were named, for the flowers varied considerably in odour (as do those of the modern H.T.'s) and some had no perfume at all." [EER] "Taken from China to England by Joseph Banks in 1809, this rose flowered for the first time in the nursery of Mr. Colville, who mentioned it as a variety in which the flower had the aroma of tea, which, Redouté says, is not quite the case." [Gx] "*Stems*, 0.3-0.4 (-0.6) meters tall [ca. 2-3 ft], with sparse, reddish, almost straight *prickles. Leaflets* 3-5, ovate, acute, glabrous, denticulate, a little purplish beneath; petiole with small recurved prickles. *Flowers* 7 centimeters or more in diameter [ca. 2 ¾ + inches], nodding; pedicels slightly hispid; *petals* flesh-white, as if transparent, in many rows, irregularly notched above; *receptacles* globose, and *sepals* nearly always entire, the both of them glabrous. This is notable among the many China roses by way of the size and transparency of the petals, and the perfume, especially when the flower is opening. Introduced from the East Indies to England in 1809, it flowered for the first time in the nursery of Colville, who distributed it under the imprecise name of tea-scented rose. It spends the Winter in the orangery, and is easily propagated by cuttings or, better, budded on the Common China. It is often attacked by mildew caused by cold wet weather in Spring. According to Monsieur Boursault, this can be cured by rubbing all the affected parts with a sponge soaked in vinegar. Perhaps rust and all similar rose ailments could be cured in this way." [T&R] "Voila, the charming sister of ['*La Spécieuse*'], and from the same land [*China*]. Its growth is lower and as slender, leaves a little larger and much more delicate—but don't despair of acclimating it—graft it on the Briar, which gives its growth vigor, which it lacks from cuttings. In order to produce strong shoots with roots, it is necessary to put it into the frame early, because otherwise it starts to bloom, leaving no hope for the graft. Its blossom is as big as that of the Centifolia, and it has the same form as well; its petals are large and quite thick. Its color is diaphanous delicate pink, or with some nankeen. Late to [...*word illegible in manuscript, probably to the effect of* "commence growth" *or* "commence bloom"...], late to finish, its India Tea scent perfumes the sitting-room. Summing up, this is an extraordinary flower which looks like no other and which is always in bloom throughout the year for its owner with neatly charming blossoms." [LeR]

Hyménée (Hardy,-1829)
"White, yellowish center." [TCN] "White, with fawn centre." [JWa] "Bush of moderate growth, with outspread canes armed with not very numerous thorns, which are equal, straight, compressed at the base, sparse; leaves of a bright green, composed of three to five oblong leaflets; flowers often solitary, sometimes clustered in twos or threes, fairly well formed, large, of a yellowish white at the edge, pale yellow towards the center, with petals fairly regularly arranged." [MaCo] This early Tea traveled widely, having been recorded as far afield as California! Hymen, the god of marriage.

[Impératrice Maria Féodorowna de Russie] (Nabonnand, 1883) syn., 'Empress Marie of Russia'; trans., "Empress Maria Feodorovna of Russia" "Fine, stately flowers, extra large, very full, and delightfully sweet; color, fine canary yellow, passing to white, delicately tinged with pale lemon; very beautiful." [CA90] "Very vigorous, with large thorns; flower very large, imbricated, with very large petals, full, well formed; color, yellowish white, marbled pink, nuanced, picoteed." [JR7/183]

[Improved Rainbow] (Burbank?, ca. 1893)
Sport or seedling of 'Rainbow' (T).
"Entirely distinct in its markings. The 'Improved Rainbow' instead of being broadly marked like its parent, the 'Rainbow', is penciled with brightest '[Papa] Gontier] color, every petal in every flower, and base of petals of bright amber color, making a very distinct and charming flower." [CA96] "Just what the old 'Rainbow' ought to have been but never was. The color is a lovely shade of deep coral pink elegantly striped and mottled with intense shining crimson; finely colored at center with rich glowing amber, makes beautiful buds, and the flowers are extra large, very

sweet and of greatest depth and substance." [C&Js98] "Fair growth and good foliage; distinct color." [ARA18/118]

[Innocente Pirola] (Widow Ducher, 1878)
"A very perfect-shaped white rose. A little liable to mildew, and it likes a rich soil." [HmC] "Clouded white, medium size, full, well-formed buds. In the style of 'Niphetos', but is inferior to it in all respects save mere vigor of growth." [EL] "Only fair in growth and foliage; requires rich soil and in many places does not do well as a dwarf; rather liable to mildew, but for a white Tea Rose little injured by rain. The blooms come well, and the typical shape is unique, one of the most perfect we have, something like the whorl of a shell. Fairly free in bloom, and lasting, but not often very large till overblown. A first-class Rose, fine in petal and centre, it should be a great favorite with those purists (with whom I have much in sympathy) who insist upon regularity and perfection of shape as the one thing desirable above all others." [F-M3] "Growth very vigorous; canes short and upright, perfectly held; blossom very large, full, well formed, with big long buds; color, pure white, sometimes lightly blushing. Considering its vigor and abundance, replaces 'Niphetos'." [JR2/167]

[Isaac Demole] (Nabonnand, 1895)
Seedling of 'Duchess of Edinburgh' (T).
"Flower very large, very full, erect, perfect form; color, carminy red, darker center; petal edges lined white, giving the rose a cachet of elegance all its own; bud semi-elongate, opening well; foliage dark green; thorns strong. Very vigorous bush, extremely floriferous." [JR19/180]

Isabella Sprunt (Sprunt/Buchanan, 1865)
Sport of 'Safrano' (T).
"Pale fawn yellow." [ARA40/31] "Sulphur-yellow." [P1] "Light canary-yellow flowers." [FRB] "Lemon yellow. Beautiful pointed bud." [H] "Brilliant yellow...large to medium...vigorous; needs a southern exposure...about 104 blooms per season." [ARA21/90-91] "Flower large, semi-full; very

floriferous." [S] "High-centered, medium…, double; soft-pale yellow, fading lighter…2-3 [ft; ca. 6-9 dm]." [Lg] "Flowers in clusters, soon over. Exquisite when half open." [Hn] "Flowers moderately well formed." [JC] "The many buds open without trouble; plant stays green; blooms early to late." [JR9/70] "Moderately tall, compact, hardy; foliage plentiful, healthy; bloom free, continuous." [ARA18/125] "Hardy, but not a strong grower." [F-M2] "On a west aspect quickly covers a wall 15-ft. high [ca. 4.5 m]." [NRS/17] "Growth not good. No distinguishing characteristics." [ARA18/116] "Well known as one of the most useful kinds." [EL]

[Isabelle Nabonnand] (Nabonnand, 1873)

"Its blush-centred white blooms are fairly double, and yet open freely through the winter." [J] "Flower of chamois leather tinge with darker centre, large, half full and very sweet. A very pretty and popular rose." [B&V] "Growth extremely vigorous, large and abundant foliage, large fawn-pink roses, darker at the center, delicious fragrance." [JR5/21]

[Ivory] (Durfee/American Rose Co., 1901) syn., 'White Golden Gate'
Sport of 'Golden Gate' (T).

"Large pure white flowers." [CA02] "Perfect form; ivory white, which keeps until the blossom is done; irreproachable hold and quite full." [JR25/65] "The beautiful 'Golden Gate' Rose is now so well known that to say "'Ivory' is exactly like it, only different in color,' is all the recommendation that it needed to place it in the front rank of our most beautiful Ever-blooming Roses. It is an exceedingly free bloomer, sure to be covered with buds and flowers as long as the bush is kept in growing condition. The flowers are large, full and sweet, clear ivory white, and highly valued for cutting and all kinds of florists' work." [C&Js03]

[J.-B. Varonne] (Guillot & fils, 1889)

"Vigorous bush; flowers large, full, well formed; color varies from deep China pink to very bright carmine, with a coppery yellow center." [JR13/181] "Fine long buds." [CA93] "This fine rose always shows up well. The flowers are large, full and round, very double and sweet. Color, a very pleasing shade of soft, rosy crimson. It is a vigorous grower and constant bloomer, and makes beautiful buds for cutting." [C&Js02]

Jean André (Pelletier, 1894)
From 'William Allen Richardson' (N) × 'Ma Capucine' (T).
"This pleasing variety of nearly continuous bloom was developed in 1894...It makes a bush of good vigor for a Noisette, canes semi-climbing, flowers solitary...medium size...full and fragrant, orange yellow with a darker center." [JR31/173]

Jean Ducher (Widow Ducher, 1874) syn., 'Comte de Sembui'
"Buff bordered cream." [JR11/50] "Yellow, shaded salmon and red in the center; very good grower; fine foliage, flowers large and full; very fine." [HstXXX:236] "Bronzed-rose, large, very full, globular form; not to be depended upon, but very beautiful when well grown." [EL] "Lemon to salmon-yellow, centres shaded with peach; large and full; form globular; growth vigorous. One of the best." [P1] "A blossom beyond description, of good form and substance." [JR12/180] "Perhaps the most sensitive of all Roses to wet or rain...when a fine bloom does come at least it is grand in shape, petal, centre, size, colour, and lasting qualities...a free-bloomer...colour is variable...very decorative at a distance." [F-M2] "Very vigorous, well held, not long-lasting, and too double." [JR9/70] "A magnificent tea, but it absolutely requires a dry hot season...impatient of wet." [FRB] "Strong stout stiff growth, with good foliage...not liable to mildew." [F-M2]

[Jean Pernet] (Pernet père, 1867)
"Light yellow." [JR20/149] "Light orange-yellow, outer petals paler, flowers of moderate size and double." [JC] "Flower of glossy yellow, suffused with salmon. A very beautiful variety, resembling but hardly equal to a fine example of 'Perle des Jardins'." [B&V] "Vigorous bush; canes slender, divergent, slightly nodding; bark a glaucescent green on the shady side,

reddish on the sunny side, bearing sharp blackish prickles; leaves light green, divided into 3 or 5 leaflets which are oval, acuminate, and finely dentate; petioles slender, reddish at the base and bearing three small prickles of the same color; flower from seven to eight centimeters across [ca. 3 inches], full, globular, solitary on the small branches and in twos and threes on the vigorous canes; color, a beautiful intense yellow fading to light yellow; outer petals large, peduncles long and strong. Variety of the first order, very recommendable." [S]

Jeanette Heller
Listed as 'William R. Smith'.

[Jeanne Abel] (Guillot fils, 1882)
Seedling of 'Comtesse de Labarthe' (T).
"Vigorous variety with flowers which are medium-sized, full, well formed, colored a delicate whitish pink on a lightly yellowish ground, center bright pink, very fragrant and very floriferous." [JR6/150]

Jeanne Philippe
Listed as 'Mlle. Jeanne Philippe'.

[Joseph Métral] (Bernaix, 1888)
"Extra vigorous; buds ovoid with reddish sepals tipped with a foliaceous appendage. Flower very double, opening well; form, slightly flattened; petals numerous, undulate and curled under at the edges, creped and chiffoned at the center; color, somber magenta red passing to cherry red nuanced purple; bloom abundant and continuous. Excellent for bedding." [JR12/164] "A strong, healthy grower." [CA93]

[Joseph Paquet] (Ketten Bros., 1905)
From 'G. Nabonnand' (T) × 'Margherita di Simone' (T).
"Rose on yellow ground. Loose." [ARA27/20] "China pink tinted lake red, petal bases light yellow; large, full, fragrant; bud very long. Very floriferous." [JR29/166]

[Jules Finger] (Widow Ducher, 1879)
From 'Catherine Mermet' (T) × 'Mme. de Tartas' (T).
"Red, with a silvery lustre; a promising sort." [EL] "Very large, full, fine form, splendid bright salmon-pink to red." [Hn] "Bush very vigorous, with strong and upright canes; thorns rare, recurved, red; beautiful large dark green foliage composed of 5 leaflets. Flower very large, full, very well formed, outer petals large, more muddled towards the center; color, beautiful bright red fading to nuanced light red, shaded silvery; reverse of petals darker; very floriferous." [JR3/164] "Of good growth with fair foliage; does well as a dwarf but better as a standard, not liable to mildew and can stand a shower. The blooms generally come well, but the shape is not a refined one, the centre petals being generally incurved, whereas we expect the more elegant pointed form in a Tea Rose. Pretty good as a free-bloomer and autumnal, not very large, and aggravating in colour. This is fairly good and pure when the flower first opens, but it will not hold when cut, and if kept too long, for it has a lasting shape, it turns to a livid hue, which almost tempts one to use the word 'ugly'." [F-M3]

Julius Fabianics de Misefa (Geschwind, 1902)
From 'Bardou Job' (B) × 'Souvenir du Dr. Passot' (T).
"Carmine and crimson shaded fire-red." [RR]

[Koningin Wilhelmina] (Verschuren, 1903) trans., "Queen Wilhelmina"
Either sport of 'Dr. Grill' (T); or from 'Dr. Grill' × an HT seedling.
"Coppery salmon." [LS] "Color, rose pink. Flowers said to resemble a Dahlia." [C&Js11]

[La Nankeen] (Ducher, 1871)
"Coppery-yellow, outer petals paler, large, full, and of tolerably good form." [JC] "Highly valued for its magnificent buds, which are deep orange yellow at base and rich creamy white at the point; exceedingly beautiful, and different from all others; very fragrant." [CA90] "Vigorous; canes thin and reflexing; bark pale green, with reddish brown, upright,

flattened thorns which are wider at the base; leaves smooth, light green, of 3 or 5, rarely 7, oval-pointed, finely dentate leaflets; leafstalk slender, armed with some small prickles; flower 6-7 cm across [ca. 3 inches], very full, expanded form; color, nankeen yellow, lighter at the center; outer petals long and rounded at the edge. Buds much in demand for making bouquets. Very tender." [S]

[La Princesse Vera] (Nabonnand, 1877)

"White on a coppery ground." [LS] "White, with yellow tint; very full; fine form." [CA88] "Very vigorous; flowers large, very full, yellowish coppery white on a very bright reticulated ground; big-wooded, few thorns." [JR1/12/13-14]

La Sylphide (Boyau, 1842)

"Outer petals cream, tinted with pale carmine, centre fawn, very large and full; a beautiful free blooming rose for outdoor culture." [JC] "Blush, very large and double." [P] "Yellow flesh-colour; vigorous, grows to a big size and sweet scented. In bud or half-open stage no rose in cultivation can excel it in beauty, shape, or delicacy. Filbert shaped with petals folded one on the other with remarkable regularity, the edges slightly re-curved as in the 'La France' group. Flourishes to great advantage under the protection of glass, its flowers being very delicate, wind or rain or too much sun are detrimental to the perfect opening of its flowers. Beautiful foliage of the same shade as that of 'Maréchal Niel'. Not a common rose, but one well deserving more attention and notoriety. Unfortunately a great favorite with the Rose Bug." [B&V]

[La Tulipe] (Ducher, 1868)

"Creamy white, tinted with pale carmine, handsome in the bud, but only semi-double, moderate habit." [JC] "Moderate growth; flower large, full; color, white tinted pink." [S] "For many years, having paused often enough in front of 'La Tulipe'..., I was inclined to think that I had before me a hybrid of Tea × Noisette. I took some cuttings in order to have own-root specimens to observe, and the most vigorous of them was planted in a plot which was always under one's eye. For three or four years, the specimen would stay pretty spindly, with no differences from the plant from which it was cut. But then, at the next bourgeoning of Spring, I noted, shooting out obliquely from the specimen, long canes which were slightly undulate, with matte green foliage, at the tips of which beautiful self-yellow roses opened, a yellow comparable to that of '[Mme. la] Duchesse d'Auerstädt', which grew alongside. While the blossoms were just opening, lateral canes began to develop in profusion from the upper two-thirds of the cane in a direction noticeably perpendicular to the position of the axils from which they grew, an arrangement which I understand to be characteristic of the Noisettes. The young canes—the uppermost first—would begin to bloom when cold and snow suddenly put an end to all other growth. The effect of frost on the plant was rather curious. The typical 'La Tulipe' branches were completely untouched, while the long anomalous canes were severely hurt. Due to all this, I would of course be inclined to lay the sporting of roses to the account of Hybridity. There are two strains in the Hybrid, and the characteristics of growth results from their close mixing. When a difficulty crops up in the mix for any reason, it is outwardly reflected in a change in growth." [JR24/43]

[Lady Castlereagh] (A. Dickson, 1888)

"A pure Tea producing many branches which are short and strong, with particularly thick and beautiful foliation; blooms abundantly and very late. The flowers are of good form, large and lush, always opening well; the petals are thick, round, and smooth. Their color is of a very delicate shade, pink with yellow, the pink predominating around the outer edges. This magnificent rose hasn't the least tendency to mildew, and what is more is very robust outside without protection, never suffering from cold…it blooms with astonishing profusion." [JR12/106] "Foliage large and leathery." [CA93]

Lady Hillingdon (Lowe & Shawyer, 1910)
From 'Papa Gontier' (T) × 'Mme. Hoste' (T).
"A handsome orange-vermilion." [JR35/183] "Of remarkable orange yellow colour, and possessing long, shapely buds…satisfactory in the garden."
[OM] "Deep apricot yellow,…fading…lighter…long-pointed buds open
to flat, semi-double, fragrant, flowers…continuous profusion…3-4 [ft; ca.
1-1.25 m]." [Lg] "Flowers not full, but elongated and handsome." [Hk]
"Does not open well and droops in heat; odor slight." [ARA26/94]
"Delicious fragrance." [T2] "With better growth would be one of the best
yellows." [Th] "The vigorous shrub has pretty foliage, and strong, upright
shoots covered with attractive full blossoms which have large petals and are
of a handsome light yellow which is sometimes shaded." [JR34/118]
"Gives wonderful color in Pacific South-West, if grown in shade, under
which conditions it does not bleach for several days, petals seem to increase
in substance, and stem is longer and stronger…Prune sparingly." [Th2]
"Very vigorous in warm climates, to 6 [ft; ca. 1.75 m]." [HRG] "Rather a
weak grower [*in Bermuda*]." [UB28] "3×2 [ft; ca. 9×6 dm]." [B] "Height
and compactness medium, rather weak, not very hardy; foliage sufficient,
almost free from black-spot; bloom moderate, almost continuous."
[ARA18/126] "Always on the job." [PS] "Most attractive Rose not only for
the beauty of its flowers, but also on account of the decorative effect of
flower and foliage…bright fawn yellow, suffused orange…The flowers are
carried well…though usually somewhat bent over…certainly grows
extremely well. Its stems are smooth and the young foliage is a beautiful
ruby bronze, this tint being retained, though diminishing and merging into
green while the leaves last. The flowers are thin but a beautiful shape, with
deep shell-shaped petals. It does not suffer much from mildew. The principal defect of this Rose is that in cold weather many of the flowers—sometimes nearly half of them—are apt to come of a pale washed-out apricot,
when much of their beauty and distinction is lost. Its strength lies in the
grace and beauty of flower and foliage." [NRS/13] "Far outsells all others
combined [*of yellows and apricots in Houston, Texas*]." [ET]

Lady Mary Corry (A. Dickson, 1900)

"Deep golden yellow; flower erect." [JR30/15] "Of good size, perfect form; freely produced." [P1] "An exquisite decorative Tea Rose, growth vigorous and erect branching habit, fine large bold flowers of perfect build...delightfully tea-scented." [C&Js02]

Lady Plymouth (A. Dickson, 1914)

"Deep ivory-cream (sometimes yellow). Balls in wet weather." [Capt27] "The best of the light yellow type found among the Teas." [Th] "A meritorious Rose, of the 'Souvenir de Pierre Notting' type, whose pearly cream petals are very faintly flushed, giving it a most piquant finish. Delicately tea-perfumed." [C&Js16] "Lovely...Ivory white flushed cream and blush on a dense plant. Slightly fragrant...3×3 [ft; ca. 1×1 m]." [B] "Well-formed, semi-double." [HRG] "Good in color, form, and lasting qualities; foliage especially fine...fair in blooming." [ARA18/111] "A good addition to the Teas—spiral or conical shape with a nice recurved outer petal. Colour, deep cream with almost yolk of egg centre. Foliage a good contrast; a good grower and fragrant; a very beautiful Rose." [NRS/14] "Mild perfume...growth bushy, with good number of canes, but not exceptionally tall. A good rose." [ARA17/25]

Lady Roberts (F. Cant, 1902)

Sport of 'Anna Olivier' (T).

"Rich apricot, base of petals coppery red, edges of petals shaded orange, long pointed bud and large full flowers." [P1] "Cream and orange." [JR34/10] "Orange-apricot to fawn. Weak stems." [Capt27] "Its pretty flowers of reddish apricot shaded salmon, its petals often bordered with orange, with coppery-red nubs and metallic reflections, and a pretty pointed bud, make this a rose of the first merit. The plant is vigorous and very floriferous." [JR37/13] "Small, of good form...One of the best Tea roses." [OM] "Flowers large and perfect in shape, with long, pointed buds; colour variable." [Hn] "Does not spoil in rain or ball in damp winds, but becomes smaller in heat. Foliage very fine and lasts well."

[Th2] "An apricot-coloured sport from 'Anna Olivier', which Rose it resembles in habit…a fair amount of glossy olive green foliage. The carriage of the flowers is good, and as a rule erect, but bug flowers will sometimes droop. The blossoms are as a rule medium sized, having an apricot centre with coppery base to the petals, the edges becoming pale yellow, but the colour varies a good deal…It is not much affected by mildew…exceptional continuity of its flowers." [NRS/13] "A quite pretty rose, having leaves and flowers in abundance during the Fall." [JR36/188]

[**Lady Stanley**] (Nabonnand, 1886)
"Very vigorous; flower very large, very full, globular, imbricated, of perfect form; color, lilac on a ground of yellow, petal edges purple. Very floriferous." [JR10/169] Not to be confused with Dubos's 1849 pink Bourbon of the same name.

[**Lady Zoë Brougham**] (Nabonnand, 1886)
Seedling of 'Isabelle Nabonnand' (T).
"Very vigorous bush…flower large, full, imbricated, of beautiful form; color, extraordinarily bright chamois yellow, darker at the petal edges; bud quite long. Unique." [JR10/169] "Yellow to chamois-leather colour, edges of petals rather darker, good elongated bud, vigorous, floriferous and grows to a large size. Does not like the sun, which very rapidly sucks all colour from the blooms; it does better in every respect when the sky is clouded. Have seen some very fine examples of this rose which were flowered at Wimbledon, superior in colour and texture to what we can grow here [*on the French Riviera*]." [B&V]

Laurette (Robert, 1853)
"Seven to eight cm. [ca. 3 inches], full, salmony flesh, peduncles strong, bearing their blossoms well, wood not very thorny, vigorous." [M-L53/323] "Bush vigorous, climbing canes; flower large, full; color, salmony yellow." [S] "Insignificant." [JDR56/49] "Pretty good variety, though ordinary." [l'H56/246]

[Le Pactole] (Miellez, 1840)

"Lemon, bright yellow centre." [JWa] "Silky yellow, full, large." [LF] "Flowers cream, their centres yellow, large and full; form, cupped." Growth, moderate. A beautiful Rose." [P] "Creamy white to pale yellow. Low growing, is quite a desirable variety, with especially beautiful buds." [B&V] The Pactolus, in Lydia, Asia Minor, was the river in which King Midas immersed himself in order to *lose* his ability to turn things into gold, a process which writers call "publication"; in ancient times—indeed, up until the Christian era—gold could be found in the river's bed. The Pactolus's modern name is "Sarabat."

[Lena] (A. Dickson, 1906)

"Glowing apricot. The flowers are freely produced, frequently showing sprays of from seven to nine perfect blooms. An exquisite garden rose." [C&Js08]

[Léon XII] (Soupert & Notting, 1892)

From 'Anna Olivier' (T) × 'Earl of Eldon' (N).

"Very vigorous, foliage large and beautiful; flower large, full; petals large and well rounded; bud long like that of 'Niphetos'; color white, lightly shaded straw yellow, the center light ochre." [JR16/139] Pope Leo XIII; lived 1810-1903.

[Léon de Bruyn] (Soupert I Notting, 1895)

From 'Maréchal Robert' (T) × 'Rubens' (T).

"Plant bushy, like 'Perle de Lyon'; flower large, full, Centifolia-form; exterior petals large; color, light straw yellow, center Naples yellow. Very floriferous." [JR19/148] "Highest in the center with petals over-lapping like shingles on a roof...very free and fragrant." [C&Js98]

[Léonie Osterrieth] (Soupert & Notting, 1892)

From 'La Sylphide' (T) × 'Mme. Bravy' (T).

"Vigorous; foliage light green; flower large, full; blooms in clusters of 5-6 cupped blossoms; color, bright porcelain white nuanced very delicate

yellow towards the center. Fragrant and very floriferous." [JR16/139]
"In freedom of bloom this variety rivals a Polyantha." [CA95]

[Letty Coles] (Keynes/Coles, 1876)
Sport or seedling of 'Mme. Mélanie Willermoz' (T).
"Still regarded as one of the finest roses of its color; soft rosy pink, shaded
with intense crimson; extra large, full, globular form; very double; exceedingly sweet tea fragrance." [CA88] "Very vigorous; flower large, full; color,
beautiful delicate pink." 'JR1/6/10] "An abundant bloomer, too; large,
double flowers of a deep, globular form, and borne on strong, stiff stems;
in fact, one of the strongest and finest growing roses in its class."
[C&Js02] "Low-growing, bushy, not very hardy; foliage sufficient,
healthy; bloom sparse, occasional during midsummer." [ARA18/126]

Lorraine Lee (A. Clark, 1924)
From 'Jessy Clark' (pink Hybrid Gigantea from A. Clark, 1924, the
parentage of which was *R. gigantea* × 'Mme. Martignier' [Cl. Tea]) ×
'Capitaine Millet' (T).
"Terra-cotta tint...a length of petal that bears comparison with anything
seen elsewhere...freedom of flower...long buds, rich tea scent...disease
resistant...semi-double." [TS] "Bud long-pointed; flower medium-size,
double, open, cupped, lasting; warm rosy-apricot-pink; moderate fragrance. Foliage disease-resistant. Vigorous, upright; continuous bloomer."
[ARA24/176] "Foliage rich green and glossy...Needs extra care...2×2 [ft;
ca. 6×6 dm]." [B] "I hear of 'Lorraine Lee' as a spectacular hedge-plant in
Australia." [T2]

Louis Faure
Listed as 'Lucie Faure'.

Louis Lévêque
Listed as 'Erzherzog Franz Ferdinand'.

Louis Richard (Widow Ducher, 1877)
"Vigorous, flower large, full, coppery pink with a dark red center."
[JR1/12/12] "This is a grand bedding rose, extra large, full and double,
and richly tea scented. Color clear rosy flesh, passing to creamy pink; a
tremendous bloomer, very handsome and desirable in every way."
[C&Js04] *Cf.* 'Helvetia'.

[**Louise de Savoie**] (Ducher, 1854)
"Pale canary yellow." [CA90] "Plant vigorous; foliage glaucous green;
flower very large, quite full; color, sulphur yellow, sometimes light yellow,
taking on a buff tint. Tender." [S] "Clear pale yellow, very large and full,
fine shape, habit vigorous; does not always open freely out of doors, but
under glass it is superb." [JC]

[**Lucie Faure**] (Nabonnand, 1898) syn. 'Louis Faure'
From 'Mme. Léon Février' (T) × 'Niphetos' (T).
"Flower large, full, solitary, exquisite form, outer petals larger, recurving
gracefully; color, ivory white on an amber ground; pretty long bud, perfectly held; long stem; vigorous bush; very floriferous." [JR22/165] "A
neat compact grower, pretty buds and round full flowers, pure French
white sometimes tinted with salmon and pink; profuse bloomer all
Summer and Fall, hardy and good." [C&Js02]

[**Luciole**] (Guillot & fils, 1886)
Seedling of 'Safrano à Fleurs Rouges' (T).
"Large, full, well-formed; bud long; color, china pink with carmine, very
intense, tinted saffron yellow, on a ground of coppery yellow; reverse of
petals bronze. Very fragrant." [JR10/123] "A button-hole Tea Rose of very
poor growth, with good long buds most charmingly tinted." [F-M2] "A
large long bud. Strong rose, with red stiff stalk…The books call it a buttonhole rose, and I do not agree with them! [HmC]

[**Lucy Carnegie**] (Nabonnand, 1898)
Seedling of 'Trioomphe du Luxembroug' (T).
"Flower large, full, erect, reverse of petals carminy coppery pink, center salmony dawn-pink; bud elongate, very elegant, erect on a strong peduncle; bush very vigorous and very floriferous. From 'Triomphe du Luxembourg', but much more vigorous." [JR22/165]

[**Lutea Flora**] (Touvais, 1874) trans., "Yellow Flower"
"Moderate growth; flower large, full; color, brilliant yellow fading to white." [S]

[**Ma Capucine**] (Levet, 1871) trans., "My Nasturtium"
From 'Ophirie' (N) × *R. foetida*.
"Bronzy yellow, shaded red. Distinct and beautiful in bud." [H] "Flower medium-sized, nearly full, coppery nasturtium yellow." [S] "Moderate vigor, and very floriferous; it produces very pretty pointed buds. The blossoms are large, full, nasturtium yellow when opening, fading to white when fully open." [JR28/125] "Beautiful buds; a very distinct rose, which, from its delicate habit, is useless for ordinary cultivators to attempt growing." [EL] "Another weakly growing buttonhole Tea Rose, most charming in colour. The buds are quite small, and not particularly long or pointed, but sure to attract notice." [F-M2]

[**Madeleine Guillaumez**] (Bonnaire, 1892)
From crossing an unnamed Tea × 'Mlle. de Sombreuil' (T).
"Vigorous with upright canes; flower medium-sized or large; stiff stem; form globular, beautiful white with a salmony center, nuanced orange yellow. Very beautiful plant; very floriferous." [JR16/152]

[**Madison**] (Brandt-Hentz, 1912)
From 'Perle des Jaunes' (T) × a seedling (of 'The Bride' (T) and 'The Meteor' (HT)).
"The flower is large, perfectly double and fragrant. Color is rich creamy white." [C&Js14] "Low, weak-growing, winterkills some; foliage plentiful;

bloom moderate, best spring and fall." [ARA18/126] Madison, the city in New Jersey, U.S.A., where the Brandt-Hentz Co. was headquartered.

Magnolia Rose
Listed as 'Devoniensis'.

[Maid of Honour] (Hofmeister, 1899)
Sport of 'Catherine Mermet' (T).
"The petals are extra large, full regular form and very sweet, petals thick and of good substance, color soft rosy pink or delicate flesh-color; a splendid variety, first-class in every way." [C&Js02]

Maman Cochet (S. Cochet, 1892) trans., "Mama Cochet"
From 'Marie Van Houtte' (T) × 'Mme. Lambard' (T).
"The admirable Tea Rose 'Catherine Mermet'...is surpassed in size, poise, form, and vivacity of color by a pretty hybrid which Monsieur Scipion Cochet has bred and will offer to commerce this Fall [*1889*]. This remarkable introduction...: 'Maman Cochet', which is dedicated to the mother and grandmother of the rose-breeders in Suisnes of that ilk...the widow of Pierre Cochet, in her 87th year...[I]t is a very vigorous shrub, though not climbing, giving an abundance of flowers which are large or very large for the sort, of flesh-pink washed with a more-or-less light carmine, with salmon nankeen-yellow mixed in...very full; the outer petals are large and do not reflex like those of 'Catherine Mermet'; those of the center are sometimes formed into a rosette, or 'quartered.' It is nearly always held upright on its stem despite its size and fulness if it isn't on smaller branches or branchlets...Among the best of its sort." [JR13/137] "Pink shaded lemon-yellow." [H] "Rose." [E] "Flesh-coloured rose shaded with carmine and salmon yellow, large and full, fine large bud. A magnificent rose of vigorous growth." [P1] "Carmine rose to cream and fawn. Balls in dampness." [Capt27] "Beautiful blooms that...never ball [*in Bermuda*]." [UB28] "Large, well-filled, tulip-like form, flesh-coloured pink, changing to coppery colour. Growth strong, flowers solitary, very fine." [Hn] "Very

recommendable as an autumnal, giving enormous blossoms lasting, cupped, 8-10 days without fading or discoloring." [JR16/179] "Blooms are very large, stout and lasting...well shaped, but have often some little imperfection...the colours...in fine hot weather sometimes beautiful but often undecided and weak." [F-M2] "'Maman Cochet' and 'White Maman Cochet' are, without question, the best garden roses for southern Kansas...perfect blooms which are never malformed or blighted." [ARA21/171] "Only an occasional perfect bloom." [PS] "Lacks quality in the flower." [ARA25/105] "Large shapely blooms...to 4 [ft; ca. 1.25 m]." [B] "The flower...measures nearly four inches [ca. 1 dm], and is thus one of the largest blossoms in the Teas." [JR17/103] "Most attractive in form and color; lasts well; good growth and foliage; a shy bloomer." [ARA18/112] "A heavy constant bloomer, with long fine buds of a pearl-pink." [BSA] "Fragrant. Vigorous with few thorns...3×3 [ft; ca. 1×1 m]." [B] "Tall, compact, vigorous, hardy; foliage plentiful, black-spots some-what." [ARA18/126] "Growth is very strong...foliage is good, but has attacks of...'silver-leaf.'" [F-M2] "Resistant to mildew." [JR33/37] "Succeeds best in rather poor soil." [OM] "As good a border rose as one can find. It was in flower here last year from June to mid-October, its enormous blossoms the admiration of all who saw it." [K1] "One of the best Tea roses offered for many years." [JR22/107] "A variety to study and to recommend." [JR17/149]

[**Maréchal Bugeaud**] (Breeder unknown, 1843)
"Flowers bright rose, large and very double; form, cupped. Very good." [P] "Flower large, full, opening wide; color, lilac pink, nuanced chamois." [S] "A large and superb new French variety, yet quite rare; the flower is deep rosy, with a deeper rosette centre, and very double; this is one of the most desirable of the whole family." [WRP] "A new and splendid variety, with a remarkably robust and vigorous habit; its shoots are covered with large thorns: they are stout and erect, and altogether unlike any other rose of this class; its flowers are of a bright rose colour, large, cupped, finely shaped, and very double; and, like all in this family, they are highly fragrant." [R9]

[**Maréchal Robert**] (Widow Ducher, 1875) trans., "Marshal Robert"
"Flower very large, full, well-formed, globular; color, yellow within, blushing slightly along the edges." [S]

[**Margherita di Simone**] (P. Guillot, 1898)
"Vigorous bush, very floriferous, bud very elegant, carmine orange yellow; flower large, full, well-formed, varying from bright China pink to carmine nuanced with deep yellow, reverse of petals orange yellow flamed with gold-pink on a more or less deep carmine ground, depending upon the temperature and the exposure; very fragrant; of the 'Luciole' sort. To be recommended for bedding." [JR22/179]

[**Marguerite Gigandet**] (Nabonnand, 1902)
From. 'Mlle. Franziska Krüger' (T) × 'Reine Emma des Pays-Bas' (T).
"Reddish coppery yellow, passing to golden yellow." [C&Js06] "Flower very large, very full; color, coppery yellow with grenadine reflections or tints; center a sparkling mélange; bud well formed, coppery yellow tinted blood red while opening; very beautiful foliage; bush very vigorous, very floriferous. Fragrant." [JR26/148]

[**Marguerite Ketten**] (Ketten Bros., 1897)
From 'Mme. Caro' (T) × 'Georges Farber' (T).
"Flower yellowish peach red, petal edges tinted icy pink; golden reflections; large, full fragrant. Bush medium-sized and vigorous; floriferous." [JR21/136] "A fine, large, beautifully formed rose; makes elegant buds, deliciously sweet…constant and profuse bloomer." [C&Js99]

Maria Star (Gravereaux, 1913)
From 'Mme. Gustave Henry' (T) × 'Mme. Jules Gravereaux' (Cl. T).
Salmon-gold. Breeder Perny possibly contributed to production of this variety.

Marie d'Orléans (Nabonnand, 1883)

"Rich coppery red, with pink centre." [CA93] "Bright rose shaded, large and full." [P1] "Brick-red washed pink;…fragrant; very floriferous; very vigorous." [Cx] "At the center of the blossom, the muddled [*étroites lanières*] form." [JR23/118] "Continuous bloom; flower very large, full, flat, very well formed, well held; color, bright pink, shaded." [S] "Very pretty." [JR22/81] "Hardy and free." [TW] "A 'top of the line' variety." [JR7/184]

[Marie Guillot] (Guillot fils, 1874)

"Greenish white." [LS] "A pure, snowy-white rose…constant bloomer." [C&Js05] "Vigorous bush; flower large, very full, imbricated; white, tinted yellowish." [S]

Marie Lambert (E. Lambert, 1886) syn., 'White Hermosa'
Sport of 'Mme. Bravy' (T).

"Medium-sized, full, pure white." [LR] "Beautiful pale flesh color, passing to rich, creamy white; large, regular flowers, full and well formed buds, delightfully perfumed." [CA90] "Has the vigor of its parent 'Mme. Bravy'. Color, pure white; flower of medium size; this variety takes well to pot culture. A very beautiful variety." [JR10/171] "Habit of growth, free; flower, globular." [TW] "Tall, bushy, hardy; foliage very plentiful, healthy; bloom free, continuous." [ARA18/126] "Without a doubt an excellent acquisition…pretty." [JR25/65]

Marie Legonde
Listed as 'Marie Segond'.

Marie Segond (Nabonnand, 1902)
From 'Mme. la Comtesse de Leusse' (T) × 'Mlle. Lazarine Poizeau' (T).

"Flower medium sized, full, well formed; warm coloration, light or bright pink tinted flame, nub brilliant coppery carmine without, golden within; center flame; pretty elongated bud, coppery tinted carmine; very pretty foliage; very vigorous and bushy, constantly in bloom. Fragrant." [JR26/148]

[Marie Sisley] (Guillot fils, 1868)
"Cream, deeply margined and shaded with rosy-salmon, flowers full size and very fragrant; a distinct and good rose, habit free." [JC] "Large and double flowers, delicious tea scent; color exquisite shade of pale yellow, broadly margined with bright rose." [CA93] "Bush vigorous; flower large, full, globular." [S]

[Marie Soleau] (Nabonnand, 1895)
Seedling of 'Mlle. Suzanne Blanchet' (T).
"Blossom large, full, admirably formed, elegantly held; color, ravishing silvery pink; pretty bud; elegant foliage. Very vigorous bush; extremely floriferous." [JR19/180] "Very sweet." [C&Js98]

Marie Van Houtte (Ducher, 1871)
From 'Mme. de Tartas' (T) × 'Mme. Falcot' (T).
"Light yellow edged with pink, an universal favorite, and a magnificent grower...It is a very fine exhibition variety, particularly in moist weather." [FRB] "Yellow canary, deeper center, border of petals tipped with bright rose. An old favorite." [Th] "White slightly tinted with yellow, often edged with rose; large, full, and good; growth vigorous." [P1] "Medium-sized or large, slightly quilled, of perfect form and poise, particularly while opening; additionally, it is of a superb shade of light yellow at the center, which enhances the ample border of rose-pink which appears only on the outer petals, where also may be seen patches of milk-white." [S] "The consensus of opinion among professional gardeners is that this is the most valuable white rose for garden growth anywhere." [Dr] "Cream flesh to light peach, edged rose. Balls easily." [Capt27] "Large, very double...of gold and cream, suffused with carmine-pink and fragrant." [HRG] "White slightly tinted with yellow, border of the petals tinted with rose, flowers quite full and well formed." [JC] "Blooms from May to frost. The flower is large, full, globular, lightly fragrant...In southern climes, we have sometimes seen blossoms which were nearly white, and in the Lyon area, when positioned in full sun, it takes on a pink tint which is very delicate

and bewitching; other times, it is a dull porcelain white." [JR16/141] "Bright pink tinged orange and cream. Fragrant. Rich, green foliage…sprawling habit…3×3 [ft; ca. 1×1 m]." [B] "Of a reversed bell shape (like a bell as the ringer jerks it upward for a good peal of joy)…a supremely lovely flower, with the faintest suggestion of a tulip in it, and a breath of quite peculiar sweetness." [HstXXX:288] "Noteworthy in color and lasting qualities; growth and form good; quite a bloomer." [ARA18/113] "The flowers droop, it is true, but very gracefully…free from mildew and other diseases." [NRS/13] "The white, waxy buds are exquisite and open better than most Teas, and although the open flower is rather flat, its full petalage and peach-colored center make up for that fault. It is the most vigorous of my Teas…more upright than most of its class, with a zigzagging, slantwise growth that never permits the blossoms to trail in the dust, like 'Maman Cochet'. It has a distinct perfume, good foliage, and superb stems." [ARA29/70] "Constantly in bloom. One year a three-year-old bush here displayed sixty-two well-shaped blossoms in the middle of October." [K1]

"'Marie Van Houtte' is quite one of the freest, prettiest 'Teas' in cultivation. A small plant, which only came to me last April (a gift from Mr. Bennett, of Salisbury), is just now finishing a second crop of flowers, and growing away in all directions for another efflorescence." [R3/329] "Almost tall, compact, vigorous, hardy; foliage very plentiful, healthy; bloom free through summer, moderate in fall, almost continuous." [ARA18/126] "A free bloomer which does fine work after cool weather comes…vigorous and healthy but inclined to sprawl." [ARA29/88] "In the splendid line of Tea Roses, that which is dedicated to Mlle. Marie Van Houtte, of Ghent (Belgium), is assuredly one of the most beautiful…very vigorous, strong, and upright branches, with hooked thorns. The ample foliage, composed of five to seven leaflets, is of a light bright green; the stem is strong. The flowers are very large, full, and well formed, in clusters of two or three at the ends of the branches, though sometimes they are solitary…yellowish-white edged bright pink, aging to a light pink throughout…very fragrant."

[JR4/57] "Fine growth and production...best for interior South." [Capt28] "Developed into a huge plant [*in Brazil*], always in bloom." [PS] "Needs light pruning." [DO] "Of good habit, and in every respect a most charming sort. The finest of all Teas for out-door culture." [EL] "One of the strongest and best...at all times a beautiful flower...first-class autumnal...no one should be without." [F-M2]

[Marion Dingee] (J. Cook, 1889)

Two parentages are reported: (1) 'Mme. la Comtesse de Caserta' (T) × 'Duchess of Edinburgh' (T); or, (2), 'Mme. la Comtesse de Caserta' × a seedling (of 'Général Jacqueminot' (HP) × 'Safrano' (T)).

"Bright carmine." [LS] "Deep rich crimson, one of the darkest colored ever-blooming roses we have." [C&Jf97] "Beautiful cup-shaped flowers, quite full and fragrant and borne in great profusion all through the growing season; excellent for garden planting." [C&Js98] "A splendid red Rose, and one of the finest additions to our list of bedding Roses we have had in many years; flowers of good size, nicely cup-shaped, and borne in wonderful profusion all through the growing season. Color, deep crimson, changing to carmine in the matured flowers." [CA96]

[Marquise de Querhoënt] (Godard, 1901)

From 'G. Nabonnand' (T) × 'Mme. Laurette Messimy' (Ch).

"Coppery China pink on a golden yellow ground." [JR32/139] "Carmine on flesh or yellow ground." [CA17] "Salmon red to saffron. Decorative; mildews badly." [ARA27/20] "Persistent bloomer, bloom of good size, prime substance, full and sweet; color, beautiful china rose, salmon, copper and golden yellow. A combination rarely seen." [C&Js13] "Medium height, bushy, hardy, foliage very plentiful, healthy; bloom moderate; almost continuous." [ARA18/126]

[Marquise de Vivens] (Dubreuil, 1885)

"Pale rose, centres shaded with yellow; semi-double." [P1] "Carmine and pink." [LS] "Novel shade of violet crimson, with center and base of petals creamy yellow; large, full flowers; a constant and profuse bloomer." [CA90] "Not climbing, with hooked thorns; large leaves with 5-7 leaflets which are bright, glossy, dark green; bud very long; flower large, bicolored, fading in age; calyx with long glabrous sepals, dark green without, whitish and chalky within; petals rounded-obovate, cuneate, gracefully rolled…; upper surface bright carmine along the edge, attenuating to China pink in the middle and finally to straw yellow at the nub; lower surface flesh white nuanced sulphur." [JR9/166]

Mathilde
Listed as 'Niphetos'.

[Maud Little] (Dingee & Conard, 1891)
From 'Pierre de St.-Cyr' (B) × 'Comtesse de Labarthe' (T).
"Of moderate growth, satisfactory stature, medium culture; flowers beautiful and full; color, China pink, delicate with a distinctly bright tint; distinctive and notably beautiful." [JR15/88]

[Maurice Rouvier] (Nabonnand, 1890)
"Of remarkable vigor making an enormous bush; flower very large, very full, enormous, of perfect form; bud long, opens very well, firmly held; wood reddish brown; thorns medium; foliage light green. Bloom continuous and very abundant. Color, beautiful delicate pink, very lightly veined red, pale on the outer edge." [JR14/165]

[Medea] (W. Paul, 1890)
"Light canary-yellow; large, of good form. Vigorous grower in Southern zones and especially adapted to warm weather." [Th2] "Lemon yellow with a silk-yellow center, and light, bright tintings; large, very full, buds somewhat disposed to proliferity, but blossoms opening in a ball; a vigorous hybrid. It is a magnificent Tea rose." [JR15/87] "High centers; foliage dark and thick." [CA96] "Of stout stiff growth, but tender against frost, not very free-blooming, a fine Rose for exhibition, but not well suited for general cultivation. The blooms are particularly full, with the rounded

centres which require a hot season or situation for their full development. They are sometimes very large, and in perfect blooms the outer petals reflex well, making a very fine shape." [F-M2]

Mélanie Willermoz
Listed as 'Mme. Mélanie Willermoz'.

[Meta] (A. Dickson, 1898)
"Strawberry red touched saffron yellow." [JR32/139] "Crushed strawberry to coppery yellow. Poor growth." [ARA27/20] "Small growth; winterkilled." [ARA27/20] Meta Weldon, Irish rosarian.

[Mevrouw Boreel van Hogelander] (Leenders, 1918)
From 'Mme. Léon Pain' (HT) × 'Mme. Antoine Mari' (T).
"Fine growth, good foliage, and nice double. Flesh, shaded carmine and pink." [ARA28/102] "Bud medium size, globular; flower medium size, globular, borne several together, on average-length stems; very lasting; strong fragrance. Color rosy white and carmine. Foliage abundant, medium size, leathery, dark green. A vigorous grower of bushy habit and a profuse bloomer." [ARA20/135]

Minnie Francis (Noisette/Griffing, 1905)
"This is a new Tea rose, originating on the Noisette farm at Charleston…It is the best-growing Tea rose we have ever seen, making a very large strong bush in one season, and in two or three years will make a spread of from four to six feet [ca. 1.25-1.75 m]. Flowers are extra large and full; buds long and pointed; color fine chamois-red, richly shaded with velvety crimson; very sweet and a constant bloomer…" [*quoted from the 1905 Griffing catalog in* ARA26/212] "Open flowers." [G] "[*Good in Florida*]…like an improved and somewhat darker 'Mme. Lambard'. It grows to considerable height…and is apparently of much value." [ARA24/85]

Miss Agnes C. Sherman (Nabonnand, 1901)

From 'Paul Nabonnand' (T) × 'Catherine Mermet' (T).

"Peach." [LS] "Soft rose, centre brighter rose tinted with salmon red, large and full, perfect shape; growth vigorous." [P1]

Miss Alice de Rothschild (A. Dickson, 1910)

"Canary to citron-yellow. Mildews." [ARA27/19] "Fine double, canary-yellow Tea. Large flower with good stem, lasting. Growth fair and foliage mildews in dampness. Best for interior South." [ARA28/102] "Delicious fragrance ('Maréchal Niel' perfume)." [C&Js12] "Evidently the best yellow garden rose since 'Maréchal Niel'. Its color is a rich lemon yellow becoming darker as the blossom expands. The growth is very vigorous; floriferous; long-lasting, large, full, perfectly-formed blossoms, with a scent quite as delicate as that of 'Maréchal Niel', on rigid stems. The very erect bud is pointed and opens easily outside as well as under glass." [JR34/103] "Beautiful color; growth and foliage only fair; hardiness varies; form good; blooming fairly good. Needs time to become established." [ARA18/113]

[Miss Ethel Brownlow] (A. Dickson, 1887)

"Salmon pink." [LS] "Of robust nature, with rich glossy foliage, blooming very freely and abundantly. Flowers large, of strong substance, opening well, and perfectly formed; petals very thick, long, round, and very smooth. Color, bright salmon red shaded yellow at the base of the petals." [JR11/93] "Not a very strong grower, but in this and other respects it seems to have decidedly improved, for it was by no means a general success with amateurs for the first three or four years. Now it is fast rising in reputation, and it was plain, when first shown, that it was the best example of the imbricated form among Teas, if not among all Roses. The blooms come generally regular, and the well-formed point in the centre of good perfectly imbricated petals, which is the typical form but unfortunately seldom attained by the full-sized flowers, makes it a great favorite with those to whom shape is the first thing. It has very good lasting qualities in form, but the freshness of the first colour is very difficult to maintain and shading will destroy it. Rather late, and best as a standard, it requires fine hot weather, and needs protection against rain. Very free-flowering, the buds must be well thinned to get exhibition blooms, but are charming half-open in themselves." [F-M3] "Dedicated to the well-known English novelist." [JR17/177]

[**Miss Marston**] (Pries/Ketten Bros., 1889)
"Pink and yellow." [LS] "A light-colored Tea. Should be grown through Southern zones." [ARA28/102] "Flower yellowish blushy white, bordered very deep pink, center yellow peach red; large, full, delicious violet scent; bush of moderate vigor; extremely floriferous. A distinct variety and of the first merit. Superb!" [JR13/147] "Bushy growth; not a profuse bloomer." [ARA18/117]

[**Miss Wenn**] (Guillot & fils, 1890)
"Vigorous; flower large, full, well formed, beautiful China pink; beautiful and very floriferous." [JR14/146] "Moderate growth." [CA96]

[**Mlle. Anna Charron**] (Widow Schwartz, 1896) syn., 'Mlle. Anna Chartron' From 'Kaiserin Auguste Viktoria' (HT) × 'Luciole' (T).
"Cram and crimson." [LS] "Cream-yellow, washed lilac-rose. Loose." [ARA27/20] "Vigorous bush, very floriferous, foliage somber green edged purple; flower large, full, well formed, borne on a long, strong stem, usually solitary. The large petals are folded back into a point, giving the flower a starry look; cream tinted and edged bright carmine, center very delicate pink. The very long bud, which is very graceful, shows darker shades of the open blossom. Quite distinct, very good for cutting." [JR20/163]

Mlle. Anna Chartron
Listed as 'Mlle. Anna Charron'.

Mlle. Blanche Durrschmidt (Guillot fils, 1878)
Seedling of 'Mme. Falcot' (T).
"Flesh colour, of medium size, double, free flowering and effective; growth vigorous." [P1] "Very vigorous, flowers large or medium, double or full, well formed; color, flesh white, tinted salmon pink fading to white; blooms in clusters or solitary...very pretty for bedding." [JR1/12/14] "Semi-double, worthless." [EL] "Canes olive green tinted red, lower sections with violet tints; thorns hooked, not very numerous, flat; leaves of 3-5 glossy green, finely dentate leaflets." [S]

Mlle. Blanche Martignat (Gamon, 1903)
Possibly a seedling of 'Marie Van Houtte' (T).
"Salmon-yellow, with pink glow. Globular." [Capt27] "Salmon nuanced dawn-pink." [LS] "Vigorous without being climbing, giving at the end of every sufficiently-strong branch long buds producing very large creped blossoms with dawn-gold centers, outermost petals salmon pink, sometimes completely pink...very fragrant." [JR32/77]

[Mlle. Christine de Noué] (Guillot & fils, 1890)
"Carmine-lake shaded salmon. Mildews slightly." [ARA27/19] "An elegant deep red rose of fine texture and size." [CA95] "In form, conical; in appearance, hazy. The plant is strong and floriferous." [JR20/58] "Flower very large, full, well formed and of good hold; outer petals imbricated, deep maroon purple-red; center petals more muddled, lake pink and light purple, nuanced icy silvery white; fragrant; very beautiful variety." [JR14/146]

[Mlle. Claudine Perreau] (E. Lambert, 1886) syn., 'Mlle. Claudine Perreault'
Seedling of 'Souvenir d'un Ami' (T).
"Extra large, full, perfectly double flowers; color, rosy flesh on white ground, with rich crimson center, free bloomer." [CA90] "From 'Souvenir d'un Ami', but much more vigorous without being climbing. Color, very

bright pink, sometimes delicate pink; canes upright, peduncle very strong. Of premier merit." [JR10/171]

Mlle. Claudine Perreault
Listed as 'Mlle. Claudine Perreau'.

Mlle. de Sombreuil (Robert, 1851) syn., 'Sombreuil'
Seedling of 'Gigantesque' (T).
"White with some salmon." [JR1/28] "Flowers of a pale straw color." [SBP] "White, tinged with rose, very large and full; form cupped; growth vigorous. A good hardy free flowering sort." [P1] "A fine large blush with a yellowish tint, of the right form." [WHoIII] "Flower from 8-9 cm [nearly 4 inches], quite double, lightly blushing, beautiful form, strong peduncles." [VH51/112] "Vigorous plant; flowers large, nearly full, white touched salmon." [l'H53/223] "Vigorous, hardy...blooms in panicles." [S] "Evidently of Bourbon parentage on one side...the hardiest and most vigorous of the white Teas, and free from mildew. A valuable sort for the open air." [EL] "Short, ovoid bud, opening quickly to a double flower of large size, but somewhat flat. Plant of strong growth...Foliage holds well and is usually free from disease. Discolors in damp winds." [Th2] "Creamy white, tinted with pink, large, full, and well formed, hardy and vigorous, producing large quantities of flowers. It is very effective growing up trees. Has a resemblance to the Bourbon type." [B&V] "This rose is dedicated to Mlle. de Sombreuil, the heroine who, during the Terror, locked herself up with her father, the Count Sombreuil, governor of Les Invalides, prisoner of the Abbaye, in Paris, and who stopped the September assassins' arms by her supplications; and, according to legend, who drank a glass of human blood, a glass which she then offered to the assailants!" [JR34/15] "Or note old Monsieur de Sombreuil, who also had a Daughter: —My Father is not an aristocrat: O good gentlemen, I will swear it, and testify it, and in all ways prove it; we are not; we hate aristocrats! 'Wilt thou drink Aristocrats' blood?' The man lifts blood (if universal Rumour can be credited); the poor maiden does drink. 'This Sombreuil is

innocent then!' Yes, indeed,—and now note, most of all, how the bloody pikes, at this news, do rattle to the ground." [Cy] "Monsieur Robert, Monsieur Vibert's gardener [*in 1846, later to succeed Vibert in ownership of the firm*]." [M-L46/273] The beautiful very-climbing rose which has been frequently offered and illustrated as 'Sombreuil' in the latter part of the 20th century, particularly in the U.S.A., differs in several particulars from descriptions of Robert's 1851 Tea 'Mlle. de Sombreuil'. See the color plate—dating from the 1850s—of Robert's original 'Mlle. de Sombreuil', in *The Old Rose Adventurer*.

Mlle. Emma Vercellone (A. Schwartz, 1901)
From 'Chamoïs' (T) × 'Mme. Laurette Messimy' (Ch).
"Vigorous, bushy, foliage purple red, long bud, flower large, full, bright coppery red on a golden yellow ground fading to coppery salmon pink nuanced dawn-gold. Beautiful; very floriferous." [JR25/163] "Small growth; no special merit." [ARA18/116]

Mlle. Franziska Krüger (Nabonnand, 1879)
From 'Catherine Mermet' (T) × 'Général Schablikine' (T).
"Peachy pink with soft shades of sunset and twilight lavender." [ARA36/19] "Exterior petals are white bordered with flesh and fawn; the inner ones change from yellow to pink." [JR12/180] "Coppery yellow, shaded peach." [H] "Cream flesh to apricot-copper. Balls easily; mildews." [Capt27] "Very double, large blooms of coppery yellow with pink, green pip in center, fragrant." [HRG] "Often very perfect in form…good growth and foliage, not much liable to mildew…anything but robust." [F-M2] "An extremely attractive bloom, either in bud or fully open." [ARA29/88] "Handsome green foliage which lasts and is very resistant to disease. The blossoms are large, very full, well formed." [JR12/24] "Bush vigorous, as is the growth;…very free; color, coppery flesh-white shaded yellow and pink, fading into pink reflections and washed with the shades already mentioned; planted at the foot of a banked wall, it promptly grows to perhaps five feet in height [ca. 1.75 m], and its blossoms take on a coloration impossible to

describe, but of great charm…the flower stems nod under the weight of the blossoms." [S] "Moderate height, compact, hardy; foliage plentiful, healthy; bloom profuse and continuous till September, after that liberal and continuous." [ARA18/125] "Foliage of a leathery texture. Low to medium height, spreading…25 to 54 blooms per season." [ARA21/92] "A good hot weather rose." [L] "Much appreciated in the North." [JR5/21] "Should be in every collection. Very showy." [Dr] "An excellent Tea in every way." [FRB]

Mlle. Jeanne Guillaumez (Bonnaire, 1889)
"Very vigorous, with erect branches; foliage…evergreen; flower large, full, well formed; beautiful long buds, of a pretty dark rose color. When partially open, this rose is brick red, with much salmon and metallic red in the interior, on a ground of dark straw yellow after opening. A superb variety of novel coloration." [JR13/162]

Mlle. Jeanne Philippe (Godard, 1898) syn., 'Jeanne Philippe', 'Mme. J. Phillips'
"Nankeen, bordered carmine. Mildews slightly." [ARA27/20] "Very vigorous and compact, with upright, strong branches; foliage bronzy red, wood smooth and nearly thornless; flowers very large, full, beautiful nankeen yellow with chamois reflections, petal edges lightly touched carmine." [JR23/2] "The buds are long and open quite well…perfectly formed flowers…moderate vigor…blooms abundantly from late frosts to fall." [JR27/119] "Weak; winterkills." [ARA18/116]

Mlle. la Comtesse de Leusse (Nabonnand, 1878)
"Very vigorous, flowers large, semi-double, cupped, very large imbricated petals. Color, delicate pink with saffron reflections at the center; bud, bright pink." [JR3/9]

[Mlle. Lazarine Poizeau] (Levet, 1876)
"Fine orange-yellow, of medium size, full, fine form, growth vigorous, free bloomer." [JC] "Vigorous Tea rose, flower medium-sized, full, well formed,

and well held; color, beautiful orange-yellow. Very floriferous." [JR1/1/7] "Small size, very pretty in the bud." [EL] "Branches dusky reddish green; few thorns; leaves glossy, olive green; young leaves reddish." [S]

[Mlle. Marie-Louise Oger] (Lévêque, 1895)
"Vigorous bush; flower very large, beautiful dark green foliage; beautiful milk white, shaded—very lightly—yellowish. Very beautiful. *Note:* This rose is dedicated to the daughter of a businessman from La Fère." [JR19/163] The writer is evidently trying to assure readers that the rose is not dedicated to anyone related to rosiériste Pierre Oger of Caen, France! "Abundant bloomer." [C&Js98]

[Mlle. Marie Moreau] (Nabonnand, 1879) syn. 'Mme. Marie Moreau'
"Pale silvery white, elegantly flushed with crimson and yellow; petals margined with rich carmine; large, finely formed flowers; full and sweet." [CA88] "Vigorous bush; compact growth, well formed; flower medium-sized, full, well formed; color, bright pink, shaded, lighter at the center; bloom abundant and very early; good for making wonderful beds." [S]

[Mlle. Marie-Thérèse Molinier] (Widow Schwartz, 1896)
From 'Mme. Chédane-Guinoisseau' (T) × 'Mme. Laurette Messimy' (Ch). "Bush medium-sized, foliage graceful, small for the sort; flower solitary, medium-sized, well formed; color one of great freshness, passing to satiny tender pink nuanced cream. Nub yellowish white." [JR20/164]

[Mlle. Suzanne Blanchet] (Nabonnand, 1885)
"Rose tinted with flesh color; large and of fine form; very fragrant." [CA90] "Very vigorous, big-wooded, thorns rare; flower very large, very full, imbricated, erect, cupped; splendid coloration: A novel flesh pink; bloom continuous; very fragrant." [JR9/166]

[Mme. A. Étienne] (Bernaix, 1886)
"Bright rosy flesh." [CA93] "Wine-pink." [LS] "Wine-red and paler red, with white centre." [RR] "Of moderate vigor; long bud; calyx with long,

pointed sepals; flower large, full, well-formed, cupped, fragrant; color, vinous pink at the petals' edges, passing gradually through pale pink to white at the center; central petals smaller, muddled before the flower is completely open; fresh and intense pink which, by its brightness, sets off the paler pink of the outer petals. A very fetching coloration." [JR10/172]

Mme. Achille Fould (Lévêque, 1903)
"Very vigorous, leaves dark green, flowers very large, well formed, globular, yellow nuanced bright carmine pink, shaded red-copper and salmon, sometimes light salmon pink throughout, or carmine pink nuanced yellow; magnificent colors, superb." [JR27/165]

[Mme. Ada Carmody] (W. Paul, 1898)
"Ivory white bordered with pink tints, center of the blossom a little yellowish as with 'Cleopatra'. The flower is large and full, with very long buds. Without being extremely vigorous, the bush grows well and blooms abundantly." [JR22/56]

Mme. Adolphe Dahair
Listed as 'Mme. Adolphe Dohair'.

Mme. Adolphe Dohair (Puyravaud, 1900) syn., 'Mme. Adolphe Dahair'
From 'Général Schablikine' (T) × 'Mlle. Lazarine Poizeau' (T).
"Flower white lightly nuanced cream, large, full, satiny, plump center, cupped, fragrant, staying in bloom a long time. Growth vigorous, exhibiting the blossom well on a rigid stem; very floriferous...dedicated to the wife of a horticulturist of Niort." [JR24/135]

[Mme. Agathe Nabonnand] (Nabonnand, 1886)
"Rosy flesh, bathed in golden amber; immense buds, broad, shell-like petals, and large, full flowers." [CA90] "Carmine-magenta." [LS] "Flesh-coloured flowers of great size, slightly margined with a darker shade; buds are egg-shaped, very large and heavy, easily affected by damp; vigorous, grows to large size and very floriferous, a really magnificent rose, but very difficult to

obtain from it perfect flowers; the plant seems unequal to the task of open-ing these great fleshy buds." [B&V] "Very vigorous, continuously covered with flowers; flower very large, full, splendid." [JR10/169] "Attractive color; fairly good in growth, foliage, and blooming." [ARA18/112]

Mme. Albert Bernardin (Mari/Jupeau, 1904)
From 'Comtesse de Frigneuse' (T) × 'Marie Van Houtte' (T).
"Vigorous, slender branches, wood smooth, small thorns, flower medium or large, center canary yellow, exterior white washed bright carmine, very well formed, like a beautiful Camellia." [JR28/168]

[Mme. Angèle Jacquier] (Guillot fils, 1879)
"Vigorous bush; flowers large, full, very well formed, well held; veined, colored very bright pink at the center on a ground of coppery yellow, outer petals large and white, sometimes varying to pink, very fragrant, extra beautiful variety, sellable as a medium-sized specimen." [JR3/164] "Very fragrant, held well on its stem; remains in the partially open stage several days before opening completely." [S] "Of fair average growth, doing pretty well as a dwarf but better as a standard, and requiring rich soil and high culture for show uses. The blooms come pretty well, though sometimes divided, and a good exhibition flower may often be obtained, of fine petals, nice pointed shape, and full size. The colour is not striking, and however it may be described it is more white than anything else when grown out of doors. At one time this Rose was highly esteemed, but it has, probably from its feeble colour, gone out of favour and dropped out of the N.R.S. catalogue." [F-M3]

Mme. Antoine Mari (Mari/Jupeau, 1901)
"Rose-pink to flesh. Loose." [Capt27] "The flowers are numerous, open well, of a rich pink often tinted with white; the bud is large and elon-gated." [JR28/30]. "Blush-white; moderate, bushy." [ARA17/31] "Ground colour rose, freely washed and shaded with white; very hand-some buds which open well; growth extra vigorous and free from mildew."

[P1] "Pink on a ground of white; flower large, full, cupped; very floriferous, very vigorous." [Cx] "Pretty bud of a lightly blushing white, carmine at the edge. In Winter, this rose is nearly white, and in form resembles a Camellia." [JR24/113] "Nice shape, but small flowers; balls and discolors in damp winds. Foliage nearly evergreen, without disease. Growth very good, stem weak." [Th2] "Fine dark green foliage,…though almost crimson when it first starts into growth. The flowers are a pale rose, shaded white, of a very creamy appearance, and most delicate colouring…The carriage of the flowers is rather drooping, but not objectionably so, unless they get much rain upon them…good free growth…Flowers well and continuously…practically free from mildew…a tendency to produce rather too many weak side branches." [NRS/13] "[*One of*] those which approach more nearly in habit of growth to the Chinas." [NRS/14] "It is, as a bedding Rose, the most nearly perfect Tea Rose in my garden. Whether we regard its hardiness, its habit of growth, its beautiful foliage, its distinctive pink buds, its shapely flowers and the creamy texture of its petals, or the delicacy of its varying tints of flesh pink colouring, it is alike excellent…from 2-ft. to 2-ft. 6-inches high [ca. 6-7.5 dm]. The flowers are pointed and freely borne, of fair substance, but not full enough for exhibition, nor to give any sense of heaviness." [NRS/11] "Beautiful Camellia, immortal plant, always blooming." [JR37/172] "Never so nice as in this [*Fall*] season; it is, what is more, a Camellia which celebrates a new Spring every six months; the bud and half-open flower are pretty…Never sick, never moribund." [JR36/187] "Monsieur Mari has grown this superb rose for some six years [*i.e., since 1895*]." [JR24/146] "I adore it, and want always to possess it." [JR38/48]

Mme. Antoine Rébé (Laperrière, 1900)
From 'Alphonse Karr' (T) × 'Princesse de Sagan' (Ch).
"Dwarf and stocky, of good vigor. Buds quite long, opening easily. Flower bright sparkling red…of the first order for bedding." [JR25/5]

Mme. Azélie Imbert (Levet, 1870)

Seedling of 'Mme. Falcot' (T).

"Pale yellow." [EL] "The English consider it good for exhibitions because of the size and beauty of the blossom; the growth is very vigorous, and the flowers large, full, well formed, and beautifully colored salmon yellow." [JR7/104]

[Mme. Barriglione] (Breeder unknown,-1912)

"Coppery-carmine-rose." [D&C12]

[Mme. Barthélemy Levet] (Levet, 1879)

Seedling of 'Gloire de Dijon' (N).

"Very vigorous; foliage of 5-7 brilliant green leaflets; flower medium-sized to large, full, well-formed, with rounded petals; color, a handsome canary yellow; very remontant, very beautiful." [JR3/165] "Pretty in color, but too small." [JR13/43] "Semi-climbing." [JR10/44]

Mme. Berkeley (Bernaix fils, 1898)

"Salmon washed, pink shaded; flower large, full, imbricated; very floriferous; moderate vigor." [Cx] "Salmon-white, fine petals, semi-double, but very good; growth robust." [P1] "Foliage sumptuous, branches of moderate size, bud very elongate-ovoid, gradually narrowing from the base to the tip. Exterior color, pale blush washed violet pink. Flower large, flesh, salmon at the center, washed pink, pale violet on the exterior petals, which are notable for their size." [JR22/162]

Mme. Bravy (Guillot père, 1844)

"White, pink centre, a beautiful tea, quite distinct in form to any other tea variety." [FRB] "Full, creamy-white with pink markings, fragrant." [HRG] "Cream, centre blush, exquisitely formed; in dry weather, superb." [JC] "Large, full, of very symmetrical form and great fragrance; one of the most beautiful and useful in the class." [EL] "Form, cupped." [P] "Globular, not very regular in form." [Hk] "Pretty white buds. Full blown flowers lacking in substance." [Dr] "Blooms come very well…globular…almost like an incurved chrysanthemum. Blooms…pendant." [F-M2] "Raspberry-scented." [JR33/101] "Strong fragrance…3×3 [ft; ca. 1×1 m]." [B] "Free-flowering. Growth moderate." [Hn] "Growth vigorous." [P1] "Average growth and fair foliage." [F-M2] "The best of white Teas known." [S] Phillips & Rix report that 'Mme. Bravy' was "raised by Guillot of Pont Cherin in 1846 and introduced by Guillot of Lyon in 1848" (source of their quote unspecified); however, we find from the *Catalogue et Choix des Plus Belles Roses Remontants*…Chez Étienne Armand, "Propriétaire Horticulteur à Ecully-les-Lyon," that it is already being offered to the public in 1845—and indeed appears to have been released in 1844; Jean Sisley, one of the most respected and significant *rosiéristes* of the 1800s, reports that 'Mme. Bravy' was raised "from seed by Monsieur Guillot, gardener at the Château d'Azelles, and delivered into commerce by Guillot père." [JR3/53] The many supposed synonyms formerly reported ('Alba Rosea', 'Adèle Pradel', etc., etc.) appear not to be synonyms at all, but rather now-extinct rose varieties in their own right. We can, at any rate, also remember Mme.'s husband, "G. Bravy, of the Société d'Horticulture d'Hérault." [l'H64/75]

Mme. C. Liger (Berland/Chauvry, 1899) syn. 'Mme. C. Ligier'
"Semi-climbing; bud round and very large; flower large, very full, well formed, cupped, varying from delicate pink to deep pink, center dark red; penetrating fragrance." [JR24/2]

Mme. C. Ligier
Listed as 'Mme. C. Liger'.

[Mme. C.P. Strassheim] (Soupert & Notting, 1897)
From 'Mlle. Adèle Jougant' (T) × 'Mme. la Princesse de Bessaraba de Brancovan' (T).
"Very vigorous without being climbing; the abundant coppery red glossy foliage gives a good look to the plant. The bud is held upright on a pretty strong stem…The blossom is medium to large, full, yellowish-white in the

Summer bloom period, sulphur-yellow passing to chamois in the second blossoming...very fragrant." [JR24/72] "A good hardy grower and very free bloomer; excellent for bedding and borders." [C&Js99] C.P. Strassheim, rosarian and editor of the German periodical *Rosen-Zeitung*.

Mme. Camille (Guillot fils, 1871)
"Delicate rose, violet shade, flowers veined, very large and full...habit free." [JC] "Salmon-pink, large and full; form cupped; growth vigorous." [P1] "Vigorous; flower large, full, well formed; delicate pink with dawn gold, veined, whitish reflections." [S] "Mushroom-color, large, coarse flowers; not worthy of cultivation." [EL] "A magnificent rose; extra large size; very double and full; immense buds; color delicate rosy flesh, changing to salmon rose, elegantly shaded and suffused with deep carmine." [CA88] "A splendid garden Rose, extra large, full and sweet; clear, rosy-flesh, passing to salmon pink; good, free bloomer, very handsome and one of the Roses you can always depend upon." [C&Js11]

[Mme. Caro] (Levet, 1880)
Seedling of 'Gloire de Dijon' (N).
"Growth very weak; foliage dark green, purple beneath; thorns occasional; blossom well formed, very full, medium size, salmon-yellow." [S] "Bush with strong wood." [JR4/167]

Mme. Caroline Küster (Pernet père, 1872)
Seedling of 'Le Pactole' (T).
"Pale yellow, often mottled with rose; a free blooming, excellent shrub rose, one of the best bedding kinds." [EL] "Very vigorous, with upright canes; flower globular, full, large, beautiful orange yellow." [JR3/29] "Centre canary yellow, outer petals pale lemon, flowers large...a very beautiful rose." [JC] "Lemon-yellow fading to white." [S] "Not of climbing growth...strong good growth...small foliage; the blooms sometimes come divided, especially the strongest ones, and they are weak in colour, but good in petal, shape, fulness, lasting qualities, and size. This is an

accommodating Rose; a strong established plant in good soil may be cultivated…as a most useful bush to 'cut and come again'…It is very free
blooming and a good autumnal." [F-M2] "Vigorous with green wood
armed with red thorns; leaves of five leaflets, glossy, oval, much serrated;
leafstalk very prickly; flower stalk green or reddish, bristly, ovary cylindrical; flower very beautiful; very remontant; blooms in clusters…Mme.
Caroline Küster is a native of Germany. Being in Lyon, she visited the
premises of Monsieur Pernet, and was so ravished by this new rose that
Monsieur Pernet was pleased to give it her name." [JR10/78]

[Mme. Céline Noirey] (Guillot fils, 1868)
"Salmon-rose, flowers large and double; very beautiful." [JC] "A fine large
rose, very double, full and sweet; color, soft rosy blush, beautifully shaded
with deep purplish red; one of the best." [CA88] "Bush vigorous; flower
large, full, well formed; color, salmon-pink; reverse of petals purple red."
[S] "From Guillot fils' 1865 seedlings, released to commerce in 1868. Very
curious in its delicate salmony pink color, with purple red on the petal-
backs. The growth is vigorous; but the canes are weak, flexile, and bending
under the weight of the blossom, which is full, well-formed, solitary or in
a cluster, and able to attain 6-7 cm across [ca. 3 inches]; the leaves, composed of 3 or 5 oval-acuminate leaflets, are a light shiny green; petiole reddish and prickly; peduncle long and purplish. This beautiful variety was
obtained by open pollination; its origin is unknown…Can't withstand
more than 8] (Guillot fils, 1868)
"Salmon-rose, flowers large and double; very beautiful." [JC] "A fine large
rose, very double, full and sweet; color, soft rosy blush, beautifully shaded
with deep purplish red; one of the best." [CA88] "Bush vigorous; flower
large, full, well formed; color, salmon-pink; reverse of petals purple red."
[S] "From Guillot fils' 1865 seedlings, released to commerce in 1868. Very
curious in its delicate salmony pink color, with purple red on the petal-
backs. The growth is vigorous; but the canes are weak, flexile, and bending
under the weight of the blossom, which is full, well-formed, solitary or in

a cluster, and able to attain 6-7 cm across [ca. 3 inches]; the leaves, composed of 3 or 5 oval-acuminate leaflets, are a light shiny green; petiole reddish and prickly; peduncle long and purplish. This beautiful variety was obtained by open pollination; its origin is unknown...Can't withstand more than 8° or 10° of frost. Prune short." [JR10/93]

Mme. Charles (Damaizin, 1864)
Seedling of 'Mme. Damaizin' (T).
"Flowers sulphur or yellow, their centre salmon; large, full, of good form, and very abundant; growth vigorous." [FP] "Deep orange-yellow or apricot; beautiful colour and handsome in bud." [JC] "Very pretty flowers of a pure color, a lightly coppery nankeen yellow; vigorous." [JR10/46] "Medium growth, floriferous...flower large, nearly full, semi-globular." [S] "Very well clothed with leaves, dwarfish, blooms abundantly." [JR9/70] "Brown foliage, and one I do not disbud." [HmC] "An improved strain of 'Safrano'." [F-M2]

[Mme. Charles Franchet] (Liabaud, 1894)
"Bush extremely vigorous, of good habit, beautiful metallic green foliage; flower medium-sized or large, form globular, color very fresh pink nuanced coppery yellow, all the petals broadly margined with bright pink, a thoroughly new coloration." [JR18/146]

[Mme. Charles Singer] (Nabonnand, 1916)
"Flower large, double, erect, garnet on opening, dark velvety purple-garnet when expanded, keeps a long time; very vigorous." [ARA18/108] "Fine medium-sized red with nice form; good stem; immune foliage' medium growth." [CaRoII/3/2] "Flowers come singly on a strong stem...Valuable in the southern seacoast districts because it does not ball or mildew, and worth growing in heated areas because of its lasting qualities." [ARA28/103]

Mme. Chédane-Guinoisseau (Chédane-Guinoisseau/Lévêque, 1880)
Variously described as a seedling or sport of 'Safrano' (T) or 'Mme. Falcot' (T).
"Extremely floriferous, and its beautiful silky yellow flowers are well formed." [JR8/156] "Canary. Fair growth." [ARA27/20] "Moderate growth. The buds are pointed and well shaped, and the colour is bright yellow." [F-M2] "Very vigorous; foliage a handsome shiny glaucous green; flower large, full, very well formed, sulphurous canary yellow; buds long, like 'Mme. Falcot' or 'Safrano', but larger." [JR4/164]

[Mme. Claire Jaubert] (Nabonnand, 1887)
"Very vigorous, with big wood; flower very large, semi-double, in a cluster, with very large petals, imbricated, erect; color, brick yellow, nuanced, novel...Very floriferous." [JR11/165] "Yellow brick colour shaded to a fine rose-pink. Vigorous, grows to a great size, very free flowering, the blooms being of large size, good form and showing great uniformity." [B&V]

Mme. Clémence Marchix (Bernaix fils, 1899)
"Crimson and light pink." [LS] "Cochineal red tinted with rose, handsome deep cherry red buds; growth vigorous." [P1] "Very remontant, branches bearing 1-5 blossoms at their tips. Bud ovoid, pretty form, matte cerise red, very vigorous. Flower cupped." [JR23/168]

Mme. Constant Soupert (Soupert & Notting, 1905)
"Deep yellow shaded peach...Vigorous; best in Autumn." [Au] "Yellow tinted red." [LS] "The best and most beautiful Tea put into commerce over the past ten years. Many breeders have neglected the Tea Rose for a long time to devote themselves to HTs...'Mme. Constant Soupert' proves that there are yet pearls of rare beauty to be had from the Teas...[V]igorous and stocky; foliage dark green and much serrated; the long bud is pointed and upright on a long, erect stem; its color is a deep golden yellow strongly tinted and touched peach pink; the large blossom is very full,

opens slowly, and is beautiful pinkish yellow when fully open." [JR29/135] "Slender buds, opening to large, full flowers; odor slight. Bush small and weak. 13 blooms." [ARA26/94] "Attractive color; growth and blooming qualities not good. Being tested on 'Gloire des Rosomanes' stock, where it seems to be improving." [ARA18/112]

[Mme. Crombez] (Nabonnand, 1882)

"Vigorous bush, dwarf, very large flower, very full, very well formed, imbricated, perfectly held; color, yellow slightly nuanced coppery. This magnificent variety is one of the most beautiful nuanced yellow roses known till now." [JR6/186] "A large, finely formed rose, very fragrant; double and full, petals prettily imbricated; color, rich rosy buff, dashed and tinged with bronze and pale blush." [CA90] "A pure yellow, good sized flower, full, imbricated with outside petals reflexed after the manner of 'La France'. When well done this is one of the most beautiful of all roses; it seems to be capricious, hence not too popular among the growers; satisfactory for cutting, as it lives in perfect condition a long time in water. One of our greatest favorites." [B&V]

[Mme. Cusin] (Guillot fils, 1881)

"Violet rose, base of petals of a yellow tint, free-flowering, very distinct, has large flowers, full and the form very perfect. Of moderate growth and good habit. Very desirable." [B&V] "Crimson, with light center, slightly tinted with yellowish white; medium size, good form and quite distinct." [CA90] "Vigorous, of a pretty deportment, with upright, light green canes; leaves light green, composed of 5 leaflets; flowers large or medium, well formed, well held; color, purplish pink on a slightly yellowish white ground, sometimes a beautiful violet red; superb, very floriferous, novel coloration." [JR5/116] "Of short, thick, and often weak growth, with distinct wood and small foliage. It is rather liable to mildew and requires hot dry weather…The blooms almost always come well, though they are often undersized, and the shape is unique and very good, with a fine point in the centre, and the petals arranged in imbricated form, but standing well apart from one another. This is the true form, but large flowers sometimes do not show it…Very free-flowering; it must be well thinned for the production of exhibition blooms, but even the small flowers are lovely and of good lasting quality. A fine colour sometimes, but this is not often very lasting." [F-M3] "L. Cusin, Secretary of the Société d'Horticulture pratique du Rhône." [JR5/118]

Mme. Damaizin (Damaizin, 1858)
Possibly from a cross between 'Caroline' (T) and 'Safrano' (T).
"Buff with salmon tint, outer petals cream; a distinct and very beautiful rose; habit vigorous." [JC] "Creamy-white, shaded salmon, very large, double; not well formed." [EL] "Called a perfected 'Safrano'. Such perfection, however, is not to be had without hybridization, as is abundantly shown by the manner of branching, the globular form of the flower, the concave form of the petals, and the nearly white shade of yellow." [JR24/42] "Very full, pretty form; color salmon-flesh, abundant bloom." [S] "Very vigorous; foliage thick; flower globular, flesh nuanced salmon, abundant bloom." [l'H58/128] "Monsieur Frédéric Damaizin began raising roses in 185…[and] was the first in Lyon to undertake forcing roses." [JR3/55] It seems that Damaizin sold his firm to one Monsieur Charton in 1876 (see JR3/56).

[Mme. David] (Pernet père, 1885)
"A beautiful and promising sort; full, medium size; somewhat flat form; very double and finely scented; color, soft pale flesh, deepest in center; petals elegantly margined with silver rose." [CA90] "Vigorous bush, with smooth wood and upright canes; flower very large, nearly full; stem upright and strong; color, delicate pink edged white, sometimes salmon pink." [JR9/148]

[Mme. de St.-Joseph] (Breeder/Introducer unknown, 1846)
"Pale salmon tinted with pink…nearly unique in colour; but its flowers are often very irregular in their shape." [R8] "Fawn, shaded with salmon,

large and beautiful." [JC] "Very sweet." [FP] "Not well formed." [EL] "Pale pink, with deeper centre, sometimes dying off apricot colour, very large and double; form, expanded. Growth, vigorous." [P]

Mme. de Tartas (Bernède, 1859)

"Intense pink; flower large, full, cupped; very vigorous." [Cx] "Blossom moderate in size, pretty full; color, light pink." [S] "Bright rose, large, full, and produced abundantly; growth moderate." [P1] "Blowsy pink blooms." [Hk] "Blush pink...scented...sprawly in habit...3×3 [ft; ca. 1 m]." [B] "Coarse in growth." [Hk] Seemingly of the 'Comtesse de Labarthe' tribe.

[Mme. de Vatry] (Guérin, 1855)

"Deep rose, large and full." [FP] "Centre bright pink slightly tinted, outer petals paler, full, of good size, and free habit; an excellent hardy rose." [JC] "A splendid rose; large full form very double and sweet; color rich crimson scarlet; very bright." [CA88] "A good healthy grower and makes a fine supply of lovely buds and large fragrant flowers the whole season." [C&Js02] "Vigorous bush; flower large, full, fragrant. According to Monsieur Petit-Coq [*alias Scipion Cochet*], this rose, with robust canes, growing quite as large as '[Souvenir de la] Malmaison', is nevertheless stocky in habit. No matter what the site or exposure, you'll see it prosper; it resists frost better than other teas. Its wood is pretty big, with thorns here and there. Its dull green leaves, well-filled by leaflets of a good size, [*clothe nicely*] the plant which bears them; its upright flowers, on pretty long, thick, and usually uni-floral stems, are large or robustly medium-sized, slightly cupped, full, deep pink, slightly paler at the center, and fragrant. We recommend it because of its robustness, its elegant stature, its bloom which is prolonged and gives very beautiful flowers up to heavy frost, and, finally, for its bud, which may be used in making bouquets." [S]

Mme. de Watteville (Guillot fils, 1883)
Affiliated with 'Adam' (T).
"Cream bordered rose. Distinct, tender, fragrant." [H] "Lovely coral pink and canary." [Dr] "Very distinct pale lemon, with distinct margin of pink; large, full, and free." [DO] "Vigorous; large flowers, full, well-formed, very fragrant, well held; buds are long; color is white with some salmon, each petal fairly well edged pink. This wonderful variety is quite notable for the shading of the blossoms, resembling a tulip." [JR7/158] "Requires dry weather." [FRB] "Needs careful disbudding." [DO] "Has never been wholly satisfactory with me; but where the buds have been well thinned...I by no means despise a bunch of its lovely blossoms on long stalks." [K1] "Liable to mildew...weak." [F-M] "Branching habit of growth." [B] "Growth fair; not distinct." [ARA18/116]

[**Mme. Derepas-Matrat**] (Buatois, 1897) syn., 'Yellow Maman Cochet'
From 'Mme. Hoste' (T) × 'Marie Van Houtte' (T).
"A new and beautiful Hardy Tea Rose, throwing up fine strong stems bearing large solitary buds of grand size, and beautiful sulphur-yellow; flowers perfectly double, splendid form and freely borne." [C&Js05] "Flower solitary, borne on a long peduncle, very large, very full, opening well; color, sulphur yellow, center darker, lightly nuanced carmine while opening; growth vigorous, nearly thornless." [JR21/148]

[**Mme. Devoucoux**] (Widow Ducher, 1874)
"A magnificent rose; beautiful, clear canary yellow; delicious tea fragrance; large, very double and full; beautiful in bud and flower." [CA90] "Flower medium-sized, full, very well formed; color, bright yellow; vigorous." [S]

[**Mme. Dr. Jutté**] (Levet, 1872)
Seedling of 'Ophirie' (N)
"Flower grenadine yellow, very fragrant." [S] "Salmon, orange, and copper, very peculiar color, flowers rather loose." [JC]

[**Mme. Dubroca**] (Nabonnand, 1882)
"Very vigorous; flower large, full, well formed, perfect hold; color, delicate pink brightened with pink at the base of the petals. Novel coloration, constant bloom." [JR6/186] "A splendid rose; extra large, full flowers and finely formed buds; color clear salmon, delicately tinted and shaded with rich carmine; very beautiful." [CA90]

[**Mme. E. Vicaro**] (Breeder unknown,-1912)
"Brilliant carmine." [D&C12]

[**Mme. Édouard Helfenbein**] (P. Guillot, 1893)
Seedling of 'Anna Olivier' (T).
"Vigorous bush, flower large, full, well-formed, apricot chamois yellow nuanced with a clear deep carminy China pink; the color of each petal varies from apricot chamois yellow to carminy China pink, and is striped and veined with a darker shade of the same color...Very beautiful and very noticeable." [JR17/131]

[**Mme. Elie Lambert**] (E. Lambert, 1890)
From 'Anna Olivier' (T) × 'Souvenir de Paul Neyron' (T).
"Flowers extra large, fine globular form, very full and well built up. Color a rich creamy white, faintly tinted with pale golden yellow, and exquisitely bordered with soft rosy flesh." [CA96] "In clusters of 4-7 blossoms." [JR13/120] "Extremely floriferous and of uncommon vigor, though of moderate height. Buds elegantly borne on upright, rigid stems; flower cupped, globular, of a rare perfection, absolutely novel in color, having a center of the most beautiful blush pink, in which the flirtatious and delicate sweetness is further enhanced by the pure white found nuanced in the outer petals. The so-delicate tints of this rose—so distinct—as well as its perfection of form, will make all fanciers want to seek it out." [JR14/163]

Mme. Emilie Charrin (Perrier, 1895)
"Released to commerce in 1895 by its Lyonnais breeder, Monsieur Perrier. It appeared in a group of pink-flowered Teas, among the most beautiful varieties…[M]oderate vigor, grows pretty well, and gives many easily-opening blossoms of medium size, very double, China pink shading to bright blush." [JR32/46]

Mme. Ernest Perrin (Widow Schwartz, 1900)
"Large flower, coppery yellow, base of petals creamy white, shaded with yellow and mauve. Fine in a hot season." [P1] "Vigorous, foliage cheerful green edged purple; enormous bud; flower very large, ground color apricot nuanced yellow; petals largely tinted creamy blush, bordered mauve and peachblossom pink. A magnificent variety due to its many tints." [JR24/163]

[Mme. Ernestine Verdier] (Perny/Aschery, 1894)
"Mauve-rose, shaded salmon. Medium size." [ARA27/20] "Extra vigorous, with thorny, upright canes; the very large flower, possibly the largest of this sort, is very full, and opens with great ease. The form is very graceful, and the erect hold perfect. The wonderful buds are a pretty nuanced pink shade, varying according to exposure and season. As for the blossom's color, it is a mixture of pink, white, and red which is not easy to describe." [JR18/3-4]

Mme. Errera (Soupert & Notting, 1899)
From 'Mme. Lambard' (T) × 'Luciole' (T).
"Variable, base of petals coppery orange, outer petals flushed and veined with rose, large and full." [P1] "Very great vigor, handsome foliage, beautifully formed bud; flower large, full, well-held; color, salmon yellow, sometimes bright cerise nuanced light yellow…Floriferous and very fragrant." [JR23/170]

[Mme. Eugène Verdier] (Levet, 1882)
From 'Gloire de Dijon' (N), possibly hybridized with 'Mme. Barthélemy Levet' (T).
"Branches strong, very handsome icy-green foliage, flower large and well formed, surpassing all others of the 'Gloire de Dijon' sort; thorns straight and light; deep fawn color, very fragrant; a novel coloration." [JR6/149] Possibly a climber.

[Mme. F. Brassac] (Nabonnand/Brassac, 1883)
"Flowers and buds extra large, very double and full; color, a novel shade of bronze red, delicately tinted with coppery yellow; entirely distinct, and justly considered a very excellent rose." [CA90] "Very vigorous; flower large, full, well formed, very large petals; novel coloration, bright red, splendid for this genre. Will be much besought for its unique color." [JR7/184] "Prune to 5-7 eyes. Mme. Brassac is the wife of the distinguished Toulouse horticulturist." [JR10/61]

Mme. Falcot (Guillot fils, 1858)
Seedling of 'Safrano' (T).
"Buff yellow." [SBP] "Deep rich orange-yellow, petals large and of good substance, flowers not full, buds exquisitely beautiful, rich dark foliage; habit free." [JC] "Exterior of the outer petals having often the most charming combination of red and yellow, the inner petals being of a beautiful self-yellow. A good autumnal." [F-M2] "Flower medium or large, double, sometimes full; color, nankeen yellow fading to lighter yellow. Plant vigorous." [l'H58/98] "Deep apricot; resembles ['Safrano'], but is somewhat larger, more double, of deeper shade, less productive." [EL] "A word in passing on the subject of 'Mme. Falcot'; one errs considerably if one judges from the young plant; [*at that stage of the plant's life,*] the blossoms bear a great resemblance to 'Safrano', while the plant is less productive; but this is not the case after three, four, five, or six years; it blooms at that point quite as much as 'Safrano', and is much more brilliant and double. Fortunate shrubs! Age only increases their beauty!" [JR2/5] "Beautiful

fawn-color…a charming variety." [R8] "Medium to large in size, nankeen yellow, darker in the centre; beautiful tulip-like form. Free-flowering with moderate growth. The most perfect flowers appear in autumn." [Hn] "Loose." [Capt27] "Rich saffron-yellow, large and very double; petals large and thick; growth moderate. In the way of 'Safrano', but of a higher colour…Introduced in 1858 and still one of the best." [P1] "It has all the Tea-rose characteristics except that of having its young growths a maroon-red color. Its blossom of 2-3 inches [ca. 5-7.5 cm] doesn't have any scent—or has very little—and opens very quickly; its colors are nankeen yellow fading to plain yellow…when completely open, the flower is flat and a disgrace." [JR20/60]

"Fair growth and foliage." [F-M2] "Vigorous; reddish branches; hooked thorns, numerous and large; foliage of 5-7 lanceolate, finely toothed, shiny green leaflets; good autumn bloom;…color, moroccan yellow fading to light yellow." [S] "Pretty vigorous; branches slender and nodding; bark smooth, reddish with similarly colored thorns which are straight and pointed. The young growth is a handsome maroon red. Leaves of medium size, pale green…borne on a reddish leafstalk armed with a number of slightly hooked prickles. Flowers about 2.5 inches across [ca. 6 cm], fairly full, cupped, solitary;…outer petals large, those of the center folded and rumpled; flower stem glabrous, reddish, slender, and nodding. Calyx rounded…the bud is long and well formed." [JF] "More feeble [*than 'Safrano'*]." [EL] "I planted many specimens of 'Safrano', of which variety I would take many cuttings, because I knew they would give good seeds. That same year, I gathered fiftyish of such seeds, which I planted. Many didn't germinate. Nevertheless, among the resulting seedlings I noticed one which had semi-double blossoms of a nankeen yellow, new for that time. [*This was to become 'Mme. Falcot'*]." [JR4/88-89]

Mme. Fanny Pauwels (Soupert & Notting, 1884)
"Flower medium sized, full, bright yellow shaded light yellow, yolk-yellow in the center, sometimes reddish gold. This magnificent rose is one of the most floriferous." [JR8/164] "Growth vigorous and bushy; flower medium-sized or small, light yellow." [JR10/154]

Mme. Gamon (Gamon, 1905)
"Vigorous, bushy, flower large, full; long bud; apricot, nuanced dawn, on a golden yellow ground; very floriferous and fragrant." [JR30/24] "Apricot yellow. Mildews." [ARA27/20] "Very graceful globular form." [JR31/73]

[Mme. Gustave Henry] (Buatois, 1899)
"Bright pink with orange nubs." [LS] "Vigorous, bushy, flower very large, bud well formed; color, bright coppery pink, nubs golden yellow, extra floriferous." [JR23/169]

[Mme. Henry Graire] (Lévêque, 1895) syn. 'Mme. Henri Graire'
"Bright rose shaded vermilion, tinted bronze, large, full and sweet." [C&Js98] "Vigorous bush; very beautiful, ample, dark green leaves; superbly colored chamois yellow shaded with pink, and with light carmine; often the center is deep peach." [JR19/163]

Mme. Honoré Defresne (C. Levet, 1886)
Possibly a seedling of 'Mme. Falcot' (T).
"Sparkling yellow." [LS] "Vigorous, seemingly from 'Mme. Falcot'; flowers large, full, very well formed; color, beautiful dark yellow with coppery reflections; superb." [JR10/182] "Petals elegantly reflexed. A strong, vigorous grower, with thick foliage." [CA90] "Floriferous...Dedicated to the wife of the great French nurseryman." [JR28/157]

[Mme. Hoste] (Guillot & fils, 1887)
Seedling of 'Victor Pulliat' (T).
"Creamy color." [OM] "Flushed with rose." [C&Js00] "An exceedingly beautiful Rose; extra large, full, flowers of excellent substance; color fine

canary yellow, deepening at center to rich golden yellow. Grand for forcing." [CA93] "Fragrant." [Cx] "Vigorous; flower very large, full, very well formed, with large, thick, imbricated petals; well held." [JR11/149] "Of good growth and fine foliage.... The flowers are rather thin, and though they stand a long time in the advanced bud stage, when once they open they soon go, showing a weak centre. They are, however, very large and of very fine shape, and produced in great abundance, often very fine in the autumn...the stems are stiff and straight and the buds long and clean." [F-M2] "After serious study, the fortunate raiser of this beautiful introduction, recognizing what it was—in all ways a beautiful plant—released it to commerce in Fall, 1887. Dedicated to the wife of a Lyonnais horticulturist well known for his work with Dahlias, Chrysanthemums, Pelargoniums, etc...it is propagated on a large scale, notably in North America, where it is in great demand because of its cupped flowers. It is a vigorous plant, blooming very well, and giving an abundance of very pretty, very large blossoms, which are imbricated, and yellowish-white on a ground washed dark yellow. The large buds are long and borne on very firm stems. The plant is excellent as a garden rose." [JR17/9] Not to be confused with the flesh-white Hybrid Perpetual of the same name from Gonod in 1865.

Mme. J. Phillips
Listed as 'Mlle. Jeanne Philippe'.

[Mme. Jacques Charreton] (Bonnaire, 1897)
"Very vigorous and floriferous bush with strong canes holding large or very large flowers with oval long buds pointed at the tip; flowers very beautiful half-open. The exterior petals are milky white, center petals beautiful coppery salmon; very distinct and curious." [JR22/147]

Mme. Jean Dupuy (Lambert, 1901)
"Yellowish rose with reddish golden yellow centres, outer petals edged with rose. Large and full, opening well; growth vigorous; almost thornless." [P1]

"Deep yellow-fawn, edged rose. Mildews." [ARA27/20] "Dedicated to the wife of the simpatico French minister of Agriculture...vigorous, well covered with beautiful foliage, and its branches are partially thornless...Its deportment is that of 'Maman Cochet' or '[Mlle.] Franziska Krüger'. Its buds are long and solitary, and develop at the ends of the long branches, and are more or less erect. The blossoms are large and well formed, coppery red without and pinkish yellow within...freely remontant...delicious perfume." [JR25/170] "A good healthy grower. Makes a neat compact bush." [C&Js04]

[Mme. Joseph Godier] (Pernet-Ducher, 1887)
Seedling of 'Souvenir de Marie Detrey' (T).
"Very vigorous budsh, dwarf and bushy; young foliage reddish green, becoming dark green; flowers large, very pretty form, well held, carminy China pink at the center mingled and shaded with coppery yellow, sometimes entirely dawn yellow, lightly blushing; coloration novel and very distinct by way of the contrast of the various colors; very floriferous." [JR11/164]

[Mme. Joseph Laperrière] (Laperrière, 1898)
"Compact bush, very floriferous. Bud very long and usually solitary, of a beautiful China pink with silvery reflections on the outer petals; center darker when completely open; peduncles strong; flower large and well formed, very fragrant." [JR22/178]

Mme. Joseph Schwartz (Schwartz, 1880) syn., 'White Duchesse de Brabant'
Sport of 'Comtesse de Labarthe' (T).
"Blush, the edge of the petals tinged with carmine." [EL] "Flesh." [LS] "Lightly blushed white; flower cupped, medium-sized; vigorous." [Cx] "A new rose; flower of medium size, full, well formed, white washed flesh-pink fading to pale flesh, from the Tea 'Comtesse de Labarthe', a plant of the highest merit." [JR4/165] "Deliciously sweet." [CA90] "Double; white, tinged with pink in cool weather. Continuous...2-3 [ft; ca. 6-9

dm]. Supposedly a seedling of ['Comtesse de Labarthe']; evidence proves rather that it is definitely a color sport." [Lg] "Low growing, moderately compact and hardy; foliage plentiful, healthy; bloom free, almost continuous." [ARA18/126]

Mme. Joséphine Mühle
Listed as 'Safrano à Fleurs Rouges'.

[Mme. Jules Cambon] (Bernaix, 1888)
"Flesh color, reverse of petals magenta; of medium size, full; growth moderate." [CA93] "Moderate vigor. Elegant flower with firm petals, mostly oval; color, fresh incarnate pink with the petal edges carmine, having magenta reflections grading insensibly into the straw yellow nub...This variety exhibits, at the same time, stronger or weaker coloration, giving it a mutable character which is quite striking." [JR12/164]

[Mme. la Baronne Berge] (Pernet père, 1892) syn., 'Baronne Berge'
"Beautiful light rose, shaded with cream and yellow. Very free and constant bloomer." [CA95] "Vigorous, shooting out upright canes; flower large or medium-sized; petal edges bright pink, center light yellow, very fragrant; variety notable due to its coloration and good growth. Bloom is continuous." [JR16/154] "A most lovely rose, large full flowers, very double and sweet, color bright rosy red, with clear golden-yellow centre, very full and continuous bloomer, plants begin to bloom while very young; grand for bedding; very bright and sweetly scented." [C&Js98]

Mme. la Comtesse de Caserta (Nabonnand, 1877) syn., 'Comtesse de Caserta'
"A pretty cherry-pink, veined red." [JR5/21] "Large and very beautiful flowers; fine full form, very double and fragrant; color dark purplish red, elegantly clouded with a pale coppery yellow." [CA93] "Flower large, petals thick, not very full, showy, imbricated, coppery red; heavy, vigorous wood with large thorns. A quite new sort." [JR1/12/14] "Vigorous;

branches greenish red; thorns hooked, occasional, pretty large…effective, very fragrant." [S]

Mme. la Duchesse de Vallombrosa (Nabonnand, 1879)
"Coppery red, distinct." [EL] "Coppery pink." [Ÿ] "Very vigorous, flower very large, full, well formed, blooms in clusters, dark brick red with copper." [JR3/179] "Very floriferous; a new coloration." [S]

[Mme. la Princesse de Bessaraba de Brancovan] (Bernaix, 1890)
"Pink and yellow." [LS] "Growth moderate in size, branching, vigorous, very floriferous, bud subglobular to slightly ovoid; flower of middle size and fulness; in color, changeable, very fresh carmine, shading to blush at the edge, irradiated with canary yellow to pale chrome when opening." [JR14/163]

[Mme. la Princesse de Radziwill] (Nabonnand, 1886)
Seedling of 'Isabelle Nabonnand' (T).
"Red, coppery tinted, large and full flower, grows vigorously and very free-flowering, effective but not distinct, there being many varieties which bear to it a strong family likeness." [B&V] "Vigorous bush…, flower very large, full, erect; bud an elongate cone; color, red, shaded coppery." [JR10/169]

Mme. Lambard (Lacharme, 1877) syn., 'Mme. Lombard'
Supposedly from a cross between 'Mme. de Tartas' (T) and a rose of the 'Safrano' (T) sort.
"Salmon, shaded rose…variable on colour." [H] "Flower large, full, intense red. Very fragrant." [LR] "Rich cream and gold, flushed with rose-pink, very double and vigorous to 5 [ft; ca. 1.5 m]." [HRG] "Large, double, fragrant; flesh pink with salmon center. Repeats…2-3 [ft; ca. 6-9 dm]." [Lg] "Very vigorous; large flowers, beautiful bright red at the first bloom, more pale at the last." [JR1/12/13] "A pink rose that deepens on opening fully." [ARA39/48] "A somewhat coppery pink; flower large, full, cupped." [Cx] "Long considered to be the best all-around Tea…at its best

in the fall. Whereas the flowers are light salmon-pink in the spring and summer, in the fall they deepen into carmine, almost red, and bloom right on in a mild winter until stopped by heavy frosts." [SHj] "Salmon-pink, shaded with rose and yellow, sometimes the pink and sometimes the yellow colour predominating;…globular, perfect in shape, and petals fine." [P1] "Good both early and late, and is not too full to open in bad weather. The flowers are very variable in colour; I think a typical blossom may be described as a deep coral pink with a tinge of copper, but some may be found almost salmon, and others light rosy buff; quite a fair number of them come of good form, and the plant is very free, flowering almost continuously through the season." [NRS/11] "As to red Tea Roses we have travelled far and fast since I first saw 'Mme. Lambard' at the Paris Exhibition of 1878. It had appeared the year before, and was described as the 'finest deep-red Tea Rose in cultivation'. I shall not soon forget the excitement she created. Doubtless her colour in France is deeper than in England; for even here one sees the difference sun and warmth make to her, the first blooms in July being much darker in colour than the charming, rather pale blossoms I see from the window on an early October day. Few Teas, whether old or new, surpass her; strong, hardy, always in flower, she is hard to beat. But of course for deep vivid colour she cannot now compare with some of her modern rivals." [K1] "Scentless. The best and hardiest of the light red Teas." [S] "Large double flowers on stiff stems." [SHj] "Stems only fair." [Capt27] "Showy pink…rather round buds." [BSA] "Such a free bloomer that it adds much to the appearance of a garden." [ARA29/88] "Nearly perpetual through the season, always blooming some, and staying green till winter." [JR9/69] "Free bloomer of good growth [*in Bermuda*]." [UB28] "Small plants; winterkills." [ARA18/116] "Tall, compact, hardy; foliage very plentiful, black-spots slightly." [ARA18/126] "Liable to mildew…a cool season rose." [F-M2] "Foliage is well retained." [Th2] "A truly magnificent variety." [FRB]

Mme. Lombard
Listed as 'Mme. Lambard'.

Mme. Laurent Simons (Lévêque, 1894)
"Very vigorous, foliage ample, glossy green; flowers very large, full, handsome long bud; color, coppery pinkish yellow nuanced chrome red and tinted blush pink. Sometimes the same plant will bear coppery red blossoms shaded yellow." [JR18/150]

[Mme. Léon Février] (Nabonnand, 1882)
"A pretty and desirable variety; color a rare shade of silver rose, beautifully clouded with rich ruby crimson; flowers large, moderately full, very regular in form and exceedingly sweet." [CA90] "Very vigorous; flower very large, semi-double, perfect bud, superb hold; flesh-white, blooms in Winter." [JR6/186]

Mme. Lucien Duranthon (Bonnaire, 1898)
"Bush of great vigor without being climbing, with strong, rigid canes and peduncles; blossom solitary; bloom abundant and continuous; blossom large, cupped, colored cream white around the edge, center coppery and salmony; very distinct variety." [JR22/147]

[Mme. Margottin] (Guillot fils, 1866)
"Rich citron-red, shaded apricot; large, full flowers; profuse bloomer." [C&Js98] "Flowers large or medium-sized, very full, slightly globular, a beautiful deep citron yellow with a peach pink center, petal edges white." "Vigorous bush...the fairly long and feeble peduncle lets the flower nod a little too much—but this is not always the case." [S]

Mme. Marie Moreau
Listed as 'Mlle. Marie Moreau'.

[Mme. Marthe du Bourg] (Bernaix, 1889)
"Large, nearly double, nicely pointed centre; creamy white with carmine on the edges; very pretty." [CA93] "Fine cup shaped roses with prettily

crimped petals, creamy pink with rose center." [C&Js98] "Of good vigor, covered continuously with flowers during the height of the season. Flower pretty big, well formed, with thick petals; outer petals very large, recurved, spread out in back; center petals stiff and concave; color, white washed violet-carmine with a blush border—at first—then passing upon expansion of the blossom to pale chrome yellow washed blush. Very fresh color." [JR13/162]

[Mme. Maurice Kuppenheim] (Widow Ducher, 1877)
"Pale yellow, shaded with apricot." [EL] "Vigorous; flower large, full, salmon yellow, sometimes light pink." [JR1/12/12] "A remarkably pretty rose; flowers of elegant form, large, full and double; color pale canary yellow, faintly tinged with pink, shaded with coppery rose, sometimes soft rosy flesh; very sweet." [CA90]

Mme. Mélanie Willermoz (Lacharme, 1845)
"Creamy-white, centre tinted with fawn, petals very thick and finely formed, handsome large foliage, and moderately robust." [JC] "Vigorous; flower large, full, white shaded salmon at the center; one of the oldest and most esteemed Tea Roses." [S] "Of very sturdy stout growth with splendid foliage: an old Rose, formerly of considerable repute, but getting fast superseded by those of better manners…generally sadly lacking in the production of handsomely shaped useful blooms…The petals are very fine but the form is not good…a well-defined point in the centre being often absent…On rare occasions it does open well in hot weather with a good point in the centre, and is then very fine. It does well as a dwarf, the stiff upright character of the wood being well suited to this form of culture. It cannot be called a free bloomer or good autumnal." [F-M3] "Wood, strong, stout, glaucous green tinted violet, long internodes…Foliage, ample, rather long-stemmed…somber green, glossy above, glaucous green beneath. Flower stems long, strong, with two, three, or four foliaceous stipules around the point of attachment to the branch…Color, delicate pink at the center, white around the edges; the

petal-edge is often marbled pink. Blossom very large (to four inches [ca. 1 dm]), full, rounded, cupped, deep, regular, perfect, sexual organs evident, always opens easily. Scent, very weak…This rose grows rapidly and energetically…one of the hardiest of this delicate section. The large and beautiful flowers of '[Mme.] Mélanie Willermoz' appear abundantly throughout its period of active growth on its robust branches, and stand out elegantly by their delicate shading against the bright and lustrous green of the handsome foliage." [PlB] "An excellent sort of out-of-door culture." [EL]

[Mme. Nabonnand] (Nabonnand, 1877)
"Blossom very large, full, well formed, flesh white shaded pink, canes upright and big, perfect hold." [JR1/12/14] "White, shaded to light carmine, free-flowering and very attractive when in good condition and well grown. Grows more tall than bushy, and cannot boast of a strong constitution." [B&V] "Bush able, in two or three years, to make a plant a yard high [ca.1 m], having pretty numerous sub-branches divided into flowering branchlets, sometimes multifloral, but usually terminating in one blossom nodding slightly on its stem." [S]

[Mme. Ocker Ferencz] (Bernaix, 1892)
"Canary yellow washed carminy pink; blossom large, full, imbricated, vigorous." [Cx] "Beautiful bush of moderate size. Buds long, washed outside with violet pink. Flower of very beautiful form, with petals which are thick, satiny, glossy, and colored a very light pale canary yellow—nearly white—tinted chrome, fading towards the nub. Outer petals often washed along the edges with carminy pink." [JR16/164]

[Mme. Olga] (Lévêque, 1889)
"Beautiful large buds and flowers, cream white, shaded carmine, very sweet." [C&Js98] "Vigorous bush; foliage ample, dark green; flower large, full, very well formed, held well and firmly; beautifully colored white very finely and delicately shaded yellow nuanced greenish. Very distinct and beautiful." [JR13/164]

Mme. P. Perny (Nabonnand, 1879) syn., 'Mme. Pierre Perny'
"Saffron-yellow. Beautiful bud." [H] "Moderate vigor, nearly thornless, with semi-double flowers, well-formed, with a saffron-yellow elongated bud." [JR5/21]

[**Mme. Paul Varin-Bernier**] (Soupert & Notting, 1906)
From 'Mme. C.P. Strassheim' (T) × 'Mme. Dr. Jutté' (T).
"Melon color in the different shadings; good size and perfect form." [C&Js10] "The plant is of a healthy vigor and bears dark foliage. The flower is lightly double and large. The bud is absolutely charming and resembles…[*that of*] 'Richmond'. One could call 'Mme. Paul Varin-Bernier' a 'Richmond with Yellow Flowers'. It forces easily, easily producing solitary buds held proudly, same as outside…No matter what the season, [*the buds*] open well; bloom doesn't abate until frost; it blooms in clusters late in the season. The color is melon in the various shades; center and buds are dark yellow, petal edges light silvery yellow…Captivating perfume." [JR30/152]

[**Mme. Pauline Labonté**] (Pradel, 1852)
"Salmon rose; large, full and good in the bud; an excellent sort." [CA88] "Vigorous bush; flower large, full, fragrant; color, salmony pink." [S] "Outer petals flesh tinted with cream, centre deep salmon-buff, very large and full, sometimes peculiarly mottled; a superb and distinct rose." [JC] The mottling is reminiscent of 'David Pradel'.

[**Mme. Pelisson**] (Brosse, 1891)
"This new variety…is distinguished by its abundant and continuous bloom; the bush is vigorous and compact; the blossom is colored light citron with exterior petals being white on the outside; always growing and always covered with flowers until frost comes to destroy them; it's the first rose to open, and the last to come out; in a cluster of six to twelve double blossoms, they are of sparkling beauty. Delicious perfume; flower of medium size; having a pretty long stem which allows one to cull them

without cutting the whole group." [JR15/179] "Fine tulip form, very sweet." [C&Js98]

[Mme. Philémon Cochet] (S. Cochet, 1887)
Seedling of 'La Sylphide' (T).

"Bright, rich rosy pink, beautiful buds and large, well-filled flowers, very fragrant and constant bloomer." [C&Js99] "Bush of good vigor, with thick fairly upright canes of a pale purple brown, having somewhat triangular occasional or paired thorns. Leaves of 5-7 leaflets, of medium size, bright green and staying purple for a long time underneath. Peduncle very thick and smooth. The solitary bud is of a good size, being however not very conical but rather truncated-obtuse at the tip, very light flesh pink in color; some petal-bases are sometimes tinted a lightly carmined pink. Flowers medium-sized or large, of a slightly hollowed cup-shape, outer petals relatively large, extremely light pink, often marked on the outside with large blotches of a lightly salmoned pink. The base of this blossom is light pink nuanced pale salmon with a *soupçon* of bluish violet, which gains in intensity around the petal-tips...This rose, of beautiful form, is also fragrant...issued in 1884 from '[La] Sylphide', and has the wonderful trait of being extremely floriferous even towards the end of the season." [JR11/167]

[Mme. Philippe Kuntz] (Bernaix, 1889)
From 'Georges Farber' (T) × 'Joseph Métral' (T).

"Large, full, bright pink or China rose, finely formed and fragrant; free bloomer." [CA93] "Vigorous; beautiful brilliant green foliage. Flowers borne on thick stems, cupped, with large outer petals held out strongly; color, cerise red fading to delicate blush. This variety is notable for the contrast of colors in the flower which, delicate salmon pink upon opening, very rapidly becomes velvety crimson." [JR13/162]

[**Mme. Pierre Guillot**] (Guillot & fils, 1888)
Seedling 'Perle des Jardins' (T).
"Vigorous; flower large, quite full, opening well, very well formed, nearly always solitary; stem strong; color, a ground of coppery orange yellow grading insensibly to a lighter shade at the tip; petals bordered and tipped distinctly with carmine pink, with a yellowish white reverse; fragrant; unique coloration; extra beautiful." [JR12/146] "Free bloomer." [CA93]

Mme. Pierre Perny
Listed as 'Mme. P. Perny'.

[**Mme. Remond**] (E. Lambert, 1882)
From 'Comtesse de Labarthe' (T) × 'Anna Olivier' (T).
"A charming and valuable new rose, very double and full, fragrant, color pale sulphur yellow; petals broadly margined with bright red; very striking and remarkably beautiful." [CA88] "Vigorous, having medium-sized, full flowers which are yellow with the petal edges nasturtium; canes green, nearly thornless." [JR6/163]

Mme. Scipion Cochet (Bernaix, 1886)
From 'Anna Olivier' (T) × 'Comtesse de Labarthe' (T).
"Pale pink shaded whiteon a ground of yellow, center canary; flower large, full, cupped, fragrant; very floriferous; very vigorous." [Cx] "Beautiful creamy rose with deep crimson center; flowers large, somewhat tulip shaped, quite full, and very sweet; a good, constant bloomer." [CA90] "Thick, glossy foliage...Bush grows to about 2.5 feet [ca. 7.5 dm], branching from the base...branches not of the climbing sort, reddish, bearing doughty thorns top to bottom...Leaves numerous, thick, of 3-5-7 leaflets...somber green, glossy, like those of a Camellia above, lighter beneath. Flower solitary, erect at the summit of the stem...very double; bud ovoid, abruptly more slender towards the tip...; exterior petals regularly concave lengthwise, perfectly imbricated, pale pink with hints of flat white, and, towards the base, light yellow; center petals more irregular,

apricot/canary yellow, with touches of deep pink." [JR10/138] "A strong healthy grower and constant and profuse bloomer." [C&Js05] "A plant of the first rank." [JR14/93]

[**Mme. Thérèse Deschamps**] (Nabonnand, 1888)
"Flowers red, reverse of petals whitish; large, semi-double; growth vigorous." [CA93] "Very vigorous; big-wooded; small thorns; foliage very thick, matte bronze-green; flower large, erect, in clusters of 5-6; color, a veined red with white reflections towards the petal edges." [JR12/148] "Growth spreading, branching, with canes horizontal or indeed pendulous. Wood—old, greenish brown striped grayish; new, brownish green on the sunny side, paler on the shaded. Thorns occasional, some of them small; decurrent sometimes, to a lesser degree than they are high; hooked, the upper edge convex; grayish on the old wood, brown on the lower part of the [*present-season's*] branch, pink above. Foliage plain matte green, the reverse a little purplish at the head; leaves somewhat spaced-out. Short rachis bearing hooked prickles beneath, and, on the sides, very rare glandular hairs, branched or reflexed at the summit. Leaflets five or seven, the side ones neatly petiolate; all longly oval-lanceolate, often acuminate; toothed, the dentations slanting somewhat. Inflorescence few-flowered— 2, 3, or 4 blossoms—the secondary floral axes extremely short, growing from the axil; either with one simple bract and one leaf or three leaflets; or with one simple bract, one foliaceous bract, and one leaf of three leaflets. Peduncle long, smooth or pubescent, obscurely articulate, rather abruptly inflated into a conical-cylindrical calyx-tube. Calyx-segments barely longer than the bud; outer edges with filiform auricles; reflexing. Bud crimson; imbricated with—at the center—obscure bundles of petals. Flower semi-double, very bright pink; petals striped on the upper surface with carmine lines along the nerves, yellowish-white on the reverse. Styles numerous, long, pubescent, pink. Stigmata yellowish." [JR23/162-163] Author of the immediately preceding quotation places 'Mme. Thérèse Deschamps' in the Noisette camp; could there be confusion with

'Deschamps', alias 'Longworth Rambler', the Noisette offered by Monsieur Deschamps in 1877?

[**Mme. Therese Roswell**] (California Nursery Co.?,-1906) syn., 'Mme. Rathswell', 'Rathswell'?
"Rose-colored; small bloom; good growth; perfect and retained foliage; thornless." [CaRoII/3/2] "Bud carmine, opening rose, with deeper shadings, somewhat short; open flower double and holds center well; though small, often of value as a cut-flower. A climber or semi-climber with perfect foliage, which stands the dampest conditions without mildew. Blooms practically the whole year in Pacific South-West. Most valuable because it neither balls in dampness nor opens too quickly in heat and retains color well." [Th2] "A most valuable light red Tea for seacoast areas." [ARA28/103] It is by sheer conjecture that we connect the mysterious 'Rathswell' of Capt. Thomas to the equally mysterious 'Mme. Therese Roswell' of the California Nursery Company.

Mme. Tixier
Listed as 'Souvenir d'un Ami'.

[**Mme. Vermorel**] (Mari/Jupeau, 1901)
"Apricot yellow." [LS] "Dark, coppery yellow with bronze center; double; good size; lasting; fine cutting rose, with long stem; will ball in wet; splendid foliage." [CaRoII/3/3] "Attractive in color; form of rose varies; good growth and foliage; fair bloomer. Does well in hot weather." [ARA18/112]

[**Mme. Victor Caillet**] (Bernaix,1891)
"Bush very floriferous and of good vigor. Blossom rather larger than medium, pretty double. Exterior petals concave, cupped, thick, separate, inner petals ragged and muddled, all of a peony pink with carmine reflections nuanced salmon. Novel coloration, notably, having the singular quality of fading to white in age, and thus showing on the same plant both red and white flowers." [JR15/150]

[Mme. von Siemans] (Nabonnand, 1895)
Seedling of 'Mme. Nabonnand' (T).
"Perfect form, fine rosy flesh color, beautifully shaded, very sweet, constant and abundant bloomer." [C&Js98] "Flower very large, full, perfect hold; color, flesh pink; very beautiful long bud; very pretty foliage. Very vigorous bush, very floriferous, very beautiful variety." [JR19/180] Statisticians may wish to note that one-quarter of the previous quote is comprised of the word "very."

[Mme. Welche] (Widow Ducher/Bennett, 1876)
From 'Devoniensis' (T) × 'Souvenir d'un Ami' (T).
"Pale yellow, deep orange center, often shaded with reddish copper; flowers large, well formed and very double." [CA88] "Large, full globular flowers, and long, finely pointed buds; color soft peachy yellow, delicately clouded with pale rose; very sweet and handsome; blooms freely during the whole season." [C&Js98] "Vigorous bush; floriferous; flower large, full, flat, very fragrant; color, coppery orange yellow within; outer petals pale yellow." [S] "Height and compactness medium, hardy; foliage sufficient to plentiful, healthy; bloom moderate, almost continuous spring and fall, about half time in July and August." [ARA18/126] "The ownership of the beautiful Tea Rose bearing the name of Mme. Welche, the wife of the prefect of Lyon,…was sold to Mr. Henry Bennett." [JR1/1/8]

Molly Sharman-Crawford (A. Dickson, 1908)
"A beautiful rose…large, with a good centre…a pleasing shade of white, with a slight suggestion of eau de nil." [F-M] "Very double, greenish white, fading to white…2-3 [ft; ca. 6-9 dm]. Repeats." [Lg] "Bridal white. Large and full, with high, pointed centre. Broad, smooth petals. Delightful perfume. Very free and constant. A rose of entrancing loveliness." [Dr] "Good color; only fair in other qualities." [ARA18/117] "Medium to large…little perfume. Blooms all year. Foliage well-held; slight mildew in dampness on young foliage. Good growth. Distinct." [Capt28] "Low-growing, slim, hardy; foliage sufficient, healthy; bloom

moderate to free, almost continuous." [ARA18/127] "Beautiful foliage and a rather upright habit of growth, holding its head well, and always giving a shapely flower." [NRS/11] "Sometimes ill-shaped." [Capt27] "Its foliage is a fine ruddy colour when young, and this tint is more or less preserved for some time. Its flowers are charming, large and full, and produced in quantity from one end of the season to the other. They are well formed and nearly white, but have a little cream colour with the faintest tinge of pale green. It is customary to call them 'Eau-de-nil white', but from my recollection of the time when I took an interest in ladies' ball dresses, I should say the colour eau-de-nil has a considerable amount of blue in it, and this, I think, 'Molly Sharman-Crawford' has not got. The contrast between the flowers and foliage is very effective and pleasing. The blossoms are carried very erect for a Tea Rose...not free from mildew, but suffers very little from this trouble." [NRS/13] "The prettiest white rose on Earth." [JR32/56]

[Monsieur Charles de Thézillat] (Nabonnand, 1888)

"Flowers creamy yellow, centres chamois; very large, full, globular form." [CA93] "Very vigorous; flower very large, very full, globular, imbricated, erect, a true Tea, large petals; splendid color of creamy yellow, with a center of nuanced buff." [JR12/148]

[Monsieur Édouard Littaye] (Bernaix, 1891)

"Buds large, long, and of very fine shape; full and double when open; color rosy carmine, tinted light pink, often shaded with violet pink." [CA95] "Non-climbing; flowers abundant, of good hold; buds wonderful in form, conical-ovoid; color, carmine pink tinted amaranth during expansion, paler pink when the flower is open, the center being violet red." [JR15/150]

[Monsieur le Chevalier Angelo Ferrario] (Bernaix, 1894)
"Buds of great freshness, ovoid; petals thick, very large; flowers large, of perfect form, beautifully held, borne on long thick peduncles; in color, crimson purple red lightened around the nubs with lighter carmine." [JR18/163]

Monsieur Tillier (Bernaix, 1891)
Affiliated with 'Safrano à Fleurs Rouges' (T).
"A handsome carmine-red shaded brick, passing to violet-shaded red." [JR15/106] "An absolutely thrilling sight. This thoroughly novel color among roses makes it easy to distinguish from others…The bush is vigorous, thick, pretty hardy, and—above all—floriferous." [JR22/24-25] "It is a rare dark rose among the autumn roses which are pretty nearly always light." [JR36/187] "The tints resemble those of 'Mlle. Franziska Krüger'. Beautiful." [JR16/21] "Flower large, flat; good bedder." [Cx] "Seems to be a full-blooded Tea, but with small, double red blooms." [SHj] "Bush not climbing, very floriferous, of moderate size, with bright brownish-green leaves. The blossom is quite double, with numerous petals, often imbricated in the Camellia fashion." [JR15/150] "Looked as if its sturdy flowers would go on till Christmas." [K1] "But why is not that beautiful Rose, 'Monsieur Tillier',…seen oftener here?…It is simply invaluable for cutting, never out of bloom from June to November, and bearing heads of medium-sized flowers in such abundance, that a group of two or three plants makes a vivid splash of colour right across my garden. I first saw it at the Paris Exhibition of 1900, and have planted it freely ever since with great success, as it is quite hardy and even more effective than a China Rose, and lasts for many days in water." [K1] "L. Tillier, former head of the National School of Horticulture in Versailles." [JR11/158] "The bookstore *Octave Doin* is going to publish a charming work by Monsieur L. Tillier, the title of which is *l'Année Horticole*. It's a review of the novelties released to commerce in 1892." [JR17/63]

[**Mont Rosa**] (Ducher, 1892)
"Dawn gold." [LS] "Vigorous; flower medium-sized, full; flesh pink."

[**Morning Glow**] (W. Paul, 1902)
"Rose glow, deepening towards center." [CA06] "Carmine and orange."
[LS] "Flower large, full; petals thick; color, bright crimson pink tinted
orange and maroon." [JR26/87] "These varieties [*of which 'Morning Glow'
is one*], say the breeders, are a selection of our seedling from [the] Riviera,
born from the Tea-scented and China sorts grown in quantity in the south
of Europe for cutting. They continue the beautiful series which we began
several years ago with the now well-known roses 'Enchantress' and 'Queen
Mab'." [JR26/86]

[**Mrs. Alice Broomhall**] (A. Schwartz, 1910)
From 'Dr. Grill' (T) × either 'G. Nabonnand' (T) or 'Mme. Constant
Soupert' (T).
"Vigorous bush; flower large, double; opens well; bud long; color, salmon
apricot nuanced and tinted coppery orange yellow fading to pale pink
tinted cream, pretty coloration, very elegant bud, very floriferous."
[JR34/169] "A nice Tea, much like 'Souvenir of Stella Gray', with better
stem and good foliage." [ARA28/100]

Mrs. B. R. Cant (B.R. Cant, 1901)
Affiliated with 'Safrano à Fleurs Rouges' (T).
"Deep rose on the outer petals, and in the Autumn frequently a rich red,
inner petals soft silvery rose suffused with buff at the base, of good substance and symmetrical in form; a hardy variety and a vigorous grower."
[P1] "Sparkling pink, brighter than the usual Tea." [ARA29/95] "Deep
rose fading to light rose." [JR32/139] "Beautiful...with silvery inner
petals suffused with buff...worthy of a place in the front rank of the many
pink and salmon Tea Roses." [K1] "A good rose. Unique color; excellent
foliage; blooms very well; growth good." [ARA18/113] "Perfume mild...
best of the red Teas." [ARA17/24] "Grows vigorously all season and

blooms continuously. Not so much character but gives fine big blooms of typical rose color; also blooms well in the fall when most of the roses are off duty." [ARA29/88] "Most beautiful in the fall." [SHj] "A very free-flowering Tea, with rose-red blooms that make a good display in the garden, but have few claims to fine form." [OM] "Flowers full and globular." [W/Hn] "Form varies, being flat in the East, yet without open center and is of good size. Does not ball and holds its color well, even in heat. Has beautiful foliage and long stems. Of splendid growth, and blooms constantly." [Th2] "Medium height, compact, fairly hardy; foliage plentiful, healthy; bloom moderate, intermittent." [ARA18/127] "Resistant to mildew." [JR33/37] "To 4 [ft; ca. 1.25 m]." [HRG] "Seems in vigour, hardiness, freedom of flower…sweetness, colour, fulness and shape to be…a most valuable introduction." [F-M2]

Mrs. Campbell Hall (Hall/A. Dickson, 1914)

"Delicate creamy buff, edged or suffused rosy carmine. Of fair hardiness in Central Zone, but of small growth there. Valuable for its color. A collector's rose, and suggested for the South-East Zone only." [Th2] "The center of the bloom is warm cerise-coral-fawn…Deliciously tea-perfumed." [C&Js15] "Very fine…of excellent constitution; habit similar to 'Maman Cochet'; very free-flowering…of exquisite shape and colour." [F-M] "Large and high-centred in bud, opening full and somewhat blowsy. Dark, leathery foliage on a vigorous bush…4×3 [ft.; ca. 1.25 m × 9 dm]." [B1]

Mrs. Dudley Cross (W. Paul, 1907)

"Chamois-yellow, blushing pink in cool weather." [HRG] "Colors in warm weather and is hidden with blushes." [ET] "Flower very large, light chamois yellow, pink and crimson in the Fall. A very beautiful variety." [JR35/14] "Improved 'Marie Van Houtte'. Good growth, form, and color, although not of best; fair bloomer." [ARA18/113] "A superb light yellow rose. Large, full, and of elegant form." [Dr] "A fascinating rose, producing large double flowers on stiff, absolutely thornless stems. When used as a cut flower it is first light yellow, then becomes two-tone, and finally all pink."

[SHj] "Good growth and stem, but foliage mildews badly. Flower lasts well, and is fine for cutting. Especially adapted to dry southern climates." [Th2]

[**Mrs. Edward Mawley**] (A. Dickson, 1899)
"Bright rich pink, shading to tender rose or flesh color, very large and full, long plump buds on very long stems; a superb garden rose of grand size and substance, a vigorous grower, abundant bloomer, and quite hardy." [C&Js02] "Pink, tinted carmine.—Moderately vigorous…One of the best exhibition Teas. Fragrant." [Cat12]

Mrs. Foley-Hobbs (A. Dickson, 1910)
"Ivory white." [Bk] "Purely an exhibition variety, in creamy white with some variable pink at the tips. It has magnificent flower form and substance, more than the stems can hold upright." [Hk] "Good in color and growth; blooming below the average." [ARA18/117] "Vigorous and very robust, each branch developing a bud which matures into a magnificent, enormous blossom." [JR34/103]

Mrs. Herbert Hawksworth (A. Dickson, 1912)
"Deeply zoned, delicate ecru on milk white. With us, something on the order of 'Kaiserin Auguste Viktoria'. Practically no disbudding." [Th] "Very pretty, globular, very large, velvety petals, numerous and gracefully arranged…the growth is very vigorous, extremely floriferous…The color is, at first, dull white; then, as the rose opens, it becomes silvery white…delicious Tea scent." [JR36/91] "Growth good, hardy; good foliage and stem; medium to large size, lasts well…thirty blooms in 1915." [ARA16/20] "Low-growing, moderately compact, hardy; foliage sufficient, black-spots; bloom moderate, almost continuous." [ARA18/127] "Perfume mild; thirty-four blooms throughout the season; growth average. A fair rose for all purposes." [ARA17/22]

Mrs. Herbert Stevens
Listed as a Hybrid Tea.

Mrs. Hubert Taylor (A. Dickson, 1910)
"Shell-pink, the edges of the petals being ivory-white; a really superb Rose, of perfect formation and finish. Distinct and fine." [C&Js14] "A beautiful Tea, with a flower…nearly white in colour." [F-M] "Good grower and bloomer; color fair; foliage susceptible to mildew. Without these faults would be a good fall decorative." [ARA18/117]

[**Mrs. J. Pierpont Morgan**] (May/Dingee & Conard, 1895)
Sport of 'Mme. Cusin' (T).
"A sport from 'Mme. Cusin'; in every way much superior to that variety. The flowers are much larger and very double, petals are broad and massive; prolific bloomer; color intensely bright cerise or rose pink. Considered one of the finest and most beautiful in form, color, and substance ever produced." [CA95]

[**Mrs. James Wilson**] (A. Dickson, 1889)
"Pale yellow tipped with rose pink." [CA93] "In form, this beautiful novelty resembles the superb 'Catherine Mermet'. The flowers are a deep lemon yellow. The petals are edged pink. They are very large, full, of perfect form, and delicious perfume; petals thick and smooth. The growth is vigorous, putting forth many canes, and the blossoms which are produced profusely all season are borne on upright stems, which shows off the blossom's good point and keeps it in good condition for an extremely long time. Splendid for exhibition." [JR13/90] "Of good growth when established, and fair foliage. The habit is peculiar, in that the centre or crown bud is quite overwhelmed and starved out by the growth of the side flower buds unless these be thinned out at once; and even when this is done, the bud does not grow proportionately to the thickness of the shoot, and the blooms are rather undersized and disappointing. The petals are good and the shape nicely pointed: it is late in blooming, and not many flowers come to perfection on one plant. A pretty colour, sometimes a little like that of 'Marie Van Houtte'." [F-M3]

[**Mrs. Jessie Fremont**] (Dingee & Conard, 1891)
Seedling of 'Comtesse de Labarthe' (T).
"A seedling of 'Duchesse de Brabant' [*alias 'Comtesse de Labarthe*'], its buds
are not quite as big, but they are more double and more substantial; the
color is white, passing to deep flesh pink, sometimes nuanced coppery red
of a very delicate appearance; this is a vigorous hybrid which blooms very
freely." [JR15/88] "Often taking on nuances of coppery red or of old rose."
[JR16/38]

Mrs. Myles Kennedy (A. Dickson, 1906)
"Silvery-white, shaded light peach-buff. Mildews." [ARA27/20]
"Surpasses 'Souvenir d'Elise Vardon', favored in its time, because this new
variety is more vigorous. The color is beautiful silvery white with chamois
shading." [JR31/73] "Deeper pink in centre with back edge of petals a
slightly deeper shade of pink." [C&Js08] "Fair growth; very shy bloomer."
[ARA18/117] "Flowers of great size. Colour silvery white, with a delicate
picotee edging to the petal. It is purely an exhibitor's Rose, and requires
high culture. A fairly vigorous grower for this class." [F-M]

[**Mrs. Oliver Ames**] (R. Montgomery, 1898)
Sport of 'Mrs. J. Pierpont Morgan' (T).
"Delicate pink, the petals edged deep pink at their tips white being nearly
white at their base." [JR26/5] "Creamy yellow and soft glowing rose."
[C&Js03] "Round full flowers with lovely shell shaped petals, elegantly
ruffled...The plant is a neat bushy grower, and a most constant and abundant bloomer, particularly fine for bedding, as it is a strong robust grower,
and a tremendous bloomer, the buds are very beautiful and borne in great
profusion all through the Summer and Fall. Delightfully fragrant."
[C&Js05]

Mrs. Reynolds Hole (Nabonnand, 1900)
From 'Archiduc Joseph' (T) × 'André Schwartz' (T).
"Blossom very large, very full; color, deep purplish pink, interior tinted crimson; very handsome solitary bud borne on a long stem; growth very vigorous, wood thorny, bronze-red; very pretty foliage; very floriferous. Fragrant." [JR25/4]

Mrs. S.T. Wright (A. Dickson, 1914)
Sport of 'Harry Kirk' (T).
"Cadmium yellow." [Ÿ] "The guard petals are delicate old-gold; the center petals have a delicate and charming suffusion of delightful pure rose-pink on orange-chrome. The uniquely colored blooms have a deliciously pervading perfume. It is very floriferous." [C&Js16] "Good color; lacks in growth and blooming." [ARA18/117]

[Muriel Grahame] (A. Dickson, 1898) syn., 'Yellow Mermet'
Sport of 'Catherine Mermet' (T).
"Pale cream." [Cat12] "Similar to 'Catherine Mermet'; fine canary yellow, tipped with rosy pink. A healthy vigorous grower and abundant bloomer. Flowers are among the very largest in the ever-blooming class." [C&Js06]

Mystère (Nabonnand, 1877) trans., "Mystery"
"Vigorous, flowers very large, full, well-formed, upright, cupped, pink veined and marbled darker. Unique in color." [JR1/12/14]

[Namenlose Schöne] (Deegen, 1886) trans., "Nameless Beauty"
"Upon presenting a number of cut flowers [*from 'Namenlose Schöne'*], I asked the first convention of the society of German rose hobbyists in Darmstadt—on June 19, 1885—for an identification of this valuable cultivar…and I told them, 'About 33 years ago, we received among other rose shipments this rose as a single specimen without name or number; because it was unlabeled, it was ignored at first, and the shipper was not noted. Later, however, because of its bloom, advantages, and beauty, it caught our attention. It is a Noisette-Tea, extraordinarily rich in bloom

and very regularly remontant, such that a person can easily and readily have it quickly and perpetually in bloom. The bud and blossom are of high quality, pleasingly formed, and double, blooming in exquisite pure white, only occasionally tinted a slight flesh-red in the open air. With less light outside, it is softly imbued with sulphur yellow of the finest hue. The blossom changes, in its further development, from the loveliest double closed form to, finally, the open bowl of the rose 'Souvenir de la Malmaison', and nearly the same size. The flower has a remarkably strong but nevertheless sweet and mild fragrance, and is not likely to be surpassed by any other sort of rose in that respect. The blossom is perched upon a slender stem, and is surrounded by many buds. On the leafstalks of the plant are five elongate, elegantly-formed leaves of a vivid green coloration. Never is a flower scorched, even in the most intense heat of the sun; indeed, the more intense the sun's rays on this rose, the more flawlessly pure white it is, the more rapidly it reblooms, the more aromatic the pleasant fragrance, and the more splendid the bud and flower form. Its inexhaustible bloom, both ready and early from even the smallest plants, is not even surpassed by 'Hermosa'. As is well known, we have managed large, extensive, rose collections for about 33 years; but neither I nor the local rosarians Franz Deegen jr. and Ernst Herger—nor the foreign rose concerns—have gotten to know this rose, except from this one, now old, specimen. Further, no one anywhere else has come across it. To be sure, however, its high value has become recognized by the above-mentioned experts as well as by the nurseries. The old plant is still in my possession, recently propagated; but, because it was nameless, starts of it have not been distributed'." [RZ86/23-24] "Held in high consideration by German growers. It is white, tinged with sulphur yellow; very fragrant; buds and flowers large and well formed; very free blooming." [CA90]

[**Narcisse**] (Avoix & Crozy, 1858)
"Pale lemon yellow, tinged with salmon rose; medium size, full and double; very fragrant." [CA90] "Flower large, full, beautiful yellow fading to

straw yellow; much to be recommended." [S] "Fine pale yellow, habit of a Noisette; a beautiful abundant blooming rose, moderate in habit, and tolerably hardy." [JC] "A small bush, much in the way of 'Narcisse' and '[Le] Pactole'." [l'H57/98] There is confusion between this cultivar and the 1845 Noisette 'Narcisse' of Mansais. Narcisse, which is to say *Narcissus*, the genus of the Daffodil, and, more remotely, the self-absorbed male beauty of classic mythology.

[Nelly Johnstone] (G. Paul, 1906)
Seedling of 'Mme. Berkeley' (T).
"Pure rose pink often shot with light pale violet on the outside; blooms fairly double with fine light petals. Free flowering and deliciously fragrant." [C&Js08] "Vigorous bush, beautiful long bud, flower large, full; color, carnation pink, sometimes tinted violet on the outside. [JR33/184-185]

Niles Cochet (California Nursery Company, 1911) syn., 'Red Maman Cochet'
Sport of 'Maman Cochet' (T).
"Red on edge of petals, pink at base…Thorough tests have demonstrated that it is unquestionably far superior to any of the other Cochet varieties, being a much better bloomer and of finer color and substance." [CA11] "Deep claret to cream. Balls in dampness." [Capt27] "A variegated rather than a solid red." [Capt28] "Large, double, sometimes irregularly shaped; cherry-red with lighter center." [Lg] "Form almost identical with its parent, but claimed to be a trifle smaller and with better stems; slight fragrance. Fine foliage, and otherwise like its parent." [Th2]

[Nita Weldon] (A. Dickson, 1908)
"Ivory-white with each petal edged light pink; perfect." [C&Js12] "White, tinted blush.—Vigorous.—[*For the*] garden." [Cat12]

Niphetos (Bougère, 1841 [poss. before]) syn., 'Mathilde'; trans., "Snowy"
"Of a pale lemon, turning to snow-white." [FP] "White, centre pale straw, long handsome buds, large Magnolia-like petals; in dry weather superb."

[JC] "Suffers much from rain; the blossoms open poorly…in essence, it is a greenhouse rose." [JR7/3] "Large, full, tulip-like form, pure white; buds long, tapering, drooping. A delightful rose." [Hn] "Very large, very floriferous, large petals." [R-H42] "No white Tea can beat it for purity of colour." [FRB] "Large, globular, fragrant white. Repeats…2-3 [ft; ca. 6-9 dm]." [Lg] "Frequently malformed." [F-M] "Delicate long-pointed buds…not very strong in growth." [BSA] "Remarkable for its large taper formed flower bud, and till it is fully open is very splendid…when fully expanded, it is not at all attractive; the wood is strong." [Bu] "Flower of medium size, full; color, pure white; form, pointed; the most tender of white roses…the leaves are light green, rather dense, sufficient unto the blossom, which itself is just the thing to cut a fine figure in the open garden; but it is primarily grown under glass, giving excellent results." [S] "The bush is small, stocky, with light green serrated leaflets. The young wood is green, and is sometimes covered with rust-colored spots. The thorns are solitary, much hooked, and very thick. The marvelous buds are greenish-white; their stem is long; long sepals; when the blossom opens, its petals are pure white, reflexing to the stem à la 'Maréchal Niel'; this characteristic keeps the flower in an attractive bell-like form from first to last. As the final petals unfurl, they take on a tint of pale pink intermingled with little lines." [JR4/174] "Created as great a sensation as any rose that ever appeared. The peculiar elongated, oval, pure white bud had not been seen among roses." [Dr] "It occurred during the sixties [*i.e., 1860s*] that 'Niphetos' was entirely lost to culture. The most diligent search failed to recover a single 'Niphetos' rose-bush. It was universally regretted. Accidentally, a Northern tourist came across a garden of the Blue Ridge, Virginia, that had in it a rose-bush full of unmistakable elongated, oval, snow-white 'Niphetos' buds. The prize was secured and taken to Philadelphia. 'Niphetos' was restored to its own." [Dr] "Represents, among roses, a perfect distinction, a supreme elegance, finesse, and—finally—nobility." [JR13/152]

[**Number 27**] (Dingee & Conard, 1912)
Sport of 'Bridesmaid' (T).
"A deeper pink sport of 'Bridesmaid'." [D&C12]

[**Palo Alto**] (Conard & Jones, 1898)
"This is a splendid new rose from California. It is large, full and very sweet; the color is a lovely chamois rose, delicately tinged at centre with golden-yellow and creamy white. The bush is a strong healthy grower, and constant and abundant bloomer; it is a rose sure to please and give satisfaction in every way; bears beautiful large sweet roses all through the season." [C&Js98] Possibly originated by Luther Burbank. Palo Alto, city in California.

Papa Gontier (Nabonnand, 1882)
Seedling of 'Duchess of Edinburgh' (T).
"Intense pink; reverse, carmine-red; flower large, imbricated; very floriferous; fairly vigorous." [Cx] "Rosy crimson, pointed bud, free." [H] "Rich pink rose of striking color for a Tea." [ARA29/95] "Vigorous, very large thorns,...large flower, semi-double, well-formed, bright pink at the center, shaded yellow, the reverse of the petals being purplish red; winter-flowering." [JR6/186] "Lovely color." [Capt28] "Red flowers during the regular season, giving blossoms which are more pale but more profuse in the Fall." [JR16/179] "An old favourite Tea rose, with lovely rose-crimson buds that too soon become full-blown flowers. It is only fairly strong-growing, though it blooms freely." [OM] "Somewhat thin petals, and not very many of them." [F-M2] "Splendid buds and good habits." [BSA] "Buds long, clean, and handsome; not double enough for a show Rose, but excellent for cutting." [P1] "Very pretty in color and foliage, but subject to malformation; also, sometimes it lets fall its leaves, proving Bourbon descent...no scent." [JR13/92] "Resistant to mildew." [JR33/37] "Beautiful bud, but opens loose, with scanty petalage in heat; fine substance; fragrant; does not ball or discolor in heavy winds, but bleaches somewhat in heat. Has

fine foliage and blooms constantly…beautiful bush in the garden."
[Th2] "Free-flowering, especially on loamy soil." [Hn] "Without rival
in its class…The bud…is a splendid floral marvel; it grows to about
2.25 inches [ca. 5.25 cm] and more, in length; its elongated, elegant
form is always graceful…color, very bright deep rose, quite extraordinary, sumptuously shaded carmine; it is hardly possible to imagine anything more attractive…does not 'blue'…of great vigor…wood, somber
red or bronze green depending upon its age, large and robust; amply
furnished with thorns both large and small, fairly upright. Its foliage is
a handsome somber green, quite shiny, and is large and full…it is
nearly inexhaustibly floriferous, comparable to the noble 'Safrano' in
this regard." [JR14/72-73] "One of the most remarkable of the many
varieties which flourish on the Riviera. The flat filbert shaped bud, produced at the extremity of an unusually long and strong stem, is of clear
carmine rose; as such and until half expanded is beautiful in the
extreme, nothing in the rose-world can well be superior; with greater
maturity alas! This excellence of form and colour vanishes. The flower
when fully expanded is large and loose, in very short time owing to the
flaccidity of its petals is deprived of all elegance of appearance; the
colour, truly splendid in the earlier stages of flowering, degenerates into
a mixture of mauve and purple, a false and unpleasant tint. Cut flowers
allowed to open indoors are very superior to those which have been
exposed to the sun. When planted in a strong rich loam it flourishes
and grows in a manner truly surprising, two or three years suffice to
turn a single little plant into a large tree or bush." [B&V] "So tremendous a philanthropist is 'Papa Gontier' that it seems almost disrespect-
ful to name him with such familiar brevity. Anyhow, he loves the north
as he loves the warm land of his raising; and rejoices in our [*British*]
green summers and rain as much as ever in the sun-baked slopes and
torrid seasons of Golfe Juan [*France, where it was raised*]; always, everywhere, of a temper that you can absolutely rely on, and a beauty that no
poor words of yours can ever hope to realise or express." [Fa]

"While visiting the wonderful nurseries of Monsieur Gontier père, green-house produce expert, on the Orléans road at Montrouge, one can be convinced that Horticulture is a science requiring intelligence to succeed. Monsieur Gontier is indeed one of our most able horticulturists. And for Monsieur Gontier, there are no seasons—he is able to produce in Winter what nature gives us in Summer...Monsieur Gontier's establishment has become a sort of horticultural laboratory in which he can create, at will, the most delicious fruits...In seeing his establishment run so intelligently, in recalling the services rendered, I can only ask myself why this able horticulturist has not yet received the high honors which have already been given to many of his associates. His work, so knowledgeably undertaken, so replete with judicious observation, is beyond all praise...It is hard to understand how the *Société impériale d'horticulture de Paris*, which for several years has had several chevalierships in the Legion of Honor at its disposal, has been able to forget one of our celebrated horticulturists; we hope that it will quickly repair this omission." [l'H59/219]

Parks' Yellow Tea-Scented China (China/Parks, 1824)

"By the bye, I have had a Tea Rose in blossom in the vinery—of a sort I rarely see, and of which I really do not know the proper name. It used to grow over a cottage in Hertfordshire, which I knew many years ago, and the Hertfordshire nurseryman, from whom I got my standard, called it 'the old yellow China'. Is this the right name, and is the Rose more common than I imagine? Its petals are loose and thin, and of a pale primrose colour, and before it is fully out is at its best. Its leaves are large and handsome, and of glossy green. Its blossom has a certain half-bitter scent of Tea about it, to which the scent of no other Tea Rose can at all compare—it is so strong and aromatic." [Br] "Yellowish." [V3] "Pale straw colour, extremely large bold petals; it is very splendid when half expanded, but when full blown is loose and not fully double; it bears an abundance of seed, but we have never produced a good rose from it...In fresh sandy rich soil it grows very strong, and flowers profusely, but does not thrive in heavy soils." [Bu] "Light yellow, long, fine buds, fragrant. This has been the parent of many of our finest yellow Teas." [EL] "*Ovary* large and very short. *Corolla* from three and a half to five inches in diameter [ca. .09-1.3 dm], double, sulphur yellow, becoming nearly white. *Petals* 25 to 40, interior ones unguiculate. *Styles* 30 to 40, salient, equal, bristly, yellowish green." [Pf] "Vigorous; strong branches; large flower, full, globular; bud, remarkably handsome, elongated; same shade as 'Maréchal Niel'; color, bright yellow bordered sulphur; one of the best old Tea roses." [S] "Smooth glossy leaves and faint Tea-odour sufficiently show its affinity." [WRP] "Many of these lovely Roses very distinctly show the effect of the old Yellow Tea Rose upon the race, in the golden and sulphur base which adds such richness of tone to their countless shades of white, pink, crimson and copper." [K1] "In France the Yellow Tea Rose is exceedingly popular, and in the summer and autumnal months hundreds of plants are sold in the flower markets of Paris, principally worked on little stems or 'demitiges'. They are brought to market in pots, with their heads partially enveloped in coloured paper in such an elegant and effective mode that it is scarcely possible to avoid being tempted to give two or three francs for such a pretty object." [R8] "For delicacy of color, delightful fragrance and beauty of bud, has scarcely a peer, and, in my judgment, has never been excelled." [HstXXX:143]

"Brought to England by John Damper Parks in 1824, who was then collecting for the Royal Horticultural Society in China and Java." [EER] "Messieurs DuBourg, Hardi [*sic*], and Grandidier saw it in bloom last year in London, and now (May 24, 1826) fanciers can see it bloom at the Luxembourg." [J-A] "[*Pirolle's*] malicious envy can even be noted in the most inconsequential things. Thus it is that…we read, in italics, in a discussion of the sulphur-yellow China [*i.e., 'Parks' Yellow Tea-Scented China'*] *that this rose is not an Arvensis*. Now, I had said, four or five years ago, that I had received and grown the Arvensis rose under the name 'Yellow China' [*Vibert had been discussing the tricks that rose vendors play on customers*]; this remark had nothing to do with the sulphur yellow China. The author, however, wanted people to think that I had confused the two roses, much as this latter did not yet exist on the Continent. What is more, still talking about the sulphur-yellow China, he adds, *some others have also sought to obtain it, and lit upon it so well that he will soon he selling it at four and five francs, and less.* We see at once that Monsieur Pirolle seems to be ignorant of the fact that this rose is not the result of a sowing made in Europe [*"obtain" was used in the sense of "obtain in a crop of seed," i.e., "raise"*]— rather, it was sent from the Indies to the garden of the London Horticultural Society. I well understand that he does not stoop to concern himself with these petty details; but why talk of things of which you are ignorant? And can't he hold me up to ridicule without blundering? As to the price of this China, he has known about that all along. He says that, in 1825, this rose was sold in London at the price of only one guinea. As bad luck would have it, it was in the Fall of that same year that I was there. I took home twelve specimens [*evidently the first in France*], which cost me between one-and-a-half guineas and three, apiece. In Fall of 1826, a [*British*] firm which treats me well, and with whose good will I am honored, sent me five specimens at a guinea apiece, specimens only a year old. As to this business of the rose being sold this Fall [*1827*] at four francs or less—perhaps we should let him know that these details are somewhat inconsequential. Had he deigned to consult Monsieur Noisette on this head, that honorable nurseryman—much more competent than Monsieur Pirolle to judge the question—would have told him, as he did me, that, if true, it indeed only makes sense: [*We have been able to propagate so many specimens that*] we are exporting them back to England." [Vrp] "My [*Buist's*] late partner, Mr. Hibbert, introduced this rose and the *White China* into this country [*the U.S.A.*] in 1828, and the first plants that were sold of them was in 1830; they are found in thousands over every part of the United States." [Bu]

Paul Nabonnand (Nabonnand, 1877)

"Satiny-rose." [EL] "Bright rose." [ARA27/20] "Pure rose colour, large and full, beautiful bud, vigorous, free-flowering and fine. It is very popular with the nurserymen who cultivate its flowers largely for export." [B&V] "Very vigorous; flower very large, very full, form and hold perfect." [JR1/12/14] "Large growth; very fine foliage, well held; no mildew. Flowers of medium size, double, opens well, light rose to strawberry in the center. Good on seacoast. Decorative." [ARA28/103] "Vigorous, with dark green branches touched with red; thorns hooked, often flat, pretty big; leaves olive green, finely dentate; flower very large, very full, Hydrangea pink. This variety is wonderful in all respects, and should not be left out of any collection." [S]

[**Peace**] (Piper, 1902)

"This ravishing newcomer will be released to commerce at the end of November 1902 by its breeder Mr. G.W. Piper, horticulturist at Uckfield, Sussex (England). It opens well and will be an excellent rose for forcing in Winter…'Peace' is a variety which opens well; its pale lemon coloration, its very long buds, its solitary flower on a very straight and strong stem, the many flowers which make the plant a veritable mass of flowers, the very large petals solidly attached to the blossom, its magnificent foliage, and its delicious scent—all of these unite to make it an absolutely elite variety." [JR26/162-163]

[**Peach Blossom**] (Conard & Jones, 1898)

"A superb new Tea Rose introduced from California; the flowers are of exquisite form, with broad deep petals of excellent substance, and deliciously sweet; the color is a rich shade of golden rose or peach blossom; very rare and beautiful. All we have seen of this rose leads us to believe it is a variety of the very first quality." [C&Js98] Possibly originated by Luther Burbank.

[**Pearl Rivers**] (Dingee & Conard, 1890)
From 'Devoniensis' (T) × 'Mme. de Watteville' (T).
"Obtained by crossing 'Devoniensis' and 'Mme. [de] Watteville', this variety partakes of the distinctive characteristics of these two varieties, but the stature of its growth is better and its blossoms open more freely. Its color is an ivory white delicately nuanced and bordered light pink; very fragrant and of an exquisite beauty." [JR15/88] "The flowers are large and full with peachy-red buds...very beautiful and deliciously sweet." [C&Js98]

Penelope (J. Williams, 1906)
Red with an ivory center. Penelope, the loyal and wily wife of Odysseus.

Perfection de Monplaisir (Levet, 1871)
Seedling of 'Canari' (T).
"Clear lemon, form of the flowers similar to [*that of 'Parks' Yellow Tea-Scented China*], very pretty, habit moderate." [JC] "Flower medium-sized, full, fragrant; color, bright canary yellow." [S] "A good Tea, which may be described as an improved 'Canari'; like that sort it is delicate." [EL] "[*Of 'Perfection de Monplaisir', 'Jean Pernet', and 'Perle des Jardins',*] 'Perfection de Montplaisir' [*sic*] has the lightest color." [JR10/45] Monplaisir was Levet's home community in Lyon.

[**Perle de Feu**] (Dubreuil, 1893) trans., "Fire-Pearl"
From 'Mme. Falcot' (T) × 'Mme. Claire Carnot' (N).
"Chinese-yellow. Small." [ARA27/20] "Bushy plant, very vigorous and very floriferous; medium-sized flower; graceful, pretty form; a most remarkable color...copper-red nuanced nankeen yellow, with purplish chamois reflections. Sometimes in the Spring it is incarnadine with chamois reflections." [JR17/166] "This is a perfect little gem; flowers are only of medium size, but the buds are large in proportion and of beautiful, perfect form, and the color is so intense that its name, 'The Fire Pearl', is a better description than any we can write." [C&Js99]

[**Perle de Lyon**] (Ducher, 1872) trans., "Lyon's Pearl"
"Deep fawn and apricot, colour of 'Mme. Falcot', petals large, flowers globular, exquisitely formed; a superb rose." [JC] "Here is what Monsieur Petit-Cog says of 'Perle de Lyon': We have seen some flowers which measure more than 8 centimeters in diameter [ca. 3½ inches] though still not completely open; of a faultless form, well packed with petals which are uniformly very brilliant dark yellow, or sometimes nuanced with apricot at the center, this rose is held gracefully erect on a unifloral [*correcting "uniforme"*] peduncle, or, if the specimen is vigorous, on a pedicel which supports a sparsely branched peduncle; canes short, thick, and compact, moderately leafed, tending away from the vertical; the bush is hard-pressed to attain sixty centimeters in height [ca. two feet] out in the open; rain or a drop in temperature of some duration impedes the development of the flower in our climate; it only gives a good bloom in good weather; this variety is of a fairly delicate constitution which doesn't allow it to bear the merest chills of Autumn; an excellent variety for forcing in March." [S]

Perle des Jardins (Levet, 1874) trans., "Garden-Pearl"
Seedling of 'Mme. Falcot' (T).
"Bright straw-color, uncertain in form." [H] "Apricot suffused light buff." [Capt27] "Canary yellow, centres orange yellow, large and full...One of the best." [P1] "Full...much copper and a little pink in the center." [ARA36/19] "Said to be of the highest merit; the flowers are very large, full, and well formed; it is vigorous in growth, color varying from pale yellow to deep canary-yellow. This will be a formidable rival to 'Maréchal Niel' because of its rich color and the continuous manner in which its flowers are produced." [HstXXX:236] "Flower large, full, globular, high-centered, opening well, coppery chrome yellow, with the petals' exteriors fading to cream yellow." [JR38/41] "Fragrant, shapely, sulphur to buff...wiry plant...3×2 [ft; ca. 9×6 dm]." [B] "Canary–yellow, large or very large, full, well formed, stiff stems, very free; the leaflets are five to seven in number, deeply serrated, very dark and glaucous...fine...in open

air." [EL] "Shows a high production of blooms..., but until a few weeks ago I had never seen a perfect one. The outer petals have always shriveled before the buds were ready to cut." [ARA25/99] "Fades too easily." [ARA25/105] "Needs warmth." [HRG] "As a rule balls in wet and damp." [Capt28] "Sometimes opening badly in centre." [DO] "A rose of shocking bad manners." [F-M2] "Very vigorous and persistent, and very good in a warmer climate, but a little too double for here [*England*]." [JR9/70] "Growth small; superseded by better roses." [ARA18/117] "Growth moderate; very fragrant." [Hn] "Tall, bushy, hardy; foliage very plentiful, black-spots slightly; bloom abundant in June, moderate in July, none later." [ARA18/127] "Exquisite tea-fragrance; a free-grower and bloomer...excellent in the open ground." [SBP] "Valuable for winter blooming." [Dr] "Foliage attractive and good. Stem fairly good...there seems to be a general opinion that it is better to grow the climbing sport rather than the bush form of this rose. Is found useful in Gulf Coast regions, but balls in damp winds." [Th2] "The most elegant and cherished rose for bouquets, it blooms the whole year [*in Havana*] without being pruned." [JR6/43]

Perle des Jaunes (Reymond, 1903) trans., "Pearl of the Yellows"
"Deep orange yellow, tinted salmon" [K2] "Very vigorous, with twiggy growth, handsome foliage, large and full flowers; superbly colored dark golden yellow, with orange and carmine. Remarkable for the pretty shade of yellow, and for the flowers, which are just as large as those of 'Mme. Falcot, but fuller. This rose forms a bush which is compact, a quality which will make it much desired for bedding; very floriferous." [JR27/131] "Fair growth; no special distinction." [ARA18/117]

Primrose (Dingee & Conard, 1908)
Primrose yellow. "Poor growth and foliage; shy bloomer." [ARA18/117]

Prince Wasiltchikoff
Listed as 'Duchess of Edinburgh'.

[**Princess Beatrix**] (Bennett/Schultheis, 1887)
"Flower large, full, held well on upright peduncles, and further has the most perfect form; large petals, well rounded, the exterior of which is light yellow, and the interior rich golden yellow, while the edge of the petals is delicately bordered bright pink." [JR11/92]

[**Princess Bonnie**] (Dingee & Conard, 1896)
From 'Bon Silène' (T) × "William Francis Bennett' (HT).
"Rich vivid crimson, large, semi-double with fine petals, exceedingly fragrant, beautiful long buds." [CA97] "The flowers are extra large and full, perfectly double, and deliciously sweet; the color is solid rich crimson, exquisitely shaded; a constant and abundant bloomer, loaded with flowers the whole season; a hardy vigorous grower, and one of the sweetest and most beautiful ever-blooming roses you can possibly have." [C&Js98] "This rose would seem to be of very abundant bloom, nearly continuous. The flowers are borne on upright, strong stems; they are large, pretty full, and a beautiful crimson which is more pronounced than that of 'William Francis Bennett'. The reverse of the petals has the same color as those of 'Général Jacqueminot', while the interior is lightly striped white. The perfume is penetrating and sweet though not as strong as that of the HPs." [JR20/98] "Moderately high and compact, fairly hardy; foliage sufficient, black-spots somewhat; bloom free, continuous." [ARA18/127]

[**Princess of Wales**] (Bennett, 1882)
From 'Adam] (T) × 'Elise Sauvage' (T).
"Moderate vigor; flower large, well formed; exterior petals pink yellow; those of the center, deep rich waxy yellow; distinct; opens well; buds long and pointed...Very floriferous, and well held." [S] "Well cupped handsome flower of good size and form. In habit this rose resembles 'Comtesse de Nadaillac'." [B&V] "Of small dwarf growth and foliage, requiring fine weather...A small stem will sometimes grow, stiffen, and swell for a long time without opening the bud, which when it does come will be a great and probably a good Rose, while a much stronger shoot of three times its

length perhaps remains pliable, opens quickly, and produces a much inferior bloom. The shape of the smaller flowers is weak and undecided, but there is no doubt about its beauty in form and every other quality when it does come good, though it is seldom very large. It is variable in colour, and is somewhat capricious, doing well in some soils and badly in others, but generally best as a standard." [F-M3]

[Princesse Alice de Monaco] (Weber, 1893)
"Blush pink." [JR20/7] "Creamy yellow edged with rose, centre peach colour, handsome buds; very free and effective; one of the most beautiful decorative Tea Roses." [P1]

Princesse de Bessaraba de Brancovan
Listed as 'Mme. la Princesse de Bessaraba de Brancovan'.

Princesse de Venosa (Dubreuil, 1895)
"Non-climbing, wood dark, foliage very bright, bud a beautiful long ovoid form, white tinted blush nuanced yellow upon opening. Flower...well formed, opens well, very fragrant, golden nankeen yellow nuanced carmined with amethyst violet glimmerings." [JR19/147]

Princesse Étienne de Croy (Ketten Bros., 1898)
From 'Comtesse de Labarthe' (T) × 'Mme. Eugène Verdier' (T).
"Lilac peach carmine, tinted China pink, on a ground of pale orange, very large, very full, opens well, erect, firm stem. Vigorous and floriferous." [JR22/133]

Princesse Hohenzollern
Listed as 'S.A.R. Mme. la Princesse de Hohenzollern, Infante de Portugal'.

Principessa di Napoli (Bonfiglioli, 1897; or Bräuer/Ketten Bros., 1898)
From 'Duc de Magenta' (T) × 'Safrano' (T).
"Fresh pink with lilac." [Ÿ] "Pale rose, base of petals cream colour, fine long buds; hardy and free; vigorous." [P1] "Flower pale pink on a cream ground, large, full, solitary, long stem, scent of 'Maréchal Niel'. Bush floriferous and vigorous." [JR22/133]

[Professeur d'André] (Nabonnand, 1902)
From 'Papa Gontier' (T) × 'Gloire de Dijon' (N).
"Flower very large, semi-full; petals thick, form perfect; color, deep carminy pink marbled white; beautiful solitary deep carmine bud; petal edges silvery when opening; bush very vigorous and floriferous." [JR26/148]

Professeur Ganiviat (Perrier, 1890)
"Shaded fire-red." [RR] "Dark red." [LS] "Fair growth; good foliage. Medium sized wine-color blooms with orange glow in center; has cutting value." [ARA28/103] "Seems to be very floriferous; the flower is medium-sized, very full, a pretty color of cherry-red, and the bud is well formed." [JR14/166] "Growth very vigorous, very floriferous, flower well formed, large, full, stem firm, color poppy-red, shaded, not as dark as 'Souvenir de Thérèse Levet'." [JR14/164]

Queen Victoria
Listed as 'Souvenir d'un Ami'.

Rainbow (Sievers/Dingee & Conard, 1891)
Sport of 'Papa Gontier' (T).
"The color of this lovely rose is a deep Mermet pink, striped and splashed in the most fanciful way with rich Gontier shades, just sufficient to add greatly to its beauty; the base of the petals in of a rich amber. The flowers are well carried on long stiff stems of the same general character as those of the 'Papa Gontier', but are most decidedly larger, sweeter, of greater substance, and produced much more freely." [CA93] "Semi-double pale pink blooms striped with carmine-red." [HRG] "Rosy flesh, splashed crimson. Distinct and free." [H] "Originated in California, and resembles its parent in all features, even in color, which is a light yellow at the base, shading upwards to a bright red, while on the exterior of the petals there are silvery stripes." [JR16/38] "Has a resemblance to 'Mme. de Tartas'." [JR28/183] "Pretty; growth vigorous." [P1] "Though delicate, very nice." [JR36/188] Not to be confused with 'Improved Rainbow'.

[**Raoul Chauvry**] (Chauvry, 1896)
Seedling of 'Mme. Lambard' (T).
"Bush vigorous, compact, with erect canes, wood reddish. Thorns straight and few. Foliage soft and elegant; new shoots purple-red, which passes to reddish-green; buds very elongate; color, Nasturtium when opening; flowers large and double, fawn coppery yellow with copper tints, center sometimes apricot, fragrant." [JR20/163]

Rathswell
Listed as 'Mme. Therese Roswell'.

[**Recuerdo di Antonio Peluffo**] (Soupert & Notting, 1910)
From 'Mélanie Soupert' (N) × 'Mme. Constant Soupert' (T).
"Diaphanous light yellow, washed delicate pink along the edges. Flowers extremely large, of perfect form, produced continuously until late in the autumn...The plant is vigorous with quite decorative foliage; it produces long and elegant buds." [JR34/183] "An old Tea which rivals the best of the Hybrid Teas in size and cutting value. Variegated light yellow and pink. Strongly recommended for all southern climates." [ARA28/103] "Medium growth." [CaRoII/3/3]

Red Maman Cochet
Listed as 'Niles Cochet'.

Red Safrano
Listed as 'Safrano à Fleurs Rouges'.

Regulus (Robert & Moreau, 1860)
"Bright rose, shaded with copper, large and full." [FP] "Bright coppery and rose; pretty, habit vigorous." [JC] "Large regularly formed solid flowers, borne in great abundance on stout hardy bushes all through the growing season; color, clear rosy pink, very fragrant and desirable. A fine garden rose." [C&Js06] "Growth very vigorous; flower medium-sized, full, flat; petals fluted; very fragrant; color, intense coppery-pink, center darker." [S] Marcus Atilius Regulus, fl. 240 BC, Roman consul and general.

[Reichgraf E. von Kesselstatt] (Lambert, 1898)
From 'Princesse Alice de Monaco' (T) × 'Duchesse Marie Salviati' (T).
"Flowers extra large and quite full, petals broad and nicely arched, color brilliant carmine, passing to rose-pink on pure white ground; petals edged with rich crimson, very fragrant. The bush is a handsome erect grower and abundant bloomer." [C&Js99]

Reine des Fées
Listed as 'Rosalie'.

[Reine Emma des Pays-Bas] (Nabonnand, 1879) trans., "Queen Emma of The Netherlands"
"Yellow, shaded with reddish salmon." [EL] "Yellow, orange, red—looking just like a sunrise. It is large, full, very well formed, and well held." [JR3/156] "Its medium-sized flowers are semi-double, and divided into two parts; its color is sharp." [JR10/46] "Vigorous, nice foliage; flower very large, full, imbricated, perfect form, measuring as much as five inches across [ca. 1.25 dm]; color, gold tinted salmon with dawn-gold reflections, singularly beautiful; same coloration as 'Fortune's Double Yellow', but bigger and fuller." [S] "Reverse of petals almost flame-coloured, free growing, full size, vigorous and floriferous. Although quite distinct, the metallic blush of its flowers is remindful of 'L'Idéal'. A valuable and most desirable variety." [B&V]

[Reine Olga] (Nabonnand, 1885)
"Soft rosy pink, shaded with golden yellow; edge of petals silver rose." [C&Js07] "Full flowers; an exceedingly free bloomer." [C&Js11] "Very vigorous bush, with not very thorny big wood; flower large, full, imbricated, perfect form; color, nuanced coppery red; novel coloration; very fragrant." [JR9/166]

Rhodologue Jules Gravereaux (Dr. Fontes, 1908)
From 'Marie Van Houtte' (T) × 'Mme. Abel Chatenay' (HT).
"Yellowish pink, medium size, very full, light scent, moderate height." [Sn]

Rival de Pæstum (Beluze, 1841) trans., "Pæstum's Rival"
Considered a hybrid of China and Tea.
"Yellowish white, large, superb." [WRP] "Flower medium, full; floriferous; moderate vigor." [Cx] "Flower small, full." [S] "Beautiful, the flowers abundant, not full, but of charming purity and form." [Ro] "Bud tinged pink...white with blush and ivory base. Foliage dark...3×2 [ft; ca. 9×6 dm]." [B] "Young shoots, thorns, and leaves rich glaucous plum colour. Long creamy buds are borne erect, but nod to open into loose, semi-double, ivory-white blooms. Gracious and floriferous. Slight tea-scent. 4 ft [ca. 1.25 m]." [T3] Pæstum, in Italy, where in Augustan times the gardens were said by the poetically-inclined to bloom and bloom again.

[**Roi de Siam**] (Laffay, 1825)
"Pink." [RG] "Pinkish-yellow." [EER] "*Ovary*, ovoid. *Flower*, large, double, pale pink. Inner *petals*, narrow, with revolute edges." [Pf]

[**Rosa Mundi**] (Conard & Jones, 1898)
"Deep rich crimson, large cupped form, very free bloomer. A splendid rose that ought to be better known. Scarce and rare." [C&Js98]

[**Rosalie**] (Ellwanger & Barry, 1884) syn., 'Fairy Queen', 'Reine des Fées'
Seedling of 'Marie Van Houtte' (T).
"Medium-sized flowers, very full and regular; color clear, bright pink; deliciously scented; a profuse bloomer." [CA90] "Moderate growth, but very healthy. Its flowers are small, it is true, but of luxuriant bloom and well-scented. Carnation pink." [JR16/36] "Canes thin but vigorous; flower small but a little larger than 'Paquer-Lambard' [*???—evidently an early unreleased or re-named Polyantha cross of 'Paquerette' and 'Mme. Lambard'*]. In bud, it is very pretty; once open, it is robust and lasts a long time with a very elegant scent. One of its precious qualities is that it blooms well outside, and that each branch bears a flower. We regard it—its breeders say—as a charming rose in miniature, which, moreover, can be forced." [JR8/29-30]

[Rose d'Evian] (Bernaix, 1894)

"Pink, carmine center." [LS] "Long buds of a beautiful magenta red before expansion. Flower very large, quite double, cupped; petals numerous, thick, beautiful China pink, blush on the reverse, carminy on the obverse. Very fresh coloration." [JR18/163-164] "Stout stems and thick glossy green leaves. The flowers are large and handsome, somewhat cup-shaped, but well filled and very sweet. The color is deep rich rosy red, reverse of petals pale amaranth; makes extra long pointed buds, and blooms abundantly all through the Summer and Fall. 15 cts." [C&Js99] "D'Evian" refers to a French town in Haute Saône which had a yearly rose festival (those interested may see JR28/89, etc.).

Rose Nabonnand (Nabonnand, 1882)

"Large and beautiful; flowers quite full and regular; color, soft satiny rose, changing to salmon, elegantly tinted with amber and pale yellow; very pretty and highly scented." [CA90] "Very vigorous bush, big-wooded; thorns rare, but protrusive; flower very large, very full, imbricated; color, delicate pink towards the center...very floriferous; good variety for the North." [JR6/186]

Rosette Delizy (P. Nabonnand, 1922)

From 'Général Galliéni' (T) × 'Comtesse Bardi' (T).

"Yellow blooms with petals blushing pink to chestnut red as they open, pronounced tea fragrance." [HRG] "Flower large, full, well-formed; cadmium-yellow, with apricot reflexes, outer petals dark carmine. Very vigorous; profuse bloomer." [ARA23/152] "Although called yellow by its introducer, this nice little rose reminded us very much of 'Mrs. B.R. Cant', with much exaggerated light shadings." [ARA27/143] "Rose-pink, buff and apricot...deeper colouring on the outside...vigorous...4×3 [ft; ca. 1.25 × 9 dm]." [B] "Perfect foliage, immune to mildew...strongly recommended." [Capt28] "The combination of colors (yellow, buff, gold, coral, pink, rose) and form often attain a singular perfection of beauty, particularly during the cooler months when the coloration is more delicate. The blossoms unfurl slowly, meanwhile wafting a delicious 'tropical fruit punch' perfume. The flower stems are strong and hold the blossoms upright if not beaten down by the rain. The plant blooms abundantly, in bursts, and grows vigorously, quickly reaching six feet or so [ca. 1.75+ m]. One hears that there are several slightly differing roses under this name on the market; the vendor should be quizzed as to the vigor and appearance of the particular 'Rosette Delizy' being sold, though it should be kept in mind that some variance is caused by whether the specimen is own-root or on a rootstock, and, in the latter case, what rootstock was used." [BCD]

Rosomane Narcisse Thomas (Bernaix fils, 1908) trans., "Rose-Enthusiast Narcisse Thomas"
"Crimson to burnt orange. Small." [ARA27/19] "Fine variegated copper, orange and red blooms. Very prolific. Most valuable for southern zones." [ARA28/104] "Wonderful color; good growth, foliage, and blooming qualities; flowers small, most attractive in bud-form." [ARA18/114] "Vigorous, beautiful brilliant foliage, bud develops an unusual intensity of color. Flower medium, scarlet with dawn copper red upon opening, large nub of apricot yellow. Outermost petals colored reddish violet at the tip. This variety has quite novel tintings; a thoroughly curious coloration." [JR32/135]

Rubens (Robert & Moreau, 1859)
"Creamy-white with pale gold base, very double...blushing pink on edge." [HRG] "Rosy-flesh, deeper at centre, large, full, well formed, fine in the bud. An excellent variety." [EL] "White, shaded with rose, centres bronzy yellow, large and full; form cupped, fine; growth vigorous. A good and distinct sort." [P1] "Fragrant; moderate vigor." [Cx] "White shaded rose...and if it can be grown with that delicate shade of pink it is magnificent. A red sandstone loam suits this variety best." [FRB] "Resembles ['Souvenir de la Malmaison'] a little in form, but its color is white washed with pink and not flesh." [JR20/44] "Of elegant bearing, very remontant, and delicately colored." [JF] "A good grower, producing strong clean

shoots with very fine foliage, and quite capable as a short standard of covering the wall of a one-storied building. It is not liable to mildew, and the blooms, which are slightly pendant, can stand a little rain. They can be generally relied on to come of good shape, but the petals are thin and the form fleeting. The fine half-open buds are well supported by grand foliage, but the flowers are difficult to exhibit well, as they look weak and unsubstantial when shown with other Teas. It is pretty hardy, best as a standard and in cool weather; capital, early and late, against a dwarf wall: very free blooming and a good autumnal, thriving well on lightish soil." [F-M2] "Vigorous, with slender, nodding branches; bark smooth, light green; prickles reddish, elongate, compressed, enlarged at the base, upright, pointed; foliage glossy, of a handsome green, of 3-5 rounded-acuminate, finely dentate leaflets; leafstalk green, armed with several very fine little prickles; flower to 3.5 inches across [ca. 8 cm], full, globular, solitary, sometimes in twos or threes on vigorous branches…petals large, those of the center small and folded; flower stalk smooth, green, slender and nodding; very remontant; tender." [S] "Old but still pretty, and almost certain to give the first blossom of the season." [JR12/180] Not to be confused with Laffay's amaranthine HP of 1859, nor with Verdier's "pansy-colored" HP of 1864. Peter Paul Rubens, Flemish painter; lived 1577-1640.

[S.A.R. Mme. la Princesse de Hohenzollern, Infante de Portugal] (Nabonnand, 1886) syn., 'Princesse Hohenzollern'; trans., "Her Royal Highness the Princess of Hohenzollern, Royal-Daughter of Portugal"
"Extra large, perfectly formed flowers, very full and double; color, a handsome shade of bright peachy red, passing to rich crimson." [CA90] "Very vigorous; flower very large, full, of perfect form; color, bright red, sparkling, outer petals darker than the central ones…Flower very fragrant, very floriferous." [JR10/169] "Noted for strong vigorous growth and beautiful dark green foliage…[*flowers*] often borne in clusters.

Safrano (Beauregard, 1839; poss. 1837)

Seedling from 'Parks' Yellow Tea-Scented China'. (Fatherhood ascribed to the Bourbon 'Mme. Desprez' is supposititious and doubtful.)

"Apricot yellow. Very free." [H] "Bright fawn." [HoBoIV/320] "When the bud opens in the morning, [it] is a fine saffron or dark orange colour, and is beautiful; in the forenoon it is blush, and in the afternoon a very poor white not worth notice." [Bu] "Large, double, dark yellow, copper towards the center." [JR1/2/8] "A fresh butter-yellow, washed carmine; flower large, imbricated, fragrant; very floriferous, vigorous." [Cx] "Pale apricot-buff with peach." [HRG] "Pointed flowers, semi-double...4×3 [ft; ca. 1.25 × .9 m]." [B] "Lovely buds of sunset coloring." [ARA29/95] "Saffron to apricot in the bud, changing to pale buff, large and double; form cupped. A pretty and hardy variety, worthy of a place in every collection; growth vigorous." [P1] "Scarcely excelled by any [*other*] rose. Its half-opened bud is very beautiful, and of a rich, deep fawn color. When open, its form is poor, and its color a much lighter fawn. These fawn-colored roses have peculiar charms for us; and of them all, there are none more beautiful or richer than 'Safrano'." [SBP] "The action of light on the buds at an early stage is very remarkable in this Rose; frequently giving to the backs of half unfolded petals a perfectly rosy hue, distinctly defined by the expansion of the overlapping ones." [C] "Opens pale, with a poor centre of short petals." [Hk] "Does not last." [Capt27] "Carnation-scented." [JR33/101] "The seed organs are better developed than in almost any other kind." [EL] "Continuous supply of flowers." [L] "Never ceases blooming till the frosts." [K1] "Useful as a low decorative. Good growth and foliage; color pretty, not of best; excellent blooming qualities." [ARA18/114] "Foliage mildews, but it is a profuse and constant bloomer in Southern Zones." [Th2] "Bronze foliage." [ARA40/36] "Good, early, vigorous—but less good late in the season; it loses its leaves." [JR9/70] "A certain amount of shade during part of the day can promote production of semi-climbing canes—no doubt a remembrance of its parent's habit." [BCD]

"It is to a devoted rose amateur, Monsieur de Beauregard—reserve officer, chevalier in the Legion of Honor—that we owe the development of the beautiful Tea rose 'Safrano'...This variety so precious to florists dates to 1839, and came most probably, according to particular information, from the seed of ['Parks' Yellow Tea-Scented China'], the one rose which set seed in those days." [JF] "Suffice it to say that 'Safrano', raised at Angers by Monsieur de Beauregard in 1837, is one of the prettiest yellow varieties known; it came from our old Yellow Tea, and was entered into commerce in the Autumn without much hoopla; the journals of the time don't mention it...Branches smooth, furnished with occasional thorns which are short and purple; very ample foliage, dark green above, glaucous beneath, on the old wood, and a very elegant purple—quite bright—on the young branches, particularly beneath. Leaves of five elliptical leaflets, very slightly dentate, slightly stalked; stipules smooth, narrow, finely and delicately ciliate; leafstalk articulated at the second pair of leaflets, and bearing two or three prickles beneath, as well as numerous stiff hairs. Flower stem feeble, light red, bristling with glandular hairs, long, nearly 2 inches [ca. 6 cm]; it its position on an aborted branch adds as much again to its length...the ovary is short, inflated, smooth, purplish; the sepals short, often entire, or with only two very small projections like long teeth; they are slightly rugose, ciliate, lanate within; bud elongate, ovoid. Bush vigorous, easily recognized in the Spring by the purple of its young foliage. The beauty, the delicious scent, the elegant poise of the Tea Rose 'Safrano' assure it a foremost place in all collections." [PlB]

[**Safrano à Fleurs Rouges**] (Oger, 1867) syn., 'Mme. Joséphine Mühle', 'Red Safrano'; trans., "Safrano with Red Flowers"
Seemingly a sport of 'Safrano' (T)?
"Saffron yellow, shaded with coppery red, semi-double; a peculiar scent, not pleasing." [EL] "Medium growth; flower medium-sized, fairly full; color, shining red nuanced copper-yellow. Cultivated in America on a grand scale for its attractive bud which wafts a delicious aroma." [S]

Santa Rosa (Burbank, 1899)

From 'Hermosa' (B) × a seedling of 'Bon Silène' (T); *or* from a seedling of 'Hermosa' (B) × 'Bon Silène' (T).

"Shell pink, inclining to crimson." [CA02] "An elegant new Tea Rose from California. It somewhat resembles 'Hermosa', but is larger and more beautiful. The flowers are large, round, full and sweet; the color is rich rosy pink, shading to coppery red. It is a constant and abundant bloomer and quite hardy." [C&Js99] "Another exceptional quality…is the power of resistance…to those ever-present foes of the rose family, mildew and rust." [Lu]

[**Sappho**] (W. Paul, 1889)

"Large, full and globular flowers; rich apricot yellow, delicately tinged with fawn and pale rose; strong and vigorous grower." [CA93] "Buds peacock [*sic: "paon"; prob. "peony"/"pivoine" was intended*] in color, with a pink nuance; flowers open with a shade of yellow and hazel-buff-yellow, large and full; this pretty and distinctive rose is of strong build, stronger than 'Homère'; it produces its flowers with a profusion which is extraordinary for a Tea; petals large and of good substance, and we know of no other variety which keeps so long in a good state, as well on the plant as when cut…'beautiful, very full and thick blossoms of an apricot-yellow, with a delicious 'Gloire de Dijon' scent'." [JR13/70-71] Sappho, Greek poetess long thought—ev. incorrectly—to be the first to bestow on roses their title of "Queen of Flowers."

[**Sénateur Loubet**] (Reboul, 1891)

"Dwarf, but vigorous; very large, finely formed flowers. Outer petals light tender rose; center, metal yellow color, heightening sometimes to crimson." [CA96] "Very floriferous; flowers large, very full, center petals finely serrated, [*serration*] gradually enlarging around the exterior petals; petal-color delicate pink, on a ground of metallic yellow towards the center, changing to poppy red when fully open. Novel coloration." [JR15/165-166]

[**Senator McNaughton**] (California Nursery Co.?, by 1895)
Sport of 'Perle des Jardins' (T).
"A sport of 'Perle des Jardins', to which it is similar in every respect except-
ing color; rich glossy foliage, sturdy habit of growth, and extremely free-
flowering. The flowers are very large and full, with excellent shaped buds.
Color, a delicate creamy white." [CA95]

[**Shirley Hibberd**] (Levet, 1874)
Seedling of 'Mme. Falcot' (T).
"Moderate growth, floriferous; blossom medium-sized, full; color, buff
nankeen yellow." [S]

[**Simone Thomas**] (Introducer unknown, by 1927)
"Carmine to coppery red. Mildews." [ARA27/19] Otherwise unknown.
Probably 'Margherita di *Simone*' grown by Capt. *Thomas*.

[**Smith's Yellow China**] (Smith, 1834) syn., 'Smithii'
From 'Blush Noisette' (N) × 'Parks' Yellow Tea-Scented China' (T).
"Sulphur yellow, full, cupped, large beautiful." [LF] "Fine straw-color; a
beautiful rose." [HstI:308] "White, center yellow." [R-H56] "Lemon,
center yellow, large and very full, a superb rose, but often disfigured by a
green centre; only fit for forcing." [JC] "Pale straw colour, large and full;
form, globular. A fine forcing Rose, but seldom opens well out of doors."
[P] "Growing freely...opening in great profusion, except in time of
rain...pale lemon-yellow before the sun destroys it...delightfully fragrant." [Bu] "Vigorous; branches green, touched with violet where the sun
hits them; flower...sulphur yellow." [S] "Vigorous bush; wood brownish
with dark purple thorns which are remote, wide, short, and upright; leaves
petiolate, alternate, with five oval, nearly rounded leaflets, which are dentate, which terminate in a more or less sharp point, and which are a fresh
green. Purplish bracts. Blossoms well formed, lemon yellow, very full and
fragrant, 130-160 short petals, which are slightly rolled and well arranged.
We received this rose from England last month under the name 'Noisette

Jaune', a name we believe should be kept for it, despite certain persons who claim that it comes from the Chinas. These people base their belief on the fact that, previously, it hadn't bloomed in a cluster. Hopefully, the weak specimen I have received will show that particular characteristic in due course. Furthermore, the doubleness of the blossom is such that we haven't been able to tell if the stamens' filaments are free or united. Whatever the case, should there be an error in its classification, we won't fail to put it right once we have a chance to study it more closely. Setting aside such matters—this rose, which blooms all year, is a precious introduction, and will certainly pique the curiosity of fanciers. We think that it will endure the Winter out in the open; however, as it is indeed a rarity, we advise its possessors to let it spend that season in a greenhouse or frame. Propagated by graft, budding, and layering." [An33/19-20]

Smithii
Listed as 'Smith's Yellow China'.

Snowbird
Listed as a Hybrid Tea.

Socrate (Robert & Moreau, 1858)
"Pink, center peach." [LS] "Large, full, deep pink, apricot at the center." [JR3/28] "Dark rose with an apricot yellow heart." [JR10/47] "Deep rose, tinged with fawn, large or medium size, double or full. Quite a good Tea." [EL] "Vigorous; flower large, full, flat, very pronounced peach scent." [S] "Bright salmon and fawn, large and full, habit free; a most distinct and beautiful rose." [JC] Socrates, the great Athenian philosopher; lived 470?-399 BC.

Souvenir d'Auguste Legros (Bonnaire, 1889) trans., "In Memory of Auguste Legros"
"Growth very vigorous, somewhat bushy, of the 'Souvenir de Thérèse Levet' sort, but developing larger, erect branches; foliage glossy green; flower handsome fiery red mixed with dark crimson; blossom very large;

beautiful elongated bud, one of the largest among the Teas. Flower stem strong." [JR13/162]

Souvenir d'Elisa Vardon (Marest, 1854) trans., "In Memory of Elisa Vardon" "Outer petals cream, centre salmon and fawn, petals large, flowers full and generally perfect, though occasionally producing a hard centre; a most superb rose." [JC] "High centre…pale rosy salmon, more cream inside." [Hk] "Medium-sized, full, well-formed, soft salmon-pink." [JR2/142] "Yellowish-rose centre; very large and globular; foliage copper-coloured. Although at times difficult to grow, this beautiful rose should not be left out." [DO] "Fragrant, coppery-yellow overlaid with cream…3×3 [ft; ca. 1×1 m]." [B] "Flesh color, shaded with rosy salmon, large, full; highly esteemed in England, but we have never admired it; refinement is lacking in the flower." [EL] "The petals are shell-shaped, of notable substance; its form is wonderful, and lasts in good condition for a long time…Its color is a very light straw-yellow with yellowish-white, a little darker at the center, and lightly tinted pink around the edges of the young flowers. This variety has only moderate growth, but each bud formed will produce a pretty flower." [JR15/120] "Cream with rosy tint, a magnificent tea, if it is grown well. Unfortunately, it lacks vigor." [FRB] "Of great substance; the flowers are usually few but fine." [P2] "Not perpetual enough." [JR9/70] "Massive roses. Heavy foliage." [Dr] "Not liable to mildew, but easily injured by rain…when fine, the finest of all show roses…not for general cultivation." [F-M2] "Seems to be very hardy." [l'H55/31] "Wood big, strong; long internodes. The smooth epidermis is, when young, reddish purple and covered with a bloom…Thorns, fairly numerous…Leaves, pretty ample…smooth and a slightly yellowish light green, glossy, when growing frequently tinted purple above; beneath, whitish green, having a cottony appearance…Flower stems thick, long, strong, firmly supporting the blossoms…Buds, fairly large, long, usually solitary at the branch-ends, flesh-pink and maroon-red when the sepals open…Flowers large (about 3.5 inches [ca. 8 cm]), very full, quite regular; outer petals very large, thick, compressed slightly, concave, reflexing strongly, however, at the tip, containing numerous smaller petals, crowded, also concave, but only with difficulty reflexing at the tip, giving the blossom a lightness, the form of an elegant cup, the edges of which are recurved; always opens well, whatever the weather; color, delicate flesh-pink shaded chamois-yellow, becoming a nearly white flesh around the edges; center, a pronounced coppery pink; the petal tips are often a brighter purplish-pink than the petal reverse. Scent, the usual tea-scent, but weaker…The growth of this rose, which is vigorous and easy, assures it a flowering both abundant and prolonged…Placed under the protection of a young girl, 'Souvenir d'Elisa Vardon' offers a touching and symbolic reminder of grace and charm, qualities which it so effectively brings to mind." [PlB] "Exquisite." [H]

Souvenir d'un Ami (Bélot-Défougère, 1846) syn., 'Mme. Tixier', 'Queen Victoria'; trans., "In Remembrance of a Friend"
Affiliated with 'Adam' (T).
"We have just received from Monsieur Bélot-Défougère, horticulturist at Moulins, some samples of his magnificent Tea Rose 'Souvenir d'un Ami'; it is a wonderful introduction, considering its form and size, its typical Tea Rose fragrance, and its color, a beautiful dark delicate pink. I believe it to be the most beautiful Tea yet, with its abundant and lasting bloom-period…This rose, as with all Teas, gives better blossoms in September than during its first bloom in June." [R-H46] "Variable somewhat as to colour, but usually a pale or a deep rose; large, well-formed, and free." [DO] "One of the largest…a clear pale flesh, and may be termed of robust habit." [WHoIII] "Moderately full, globular, delicate pink, flowers drooping on long stalks. Growth regular; fragrant." [Hn] "Very full; fine handsome foliage; a most superb rose for forcing or out of doors." [JC] "The queen of the tea-scented roses, and will rank the very first among them. Its habit is good, it blooms freely, and its large and beautifully imbricated flowers, when open, much resemble those of 'Souvenir de la Malmaison'. Its color is a delicate salmon, shaded with rose, and its general character

highly recommends it as first-rate in every respect." [SBP] "Petals of the circumference are large, those of the center muddled and folded; flower stem pretty thick; brown. Calyx rounded. Much recommended; one of the most vigorous of the Teas; flowers well formed; very beautiful bud; very attractive tea scent." [JF] "Flower soon loses its colour and is apt to look dirty." [F-M2] "Vigorous; branches slender and flexuous; bark reddish-green, primarily where the sun strikes; thorns brownish-red, very clinging, hooked, and very sharp; leaves olive green, lustrous, of 3-5 oval, rounded, pointed leaflets; leafstalks reddish, long, flexible, armed with a few sharp, hooked prickles; flower to three inches across [ca. 7.5 cm], globular, concave, often solitary; color, light flesh-pink." [S] "Constitution is hardy, the foliage fine." [P2] "One of the brightest and most refreshing of the Teas." [Wr]
"One of the roses for memory. Bright pink, sweet-scented, hopeful, and as constant as the summer days, equally as interesting as its claims of beauty, life, and strength, is its tender history...not a line of prose or poetry has ever revealed the secret of its name...Motives of delicacy seem to have prompted withholding the name of the friend. Was it death or estrangement? Was it a name under political ban? The name of the remembered friend folded forever in the heart of the rose; by whom and for whom named a mystery." [Dr] "The rose in question is still new...It was two months or more ago that this Rose was added to our catalog of species and varieties in our trial garden...We have been able to judge and predict for this rose the success which it merits. It is an introduction raised at Moulins...by an amateur, and which was sold to Monsieur Bélot-Défougère, who brought it into commerce. The name of the plant alludes to the friend who negotiated the deal...A superb flower of the most beautiful intense flesh that one could hope to see. Petals numerous, imbricated, and in a rosette as with the Centifolia, substantial, one could call it immortal, giving this pretty rose a charm and a perfect form...flower stem brown, thick, strong. Ovary short, green; sepals entire, elongate, ciliated with small glandular hairs...In 'Souvenir d'un Ami', the delicacy of the

tints and the brilliant sparkle of the nuances last as long as the blossom, and thus prolong the Spring-like charms up to the hoarfrost of Winter." [PlB] "One of the wonders and delights of my childhood was a fine plant...which grew up a pillar in the conservatory in Fir Grove near by. And when once the dear owners bestowed one of its flowers upon me, I think there was not a happier little girl in all Hampshire...I determined it should be the first Tea Rose I planted when I made my garden here...It never gets any special attention...But each year its great bell-shaped fragrant flowers on their long slender stems show grandly against the Rhododendrons." [K1] "Monsieur Bélot-Défougère, having sold his nursery, has kept his seed business." [l'H52/188] "A distinguished horticulturist, Monsieur Belot-Défougères [*sic*], died January 13 [,1868,] at Moulins (Allier), where he had a horticultural establishment. He was 69 years old. Monsieur Belot-Défougères had retired a long time since, and had turned over his firm to Monsieur Marie, who still maintains the premises." [R-H68]

[**Souvenir d'Espagne**] (Pries/Ketten Bros., 1888) trans., "Recollection of Spain"
"Yellow, pink, and white." [LS] "A grand new Tea Rose; color coppery yellow and rose beautifully blended; very fine in bud; a strong grower and free bloomer." [CA93] "Flower reddish orange on a yellow orange ground; petals edged with a large border of pinkish carmine; reverse of petals blush white; medium-sized or large; pretty full, cupped, very fragrant, opening well. Moderate bush with very rich and continuous bloom. Coloration novel and ravishing." [JR12/181] "Hybrid of Tea and China." [JR24/44]

Souvenir de Catherine Guillot
Listed as a China.

[**Souvenir de Clairvaux**] (E. Verdier, 1890) trans., "Recollection of Clairvaux"
"Bush of good vigor with strong, erect canes; leaves composed of five undulate leaflets which are glossy, deep green, reddish in youth, and irregularly

but fairly deeply toothed; thorns not very numerous, strong, hooked, blackish; flowers medium to large, quite full, well formed, borne on a strong and rigid stem; color, very fresh, a beautiful China pink shade, petal bases apricot yellow washed nankeen and tinted carmine; excellent variety, very floriferous, very nice scent." [JR14/163] "Color of '[Mlle.] Thérèse Levet' [*the HP*]." [CA96]

[**Souvenir de David d'Angers**] (Moreau-Robert, 1856) trans., "In Memory of David d'Angers"
Reputedly descended from 'Caroline' (T).
"Glistening dark red, shaded maroon." [RR] "Rosy-salmon, fine petal, flowers very large and double; a most deliciously fragrant rose, and very beautiful." [JC] "Bright cherry-color, distinct and good." [FP] "Double, bright cerise, in clusters." [JDR56/41] "Flower large, full, well-formed; color, dark red nuanced maroon and violet. Growth moderate." [S] Pierre Jean David d'Angers, sculptor; lived 1788-1856.

Souvenir de François Gaulain (Guillot & fils, 1889) trans., "In Memory of François Gaulain"
"Vigorous growth; flowers large, full, well-formed; varies from magenta red nuanced violet to dark violet shaded crimson." [JR13/181]

[**Souvenir de Gabrielle Drevet**] (Guillot & fils, 1884) trans., "In Memory of Gabrielle Drevet"
"A rare shade of salmon, red, or terra cotta, delicately toned with violet crimson; a very striking and novel color; deliciously fragrant and very beautiful." [CA90] "Vigorous, flowers large, full, well formed and well held; color, whitish salmon, center bright pink, on a ground of coppery yellow, passing to light salmon; very fragrant." [JR8/133] "Fair form and very sweet." [B&V]

Souvenir de Geneviève Godard (Godard, 1893) trans., "In Memory of Geneviève Godard"
"China pink." [Ÿ]

[**Souvenir de George Sand**] (Widow Ducher, 1876) trans., "In Memory of George Sand"

"Very vigorous, short canes, flower very large, full, very well formed, tulip-form; color, salmony yellow, reverse of petals ribboned lilac." [JR1/1/8] "Fine, large full flowers; bright carmine buds, changing when open to reddish amber, veined with brilliant crimson; very fragrant." [CA90] "Flower large, full, tulip-formed; color, salmon pink, sometimes light coppery pink; much to be recommended for forcing; the bud is generally used like that of 'Safrano' for making bouquets." [S] George Sand, *nom de plume* of Amandine Aurore Lucie (née Dupin), Baronne Dudevant; French novelist; lived 1804-1876.

Souvenir de Germain de Saint-Pierre (Nabonnand, 1882) trans., "In Memory of Germain de Saint-Pierre"

"Very vigorous, blooms in clusters, flower very large, semi-double, with very large petals of purple-red, unique in the sort. Constant bloom, at least as abundant as 'Safrano'. This wonderful rose for Winter bloom is named in memory of our late collaborator [*on the Journal des Roses*]." "Very showy and attractive...large, full and sweet." [CA90] "Germain de Saint-Pierre, Commandeur de l'Ordeur Impérial de la Rose. President (1870-1872) of the Société Botanique de France." [JR2/40]

Souvenir de Gilbert Nabonnand (P. Nabonnand, 1920) trans., "In Memory of Gilbert Nabonnand"

"Fire-red to apricot-yellow. Shy bloomer in late fall." [ARA27/19] "Variegated copper and pink, fine growth; foliage immune to mildew; good cutting value; continuous and prolific bloomer; holds foliage tenaciously. Entirely distinct, and strongly recommended for southern seacoast climates." [ARA28/104] "Gilbert Nabonnand, who died at Golfe-Juan last January 6 [1902] in his 76th year. Born at Grézolles, near Roanne (Loire) May 20, 1829, he worked in the fields as a laborer until he was 16. The love of flowers which he had made him enter into a two-year apprenticeship at Vienne (Isère) at a nursery where he began his horticultural education. After two more years at a tree-farm in Lyon, he was 20, and entered the establishment of Monsieur Guillot...After completing his education at various other firms, he was at the age at which it is necessary to decide upon which road to take in life. He established himself at Sorgues (Vaucluse), where he grew fruit-trees, conifers, and shrubs. Then, in 1858, he moved to Avignon, where he took up roses exclusively. Finally, in 1864, having been tempted by the luxuriant vegetation and enchanting venues offered by the coastal Mediterranean area, he fixed on Golfe-Juan, in the Alpes-Maritimes, where he created a horticultural establishment of the first rank." [JR27/23]

Souvenir de J.-B. Guillot
Listed as a China.

[**Souvenir de Jeanne Cabaud**] (P. Guillot, 1896) syn., 'Yellow Maman Cochet'; trans., "In Memory of Jeanne Cabaud"
"A grand new rose, producing in the greatest profusion extra large fully double flowers, beautiful coppery yellow, finely tinted with apricot and rosy carmine, exceedingly beautiful and a good healthy grower; quite hardy." [C&Js06] "Vigorous bush; flower large, full, well formed; exterior petals coppery yellow, center petals carminy apricot yellow. Fragrant, very beautiful." [JR20/147]

[**Souvenir de l'Amiral Courbet**] (Pernet père, 1885) trans., "In Memory of Admiral Courbet"
"Round, globular flowers, very solid and compact, and borne in large clusters; color, bright fiery red, very lively and striking; highly scented." [CA90] "Moderately vigorous, with strong and upright canes; flower medium-sized, nearly full, bright red; flower-stem upright and strong; abundant bloom. This variety will be of much merit for borders and bedding as well as pot culture; at first bloom, average stems bear 20-25 buds on the same shoot—better than the Polyanthas." [JR9/148]

[**Souvenir de Lady Ashburton**] (C. Verdier, 1890) trans., "In Memory of Lady Ashburton"
"A fine shade of rich coppery red, delicately suffused with pale orange yellow; highly scented with true Tea Rose odor." [CA96] "Flower very variable, coppery red, salmon yellow, sometimes red, sometimes bright red, light yellow, showing all shades, sometimes separate, sometimes mixed, depending upon the stage of bloom." [JR16/156]

Souvenir de Laurent Guillot (Bonnaire, 1894) trans., "In Memory of Laurent Guillot"
"Very vigorous, beautiful bronze-green foliage; thorns pink; flower large, very full, beautiful China pink with a peach yellow center, petal edges carmine. Very pretty." [JR18/130]

[**Souvenir de Marie Detrey**] (Widow Ducher, 1877)
"Bush vigorous, flower large, full, well-formed, delicate salmony pink, sometimes bright pink." [JR1/12/12] "Canes deep green at the base, olive green on the young branches; thorns flat, irregular, and not very numerous; flower large, well-formed, petals thick, making the flower substantial; color, delicate salmony pink." [S]

[**Souvenir de Mme. Lambard**] (California Nursery Co.?, by 1890) trans., "In Memory of Mme. Lambard"
Conjecturally, a sport of 'Mme. Lambard' (T).
"Large canary colored flowers, exquisitely shaded and tinted with salmon rose; a fine vigorous grower and free bloomer." [CA90]

[**Souvenir de Mme. Levet**] (E. Levet, 1891) trans., "In Memory of Mme. Levet"
From 'Mme. Caro' (T) × 'Mme. Eugène Verdier' (T).
"Vigorous bush, blossom large, full, well formed, opening very well, stem very strong; color, beautiful deep orange yellow, very fragrant; petals very thick, keeping their tints well. Heavy wood, few thorns, growing to 4-5 dm [ca. 1.5 feet]; its beautiful dark green foliage attracts notice because of its shade and good poise. The plant is extra floriferous." [JR15/164]

Souvenir de Mme. Sablayrolles (Bonnaire, 1890) trans., "In Memory of Mme. Sablayrolles"
From 'Devoniensis' (T) × 'Souvenir d'Elisa Vardon' (T).
"Growth very vigorous, with erect branches having handsome somber green foliage; flower stem very strong, flower large, full, beautiful globular form, nearly always solitary; color, apricot pink nuanced yellow, the edge of the petals bordered carmine fading to cream white." [JR14/146]

[**Souvenir de Paul Neyron**] (Levet, 1871) trans., "In Memory of Paul Neyron"
Two parentages are given: (1) From 'Devoniensis' (T) × 'Souvenir de la Malmaison' (B); (2) Seedling of 'Ophirie' (N)
"White, with rose and buff tint, flowers large, full, and very distinct; a first-rate rose, habit free." [JC] "An elegant sort; color white, beautifully tinged with clear golden yellow, each petal edged with bright rosy crimson; very distinct and fine; the flowers are of medium size, very full and double, with delicious tea scent; a profuse bloomer." [CA88] "Very vigorous, very floriferous…Flower large, full, semi-globular, very fragrant; color, salmon yellow bordered pink." [S] "Of rather weak growth with small foliage, though occasionally a plant will grow pretty well…It is a good autumnal where it will grow sufficiently, and very free-flowering in the season, every wood bud over the plant trying to grow as soon as the flower buds are formed." [F-M3]

Souvenir de Pierre Notting (Soupert & Notting, 1902) trans., "In Memory of Pierre Notting"
From 'Maréchal Niel' (N) × 'Maman Cochet' (T).
"Beautiful apricot yellow; flower very large, very full, quartered; very floriferous; very vigorous." [Cx] "Dark yellow to apricot. Discolors in wet weather." [Capt27] "Large, very double, high centered; pale yellow tipped w/pinkish and red. Profuse, continuous bloom…2-4 [ft; ca. 6 dm-1.25 dm]." [Lg] "Fragrant, double, orange-copper." [ARA29/95] "Often with lilac splashes near edges; form full…Foliage generally well retained and

immune from mildew under worst conditions." [Th2] "Small and delicate; delicious Tea odor. Bush slim." [ARA26/96] "Large, finely formed buds and flowers...Good foliage. Strong bushy grower. Averages 50 blooms per season." [ARA21/92] "The bush is compact, with glossy foliage, and produces an abundance of flowers of a thrilling beauty. The bud is much bigger and longer than that of 'Maman Cochet'." [JR22/181] "The buds...are long and shapely, and of apricot-yellow colouring, though they are none too double, and in hot weather quickly open to full flowers. It grows well, and is quite a good Tea rose for the garden." [OM] "Weak outside petal...free flowering." [F-M] "The cross was made in May, 1894, and yielded 26 seeds which were sown November 17 of the same year. Of those, 12 successfully sprouted in March and April, 1895. One of these plants bloomed at the end of April, and was noted down as 'bud and flower very elongated' in the way of 'Maman Cochet'. Four open-air stocks were grafted from this mother plant, and bloomed magnificently in August, 1895. Ravishing in the beauty of their blossoms, we referred to them by the name 'Yellow Maman Cochet'. The plant is of great vigor without being climbing; the wood is reddish, the foliage large and of a pretty somber green, and isn't attacked by silver-leaf or mildew. The blossoms, of exceptional size, are full, of an admirable elongated form, and well-held...I might add to the distinction of this flower by mentioning that it is of quite long duration, ordinarily 10-15 days...The color is a very delicate China pink strongly tinted saffron, the center pure golden yellow...In floriferousness it surpasses all the varieties which might be mentioned...[under glass,] the exterior petals do not fall—they dry up, and the inner petals grow and renew the blossom...Sometimes neither pistils nor stamens but rather small petals are found in the center of the blossom. These develop slowly, and thus help the duration of the flower." [JR23/109] "Excellent in every way." [K2]

Souvenir de Thérèse Levet (Levet, 1882) trans., "In Memory of Thérèse Levet"
From 'Adam' (T) × ? 'Safrano à Fleurs Rouges' (T).
"Crimson-maroon. Medium size." [ARA27/19] "Crimson, shaded pink at the center, beautiful in bud." [JR11/50] "A magnificent variety with large pink blossoms." [JR8/146] "Wood strong; foliage dark green; large, hooked thorns; flower large, poppy red, shaded." [S] "Pretty good growth and foliage…late in blooming and fairly hardy…remarkable for its colour, which is a deep, dull, and sometimes blotchy crimson, forming a great contrast to the bright light colours common to the rest of this section. The blooms do not often come perfect, but are fine when they do, and very lasting. If the colour were bright, pure, and velvety, it would be much better, but as it is it does not show well against the pure whites, pinks, and yellows of its sisters in a stand of Teas. Perhaps it ought to be more cultivated, but most fanciers of Tea Roses seem half ashamed of it, as if it had no business to be dark red; and it is not in general highly esteemed in this country, but does much better in hot climates, being very popular in Australia. 'Francis Dubreuil'…is very like this Rose, and perhaps in some respects a little improvement on it." [F-M2] Inexplicably, this is often seen with the Levet transformed into "Lovet."

Souvenir de Victor Hugo (Bonnaire, 1885) trans., "In Memory of Victor Hugo"
From 'Comtesse de Labarthe' (T) × 'Regulus' (T).
"Vigorous with upright branches; flower-stem strong; flower large, full, very well formed, beautiful intense sparkling China pink, center nasturtium yellow; reverse of petals silvery, bright carmine red at the edge." [JR9/136] Victor Marie Hugo, novelist and dramatist; lived 1802-1885.

[**Souvenir de William Robinson**] (Bernaix fils, 1899) trans., "In Memory of William Robinson"
"Salmon-carmine to nankeen. Mildews." [ARA27/20] "Very graceful ovoid bud, middle chamois to the base, and pale blush yellow in the outer

two rows, like 'William Allen Richardson'. Flower well formed, variegated, nearly quadri-colored, peony-pink—very freshly so, or with salmon—partly cream white, and apricot yellow with violet veins." [JR23/168] "Vigorous…This variety often varies in its shadings." [JR25/10]

[**Souvenir du Dr. Passot**] (Godard/E. Verdier, 1889) trans., "In Memory of Dr. Passot"
"Velvet carmine." [RR] "Vigorous growth; flowers large, full; color, velvety crimson red fading lighter." [JR13/181]

[**Souvenir du Général Charreton**] (Reboul, 1887) trans., "In Memory of General Charreton"
"Bush vigorous, with upright branches; foliage light green, the young growths being bronzy green; flower large, full, opening well, exterior petals white lightly edged with delicate pink; flower-center is China pink, sometimes nuanced with red, with a yellow nub at the base." [JR11/165]

[**Souvenir du père Lalanne**] (Nabonnand, 1895) trans., "In Memory of father Lalanne"
"Flower large, full, with large petals; color, bright carmine rd, golden center; beautiful long deep carmine bud; beautiful foliage. Bush very vigorous, very floriferous. Very beautiful variety." [JR19/180]

Souvenir du Rosiériste Rambaux (Rambaux/Dubreuil, 1883) trans., "In Memory of Rose-Grower Rambaux"
Seedling of 'Goubault' (T).
"This graceful gem should be a part of every collection, possessing as it does everything that one could wish for, beautiful form and color, straw yellow, heavily bordered bright rose, tints which, together, are very effective. Its tea scent is very pronounced and elegant." [JR10/46] "Very vigorous and floriferous; leaves medium sized, glossy above, glaucous beneath; buds ovoid; flower erect, cupped; petals streamlined, concave at the base, folding back elegantly at the tip; carmine pink within, with a large straw yellow nub; exterior bordered bright pink on a ground of pale

canary yellow. Very engaging because of its fresh appearance, and the contrast of its colors—a unique feature; very fragrant." [JR7/169] "Makes a handsome bush." [JR8/24]

[Souvenir of Stella Gray] (A. Dickson, 1907)
"Light to deep orange, beautifully variegated by apricot and crimson shadings; buds and open flower short, loose, and of only fair size; fragrant. Foliage very fine." [Th2] "Flower medium-sized, very full, perfect form, deep orange veined yellow-apricot-salmon and crimson. Very beautiful variety; lacks something in the way of vigor, but remarkable due to its rich coloration." [JR35/14] "Hard to establish." [ARA27/19]

[Sulphurea] (W. Paul, 1900)
"Bright sulphur yellow, fine buds and large full flowers. Very fragrant; a good bloomer." [C&Js07]

[Sunrise] (Piper, 1899)
Sport of 'Sunset' (T).
"Salmon-rose, center yellow, salmon, and orange." [ARA27/20] "This is a sport of smaller size from 'Sunset'…a button-hole Rose of most varied and beautiful colours when grown under glass. It appears to be even more tender than the variety from which it sported, and a worse grower, and I fear it may be apt to give disappointment out of doors." [F-M4] "The flowers are extra large, perfectly double, and of excellent form and texture. The foliage is thick and glossy, and the new growth is the darkest and most beautiful found among roses. The buds are long and pointed, beautifully colored with scarlet and yellow. The flowers are large and full, with broad shell-shaped petals, and delightfully sweet. The color is dark coppery-red, beautifully shaded with rich orange, exceedingly beautiful. The bush is a strong, healthy grower, and most abundant bloomer." [C&Js02] "Pretty color; lacks in growth." [ARA18/118]

Sunset (Henderson, 1883)
Sport of 'Perle des Jardins' (T).
"Orange." [LS] "Apricot, shaded yellow. Good in autumn; bronzy foliage." [H] "A yellow tawny rose. In some places it grows yellower than in others; perhaps it fades a little in the sun. It is always covered with bloom and is very strong." [HmC] "One of the most fragrant and beautiful roses in cultivation. The flowers are extra large size, fine full form, and delightfully perfumed; color rich, coppery yellow or real old gold, elegantly clouded with dark, ruddy crimson, true sunset tints; robust and vigorous, and a constant bloomer." [C&Js00] "A sport from 'Perle des Jardins', of the same colour as 'Rêve d'Or': a handsome, useful, strong-growing Rose, with foliage of a beautiful red colour in the spring. It comes a little better than its progenitor, and is a very good autumnal, but the blooms are always small compared with the size and stoutness of the shoots, the plant is tender to frost, and like the parent variety this tenderness is shown by the summer blooms coming malformed when the plant is grown out of doors. Like the original, it does well and is much esteemed in Australia." [F-M2] "In all ways it is like its parent, except in color, which is, instead of canary yellow, saffron orange, like 'Mme. Falcot', only darker. It also differs in its leaves, which when young are a dark crimson which contrasts nicely with the flowers." [JR7/172] "Fairly vigorous, giving lots of flowers, more often medium-sized than large, and wafting a delicious Tea-rose scent." [JR17/40-41] "Moderate growth; branches not very vigorous, green touched sometimes with violet." [S] "Weak growth; winterkills." [ARA18/118]

Susan Louise (Adams/Stocking, 1929)
Seedling of 'Belle Portugaise' (HGig).
"Bud medium size, long-pointed, deep pink; flower medium size, semi-double, open, fairly lasting, slightly fragrant, flesh-pink, borne singly on average-length and strength stem. Foliage sufficient, disease-resistant. Growth very vigorous (4 to 5 ft. [ca. 1.25-1.5 m]), upright, bushy; profuse

blooms (40-50), intermittent bloomer (about every six weeks)." [ARA30/220] "Blooms from the time of the first bloom until freezing weather...never without buds or blossoms." [ARA34/213] "A strong grower and free bloomer, with slight mildew...attractive bronzy foliage...very long buds and flowers of dainty coloring." [ARA36/216-217] "In a bad year, a good deal of mildew...it has been a real joy at Breeze Hill for several years; its long bud reminds the Editor of its distinctive parent 'Belle of Portugal'." [ARA35/204] "Blooms mid-winter in warm areas." [Lg] "A joy to all who have grown it." [ARA31/208]

Sweet Passion (Starnes, not yet introduced)
From 'Comtesse de Labarthe' (T) × 'Francis Dubreuil' (T).
"This modern Tea is makes an unusually handsome compact plant to four feet [ca. 1.3 m] with healthy, dark green foliage. The variety is very floriferous, in Southern California easily blooming through the Winter. The flowers unfurl into a beautiful full blossom which at length is shaped rather like that of the Bourbon 'Souvenir de la Malmaison'. The color of the blossom varies, depending upon the weather, from a dark red about the color of that of the modern Hybrid Tea 'Chrysler Imperial' to a wonderful steely rose-pink, meantime wafting a powerful citrusy fragrance, most especially in humid periods. Those fortunate enough to possess it will find it to be the perfect 'flower-border' Tea, as its coloration, health, and productivity make it ever-ornamental, while its health and good 'vigorously compact' growth make it easy to care for and a good neighbor to other plants. We hope that discerning nurserymen make it widely available soon; it proves that continued breeding with Teas can still yield valuable roses." [BCD]

Sylph (W. Paul, 1895)
"Ivory white tinted with peach colour, centre creamy pink, a very lovely blending of colours; large, high-centred, and deep stiff petals; habit erect, a magnificent exhibition Rose, also good for garden decoration; hardy and vigorous." [P1] "Large and very free-flowering." [DO] "Free blooming,

requiring fine weather and liberal treatment...large, of good pointed shape...white, tinted with pink and in some cases...violet...many do not come good...fair growth and habit with stiff wood." [F-M2] Not to be confused with Vibert's yellowish-flesh Tea of 1838, nor with Boyau's flesh and lilac Tea of 1842, both named 'La Sylphide'.

Sylphide
Listed as 'La Sylphide'. See also 'Sylph'.

The Alexandra (W. Paul, 1900)
"Beautiful rosy buff flowers." [C&Js02] "Pale buff with orange yellow centres shaded with apricot and bronze; very beautifully shaped, exceedingly attractive." [P1] "Flower large, full, and very well formed." [JR30/15] "Small growth; winterkills." [ARA18/115] Queen Alexandra of Great Britain, wife of Edward VII; lived 1844-1925.

The Bride (May, 1885)
Sport of 'Catherine Mermet' (T).
"White, suffused with lemon, a magnificent tea...sometimes the flowers have a slight pink shade at the extremity of the petals, which has a charming effect...a moderate grower." [FRB] "An ever blooming pure white Tea Rose, of large size and most perfect form. The buds are pointed and the ends of the petals are slightly curved back. It is a very free blooming variety and has the most delicious tea fragrance." [CA88] "Large, well-filled, cupped, creamy-white with a greenish-yellow high centre, the outer petals often tinted with pink. Growth moderately strong. A charming rose." [Hn] "This newcomer is without a doubt the most beautiful white rose ever offered to the public. It is a sport of 'Catherine Mermet', which it resembles except in color, which is pure white. The blossoms are beautiful and strong, and have the advantage of staying fresh, once cut, longer than any other variety. It is more floriferous than its mother." [May being quoted in JR10/71] "The flowers are equal in quality to those of the parent rose, and are carried well above the foliage. In all respects a first-class

Rose." [P1] "Better form [*than 'Catherine Mermet'*]." [Hk] "Very fragrant; very floriferous." [Cx] "Weak-growing, tender." [ARA18/124] "The plant is vigorous and very pretty when left to develop its natural form." [JR20/57] "Foliage slightly liable to mildew." [Th2] "The best import from America...it surpasses 'Niphetos' easily." [JR16/37] "Of great value. It speedily took a high rank, and gained a great reputation quite equal to that of the type, and is generally acknowledged as being one of the best half-dozen. In manners and customs it is similar to C. Mermet, but, like its sister sports, 'Bridesmaid' and 'Muriel Grahame', differs from it a little in form as well as colour. The true form of 'The Bride' is perhaps the nearest approach to globular, yet with a point, that we have...white with occasionally in a young bloom a greenish lemon tinge at the base of the petals. There are very few, if any, white Roses which are more lovely than a perfect flower of 'The Bride'." [F-M2]

The Hughes
Listed as 'Bridesmaid'.

[The Queen] (Dingee & Conard, 1889)
Sport of 'Souvenir d'un Ami' (T).
"White, of peculiar delicacy; good sized flowers of perfect globular form. Most attractive and of extreme elegance." [B&V] "Good pointed form...I cannot get the blooms to come as large as those of the type." [F-M3] "A pure white kind of 'Souvenir d'un Ami', well formed, vigorous plant, always in bloom. It gives a large amount of buds and flowers the whole season; buds, well-formed; petals, strong and of good substance. It opens well and keeps well." [JR13/71] "A vigorous, healthy grower, and one of the heaviest and most continuous bloomers we know. The flowers are large, full and well filled; color, pure snow white and very sweet. A remarkably early forcer; makes fine buds; opens well, has plenty of substance, and is a good keeper." [CA91] "Can't be recommended as a nursery flower, but as a garden flower it is splendid." [JR16/38]

[**The Sweet Little Queen of Holland**] (Soupert & Notting, 1897)
From 'Céline Forestier' (N) × 'Mme. Hoste' (T).
"A very dainty and attractive Rose, grows neat and compact, and is a quick and most abundant bloomer, scarcely ever without flowers during the whole season, makes elegant buds, and the flowers are large, full and double. Color, bright rich golden yellow, centre shaded with orange and blush, very sweet and a really charming rose." [C&Js02] "Vigorous bush, beautiful glaucous green foliage, long bud, flower very large, full, good form, outer petals large, center petals narrower; color, shining daffodil yellow, the centre ochre yellow mixed with pink and bright orange yellow. The petals are pointed like those of the Chrysanthemum, giving the blossom a look all its own. Very fragrant and floriferous. Color and form novel among Teas. Excellent for forcing." [JR22/20]

[**Thérèse Lambert**] (Soupert & Notting, 1887)
From 'Mme. Lambard' (T) × 'Socrate' (T).
"Elegant and very handsome in color and form; delicate rose, base of petals finely tinged with old gold, center pale silvery salmon; very large and full." [CA93] "Good hold; color, delicate pink on a yellowish red ground; center silvery salmon gold. Very fragrant." [JR11/152]

Therese Welter
Listed as 'Baronne Henriette de Loew'.

[**Triomphe de Milan**] (Widow Ducher, 1877) trans., "Milanese Triumph"
"White, suffused with pale yellow, without fragrance; a fine rose, similar, but inferior to, 'Marie Guillot'." [EL] "Flower large, full, well-formed; color, white with a deep yellow center. Good exhibition rose, and recommendable for bouquets, particularly before expansion; bush vigorous, with short, upright branches." [S]

Triomphe du Luxembourg (Hardy/Sylvain-Péan, 1835) trans., "Triumph of the Luxembourg [Palace]"
"Salmon-pink blooms changing to buff-pink." [HRG] "Fire-red." [RR] "Flower full, having a coppery-red color." [R-H35] "Large, aurora shaded with pink." [JWa] "Flesh colour, tinged with fawn and rose, very large and full; form, globular. Growth, vigorous. A beautiful Rose, and very sweet." [P] "Rosy blush." [Sx] "Buff-rose, large, good in the bud, of healthy habit; a desirable sort." [EL] "Fiery dawn red; flower very large, full; very vigorous." [Cx] "Bronzed rose." [JC] "Rosy pink, with fawn shading. Remarkably fine, handsome buds. Without a fault except that it is not a profuse bloomer. Popular since 1836. Magnificent form of growth. Abundant dark, leathery foliage." [Dr] "The flowers are often six inches in diameter [ca. 1.5 dm], of peculiar rosy-buff colour, and may be frequently seen of a yellowish-white or deep rose, according to season and situation; its growth is remarkably strong, in some soils producing shoots five feet long [ca. 1.5 m] in one season, flowering freely and perfectly, and is possessed of considerable fragrance." [Bu] "This very large and imposing flower has probably attracted more attention and been more extensively disseminated during the ten years of its existence, than any other of the Perpetual flowering classes, and at first it was sold as high as thirty to forty francs at Paris; the bud and flower are very large and distinct, the latter often five inches or more in diameter [ca. 1.25 dm +], of globular form, fragrant, usually of aurora hue shaded with pink, but varying somewhat." [WRP] "Bush vigorous, with horizontal branches which are violet in the new growth; thorns equal, not numerous, wider at the base; leaves of three cordiform leaflets, glossy, margined reddish, pretty regularly dentate; flowers fairly numerous, well formed, in a cluster, often solitary, four inches across [ca. 1 dm], borne on a strong, upright, glabrous stem; petals large, fawn mixed with pink, very nice scent. The calyx-tube is very short and bears some glandular hairs at its base. This superb variety, born at the Luxembourg Palace, is one of the most beautiful teas known." [An35/51] Alexandre Hardy, 1787-1876; chief horticulturist at the gardens of the

Luxembourg Palace in Paris: "M. Hardy is no stranger in the Rose world: One of his varieties alone ('Mme. Hardy') would have sufficed to render his name popular; but he has been fortunate enough to raise many others of first-rate properties, some bearing the after appellation of 'Du Luxembourg'. And how could it be otherwise, when he has devoted so many years to the cultivation of his flowers, and raised so many thousands of seedlings? He has never practised selling his Roses, but exchanges them with his friends for other plants. The Roses in the Gardens of the Luxembourg are seen from the public promenades; and M. Hardy is very courteous to foreigners. It is necessary to visit him early in the morning during the Rose season." [P] A gentleman in New Zealand, Mr. Francis J. Nettleingham, has shared some family history which had been passed down through the years, several elements of which we would like in turn to share with the Reader just as he related it. Mr. Nettleingham is a distant relation of one Mary Hardy, who herself was the great-niece of Alexander/Alexandre Hardy. "Mary Hardy's grandfather was Capt. Thomas Masterson Hardy, who was in charge of the blockade of France under Nelson and commanded at the Battle of Trafalgar. The Hardys had a nursery in England but my father could not remember just where. He and his brothers worked as subcontractors to the Hardy Boatbuilding Yard at Gravesend before coming to New Zealand." Concerning Alexander, Mr. Nettleingham continues, "Born in Aberdeen 30 July 1787. Parents Alexander and Ellen Hardy. Was sent at an early age to Holland to learn about roses and their culture. His ability to propagate roses was noted by Dupont when he was in Holland looking for roses for Malmaison so he hired Hardy to propagate roses at the Luxembourg Palace and at Malmaison. At Malmaison he grew a number of roses. Marie Joseph was one which Dupont changed to Marie Louise when Napoleon married again [...] When Mary Hardy his great niece married in 1872 he gave her five roses with green centres, which because she and William were renting a flat at No. 5 London Road Stone in Kent, England, they were planted at 'Stonewood Farm' on the Old Kent Road, the family place of work. This Family story was passed to us by my Father's sister Mildred Curry of Dartford England, who died at 96 years in 1976."

[**True Friend**] (California Nursery Co.?, by 1905)
"Light yellow." [CA05]

[**Uncle John**] (Thorpe, 1904)
Sport of 'Golden Gate' (T).
"Blush white." [LS] "Creamy yellow." [CA07] "A very pleasing constant blooming rose; never out of bloom during the whole growing season, pretty buff yellow flowers shading to white and pink, large, full and fragrant; a strong bushy grower, splendid for garden planting." [C&Js06]

[**V. Viviand-Morel**] (Bernaix, 1887)
Seedling of 'Safrano à Fleurs Rouges' (T).
"Bright cherry pink, shaded salmon, very large and double, long plump buds on strong stems; a fine garden rose, and a strong healthy grower and free bloomer." [C&Js06] "Bush with thick canes, upright, robust, purplish; leaves outspread; leaflets leathery, glossy above, glaucescent and reddish beneath; stems long, strong, and very rigid, holding the blossom upright without bending, 5-7 cm long [ca. 2.5 inches], measuring from the base of the last leaflet to the base of the ovary; calyx and ovary nearly smooth; bud long before expansion; petals thick, firm, veined, reticulated with flattened anastomical stripes; exterior petals very large, revolute; inner petals wedge-shaped, large, rounded at the tip; flower crimson red, nuanced oriental matte grenadine while opening; very large when completely open; moderately double; shimmering, passing from crimson to poppy-red, lightening gradually to carmine nuanced saffron red." [JR11/151]

[V. Vivo é Hijos] (Bernaix, 1894)
"A new coloration, quite double, exterior petals large, carmine pink, paler at the center and base, middle petals numerous, ragged, bright dawn yellow with salmon, apricot, and often tinted incarnadine." [JR18/163-164] "Medium size." [CaRoII/3/3] "Carmine-salmon and apricot-yellow. Medium growth." [ARA27/20] "A variegated pink Tea, verging on salmon and apricot. Good growth; very floriferous; perfect foliage. Strongly recommended for southern zones." [ARA28/104]

[Vallée de Chamonix] (Ducher, 1872) trans., "Chamonix Valley"
Affiliated with the Noisettes in JR23/163.
"Copper, afterwards yellow and rose, very variable." [JC] "Bud pink [*and*] orange pink. Flower semi-double. Color, pinkish yellow, lightly coppery at the center." [JR23/163] "A very beautiful rose; good size, very double, full and sweet; color coppery yellow, elegantly shaded and tinged with rosy blush." [CA90] "Vigorous; flower medium-sized, full, flat." [S]

[Vicomtesse de Bernis] (Nabonnand, 1883)
"Striped pink." [LS] "Fine, large, full flowers; very fragrant; color rich coppery rose, passing to fawn and deep salmon; showy and handsome." [CA90] "Very vigorous; flower very large, full, imbricated, with very large petals, perfect form, good hold; color, delicate pink towards the edge, bright pink towards the center." [JR7/184]

[Vicomtesse de Wauthier] (Bernaix, 1886)
'Mme. de Tartas' (T) × 'Anna Olivier' (T).
"Bright carmine red; center and reverse of petals silver rose." [CA90] "Pretty vigorous; long bud; flower large, full, pretty well formed; beautifully colored pink tinted yellowish on the exterior of the petals and blush white within. The blush white is often striped pink. The flower's middle is a very deep pink, which produces a superb effect. Novel coloration." [JR10/172]

[**Victor Pulliat**] (Ducher, 1870)
Seedling of 'Mme. Mélanie Willermoz' (T).
"Yellowish-white, large, full and clustering; habit moderate." [JC] "Flower medium-sized, full, flat." [S] "Pale yellow, long buds, quite a good Tea." [EL] "Victor Pulliat, the vinologist known to all grape-vine growers." [JR22/160]

Victor Velidan (Breeder unknown, date uncertain)
One runs across this name here and there; and it is, we think, a mishearing, mispronunciation, or misremembrance of some other variety, perhaps 'Victor Waddilove', McGredy's 1925 Pernetiana-HT which didn't generate very much enthusiasm. 'Victor Waddilove' varied in color from pink to yellow much as the blossoms of many Teas do.

[**Virginia**] (Dingee & Conard, 1894)
From 'Safrano' (T) × 'Maréchal Niel' (N).
"A very beautiful Tea Rose, pure deep yellow, both buds and flowers, are very handsome and borne in great profusion all through the season; richly tea scented." [C&Js98] Also attributed to Nanz & Neuner, 1896.

[**Waban**] (Wood, 1891)
Sport of 'Catherine Mermet' (T).
"Originated at the Waban Conservatories, Massachusetts, from whence it takes its name. It is a sport from that excellent old rose, 'Catherine Mermet', and identical with it in every characteristic except color, which is a rich, deep bright pink, much brighter and more durable than 'Mermet', but has the same beauty of form, and is a more abundant bloomer." [CA93] "In foliage and vigor, 'Waban' takes after its parents [*sic*]; the flowers are borne on long, strong stems, and the petals are a little larger and more numerous than those of 'Catherine Mermet'. Its color is carmine pink…plumed with fiery madder red, brightly nuanced on the outer petals." [JR15/88] "Does not often come good." [F-M3]

[**White Bon Silène**] (Morrat, 1884)
Presumably a sport of 'Bon Silène' (T).
"Flower medium-sized, full; color, virginal white. Much to be recommended for its good bloom." [S] "This elegant new variety is valued particularly for its splendid buds, which are remarkably large and handsome; the color is pale lemon yellow, passing to rich creamy white; very beautiful." [CA90] "Its color is not perfectly white, which is why it isn't much liked as a nursery rose; nevertheless, its fragrance is exquisite, making it perfectly precious as a garden plant, where it surpasses all other white roses." [JR16/38]

[**White Catherine Mermet**] (Forrest, 1887)
Presumably a sport from 'Catherine Mermet' (T).
"White." [LS] Possibly synonymous with 'The Bride'.

White Duchesse de Brabant
Listed as 'Mme. Joseph Schwartz'.

White Hermosa
Listed as 'Marie Lambert'.

White Maman Cochet (J. Cook, 1896)
Sport of 'Maman Cochet' (T).
"Cream white, lightly pink at the edge of the petals; flower large, full, globular, fragrant; very floriferous; vigorous." [Cx] "Light lemon to cream-flesh, edged rose. Weak stems." [Capt27] "Large double flowers on stiff stems." [SHj] "White blushing pink in cool weather." [HRG] "A beautiful rose, nearly hardy, not always opening well. Affected by rain, when it looks bad, getting eaten into…it breaks off at the stem." [JR37/171] "It opens its flowers easily." [JR24/102] "Wonderful vigor…beautiful blooms that…never ball [*in Bermuda*]." [UB28] "'Maman Cochet' and 'White Maman Cochet' are, without question, the best garden roses for southern Kansas…perfect blooms which are never malformed or blighted." [ARA21/171] "Of growth free and vigorous…the habit of the plant is very

spreading, but often unequally balanced…The foliage is dark green, glossy and good, free from mildew, but some of my friends have found it suffer from black spot…The flowers are a grand pointed shape, and most beautiful when perfect, but rather too liable to come with a split centre…The petals are of fine lasting substance, very pale lemon with rose on the edges of the outer petals…if the weather be wet they rot wholesale in a woeful fashion. They have a slight Tea fragrance." [NRS/10] "Has the advantage over its mother of opening more easily even during rainy periods." [JR22/19] "Medium height, spreading, almost hardy; foliage very plentiful, black-spots somewhat; bloom almost abundant, continuous." [ARA18/128] "Does not fade easily, being one of the best of its color in this respect…does well on 'Mme. Plantier' stock, and does not ball." [Th2] "The half-open buds are particularly lovely." [Hn] "Lacks quality in the flower." [ARA25/105] "Must be lightly pruned." [DO] "Quite the finest and best white Tea Rose of the pure pointed shape we have at present." [F-M2]

[**White Pearl**] (Ritter/Nanz & Neuner, 1889)
Sport of 'Perle des Jardins' (T).
"A white product of 'Perle des Jardins', of very vigorous growth, blooming easily under glass, and profusely. Not recommendable as a nursery rose." [JR16/38] "Blooms in great abundance; stems quite upright, buds very pretty, foliage large and very well formed. Excellent for pot culture and for open air where Teas will grow." [JR13/71] "Low-growing, compact, winterkills some; foliage sufficient to plentiful; bloom moderate, almost continuous." [ARA18/128]

William R. Smith (Bagg, 1908) syn., 'Charles Dingee', 'Jeanette Heller'
From 'Maman Cochet' (T) × 'Mme. Hoste' (T).
"Silver-flesh to cream-peach edged lilac. Balls in cold and dampness." [Capt27] "Exceedingly promising…excellent growth and habit…creamy white, the outside petals of the younger flowers being tinged a delicate pink…good shape and size…develops a split." [F-M] "Blooms medium to

large, full, of excellent form, lasting five to seven days;...strong enduring fragrance. Excellent foliage...vigorous...Averages 36 blooms per season. Very fine autumn bloomer. Hardy." [ARA21/91] "Large double flowers on stiff stems." [SHj] "Form lovely; fine size; lasting quality is almost perfect. Stem strong; growth good. Hardy for a Tea...Immune from mildew under worst conditions." [Th2] "The plant is spreading in growth, the foliage is exceptionally fine, a deep olive-green in color, it is thick and leathery and exceptionally free from disease. The buds and blooms are simply perfect in the fall." [C-Ps28] "Its growth is pretty much the same as 'Kaiserin Auguste Viktoria'; its solitary buds are long; its double flowers are of good size and a nice pale pink. It has the same foliage as 'Maman Cochet'." [JR32/22] "It grows well, and gives freely of good blooms. One of the best new Teas. The bloom is liable to come divided." [OM] "An extra fine late summer and autumn rose." [Dr] "Most attractive in color and form; growth and foliage good; lacks in blooming qualities." [ARA18/114] "Whether you live East, West, North or South, whether you wish one Rose or 1000, *here is a Rose which has our unqualified endorsement.* It will thrive abundantly in almost any reasonable location. The flowers are large, full and double and most exquisitely formed. The petals are so firm they look like wax, softly curled, colored cream with flesh tint tips, buff yellow base and the center a heart of deep pink. Perfect buds. The flowers are borne on long, strong stems, just right for making bouquets. Fragrance is delightful. You will admire the foliage too, deep green leaves on red stems and the new growth of rich garnet; the plant will grow for you vigorously, is among the hardiest in this class and blooms abundantly. TRY A ROSE BED FULL OF THIS ONE KIND." [C&Js10]

"Very likely it would interest you and others to know exactly how the rose 'William R. Smith' was produced. It happened years ago in my greenhouses, in Bridgeton, N.J. One morning, late in September or early in October, I noticed among a few roses in pots a 'Maman Cochet' in bloom, with fewer petals than usual but a perfect set of pistils. This was an opportunity that had never occurred before, or since for that matter, so I immediately began a search for pollen, and was quite provoked because the only rose with pollen to be found was a 'Mme. Hoste', so I used that. When the hip was ripe the seeds were planted; five or six germinated and grew; one went ahead of all the rest and soon produced a fine little double flower. The rest of the plants were about half the size of this one, and had little, single, pink flowers. *This little double one was afterwards named 'William R. Smith'*. That fall I moved to Philadelphia and kept it in the greenhouse of a friend. It would not do anything as a winter rose, so I lost a good bit of my interest in it. Afterwards I was told by a reliable party that my friend sold it for $500, but he never paid me a cent of it...Mr. John Shellem, at a dinner party, sold the rose 'William R. Smith' to E.G. Hill for $500. The trouble with me was, that I lost my property in Bridgeton. I had to get work somewhere and struck it with Mr. Shellem. I went there in the fall and took two or three little seedling roses with me, and he let me plant them on a bench where some of his roses had died out...Yes, I know that 'William R. Smith' has been renamed by several. One of the names is 'Charles Dingee'. Just a swindle! Why cannot people deal square? Sincerely yours, Richard Bagg." [ARA30/206] "Mr. John Shellum, of Philadelphia, never claimed to have originated the variety named 'William R. Smith', but I could never get from him the information as to who did originate the rose...I bought the variety...with the understanding that I was to have all stock of the said rose. I had understood that Mr. Robert Craig had a few plants of the variety on trial, but these and all other plants of the same were to be given into my possession on the payment of $500, and as Mr. Shellum was being hard pressed for money at the time, I advanced him the amount ($500) in good faith, and he later sent me a considerable number of plants which, I supposed, were all of the variety, but I afterward found that he had let out plants on trial to five or six other parties...The rose was christened at a dinner party in Philadelphia, by blooms furnished by Mr. Shellum. Mr. [Robert] Craig, I believe, was the principal mover in the affair, and thought it would be nice for it to bear the name of his old Scotch friend, William R. Smith...We found that other parties had this rose and we never exploited it as a novelty. Very truly yours, E.G. Hill." [ARA30/207]

[**Winnie Davis**] (Little, 1892)
From 'Devoniensis' (T) × 'Mme. de Watteville' (T).
"Flesh pink, outer petals silvery blush." [CA17] "Growth seems quite fair, blooms of good size and nice color." [ARA18/114] "Named in honor of the daughter of the Confederacy. The buds are long, heavy, and splendidly formed. Color is apricot-pink, shading to flesh tint at the base of petals." [C&Js07]

[**Winter Gem**] (Childs, 1898)
"Lovely creamy pink and a tremendous bloomer." [C&Js03] "This is a very beautiful Winter-blooming Rose, a perfectly wonderful bloomer, continuing covered with lovely buds and flowers as long as kept in a growing condition. The blossoms are borne on long graceful stems, and are large, full and double...Very sweet and beautiful. It is a strong rapid grower, and blooms nearly all the time, particularly in Winter." [C&Jf03] "Very low-growing, moderately compact, winterkills some; foliage plentiful, healthy; bloom free, almost continuous." [ARA18/128]

Yellow Maman Cochet
Listed as 'Alexander Hill Gray'. See also 'Souvenir de Jeanne Cabaud' and 'Souvenir de Pierre Notting'.

[**Zephyr**] (W. Paul, 1895)
"A beautiful sulphur yellow with beautiful white reflections; the flowers are large, full, and cupped, and open very well. The bush grows vigorously, and is very floriferous. Much to be recommended for cut-flowers." [JR19/67] "A truly elegant rose of vigorous growth and good habit. Extra large flowers of beautiful cupped form; pale sulphur yellow passing to creamy white; large broad petals; very deep and deliciously tea scented." [C&Js98]

Chapter Five

Bourbons

"It is now about thirty years since a beautiful semi-double rose, with brilliant rose-coloured flowers, prominent buds, and nearly evergreen foliage, made its appearance in this country [*England*] under the name of 'L'Ile de Bourbon Rose', said to have been imported from the Mauritius to France, in 1822, by Monsieur Noisette. It attracted attention by its peculiar habit, but more particularly by its abundant autumnal flowering; still, such was the lukewarmness of English rose amateurs, that no attempts were made to improve this pretty imperfect rose, by raising seedlings from it, although it bore seed in large quantities. This pleasing task was left to our rose-loving neighbors the French, who have been very industrious, and, as a matter of course, have originated some very beautiful and striking varieties, and also, as usual in such cases, have given us rather too many distinct and fine-sounding names attached to flowers without distinctive characters. In a little time we shall be able to rectify this very common floricultural error. Many fables have been told by the French respecting the origin of this rose. The most generally received version of one of these is, that a French naval officer was requested by the widow of a Monsieur Edouard, residing in the island, to find, on his voyage to India, some rare rose, and that, on his return to l'Île de Bourbon, he brought with him this rose, which she planted on her husband's grave: It was then called 'Rose Edouard', and sent to France as 'Rose de l'Île Bourbon'. This is pretty enough, but entirely devoid of truth. Monsieur Breon, a French botanist, gives the following account, for the truth of which he vouches:—'At the Isle of Bourbon, the inhabitants generally enclose their land with hedges made of two rows of roses, one row of the common China rose [*'Parsons' Pink China'*], the other of the Red Four-Seasons [*the 'Monthly Rose' Damask Perpetual*]. Monsieur Perichon, a proprietor at Saint Benoist, in the Isle, in planting one of these hedges, found among his young plants one very different from the others in its shoots and foliage. This induced him to plant it in his garden. It flowered the following year; and, as he anticipated, proved to be quite a new race, and differing much from the above two roses, which, at the time, were the only two sorts known in the island.' Monsieur Breon arrived at Bourbon in 1817, as botanical traveller for the government of France, and curator of the Botanical and Naturalization Garden there. He propagated this rose very largely, and sent plants and seeds of it, in 1822, to Monsieur Jacques, gardener at the Château de Neuilly, near Paris, who distributed them among the rose cultivators of France. (Whence the name often given to the Common Bourbon Rose of 'Bourbon Jacques'.) Monsieur Breon named it 'Rose de l'Île de Bourbon'; and is convinced that it is a hybrid from one of the above roses, and a native of the island." [R8]

"In October or November 1819, I [*Monsieur Jacques*] received from the Île-Bourbon a large collection of seeds of trees and shrubs; they were sent to me by Monsieur Breon, then chief gardener of the isle's royal possessions, and one of my good friends. In the number were found five rose-hips without any name other than that of 'Rosier de l'Île Bourbon'. At the end of November, I sowed all the seeds in hot-beds, and, along with the others, the roses. Come Spring, five individuals came up and, after having been pricked out, raised in pots, and having passed the Winter in a cold-frame, two bloomed and rebloomed well enough in the Spring of 1821; one had semi-double flowers of a brilliant pink, and served that same year as a model for Redouté's picture, and was then propagated under the name 'Rosier de Bourbon'; the other was also propagated, but wasn't drawn." [JR17/158] "It was introduced first, in 1819, in the form of seeds sent to Monsieur Jacques…; second, in 1821, by Monsieur Neumann, in the form of cuttings from this same 'Rose Edouard'. It was distributed, soon after this last introduction, under the name 'Rose Neumann' and 'Rose Dubreuil'." [JR25/137] "It was Monsieur Grandidier who brought it to Europe." [Hd] "It was introduced to this country [*the U.S.A.*], in 1828, by the later Mr. Thomas Hibbert, whose name will always be associated in the memory of many with rose culture." [Bu]

"Whatever the case, the new rose attracted attention by its vigor as well as by the novelty of its characteristics; its bright pink flowers of a shade all its own…its long wood which could be distinguished by the strong thorns which armed it. Its arrival was much celebrated, and it was grown by practically everyone—and then it was removed from the gardens because it took up too much room. This rose gave a great quantity of seed, giving rise to many seedlings—which at first were not so good: The plants arising from them were single, or perhaps too full, always aborting as with the Bourbon 'Neumann', for example, from which one had to content one's self with gathering buds only…the future looked bleak." [VH51/77-78] "In 1831, Monsieur Desprez, amateur from Yèbles…indefatigable hybridist, raised two plants from the original type. They were two varieties which, by their good qualities, still hold a place in the catalogs. I speak of the Bourbons 'Charles Desprez' and 'Mme.

Desprez', which had, particularly the latter, an immense vogue which was well-deserved. By this, then, the future of the class was decided." [JR23/125]

"Owing to the original being a hybrid, the roses of this family vary much in their characters." [WRP] "The Roses of this section are, in general, vigorous; the branches, often short and ordinarily stouter than those of the Teas or Chinas, terminate in one sole bloom; but when growing vigorously, it will attain a great length and end in a more or less great number of flowers per cluster; the bark is very smooth; the thorns, short, strong, and enlarged at the base, are curved at the tip, and are occasional; the leaflets, oval-rounded, toothed, shiny somber green, are in 3's, 5's, or 7's; the ovary is rounded, often short, and inflated." [BJ] "The Bourbon roses have one feature that is seldom found in another class—the opalescence or translucence of the petals—the hues seem to shimmer around according to the angle from which you look at it." [K]

"This class does not possess the hardiness of the Remontants, nor the free blooming properties of the Bengales, Teas, and Noisettes, and therefore can never compete with the former for the North, nor with the latter for the South. In it, however, are varieties like 'Hermosa', 'Souvenir de la Malmaison', and others, which are scarcely surpassed in any class. The Bourbon Rose has also qualities which make many varieties favorites. These qualities are its greater hardiness than the Tea Rose, its very thick, leathery foliage, its luxuriant growth, its more constant bloom than the Remontants, and its thick, velvety petals, of a consistency to endure the summer's sun." [SBP]

Acidalie (Rousseau/V. Verdier, 1837)
"White, center flesh, full, medium-sized, beautiful." [LF] "White, in dry weather beautifully tinted; a very good white rose, suitable for a pillar, wall, or tall standard." [JC] "Who that has seen this beautiful rose in fine calm weather in September, has been able to withhold intense admiration? Its large globular finely-shaped flowers of the purest white, delicately

tinted with purplish rose, seem always to be drooping with beauty. Yes, it is indeed unique and charming." [R8] "Has been in cultivation for several years, but is only now coming into notice for its distinct pale rose-white colour; the flower is perfect in form, large, and a little fragrant; the plant is quite hardy, and grows well." [Bu] "Vigorous, with long, robust canes of a violet maroon green on the sunny side; thorns somewhat numerous, large, short, enlarged at the base and strongly recurved; leaves somber green, slightly dentate; flower large, full; bowl-shaped; color, white shaded light pink; very fragrant. Of the first order." [S] "Canes big, green, thorny; thorns close-set, large at the base, pointed, purplish, nearly straight. Leaves comprised of five or seven medium-sized, oval, dentate, fresh green leaflets, petiole prickly, wider at the base; young growths purplish yellow-ish-green. Blossom solitary, 7 cm across [ca. 2.5 inches], petals large, twisted, and rounded, flesh at first, then pure white, then pink at the edge, rolled; light scent." [An41/14-15] "A beautiful Rose in fine weather. Very sweet." [P1]

Adam Messerich (Lambert, 1920)
From 'Frau Oberhofgärtner Singer' (HT) × an unnamed seedling (result-ing from crossing the Bourbon 'Louise Odier' with the China 'Louis Philippe').
"Bright pink to rosy red...5 × 4 [feet; ca. 1.5 × 1.25 m]." [B] "Rich rasp-berry fragrance." [T3] "Bud ovoid, rose-red; flower medium size, semi-double, clear rose-red...; open cupped, borne singly or several together...lasting. Very vigorous; trailing; bushy; blooms abundantly and continuously from May to October." [ARA21/163]

Adrienne de Cardoville (Guillot père, 1864)
"Flowers delicate rose." [FP] "Flower medium sized, perfect form, very full, opening well, delicate pink." [l'H64/328] "Not very vigorous; canes weak, green; thorns occasional, slightly hooked, nearly straight; leaves dis-tinctly pointed, dark green." [S]

Alexandre Chomer
Listed as a Hybrid Perpetual.

Alexandre Pelletier
Listed as 'Monsieur Alexandre Pelletier'.

Aline Rozey (Schwartz, 1884)
"Vigorous, flower medium-sized, full, imbricated, very perfect form, color flesh-pink fading to white. Abundantly floriferous." [JR8/133] Sometimes called an HP or even a Hybrid Noisette, it is in the 'Mme. Alfred de Rougemont' and 'Boule de Neige' group of Bourbons, and most probably had the same or similar parentage.

Amarante (Page, 1859) trans., "Amaranth"
"Crimson purple." [LS] "Blossom medium-sized, full, cup-shaped; color, bright cerise red." [S] "Carmine purple, with cherry red, medium size." [Jg]

Amédée de Langlois (Vigneron, 1871)
"Flower medium-sized, full, growing in a cluster; dark velvety purple." [S]

Apolline (V. Verdier, 1848)
Seedling of 'Pierre de St.-Cyr' (B).
"Flower large, intensely shaded delicate pink. This variety was developed from seed gathered from 'Pierre de St.-Cyr', which it resembles in its growth." [R-H48] "A beautiful and glossy rose colour." [R8] "The most valuable [*of Bourbons*]...large cup-shaped blossoms of rosy-carmine that are very attractive." [EL] "Large flower, full; delicate pink shaded bright rose." [S] "A most lovely fall rose, growing in good ground from ten to fifteen feet [ca. 3-4.5 m], and glorious from September to November. It blooms profusely during the summer, but as the fall advances its color is of the most vivid pink." [HstXXVIII:193-194] "A beautiful rose, and a good weeper, pillar or wall rose." [JC]

Armosa
Listed as 'Hermosa'.

Bardou Job (Nabonnand, 1887)

From 'Gloire des Rosomanes' (B) × 'Général Jacqueminot' (HP).

"Deep scarlet shaded to yellow, reverse of petals a darker hue, surface of velvety down, beautiful in the extreme. This rose is impatient of the sun, when well grown and protected from its direct rays, every shade from dark beetroot to golden yellow may be observed on its lovely petals; the flowers greatly vary, some being so much darker than others, that surprise is felt that all could be attached to the same growth. Semi-double, indeed almost a single rose, centre brilliant yellow, generally bearing an excessive quantity of pollen. Likes to climb, is most attractive." [B&V] "Very vigorous; flower large, semi-double, of perfect form, erect; bud conical, elongated, perfect; large leaves of a splendid dark green; color, velvety scarlet on a ground of black, reverse of petals darkly velvety…Very fragrant…always in bloom." [JR11/164] "Of good growth requiring but little pruning. This is almost, if not quite, a single Rose…I do not know of one to beat it for size of petal, freedom of flower, and brightness of crimson colour." [F-M2]

Baron G.-B. Gonella (Guillot père, 1859)

Seedling of 'Louise Odier' (B).

"Pink and lilac shaded, large, full, and fine." [FP] "Bright cherry-coloured…blooms in large corymbs, and is distinct and beautiful." [R8] "Bronzed rose, well formed, fragrant; non-autumnal." [EL] "Very vigorous, flower large, full, beautiful form, reverse of petals violet pink, white in the center." [JDR59/28] "Bright cerise, with a fine bronzy hue, petals large, smooth, thick, and beautifully disposed; flowers large, double, and exquisitely formed; a superb rose of free habit." [JC] "Growth moderate." [P1] "Growth pretty vigorous; canes of medium vigor, upright or branching; bark smooth, somber green, with some reddish thorns which are unequal, much compressed, and somewhat hooked. Leaves somber green, divided into 3 or 5 rounded and finely dentate leaflets; leafstalk pretty strong, no prickles. Blossoms about three inches across [ca. 7.5 cm], full, cupped, well formed, solitary or in a cluster of two or three on the stronger branches;

color, light pink, center silvery; reverse of petals violet pink; outer petals convex and very thick, center petals ruffled; flower stalk strong, upright, holding the blossom well. Calyx globular. A variety of the first order, well poised and very remontant, but with little fragrance; it is proof against such Winters as Paris has." [JF] The Baron has picked up many variations of his initials in his travels; the above is the name as introduced.

Baronne de Maynard (Lacharme, 1865)
From 'Mlle. Blanche Laffitte' (B) × 'Sapho' (DP).
"French white, beautifully cupped." [FP] "Very beautiful blossom, much to be recommended, very floriferous, bearing flowers until October; flower medium-sized, full, in a cluster; color, virginal white; growth vigorous." [S]

Baronne de Noirmont (Granger, 1861)
"Pale, shaded rose, compact and good." [FP] "Flower medium-sized, full, cupped, very bright purplish-pink, blooming in clusters of five or six." [JR1/2/7] "Rose, large, full, and very sweet; form cupped, fine; growth moderate." [P1] "Fresh rosy-pink, petals of good substance, flowers large, full, and beautifully formed; with a delicious violet scent; a very fine rose, habit robust." [JC] "Very vigorous; canes upright, bearing flat thorns which are straight and violet green; blossom medium sized, full, very beautiful in form; color, delicate but very bright pink." [S]

Béatrix (Cherpin, 1865)
Seedling of 'Louise Odier' (B).
"Flower large, full, centifolia form; bright carmine red." [S] "*Béatrix* is the name of the beloved of Dante to whom a statue is going to be raised in Florence. It is a felicitous appellation…The bush is vigorous and remontant, with upright, smooth stems, nearly thornless; foliage elegant, blossoms solitary, sometimes in twos or threes. The blossom is upright on its stem; it is of the globular [*pommée*] form, medium to large depending upon the exposure. The exterior is a whitish pink. Upon opening, it takes on carmine tints deep within. It has neither stamens nor pistils. All of its

short petals are arranged like steps to the interior, forming a cup. This cup opens little by little, but without breaking." [RJC65/155] "The rose propagators…of Paris sold, this Spring, an old rose named Gulino [*i.e., 'Louis Gulino', HP*] as the new variety 'Béatrix'. These two varieties are about as like each other as an oak and a fir tree! The first has big wood and a big flower; the second, a Bourbon hybrid from 'Louise Odier', has long canes which are completely or nearly thornless. The blossom, rather small than medium, opens like a Centifolia, like which it has the form and coloration." [RJC66/159-160]

Beauté de Versailles
Listed as 'Georges Cuvier'.

Belle Nanon (Lartay, 1872) trans., "Beautiful Nanon"
"Carmine." [Ÿ]

Bijou de Royat-les-Bains (Veysset, 1891) trans., "Royal-les-Bains Gem"
Seedling of 'Hermosa' (B).
"'Hermosa' marbled carmine pink." [JR16/21] "Flower silvery pink, exterior and interior striped bright pink and bright carmine; medium-sized, well-formed; vigorous; very bushy and floriferous." [JR15/149]

Blanche Laffitte
Listed as 'Mlle. Blanche Laffitte'.

Boule de Neige (Lacharme, 1867) trans., "Snowball"
From 'Mlle. Blanche Laffitte' (B) × 'Sapho' (DP)
"Pure white, centre delicately shaded with cream, flowers medium size, beautifully imbricated and very perfect; habit vigorous." [JC] "Full, cupped. Flowers white, tinted with greenish-yellow. Blooms freely in clusters. A good autumnal rose." [Hn] "Imbricated, perfect rosettes…charmingly shaped." [F-M2] "Flower about two inches across [ca. 5 cm], full, globular, well formed, pure white; the blossom tends to nod…incontestably one of the best roses for the garden as it is very floriferous and remontant." [JR10/59]

"Petals large, quite convex, those of the center being smaller…not entirely hardy." [S] "Petals of great substance…good habit, hardy and free; growth vigorous. One of the best." [P1] "Perhaps the most floriferous of all the whites; undoubtedly, not the most beautiful, but it blooms through the Fall nearly to Winter." [JR32/34] "Elegant upright shrub, 4×3 [feet; ca. 1.25 m × 9 dm]." [HRG] "Glossy foliage…strong fragrance…5×4 [feet; ca. 1.5×1.25 m]." [B] "8-10 [feet; ca. 2.25-3 m]. Attractive dark foliage." [Lg] "Should not be…pruned closely." [F-M2] "From the work of Lacharme, the able and fortunate Lyonnais breeder whom all the horticultural world knows and who fills our gardens with wonderful introductions. This one is of the highest merit; its growth is to perhaps 4 and a half or so feet [ca. 1.3 m]. Its blossoms are pure white, but the exterior petals are sometimes tinted pink; it makes numerous clusters of blossoms…not an exhibition rose, but in the garden it deserves a place among the best…the abundance of its handsome shiny green foliage…sorts well with the snowy white of the flowers." [JR18/136] "Pretty vigorous; canes of moderate size, sometimes slightly slender, branching; bark smooth, pale green, with numerous reddish, hooked, sharp thorns. The wavy leaves are light green, sometimes bordered red, divided into five or seven nearly round leaflets which are acuminate and finely dentate; leafstalk, slender and nodding. Flower about 2.5 inches across [ca. 6.5 cm], full, globular, very well formed, often solitary; color, pure white; petals large, scalloped, those of the center smaller; flower stalk slender, reflexing under the weight of the blossom. Calyx rounded, pear-shaped; sepals leaf-like…one of the most beautiful white roses in the HPs." [JF] "It is said that this rose cannot be propagated from cuttings." [B&V] "Very much in vogue in England where it is considered as one of the best Hybrid Noisettes." [JR27/152] The association of 'Boule de Neige' with the Noisettes is perplexing, as it has no Noisettes in its ancestry; parentage of Bourbon × Damask Perpetual argues proper placement among the Bourbons.

Bouquet de Flore (Bizard, 1839) trans., "Flora's Bouquet"
"Bright light red, full, superb." [LF] "Light carmine." [HoBoIV] "Bright rosy carmine." [FP] "A great favorite…the flowers are very large, perfectly double, with large round firm petals, blooming very profusely; it possesses considerable fragrance, is a strong grower, and quite hardy." [Bu] "Canes amply furnished with handsome dark green foliage; flower large, full, cupped; bright carmine pink." [S] "Light glossy carmine, very large and double; form, cupped, exquisite. Growth, vigorous. Foliage and petals particularly elegant. Flowers, sweet. Forms a fine Standard or Pillar; good also for Pot-culture. A good seed-bearer." [P]

Bourbon Queen
Listed as 'Reine des Île-Bourbons'.

[Burboniana] (Jacques, ca. 1821) syn., 'Jacques', 'Rose Jacques', 'Rosier de Bourbon'
Seedling of 'Rose Édouard' (B).
"Bright rosy." [JWa] "*Shrub*, tall, vigorous, branched, bushy. *Prickles* large, hooked, wide, reddish. *Leaflets* 5 or 7, base rounded, acute at the tip, glabrous on both surfaces, simply dentate, glossy green above, paler beneath; petioles villose, with small sessile glands and tiny prickles; stipules decurrent, acute, denticulate. *Flowers* sweetly scented, many together at the ends of the laterals; pedicels finely glandulose; bracts elongate, ciliate, glandulose; *receptacles* ovoid, glabrous; *sepals* pinnatifid with subsetaceous prickles; *petals* 3-4 seriate, cordately notched, bright pink. *Hips* somewhat rounded, ovoid, red. According to the Duc d'Orléans, this rose [*meaning by "this rose," confusingly, the* parent *of the rose just described, as close reading will show*] grows in waste places on Réunion Island. Seeds brought from there some years ago produced the plants in the Neuilly gardens from which our painting [*accompanying the description*] was made. It has a good habit, and the abundance of its blooms, sometimes almost single but mostly semi-double, and their fine color and perfume, make it a worthwhile adornment for landscape gardens." [T&R]

Capitaine Dyel, de Graville (Boutigny, 1905) trans., "Captain Dyel, from Graville"
Sport of 'Souvenir de la Malmaison' (B).
"Flower very large, very full, a fresh beautiful pink with a darker center; well-held, very remontant, opens perfectly...Dedicated to a valiant captain of [*the Franco-Prussian War in*] 1870." [JR30/153]

Catherine Guillot (Guillot fils, 1860) syn., 'Michel Bonnet'
Seedling of 'Louise Odier' (B).
"Flower large, perfect form, purplish pink." [JR1/2/7] "Carmine-rose, beautiful even smooth petal, flowers large and beautifully formed...vigorous." [JC] "Intense purple illuminated by carmine...fragrant." [Cx] "Beautiful rosy-peach, large, full, and of fine form; blooms freely...Growth vigorous." [P1] "The bud doesn't open [*in Havana*]." [JR6/44] "Crimson...to about 2 metres [ca. 6 feet]...quartered and fragrant." [G] "From seedlings grown in 1857...vigorous, of the 'Louise Odier' sort, whence it sprang." [JR10/91]

Champion of the World (Woodhouse, 1894)
From 'Hermosa' (B) × 'Magna Charta' (HP)
"Pale pink with lilac." [T1] "Deep rose-pink, double...scented...4×3 [feet; ca. 1.25×1 m]." [B] "Dark red." [LS] "Ever free and constant blooming...One of the finest roses an amateur can have, blooming when quite young, it continues for years; the older the bush, the more and better the roses. The colour is bright pink; the roses large and double." [Dr] "Dainty bearing...small, light green, neat leaves." [T1] "The plant is vigorous and thrifty, and produces flowers abundantly all through the growing season." [C&Js98] Conard & Jones, as well as more recently Phillips & Rix, equate this cultivar with 'Mrs. Degraw', which is however an HB released by Burgess in 1885.

Charles XII (Dickerson/Sequoia, 2001)
Seedling of 'Souvenir de Victor Landeau' (B).
"Beautiful large very double pink blossoms of the same form as those of 'Souvenir de la Malmaison', only more deeply cupped. The plant is extremely robust, sending up thick canes not only from the base but also as laterals from the basal canes; the epidermis of the canes is often reddish-brown on the sunny side. The foliage, burgundy when young, matures to a dark green, and is large, healthy, and robust, sorting well with the size of the plant. The blossoms are large (4-5 inches [ca. 1-1.25 dm]), and come both singly and in small paucifloral clusters when the plant is established. They have a rich but not strong scent. Its habit makes it the perfect rose for fences or walls, as the long-growing canes (to eight feet [ca. 2.6 m] or more), though very thick, are supple in maturity, and can be trained to follow the peak of the fence, or the cross-bars of trellises against a wall. The hips are large, reddish-orange, and globular. The extreme vigor and commanding presence of this rose suggested its name, which commemorates the Swedish king Charles XII, who lived 1682-1718." [BCD]

[Charles Desprez] (Desprez, 1831)
"Delicate roseate." [WRP] "Rose colour. Worthless." [P] "Delicate pink, full, medium sized, beautiful." [LF]

Charles Lawson
Listed as a Hybrid Bourbon.

Claire Truffaut
Listed as 'Mlle. Claire Truffaut'.

[Comice de Seine-et-Marne] (Desprez, 1842) trans., "Seine-et-Marne Agricultural Committee"
"[A] fine variety, with flowers of the most brilliant crimson, not quite so deep in color as ['Proserpine'], and not tinted with purple; this is a most splendid rose." [WRP] "Flowers large, very full, somewhat forming a cup, of a pretty violet red color." [An42/331] "Growth vigorous; canes flexile,

light green, not much clothed with thorns; flower medium-sized, full, cup-form, growing in clusters; color scarlet, shaded with crimson." [S] "Flowers crimson scarlet when first opening, changing to rosy purple, produced in clusters of medium size, very double; form, cupped. Growth, moderate. One of the most beautiful of the group, especially when grown as a Standard. A good seed-bearer." [P]

Comice de Tarn-et-Garonne (Pradel, 1852) trans., "Tarn-et-Garonne Agricultural Committee"
"Cherry-color." [FP] "Carmine-red, well formed." [EL] "Color, very brilliant red." [S] "Moderate vigor; flowers medium-sized, full, intense brilliant deep pink." [l'H56/198]

Commandant Beaurepaire
Listed, as earnestly desired by its originator, as 'Panachée d'Angers', among the HPs.

Comtesse de Barbantane (Guillot père & Clément, 1858)
From 'Reine des Île-Bourbons' (B) × 'Louise Odier' (B).
"Blush, shaded with rose." [EL] "Flesh colour, large and full; form cupped; growth vigorous. A good useful Rose." [P1] "Moderate vigor...flesh white shaded pink." [JR26/137] "Flowers of medium size...blooms in clusters. Of the 'Louise Odier' sort." [S] "Very floriferous." [JR3/28]

Comtesse de Rocquigny (Vaurin, 1874)
"White; tinted with rosy salmon, beautiful." [P1] "Flower medium-sized, full, globular." [S]

Coquette des Alpes (Lacharme, 1867) trans., "Alpine Flirt"
From 'Mlle. Blanche Laffitte' (B) × 'Sapho' (DP).
"White, centre rose shaded, of medium size, full, form fine; growth vigorous." [P1] "Moderate vigor; flower...full, demi-globular." [S] "White, tinged with blush; size, medium to large; semi-cupped form, the wood is long-jointed. A very desirable white rose." [EL] "Fragrant, medium stem. Good

foliage, sufficient. Growth tall; hardy." [ARA23/159] "Clustering...habit free." [JC] "Profuse and constant. Iron-clad in constitution." [Dr]

Coquette des Blanches (Lacharme, 1865) trans., "Albine Flirt"
From 'Mlle. Blanche Laffitte' (B) × 'Sapho' (DP).
"Pure white with greenish reflections." [S] "White lightly washed pink; flower medium-sized, full, cupped, fragrant; vigorous, with erect branches." [Cx] "Pure white, large and globular; growth vigorous. One of the best." [P1] "Flowers freely in trusses." [Hn] "Very full, somewhat flat, but pretty; growth bushy. An improvement on...'Mme. Alfred de Rougemont'." [EL] "Free growth. Elegant foliage. Symmetrical bush. Beautiful cemetery rose." [Dr] "Of a robust constitution...it quickly forms and fine bush...on which are borne quantities of Centifolia-form flowers, medium to large in size, well held, and of a sparkling white sorting well with the handsome green foliage." [JR9/88-89] "Always green, consequently blooming continually. Its foliage is a very beautiful green, and its wood vigorous, presenting nothing to speak of in the way of thorns. The poise of the blossoms is perfect; they are of medium size, and borne gracefully on long stems...beautiful shaded pearly white, lightly tinted at the center with pink when they open in the sun...Today, February 25 [*in Havana*], our specimens of 'Coquette' are covered with a multitude of flowers, veritable snowballs...the semi-open buds somewhat resemble a white Camellia...'Coquette des Blanches' is not sufficiently known; it is lost in a crowd of novelties." [JR10/57-58]

Coupe d'Hébé
Listed as a Hybrid Bourbon.

Delille (Breeder unknown,-1848)
"Flesh." [LS] "Rosy lilac, large and very double; form, compact. Growth moderate. Uncertain." [P]

Deuil du Dr. Raynaud (Pradel, 1862) trans., "Mourning for Dr. Raynaud"
"Crimson, shaded." [Ÿ] "Vigorous; flower large, nearly full; velvety crimson black." [S]

Deuil du Duc d'Orléans (Lacharme, 1844) trans., "Mourning for the Duc d'Orléans"
"Flowers clouded purple, large and very double; form, expanded. Growth, vigorous." [P] "Very vigorous; branches climbing, nearly thornless; leaves dark green lightly touched yellowish green; flower large, full, very well formed; color, deep purple." [S]

Dr. Brière (Vigneron, 1860)
"Cerise." [Ÿ]

Dr. Leprestre (Oger, 1852)
"Bright purplish-red, shaded." [FP] "Very vigorous; foliage olive green; flower large, full, well formed; quite remontant; velvety purple." [S] "Moderate vigor; flower medium-sized, full, very intense velvety purple red, superb." [l]H56/198]

Duc de Crillon (Moreau-Robert, 1860)
"Brilliant red, changing to bright rose, large and full." [FP] "Vigorous; flower large, full, flat; fiery red passing to bright pink." [S]

[**Duchesse de Thuringe**] (Guillot père, 1847) trans., "Duchess of Thuringia"
"Flower large, full, growing in cluster; color, blush white, tinged lilac." [S]

Dunkelrote Hermosa (Geissler, 1899) trans., "Deep Red Hermosa"
From 'Reine Marie Henriette' (Cl. HT) × 'Hermosa' (B).
"Cerise red." [JR25/177] "Dark carmine." [LS] "Has the vigor of growth and profuse blooming habit of the well-known 'Hermosa' Rose, with bright glossy green foliage and beautiful vinous crimson flowers; a beautiful new variety which must soon become very popular, as it is quite hardy and a constant bloomer." [C&Js02]

Edith de Murat (Ducher, 1858)
"Flesh-color, changing to white, of fine form." [FP] "Good form, medium-sized, white lightly tinted pink." [l'H58/128] "Growth vigorous; flower medium-sized, full, well formed; color, a lightly blushing white."

[S] "Palest pink double blooms with rather fringed petals, tidy upright shrub to 4 [feet; ca. 1.3 m]." [HRG87]

[Émile Courtier] (Portemer/V. Verdier, 1837)
"Deep rose, perfect." [JWa] "Lilac-pink or sometimes light red...very good seed-bearer." [PlB] "Medium sized, full, well-formed, light red, shaded." [R-H42] "Pale rose, large." [HoBoIV] "Form, compact. Growth, moderate. A free flowerer, of fine habit, often splendid in the autumn. Excellent for a Standard." [P] "Wood vigorous, canes large, green, thorny; thorns short, wide at the base, red, pointed. Leaves comprised of five oval-pointed leaflets which are deeply toothed, dark green, and borne on a prickly leafstalk. Blooms in a bouquet of four or five, stem thick, green, glabrous, with short, lacinate, purplish bracts at the base. Calyx rounded; sepals short, entire, pointed. Bud round. Blossom flat, full, large to 6 or 7 cm [ca. 2.5 inches], outer petals round, inner ones ragged, lilac pink." [An41/13-14]

Emilia Plantier (Schwartz, 1878)
"A vigorous Noisette [*so-called*] with semi-double, yellowish white flowers. There is a dwarf Bourbon of the same name [*'Emilie Plantier'*, Plantier, ca. 1845, pink]." [GAS] "Semi-double, sometimes double, ill formed; utterly worthless." [EL] "Medium scent." [Sn] "Very vigorous, beautiful distinctive foliage, purplish green becoming glossy green; blossom medium to large, full, light coppery yellow, developing a yellowish-white tint—new in the Noisettes." [S] The references to Noisettes are in relation to the line of Bourbons such as 'Mme. Alfred de Rougemont' and 'Boule de Neige' being called Hybrid Noisettes by some for no reason which can be discerned today, as their parentage was Bourbon × Damask Perpetual.

[Emotion] (Guillot père, 1862)
"Pinkish-white." [BJ] "White, here and there touched light pink, beautiful virginal pink." [JR3/28] "Flower medium-sized, full; light flesh, with silvery white reflections." [S] "Delicate shaded blush, compact and good."

[FP] "Vigorous growth." [l'H62/276] Not to be confused with Fontaine's 1879 salmony Bourbon of the same name.

Eugène E. Marlitt
Listed as 'Mme. Eugène E. Marlitt'.

Euphémie (Vibert, 1847)
"Delicate rose, of medium size, full." [P] "7 cm [ca. 2 ¾ inches], full, delicate pink, mucronate." [M-L47/362] "Flower full, large; petals very pointed, giving a particular form to this rose; color, delicate pink." [S]

Fellemberg
Listed as a Noisette.

Frau Dr. Schricker (Felberg-Leclerc, 1927) trans., "Mrs. Dr. Schricker"
From 'Gruss an Teplitz' (B) × 'Souvenir de Mme. Eugène Verdier' (HT).
"Flower large, double, full, very fragrant, bright fiery crimson and coppery red. Foliage dark green. Growth vigorous, upright; very free-flowering." [ARA28/242] "The Bengale blood in this Rose gives it greater hardiness than the Hybrid Teas, so this recommends it to people in the North who want a continuous-flowering Rose that is hardy. The luminous, carmine-red flowers are of medium size but well formed. They come abundantly throughout the entire season. Fragrance also noteworthy." [C-P31]

Frau O. Plegg (P. Nabonnand, 1909) trans., "Mrs. O. Plegg"
"Deep red, medium size, full, very fragrant, tall." [Sn] Not to be confused with Jacobs' yellow HT of 1911, 'Frau Oberbürgermeister Piecq'.

Garibaldi (Pradel, 1860)
"Flower large, full, cerise red nuanced lilac." [S] Not to be confused with Damaizin's similarly-named lilac-pink HP of 1859. Giuseppi Garibaldi, 1807-1882; promoted the unification of Italy.

Georges Cuvier (Souchet/V. Verdier, 1842) syn., 'Beauté de Versailles'
"Bright cerise, shaded pink." [S] "4-6 cm [ca. 2 inches], outer petals concave." [dH44/334] "Bright rose, fine form, large and full." [FP] "Vigorous; canes weak, deep olive green, violet on the sunny side; thorns straight, flattened at the base; leaves very dark intense green; flower full, cupped; carmine pink." [S] "Rosy cherry, beautifully tinted with light purple. Large and full; form, compact. Growth, moderate. A splendid Autumn Rose. Habit and foliage fine." [P]

Gloire d'Olivet (Vigneron, 1886) trans., "Olivet Glory"
Seedling of 'Monsieur Dubost' (B).
"Vigorous, upright, pretty numerous chestnut-colored thorns; flower large, full, globular, beautiful delicate lilac-flesh; perfectly poised; beautiful long bud. Very floriferous." [JR10/147] Olivet was Vigneron's community in the département of Loiret.

Gloire des Rosomanes (Plantier/Vibert, 1825) syn., 'Ragged Robin', 'Red Robin'; trans., "Glory of the Rose-Maniacs"
"Glory isn't lacking in the world of Roses. Open any commercial catalog of consequence, and you will see *Gloire de Guérin, Gloire des Héllènes, Gloire de Paris, Gloire d'Auteuil, Gloire des Perpétuelles, Gloire de France, Gloire de Colmar, Gloire d'un Parterre, Gloire de Pelay, Gloire des Lawrenceanas, Gloire d'Angers, Gloire de la Guillotière*, and a thousand other Glories; but you will not always find *Gloire des Rosomanes*. It is not that the rose is mediocre—far from it; it is only that it is old...'Gloire des Rosomanes' was raised at Lyon about fifteen years ago by Monsieur Plantier, who had the good sense to give it a name it deserves so well, as it is the glory of the fanciers who possess it. It appeared in a section of mixed remontant hybrids...Branches long, of notable vigor, climbing, bark smooth, glaucous green; thorns occasional, of a flesh-shaded yellow, very strong, elongate, hooked, very sharp, pretty regularly distributed two-by-two at the base of the leaves, which are themselves composed of seven large leaflets, rounded, curled pretty much like those of the Elm, with long

much-tapered dentations, and hints of purple, a shade infusing the leaf as a whole; the leafstalk is lightly pubescent above, and furnished beneath with 6-10 prickles of the sort found on the branches, but shorter and smaller. The blossoms come in clusters at the ends of the canes; they are borne on long stalks of 1-1.5 inches [ca. 2.5-3 cm], bristling with purplish glandular hairs, as are the ovary and sepals, which have the distinctive characteristic of having cottony pubescence, and are much tapered, some-times extending into smaller divisions, making them lyrate-filiform. The ovary is small, and narrowed at the summit. The flower is 'hollow'—or (in common parlance) single—but, to be precise, it is double, because it is composed of two rows of petals instead of the one found in single blos-soms...Its fragrance is delicious, and its color a sparkling maroon, at the center of which one sees its numerous sulphur-yellow stamens. Examining the separate petals, one notes that they are whitish at the nub, violet-red beneath, and velvety maroon above. They are cordiform and number about five rows." [PlB]

"Single, dark crimson, and very sweet-scented...the foliage is not dense, and it straggles." [BSA] "Brilliant crimson, semi-double." [EL] "Intense red with a white nub; flowers large, full." [Cx] "Purpling in heat." [Th2] "Hard, almost unpleasant color." [Capt 28] "A most brilliant and beauti-ful variety...deficient in fullness...they fade very quickly in hot weather; it is only in the cool cloudy days of autumn, when their flowers never fully expand, that they are seen in perfection." [R8] "We find in our archives the following description of this old and beautiful rose: 'No. 109.—Gloire des Rosomanes (Hybrid Remontant), Vibert 1825, flower nearly single, brilliant intense red.' Such is the description of its introducer.—But we hasten to add that this plant is assuredly a China hybrid." [JR31/69] "Unlike the Bourbon rose in everything." [Sx] "Vigorous; flower large, semi-double, widely cupped; very floriferous; blooms up to Winter." [S] "Never flowerless." [J] "The only stock at the Knoxville station which blooms in both the spring and the fall." [ARA30/73] "For profusion of bloom from June till severe frost, has not an equal; the flowers are nearly bright scarlet, produced in large clusters, but are not fully double, of rampant growth...clothed with large foliage from bottom to top." [Bu] "A hybrid of most remarkable habits. Its large foliage, luxuriant growth, and showy semi-double crimson flowers, make it one of the most desirable of this division...I cannot imagine anything more imposing in floriculture than a pillar, from twelve to fifteen feet high [ca. 3.5-4.5 m] covered with the splendid flowers of this rose from June till October." [WRP] "This variety is above all notable for its dark green foliage; the canes are armed with strong thorns, the blossoms are very large, flat, of a vermilion red, and nearly single. This variety, of moderate growth in our climate, blooms well enough, but prefers warmer regions. In le Midi, where it may grow ten to fifteen feet high [ca. 3-4.5 m], it is much sought out as a beautiful and profuse bloomer, flowering once in the year." [JR2/44] "Continuous supply of flowers." [L] "Does well everywhere." [Capt28]

Gourdault
Listed as 'Monsieur Gourdault'.

Great Western
Listed as a Hybrid Bourbon.

Gruss an Teplitz (Geschwind/Lambert, 1897) syn., 'Virginia R. Coxe'; trans., "Greetings to Teplitz"
Parentage rather complicated! An unnamed seedling (parentage: 'Sir Joseph Paxton' (HB) × 'Fellemberg' (N)) was crossed with 'Papa Gontier' (T); the resulting seedling was crossed with 'Gloire des Rosomanes' (B), thus producing 'Gruss an Teplitz'.
"Brilliant cinnabar scarlet shaded with velvety fiery red...Very vigorous." [P1] "Iron red; flower medium-sized, cupped, fragrant." [Cx] "Flowers fairly large, some solitary, some in small clusters, bright orange-scarlet cherry-red...often flowers well in autumn." [Hn] "Crimson...deepening with age...strong spicy scent...6×4 [feet; ca. 2×1.3 m]." [B] "Unequalled as a free-flowering...rose." [J] "Little or no rebloom in Fall." [JR33/93] "A

favorite variety, with semi-double, bright crimson blooms that are especially freely produced in autumn." [OM] "Foliage is dark." [W]
"Leaves…small." [Hk] "For…districts without dampness…mildews."
[Capt28] "Foliage, immune from mildew; slightly susceptible to [black-]
spot." [Th] "Growth perfect." [ARA17/24] "Moderate height, rather
stocky, vigorous, hardy; foliage very abundant." [ARA18/125] "It is
absolutely one of the most valuable roses of the last ten years…From June
to November it is always in flower here." [K1] "It thrives splendidly when
not trained in any way, and it is especially valuable because it comes into
flower rather late, and in September is at its best. The blooms are in big
loose bunches, chiefly on the upper part of the stems; they are only semi-
double, but of vivid crimson-red colouring, and most fragrant…It thrives
with me in a half-shady corner, and there flowers quite freely, though it is
certainly worth a place in the sunshine." [OM] "Ornamented with large,
shiny, coppery foliage…One of the great advantages of this flower is that
it doesn't blue after being cut, and lasts a long time in a vase." [JR23/138]
"This Rose has good and attractive foliage and a strong semi-climbing
habit, growing readily into a good symmetrical, rather upright bush…The
flowers, which are produced in loose clusters, are semi-double and not
well-shaped, but very brilliant in the garden. The colour is normally a
bright crimson, occasionally tending towards maroon. They are not well
carried, and much inclined to hang their heads. They are produced in considerable quantity and very continuously, the autumn crop being especially good. The flowers are fragrant, and the plants have a magnificent
constitution." {NRS/12] "Blooms early and has all the Tea and Hybrid
Tea characteristics. The shrub is quite large, with brilliant foliage, and very
leathery leaves; the young growths are very distinctly a bronzy reddish-
green. The large blossoms, nearly always solitary, are sometimes in clusters
of two or three, and are upright and cupped; the color is a rusty cinnabar
illumined with fiery red and brown. The flower has no bluish tone. The
scent is of an incomparable sweetness. This variety is of easy culture,
blooms abundantly both early and late, and maybe in Winter as well!"

[JR21/67] "Happy, cheery, and most friendly of all roses! A great big lusty fellow, always nodding 'howdy-do' with bunches of red posies." [C-Ps27]

Gypsy Boy
Listed as 'Ziguenerknabe' among the Hybrid Bourbons.

Hermosa (Marcheseau/Rousseau, 1834) syn., 'Armosa', 'Mélanie Lemaire'; trans., "Beautiful"
"Deep pink, of medium size, full. Growth, moderate. A most abundant bloomer." [P] "Well formed, intense flesh." [R-H42] "Lilac pin, fragrant." [G] "Bright rose...constantly in flower, bushy habit." [EL] "Delicate pal pink cupped blooms...3×2 [feet; ca. 9×6 dm]." [B] "Sweet, small, full, China-pink rose beloved by everyone who knows it." [ARA36/19] "Fades in heat." [Th2] "Has been cultivated these ten years, and is still a favorite; the flowers are of the most exquisite form, perfectly cupped; though under the medium size, the deficiency is made up in the profusion of pale rose coloured flowers. It is a dwarf grower." [Bu] "Its beauty of form and color strongly recommend its being in every collection, independently of its profuseness of autumnal flowering and perfect hardihood...will bloom abundantly where China Roses, to which it bears a strong resemblance, will scarcely exist." [C] "Has China growth characteristics, and Bourbon floral characteristics; it is a hybrid of China and Bourbon." [JR23/56] "Quite ordinary and unexciting, but liberal in yield." [ARA20/16] "A distinctive and free bloomer." [ARA31/31] "Truly a jewel; always in bloom [*in Brazil*]." [PS] "Good decorative rose...Foliage, very good." [Th] "Leaves, greyish-green." [B1] "Requires little or no pruning." [JP] "Vigorous; branches thin and divergent...bark, dark green, glabrous, armed with the occasional brownish thorn, perhaps a little reddish; smooth foliage is a handsome green; flower, about 2.5 inches across [ca. 6.25 cm], globular, slightly cupped." [S] "Branches thin, boding a sickly constitution, but nevertheless growing with vigor, glabrous, shiny, olive green; armed with some remote, abruptly narrowed sharp thorns; [leaves] composed of five or rarely three unequal leaflets which are glabrous,

smooth, shiny, fairly strongly dentate, dark olive green above, paler and glaucescent beneath...Flowers ordinarily solitary at the ends of the branches, loosely full, very well formed in a rosette, of medium size, a pretty pale pink, darker at the edge. Flower stalk to two inches [ca. 5 cm], glandular-pilose, somewhat flexile...Calyx with glaucous green tube, glabrous, hemispherical, slightly elongated, not contracted at the mouth...Bud ovoid, pointed, intense pink, ordinarily with five darker lines. Petals obovate, spoon-shaped, nearly white at the base; outer ones large drawn up, well imbricated; outer petals pink to the base on the reverse; those of the center are folded or weakly curled, showing some anthers...'Hermosa' is a very graceful rose, even stylish, and of a delicate color. Its bud opens easily and with perfect regularity, giving birth to a flower which is exactly in the form of a cup during the first moments of opening, after which the outer petals reflex, drawn aside as if by design; at that point, their brilliant color begins to lose its freshness, and indeed the delicate pink which it had takes on a flat tint which foretells the end of this ephemeral beauty. This variety was raised by Monsieur Marcheseau...During recent years, it has been again released to commerce under the name 'Mélanie Lemarie' [*sic*]." [PlB] "Calyx nearly pear-shaped, glabrous; sepals narrow." [JF] "An old variety, but still one of the very best of this group." [SBP]

Héroïne de Vaucluse (Moreau-Robert, 1863) trans., "Vaucluse Heroine" "Velvety pink." [Ÿ] "Vigorous, blooming in clusters; flower large, full, globular; color, bright pink, sometimes washed with carmine." [S] Not to be confused with Cherpin/Guillot's 1844 Tea of the same name, which was pink marbled white. We are advised by my colleague Monsieur Massiot that the Heroine of Vaucluse was Laure de Noves of the town of Vaucluse near Avignon, the object of Petrarch's love from afar, who however remained true—alas! (but so much the better)—to her husband.

Hofgärtner Kalb (Felberg-Leclerc, 1913) trans., "Court-Gardener Kalb"
From 'Souvenir de Mme. Eugène Verdier' (HT) × 'Gruss an Teplitz' (B).
"Semi-double, delicate pink, very floriferous." [JR38/30] "Growth vigorous, bushy, upright, about three feet in height [ca. 9 dm]; foliage copper-colored. Very full, large blossoms, fragrant, of good form. The color is brilliant carmine, with a yellow center; the exterior petals are somber carmine, sprinkled with brilliant red. 'Hofgärtner Kalb' blooms up to frost without interruption, giving 20-25 blossoms on each stem. This newcomer, by its even height and flowers of noteworthy hue, is just the thing for bedding." [JR37/137] "Balls and mildews badly. Vigorous. [*Best in*] Interior South." [Th2]

Honorine de Brabant (Breeder unknown, date uncertain)
"Double blush-pink, mottled and striped with violet and mauve. To 4 [ft; ca. 1.25 m]." [HRG] "Loose…well scented." [G] "Large, full, cupped, fragrant; lilac-pink striped crimson and red…Repeats…common, but excellent." [Lg] "Main crop at midsummer." [T1] "Especially good in Autumn…5×4 [ft; ca. 1.5×2.5 m]." [B] "Mid-green foliage on a vigorous plant." [G]

[Impératrice Eugénie] (Plantier, 1855) trans., "Empress Eugénie"
"Purple pink." [LS] "Medium-sized, full, lilac-y pink nuanced silvery at the center, very floriferous." [R-M62] As with many Bourbons, sometimes listed as a China.

[Impératrice Eugénie] (Avoux & Crozy, 1856) trans., "Empress Eugénie"
"Vigorous bush; flower medium-sized, full, globular; color, lightly blushing white passing to snow-white." [S]

J.B.M. Camm (G. Paul, 1900)
From 'Mme. Gabriel Luizet' (HP) × 'Mrs. Paul' (B).
"Opaque salmon pink." [LS] "Light pink, large, very full, medium scent, medium height." [Sn] "Resembles the hardy perpetuals in foliage and habit of growth…Flowers very large and remarkably full, perfectly double

and delightfully sweet, color soft flesh pink; a fine out-door rose, entirely hardy." [C&Js02] "I [*exhibitor Arthur Soames*] was specially complimented...by the Rev. J.B.M. Camm in the *Journal of Horticulture*, to which, under the pseudonym of 'Wyld Savage', he contributed articles so long as Rose Shows were in progress." [NRS28/114]

Jacques
Listed as 'Burboniana'.

Jean Rameau (Darclanne/Turbat, 1918)
Sport of 'Mme. Isaac Pereire' (B).
"Pink, large, full, tall." [Sn] "Sport of 'Mme. Isaac Pereire', and a great improvement over it in color. Long, full bud of tender pink; flower double, the reverse of the petals rose Nilson, interior iridescent rose. Very hardy." [ARA19/100]

Joseph Gourdon
Listed as a Hybrid Bourbon.

Kathleen Harrop (A. Dickson, 1919)
Sport of 'Zéphirine Drouhin' (B).
"Delicate pink." [Cw] "Soft shell-pink...6×5 [ft; ca. 1.75×1.5m]." [B] "Not so vigorous [*as 'Zéphirine Drouhin'*], but makes a very pleasing bush with flowers of bright, light pink, the petals being much darker on the reverse...beautifully marked with transparent veins." [T1] "Bud large; flower large, semi-double; moderate fragrance." [ARA20/128] "An effective hedge background." [ARA33/18]

Kronprinzessin Viktoria von Preussen (Volvert/Späth, 1888) trans., "Crown-Princess Victoria of Prussia"
Sport of 'Souvenir de la Malmaison' (B).
"Milk white, tinted with sulphur-yellow. Good." [P1] "Of all the new roses introduced to commerce in 1888, the present subject is certainly one of the best, and when it becomes well known, it will take a place in the

forefront of cultivated varieties for its abundant bloom...originated in Germany...a sport of 'Souvenir de la Malmaison', and has the same bearing and growth...As for the flower, it is quite beautiful; the bud is slightly oval and is a handsome pure white; once open, the edges of the petals remain white while the center of the blossom has shadings of pale yellow. The flowers have the precious advantage of staying open a long time, and take on the appearance of a pretty Camellia." [JR15/6] "Over the entire Summer and Fall, it never stops bearing flowers abundantly." [JR32/34] "Very vigorous, with branches usually short and erect, bearing unequal thorns, few in number; the leaves are soft green and oval; the blossoms, large rather than medium in size, are about four inches across [ca. 1 dm], full, with large, rounded petals around the circumference, those of the center being shorter and more narrow; cupped, ruffled, perfect and graceful; very delicate sulphur-white, evenly throughout; strong Alba fragrance...very floriferous and remontant, as the short Bourbons tend to be; opens well, from a tapered bud." [JR12/120] "Good vigor, upright branches; leaves of a handsome dark green, sometimes brushed on the edges with light pink...The bud is of good oval form and lasts a long time." [JR11/166]

La France (Guillot fils, 1867) trans., "France"
Supp. seedling of 'Mme. Falcot' (T).
"Silvery-rose, with pale lilac shading...most abundant...highly fragrant." [H] "Now, upon examination, 'La France' corresponds exactly in its details to the Bourbon: its spination, with fairly numerous thorns intermingled with prickles, bristly and glandular on the young canes, and especially around the flower-stems before the blossom opens...it was declared by the introducer himself, Monsieur Guillot fils [*to be a*] hybrid Bourbon." [JR31/126] "Pronounced somewhat suddenly by the [*British*] National Rose Society to be a Hybrid Tea. There does not seem to be sufficient evidence or authority for this distinction, and opinions on the matter are divided; but some signs of affinity to the China race are to be seen

in the habit and freedom of bloom." [F-M3] "An invaluable rose for its hardiness, and its constant blooming qualities. Its color is pale peach, with rosy center; its form is globular, full, and very large." [SBP "Silvery-rose, changing to pink...the sweetest of all roses. If the buds remain firm, by gently pressing the point and blowing into the center, the flowers will, almost invariably, expand. An invaluable sort." [EL] "Beautiful shining lilac-rose on the interior." [JR1/2/8] "Blush, shaded peach; a superb Rose, one of the best for all purposes, except for walls." [WD] "It blooms perpetually, the end of each shoot always carrying a flower-bud, and these shoots constantly pushing forth." [ElC] "Globular, with pointed centre; free and very sweet." [DO] "Tight with petals, of attractive form...flowers...float gracefully above the foliage." [Hk] "Monster size." [L] "The most odiferous of roses." [JR1/11/2] "Tea-scented...and generally satisfactory...should not be too closely pruned." [HRH] "Fragrance just like that of the Centifolias." [JR1/3/4] "Blend of Musk and Damask [*perfumes*]." [NRS/17] "A good hot weather rose." [L] "Not a good laster in very hot weather...scent distinct and exquisite." [F-M2] "Best on own root in Southern zones." [Th2] "Practically worthless in this section [*Texas*]." [ARA18/79] "Of great beauty, except in wet weather...3×3 [ft; ca. 9×9 dm]." [B] "Often 'balls' in our 'liquid summers'...a charm and silvery subtlety." [RP] "Bright pink...blues slightly...bud is not long and tends to ball...susceptible to mildew and [black-] spot...if not properly grown has bad faults which are especially noticeable in wet seasons. If planted in poor ground in a bed which drains readily and not fed, it is well worth cultivating." [Th]

"Growth very vigorous; flowers very large, full, beautiful form and well held, with large petals; the center of the flower is a silvery white, the exterior a beautiful shining lilac pink its scent surpasses that of the Centifolia; this introduction will be of great merit for bedding." [l'H67/286, classified as a "freely remontant Bourbon hybrid."] "Grows better in soil that is not too rich." [M-P] "Growth well above the average...worthy of cultivation if planted in poor ground." [ARA17/23] "Medium height, compact, moderate in growth and hardiness; foliage sufficient to plentiful, black-spots slightly; bloom moderate, almost continuous." [ARA18/125] "Vigorous; canes pretty large, and, when so, straight and upright; smaller ones branch; bark, pale green, reddish on the sunny side; thorns short, very large and clinging, terminating in sharp points; foliage large, light green, slightly bullate, divided into 3-5 rounded leaflets, which are pointed and toothed; leafstalks are strong, reflexed, bearing numerous small prickles; flower, between three and four inches across [ca. 7.5 cm-1 dm], full, globular, solitary on the small branches and in a bouquet of 3-5 on vigorous branches; color, light pink, silvery on the interior, and lilac on the exterior; outer petals tight, large, and reflexed, those of the center smaller; flower stalks slender, nodding under the weight of the flower. A very pretty variety in all ways, and quite hardy." [S] "The growth is free and vigorous, making a bush from 3-4 feet high [ca. 9 dm-1.25 m], the habit branching; the foliage is thick and good, seldom affected by mildew, and the flowering period continuous from late June to early Autumn. The flowers are produced freely and borne on fairly stiff stems, but full blos-soms are apt to droop...At its best it is a beautiful flower and still one of the sweetest, free-flowering and most fragrant Roses we have...a good bedding rose...plants on their own roots being, I suppose, less vigorous will often give excellent flowers of the beautiful Rose in a wet season, when those on the briar have become nothing but melancholy sopping balls. It has the advantage, too, of rooting from autumn cuttings more readily than most garden Roses." [NRS/10]

"Calyx tubular, only slightly apparent." [JF] "Always blooming, but never sets seeds." [JR12/47] "I have made use of 'La France' often enough in my hybridizing, but I have never been able to get any seeds from it." [JR26/100-101] "It seems that this rose has decided to become produc-tive, and that it bore seeds at the home of Herr Dienemann, of Klein-Furra, in Thuringia. From three hips gathered, Dienemann obtained one rose which was single, another a lot like 'Mme. Julie Wiedmann', but paler. Finally, a third seedling, a climber, absolutely refused to bloom.

Though the results have heretofore been negative, we nevertheless believe that it will be good to try to breed with 'La France' in hopes of better success." [JR27/17-18] "'La France' blooms itself to death. *Mea culpa*, if others do not find it a short-lived rose. It is remarkably free in growth, almost immune from diseases and blemishes. In all nature, I know nothing to surpass 'La France' in full bloom." [Dr]

Lady Ardilaun
See 'Souvenir de St. Anne's'.

Lady Emily Peel (Lacharme, 1862)
From 'Mlle. Blanche Laffitte' (B) × 'Sapho' (DP)
"White tinged with blush." [EL] "Shaded French white." [FP] "White, slightly shaded with rose, large and full; growth vigorous." [P1] "Vigorous, blooming in large clusters; flower medium-sized, full; color, white edged with carmine; floriferous. One of the most beautiful white roses developed up till now." [S]

Las-Cases
Listed as a Hybrid Bourbon.

Le Bienheureux de la Salle
Listed as 'Mme. Isaac Pereire'. Our best wishes to those who use this synonym.

Le Roitelet (Soupert & Notting, 1868) trans., "The King-ling"
"Flower small, full; color, silky pink; growth moderately vigorous." [S]

[Leuchtfeuer] (Türke/Kiese, 1909) trans., "Beacon-Fire"
From 'Gruss an Teplitz' (B) × 'Cramoisi Supérieur' (Ch).
"Flower bright red, large, full, sweetly scented. Growth vigorous, free." [GeH]

Leveson-Gower (Beluze, 1846) syn., 'Leweson Gower', 'Malmaison Rose'
"Deep rose, tinged with salmon, the flowers are of the same character as Malmaison." [EL] "Fresh satiny pink." [JR9/12] "Blossom very large;

color, violet pink." [S] "Large, full, beautiful pink. Fragrant." [LR] "Rosy salmon." [TW] "Purplish pink." [Cw] "Bright pink to red...4×3 [ft; ca. 1.25×1 m]." [B] "Rose, shaded with salmon, very large and full; form, cupped. Growth, robust. Partakes of the nature of the Tea-scented." [P] "Something of a hybrid tea." [JR2/104] Confusion exists between this variety and 'Malmaison Rouge'. The problem is further complicated by confusion between 'Leveson-Gower', the deep pink Bourbon, and 'Souvenir de Leveson-Gower', a "deep purple" HP. The Bourbon 'Leveson-Gower' was not stated to be a sport of 'Souvenir de la Malmaison' by its introducer; and, considering their respective dates of introduction, 'Leveson-Gower' could be perhaps a sibling or, more likely a related cross. Contrariwise, 'Souvenir de la Malmaison Rouge', from nearly forty years later, was indeed a sport of 'Souvenir de la Malmaison'. George Granville Leveson-Gower, 1773-1846, 1st Earl Granville, Ambassador at Paris. Or perhaps "W. Leveson Gower, Esq., whose Roses at Titsey, near Godstone, are well known for their beauty." [P]

Leweson Gower
Listed as 'Leveson-Gower'.

Lorna Doone (W. Paul, 1894)
"The blossoms of this variety are magenta carmine, shaded with scarlet; they are large, globular, well formed, and very abundant. The bush is very vigorous for the sort." [JR18/4] "The flowers have a sweet perfume; they bloom just as well out in the open in the Fall. This is a desirable addition to the roses which bloom late...The buds are very large and of good substance." [JR18/67]

Louise d'Arzens (Lacharme, 1861)
"Creamy-white, beautifully cupped and well formed, flowers rather too small, though distinct, and very pretty; habit moderate." [JC] "White with yellowish reflections." [JR1/2/8] "Pure white, medium size, full, and of fine form; growth moderate; one of the best." [P1] "Quite a gem, producing its

pure white exquisitely formed flowers in great abundance; it might almost be called a perpetual 'Mme. Hardy' [*i.e., 'Félicité Hardy', Damask*]." [P2] "One of the best for massing." [FP] "Of moderate vigor, floriferous…one of the prettiest white roses." [S] Parentage consisting of 'Mlle. Blanche Laffitte' (B) × 'Sapho' (DP) may be suspected.

Louise Odier (Margottin, 1851)
Seedling of an unnamed seedling of 'Émile Courtier' (B).
"A bright rose-color, of a beautiful cupped form…it has a tendency to bloom in clusters." [FP] "Very double, full; bright soft pink with lavender shadings. Repeats…Excellent soft green foliage…6-10 [ft; ca. 1.75-3 m]." [Lg] "Camellia-like…vigorous and perpetual…4×4 [ft; ca. 1.25×1.25 m]." [B] "Almost equal to 'Coupe d'Hébé' in the shape of its bright rose-coloured flowers." [R8] "Good centifolia form." [Hn] "Very floriferous." [Cx] "Branches vigorous, somewhat thin, olive green…Leaves generally of five leaflets tinted brownish red when young, later turning a beautiful olive green above and pale green beneath…Flowers large, very full, perfectly formed, beautiful intense pink, solitary or in twos or threes at the end of the cane. Bud rounded-oval, handsome red. Flower stem glandular, thick, fairly long, very stiff, holding the blossom well…Exterior petals wider than long, upright, well imbricated, nubless, shell-like, rounded at the outer edge; center petals narrower or ragged and folded." [PlB] "Calyx pear-shaped and quite glabrous." [JF] "Branches fairly slender and divergent; bark, a somewhat yellowish green, armed with occasional maroon thorns, hooked and quite large; leaves smooth, olive green, in three to five acuminate irregularly dentate oval leaflets; strong leafstalks, bearing four to five little prickles; flower, about 2.5 inches across [ca. 6.25 cm], very full, cupped, solitary on the smaller branches…one of the best Bourbons; hardy." [S] "Very beautiful variety both grafted and own-root; its only problem is that it grows a little too high." [l'H53/224] "A free growing and beautiful rose." [JC] Possibly named after the wife or daughter of James Odier, nurseryman of Bellevue, near Paris, active at the time 'Louise

Odier' was introduced. Monsieur Odier was indeed also a rose breeder, having bred and introduced the early (1849) Hybrid Tea 'Gigantesque'. He thus may well have been the actual breeder of 'Louise Odier', Margottin later purchasing full proprietary rights to it from him.

Madeleine de Vauzelles
Listed as 'Mlle. Madeleine de Vauzelles'.

Malmaison Rose
Listed as 'Leveson-Gower'.

Malmaison Rouge
Listed as 'Souvenir de la Malmaison Rouge'.

Maréchal du Palais (Beluze, 1846) trans., "Palace Marshal"
"Delicate rosy blush, large; form, cupped." [P] "Flower large, full, flared; color, pale pink." [S] "A delicate pink, plump, full, large." [dH46/258]

Marie Dermar (Geschwind, 1889)
Seedling of 'Louise d'Arzens' (B).
"Cream and flesh." [LS] "Yellowish white, medium size, full, medium scent, tall." [Sn]

Marquis de Balbiano (Lacharme, 1855)
"Rose, tinged with silver, full, fine form, distinct." [FP] "Tinged with lilac, large and full; form cupped, fine; growth vigorous, well furnished with handsome foliage." [P1] "Flower medium-sized, full, very beautiful form; color, crimson nuanced satiny pink." [S] "Growth vigorous, looking much like a hybrid; flower full, well formed, carmine pink nuanced silvery." [l'H56/2]

Martha (Knudsen/Zeiner-Lassen & Dithmer, 1912)
Sport of 'Zéphirine Drouhin' (B).
"Double deep pink fragrant flowers of medium size." [G] "Unusual mauve-pink shapely flowers, very free-flowering on a vigorous shrub, 5×4

[ft; ca. 1.5×1.25 m].” [HRG] “Vigorous…The blossom is of an irregular form, intense pink on a yellow ground, brilliant. Very floriferous, this variety blooms until frost. Foliage, dark green with metallic reflections. Resistant to all maladies and insensible to cold, ‘Martha’ is, because of its many good points, an excellent introduction for bedding.” [JR37/25] Not to be confused with Lambert’s coppery pink Polyantha of 1905.

Mélanie Lemaire
Listed as ‘Hermosa’.

Michel Bonnet
Listed as ‘Catherine Guillot’.

Mlle. Alice Marchand (Vigneron, 1891)
Seedling (or sport?) from ‘Reine Victoria’ (B).
“Very vigorous and floriferous, blossom medium to large, full, globular, perfectly held, beautifully colored very delicate pink shading to blush white at the petal edges; very pretty variety.” [JR15/148]

Mlle. Andrée Worth (Lévêque, 1890)
“Very vigorous, flower large, full, extremely well formed, light pinkish white or washed pure carmine, very delicately nuanced, vigorous, quite remontant; foliage ample, glaucous green.” [JR14/179]

Mlle. Berger (Pernet père, 1884)
“Moderately vigorous, canes upright, well intermingled, thorns protrusive and numerous, handsome somber green foliage, flower medium-sized or large, full, beautiful delicate pink, autumn bloom much brighter, very well held, quite remontant, always opens well.” [JR8/151]

[Mlle. Berthe Clavel] (Chauvry, 1891)
Sport of ‘Souvenir de la Malmaison’ (B).
“Flower white, on a yellowish ground, pink center, reverse of petals marbled and striped with violet and bright pink. Variety enfixed from a cane of ‘Souvenir de la Malmaison’. This beautiful variety, over the five years I

have grown it (says the raiser), has always maintained its much striped and marbled characteristic; also, the bush is as vigorous as the Type, but more floriferous." [JR15/166]

Mlle. Blanche Laffitte (Pradel, 1851) syn., 'Blanche Lafitte'
"Faintly tinged with flesh-color." [FP] "Vigorous, blooms in clusters; blossom medium-sized, full; color, flesh-white. A pretty, very floriferous variety both grafted and own-root." [l'H53/224] "Autumn-blooming." [S]

Mlle. Claire Truffaut (E. Verdier, 1887)
"Vigorous, short-wooded; continuously in bloom; thorns hooked, pink; leaves composed of 3-5 leaflets of a delicate green, with shallow and irregular pink dentation; flowers medium-sized, full, very elegant and fetching in form; charming silvery pink, very delicate and fresh." [JR11/167]

Mlle. Favart (Lévêque, 1869)
"Bright pink." [Ÿ] "A charming rose of perfect form; very light satiny pink lightly edged white...very floriferous." [l'H70/125] "Flower medium-sized, full; color, silky flesh pink." [S] Pierette-Maria Pingaud, stage name "Mlle. Favart"; lived 1833-1899.

Mlle. Joséphine Guyet (Touvais, 1863) syn., 'Mlle. Joséphine Guyot'
"Deep red." [FP] "Flower medium-sized, full; color, bright velvety red." [S] "Red, exterior petals deep red." [S] "Rich violet-crimson, petals smooth, shell-shaped, flowers globular, large, full, and exquisitely formed; habit moderate." [JC]

Mlle. Madeleine de Vauzelles (Vigneron, 1881)
"Very vigorous, with upright canes, few thorns, light green foliage, flower large, full, beautiful delicate pink, center brighter, perfect form, well held, quite remontant, of the first merit." [JR5/185]

Mlle. Marie Dauvesse
Listed as a Hybrid Perpetual.

Mlle. Marie Drivon (Widow Schwartz, 1887)
Seedling of 'Apolline' (B).
"Poppy-pink." [Ÿ] "Very vigorous, leaves cheerful green, of 3-5 twisted leaflets. Flower medium-sized, perfect form, very full, petals large and rounded at the edge, arranged around a muddled center of pointed and seemingly ligulate petals. The color varies from bright pink nuanced peachblossom, marbled, spotted carmine or lilac pink...extremely floriferous and freely remontant." [JR11/150]

[Mlle. Marie-Thérèse de la Devansaye] (Chédane-Guinoisseau, 1895)
Sport of 'Souvenir de la Malmaison' (B).
"Vigorous bush, very floriferous, canes bushy, foliage light green; thorns occasional, short, and hooked; flower large, full, well formed, pure white, long bud, blooming abundantly, very fragrant. This variety is very recommendable for cut flowers, forces easily, and resembles 'Souvenir de la Malmaison' in habit and bloom." [JR19/130]

Mme. Adélaïde Ristori (Pradel, 1861)
"Flower full; color, deep cerise red with coppery reflections." [S]

Mme. Alfred de Rougemont (Lacharme, 1862)
From 'Mlle. Blanche Laffitte' (B) × 'Sapho' (DP).
"Pure white, lightly and delicately shaded with rose and carmine, large and full, shape of the Cabbage Rose; one of the best." [FP] "My most favorite [*of this race*]. It is small, and at first pure white, then blushing pink at the edges of the petals. It blooms early and easily." [JR18/38] "Cupped, fragrant." [Cx] "Beautifully formed flower." [P2] "Of medium growth, floriferous, blooming in clusters; flower large, full, centifolia-form; color, white shaded pink and bordered carmine." [S] "Surpassed by 'Coquette des Blanches'." [EL] "A perfect little gem...covered with its delicate and lovely roses. The wood and foliage are of a light green, the growth moderately stout, and with a free and graceful habit. The roses are small in size, quite double and full; when newly opened they are most handsomely

cupped, white with a delicate tint of flesh color, deeper towards the centre. It is a most abundant bloomer, and though by no means showy, is yet exceedingly attractive in its modest loveliness." [HstXXVIII:165]

Mme. Arthur Oger (Perrin/Auguste Oger, 1899)
Seedling of 'Mme. Isaac Pereire' (B).
"Pink tinted salmon." [LS] "Bright red." [Ÿ]

Mme. Auguste Perrin (Schwartz, 1878)
"Mottled pink, small or medium size, well formed; a new color in this class. We are most favorably impressed with it." [EL] "Vigorous, beautiful olive green foliage; blossom medium sized, full, well formed; very fine coloration; beautiful pearly pink; reverse of petals whitish; very fetching." [JR2/166]

Mme. Charles Baltet (E. Verdier, 1865)
Seedling of 'Louise Odier' (B).
"Flowers large, in clusters of 4-6, imbricated, beautiful delicate pink." [l'H65/338] "Vigorous…very full, delicate pink." [S] "Charming in color and imbrication, like 'Louise Odier', whence it comes." [l'H67/54]

Mme. Chevalier (Pernet père, 1886)
"Moderately vigorous, growing with upright canes; flower large, fairly full, opens well, beautiful bright pink; bloom continuous and abundant." [JR10/183]

Mme. Cornélissen (Cornélissen, 1865)
Sport of 'Souvenir de la Malmaison' (B).
"Yellowish pink." [Ÿ] "'Souvenir de la Malmaison' with white flowers plumed pink; smaller, poorly formed, and often inconstant." [JR12/173] "Of medium growth; flower large, nearly full, flat, looking like 'Souvenir de la Malmaison', but of a less pretty form; white, with blush-pink and yellow center." [S]

Mme. d'Enfert (Widow Vilin & fils, 1904)

From 'Mme. Ernest Calvat' (B) × 'Mme. la Duchesse d'Auerstädt' (N). "Vigorous, very floriferous, canes upright, thorns not much hooked, remote; foliage delicate green; bud virginal white; flower pretty, full, very pale blushing flesh white, a little pinker towards the center." [JR28/157]

Mme. de Sévigné (Moreau-Robert, 1874)

"Vigorous; flower large, full, growing in clusters; color, pale pink, brighter towards the center, petal edges blush white." [S]

Mme. Desprez (Desprez, 1831)

"Splendid lilac rose." [JWa] "Lilac-y pink." [TCN] "Deep pink." [V4] "Violet pink, full, flat, large superb." [LF] "Rose and lilac shaded, produced in large clusters, large and full; form cupped; growth vigorous." [P1] "This fine and robust rose blooms beautifully; its large clusters of very splendid lilac roseate flowers are indeed superb." [WRP] "It is eleven years since I first imported this rose, together with 'Aimée Vibert', 'Lamarque', 'Jaune Desprez', and some others of equal celebrity…This rose originated with Monsieur Desprez…[I]t is considerably hybridized with the Noisette, and like that rose produces its bright rose coloured flowers in immense clusters; from thirty to seventy bloom in each when the plant is fully established; the foliage is a rich green, strong and handsome." [Bu] "The secondary branches come only at the ends of the canes. The shrub is branched, but not intricately." [JR23/115-116] "Vigorous…leaves purplish green passing to very dark glaucous green; flowers very full, open well, three inches across [ca. 7.5 cm], well formed, intense pink at first, then violet pink, finally lilac, such that, as it is floriferous, one can see four different shades of flowers all at once in perfect condition. This variety has won the support of the many fanciers who have seen it." [R-H33]

Mme. Doré (Fontaine, 1863)

"Vigorous; flower large, full; color, light pink." [S]

Mme. Dubost (Pernet père, 1890)
Seedling of 'Victor Verdier' (HP).
"Flesh, center pink." [LS] "Vigorous, of good growth, well branched, with branches upright and strong; blooms in clusters; flowers of medium size or larger, pretty full, white blushing at the edge and bright pink at the center; well held; very floriferous; opens easily; quite remontant." [JR14/164] Not to be confused with Pernet's 1891 HP 'Mlle. Dubost' of much the same color.

Mme. Edmond Laporte (Garçon/Boutigny, 1893)
"Very vigorous, dark green canes, leaves of 5 leaflets, very glossy dark green, flower very large, semi-globular, full, silvery white within, very fresh pink without, very remontant." [JR17/147]

Mme. Ernest Calvat (Widow Schwartz, 1888) syn., 'Mme. Ernst Calvat'
Sport of 'Mme. Isaac Pereire' (B).
"Flower very large, full, of perfect form, variable, changing from China pink to intense pink; petal nub yellowish. Very fragrant." [LR] "Ruffled." [Cx] "Many yellow anthers." [GAS] "Very vigorous, climbing-type canes, somber green foliage, reddish beneath; flower…variably tinted, fading from China pink to bright pink or lilac-pink…quite remontant." [JR12/163] "6×4 [ft; ca. 1.75×1.25 m]." [B] Ernest Calvat, died 1910; manufacturer (glover) and amateur horticulturist, particularly interested in Chrysanthemum hybridization [information from R-HC]. Though found as 'Mme. *Ernst* Calvat' for the greater part of the 20th Century, for reasons as yet undetermined, this rose was introduced as 'Mme. *Ernest* Calvat'.

Mme. Eugène E. Marlitt (Geschwind, 1900) syn. 'Eugene E. Marlitt'
"Carmine-red [*and listed as giving between 100 and 200 blossoms annually*]." [ARA20/84] "Vigorous, practically continuous blooming, very fragrant." [ARA25/112] "A beautiful rose and almost thornless; flowers large, very double and full, bright rich carmine red, does not fade or bleach so

quickly as others, but continues bright and beautiful a long time, a strong healthy grower, constant and abundant bloomer; quite hardy and delightfully fragrant, makes plenty of buds and flowers for cutting all Summer and Fall." [C&Js06] "Blooms are large, full, globular, crimson shaded with scarlet on an almost thornless plant, 4 [ft; ca. 1.25 m]." [HRG] Correct form of the name of this rose is not yet fully settled.

[Mme. Fanny de Forest] (Schwartz, 1882)
"Pure white constant bloomer, handsome and desirable." [C&Js99] "Vigorous bush with upright canes, foliage dark green; flower large, well held, of a size surpassing all others of this series [*i.e., the series begun by Lacharme comprising in the main—if not entirely—progeny of crossing 'Mlle. Blanche Laffitte' (B) and 'Sapho' (DP)*], full, well formed, salmony white upon opening, fading to white lightly tinted pink." [JR6/148]

Mme. François Pittet (Lacharme, 1877)
Seedling of 'Mlle. Blanche Laffitte' (B).
"White, small, and very double; growth vigorous. A very effective garden Rose." [P1] "Vigorous, flower medium, extremely well formed, very beautiful white, globular…the most beautiful of miniatures. Not to be forgotten!" [JR1/12/13]

Mme. Gabriel Luizet (Liabaud, 1867)
"Carmine." [Ÿ] Not to be, or indeed perhaps to be, confused with Liabaud's 1877 Hybrid Perpetual of the same name.

Mme. Isaac Pereire (Garçon/Margottin fils, 1880) syn., 'Le Bienheureux de la Salle'
"Carmine-red, very large, full, free blooming." [EL] "Rosy-carmine, extra large and full; form expanded; growth vigorous." [P1] "Revolting in colour." [Hk] "Of a pretty color of lilac-rose, and the blossoms are well formed." [JR7/157] "Weak in centre." [F-M2] "Flower enormous, full; color, bright carmine-red; imbricated; very well formed." [S] "Light carmine. Good in autumn." [H] "Huge shaggy blooms of purple crimson…free…6×4 [ft; ca.

1.75×1.25 m].” [B] “Of good growth. A splendid rose, with a wonderful blooming record all season.” [ARA18/112] “Long branches clad with dull foliage, nasty little thorns, and mildew.” [Hk] “For our part, we believe that it is not a pure Bourbon. A simple examination suffices to show that it is strongly hybrid…[W]e retain the classification which was given it by its introducer, which is to say that we place it with the Hybrid Bourbons, of which it is certainly one of the prettiest, if not indeed the prettiest, variety…it is always an excellent sort, making such a vigorous bush that one would sometimes be able to call it a climber; its numerous blossoms, in big clusters, rarely solitary, are very large, full, well-formed, imbricated, very pretty bright carmine-red, and wafting an exquisite perfume. It is furthermore an excellent seed-bearer.” [JR17/52-53]

Mme. Joséphine Guyet
Listed as ‘Mlle. Joséphine Guyet’.

Mme. Lauriol de Barney
Listed as a Hybrid Bourbon.

Mme. Létuvée de Colnet (Vigneron, 1887)
Seedling of ‘Mme. Dubost’ (B).
“Vigorous, firm and upright canes, beautiful dark green foliage, thorns chestnut brown and fairly numerous; flower very large for the class, full, beautifully colored lilac within, petal edges silvery, perfectly poised, a splendid, very floriferous variety.” [JR11/152]

Mme. Massot (Lacharme, 1856)
“Medium-sized, full, white, center flesh.” [S] “Much like ‘[Mlle.] Blanche La[f]fitte’, but with smaller flowers.” [JDR56/41]

Mme. Moser
Listed as a Hybrid Tea.

Mme. Nérard (Nérard, 1838)
Seedling of 'Rose Édouard' (B).
"Silvery-blush, centre pink." [FP] "Delicate blush, large." [HoBoIV] "A pale rose-coloured variety, is most perfect in the shape of its flowers." [R9] "Vigorous; flower…very full, flaring, very good fragrance, very good seed-bearer; delicate pink shaded bright pink." [S] "Form, cupped, fine. A beautiful Rose, of moderate growth." [P] "Flower large, flat, flesh, nearly full…This new variety has been very fecund, giving birth to a great number of other varieties." [JDR59/32]

Mme. Nobécourt (Moreau-Robert, 1893)
Seedling of 'Mme. Isaac Pereire' (B).
"Very vigorous, wood strong and robust, beautiful light green foliage, bud very large and long, flower extra large, cupped, beautiful light satiny pink, in clusters, very fragrant." [JR17/164]

Mme. Olympe Térestchenko (Lévêque, 1882)
Sport of 'Louise Odier' (B).
"Very vigorous; beautiful dark green foliage; flower large, full, extremely well formed, cupped; a lightly blushed white, or perhaps washed and marbled carmine pink; very elegant color of rare beauty." [JR6/148] Has also been called a Hybrid Perpetual.

Mme. Pierre Oger (Oger/C. Verdier, 1878)
Sport of 'Reine Victoria' (B).
"Creamy-white; petals blotched and bordered delicate lilac-pink; a new coloration." [JR2/187] "Medium size, cupped, beautiful loose form, pale pink, gradually becoming redder in colour; a particularly charming, delicately-scented rose. Vigorous growth, good in autumn." [Hn] "White, edged with lilac, distinct and pretty." [P1] "Blush, the exterior of the petals tinged with rosy lilac, cupped form, not a free bloomer." [EL] "Petals rigid, porcelain-like; very floriferous; very vigorous." [Cx] "Very pale silvery pink. Translucent cupped flowers…4×4 [ft; ca. 1.25×1.25

m]." [B] "Makes a vigorous shrub with upright branches; its abundant foliage is light green; its abundant blossoms are medium to large, full, globular, and well formed. The color is creamy-white on opening, with the outer edges of the petals taking on a nice coppery lilac-pink with age...a rose of the first order." [JR9/104]

Mme. Thiers (Pradel, 1873)
"Vigorous; flower medium-sized, full; pink, center brighter, edged violet." [S]

Monsieur A. Maillé (Moreau-Robert, 1889)
"Bright carmine red, changing to deeper red; very large and full." [P1] "The formation of the petals is nearly the same as is the case with 'Charles Lefebvre', and you could call this 'Lefebvre in carmine'; strange to say, they both have the same penetrating perfume. The growth is the same as that of 'Mme. Isaac Pereire', but the foliage is more like that of the usual Bourbon...The most suitable training for 'Monsieur A. Maillé' is most certainly as a climber." [JR23/19] "Very vigorous, big-wooded and robust, with recurved thorns, beautiful very dark green foliage, flower very large, very full, always opens well, a model in form, sparkling carmine red while opening, passing to a darker red; blooms in clusters, very floriferous, quite as much as 'Souvenir de la Malmaison', and, contrary to the usual habit of Bourbons, very fragrant...[D]edicated to the honorable Monsieur A. Maillé, former may of Angers, former député." [JR13/100]

Monsieur Alexandre Pelletier (H. Duval, 1879)
"Velvety pink." [Ÿ] "A rose of the 'Louise Odier' sort, vigorous, medium-sized flowers, full, very abundant, bright pink." [JR3/182]

Monsieur Cordeau (Moreau-Robert, 1892)
"Violet pink." [Ÿ] "Very vigorous, bid-wooded with thorns; flower very large, full, opens well, globular; color, bright carmine red shaded vermilion, very fragrant and floriferous." [JR16/153]

[**Monsieur Dubost**] (Vigneron, 1864)
"Very light salmon." [LS]

Monsieur Gourdault (Guillot père, 1859) syn., 'Gourdault'
Seedling of 'Souvenir de l'Exposition de Londres' (B).
"Rich purple, fine form, full." [FP] "Flower medium-sized or large; deep purple." [S] "Very vigorous bush; flower medium-sized, full, deep purple to good effect." [l'H59/108]

Mrs. Bosanquet (Laffay, 1832) syn., 'Mistress Bosanquet', 'Thé Sapho'
"Very soft pink flower of much charm." [E] "Pale incarnate; wax like." [JWa] "Rosy flesh, very productive." [EL] "White, their centres delicate flesh, large and full; form cupped; growth vigorous. A beautiful Rose, sweet, and an abundant bloomer." [P1] "Very delicate and beautiful, at the same time large and double." [FP] "Flat in the form of a camellia; color, white shaded peach-pink." [JR26/57] "Globular." [Cx] "Medium size, full, cupped, white tinted with pink, fragrant, flowering till autumn. An old charming Rose of moderate growth and established merit." [Hn] "One of the very best of the pale roses...perfectly double, of cup form; colour, waxy blush; the growth is strong, nearly approaching the Bourbon roses, to which it is related." [Bu] "This rose appears intermediate between the Chinese and what are called Bourbons...If possible, more unique and beautiful than any other variety. A truly splendid Rose." [HstVI:368] "Very vigorous, blooms with abandon up to frost...salmon-white." [S] "One of the most desirable of the old China roses, and there are few in any other class that are superior to it. Its growth is luxuriant, and its superb cupped, wax-like flowers are of a delicate flesh-color, and are produced in the greatest abundance." [SBP] "Yet unrivalled." [R8] "The next collection which demands our notice is that at Broxbournebury, the seat of George J. Bosanquet, Esq., where there are at the present time a great number of very fine specimens...I believe this to be the best private collection of Roses in England." [P]

Mrs. Paul (G. Paul, 1891)

Seedling of 'Mme. Isaac Pereire' (B).

"Blush white, shaded rosy peach; large open flower like a Camellia. Distinct and handsome." [P1] "Soft, pale pink to white...ample, although somewhat coarse, foliage...54 [ft; ca. 1.5×1.25 m]." [B] "Flowers white with carmine, tinted peachblossom pink." [JR17/166] "Petals thick...Strong-growing, free-flowering, well into the autumn." [Hn] "Poor autumnal...colour blotchy." [F-M2] "A charming Bourbon rose; the blossom is exquisite in form and structure, the petals are large, imbricated, and recurved. The shade is a delicate pink, blanched at the center of the old petals. The tender shade contrasts nicely with those of other roses." [JR14/174-175] "Growth very strong, foliage...not liable to mildew." [F-M2] "Mr. George Paul...who for many years has mainly been interested in raising roses from seed had the idea of breeding varieties with the great vigor and remontancy of 'Mme. Isaac Pereire', thus profiting from all the good qualities found in that variety. He turned his hand to that task, and got seeds from 'Mme. Isaac Pereire', hoping to get seedlings which kept the magnificent bearing and growth of their mother, yet producing flowers which were more perfect and of a more beautiful color. The hope was translated into reality in one of the seedlings...[T]he plant inherited the vigorous habit and handsome foliage of the parent, as well as its remontancy...The exterior petals, which form a 'guard of honor,' are large and of a form without parallel, giving it a very distinctive character, while meantime the pearl-white color, sometimes with shadings of peach, makes it very intriguing...will play a very important role in rosiculture during this fin-de-siècle." [JR17/116-117]

Olga Marix (Schwartz, 1873)

"Rosy-flesh, changing to white; inferior." [EL] "Flesh coloured, changing to pure white, of medium size, full; growth vigorous." [P1]

Omer-Pacha (Pradel, 1854)
"Purple." [JDR55/19] "Brilliant red, large, full, and good form." [FP]
"Flower medium-sized, full; delicate pink." [S] "Flower imbricated, velvety bluish purple tinted slaty; upright stem; very floriferous." [l'H55/33]

Panachée d'Angers
Listed as an HP.

Parkzierde
Listed as a Hybrid Bourbon.

Perle d'Angers (Moreau-Robert, 1879) trans., "Pearl of Angers"
"Extraordinarily vigorous, flower large, very full, opens perfectly, very well imbricated, very delicate frosty flesh-pink, nearly white, blooms frequently and in clusters." [JR3/167] "Blush." [EL]

Perle des Blanches (Lacharme, 1872) trans., "Pearl of the Whites"
From 'Mlle. Blanche Laffitte' (B) × 'Sapho' (DP).
"Creamy-white, changing to pure white, foliage of 'Boule de Neige', and flowers somewhat similar; vigorous habit." [JC] "Pure white, medium-sized, full, quite globular, blooming sumptuously in clusters, growth strong, elegant habit, a very beautiful rose." [N] "Globular, full, deep, double roses. Buds hard and round. Very hardy. Free and constant. A very fine, old, pure white rose." [Dr] "Inferior to others of the type." [EL] "Very fragrant." [LR] "To five metres [ca. 15 feet] with handsome foliage." [G]

Philémon Cochet (S. Cochet, 1895)
Seedling of 'Mme. Isaac Pereire' (B).
"Extremely vigorous, semi-climbing; wood heavy, dark green; thorns slightly recurved, reddish; foliage handsome, 5 leaflets, dark green above, light green beneath; very floriferous. Flower very large, very full, often solitary, held upright, well formed, somewhat globular, beautiful deep bright pink." [JR19/164]

[**Pierre de St.-Cyr**] (Plantier, 1838)
"Pale rose, robust." [HoBoIV/319] "Pink, large and full." [FP] "Light pink, free flowering, a fine pillar rose." [JC] "Vigorous; flower large, full, flaring, very remontant, very good seed-bearer; silvery flesh-pink." [S] "Pale glossy pink, very large and very double; form cupped, fine. Growth, vigorous. A distinct and beautiful variety, blooming and seedling freely. Grown as a Weeping Rose, it forms a beautiful umbrageous tree, laden with its elegantly-cupped flowers throughout the summer and autumn." [P] Poss. not released until 1840.

[**Pompon de Wasemmes**] (Rameau,-1828) trans., "Pompon from Wasemmes"
"Lilac-pink, double." [RG] "Flowers very full, small, and a pale pink." [AC] "Bush not growing very high, having pretty much the stature of the ordinary Pompon [*probably intending the Centifolia Pompon 'De Meaux'*]; canes diffuse, slender; thorns numerous, close-set, equal, curved; bark smooth and glossy, greenish; leaves of a shiny green. Flowers small, globular, very full, perpetual, fragrant, a pale pink." [MaCo] The foundling in commerce as 'Huilito' has much in common with this description.

Président de la Rocheterie (Vigneron, 1891)
Sport of 'Baron G.-B. Gonella' (B).
"Vigorous and very floriferous, flower very large, full, cupped, perfect poise, beautifully colored bright red, center lightly shaded purple, fragrant, a magnificent variety." [JR15/148]

Président Gausen (Pradel, 1862)
"Flower large, full, bright carmine red." [S]

Prince Albert (Fontaine/A. Paul, 1852)
Seedling of 'Comice de Seine-et-Marne' (B).
"Brilliant crimson-scarlet...its autumn bloom is abundant." [FP] "Growth vigorous; canes very long, nearly lacking thorns; flower medium-sized, full, very well formed; color, deep scarlet; beautiful exhibition rose."

[S] "Vigorous bush; medium sized flowers in a cluster; deep intense cerise, shaded darker; very floriferous." [l'H56/247] "The plant is described as pretty stocky, with very robust shoots, and well clothed with large foliage of a very rich green. Its habit is to produce its blossoms in large bouquets; but, instead of ramping when planted out, like 'Mme. Desprez', it has short, stocky canes, like 'Comice de Seine-et-Marne'...only more robust, larger in its proportions, brighter in color, and more double. Its dwarfish habit joined with the length of its bloom (from June to November) recommends it for bedding...the autumn flowers are darker but less brilliant." [VH52/158] Not to be confused with Laffay's pink to dark violet Hybrid Perpetual of 1837.

Prince Charles
Listed as a Hybrid Bourbon.

Prince Napoléon (Pernet père, 1864)
"Flowers bright rose; very large and very double; growth vigorous; very effective." [FP] "Abundant bloom; flower...nearly full; bright pink." [S]

Proserpine (Lebougre/Mondeville/V. Verdier, 1841)
"Velvety crimson flame, full, flat, medium sized, superb." [LF] "Crimson to purplish crimson, variable, sometimes velvety, beautiful, of medium size, full; form, compact, fine. A free bloomer and good seed-bearer, of dwarf growth." [P] "Forms a dense and compact bush." [R9] "Grown from seed by Count Mondeville at St.-Radégonde, near Mennecy...now owned exclusively by Victor Verdier...It seems to be a Bourbon of the 'Émile Courtier' sort, having all of that variety's characteristics as far as wood and foliage go, partaking equally of the Bengal so as to look intermediate between *Rosa bengalensis* Pers. (*R. semperflorens* Lindl.) and *R. borboniana* Desp. (*R. canina burboniana* Thory). The bush is vigorous and seems very hardy; its canes are green, glabrous, and armed with strong, hooked, pale red thorns. Its leaves are comprised of 3 or 5 leaflets which are oval-elongate, pointed, cordiform at the base, serrate, deep green

above, paler beneath, and glabrous. It bears, at the tip of the cane, flowers in threes or fours on a more or less long stem of a purplish green which bears, at nearly the half-way point, a leaf-like bract, incised at the tip; calyx glabrous, glaucous green; bud round. Flower very full, 8-9 cm across [ca. 3-3.5 inches], slightly plump; petals large, oval, rounded at the edge, smaller towards the center, uniformly colored a very dark and velvety crimson—quite beautiful. This rose, borne horizontally on its stem, is very showy, and will take a high place among the Bourbons because of its coloration. It reblooms freely, its first bloom occurring in June." [An40/281-282] Proserpine, alias Proserpina, alias Persephone, daughter of Jupiter and Ceres and wife of Pluto.

Queen of Bedders (Standish & Noble, 1877)
Seedling of 'Sir Joseph Paxton' (B).
"Rich crimson. Few recent roses have been so highly praised as this; evidently a useful free-blooming sort." [SBP] "Vigorous, full, cherry-red, very floriferous." [JR1/12/13] "Flower full, large, dark cerise-red…blooms up to the Fall; resembles 'Charles Lefèbvre'." [S] "Medium size, very full; a free flowering sort. The color is not very durable." [EL] "Short growing, compact…shapely carmine flowers produced freely…3×2 [ft; ca. 9×6 dm]." [B] "Moderate growers, like 'Queen of the Bedders' [*sic*], require their strongest shoots to be shortened to three or four inches [ca. 8 cm-1 dm], and the weaker ones to one or two inches [ca. 2.5-5 cm]." [TW]

Queen of the Bourbons
Listed as 'Reine des Île-Bourbons'.

Ragged Robin
Listed as 'Gloire des Rosomanes'.

Red Malmaison
Listed as 'Souvenir de la Malmaison Rouge'.

Red Robin
Listed as 'Gloire des Rosomanes'.

Reine des Île-Bourbons (Mauget, 1834) syn., 'Queen of the Bourbons'
"Fawn and rose, medium or small size, fragrant, very free; of delicate habit." [EL] "Moderately full, a very fresh carmine pink." [JR1/2/7] "Fawn colored." [JWa] "White with a hint of flesh." [JR8/26] "Salmon carmine pink; flower large, full; very floriferous; very vigorous." [Cx] "Semi-double magenta and pink flowers, mainly in June. Crinkled and veined." [T1] "Medium or large, full, very delicate flesh color." [R-H42] "Its petals are arranged with a beautiful regularity." [SBP] "Delicate salmon-flesh, often tinged with buff, large and very double; form cupped, fine; growth moderate. An abundant bloomer, sweet, and of fine habit." [P1] "At first it was thought to be a Bengal, the same as 'Madam Bosanquet' [*sic*]…The colour is a beautiful waxy blush, with petals perfectly formed, bold, and cup-shaped; a half-blown rose from this plant is loveliness itself…dwarf in habit." [Bu] "Peculiar compact habit of growth." [Fl] "Vigorous…64 [ft; ca. 1.75×1.25 m]." [B] "Continual and copious bloom." [WD] "Large fruit in the autumn." [G] "Vigorous, with short productive branches; wood green, bearing rust-colored prickles which are short but big; leaves of three to five rounded, dentate leaflets; numerous buds; flower semi-double or nearly full, of a salmon-carmine pink, blooming over many months." [S] "Quite unique in their colouring, and well worthy of cultivation." [R8] "A charming hardy rose of proved merit." [Hn]

Reine des Vierges (Beluze/Armand, 1844) trans., "Queen of the Virgins" "Flower medium-sized, sometimes large, semi-full; rarely grown out-of-doors; color pale pink, flesh towards the center. Very good under glass." [S] "Growth, robust. A good Forcing Rose, whose flowers do not always open out of doors." [P] "This rose surpasses 'Souvenir de la Malmaison' in form and beauty." [dh45/395] "Her flowers are not, however, of virgin-white, but they are still more pale than those of the 'Souvenir [de la Malmaison]', not quite so large, but more regular and elegant in their shape." [R9]

Reine Victoria (Labruyère/Schwartz, 1872) trans., "Queen Victoria" "Beautiful bright pink." [l/H72/261] "Flower large, full, very well formed, of a handsome rose-color. A very beautiful variety." [JR26/57] "Very vigorous; flower medium-sized or large, full; color, bright pink. Reblooms very well and flowers until Winter." [S] "Damask fragrance intense." [W] "5×3 [ft; ca. 1.5×1 m]." [B] "Beautiful, but evidently varies. For me, alas, extremely sparse recurrence. Long willowy branches which, aspiring to be upright, hang and bend forlornly with the weight of the Spring bloom, made all the worse by rain, when the beauty of the globular blossoms becomes discernible to none but observant lizards and æsthetically-inclined ants. Susceptible to attacks of mildew, suffering much. The blossoms are a smoky lilac-rose, and are overly tenacious of petal—the plant must be dead-headed. Does not set seed. In good weather, it makes a handsome specimen, something to inspire us all; and, despite its potential weaknesses, it is something to recommend as being—under favorable conditions—admirable in full bloom." [BCD] Queen Victoria, of Great Britain; lived 1819-1901; admired on both sides of the Channel.

Réveil (Guillot père & fils, 1852) trans., "Awakening" "Cherry red tinted velvety deep shaded violet, resembling 'George IV'." [l'H52/148] "Flower large, full." [S]

Réverend H. D'Ombrain (Margottin, 1863) "Large flower, full, silvery carmine red." [JR1/2/7] "Bright pink, carmine center...very beautiful." [N] "Vigorous...color, very brilliant carmine." [S] "Well-formed, cupped." [JR3/29] "Fragrant and opens flat...to 1.5 metres [ca. 4½ feet]." [G] "Matt green foliage rather prone to mildew but the bush is of quite tidy habit." [B1] Rev. H. Honywood D'Ombrain, one of the great "ecclesiastical rosarians" of the late Victorian era.

Reynolds Hole (Standish & Noble, 1862) "Lively pink, increasing in brilliancy as the flowers advance in age, large, not very full." [FP] "Medium size, very fragrant, medium height." [Sn] S.

Reynolds Hole, Dean of Rochester; delightful rose-author, and very influential British rosarian of the Victorian age.

Robusta (Soupert & Notting, 1877)
"Vigorous, flower large, full, in clusters, fiery velvety red passing to purple." [JR1/12/12] "Foliage large and superb; not very remontant." [S] "A fine Pillar Rose." [P1]

Rose Dubreuil
Listed as 'Rose Édouard'.

Rose Édouard (Perichon/Breon/Neumann, 1820) syn., 'Rose Dubreuil', 'Rose Neumann'
From 'Monthly Rose' (DP) × 'Parsons' Pink China' (Ch)
"Bright pink, shaded." [LS] "It is everblooming, and bears double blossoms of a charming pinkish color; Monsieur Richard says that he never saw single blossoms." [JR19/9] "['Souvenir de la Malmaison'] is not distinct from 'Rose Édouard', except in its flowers, which are whiter, more double, and blushing a little in the center; in other characteristics, they are the same." [JR19/9] "This was the first one brought to France, and may be considered the Type of the species. *Canes* long and divergent, armed with much-hooked thorns, which are glandular at their base. *Leaflets* oval, large, cordiform at their base. *Ovary* ovoid-oblong, glabrous and glaucous at the tip. *Corolla* medium-sized, hypocrateriform, double or lightly double, intense and bright deep pink." [Pf] "This new rose attracted attention by its vigor and the novelty of its characteristics: its bright pink blossoms of a particular sparkling and brilliant shade, its long shoots notable for strong thorns…This rose gave a great many seeds, instigating many sowings which, at first, did not meet with good fortune. The specimens which arose had single flowers, or very double blossoms which aborted." [JR23/125] "The name 'Rose Édouard' (in remembrance of Monsieur Édouard Perichon, late settler)." [JR25/137]

There is confusion between 'Rose Édouard', 'Rosier de l'Île Bourbon', and anything else called anything like 'Rose-' or 'Rosier de Bourbon'. Properly, 'Rose Édouard' is the plant, or clones of the plant, found by Monsieur Perichon among his hedgelings that fateful day on the Île Bourbon. Cuttings of this were imported to France by Monsieur Neumann and sold as 'Rose Neumann' and then by Dubreuil and others as 'Rose Dubreuil' (evidently others imported it as well at length). Meantime, the 'Rose de Bourbon' or 'Rosier de Bourbon' designation—synonym 'Rose Jacques' or just 'Jacques'—should refer to one (or the other!) of two seedlings which Monsieur Jacques sprouted from seed of 'Rose Édouard' sent him from the Île Bourbon by his friend Monsieur Breon, and which was subsequently described by Thory and illustrated by Redouté, and which consequently has 'Burboniana' as its official name. Alongside this, 'Rosier de l'Île Bourbon' was an ill-advised additional name given to 'Rose Édouard' by certain of the Bourbon islanders; and—worse and worse—early seedlings of any of these might also find themselves called either of the 'Bourbon' names. Thus, properly, the first three Bourbons would be 1. 'Rose Édouard' (the imported original); 2. 'Burboniana' (French seedling of the original, illustrated by Redouté); 3. one other little-known and evidently unnamed French seedling of 'Rose Édouard'.

Rose Neumann
Listed as 'Rose Édouard'.

Rosier de Bourbon
Listed as 'Burboniana'.

Rouge Marbrée (Breeder unknown, date uncertain) trans., "Marbled Red" "Red and violet." [Ÿ]

Scipion Cochet (S. Cochet, 1850)
"Vigorous plant; flowers medium-sized, nearly full, sparkling red." [l'H53/202] "Very vigorous; flower large, full; very floriferous; color, bright pink, sometimes deep grenadine." [S] Scipion Cochet, *rosiériste* and

one of the founders of the 1877-1914 *Journal des Roses*, a publication so important to rose research. "Born at Suisnes the first of October, 1833, Scipion Cochet had not reached the age of 63 when death called…His ancestors were gardeners. His grandfather and father were horticulturist-nurserymen…The vast works which he directed at Suisnes…were created in 1799 by Christophe Cochet, encouraged and advised by Admiral Count Bougainville, for whom he was chief gardener." [JR20/82-83]

Sir Joseph Paxton
Listed as a Hybrid Bourbon.

Sophie's Perpetual (Breeder unknown,-1928)
"Fragrant, double flowers of silvery pink, petal edges blushing deep rose." [HRG] "Cupped…8×4 [ft; ca. 2.25×1.25 m]." [B] Sophie, Countess Beckendorf.

Souchet (Souchet/V. Verdier, 1842)
"Deep crimson-purple, vivid, superb." [FP] "Deep crimson, large and full." [HoBoIV/319] "Blossom 7 cm across [ca. 3 inches]…full, carmine-purple." [dH44/335] "Flower large, full, very tightly filled, very fragrant; color, bright grenadine." [S] "Purple-red…medium height." [Sn] "Flowers bright rosy purple, sometimes brilliant crimson, glossy, very large and full; form, compact. Growth, moderate. A superb Rose, and sweet. Raised by Mons. Souchet in the vicinity of Paris. Introduced in 1843 [*1842 appears correct*]." [P] "Canes vigorous, light green, with large, hooked, red thorns; leaves with five leaflets, glossy green above, a more glaucous green beneath, finely and regularly dentate. Peduncle upright, strong; ovary smooth, short, and round; flower 10-11 cm in size [ca. 4 inches], with large petals around the circumference, more muddled towards the center, a pretty bright purple, seeming more somber than it is by the clarity of the violet shade on the backs of the petals. It is very full." [An42/337] Not to be confused with 'Charles Souchet' the deep carmine Bourbon of 1843. "Monsieur Souchet, flower gardener in Bagnolet." [An42/210]

Souvenir d'Adèle Launay (Moreau-Robert, 1872) trans., "In Memory of Adèle Launay"
"Light red." [Ÿ] "Flower large, full, opens well; color, bright pink." [S] "Pale rose, globular; a pretty well formed flower, with good foliage and vigorous habit; a good pillar or wall rose." [JC]

Souvenir d'un Frère (Oger, 1850) trans., "In Memory of a Brother"
"Purple-red and carmine." [S] "Medium-sized, full, deep red nuanced with crimson." [BJ58] "6-7 cm [ca. 2 ½ inches], nearly full, very dark red mixed with crimson." [R&M62] "Vigorous plant; blossoms medium-sized, nearly full, deep violety red sometimes having a white line down the middle of several petals." [l'H53/202]

[Souvenir de l'Exposition de Londres] (Guillot père, 1851) trans., "Remembrance of the London Exhibition"
"Flower medium-sized or large, depending upon the season and the vigor of the plant; full; color, rich velvety poppy." [VH51/112] "Plant moderately vigorous; flowers medium-sized, full; velvety bright red. Pretty both grafted and own-root." [l'H53/224]

Souvenir de la Malmaison (Beluze, 1843) trans., "In Remembrance of Malmaison"
From 'Mme. Desprez' (B) × "a Tea Rose" (possibly 'Devoniensis')
"Monsieur Beluze, horticulturist at Vaise, a suburb of Lyon, has found among his seedlings a new Bourbon rose which, as a fancier from Lyon tells us, is very beautiful. Basically flesh, the blossom, tinted violet upon opening, is full, and large to about four inches [ca. 1 dm]; the bush is, like 'Mme. Desprez', quite remontant. This rose, 'Souvenir de la Malmaison', will be available…at the beginning of June." [R-H42] "It was in 1840 that Monsieur Beluze the elder, rose-breeder in Lyon, sowed the seeds which produced the splendid and magnificent rose which I now place before the reader. Two years later, in 1842, the breeder declared that he had produced a rose which was out-of-the-ordinary, though without having been able,

up to that time, to get more than one sole blossom, which was on the one stem of the original plant, that stem having reached a foot [ca. 3 dm] or so in height. The situation was assessed by Monsieur Plantier, distinguished rosarian, who declared on sight that this was one of the most fortunate obtentions of the era…The great question to be resolved concerned which variety produced the seeds from which Malmaison sprang. Over and again the Société d'Horticulture Pratique de Rhône hoped to settle the question at its meetings…[*The Société determined*] that in all probability 'Souvenir de la Malmaison' came from the Bourbon 'Mme. Desprez', the opinion on Beluze, which was indeed shared by Plantier. In support of this, it is a fact that the seeds collected and sown were for the most part from 'Mme. Desprez'. Upon close scrutiny, one notes a great similarity between the stature and foliage of the two varieties…The original specimen of Malmaison still exists at Lyon [*in 1879*], where it continues to bloom so well that it gives offspring, despite being in a less than favorable position—a southern exposure." [JR3/73] "The blossoms…were taken to the markets of Lyon, whence they were quickly borne off; and Beluze was not of a mind to release this wonderful variety [*wanting to maintain his monopoly on its appearance in the florist trade*]…Beluze was so happy in the possession of this jewel that, whenever someone would enter his yard, he would place that person under the strictest surveillance, believing that otherwise the person would take many cuttings. The story also goes on to say that Mme. Beluze would stand, watching, in one of the windows of the house. As for Beluze himself, he would himself be lost in watching the visitor from head to toe." [JR19/9-10] "Beluze released it to commerce in June, 1843, when specimens of it sold at the price of 25 francs. It bloomed for the first time [*that is, off Beluze's premises*] at Paris in 1844…When Monsieur Beluze announced his rose, he described it as 'ground, flesh, lightly violet when opening, full, large to 3.5 inches [ca. 8 cm]'. In effect, the rose is white…As to the form, it is equally variable. If the plant is somewhat vigorous, the blossom is flat, ruffled in the center, and nearly completely white; the petals, instead of assuming a graceful round form, imbricate, resembling the scales of a pine cone…The variety is vigorous, grafted on good stock; the blossom is symmetrical; its stem is long and somewhat flexible, and the flower nods gracefully…[E]xamined closely, it is composed of rounded petals, imbricated, diminishing from the circumference to the center; taken together, they form a veritable Legion of Honor officer's medal." [PlB]

"A grand flesh-colored rose, of vigorous growth." [JP] "Creamy-white, fine." [Sx] "Soft pearly flesh-pink, large, quite flat, quartered in form, strong on its stem." [ARA36/19] "A large and splendid rose of pale incarnate hue, slightly tinged with fawn, very double, and of fine form; it is deemed one of the richest acquisitions of this class of roses." [WRP] "Unsurpassed among roses. It is very large, and beautifully formed. It is of a light, transparent flesh-color." [FP] "Satiny white flower." [Hn] "Flesh-colour…margins almost white, very large and full; form compact; growth vigorous. A magnificent Rose, with large thick petals." [P1] "Blush centre, disk circular in outline, perfectly double, though flattish. Its tendency is to bloom in corymbs, and its habit, when upon its own roots, is rather robust and straggling. The perfume is delicious, and its flowers average nearly five inches in diameter [ca. 1.25 dm]. The purity and exquisite loveliness of this old variety is unsurpassed." [WD] "Grown upon its own roots, and well mulched through the winter, it gives us, early in summer and late in autumn, the flowers so exquisite in the eve of their full development." [R1/159] "The grand old rose 'Souvenir de la Malmaison' is never so beautiful in summer as in autumn, so that it is quite worth while to sacrifice the summer blooms, and let it bloom in autumn only." [GG] "Injured by rain." [F-M2] "The petals of a kid-like texture are smoothly folded back from the centre, forming a broad, flat rose like no other except the Hybrid Perpetual 'Mme. Charles Wood'." [Dr] "Superlatively beautiful buds, blush-white with rose-pink flirtings, open slowly into fascinating blossoms which look like circlets of rumpled blush-colored satin. Dream-like sweet yeasty aroma. Has an affinity for mildew (no rust), but takes spraying well. Blooms in bursts rather than continuously." [BCD]

"Magnificent foliage—very large and distinct—a superb rose...of very robust growth...The flowers are frequently *immensely* large, borne on erect stout footstalks, with broad and beautiful foliage deeply serrated, giving to the whole plant a remarkably noble appearance." [C] "Altogether the most perfect and superb rose of this or any other class...Its flowers are cupped, and of very perfect form, very double, with thick velvety petals; they are of the largest size, often four to five inches in diameter [ca. 1-1.25 dm], and their color delicate blush, with a rich tint of cream. Its large and very luxuriant foliage, compact habit, and flowers of exceeding beauty, render this one of the very finest roses known." [SBP] "Foliage very good, holds well. Vigorous growth in Southern Zones." [Th2] "Bear in mind that vigorous growers like 'Souvenir de la Malmaison' must not be pruned too closely. Simply shorten the strongest shoots one-third and the weakest two-thirds." [TW] "Vigorous; branches pretty strong, divergent, the young growths being reddest; bark a handsome green, with slightly reddish thorns, which are short, upright, and very sharp; foliage of 3-7 leaflets, which are slightly rounded at the base, acuminate at the tip, and finely toothed; the leafstalks are thin, and armed with a few little prickles; the flower is about 3.5 inches across [ca. 9 cm], very full, cupped, flat, solitary on the branchlets, clustered on the more vigorous branches; color, salmon-white, and towards the center bright light pink with violet-pink reflections; the bud is well formed, and the color is a more pronounced flesh-pink; the outer petals are large and concave; those of the center are smaller, rumpled, and very numerous, making a muddled center; the flower stalks are short, and nod under the weight of the blossom. This variety is without rival for late bloom. Does not like harsh Winters." [S] "Calyx short, rounded, and glabrous." [JF] "We believe that it is worthy of notice that neither of these [*'Devoniensis' and 'Souvenir de la Malmaison'*] have produced seed." [WD] "Has never given me seeds." [JR26/101] "Sported 'Kronprinzessin Viktoria', 'Mme. Cornélissen', 'Mlle. Berthe Clavel', 'Mlle. Marie-Thérèse de la Devansaye', [*not to forget 'Souvenir de la Malmaison Rouge', 'Climbing Souvenir de la Malmaison', 'Capitaine Dyel, de Graville', and 'Souvenir de St. Anne's*]." [JR26/106]

"Malmaison" was of course the palace to which the Empress Joséphine retired after her divorce from Napoléon. On the grounds, she created what was then the world's most complete collection of roses, which was evidently dispersed after her death in 1814, with first attempts at reconstitution not taking place until circa 1900. One occasionally sees an interesting saga about the naming of this rose involving a Russian nobleman obtaining cuttings of this cultivar—from no less a place than the palace of Malmaison itself!—and, in the best romantic tradition, going into such transports of nostalgia that said nobleman demanded that the name of the cultivar be none other than...'*Souvenir de la Malmaison*'. As Rivers says in another connection, this is pretty enough, but entirely devoid of truth. As we have seen, Beluze knew it came from seed, and jealously guarded his cultivar prior to introduction—no cuttings to Russian noblemen, and certainly none to or from a Malmaisonian garden which had been in decay for some thirty years, and which was not due to be reconstituted for another sixty. Finally, *even prior to introduction* the name of the rose was 'Souvenir de la Malmaison', evidenced by the announcement in the 1842 *Revue-Horticole* which we offer above. We have not, however, investigated the possibility that Beluze himself was the Russian nobleman, *incognito*. "Inimitable." [JR20/23] "Like water lilies upon a dark pond." [Hk] "Always beautiful, always ravishing." [JR25/3] "Its beauty suggests a blending of the finest sculpture and the loveliest feminine complexion." [HstIII:61] "As yet unrivalled in its noble flowers, so delicate in colour and so truly beautiful." [R8] "Pale beauty and peculiar fragrance—we have nothing like it among the modern roses." [ARA29/50] "Imperial Malmaison...your memory is always alive in me." [JR38/49]

[**Souvenir de la Malmaison Rouge**] (Gonod, 1882) syn. 'Malmaison Rouge', 'Red Malmaison'; trans., "Red Souvenir de la Malmaison"
Sport of 'Souvenir de la Malmaison' (B).
"Flower medium-sized, full, beautiful dark velvety red. Fragrant." [LR] "Large flowers, beautifully imbricated; very full, perfect form; color bright, glowing crimson, very vivid, rich, and velvety; highly scented, and a very promising variety." [CA88] "Sport of 'Souvenir de la Malmaison'. This variety has the thorns of its parent; the foliage is of five leaflets which are very dark green; it blooms just like Malmaison; the blossom is of moderate size, and a dark velvety red. It is quite valuable for bouquets due to its cupped flowers. It produces a charming effect when bedded with Malmaison." [JR6/149-150] Confusion exists between this variety and 'Leveson-Gower', which see.

Souvenir de Louis Gaudin (Trouillard, 1864) trans., "In Memory of Louis Gaudin"
"Reddish-purple, shaded with black, fine form, full, abundant bloomer." [FP] "Flower medium-sized, full, purple shaded black; very floriferous, very remontant." [S]

Souvenir de Mme. Auguste Charles (Moreau-Robert, 1866) trans., "In Memory of Mme. Auguste Charles"
"Salmon-flesh." [LS] "Light pink tinged salmon, medium sized, full, well formed, petals rolled." [N] "Not…very vigorous." [G]

Souvenir de Monsieur Bruel (Levet, 1889) trans., "In Memory of Monsieur Bruel"
"Light red." [LS] "Growth vigorous, flower large, full, well-formed, brilliant light red, large thorns, heavy wood, handsome dark green foliage, very floriferous." [JR13/147]

Souvenir de Némours
Listed as a Hybrid Bourbon.

Souvenir de St. Anne's (G.S. Thomas/Hilling, 1950) syn., 'Lady Ardilaun'; trans., "Remembrance of St. Anne's"
Sport of 'Souvenir de la Malmaison' (B).
Blush. "Rich quality in [*the flower's*] delicate tints and beautiful sculptured shapes." [T1] "Semi-double...very attractive...4×3 [ft; ca. 1.25×1 m]."
[B] The sport occurred in the garden of Lady Ardilaun (otherwise Guiness) at St. Anne's, Clontarf, Ireland. According to Graham Stuart Thomas, however (*v. The Garden* of August, 1989), the sport, having occurred prior to 1916, was preserved by Lady Moore.

Souvenir de Victor Landeau (Moreau-Robert, 1890) trans., "In Memory of Victor Landeau"
"Very vigorous, handsome dark green foliage; heavy upright robust growth, thorny, flower extra large, full, cupped, bright red nuanced carmine, in clusters, very strong and numerous." [JR14/148]

Souvenir du Lieutenant Bujon (Moreau-Robert, 1891) trans., "In Memory of Lieutenant Bujon"
"Very vigorous bush, beautiful dark green foliage, big-wooded, thus bearing the enormous bud perfectly upright; blossom extra large, full, opening well, cupped; color, light red passing to carmine, very floriferous and very fragrant. A top of the line variety." [JR15/148-149]

Souvenir du Président Lincoln (Moreau-Robert, 1865) trans., "In Memory of President Lincoln"
Seedling of 'Sir Joseph Paxton' (B).
"Very vigorous; flower medium-sized, full; color, crimson red nuanced black." [S]

Thé Sapho
Listed as 'Mrs. Bosanquet'.

Toussaint-Louverture (Miellez, 1849)
"Flower medium-sized, full, well-formed; color, deep violet red." [S]
Pierre Dominique Toussaint-Louverture, 1743-1803; Haitian liberator.

Triomphe de la Duchère (Beluze, 1846) trans., "Triumph of la Duchère"
"Rosy-blush, large and full." [FP] "Pale rose, produced in large clusters, of medium size, full; form, cupped." [P] "Well formed; color, delicate pink; branches climbing; blooms in clusters." [S] "An abundant bloomer, and a good pillar or climbing rose." [JC]

Variegata di Bologna (Lodi/Bonfiglioli, 1909) trans., "The Variegated One from Bologne"
"Very pronounced stripes of purple on a creamy white background...tall...a bit sparse in foliage...5×4 [ft; ca. 1.5×1.25 m]." [B] "Very fragrant." [G] "Not profuse in the least for me—three blossoms in two years—and very subject to mildew and rust; performance must vary. The canes on mine—a budded plant—exceeded eight feet in length [ca. 2.25 m]." [BCD]

Velouté d'Orléans (Dauvesse, 1852) trans., "The Velvety One from Orléans"
"Flower large, full; light purple." [S]

Vicomte Fritz de Cussy (Margottin, 1845)
"Lively red." [FP] "Cherry colour, tinged with purple, large and very double; form, compact. Growth, moderate." [P] "Very remontant, flower well-formed, prettily colored bright pink." [An47/209] "Branches vigorous, light green; thorns large, slightly hooked, light red; leaves of 5 dark green leaflets, deeply toothed; flower stem strong, long, upright; ovary smooth, slightly rounded; sepals narrow and long; flower 7-8 cm across [ca. 3 inches], full, well-formed, beautiful bright cerise-red; blooms easily. Grown from seed by Monsieur Margottin in 1844." [dH46/270]

Victoire Fontaine (Fontaine, 1882)
Seedling of 'Catherine Guillot' (B).
"Vigorous plant; flower medium-sized or large, very full, well formed; color rich, a beautiful bright satiny purple pink...very floriferous. Flower very beautiful, opening perfectly." [JR6/164]

Virginia R. Coxe
Listed as 'Gruss an Teplitz'.

Vivid
Listed as a Hybrid Bourbon.

Zéphirine Drouhin (Bizot, 1868)
"Cerise-pink, semi-double...10×8 [ft; ca. 3.2×2.25 m]." [B] "Brilliant crimson red; flower large, full." [Cx] "Finely shaped double...of sparkling pink...true, rich, rose scent." [ARA29/98] "Beautiful soft pink...a fragrance all its own...a healthy plant which blooms for several weeks." [ARA29/50] "Long, pointed buds." [W] "Fair growth; beautiful color; good form; very occasional flowers in summer and fall." [ARA18/121] "This variety is well known for adorning walls and making arbors. In my opinion, few varieties surpass it; very vigorous and very floriferous, it is not perhaps remontant enough, but the first bloom is so abundant that it is prolonged late into the season." [JR13/33-34] "Pinkish, bronzy foliage...practically evergreen." [ARA29/101] "Lusty shrub to 10 [ft; ca. 3 m]." [HRG] "An effective hedge background." [ARA33/18] "Makes an excellent bush, and its lovely, fragrant blooms of soft rose-colour, that are freely produced for weeks together, are most welcome...The smooth, vigorous stems, richly coloured young leaves and the profusion of fragrant flowers of a most exquisite shade of rose pink, constitute its chief attractions; considered together with its accommodating nature and ease of cultivation, they should ensure its *entrée* into every rose garden worthy of the name." [OM] "Evidently does best in seacoast climates." [Th2] "The climbing and reblooming rose 'Zéphirine Drouhin' is very vigorous, of unfailing hardiness...It presents another advantage—that of being thornless. This variety is one with very persistent foliage, is hardy, vigorous, very floriferous, and particularly remontant...the many buds expand from May until late into the Fall...[D]edicated ...to Mme. Zéphirine Drouhin, the wife of an amateur horticulturist residing at Semur, on the Côte d'Or." [JR27/151-152]

Zigeunerblut (Geschwind, 1889) trans., 'Gypsy Blood'
From a Boursault × a Bourbon.
"Purple-red, large, full, tall." [Sn] "Vigorous growth, with large cup-shaped flowers of deep crimson, tinged with purple." [GAS]

Zigeunerknabe
Listed as a Hybrid Bourbon.

Chapter Six

Hybrid Bourbons, Hybrid Chinas, and Hybrid Noisettes

"The roses of this class form a series of varieties developed from 1820 to 1840…They are also the founders of the HPs." [JF] "This section owes its origin to the Bourbon, China, and Tea-Scented Noisette, crossed with the French, Provence, and other summer roses, and also to the latter crossed with the former. The varieties first obtained by this crossing arose by accident…Many of the flowers in this section combine all the properties desired in the rose—viz., size, form, fulness, and exquisite colouring. *Hybrid Bourbon*…This very splendid family of roses owes its origin to the

Bourbon rose, which is itself a hybrid. 'Coupe d'Hébé' may be given as a specimen of this family, which for the disposition and regularity of its petals is quite unique. They differ from the hybrid Chinas in the greater substance of their flowers and foliage, but, like them, are remarkable for the abundance and beauty of their flowers." [M'I] "Our Hybrid Chinas...bear fruit but rarely." [V2] Many Gallicas lie under heavy suspicion of being Hybrid Chinas or Hybrid Bourbons, and rightly so, we believe. It seems likely that non-remontant offspring generated in Hybrid Perpetual breeding would, if they were of high quality, be offered to the public now and then under the banner of a familiar class—Gallicas, perhaps—particularly if the breeder, in his indiscriminate sowing of unmarked seed from miscellaneous sources—the normal practice for many breeders—had no idea of the seedling's genetic heritage. As we, too, have no idea of the background of varieties with veiled pasts, it is difficult for us to point out a plant and declare that some particular rose is certainly (or certainly not) a Hybrid China; the differences are relative and subtle: "The Hybrid Chinese differ from the French Roses in their growth, which is more diffuse; in their foliage, which is usually smooth, shining more or less, and retained on the tree later in the year; in their thorns, which are larger, and usually more numerous; and in their flowers, which are produced in larger clusters, whose petals are less flaccid, and which remain in a perfect state a longer time after expansion." [P] "The Hybrid Bourbon Roses...are less diffuse and more robust in growth than the Hybrid Chinese, being readily distinguished from them by their broad stout foliage, the leaflets of which are more obtuse. The *tout ensemble* of these Roses is particularly fine; some are compact growers, many are abundant bloomers, and the flowers are in general large and handsome." [P] "Being certain to bloom only once in the season, [*most Hybrid Chinas*] are scarcely worthy of cultivation, compared with the Remontants." [SBP] "The superior varieties of this fine division give a combination of all that is or can be beautiful in summer roses; for, not only are their flowers of the most elegant forms and colours, their foliage of extreme luxuriance, but their branches are so vigorous and graceful, that perhaps no plant presents such a mass of beauty as a fine-grown hybrid China rose in full bloom." [R8]

Anaïse (Breeder unknown, date uncertain)
Hybrid Bourbon
"Pink, medium size, full, moderately tall." [Sn] Not to be confused with the lilac Gallica.

Arthur Young (Portemer, 1863)
Hybrid China
"Blossom large, full, very dark, velvety purple." [S]

[Athalin] (Jacques, 1829) syn., 'Général Athalin'
Hybrid Bourbon
"Bright pink." [TCN] "Cerise." [LS] "Bright red, double, large, cupped." [LF] "Rosy crimson, sometimes spotted with white, lively, of medium size, double; form, cupped. Habit, branching; growth, robust. A distinct and showy Rose, of a fine habit, blooming most abundantly; requires but little pruning. A good seed-bearer, and the parent, on one side, of many of the Hybrid Perpetual roses." [P] "'Athalin' crossed with 'Rose du Roi' later gave remontant roses having the Portland character…distinct from the first seedlings from 'Athalin', varieties feeble in growth and poorly remontant." [JF] "Divergent branches; thorns somewhat s\numerous, unequal, nearly straight; leaves comprised of 3-5 oval leaflets, light green, slightly shiny, distinctly and irregularly dentate; flower large, double, regular, bright cerise red." [S] "Sprang from the Bourbon rose." [JR31/130]

Belle de Crécy (Roeser/Hardy, 1829) trans., "Crécy Beauty"
Hybrid China
"Deep violet." [V4] "Blackish purple, full, medium-sized." [LF] "Medium-sized, very full, deep purple." [BJ53] "Purple-red, medium size, very full, very fragrant, tall." [Sn] "Flowers red, shaded with velvety p[e]uce, changing to dark slate soon after opening, exhibiting flowers of different characters on the plant at the same time, of medium size, full;

form, expanded. Habit, erect; growth, moderate, branches covered with small black spines. An abundant bloomer, and showy, but often faulty, from exhibiting a green eye in the center." [P] "*Shrub* pretty vigorous. *Branches* slender, armed with numerous thorns, slightly hooked; of a dark brown. *Leaflets* seven in number; long; irregularly and very deeply toothed. *Flowers* numerous, in clusters, full, middle-sized. *Petals*, violet; shaded and velvety, irregularly sloped at the summit, symmetrically arranged at the circumference, rolled in the centre." [Go] "Shrub with upright, slender stems; prickles fairly numerous, dark brown, slightly hooked; leaves a very dark green, composed of elongate leaflets with very pronounced, irregular dentations; blossoms arranged in corymbs, numerous, medium-sized, full; petals violet, velvety and shaded, rolled at the center, symmetrically arranged in the other parts, irregularly notched at the tip. Hybrid China." [SAP29/266] "Raised by Monsieur Roeser, a fancier in Crécy, and published by Monsieur Hardy." [BJ30]

[**Belle de Vernier**] (Breeder unknown,-1827) trans., "Vernier's Beauty" Hybrid China
"Flowers rosy crimson, marbled with dark purplish slate, more slaty towards their circumference, of medium size, full; form, cupped. Habit, erect; growth, moderate." [P] The cultivars 'Belle de Vernier', 'Belle Violette', and 'De Vergnies' are locked in a struggle concerning possible synonymy, it being quite a horse race which will turn out to be the name with priority should they all indeed be the same rose; we include entries for them all here until the situation is resolved.

[**Belle Violette**] (De Vergnies,-1830) trans., "Violet Beauty" Hybrid China
"Beautiful bright violet." [S] "Medium-sized, full, violet." [R&M62] "Dark bluish violet, large, superb." [WRP] "Flowers violet, of medium size, full. Raised at Angers. Introduced in 1845." [P, incorrect in his latter information, as BJ30 lists it (in 1830) as "'Belle Violette' de Verny," and tells us that it is a seedling from the (royal) flower nursery at Sèvres, where presumably De Vergnies worked.] *Cf.* 'Belle de Vernier' and 'De Vergnies'.

Belmont (Vibert, 1846)
Hybrid China
"Flesh, tinted pink." [Ÿ]

Bijou des Amateurs (Breeder unknown, pre-1835) trans., "Fancier's Gem"
Hybrid China
"Pinkish red." [Ÿ] "Dark cerise, large." [S-V] "Medium-sized, full, crimson." [V8] "Blossom very large, full, sparkling red, violet at the petals' edges." [S] "Flower crimson spotted, their circumference inclining to violet, of medium size, full." [P]

Brennus (Laffay, 1830)
Hybrid Bourbon
"Light poppy, large, full, flat, superb." [LF] "Bright purplish red." [TCN] "Deep carmine; a handsome old variety." [JC] "Purplish-crimson." [HstI:307] "Cup., brilliant crimson, very large." [CC] "Globular, vivid red." [Go] "Cupped, crimson-maroon." [JR9/162] "Light carmine, large and full...habit branching; growth vigorous; foliage fine." [P1] "Superb; the flowers are extra large, of a glowing red, perfectly double; it makes fine shoots, and is an excellent pillar plant." [Bu] "Finer...as a pillar rose...than as a bush; its luxuriant shoots must not be shortened too much in winter pruning, as it is then apt to produce an abundance of wood, and but very few flowers. This rose often puts forth branches in one season from eight to ten feet in length [ca. 2.25-3m]." [R8] "One of the most beautiful of the non-remontant hybrids." [JF] Brennus, the 4th century B.C. Gallic chieftan whose forces overran Rome.

Capitaine Sissolet (Breeder unknown,-1841) syn., 'Capitaine Sisolet'
Hybrid Bourbon
"Rich fulgent rose colour." [FlCa41/31] "Flower large, full, flaring, bright pink." [S] "A magnificent rich fulgent rosy lilac, and distinct." [WRP] "Rose-red, large, full, tall." [Sn] "Flowers beautiful rose, large and very double; form, cupped. Habit, branching, fine; growth, vigorous. A very showy Rose. A good seed bearer." [P]

Cardinal de Richelieu (Van Sian/Laffay, 1840)
Hybrid China
"Flower medium-sized, full; color, very deep violet, becoming blackish Parma [violet]; petal edges carmine." [S] "Vigorous, bushy, giving a great quantity of medium sized blossoms of a very dark violet in Spring, the petals lightly bordered carmine." [JR29/170] Verrier provides the information that this rose was bred by the Dutch breeder Van Sian, who provided it to Laffay, unnamed. Armand Jean du Plessis, Duc and Cardinal de Richelieu; minister of Louis XIII; lived 1585-1642.

Catherine Bonnard (Guillot fils, 1871)
Hybrid China
"Vermilion." [Ÿ] "Cerise, flowers moderate size, full and well formed; will make a good pillar rose." [JC] "Very vigorous; wood quite prickly; foliage dull green, slightly on the scant side; but its large, full blossom—well formed and well held—can be picked out among all others because of its rich scarlet-crimson color, which is very brilliant." [S] "Note that I call this a non-remontant hybrid, which means that this variety is little known to those finicky amateurs who won't buy such a thing as a rose which won't rebloom. This is a pity, because it is worthy of a place in all collections. It is a very vigorous plant...its canes are armed with numerous thorns, its blossom is very large, well-formed, very well held, and of a superb sparkling carmine red. It is a product of open pollination. It is supposed that it descends from 'Jules Margottin' or one of its tribe; but its raiser himself did not feel any confidence in making an attribution." [JR10/91]

Catherine Ghislaine (Emiliana, 1885?)
Hybrid China
"Blossom small, semi-full; color, white, marbled with violet." [S] Often called a Damask.

[**Céline**] (Laffay, 1835)
Hybrid Bourbon
"Fleshy lilac." [TCN] "A deep shaded blush, spendid." [WRP] "Deep pink." [Ÿ] "Bright pink, double, very large, cupped." [LF] "Flowers pale rose, very large and double; form, cupped. Habit, branching; growth vigorous; the flowers produced in large clusters. A loose Rose. A good seed bearer." [P]

[**Cerise Éclatante**] (Jantet/Vibert, 1816) syn., 'Cerise Élégante'; trans., "Sparkling Cerise"
Hybrid China
"Scarlet." [RG] "Flowers large, semi-double, bright red." [No26] The second Hybrid China.

[**Charles Duval**] (C. Duval, 1841)
Hybrid Bourbon
"Bright rose, large and perfect." [JWa] "Flesh pink, cupped, large, beautiful." [LF] "Rose, large, double." [HoBoIV] "Very large, full, light red, pretty form." [R-H42] "Light pink." [Pq] "Deep pink...form, cupped. Habit, erect, fine; growth, vigorous; the shoots clothed with beautiful foliage. A good Rose, either for a pot or pillar; forms also a very handsome tree. A good seed bearer." [P] "A large, finely-shaped, and very double rose, of a bright rose-colour, of the most robust habit: this when budded on a very stout stem, either as a half or full standard, soon forms a large tree, than which nothing among roses could be more ornamental." [R9]

Charles Lawson (Lawson, 1853)
Hybrid Bourbon
"Bright pink, very large, full and perfect, a noble rose, with large handsome foliage." [JC] "Flowers vivid rose shaded...form compact; growth vigorous." [P1] "Large and beautiful roses." [R1/251] "Highly scented." [Wr] "A brilliant crimson pillar rose...not easily surpassed...flowrs are borne in immense quantities." [K2] "Branches dark green; thorns unequal,

numerous, bristling, the larger ones being hooked; flower large, full, very well formed; delicate pink shaded rose." [S] "Rather ungainly habit...6×4 [ft; ca. 1.75×1.25 m]." [B1] "Another old favorite too rarely seen nowadays." [K1] "Considered by amateurs fortunate enough to possess it as one of the finest climbing roses in the world." [GAS] "Discovered amongst some Roses from the Continent, and its origin is a mystery." [NRS28/35] "Lawson and Son, Messrs., Nurserymen, Edinburgh, N.B." [P]

Charles Louis No. 1 (Foulard/V. Verdier, 1840)
Hybrid China
"Large, a bright deep cherry color, exceedingly splendid." [WRP] "Globose." [WRP] "Flowers rosy carmine, large and full; form, cupped. Habit, branching; growth, moderate. Sometimes fine, but produces too often a green bud in the centre of the flower." [P] "Medium scent, tall." [Sn] "Vigorous bush, with slightly purplish green canes; thorns thin, very pointed, purplish; flowers rounded, very regular, slightly plump, very full; petals well imbricated, erect, smaller at the center than around the edges of the blossom; the four or five last rows of petals are a pale pink, while the others are a bright purplish pink. This rose has an elegant fragrance, and is charming in effect. Its leaves are comprised of two or three pairs of leaflets with an odd one, an attractive fresh green in color, purplish when young. Monsieur Verdier, who has grown it for three years, received it from Monsieur Foulard, a fanicer in Le Mans. The bud is round, the sepals long, foliaceous, and fringed along the edge. The peduncle is strong and bears several blossoms." [An40/246] Not to be confused with the "small, of ranunculus form, rich roseate blush" 'Charles Louis No. 2' (description from WRP). Sangerhausen has a note connecting it with Guinoisseau; perhaps it was collected for Sangerhausen from the Guinoisseau nursery or breeding-grounds.

Chénédolé (Thierry, ca. 1840)
Hybrid China
"Bright carmine." [LS] "Very large, very double, cupped, light vermilion."
[JR9/163] "So called from a member of the Chamber of Deputies for
Calvados, a district in Normandy, where this fine rose was raised. It has
often been asserted that no rose could compete with 'Brennus' in size and
beauty; but I feel no hesitation in saying, that in superior brilliancy of
color, and size of flower, this variety is superior; the foliage and habit of
the plant are also much more elegant and striking; in color its flowers are
of a peculiar glowing vivid crimson, discernible at a great distance: it is
indeed an admirable rose, and cannot be too much cultivated." [WRP]

Chévrier (Laffay, ca. 1825)
Hybrid China
"Purple violet." [V4] "Vigorous growth; flower small, very full; color, very
deep violet, striped carmine." [S] "Not a large rose, but decidedly one of
the most brilliant and beautiful dark crimson roses we possess." [WRP]
"Medium height." [Sn] "*Shrub*, small, not vigorous. *Stems*, straight, armed
with very small thorns, crooked and uneven. *Leafstalks*, unarmed. *Leaflets*,
near together; some oval, some oblong, regularly toothed. *Flowers*, small,
full, regular; of a purple-black." [Go]

[Comtesse de Coutard] (E. Noisette, 1829)
Hybrid China
"A pretty pink." [MaCo] "Very vigorous shrub, canes not very numerous;
many thorns of very unequal sizes, some long and recurved, others very
slender; leaves composed of five to seven leaflets which are elongate,
glabrous, lightly dentate, slack; blossoms pink, very double, large, in a
bouquet of five to seven, borne on short peduncles." [SAP29/303]
"Raised by my brother Ét[ienne] Noisette." [No35]

Comtesse de Lacépède (C. Duval/V. Verdier, 1840)
Hybrid China

"Grown from seed by Monsieur Duval of Montmorency. Growth vigorous, with green canes bearing close-set thorns which are slender and of varying lengths. Beautiful green leaves in two or three pairs with an odd one, bordered purple when young. Flower round, very full, flat, white with some flesh; outer petals very large, inner ones smaller. Buds round, sepals large and pointed with small foliaceous processes at the base. The bud, while opening, resembles that of the Tea; its exterior petals are very flesh-colored; and, indeed, when first opening, the blossom's center shows a very pronounced flesh tint. Lightly scented, very profuse." [An40/246-247] "Growth vigorous; branches weak, slightly upright, nearly thornless; flower large, full, flesh pink." [S] "Silvery blush, their centre sometimes rosy flesh, large and full; form, cupped, delicately beautiful. Habit, branching; growth, moderate. A good rose, partaking somewhat of the nature of the Hybrid French." [P] "A most abundant bloomer and a charming rose." [JC] The Comte de Lacépède, alias Bernard Germain Étienne de la Ville sur Illon, was a naturalist (lived 1756-1825) whose great *Histoire Naturelle* was published posthumously in 1839, with a eulogy by Cuvier.

[Comtesse Molé] (Laffay, ca. 1845)
Hybrid Bourbon

"Pure flesh color, superb." [WRP] "Flowers large and double; color fine clear flesh; habit robust." [MH45/Aug.Ad.3] "Very vigorous growth; canes strong, bright green, clothed with thorns that are flattened at the base; leaves glossy dark green, regularly dentate; blossom large, full, cupped; color, very fresh pink shaded bright grenadine." [S]

Coupe d'Hébé (Laffay, 1840) trans., "Hebe's Cup"
Hybrid Bourbon

"Delicate pink lightly touched saffron, full, large, cupped, superb." [LF] "Delicate rosy-flesh, large and double; one of the most beautiful of all summer roses." [JC] "Sometimes recurrent." [W] "Good full pink colour." [J] "It is of a beautiful shaded blush, and the form and arrangement of its petals are all that can be desired. It has, however, from the very delicacy of its shade, a great tendency to fade. It should, therefore, be grown where the full power of a July sun will not be brought to bear upon it." [Ed] "Deep pink, medium or large size, cup-form; seven leaflets. A fine distinct sort." [EL] "Globular, soft pink...lush pale green foliage, free-flowering...to 6×4 [ft; ca. 1.75×1.25 m]." [HRG] "Vigorous, fairly climbing; foliage, blackish-green...delicate pink shaded cerise." [S] "Rich deep pink, exquisite in colour, large and very double...habit erect...A good seed bearer." [P1] "A delicate blush when fully expanded...a fine grower and profuse bloomer, with large glossy green foliage." [Bu] "Remarkable both for the perfection of its cup-like form, and for the delicate rose-color of its petals. Its growth is very vigorous; and, like most of its kindred, it is perfectly hardy." [FP] "The gem of this family...a beautiful wax-like pink, and in the disposition and regularity of its petals it is quite unique...soon forms a large bush." [R8] "Growth is luxuriant, and adapted for pillars." [SBP] "Foliage glossy, sub-evergreen, and abundant." [WRP] "Mildew if precautions are not taken in time." [B1] "Wonderful variety." [JR9/164] Hebe, goddess of youth and cup-bearer, with Ganymede, to the Olympian gods.

[De Vergnies] (De Vergnies, 1824)
Hybrid China
"Bluish violet purple." [TCN] "*Ovary* oval, glandulose, with a constricted neck. *Blossom* medium-sized, full, semi-globular, blackish-violet. *Petals* wavy along the edge." [Pf] *Cf.* 'Belle de Vernier' and 'Belle Violette'.

Dembrowski
Listed as 'Dombrowski'.

[Deuil du Maréchal Mortier] (Breeder unknown,-1841) trans., "Mourning for Marshal Mortier"
Hybrid China
"Velvety maroon purple. Superb." [LF] "Flower large, full, cup-shaped; color, velvety purple crimson; base of petals, pure white; towards the end of the season, the coloration alters to purple marbled with white." [S] "Flowers crimson purple, very velvety, the base of the petals white, giving to the center of the flower a whitish appearance, the flowers sometimes open of a light vivid crimson, afterwards becoming marbled with purple, large and double; form, cupped. Habit, branching; growth, vigorous; shoots, very spinous." [P] *Cf.* the Gallica 'Dumortier'.

Dombrowski (V. Verdier?,-1842) syn., 'Dembrowski'
Hybrid Bourbon
"Medium-sized, more or less floriferous, dark scarlet." [R-H42] "A beautiful flower, of a deep brilliant red due, approaching to scarlet, well worthy of the place in the [*Hybrid Bourbon*] group." [WRP] "Flowers deep scarlet, often shaded with purple, of medium size, very double; form, cupped. Habit, branching yet compact; growth, moderate. A very abundant bloomer, producing a fine effect on the tree. A good seed bearer." [P]

Duc de Sussex (Laffay,-1841)
Hybrid China
"Pale pink, center velvety ruby, full, large, flat, superb." [LF] "Large, full, plump, shaded pink." [BJ53] "Blossom large, full, globular; color, cream, nuanced pink." [S] "Yellowish white and pink, large, full, tall." [Sn] Often construed a Damask.

Duchesse de Montebello (Laffay,-1826)
Hybrid Noisette
"Delicate pink, full, flat, medium-sized, beautiful." [LF] "Medium-sized, full, pink." [V8] "Flowers rosy pink changing to flesh pink, of medium size, full; form, compact. Habit, erect; growth, moderate. Almost a French

Rose." [P] "*Tube of calyx* smooth, oval or globular. *Flowers*, full, middle-sized; flesh-coloured." [Go] The Duchess of Montebello, wife of the ennobled soldier Maréchal Lannes.

[Edward Jesse] (Laffay,-1842)
Hybrid Bourbon
"Deep purple nuanced crimson, full, large." [LF] "Deep rose, small, double." [EL] "Dark purple, shaded." [HoBoIV:319] "Rich purplish crimson, often shaded with blackish purple, of medium size, double; form, cupped. Habit, branching; growth, moderate. A good seed bearer." [P] "Vigorous; branches very limber, bearing the blossom with difficulty at the end of the cane." [S] "The well known naturalist and popular author of *Gleanings in Natural History*, Mr. Edward Jesse." [C]

Ekta (Hansen, 1927)
Hybrid China
From *R. gallica* 'Grandiflora' × 'American Beauty' (HP)
"Of tall, upright habit; very hardy and vigorous. Flowers, single, pink; blooming freely throughout June and a few days in July. Since the flowers are single, this plant may not be a hybrid. However, the flowers are pink while the flowers of the *R. gallica* parent are dark crimson. Also, it blooms much earlier than *R. gallica*. This plant sprouts freely. May be useful for screens, hedges, or as an ornamental shrub." [ARA27/226-227] "White, medium-size, single to semi-double, moderate scent, tall." [Sn]

Enfant d'Ajaccio
Listed as 'Souvenir d'Anselme'.

Frances Bloxam (G. Paul, 1892)
Hybrid China
"Salmon pink." [Ÿ]

[Francis B. Hayes] (J.M. May, 1892)
Hybrid Bourbon
"Scarlet." [CA06]

Frédéric II de Prusse (V. Verdier, 1847) trans., "Friedrich II of Prussia" "Rich crimson-purple, large and double." [FP] "Violet-purple and crimson, large, handsome and distinct; a good rose of vigorous habit." [JC] "Medium scent, tall." [Sn] Friedrich II of Prussia, called Frederick the Great; lived 1712-1786.

Fulgens
Listed as 'Malton'.

[Général Allard] (Laffay, ca. 1835)
Hybrid Bourbon
"Bright pink, full, medium sized, globular, superb." [LF] "Fine deep rose, very double." [FP] "Not very vigorous; branches very feeble; flower medium-sized, semi-double, globular; color, carmine pink." [S] "Flowers rosy crimson, of medium size, usually very double, but varies as to fulness; form, globular, exquisite. Habit, branching; growth, small. A distinct and beautiful Rose, blooming occasionally in the autumn...A tolerably good seed bearer." [P] "Although now rather an old variety, is seldom seen in perfection; it requires [*to be budded on 'Manettii' or 'Céline'*], and, when luxuriant, very often gives an abundant crop of flowers in autumn; these are globular, of a bright rosy red, and very beautiful." [R9]

Général Athalin
Listed as 'Athalin'.

George IV (Rivers, 1820)
Hybrid China
"Superb crimson" [Sx] "Velvety deep purple." [TCN] "Dark rose." [HstI:307] "Deep velvety crimson and purple, full, cupped, large, beautiful." [LF] "Glob., deep velvety crimson." [CC] "Large, full, cupped, reddish crimson with touches of dark maroon." [JR9/163] "Semi-double or double; no longer of any value." [EL] "An old rose...but is still one of the most desirable of this class. Its flowers are of a dark crimson, and its young shoots have a purple tinge. Its very luxuriant habit makes it suitable for a

pillar." [SBP] "Growth feeble; branches thin, with short, flat thorns; leaves dark green, rounded; flower large, full, flat." [S] "An old but splendid variety, of the richest crimson colour, always perfect and fully double, of cupped form, a free grower in rich soils...Mr. Rivers, of England, a celebrated rose grower, raised this variety from seed...according to his own history of the plant, it came up in a bed of seedlings, unexpected, and without any act on his part to produce it." [Bu] "As this came by accident, its origin is not so well ascertained." [R8] "Even now I have not forgotten the pleasure the discovery of this rose gave me. One morning in June I was looking over the first bed of roses I had ever raised from seed, and searching for something new among them with all the ardour of youth, when my attention was attracted to a rose in the centre of the bed, not in bloom, but growing with great vigour, its shoots offering a remarkable contrast to the plants by which it was surrounded, in their crimson purple tinge...shoots more than ten feet [ca. 3+ m] in length in one season." [R8] "A death which is a blow to horticulture, arboriculture in particular, is that of Mr. Thomas Rivers, nurseryman of Sawbridgeworth, England, which happened last October 17 [1877]...He was 69." [R-H77] King George IV of England; lived 1762-1830.

Gloire des Héllènes
Listed as 'La Nubienne'.

[**Gloriette**] (Vibert, 1836)
Hybrid Noisette
"Small, flesh, full, tender." [R&M62] "Delicate flesh colour, small and full." [P] "Bush not very vigorous; canes feeble, nearly without thorns; color, pink-white, with a bright pink center." [S]

Great Western (Laffay, 1838)
Hybrid Bourbon
"Magenta-crimson, flushed with purple." [T1] "Deep crimson, very fine." [HstI:307] "Red shaded crimson, double, fragrant; poor." [EL] "Bright

reddish crimson, beautiful." [FP] "Large, full, globular; color, ashen, marbled reddish-violet." [S] "Quartered, followed by red fruit." [G] "Not a delicate but a *grand* rose, of the habit of 'Céline', but more robust, and makes shoots 6 to 8 feet in length [ca. 1.75-2.25 m], of the diameter of a moderate sized cane. The leaves are enormous, often nine inches [ca. 2.25 dm] from base to tip, leaflets three and a half by two inches [ca. 9×5 cm]; its large clusters of flowers comprise ten to fifteen in each, but as these are frequently too much crowded to expand properly, it is better to thin out each cluster by removing about half of the buds; the color is a peculiar deep rich red, sometimes tinted with purple, variable according to the season." [WRP] "Varying exceedingly, sometimes brilliant, sometimes dark and beautiful, produced in great clusters, very large and double; form, globular. Habit, branching, fine; growth, robust. An extraordinary Rose, forming an immense tree, producing a splendid effect when in flower. A good seed bearer. Requires but little pruning." [P] *Great Western*, the notable American steamship.

Gypsy Boy
Listed as 'Zigeunerknabe'.

Impératrice Eugénie (Beluze, 1855) trans., "Empress Eugénie"
Hybrid Bourbon
"Large rose-coloured flowers." [R8] "Growth vigorous; floriferous; flower large, full, delicate silvery pink." [S] "Silvery-rose, medium size, full, fragrant; a good variety, and would be very useful had we not 'La France'. Subject to mildew; shows Bourbon character." [EL] "Vigorous canes bestrewn with occasional flat, very sharp, hooked, purple-red thorns; leaves lush, composed of 3 or 5 unequal, oval, diminishing, pointed, dentate, smooth, glossy leaves, dark green above, whitish-lanate beneath. Flowers on a pretty long stem, large to 7-8 cm [ca. 3.75 inches], cupped at first, then flattening, very full, purplish pink at the edge, carmine pink at the center." [l'H56/49] Not to be confused with the lilac pink Delhommeau/Plantier Bourbon of 1854, nor with Oger's white Bourbon

of 1858, both of the same name. Empress Eugénie; lived 1826-1920; wife of Louis Napoléon.

Jenny (Duval,-1846) syn., 'Jenny Duval'
Hybrid China
"Flowers rosy blush." [P] "In color rather a deep rose, with flowers beautifully cupped." [WRP] "Flower medium-sized, full; color, bright red." [S] "A new rose of great excellence; flowers of middle size, and of the most perfect cupped shape; colour bright rose, tinted with lilac; the habit of the plant is most robust, and its foliage glossy and beautiful." [R9]

Jenny Duval
Listed as 'Jenny'.

Joseph Gourdon (Robert, 1851)
Hybrid Bourbon
"Flower from 6-7 cm [ca. 3 inches]; full, globular, incarnate red, beautiful form." [VH51/112]

Jules Jürgensen (Schwartz, 1879)
Hybrid Bourbon
"Magenta-rose." [EL] "Very vigorous, with strong and branching canes; foliage olive green; flower large, full, well formed, magenta pink, interior violet carmine with slaty reflections, reverse of petals pale pink; very beautiful; fragrant." [JR3/165]

L'Admiration (Robert, 1856)
Hybrid China
"Light pink." [LS] "Pink, medium size, single, medium height." [Sn] Not to be confused with a Hybrid Bourbon of the same name, by Laffay a decade earlier, which was "cupped, finely shaped, and of a delicate, yet bright pink." [R9]

[**La Dauphine**] (Mauget, 1827)
Hybrid Bourbon
"Flowers clear pale flesh, slightly tinged with lavender, peculiar in colour, large and very double; form, cupped. Habit, branching; growth, robust; the branches clothed with fine broad foliage of a very dark green." [P] "Flowers nearly white, is remarkable, and worthy of attention for its large foliage of the deepest glossy green." [R9] "Very vigorous shrub; leaves brilliant dark green; flower large, quite full, in the form of a cup; color, light flesh pink, a little darker at the center." [S] The second Hybrid Bourbon.

La Nubienne (Laffay, 1825) syn., 'Gloire des Héllènes'; trans., "The Nubian Woman"
"Wine-lee." [V4] "Violet purple." [JWa] "Deep velvety purple, globular, full, beautiful." [LF] "Flowers slaty purple, of medium size, full; form, cupped. Habit, branching; growth, moderate." [P] "Very vigorous; flower large, full, widely cupped; color, bright carmine, and, at the second bloom, amaranth red marbled reddish lilac." [S] "*Tube of calyx*, hemispherical, smooth. *Flowers*, full, convex, regular; of a slate-coloured purple, often dark." [Go]

[**La Philippine**] (Jantet/Vibert, 1816)
Hybrid China
"Blackish." [RG] "Semi-double...dark violet." [Cal] "*Flower*, hypocrateriform, medium-sized, double or multiplex, velvety, black-purple." [Pf] The third Hybrid China.

[**La Pudeur**] (Laffay, ca. 1826) trans., "Modesty"
Hybrid Bourbon
"Flower small, full, flat, regular, of a pale flesh." [S] "*Canes*, slender. *Thorns*, slender, weak, straight, unequal, intermixed with bristles. *Petiole* long, slender, glandulose, prickly. *Stipules*, slender, with glandulose edges. *Leaflets*, five, slender, glabrous and smooth, acute or acuminate. *Serration*, ordinarily simple, with inclining tips. *Peduncles* short, bestrewn with

glands, in groups of 3 to 8. *Bracts*, linear-lanceolate, with glandulose edges. *Ovary* glabrous, long, narrow, fusiform. *Sepals* glandulose, long, foliaceous; three are edged with long branching appendages. *Flower* nodding, small or medium-sized, full, regular, flesh." [Pf]

La Saumonée (Margottin fils, 1877) trans., "The Salmony One"
Hybrid China
"Vigorous growth; blossom large, full, cupped; beautiful salmony pink. Sometimes reblooms in the Fall; climbing." [S]

[Lady Stuart] (Breeder unknown,-1833)
"Flesh." [TCN] "Silvery-blush, fine form, medium and full." [FP] "A delicate pink, of perfect globular form, very double, and apparently a free grower." [Bu] "Silvery blush, large and full; form, cupped, exquisite. Habit, erect; growth, small." [P] "[A] gem of the first water, for no rose can surpass it in beauty; the form of the flowers before expansion is perfectly spherical and exceedingly beautiful. This rose, for some years to come, must and will be a favorite." [WRP] The "English" name combined with the date of introduction give suspicion of Laffay being the breeder.

Las-Cases (Vibert, 1828)
Hybrid Bourbon
"Deep pink." [V9] "Pink, nuanced carmine." [S-V] "Purplish pink, full, flat, large, beautiful." [LF] "Rose, very large." [HoBoIV/318] "Carmine, shaded. Non-remontant." [LS] "Superb, very large, most magnificent rose colour." [FlCa38] "Flowers rosy pink, sometimes deep rose colour, edged with crimson, very large and full; form, cupped. Habit, branching, fine; growth, robust; the foliage particularly good. A splendid Rose in warm seasons." [P] "Something over 1.5 m [ca. 5 feet]." [G] "Of the most robust habit, producing very large flowers of a deep shaded rosy hue, nearly of the color and shape of the old Cabbage Provence rose." [WRP] "Branches very climbing, too feeble to hold the blossoms, which thus nod under their weight. Frequently used as a weeping standard budded on the Briar;

flower of medium size, very full, expanded form; color, carmine marbled grenadine." [S] "Much esteemed." [M'I] "*Thorns*, slender, unequal, sparse, intermingled with bristles. *Petiole* glandulose, prickly. *Stipules* entire, ordinarily glabrous, with glandulose edges. *Leaflets* 5, oval-rounded, close-set, pale green, glabrous and smooth above, glaucous beneath as well as glabrous, except on the main veins, which are pubescent. *Serration* sharp, usually simple, slightly glandulose. *Peduncle* short, glandulose. *Ovary* glabrous, oval-turbinate, not pinched. *Sepals* glandulose, concave, short, terminating in a subulate point, three bearing several appendages. *Flower* medium-sized or large, semi-globular, very full, very regular, an even pink with is light, intense, and bright." [Pf] *Emmanuel*, Comte de Las-Cases; lived 1766-1842; historian, companion of Napoléon's on St. Helena. *Not* Bartolomé de Las Casas; lived 1474-1566; interesting if occasionally misguided Spanish prelate, companion of Columbus; in his humane efforts to protect the Indians and their liberty, he alas helped found the African slave trade; chronicled the Spanish discoveries of 1492-1520.

Le Météore (Thierry,-1846) trans., "The Meteor"
Hybrid China
"Blossom very large, full; color, carmine, nuanced purple." [S] "Flowers bright red, large and semi-double. Habit, branching; growth, vigorous. A very showy Rose; good for a pillar." [P] "[B]right rosy red, very striking, and when blooming in large clusters on the plant, always much admired." [WRP]

Le Vingt-Neuf Juillet (Breeder unknown,-1834) trans., "The 29th of July"
Hybrid China
"Deep purple." [V4] "Crimson black, flame center." [TCN] "Velvety carmine, full, flat, medium-sized, superb." [LF] "Alike beautiful in its flowers and foliage; in early spring its leaves and shoots are of a most vivid red, and this appearance they retain the greater part of the summer; its flowers are brilliant in the extreme, crimson purple shaded with scarlet: the shoots of this rose must be left at nearly their full length." [WRP]

"Very vigorous bush; robust canes of a beautiful green; very climbing; flower large, full, well formed; color, deep crimson, center scarlet." [S] *Not* by Vibert or Laffay, as neither claims it in his respective catalog. My colleague Monsieur Massiot advises that the name refers in most likelihood to July 29, 1830, the capper of the three "glorious" days of revolution which eventuated in the replacement on the French throne of Charles X by Louis-Philippe the "Citizen-King" (see below); the day also saw Lafayette chosen to replace the white flag of the Bourbons with the Tricolor on the Paris City Hall. The date was also commemorated in the name of a Parisian street in the First Arrondissement; for those taking notes, we can state that this street is 116 meters in length (ca. 348 feet), and 10 meters in width (ca. 30 feet), having been first opened in 1826 with the name Duc-de-Bordeaux, the name being changed in 1830 to Vingt-Neuf Juillet. Guessers may feel confident in supposing, thus, that the rose originated about the same year.

[Louis-Philippe] (Miellez,-1835)
Hybrid Bourbon
"Deep pink, cerise center." [TCN] "Purple." [V4] "Crimson, center pinkish." [BJ40] "One of the older varieties, light reddish crimson." [WRP] "Bright pink, very large." [S-V] "Flowers purplish rose, large and very double; form, cupped. Habit, branching; growth, vigorous." [P] King Louis-Philippe, the Citizen-King; lived 1773-1850.

Malton (Guérin, 1829) syn., 'Fulgens'
Hybrid China
"Vermilion red, full, cupped, medium-sized, beautiful." [LF] "Bright scarlet." [TCN] "Crimson velvet, cupped." [HoBoV/318] "Cerise; flower large, full; very floriferous; very vigorous." [Cx] "A very old, but almost forgotten rose...its color is almost scarlet, and a charming peculiarity is that of its petals having a shell-like bloom outside, while their inside is that of a glowing red." [R8] "Very decorative, will climb to ten feet in height [ca. 3 m]. The blossoms, clustered in small close groups, are very

numerous, of medium size, quite full, a little concave, well held, of a cherry carmine red which does not fade up to the time the petals fall. It is a plant of the first order, without rival in its color. This very fine climber was obtained from a sowing made at Angers about 1830 by Monsieur Guérin who, error has it, dedicated it to his niece; however, the truth of the matter is that he dedicated it to Monsieur Malton, his brother-in-law." [JR8/126] "And so, the fortunate Guérin proclaims not only his victory, but also that of his town, in naming two of his Hybrid Chinas (which are of the greatest beauty) 'Triomphe de Guérin' and 'Triomphe d'Angers'. Another rose, probably by Monsieur Guérin, with less Glory than these other two, has received the modest name of 'Malton'." [R-H29/358] "*Shrub*, having straight, strong, numerous branches; the *bark* green, variegated with dark purple." [Go] "The shoots must not be pruned very close, for in that case it will not show a bloom." [Bu] "An excellent seed-bearer." [JF] "Played a large part in the creation of the first HPs." [JR12/45] "I [*Mauget*] have sown a lot of 'Malton', which has given me some good rebloomer pretty much of the same shade—sanguine purple—and which I am going to propagate." [SHP45/309] "Certainly one of the most brilliant and beautiful...the entire plant is also worthy of admiration, independent of its magnificent globular scarlet flowers, as its foliage is so abundant, and so finely tinted with red; its branches so vigorous, and yet spreading so gracefully, that it forms one of the very finest of standard roses." [WRP]

Mme. Auguste Rodrigues (Chauvry, 1897)
Hybrid Bourbon
From 'Souvenir de Nemours' (B) × 'Max Singer' (Pol × HP)
"Vigorous, upright, climbing; foliage dark green; very large round buds; blooms in clusters, sometimes solitary; blossom very large, very full, globular; the petals flare back in a Camellia from; very pretty color, pure frosty pink, reverse silvery; the blossoms last 8-10 days on the bush; fragrant...blooms up to the middle of July." [JR21/149]

'**Mme. Caroline Testout**' × *R. gallica* 'Splendens' (Breeder unknown, date uncertain)
Hybrid China
From 'Mme. Caroline Testout' × *R. gallica* 'Splendens'
"Pink, large, full, tall." [Sn]

Mme. Galli-Marié (E. Verdier, 1876)
Hybrid China
"Very vigorous, flower medium size, full, well-formed, beautiful bright pink; very pretty." [JR1/6/11] "Dull green canes; flower…in a cluster." [S]

Mme. Jeannine Joubert (Margottin fils, 1877)
Hybrid Bourbon
"Bright cerise." [Ÿ] "Red, medium size, non-autumnal." [EL] "Vigorous, flower large, full, beautiful carmine red, very beautiful imbricated form." [JR1/12/12]

Mme. Lauriol de Barney (Trouillard, 1868)
Hybrid Bourbon
"Light silvery pink. Most beautiful." [T1] "Quite large and fully double…quartered." [G] "Very flat…unusual fragrance…5×4 [ft; ca. 1.5×1.25 m]." [B] "Branches climbing, used for covering rocks and for forming allées." [S] Has also been called a Hybrid Arvensis.

Mme. Plantier (Plantier, 1835)
Hybrid Noisette
"Flowers creamy white when newly opened, changing to pure white, of medium size, full; form, compact. Habit, branching; growth, vigorous; shoots, slender; foliage of a light green. An immense bloomer, and a beautiful Rose, forming a large bush or tree, producing a sheet of white blossom, and lasting a long time in flower." [P] "A Hybrid Noisette, of vigorous growth, producing pure white double flowers of extreme beauty and in great profusion." [WRP]

Ohl (Hardy,-1835)
Hybrid China
"Velvety purple." [TCN] "Shaded lake." [MH50/421] "Large blossom, with large petals, a beautiful deep crimson." [An42/328] "Violet, red center." [Ÿ] "Flower large, full, violety bright carmine red, superb." [Gp&f] "Flowers large, very full, well formed, violet purple with a bright red center." [JR1/8/12] "Velvety-crimson, colour very rich and beautiful, flowers large and finely shaped." [JC] "Violet pink, medium size, very full, tall." [Sn] "Flowers violet purple, their centre brilliant red, large and full. Habit, branching; growth, robust. A fine show Rose." [P] Previously understood to be a Gallica with a somewhat shady background, we recently have found it listed as a Hybrid China in 1835, and so update the dating and classification given in *The Old Rose Adventurer*.

Parkzierde (Geschwind/Lambert, 1909) trans., "Park Decoration"
Hybrid Bourbon
"Very floriferous for a short period in early summer...scarlet-crimson... long stems...4×4 [ft; ca. 1.25×1.25 m]." [B] "Growth not especially good; blooms fade quickly." [ARA18/122] "Foliage dark green." [B1]

Paul Perras (Levet, 1870)
Hybrid Bourbon
"A fine, very large rose, of the most luxuriant growth...in colour it is of a fine bright rose." [R8] "Beautiful pale rose, large and very double; form compact; growth vigorous...An abundant seed bearer." [P1] "Foliage glossy dark green...a true exhibition variety." [S] Not to be confused with the pre-1843 Hybrid Bourbon of the same name and similar color.

Paul Ricault (Portemer, 1845)
Hybrid Bourbon
"Flowers rosy-crimson, large and full." [P1] "Carmine-crimson, medium size, fine globular form; one of the most beautiful summer roses." [EL] "Bright rose pink. Superb flattish sometimes quartered flowers...good

perfume. Vigorous upright...4×3 [ft; ca. 1.25×1 m]." [B] "A most desirable variety in colour; one of the most brilliant of the group." [R8] "Outer petals reflexed, inner ones recurved." [Kr] "Magnificent in its form, size, and in the rich crimson of its hue...of moderate growth." [Ed] "Brilliant carmine, often shaded with velvety-purple, flowers large and exquisitely formed, habit free, though not vigorous; one of the most beautiful roses in cultivation, and a superb show rose." [JC]

Paul's Carmine Pillar (G. Paul, 1895)
Hybrid China
Seedling of 'Gloire de Margottin' (HP).
"Blossom large, beautiful shining carmine red." [JR32/171] "Bright carmine pink, very floriferous, single." [JR35/120] "Beautiful large single flowers, soft pale pink; a vigorous grower and entirely hardy." [C&Js99] "Variously classed as a hybrid of *R. gallica*, as a Multiflora, or as a Hybrid Tea. In some ways, it resembles all three. It is moderately vigorous, fairly hardy, blooms only once a season. The large, brilliant crimson flowers are single, borne in clusters, and very effective on a pillar." [GAS]

Prince Charles (Hardy, 1842)
Hybrid Bourbon
"A fine new light crimson variety, very perfect in form, and, as well as many others of similar good qualities, is an offspring of the Luxembourg Gardens." [Bu] "Brilliant carmine, superb." [HstIV:478] "Large and globular, of a fine rosy-red." [WRP] "Bright cherry, very double." [FP] "Brilliant crimson, often suffused with light purple, of medium size, full; cupped." [P1] "Flower of medium size, full, expanded; color, brilliant carmine bordered light purple." [S] "Scented...4×3 [ft; ca. 1.25×1 m]." [B] "Noticeable veining in maroon to lilac, double...early summer only...to 5 [ft; ca. 1.5 m]." [HRG]

Purity (Cooling, 1898)
Hybrid Bourbon
Parentage said to be 'Devoniensis' (T) × 'Mme. Bravy' (T).
"Pure white. Very free and early, good Pillar Rose." [H] "Absolutely distinct from all others in its class…pure white with a lightly rosy center; the petals are firm and very regular. The medium sized blossom of is perfect form and extremely early…semi-climbing." [JR22/68] "Flowers…freely cover the plant. It is of very strong growth, not so much an actual climber as a suitable Rose to form a large bush, or to clothe a short pillar." [F-M2]

Richelieu (V. Verdier, 1845)
Hybrid China
"Beautiful delicate pink, full, cupped, superb." [LF] "Lilac-rose, large and full; form, compact, perfect. Habit, branching; growth, vigorous. A fine Pillar Rose." [P] Not to be confused with 'Cardinal de Richelieu', nor with the 'Richelieu' by Duval of circa 1843.

Riégo (Vibert, 1831)
Hybrid China (or Hybrid Rubiginosa)
"Deep pink." [TCN] "Bright pink, full, cupped, large, beautiful." [LF] "Rose, raspberry odor." [WRP] "Very vigorous bush; canes strong; foliage thick, dark green; flower large, full, globular, very fragrant; color, bright carmine." [S] "Flowers light carmine, the colour clear and beautiful, large and double, very sweet; form, globular. Habit, branching; growth, robust, forming an immense bush or tree with fine dark foliage. A little hybridized with the sweet-briar, but retains more of the features of this group [*Hybrid Chinas*] than of any other seed-bearer." [P] "Partakes of the sweet briar, might be made the parent of some beautiful briar-like roses by planting it with the 'Splendid Sweet Briar'." Rafael del Riego y Nuñez, Spanish revolutionary; lived 1785-1823.

Roxelane (Prévost, ca. 1825)
Hybrid Noisette
"Bush very floriferous, with canes that are slender and climbing; sepals glandulose; flowers small, cupped, pink, double, the interior petals often marked with a white line." [MaCo] Given in V3 as a "Hybrid of China and Noisette."

Sir Joseph Paxton
Listed as a Bourbon.

Souvenir d'Anselme (Introducer unknown,-1848) syn., 'Enfant d'Ajaccio'; trans., "Remembrance of Anselme"
Hybrid Bourbon
"Growth very vigorous; foliage thick, making a magnificent cover, dark green; young growth chocolate mixed with red; flower large, full, cupped; bright cherry red." [S]

Souvenir de Mère Fontaine (Fontaine, 1874) trans., "In Memory of Mother Fontaine"
Hybrid China
"Growth vigorous; flower very large, full; bright red, nuanced carmine, carmine-lake towards the center." [S]

Souvenir de Paul Dupuy
Listed as a Hybrid Perpetual.

[**Thisbé**] (Vibert, 1820) syn., 'À Odeur de Jacinthe'
Hybrid Noisette
"Blush-white." [RG] "Flowers white, double, very numerous, slightly flesh." [No26] "*Bush*, very vigorous and thorny. *Leaves*, with seven leaflets of a glaucous green. *Ovary*, ovoid, fusiform, villose. *Flower*, medium-sized, full, flesh, fragrant. Center *petals* folded, bullate, wavy." [Pf] "Bloom…only appearing once a year." [S] The synonym reveals that the fragrance is that of the Hyacinth. The first Hybrid Noisette.

Triomphe de Laffay (Laffay,-1831) trans., "Laffay's Triumph"
Hybrid Noisette
"Flesh white." [TCN] "Pure white, full, globular, superb." [LF] "Flower large, full, regularly formed with imbricated petals; greenish white fading to pure white." [MaCo] "A beautiful rose, not of a pure white, but rather what is called French white, the outer petals inclined to rose-color." [WRP] "Flowers delicate flesh when newly opened, changing to white, large and very double; form, expanded. Habit, pendulous; growth, moderate. A showy Rose." [P]

[Vibert] (Écoffay, 1814) syn., 'Reine des Hybrides'
Hybrid China
"Large, double, deep crimson." [No26] "*Canes*, erect, out-thrust. *Ovary*, glabrous, shortly turbinate, or hemispherical. *Flower*, medium-sized, full, regular, homogeneously purple." [Pf] The first Hybrid China, named after a young Jean-Pierre Vibert, evidently already making himself known as an enthusiast even before going into business!

Vivid (A. Paul, 1853)
Hybrid Bourbon
"Bright carmine." [LS] "Brilliant crimson, very showy." [P1] "Very bright…magenta pink. Vigorous and rather prickly. Scented…4×3 [ft; ca. 1.25×1 m]." [B] "Light grenadine towards the center." [S] "Its flowers are not large, but they are of the most vivid crimson; and the vigorous habit of the plant makes it very suitable either for a pillar or a trellis." [FP]

[William Jesse] (Laffay, 1838)
Hybrid Bourbon
"Vermilion, full, flat, very large, superb." [LF] "Very large flower of a beautiful purplish pink, nearly full. Very handsome foliage. Doesn't seem to repeat very freely." [An42/335] "Crimson, tinged with lilac, superb, very large and double." [FP] "Crimson, black tinged." [HoBoIV:319] "Red, suffused with violet, in the way of 'Pius IX'. An undesirable sort."

[EL] "Very well formed." [S] "Light crimson, tinged with purple, very large, and very double; form, cupped. Habit, erect; growth, moderate. A magnificent Rose, but an uncertain autumn bloomer. A good seed bearer." [P] "A large and superb rose, crimson, with lilac tinge. This is certainly one of the most beauitful *very large* roses that exists; its flowers always open freely." [R9] "*Rivers*, 'Light crimson—lilac tinge—very large—beautiful and cupped'; *Paul*, 'Crimson, tinged with lilac—superb—very large and double'; *Wood*, 'Bright rose—very large and highly scented—one of the finest'...; *Curtis*, '—the king of perpetuals—light crimson—backs of the petals pale lilac—magnificent in size—most beautifully cupped shape and highly fragrant.' This truly noble rose was raised by Monsieur Laffay, and named in honor of his friend Mr. Jesse, of London; brother to the well known naturalist and popular author of *Gleanings in Natural History*, Mr. Edward Jesse. 'William Jesse' was sent out as a hybrid china rose, in 1838, but after being cultivated a few seasons in the country, it commenced blooming in the autumn, and has continued to do so ever since. It has now stood the test of years, and may fairly be ranked as one of our largest and most striking show roses, a model of shape as well as size. In colour it is a light crimson with pale backs to the petals, which are very large, beautifully cupped, and exquisitely scented. Under the poorest cultivation it is a large rose, but grown under the most favourable circumstances, we have measured specimens seventeen inches in circumference [ca. 4.25 dm]. Its growth is vigorous and flexible, it makes a good half pillar rose, and is also fine for the greenhouse and for forcing. 'William Jesse' is one of our freest seed-bearing roses, yielding hips of great size, but unless they are very carefully hybridized, they are not worth sowing. We speak thus confidently from experience, having raised thousands of seedlings without producing one really better than the parent rose." [C]

Zigeunerknabe (Geschwind/Lambert, 1909) trans., "Gypsy Boy"
Hybrid Bourbon
Two parentages have been advanced: (1), seedling of 'Russelliana' (Mult); or, vaguely, (2), seedling of an unnamed 'Russelliana' seedling × an unnamed Bourbon or Rugosa seedling.
"A great bush bearing hundreds of rich purple roses at midsummer." [T1] "Light fragrance...vivid crimson-purple." [G] "Medium double...deep crimson, almost purple to black...5×3 [ft; ca. 1.5×1 m]." [B]

Chapter Seven

Hybrid Perpetuals

"This class is like Moses' serpent, it swallows up all the rest." [Hd]

Laffay having led the way with the obscure 'Hybride Remontant à Bois Lisse' in 1830, "Guérin obtained [*in 1833*] the dwarf variety 'Gloire de Guérin' from the rose 'Malton', a variety which, for that era, was a precious introduction. Up to 1835, the catalogs contained only the hybrid *non*-remontant series; soon, however, these hybrids underwent a notable physiological change. Little by little, the seedlings of these hybrids took on the characteristics of the Oriental roses, while preserving the bearing of the European roses...In 1835, one would have been able to mention an HP unknown to us, 'Sisley', developed by Monsieur Sisley of Paris; however, it is to Monsieur Laffay, horticulturist of Auteuil, then at Bellevue, that we must allow the honor of having actually created the race of Hybrid Perpetuals." [JF] "It was in 1837 that Monsieur Laffay...sent to Mr. William Paul, his friend, the first cross-bred hybrid from the old Damasks, then so much in fashion." [R-H63] "My [*William Paul's*] friend Monsieur Laffay once told me that he raised many of his splendid Hybrid Perpetual Roses from 'Athalin' and 'Céline', crossing them with the free-flowering varieties of Damask Perpetual and Bourbon." [P] "Some of this class owe their descent to the Damask Perpetual, crossed with the China or Bourbon; others, to the latter roses, crossed with the Hybrid China and Hybrid Bourbon. In many cases it is difficult to trace their true genealogy. But whatever their descent may be, their value is undisputed." [Ed] "[*Laffay*] developed, in 1837, 'Prince Albert' and 'Princesse Hélène'; then, in 1839, 'Comte de Paris', 'Mme. Laffay', and 'Louis Bonaparte'; in 1840, 'Duchesse de Sutherland' and 'Mistress Eliot'; finally, in 1843, that superb rose 'La Reine', his triumph. Several rosarians, going the same route, successfully developed worthwhile varieties...Finally given this impetus, this beautiful race of roses took the foremost place in our gardens." [JF]

"Certainly, a more beautiful and interesting class of roses does not exist; their flowers are large, very double, most fragrant, and produced till the end of autumn. Their habit is robust and vigorous in a remarkable degree, and, above all, they are perfectly hardy." [WRP] "We would advise you to plant Perpetuals instead of 'June Roses', as they have all the beauty, size, color, and fragrance of the June roses, with the advantage of blooming several times in the season." [HstV:247] "Now, the class of roses called 'Hybrid Perpetual', or 'Remontants', is not exactly rightly named—that is, they do not bloom perpetually, but only at intervals. They bloom full in June, and then give a few scattering blooms along during the summer, and a good display again in September, doing better or worse, according as they are illy or liberally treated." [HstXXVI:187] "As we look upon them, we survey a gorgeous chaos. Here are innumerable varieties of foliage and flower, perplexing us in our search for genealogies and relationships...All require rich culture and good pruning. When an abundant autumn bloom is required, a portion of the June bloom must be sacrificed by cutting back about half the flower-stems to three or four eyes as soon as the flower-buds form. When the flowers fade, these also should be cut off with the stems that bear them, in a similar manner. The formation of seed-vessels, by employing the vitality of the plant, tends greatly to diminish its autumn bloom. Give additional manure every year, and keep the ground open and free of weeds. If rank, strong shoots, full of redundant sap, form in summer, check their disproportioned growth by cutting off their tops." [FP] "And when you are advised to let the shoots grow long and then to peg them down, do not yield; it does not answer. For a year or two, it may look well, but it spoils the plants and is a mistake." [HmC]

A note on the name of the class may not be out of place. "Hybrid Perpetuals" refers to "Hybrid *Damask* Perpetuals"—which is to some degree just what the first HPs were, as we have seen: Damask Perpetuals hybridized with Bourbons, Hybrid Bourbons, Hybrid Chinas, and the like. At length, these differing ancestries enabled fanciers to split the HPs into groups (the following adapted from Cx, EL, JR25/12-15, and JR25/22-25):

Group A, 'La Reine' Type. The roses of this group are vigorous and hardy; canes upright, slightly rigid with small to medium-sized prickles; foliage ample, serrated, light green; leaflets rounded, slightly glandular; flowers profuse, globular or cupped, very large, very full, fragrant, varying in color from delicate to intense pink; petals recurved on the interior of the calyx; calyx very long and widely spreading at the tip, glandular, deep pink and cerise at maturity. They sucker with the stems arising at some distance, as is the case with the Gallicas, which they much resemble in their growth. Some examples: 'La Reine', 'Anna de Diesbach', 'François Michelon', 'Mrs. John Laing', 'Paul Neyron', 'Ulrich Brunner fils', 'Alice Dureau', 'Antoine Mouton', 'Archiduchesse Elisabeth d'Autriche'. The 1901 Congress of Rosarians at Paris discerned a 'Louise Peyronny' subgroup which includes those varieties lacking any tint of lilac, which was found endemic, varying from delicate lilac to deep lilac, to the *true* 'La Reine' group. Some of the varieties thus split off to form the 'Louise Peyronny' *non-lilac* subgroup are: 'Louise Peyronny', 'Anna de Diesbach', 'Mme. Eugène Verdier', 'Mme. Montel', 'Mrs. John Laing', 'Paul Neyron'.

Group B, 'Baronne Prévost' Type. It is generally believed that the roses of this group are only sports of the Type…They form handsome bushes of a longevity uncommon to the HPs. Their principal characteristics are: strong, slender branches which are spreading in growth, armed with numerous strong, slender thorns; foliage ample; flower flat, full, resembling those of the Centifolia, varying from pink to deep pink; bearing little fruit. 'Baronne Prévost', 'Caroline de Sansal', 'Duchesse de Sutherland', 'Dr. Hurta', 'Louis Noisette', 'Mme. Charles Verdier', 'Mme. Desirée Giraud', 'Orderic Vital', 'Triomphe d'Alençon'.

Group C, 'Géant des Batailles' Type. Bush vigorous, hardy, floriferous, and very remontant, with brown, upright (but not rigid) canes; thorns numerous, strong; foliage small, not very ample, very subject to the fungal disorders; leaflets medium-sized, lanceolate, dentate, crowded on the leaf-stalk; flower flat or cupped, small to medium-sized, ovoid, grading into the stem. 'Géant des Batailles', 'Empereur du Maroc', 'Abbé Berlèze', 'Abbé Bramerel', 'Cardinal Patrizzi', 'Claude Jacquet', 'Eugène Appert', 'Napoléon III', 'Souvenir du Président Lincoln'.

Group D, 'Victor Verdier' Type. The varieties of this group are homogeneous, different from the ordinary HPs, and are very close indeed to the Hybrid Teas. They are notable for their pretty growth and their abundant bloom. Bushes vigorous; canes upright, large, short, smooth, green; thorns not very numerous, fairly large, recurved, enlarged at the base; foliage beautiful, ample, purplish green, elegant; leaflets elongate, dentate, glossy; flower very large, cupped; petals large, pink nuanced intense carmine; calyx round, with long, dentate sepals which themselves cover the round bud which gradually lengthens until becoming magnificent as the blossom is just opening; little or no perfume. 'Victor Verdier', 'Comtesse d'Oxford', 'Hippolyte Jamain', 'Eugénie Verdier', 'Lyonnais', 'Marie Finger', 'Pride of Reigate', 'Pride of Waltham', 'Suzanne-Marie Rodocanachi'.

Group E, 'Général Jacqueminot' Type. The roses forming this group, the most important of all, are hardy, bushy plants of vigorous growth, very floriferous, and bearing much fruit. Canes long, flexile, and generally slender; thorns very numerous, sharp, hooked, variable in size and shape depending upon the cultivar; foliage dark green; leaflets oval, dentate, slightly bullate; usually blooms in clusters; flower large, full, very fragrant, cupped or ruffled, sometimes globular; color, light red to blackish maroon; fruit abundant, fairly rounded, red at maturity. 'Général Jacqueminot', 'Abel Carrière', 'Alfred K. Williams', 'Baron Girod de l'Ain', 'Duc de Montpensier', 'Éclair', 'Eugène Fürst', 'Fisher Holmes', 'Gloire de Bourg-la-Reine', 'Jean Liabaud', 'Jules Chrétien', 'Monsieur Bonçenne', 'Prince Camille de Rohan', 'Princesse de Béarn', 'Prosper Laugier', 'Roger Lambelin', 'Souvenir de William Wood'.

Group F, 'Jules Margottin' Type. Bushes of unusual vigor without being climbing, very resistant to cold. Canes upright, armed with numerous large, strong, sharp, hooked thorns; foliage ample, stiff, slightly bullate; leaflets oblong, denticulate, dark green; bloom abundant, most often in clusters; the bud surrounded with foliaceous long, green, toothed sepals; sepals inserted at the tip of the calyx; mature calyx takes on the color of the flower; flowers large, full, perfectly imbricated, varying from pink to bright red, without the dark shades; very fragrant; fruit very elongate, resembling that of the Damask Perpetuals, from which this group was probably developed. 'Jules Margottin', 'Berthe Baron', 'Catherine Soupert', 'Clio', 'Duchesse de Vallombrosa', 'Heinrich Schultheis', 'Magna Charta', 'Mme. Gabriel Luizet', 'Mme. Renard'. The 1901 Congress of Rosarians at Paris splits off a less vigorous, smaller-flowered subgroup, the thorns of which are, for the most part, replaced by "rugosities" or medium-sized thorns: 'Comtesse de Serenye', 'Heinrich Schultheis', 'Margaret Dickson', 'Mme. Gabriel Luizet', 'Mme. Lacharme', 'Violette Bouyer'.

Group G, 'Mme. Récamier' Type. Bushes not terribly vigorous, but very floriferous; branches more upright than branching, resembling those of 'Général Jacqueminot'; very numerous thorns; foliage dense, glaucous green; leaflets oblong, dentate, rugose; flower pretty big, cupped or nearly globular, not very fragrant, white to blush white; fruit short, small, slightly conical, tinted pink at maturity, not very abundant. 'Mme. Récamier', 'Elisa Boëlle'.

Group H, 'Triomphe de l'Exposition' Type. The roses of this group are very vigorous, hardy, and fairly floriferous. Canes long, sometimes climbing, with extended internodes, glandulose; thorns not very numerous, variable in form and size; foliage ample, dark brownish green, purple when young; leaflets spaced out, dentate, rounded at the base and pointed at the tip; flower large, very full, generally flat, sometimes bulging, fragrant, often tripartite, varying from red to dark red to velvety crimson or violet; fruit variable in form, generally round or avoid, colored carmine cherry red at maturity. Its descendants are somewhat variable, though not enough so to form any subgroups. 'Triomphe de l'Exposition', 'Achille Gonod', 'Captain Hayward', 'Clémence Joigneaux', 'Comte Adrien de Germiny', 'Duhamel-Dumonceau', 'Éclaireur', 'Jean Goujon'.

Group I, 'Mme. Victor Verdier' Type. This group is much like Group J, in that the constituent roses are like 'Général Jacqueminot', but with smoother wood, and longer and more flexile canes; thorns often wider at the base and colored purple on a ground of greenish brown at the tip; the plants are very vigorous, very floriferous, hardy, bushier than is the case with Group J, and quite remontant. Branches smooth, green; thorns small and rare; foliage green, medium sized; flower large, globular or cupped, full, well-formed, well-held, very fragrant, and blooming most often in clusters of 3-12, depending upon the vigor of the plant's growth; the calyx more ovoid than those in Group J, sometimes takes on the form of an elongated cone at maturity; the bud is round, well-formed, and opens easily; most of the varieties in this group are characterized by the habit their axillary growth-buds have of sprouting very quickly, sometimes making it difficult with certain varieties to find buds for propagating. Here one finds the greatest variety of colors, from pink to blackish maroon: 'Mme. Victor Verdier', 'Alfred Colomb', 'André Leroy d'Angers', 'Bernard Verlot', 'Beauty of Waltham', 'Countess of Rosebery', 'Crimson Bedder', 'Duchesse de Galliera', 'Duke of Edinburgh', 'Duke of Teck', 'Dupuy-Jamain', 'Earl of Dufferin', 'Eugène Verdier', 'Général Duc d'Aumale', 'Louis Van Houtte', 'Paul de la Meilleraye', 'Reynolds Hole', 'Souvenir de Spa', 'Victor Hugo'.

Group J, 'Charles Lefebvre' Type. As mentioned above, the roses of this group are like the preceding. The plant is vigorous and hardy; canes pretty strong, long, not very branching, brownish or purplish-green, smooth; thorns large, sharp, hooked, pretty strong, and rare; foliage ample; leaves very large; leaflets oval, dentate, deep purple-green; flower large, full, very well formed, globular, cupped, or imbricated, deeply colored from red to blackish red, occasionally pink; calyx small, round, inflated at maturity; sepals long, covering the bud, which is short, pretty big, and conical; the inflorescence is of 3-7 flowers, depending upon the plant's vigor. 'Charles Lefebvre', 'Aurore Boréale', 'Capitaine Peillon', 'Colonel Félix Breton', 'Dr. Andry', 'Duchesse of Fife', 'Emperor', 'Florence Paul', 'Horace Vernet', 'Lord Bacon', 'Miller-Hayes', 'Président Schlachter', 'Salamander', 'Souvenir de Laffay', 'Souvenir du Dr. Jamain'.

Group K, 'Souvenir de la Reine d'Angleterre' Type. This group is very close to the 'La Reine' group. Plants very vigorous; canes very long, very strong, thick; thorns large, short, hooked, and close together; internodes very short; foliage ample, stiff; leaflets long, dentate, dark green; blossom solitary, cupped, quite full; color, fresh or light pink, except in the sports when it is white or blush white; flower scentless; the form of the calyx resembles that in the 'La Reine' group, but is shorter. Some of the varieties diverge from the above in having short canes, and a flower on a very short stem. 'Souvenir de la Reine d'Angleterre', 'Baronne Adolphe de Rothschild', 'Mabel Morrison', 'Merveille de Lyon', 'Spencer'.

Group L, Miscellaneous HPs. Includes both those not fitting into the other groups, and those not yet grouped. 'Comtesse Cécile de Chabrillant', 'Denis Hélye', 'Frau Karl Druschki', 'Gloire de Chédane-Guinoisseau', 'Gloire de Ducher', 'Her Majesty', 'Hugh Dickson', 'Marchioness of Londonderry', 'Mme. Laffay' (with characteristics between those of the 'La Reine' group and those of the 'Jules Margottin' group), 'Mme. Scipion Cochet', 'Oskar Cordel', 'Paul's Early Blush'.

"The French cultivators have carried this division into 'groups' to excess." [R8]

"The decline of the Hybrid Perpetuals may be traced to the advent of the Hybrid Tea, and few new Hybrid Perpetuals are being introduced at present…Their greatest fault, with few exceptions…, is that they have but one short blooming period. Further, the plant becomes ungainly in the long summers of the Southeastern and the Interior Southern Zones by reason of its habit of losing foliage. Many of the Hybrid Perpetuals blue easily and are discolored by rain…This history of the Hybrid Perpetual makes it evident that great hardiness and everblooming characteristics were sacrificed abroad for more perfect beauty of flower for exhibition. Many really valuable kinds have been lost sight of in the steady advance of widely heralded new varieties." [Th2] "No rose, however queenly and however lovely, that blooms but once or even twice a year is worthy of cultivation in gardens where everblooming kinds can be induced to grow." [Dr]

"I cannot refrain from protesting against the neglect this really wonderful class is being subjected to. When all is said, it is of the easiest culture and the only hybrid rose that is safely hardy and naturally permanent without winter protection north of the Mason and Dixon Line, and if given half the attention required by the Hybrid Tea, it would give great satisfaction. Some people object to its scarcity of bloom after the June outburst, but even if none was forthcoming for the rest of the season those beautiful massive blooms repay us well for having waited a year and given the plants the little attention they require. Who would think of discarding the lilacs, peonies, or iris because they bloom but once!...Let us be fair to the most beautiful if not 'fancy' rose and the least exacting—the Hybrid Perpetual." [K]

A. Drawiel (Lévêque, 1886)

"Growth vigorous; flowers large, full, form perfect and globular, blackish poppy red, brightened with carmine; one of the most beautiful dark roses yet developed." [JR10/149] "Medium height." [Sn]

A. Geoffrey de St.-Hilaire (E. Verdier, 1878)

"Red, with a shade of crimson; medium size, full; fine, circular form, fragrant and free. Seed organs well developed; seven leaflets are common, a great rarity among dark varieties of this class." [EL] "Growth vigorous with upright, short, delicate green canes; thorns numerous, straight, pink; leaves composed of 5-7 oblong, brownish green leaflets, with irregular, deep dentations; flowers medium-sized or large, full, admirably formed into a quite regular cup-shape; color, beautiful intense cerise red, superb...very remontant and very fragrant." [JR2/186] "Exquisite scent." [S]

[A.-M. Ampère] (Liabaud, 1881)

Seedling of 'Lion des Combats' (HP).
"Fine large flowers, borne in clusters; color, rich purplish red, tinged with violet; very showy and attractive." [CA90] "Very vigorous bush, with erect canes; flower of medium size, full, cupped; color, purplish red with bluish reflection; very pretty." [JR5/171] "Canes armed with sparse red thorns; leaves comprised of 5 leaflets; petiole slightly prickly; peduncle stiff...This pretty rose may be grown own-root or grafted, but not in a pot. It can't be forced; it is hardy. Prune short. It bears the name of Monsieur André-Marie

Ampère, a knowledgeable [*physicist and*] mathematician, born at Polemieux, near Lyon, who died in 1836." [JR5]

Abbé Berlèze (Guillot fils, 1864)
Seedling of 'Géant des Batailles' (HP).
"Flowers varying from bright-reddish-cerise to rosy-carmine, large, full, and of fine form; growth vigorous." [FP] "Very vigorous growth, flowers large, very full, well formed, color varying from bright cherry red to carmine pink." [l'H64/328] "Canes somewhat slight and nearly thornless; flower pretty large; color, bright cerise red...dedicated to Monsieur l'Abbé Berlèze, a great fancier of Camellias." [JR10/9]

Abbé Bramerel (Guillot fils, 1871)
Seedling of 'Géant des Batailles' (HP).
"Rich velvety-crimson, intense deep colour, flowers large, full, and evenly formed; a handsome and distinct rose, habit robust." [JC] "One of the beautiful flowers admired at exhibitions; it opens easily and may be distinguished by its scent. Growth is vigorous; the irregularly toothed leaves are pilose. Mildews. Color, bright crimson red, nuanced a velvety deep blackish brown purple." [S]

Abbé Giraudier (Levet, 1869)
From 'Géant des Batailles' (HP) × 'Victor Verdier' (HP).
"Bright rose." [EL] "The foliage of this rose is rather becoming, being olive-green; growth is vigorous, and it makes handsome bushes. On Polyantha stock [*which is to say*, R. multiflora '*Polyantha*'], the roses attain about four inches in diameter [ca. 1 dm]; its cerise-red color is very charming." [S]

Abel Carrière (E. Verdier, 1875)
Possibly a seedling of 'Baron de Bonstetten'; but see below.
"Rich velvety maroon, shaded with violet, large, full and finely shaped. One of the best." [P1] "A dark crimson red which does not blush; flower large, full, flat, vigorous." [Cx] "One of the good roses; the blossom,

despite tints of blackish maroon, is pretty sun-proof." [S] "Blooms often 'come' bad...malformed...beautiful colour, one of the really dark ones...in some seasons the petals will burn." [F-M2] "The bush is adequately vigorous and very floriferous...Abel Carrière's advantage is that the blossoms are fairly resistant to damage by the sun's rays during hot periods while others of the same sort get quite burnt." [JR31/60] "Velvety crimson, with fiery centre; large, full flowers, fragrant; short wood, sharp red spines; shows traces of Bourbon blood...Shy in autumn." [EL] "Fine, dark maroon, imbricated; wood very thorny; rather inclined to mildew." [DO] "Refuses to grow strongly in the spring. Foliage second-rate...liable to mildew and orange fungus...should only be grown by exhibitors." [F-M2] "Upright, wood green, armed with light pink thorns; foliage of three to five leaflets irregularly serrated; blossom about four inches across [ca. 1 dm], very pretty and of good form, ordinarily in a cluster of three to five." [JR10/10] "It is not recommended as a reliable variety for the garden." [OM] "We had wished to complete our notes on 'Abel Carrière' by giving a few words on its origin—but such is not possible. Its breeder, Monsieur E. Verdier, picks out each year a considerable number of seedlings (perhaps twenty or thirty thousand), and plants them all mixed together as those which seem, comparatively, the best." [R-H75] "Carrière (Elie-Abel).—Editor-in-Chief of *Revue-Horticole*. Born at May-en-Multien (Seine-et-Marne) in 1818, died at Montreuil (Seine) in 1896. In charge of the breeding-grounds at the Museum. Published various works, among which was *Traité Général des Conifères*." [R-HC] "Carrière was always a simple man, but of boundless devotion to those he honored with the title 'friend.' He quitted this Earth after a long and sad illness at the age of 79." [JR20/144]

Abel Grand (Damaizin, 1865)
Seedling of 'Jules Margottin' (HP).
"Clear, silvery-pink, flowers large, full, and very well formed, habit robust; a large and handsome rose, and very distinct." [JC] "Foliage very dark,

irregularly dentate; flower large, full; color, delicate pink shaded with silvery streaks; one of the best exhibition roses...blooms early and abundantly." [S] "'Jules Margottin' type. Glossy rose, large and full, fragrant; unreliable as to form, often the finest in autumn." [EL] "Rosy blush...A fine Rose." [P1]

Abraham Zimmerman (Lévêque, 1879)
"Growth very vigorous; foliage dark green; beautiful large, full flowers, quite regular in form; richly colored bright red shaded poppy and nuanced purple; superb and sparkling." [JR3/167] "Light scent, tall." [Sn]

Achille Cesbron (Rousset, 1894)
Seedling of 'Mme. Eugénie Frémy' (HP).
"Sparkling poppy." [LS] "Red, very large, full, medium scent, medium height." [Sn]

Achille Gonod (Gonod, 1863)
Seedling of 'Jules Margottin' (HP).
"Rosy carmine." [EL] "Flower large, full, sparkling carmine; very fragrant." [S] "Brilliant scarlet crimson, shaded deep maroon, large, full and sweet." [C&Js02] "Flowers bright-reddish carmine...very large and full; extra fine foliage, dark green; growth vigorous." [FP]

Adélaïde de Meynot (Gonod, 1882)
"Vigorous; strong, upright canes, very dark green; numerous thorns; foliage of five finely dentate leaflets; strong stem; flower large, imbricated, with quite rounded petals; color, bright cerise pink; Centifolia fragrance; quite remontant." [JR6/149]

Adiantifolia (Cochet-Cochet, 1907)
"Pink." [Ÿ] Though seen listed as a Hybrid Perpetual, this is probably another in the series of which Cochet's 1899 'Rosa Heterophylla' (from *R. rugosa* × *R. fœtida*) was a member; and thus then it would be a hybrid Rugosa rather than a Hybrid Perpetual.

Adrien Schmitt (Schmitt, 1889)
"Carmine." [LS] "Red, large, full, tall." [Sn]

Alba Carnea (Touvais, 1867) trans., "Flesh White"
"Plant not very vigorous; branches draggle along the ground; very delicate foliage; color of the rose slightly blushing—nearly white; form of the blossom, plump; [*blossom*] pretty strong and nearly full." [S] Some have been confused by the name of this rose, and class it as an Alba.

Alba Mutabilis (E. Verdier, 1865) trans., "Changeable White"
"Blossom well formed, pretty strong, quite full; color, delicate pink clouded with [*deeper*] pink." [S] Has been seen listed as a Moss.

Albert La Blotais
Listed as 'Monsieur Albert La Blotais'; see also the climber of this name.

Albert Payé (Touvais, 1873)
"Growth vigorous; irregular branching; foliage light green; flower large, full; flesh pink, overlaid with darker pink." [S]

Alexandre Chomer (Liabaud, 1875)
"Growth strong and vigorous; thorns irregular and reddish; flower large, full; color, velvety purple, nuanced bishop's violet." [S]

Alexandre Dumas (Margottin, 1861)
"Velvety-maroon, highly scented." [FP] "Flower large, full, well formed, velvety blackish crimson, striped poppy." [l'H61/263] "Flower large, often very large, depending upon the soil; form perfect; notable for its good poise; color, velvety crimson striped deep poppy. In strong ground, the color is much blacker." [S] Alexandre Dumas, either *père* (lived 1802-1870) or *fils* (lived 1824-1895); in both cases, French novelist and dramatist.

Alexandre Dupont (Liabaud, 1882)

Seedling of 'Triomphe de l'Exposition' (HP).

"Red, shaded." [LS] "Very vigorous bush; canes with green surface; foliage ample, handsome dark green, deeply toothed, leafstalk armed with two or three white prickles; flower-stalk stiff, bristly; blossom 7-8 cm across [ca. 3 inches], quite double, well formed, velvety purple-red nuanced crimson; fragrant. This pretty variety...is better grafted on the Briar than on its own roots; good in pots and for forcing; hardy. It bears the name of a young nephew of Liabaud's. To ensure good bloom, prune long." [JR10/11] "Two pairs of leaflets. Flower very large...well-held." [JR6/150]

Alexandre Dutitre (Lévêque, 1878)

"Bright rose." [EL] "Vigorous, flower large, full, perfectly imbricated like '[Mlle.] Annie Wood'. Color, handsome light bright pink; very remontant; considering the perfection of form and beautiful coloration, this is an extra good variety." [JR2/166]

Alexis Lepère (Vigneron, 1875)

"Growth vigorous; foliage velvety, very dark; flower very large, full, globular and of notable form; color, glossy light red." [S]

Alfred Colomb (Lacharme, 1865)

Seedling of 'Général Jacqueminot' (HP).

"Bright fiery red, large and full; form globular and excellent; very effective; one of the best; growth vigorous." [P1] "One of the few perfect roses which is *toujours gai*. In colour, a rich carmine, with a crimson glow on it; in style, large, globular, symmetrical." [R1/159] "'Semi-globular, high centre': very good in petal, centre, size, lasting qualities, fragrance, and colour." [F-M2] "Has a certain look of 'Charles Lefebvre'; moderate vigor;...pink, with an underlying and handsome fiery red." [S] "Sometimes it is hardly distinguishable from 'Marie Baumann'. Very fragrant." [DO] "Late-flowering; vigorous, and fragrant." [J] "Blooms well in the Fall." [JR10/11] "Bears the name of a great Lyonnais rose fancier…esteemed by fanciers, it is of moderate vigor, but the flowers, which have the expanded Centifolia form, are large, full, well-formed, pink on the underside of the petals, which above are of a handsome fiery red. Nothing has been forgotten in the color and form of this beautiful and good HP." [JR2/72] "Needs heavy soil." [Th2] "Of fine growth and foliage in good soil but not on poor or light land. Seldom attacked by mildew and can stand some rain." [F-M2] "Green wood, with occasional pale green thorns, the foliage large and handsome. A grand rose." [EL] Not to be confused with the Cherpin/Ducher 1852 Cherpin/Ducher HP of the same name, which was red, and had "dingy" foliage.

Alfred K. Williams (Schwartz, 1877)
Sport of 'Général Jacqueminot' (HP).
"Carmine red, changing to magenta; large, full, and expanded." [P1] "Magenta-red, shaded with crimson; large, full flowers, partly imbri-cated…very beautiful…but…not constant and reliable." [EL] "Blooms nearly always come perfect…not a good bloom to last, or of the largest size…bright colour." [F-M2] "Early flowering…moderate growth…one of the most perfect in form." [J] "Free-flowering, especially towards autumn." [Hn] "Constitution is weak. Thorny, with good foliage, and will stand some rain…Plants not hardy or long-lived." [F-M2] "Does not appear to like removal, so when it is possible it should be budded where it is to remain." [DO] "A perfect bloom, of bright red colour, but the growth is weak. Indispensable to exhibitors, but of little value for garden display." [OM]

Alfred Leveau
Listed as 'Monsieur Alfred Leveau'.

Ali Pacha Chérif
Listed as 'Aly Pacha Chérif'.

Alpaïde de Rotalier (Campy/C. Verdier, 1863) syn., 'Alphaïde de Rotallier' "Fine transparent rose-color, glossy." [FP] "Flower large, full, well-formed; color, transparent light pink; good for forcing in February." [S]

Alphonse de Lamartine (Ducher, 1853)
"Light rosy-pink." [FP] "Blossom medium-sized, full, well-formed, delicate lilac-pink. Very beautiful variety." [JDR56/48] "Very vigorous, branches upright and very thorny, foliage dark green, blossom medium or large, depending upon the season, very full, delicate pin, perfect form, well held, very fragrant." [JDR54/11] "Distinctly hooked thorns; leaves…rough to the touch; flower…globular; color, white shaded lilac pink." [S] Alphonse de Lamartine, French poet and politician; lived 1790-1869.

Alphonse Soupert (Lacharme, 1883)
Seedling of 'Jules Margottin' (HP).
"Bright rose-colour, large and very showy." [P1] "Very vigorous (like 'Jules Margottin'); flower, form, and size that of 'La Reine'; color, pure bright pink, blooming very early." [JR7/160] "Very thorny growth, but not strong with me…[T]he blooms are rather loose and by no means first-class. They are large and may be valued where the first Roses may be esteemed, as they are quite among the earliest. The petals are rather thin, and the shape is somewhat uncertain; still it is said to be a 'showy' Rose, which in catalogue-English means 'showy at a distance,' *i.e.*, that it will not bear a close inspection." [F-M3] "Sepals foliaceous; flower large, well-formed…dedicated by its raiser to…the elder son of the great Luxembourgian rosarian." [JR10/12]

Alsace-Lorraine (H. Duval, 1879)
"Very vigorous, very remontant, flowers full, regular in form, borne majestically, particularly handsome foliage; color, deep velvety black." [JR3/182] "An extra-handsome variety." [S] Sometimes considered synonymous with 'Directeur Alphand'. Alsace-Lorraine, region of France on the German frontier, hotly contested over the years.

Aly Pacha Chérif (Lévêque, 1886) syn., 'Ali Pacha Chérif'
"Cinnabar." [JR20/5] "Very vigorous, flowers large, full, very well formed, beautiful fiery vermilion red nuanced blackish purple." [JR10/149]

Ambrogio Maggi (Pernet fils, 1879)
Seedling of 'John Hopper' (HP).
"Bright rose." [EL] "Growth vigorous, very large wood, canes upright; beautiful light green foliage; flower very large, nearly full, globular, beautiful very intense pink, well held, quite remontant." [JR3/165] "Tall." [Sn]

Amédée Philibert (Lévêque, 1879)
"Very vigorous, beautiful very green foliage, flowers very large, full, beautiful very regular globular form, handsome deep violet nuanced blackish purple, a superb and rich coloring." [JR3/167]

American Beauty (Cook/Bancroft/Field, 1886)
"Large, double, rich rose-pink blooms of exquisite fragrance." [ARA29/96] "Deep even rosy carmine, with very fine petals, large and full; form cupped; very sweet." [P1] "Rich rosy red, very large, fragrant, long stemmed, solitary, and well held. The bush is vigorous enough, and blooms abundantly." [JR10/39-40] "A majestic blossom of very nice color, fragrance, and growth, but not blooming with much abundance, and often giving imperfect blossoms." [JR13/92] "Free bloomer in autumn." [SBP] "Imperial pink to deep rose; remarkably fine form, very large, full, cupped; rich fragrance...Has been a disappointment as an outdoor rose in the East wherever tried, but in the arid regions of the Interior South has proved to be most valuable, blooming for a long-continued season...subject to mildew." [Th2] "Large, globular, of a dark rose shaded with carmine, with an exquisite perfume. The mystery of its origin hangs over it." [JR16/37] "The daughter of our distinguished historian, Mr. George Bancroft, first saw the rose in bloom in the rose nursery of Mr. Anthony Cook, of Baltimore. She purchased the plant and had it transplanted to her father's rose garden in Washington City. Mr. Cook is very positive that

it is one of nine hundred seedling roses that he raised. Mr. Field, the well-known florist of Washington City, obtained cuttings from Mr. Bancroft's plant. He propagated a large number of plants…The colour is difficult to describe. The unusual shade of carmine-crimson, with a brilliant underglow, has over it a soft violet tinge, as if a film of bluish smoke hovered over the red velvety petals." [Dr] "'Mme. Ferdinand Jamin' and 'American Beauty' are, in many ways, similar in color, but not in the form of the flower. The foliage of the latter is more stiff than is that of the former, and the young stalks of the American are more upright than are those of the other." [JR11/97] "The year 1916 has seen the decline of the old favorite, 'American Beauty'…our much worshipped Beauty is slowly being pushed aside." [ARA17/111]

[American Belle] (Burton, 1893)
Sport of 'American Beauty' (HP).
"Crimson." [LS] "Pleasing shade of pink; very distinct." [CA96] "'American Belle' will be…an improvement on 'American Beauty', from which it sported in 1890…'American Belle' is completely lacking the violet tint which 'American Beauty' has shown for several years. Both have nearly the same growth characteristics; however, the more recent variety is not quite as vigorous as the other, its flowers are more open, and the darker green foliage is generally somewhat longer." [JR17/38]

Ami Charmet (Dubreuil, 1900) trans., "Friend Charmet"
"Flower very large, quite double, wafting an elegant and pure Gallica-rose scent; form notably beautiful, with thick petals, wider than long, gracefully recurved and waved on the upper part, regularly and elegantly imbricated like a Camellia…color, China pink with satiny reflections. The stems…are strong and robust, bearing from one to six blossoms, depending upon their vigor. The blossoms measure up to 5.5 inches across [ca. 1.3 dm], open with a 'neck,' and recurve like a Medici vase." [JR24/164] "Pure China-rose colour, reflexed with satiny rose, very large and sweet; fine foliage." [P1]

Ami Martin (Chédane-Guinoisseau & Pajotin-Chédane, 1906) trans., "Friend Martin"

From an unnamed seedling pollinated by 'Eugène Fürst' (HP).

"Very vigorous, with rigid canes, thorny, dark green foliage; very large flower, very full, plump, petals very thick and often reticulated; color, very intense, bright vermilion red, doesn't blue, very fragrant, very floriferous." [JR30/167]

Amiral Courbet (Dubreuil, 1884) trans., "Admiral Courbet"

"Vigorous, with continuous bloom. Canes ashen with occasional thorns. Leaves large and beautiful, pale matte green, evenly colored. Buds oval. Flowers upright, cupped, perfectly held, bright carmine red with magenta reflections. Outer petals very numerous, quite concave, imbricated, inner petals shorter, muddled. Very fragrant...elegant and penetrating aroma which it wafts forth all season. A magnificent variety." [JR8/152]

Amiral Gravina (Robert & Moreau, 1860) trans., "Admiral Gravina"

"Not very vigorous; branches very flexile; leaves fall; flower blackish purple, dark amaranth around the edges. The blossom is well formed, of medium size, and full." [S] "[*The blossom*] humbly kisses the ground." [VH62/91] "Medium to tall." [Sn]

André Leroy d'Angers (Trouillard/Standish, 1866)

"Dark violet red." [JR25/14] "Crimson, with a shade of violet; an attractive color, but very transient; often ill-formed." [EL] "Purplish-crimson, fine color, large and full." [FP] "Vigorous; foliage very dark; blossom deep violet outside and dark pink within." [S]

Angèle Fontaine (Fontaine, 1877)

"Vigorous bush; flower medium-sized or large, full; bright and delicate pink, good form." [JR1/12/12]

Anna Alexieff (Margottin, 1858)
Seedling of 'Jules Margottin' (HP).
"Rose, tinted with pink, large, full, and produced in great abundance; form cupped." [P1] "Beautiful...large, full, and somewhat flat." [JR28/140] "Very vigorous; flowers full, in a tight cluster, beautiful light salmon pink." [JDR58/36] "Fresh rosy-pink, superb colour, flowers very large, well formed, habit vigorous; a fine and most abundant blooming rose." [JC]

Anna de Diesbach (Lacharme, 1858)
Seedling of 'La Reine' (HP).
"Brilliant glossy pink, colour exquisite and lasting, flowers unusually large, full, and cupped; petals broad and smooth; a fine rose of moderate habit." [JC] "Flowers large, full, beautiful carmine pink with reflections." [l'H58/128] "The most lovely shade of carmine; very large and thick; deeply cupped; growth vigorous." [P1] "Semi-globular, fragrant light crimson flowers...sometimes a few in the fall." [ARA34/78] "Carmine-pink, tinted silvery." [JR1/2/7] "Petals few and far between." [P2] "Large vulgar flowers, loose and uneven, of a vivid rose." [B&V] "Of very strong hardy growth, but has the...fault of general looseness and unevenness in the blooms. They are of the largest size and more or less of the true cupped shape, but a perfect one is a rarity." [F-M3] "Giving [*in the Fall*] fewer than before, but of an exquisite freshness." [JR16/179] "Free in autumn." [Th2] "Vigorous, upright branches armed with numerous prickles ordinarily quite small; foliage ample, thick petioles...flower stalk firm...flower of about three or so inches [ca. 7.5 cm]...of such freshness that one wonders if it isn't artificial; petals around the circumference straight and elevated, those of the center ruffled." [JR10/13] "Canes fairly large, upright; bark light green, with occasional small, hooked, sharp prickles. Leaves glaucous green, divided into three to five leaflets which are oval-elongate and pointed; leafstalk an even glaucous green, strong and long. Flowers about 4.5 inches across [ca. 1-1.25 dm], full, widely cupped,

solitary or in clusters of two or three on the most vigorous branches…Calyx tubular; sepals leaf-like. A variety of the first order, one of the biggest and most beautiful of roses." [JF] "[*Lacharme*] dedicated it to the daughter of the Countess of Diesbach, amateur rosarian of Fribourg, Switzerland. This estimable variety developed from seed from 'La Reine' produced by Monsieur Lacharme in 1849; he grew it for nearly ten years to study it well, and having developed an appreciation of its merits, he released it to commerce in November, 1858…Not overly productive of its wonderful blossoms, perhaps, it *is* very vigorous, lasts well, and the flowers are quite large, well formed, and of a handsome carmine pink tinted silver." [JR2/58] "Though old is always one of the best, as much for the size of the blossom as for its color." [JR17/101]

Anna Scharsach (Geschwind/Ketten, 1890)
From 'Baronne Adolphe de Rothschild' (HP) × 'Mme. Lauriol de Barney' (HB).
"Blossom fresh pink, center brighter and often light purple, large, full, cupped. Bush very vigorous, hardy." [JR14/147] "Very fragrant, tall." [S]

Anne Laferrère (P. Nabonnand, 1916)
"Blood red." [Ÿ]

Annie Laxton
Listed as 'Anny Laxton'.

Annie Wood
Listed as 'Mlle. Annie Wood'.

[**Anny Laxton**] (Laxton, 1869) syn., 'Annie Laxton'
Seedling of 'Jules Margottin' (HP).
"Vigorous bush; foliage delicate green; flower outstanding in form, medium sized; color, fresh pink, nuanced with crimson and bright red." [S] "A garden Rose, with good growth, unusually fine foliage, and strong constitution. Not liable to mildew or much injured by rain. One of the

earliest, sometimes good enough for exhibition, a free bloomer and good autumnal. The flowers are of fair size and bright colour, somewhat flat and often irregular in shape, with rather thin petals." [F-M2]

Antoine Ducher (Ducher, 1866)
Seedling of 'Mme. Domage' (HP).
"Bright purplish red, very large, full, and fine; growth robust." [P1] "Rich dark crimson, flowers globular, large, full, and deep; a distinct and beautiful rose; habit moderate." [JC] "Cupped, bright orange." [l'H66/369] "Violet-red; large, well shaped flowers, fragrant; wood very thorny. The color is very fleeting." [EL] "Very vigorous hybrid; flowers upright, cupped, extra-large, full and very well formed, bright red…[*In comparison with 'Mme. Domage',*] flowers prettier, darker in color; very good for forcing." [RJC66/209] This variety is the unlikely co-founder, with *R. fœtida* 'Persiana', of the Pernetiana class, a group which, crossed with the old Hybrid Teas, yielded the first modern Hybrid Teas. The orange color noted by l'H66 is thus weirdly predictive.

Antoine Mouton (Levet, 1874)
Seedling of 'La Reine' (HP).
"Deep rose, tinged with lilac, not unlike 'Paul Neyron'; it is more fragrant and more hardy, but in color and size is below that sort." [EL] "Fine bright rose, reverse of the petals silvery; a large flower, somewhat coarse, but often good." [JC] "Very full." [CA90] "Vigorous and hardy…few thorns, green canes; leaves of 3-5 leaflets which are much serrated; leafstalk bears some small white prickles; flowerstalk green, firm, pubescent, sepals appendiculate and covered with glands; blossom to four inches across [ca. 1 dm], of perfect form, bright pink, reverse of petals paler; very fragrant." [JR10/20] "One of Monsieur Levet's best; the growth is very vigorous." [S]

Antonie Schurz (Geschwind, 1890)
"Flower flesh-white, very large, full, centifolia form and fragrance. Moderate vigor; hardy." [JR13/147]

Archiduchesse Elizabeth d'Autriche (Moreau-Robert, 1881) trans., "Archduchess Elizabeth of Austria"
"Extra-vigorous, nearly thornless, with handsome dark green foliage; the blossom is very large, full, and opens well; the color is beautiful light satiny pink, shaded, the reverse lighter; extremely floriferous." [JR5/172] "Well formed, of a delightful color." [JR7/157] Archduchess Elizabeth, daughter of Emperor Franz-Josef of Austria.

Ardoisée de Lyon (Plantier/Damaizin, 1858) trans., "The Slaty One of Lyon".
"Bright red with blue reflections." [JR2/59] "Violet-rose, a poor color." [EL] "Flower very large, full; color, slate-violet with red-violet reflections; center, lively brilliant red. The blossoms may grow over four inches across [ca. 1 dm]." [S] "An extraordinarily large rose, of a very deep purple color, and will, I have not doubt, prove a splendid rose." [HstXV:426] "Fully double, quartered, flowers of rich deep pink with violet and purple shadings. Sweetly scented…4×3 [ft; ca. 1.25×1 m]." [B] "Vigorous, branches upright, beautiful dark green foliage, flower four or so inches across [ca. 1 dm +], quite slaty, center bright shining red." [JDR58/36] Compare another slate-colored cultivar, by the name of 'Impératrice Eugénie', exhibited by Delhommeau of Le Mans in 1854: "The blossom is red when it has just opened; it takes on a slaty tint—or, more precisely, a violet tint—when fading. Monsieur Delhommeau must certainly take us to be children of Mother Goose; or perhaps he hasn't seen any rose other than his own before. Let us advise him, before he propagates this wonderful novelty, to observe the various stages a rose-blossom goes through, in particular those of 'Géant des Batailles'; we, at least, know what he it would seem doesn't—that turning violet or 'slaty' is a fault and not a virtue in a rose." [l'H54/131] Tastes differ!—nowhere more than in this. It is interesting to note how some—like Ellwanger and the just-quoted writer—almost always despise the slaty or blued tints; others find them intriguing and enriching.

Aristide Dupuy (Trouillard/E. Verdier, 1867) syn., 'Aristide Dupuis'
"Purplish-rose, a muddy hue; double for full, fragrant; of no value." [EL]
"Growth vigorous; branches grow upright; flower large, full, very remontant; slaty violet bordered bright pink." [S] Also attributed to Touvais,
1866; possibly another HP?

Arrillaga (Schoener, 1929)
From an unnamed seedling (resulting from crossing a Centifolia with
'Mrs. John Laing' (HP)) × 'Frau Karl Druschki' (HP).
"Bud large, glowing pink; flower very large, double (35 petals), unusually
lasting, intensely fragrant, vivid pink, golden glow at base of petals, borne
on long, stout stem. Foliage handsome and healthy. Growth very vigorous
(8 to 10-ft. canes [ca. 2.25-3m] in season); profuse bloomer in summer,
scant in autumn." [ARA31/226] "Enormous blooms of excellent quality
nearly five inches in diameter [ca. 1.25 dm] and 3 inches deep [ca. 7.5
cm], very double…At Breeze Hill the plants grew fairly well and produced
ordinary pink flowers." [ARA32/175] "Immense, very double flowers and
a really outstanding variety." [ARA31/208]

Arthur de Sansal (Cochet père/Cochet Bros., 1855)
"Blackish maroon with fiery shadings." [BJ] "Dark velvet crimson;
superb." [HstXIII:225] "4×4 [ft; ca. 1.25×1.25 m] with flowers of rich
crimson-purple." [HRG] "Highly scented." [B] "Upright, compact
plant…Light green foliage." [G] "Vigorous; foliage very dark and velvety;
flower of medium size, very full, opening with difficulty; the buds are
much sought for bouquets." [S] "It is a seedling of the *Giant*, from which
it takes its deportment and imbrication…it is to 'Géant des Batailles' what
'Mogador' is to 'Rose du Roi'." [l'H55/207] One sees the name "Cartier"
mentioned as this variety's breeder; but: "[*It was a*] seedling of Monsieur
Pierre Cochet's, Suisnes rosiériste, sold in 1855 by his two sons Philémon
and Scipion." [JR10/20] Dedicated to the horticulturist son-in-law of
that other famous breeder, Desprez: "Before his marriage [*to Caroline
Desprez*], he lived at Combs-la-Ville, afterwards going to stay at

Dammarie-les-Lys, near Melun." [JR10/77] "Our readers doubtless know that for nearly his whole life Monsieur de Sansal was occupied with horticulture; and we who have had the opportunity to study his notable collection of conifers and other plants—Cucurbitaceæ in particular—at his property in Farcy-les-Lys, near Melun (Seine-et-Marne), are particularly able to say so. But it was the rose which he held in special esteem; and he had a large and rich collection of them. He was never content to do like the simple amateur and plant merely the varieties available through commerce; he sowed many rose seeds, and Horticulture is indebted to him for many beautiful varieties—from which he never made one cent." [R-H75] There are some ambiguities which suggest that, despite the above, this cultivar should be attributed only to Scipion Cochet, or to the Cochet Bros., not to father Pierre Cochet; research continues.

Arthur Oger (Oger, 1875)
Seedling of 'Gloire de Ducher' (HP).
"Flower very large, well formed, full, borne singly; color, velvety purple, very dark but bright." [S] "Tall." [Sn]

Arthur Weidling (Vogel, 1932)
Sport of 'Pride of Reigate' (HP).
"Dark pink, large, full, medium scent, moderately tall." [Sn]

Auguste Chaplain (Tanne, 1921)
"Red." [Ÿ]

[**Auguste Mie**] (Laffay, 1851)
Seedling of 'La Reine' (HP).
"Glossy pink, a large globular flower, very full and well formed, a very vigorous grower, forms a good pillar; it does not open freely in cold damp situations." [JC] "Flower large, very double, cupped; sparkling pink, magnificent." [VH51/111] "Very vigorous plant; flowers large, full or nearly full, bright pink. A superb variety, both grafted and own-root." [l'H53/225] "A red rose of exquisite form, resembling, in more than one

way, 'Coupe d'Hébé'." [R-H63] "Branches very strong, with abundant straight thorns; flower well formed, large; quite remontant, and blooms for a long time; glossy pink, silvery on the reverse." [S] "Growing very vigorously, and bearing flowers equal to those of its parent in beauty of form, and superior in delicacy of color." [FP]

Aurore Boréale (Oger, 1865) trans., "Aurora Borealis"
"Growth vigorous; flower perfectly formed, large, full, quite remontant and blooms until October; color, bright shining red." [S] Aurora borealis, the Northern Lights.

Aurore du Matin (Roland, 1867) trans., "Morning's Dawn"
"Flowers very large, full, beautiful dawn coloration, reverse of petals silvery." [l'H68/49] "Reverse of petals bright red; beautiful exhibition flower." [S] "Light red...very fragrant, tall." [Sn]

Avocat Duvivier (Lévêque, 1875) trans., "Barrister Duvivier"
Seedling of 'Général Jacqueminot' (HP).
"Brilliant dark crimson, a large bold flower, like 'Maréchal Vaillant' [*HP, Viennot, 1861, purple*]; fine and distinct." [JC] "Flower very large, full, very well formed, very effective; color, bright purplish red with light purple; growth vigorous; floriferous." [S] "Tall." [Sn]

Barbarossa (Welter, 1906)
From an unnamed seedling (resulting from crossing 'Frau Karl Druschki' (HP) with 'Captain Hayward' (HP)) × 'Princesse de Béarn' (HP).
"Pure carmine red; a red 'Frau Karl Druschki'; vigorous and floriferous." [JR34/25] "A superb red-flowered variety dedicated to Barbarossa, which was the well-known nickname given to the Holy Roman Emperor Friedrich I [*1123?-1190; drowned while on a Crusade*]. If one can believe the German horticultural press, this introduction will have exactly the same growth, floriferousness, and bearing as 'Frau Karl Druschki', from which it differs only in its carmine-red color. What is more, it also has a delicate perfume—unfortunately not the case with Druschki...Peter

Lambert…eminent rosarian, protests vigorously against the boasts made about the qualities of this new introduction, which in his opinion it doesn't merit." [JR31/26] "The plant is a vigorous grower with shining dark foliage, entirely hardy and best of all it is very free flowering." [C&Js09]

[Baron Chaurand] (Liabaud, 1869)
Possibly a seedling of 'Monsieur Bonçenne' (HP).
"Growth very vigorous; canes upright, with few nodes; thorns straight, very strong at the base, slightly flattened; foliage very beautiful; bushy, complementing the blossoms very well, which latter are large, full, cupped, and irreproachably shaped; color, velvety scarlet; very deep grenadine in the center." [S]

Baron de Bonstetten (Liabaud, 1871)
From 'Général Jacqueminot' (HP) × 'Géant des Batailles' (HP).
"Velvety maroon, shaded with deep crimson, somewhat lighter in shade than 'Prince Camille [de Rohan]', and rather smaller in size, but with a little more substance; shy in autumn, but a grand rose." [EL] "Rich velvety-purple, very dark, liable to burn in hot weather; a superb rose when newly opened; habit robust." [JC] "Red, black, and crimson, large, full, and good." [P1] "A bad rose." [K1] "A fine Rose, flat, but double." [WD] "Very double…4×3 [ft; ca. 1.25×1 m]." [B] "A color of the darkest, it blooms in abundance, and the blossoms bear the rays of the summer sun with ease…The flowers of 'Baron de Bonstetten' seem to us larger and of richer color than those of 'Monsieur Bonçenne'…We believe that this rose…is the product of seeds obtained from 'Monsieur Bonçenne'…vigorous and pretty hardy; the numerous, very large, and well formed blossoms are full, fragrant, and of a magnificent color of velvety-black crimson red. Much recommended." [JR17/23] "Vigorous, strong branches armed with numerous hooked prickles; foliage sparse and rough to the touch…Monsieur le Baron de Bonstetten is a wealthy Swiss estate owner, and is a great fancier of roses." [JR10/22]

Baron de Wolseley (E. Verdier, 1882)
"Vigorous, reddish-green upright canes; thorns somewhat numerous, short, pink; leaves of five oval-rounded leaflets, with regular serration, delicate green; flowers large, full, well formed, velvety bright crimson nuanced flame." [JR6/165]

Baron Elisi de St.-Albert (Widow Schwartz, 1893)
"Violet red, very large, full, medium height." [Sn] "Vigorous bush, beautiful gay green foliage; flower very large, well formed, beautiful very bright carmine red passing to lilac red; comes up to the size of 'Paul Neyron'. Very floriferous." [JR17/165]

Baron Girod de l'Ain (Reverchon, 1897) syn., 'Baron Giraud de l'Ain'
Sport of 'Eugène Fürst' (HP).
"Bright red with white edging…fragrant and healthy…4×3 [ft; ca. 1.25×1 m]." [B] "Large, full; color, varying from crimson red to bright carmine; petals scalloped, largely blotched and bordered white, giving the blossom the aspect of a Flemish carnation." [JR21/113] "[*As compared to 'Roger Lambelin'*], 'Baron Girod de l'Ain' is certainly equal, if not superior, in beauty…First of all, the flowers are larger…the white piping at the edge of the petals is larger. The bush is very vigorous." [JR30/45]

Baron Haussmann (Lévêque, 1867)
"Dark red, large, well-built flowers." [EL] "Clear carmine-crimson, flowers of good size, beautiful and full; habit vigorous." [JC] "Flower large, full, compact, blooming in clusters; color, very beautiful carmine red, touched from time to time with deep crimson. Much to be recommended." [S] Not to be confused with E. Verdier's red HP of the same year 'Baronne Haussmann'. Georges Eugène, Baron Haussmann, civic planner of Paris; lived 1809-1891.

Baron Nathaniel de Rothschild (Lévêque, 1882)
"Very vigorous; foliage ample, handsome dark green; flower large, full, extremely well formed; beautiful uniform bright crimson red...regular form." [JR6/148] "A splendid variety." [S] Not to be confused with '*Baronne* Nathaniel de Rothschild', below.

Baron Taylor (Dugat, 1879)
Sport of 'John Hopper' (HP).
"Light red, large, full, tall." [Sn] "The growth and everything about the wood and foliage are the same [*as with 'John Hopper'*]; the color of the blossom, which has the same form, is a very delicate pin; flower large, full." [S] "Does not appear to be constant [*in the sported character*]." [EL]

Baron T'Kint de Roodenbeke (Lévêque, 1897) syn., 'Baron T'Kind de Roodenbecke'
"Very vigorous bush; beautiful dark somber green foliage; flowers large, full, very well formed, deep purple, nuanced and brightened with carmine and vermilion." [JR21/163-164]

Baroness Rothschild
Listed as 'Baronne Adolphe de Rothschild'.

Baronne Adolphe de Rothschild (Pernet père, 1868) syn., 'Baroness Rothschild'
Sport of 'Souvenir de la Reine d'Angleterre' (HP).
"Fresh pink, petals' edges silvery; flower very large, very full, cupped." [Cx] "Pale rose." [ARA17/28] "Bright flesh pink, shaded white...Vigorous, erect, hardy; blooms early; the color is very clear." [S] "Light pink, large but not quite full flowers of perfectly cupped form. Robust with a fine erect habit, one of the most charming of pink roses, though without any scent. Useless to us [*on the French Riviera*] as it seldom flowers till the second week in May; a very distinct variety." [B&V] "She robes herself in glossiest satin, and draws around her the drapery of ample folds dyed with richest, yet most delicate, peach-blow tints. The

stout shoots, armed with ivory-like spines, have an air of matronly dignity…[I]t bears the fierce heat of our July sun uncommonly well." [HstXVIII:166] "Light colored blooms of idea shape with a silvery sheen, and scentless, but with age a few blooms can be expected in autumn." [ARA34/77] "Flowers freely in autumn, but is unfortunately scentless; cannot be done without." [DO] "Blooms…late…[*the blossoms*] generally come well, of a globular shape, and a beautiful pink colour…very large…come again well in the autumn…quite scentless." [F-M2] "Highly scented…upright, tidy plant with ample foliage…4×3 [ft; ca. 1.25×1 m]." [B] "One of the largest roses." [SBP] "One of the most beautiful, and, so far as I have tested it, one of the most reliable of our light-coloured roses, for though short in limb, she is strong and sturdy in constitution…[O]ne meets with strange antitheses. Of this very rose, and only the other day, a rosarian said to me, 'Ah, yes—isn't she lovely!' and then added, with a tender pensiveness, 'I do believe that I've given the Baroness more than double her share of—pig manure!." [R1/159] "The wood is short-jointed, thick, light green, armed with occasional light green thorns…A very distinct, beautiful rose, free blooming, and greatly valued, both as an exhibition and a garden sort." [EL] "Growth…'robust'…short, thick, stumpy, stiff, upright wood, with grand foliage right up to the blooms." [F-M2] "Upright sturdy plant, 6×3 [ft; ca. 1.75×1 m]." [HRG] "Calyx small, pear-shaped; sepals leaf-like." [JF] "This was considered last year in England as *the rose* of the year, and it is pleasant to learn that the experience of the present season has more than confirmed all that has been said in its favor." [HstXXIV:284-285] "One of the first of roses." [HRH] Not to be confused with Lacharme's HP 'Baron Adolphe de Rothschild' of 1862, which was a "shaded purple". [LS]

Baronne de Medem (E. Verdier, 1876)
"Very vigorous, flower large, full, globular, bright carmine cerise-red." [JR1/6/10] "Has the form of the China Aster." [S]

Baronne de Prailly (Liabaud, 1871)
Seedling of 'Victor Verdier' (HP).
"Bright red, large, very full; often does not open well." [EL] "Bright pink."
[Ÿ] "Moderate vigor…flower large, bright red, globular, too heavy for the
stems which are rather slight and flexuose…Mme. la Baronne de Prailly
lived in Hyères." [JR10/34] Attribution to Victor Verdier appears to
derive from confusion between the person Victor Verdier and the parental
Hybrid Perpetual 'Victor Verdier'.

Baronne de St.-Didier (Lévêque, 1886)
"Vigorous, flowers very large, full, crimson red or intense cerise, shaded
lilac and purple, petals often edged white." [JR10/150]

Baronne Gustave de St.-Paul (Glantenet/Bernaix, 1894)
"Flower extra large, about 4.5 inches [ca. 1.25 dm], borne on a strong
stem. Beautiful pale pink color, with silvery reflections—very effective.
Very floriferous." [JR18/164]

Baronne Maurice de Graviers (E. Verdier, 1866)
"Beautiful intense cerise red, nuanced and shaded pink and carmine,
reverse of petals whitish." [l'H66/370] "Growth very vigorous; canes
upright and very thorny; flower medium-sized, well formed, full; color,
dark crimson red." [S]

Baronne Nathaniel de Rothschild (Pernet père, 1884)
From 'Baronne Adolphe de Rothschild' (HP) × 'Souvenir de la Reine
d'Angleterre' (HP).
"Vigorous bush; foliage light green, very thick, much serrated, abundant.
From 'Baronne Adolphe de Rothschild', to which it bears a great resemblance in wood and foliage; flower very large, nearly full, plump; color,
beautiful bright pink with silvery shadings. This rose is beautiful and
much to be recommended." [S] "Canes upright…flower very large, nearly
full, globular…well held; very perfect form." [JR8/151] Not to be confused with '*Baron* Nathaniel de Rothschild', above.

Baronne Prévost (Desprez/Cochet père, 1842)

"Bright rose color, a very large flower, strong, vigorous, free grower, blooming freely from June till November. Always opens its blooms well...A most magnificent Rose." [HstVI:367] "Large, full, bright pink." [R-H43] "The prince of perpetuals—bright rose color—immensely large and magnificent...Few roses give so striking and grand an effect as this; producing in such abundance, flowers of so immense a size, frequently measuring with moderately good culture, five or six inches in diameter [ca. 1.25-1.5 dm]." [C] "Flattish...deep, rose pink. Upright and vigorous...ample foliage...4×3 [ft; ca. 1.25×1 m]." [B] "Pale rose, sweet." [P2] "Fragrant, very hardy. The shoots are stout and stiff." [EL] "Very vigorous, forming a handsome bush which is long-lived—rare enough among HPs!...The foliage is ample and well-distributed, and is of a pretty green. The blossom, despite its size and fulness, is held well, is of a perfect form, and is carmine-pink, unshaded, perhaps with some lilac, and is very fragrant." [JR3/152] "Flower about four inches across [ca. 1 dm], flat, the center petals ruffled, perfectly held." [JR10/34-35] "One of the very best of its class, blooming freely in autumn...It is also of luxuriant growth, and large, rich foliage." [SBP] "This is the first time that this rose has bloomed at Monsieur Verdier's; it seems to rebloom very freely. The blossom is large, and pretty full; the petals are large, a pretty pink with a touch of lilac; the bush is vigorous, with strong canes having very sharp reddish thorns; the canes are topped by a bouquet of five to six flowers which bloom successively; the leaves have seven leaflets which are finely dentate, fresh green, undulate, and bullate; the perfume is elegant." [An42/332] "Canes fairly large and branching; bark a pretty green, with numerous prickles which are reddish and unequal, though generally short. Foliage very elegant, and handsome gay green, divided into 5-7 leaflets which are somewhat rugose, as well as oval-rounded, barely acuminate, and quite dentate. The leafstalk is fairly slender, nodding, armed with a number of small prickles. Flower, 3½-4 inches across [to 1 dm], full, rounded, solitary or in a cluster of 3-5 on the vigorous canes; color, a handsome fresh pink; outer petals large, those of the center smaller and inter-folded; flower stem pretty long, glandular, strong, supporting the blossom well. Calyx tubular; sepals leaf-like. A variety of much effort." [JF] "Dedicated to the sister of his [*Desprez's*] friend Monsieur Guenou[x], fancier and breeder of Dahlias at Voisenon, near Melun. On July 27, 1841, Desprez relinquished ownership of this variety to Monsieur Cochet Sr. for about a hundred francs. Cochet released it to commerce in Fall, 1842." [JR3/152] "It is reliable everywhere for an abundance of its large, fresh, blushing roses." [R1/203] "If it had been raised at Rome by a Roman, and during the time of one of her luxurious emperors, a crown of laurel would have been accorded to him." [R9]

[**Baronne Prévost Marbré**] (Van Houtte, 1864) trans., "Marbled 'Baronne Prévost' "
Possibly a sport of 'Baronne Prévost' (HP).
"Shaded pink." [LS] See also 'Mme. Désirée Giraud' (HP).

Barthélemy-Joubert (Moreau-Robert, 1877)
"Very vigorous, flower large, full, very bright cerise red." [JR1/12/12]

Beauty of Beeston (Frettingham, 1882)
"Growth vigorous; canes strong, but without growing very tall; flower small, full; velvety crimson." [S]

[**Beauty of Waltham**] (W. Paul, 1862)
Seedling of 'Général Jacqueminot' (HP).
"Bright carmine, and blooms profusely." [FP] "Cherry-crimson, petals large and well disposed, flowers cupped, large and finely formed, habit free." [JC] "Fair in growth and foliage, and not much liable to injury from fungoid pests or rain. The blooms come true and well, being seldom divided or malformed. The shape varies according to situation and cultivation…the petals are very closely curved inwards in the centre in a manner that proclaims the variety at once…This Rose has the good custom of closing in and guarding the centre more tightly in hot weather when it is

most needed than at other times. Not first class, but a free bloomer, rather late, good in lasting qualities and as an autumnal, but not very large." [F-M2] "Very remontant, blooming until Winter; flower large, full, cupped; color, cerise red shaded bright carmine. Distinguished by its delicious scent." [S]

[**Belle Angevine**] (Robert, 1856) trans., "Beauty of Angers"
"Flower medium-sized, white, plumed pink, cupped." [JDR56/40] "5-6 cm [ca. 2-2¼ inches], full, white plumed with pink and lilac, cupped." [R&M56] "Medium-sized bush." [S] "The late Monsieur Vibert had raised a single-flowered, striped HP seed-bearer around 1845, which later, in 1856, produced the HP 'Belle Angevine', a rose with full, striped blossoms, but not very vigorous. The rose 'Commandant Beaurepaire' [*alias 'Panachée d'Angers'*] arose from the same seed-bearer" [JR6/72]

[**Belle de Normandy**] (California Nursery Company?, by 1890) trans., "Beauty from Normandy"
"Beautiful clear rose, shaded and clouded with rosy carmine and lilac; very large and sweet." [CA90] "A lovely rose with great large flowers of pure silvery pink; one of the most beautiful. Flowers especially fragrant. The plant is a strong erect grower and good in every way." [C&Js09] Not to be confused with 'Belle Normande'.

[**Belle Normande**] (Oger, 1864) trans., "Norman Beauty"
Sport of 'La Reine'.
"One of the beautiful white flowers that one finds in collections, for that reason called by the fanciers in Rouen *Virgin Rose*; in certain locales, people also make use of it for marriage bouquets because of its virginal whiteness; the bud, alas, is somewhat marked with pink and green, colors which disappear when it opens." [S] Not to be confused with 'Belle de Normandy'.

Belle Yvrienne (Lévêque, 1890) trans., "Ivry Beauty"
"Very vigorous, beautiful glaucous green foliage, very thick, flower very large, very full, opens perfectly, beautiful brilliant red, shaded white and carmine; very effective plant." [JR14/179]

Ben Cant (B.R. Cant, 1901)
From 'Suzanne-Marie Rodocanachi' (HP) × 'Victor Hugo' (HP).
"Deep clear crimson, with dark veining, and slightly darker flushes in the centre; large and finely formed, with stout rounded outer petals of good lasting power; growth strong and sturdy." [P1] "Of fine, clean, strong growth with grand foliage, and seems to be a splendid crimson Rose for exhibition when grown on good HP soil…only occasionally will it give a show bloom." [F-M]

Benjamin Drouet (E. Verdier, 1878)
"Red, shaded with purple." [EL] "Very vigorous with strong reddish green canes; thorns numerous, strong, and big, brownish green; leaves composed of 5-7 large and oval leaflets, somber green, toothed deeply and irregularly; flowers large or very large, clustered, full, and well-formed; color, intense purplish red brightened with fiery red, most beautiful." [JR2/186]

Benoît Pernin (Myard, 1889)
Sport of 'Duchess of Edinburgh' (HP).
"Bright velvety pink." [Ÿ]

Bernard Verlot (E. Verdier, 1874)
"Purplish crimson-red and violet." [JR25/14] "Crimson, centre deep velvety-crimson, flowers full and compact, very sweet." [JC] "Growth vigorous; flower very good under glass, large, full." [S]

Berthe Baron (Baron-Veillard, 1868)
Seedling of 'Jules Margottin' (HP).
"Delicate rose color." [EL] "Of moderate growth, from the 'Jules Margottin' clan; flower large, full; color, delicate pink nuanced white." [S] "Baron[-]Veillard, Orléans horticulturist." [JR13/101]

Berthe Du Mesnil de Mont Chaveau (Jamain, 1876)
"Silvery red." [Ÿ] "Silvery rose, long cup-shaped flowers, large deep petals; a distinct and very fine rose." [JC] "Flower very large, full; color, silvery pink, center lighter. This variety is very floriferous, and much to be recommended." [S] "Vigorous bush, flower medium-sized or large, full, beautiful silvery pink." [JR1/6/10] "Du Mesnil de Mont Chaveau, rose fancier at the Château Freslonières, near Ballon." [JR2/165].

Berthe Lévêque
Listed as 'Mlle. Berthe Lévêque'.

Berti Gimpel (Altmüller, 1913)
From 'Frau Karl Druschki' (HP) × 'Fisher Holmes' (HP).
"Pink, large, full, dwarf." [Sɪɪ]

Bessie Johnson (Curtis, 1872)
Sport of 'Abel Grand' (HP).
"Light blush, large, very double, and sweet; a fine Rose of good habit; growth vigorous." [P1] "Large, globular, full, light flesh pink, very fragrant." [JR3/26] "Growth vigorous, climbing; wood long, vining; flower well formed, and nearly pure white." [S]

Bicolor Incomparable (Touvais, 1861) trans., "Incomparable Bicolor"
"Medium-sized, full, black center, top of the petals delicate pink." [M-R65]

Bicolore (Oger, 1877) trans., "Bicolor"
"Moderate growth; flower large, nearly flat, full, white with a light pink edge, passing to frosty pink." [S]

[Bijou de Couasnon] (Vigneron, 1886) trans., "Couasnon Gem"
Seedling of 'Charles Lefebvre' (HP).
"Growth very vigorous; wood stout, upright, with few thorns; flower large, full, beautifully colored intense velvety red; well held; very floriferous; very effective plant." [JR10/147-148]

Bischof Dr. Korum (Lambert, 1921) trans., "Bishop Dr. Korum"
From 'Frau Karl Druschki' (HP) × 'Laurent Carle' (HT)
"Bud large, ovoid, red; flower very large, full, cupped, very double, lasting; yellowish rose, with silvery shade; borne singly on strong stem; strong fragrance. Foliage sufficient, glossy, rich green, disease-resistant. Vigorous, upright, bush; blooms freely in June, July, September and October; hardy." [ARA22/154] "Tall." [Sn]

Black Prince (W. Paul, 1866)
Seedling of 'Pierre Notting' (HP).
"Dark crimson shaded with black, cupped, large, full, and of fine form; growth vigorous." [P1] "Glowing crimson shaded with purple, flowers large, full and globular, fine imbricated form; a distinct and first-rate rose, habit robust." [JC] "Very dark maroon, good climber." [FP] "Gives...quite a good dark bloom...rarely." [F-M2] "Fragrant, large, cupped...rich crimson shaded almost black. Vigorous...4×3 [ft; ca. 1.25×1 m]." [B] "Fair growth and fine foliage." [F-M2] "Very vigorous; branches upright, short, amply furnished with flat thorns." [S] "Not considered a reliable sort, occasionally it is very fine." [EL] Not to be confused with the HP 'Prince Noir', *q.v.*

[**Blanche de Méru**] (C. Verdier, 1869)
Seedling of 'Jules Margottin' (HP).
"A lightly blushing white while opening, passing to pure white, and in clusters." [l'H70/125] "Large full flowers; color pure white; a good grower and free bloomer." [C&Js98] "Vigorous bush." [S]

Boccace (Moreau-Robert, 1859)
"Crimson." [Ÿ] "Growth vigorous, canes knotty; foliage dark and very rough to the touch; flower large, full, well formed; color, bright carmine." [S] Giovanni Boccaccio, Italian author; lived 1313-1375.

[**Boïldieu**] (Garçon/Margottin fils, 1877)
From 'Jules Margottin' (HP) × 'Baronne Prévost' (HP).
"Flower very flat, very large, beautiful bright cerise red;...freely remon-tant." [S] "Bush vigorous, flowers very large, beautiful bright cerise red...We have seen this rose, and particularly recommend it." [JR1/12/12] Boïldieu or Boieldieu, a French composer from Rouen.

Boileau (Moreau-Robert, 1883)
Seedling of 'Victor Verdier' (HP).
"Flower large, full, cupped; color, beautiful bright satiny pink, nuanced. Very floriferous." [S] Nicolas Boileau-Despréaux, influential French critic; lived 1636-1711.

Bouquet Blanc (Robert, 1856) trans., "White Bouquet"
"Flower medium-sized, full, plump, very floriferous; color, pure white." [S]

Bouquet de Marie (Damaizin/Touvais & Fontaine, 1858) trans., "Marie's Bouquet," though we wonder if, rather than "Marie," either "Marié" or "Mariée" (meaning "Bridesgroom" or "Bride," respectively) was intended; *cf.* the HP 'Belle Normande'.
"Very vigorous, wood very thorny, thorns short; foliage light green; flow-ers medium-sized, in clusters; color, a lightly greenish-white fading to pure white; very floriferous." [JDR58/36] "This variety should be pruned long; it is hardy to 12°-14°." [JR10/60]

Bradova Lososova Druschki (Brada, 1937)
"Salmon-pink, large, full, tall." [Sn]

Buffalo-Bill (E. Verdier, 1889)
"Vigorous, canes short, erect; flowers large, full, flat, imbricated; color, very light pink." [JR13/167] Buffalo Bill, alias William F. Cody, American frontiersman and showman; lived 1846-1917. The hyphen is part of the rose's name.

Cæcilie Scharsach (Geschwind/Ketten, 1887)
Seedling of 'Jules Margottin' (HP).
"Flesh white fading to white, large, often very large, very full, fragrant, well formed." [JR11/184] "Pinkish white...tall." [Sn]

[**California**] (California Nursery Company?, by 1905)
"Bright pink." [CA05] "Rosy pink." [CA10] The great state of California, where bowers of flowers bloom in the sun.

Camille Bernardin (Gautreau, 1865)
Seedling of either 'Général Jacqueminot' (HP) or 'Maurice Bernardin' (HP).
"Light crimson, paler on the edges. A very certain Rose; fragrant." [H]
"Bright red, large, full, and of fine form, blooms freely, very sweet." [P1]
"Flower large, full, well formed, cerise red bordered white." [JR1/2/7]
"Medium size, semi-cupped form, fragrant; does not bloom until late in the season, and then the flowers fade easily; never very productive." [EL]
"Light crimson, shaded, flowers very large and full; a well formed good rose, habit vigorous." [JC] "Camille Bernardin died at Brie-Comte-Robert last December 5th [1894] in his 64th year...Having studied with an eye towards the legal profession for quite some time, but at length preferring the country life to that of the Bar, Bernardin settled early in life at Brie-Comte-Robert, and devoted himself entirely to the interests of the Briard populace, who never referred to him by any name other than the familiar one of 'Monsieur Camille'...For many months, a cruel malady had sapped his strength...'He was the friend of the common man, and of Democracy...' Around 1860, he took up the Rose...He organized, at Brie, the first special Rose Exhibitions which have subsequently echoed throughout the entire world." [JR19/1-2]

Candeur Lyonnaise (Croibier, 1913) trans., "Lyonnais Ingenuousness"
Seedling of 'Frau Karl Druschki' (HP).
"White, sometimes shaded yellow." [NRS/15] "The blooms are large and of fine form, but they are of palest sulphur colour." [OM] "Surpasses

['*Frau Karl Druschki*'] in substance and size, and if it were not tinted pale yellow, it would at times outclass it as an exhibition rose. It naturally produces its flowers on long, strong stems, a great many singly, but not as freely as Druschki." [ARA34/76] "Of great vigor, very hardy, with upright canes branching somewhat; foliage somber green; prickles fine and not very numerous; pretty ovoid bud, usually solitary, borne on a very rigid stem; flower of extraordinary size, having attained 6½ inches across [ca. 1.5 dm]. Color, a handsome pure white, sometimes lightly tinted very light sulphur yellow…The main ways in which 'Candeur Lyonnais' differs from its mother are that this rose is very full, that it keeps until fully open without showing its stamens and pistil, which are hidden in the petals in the center of the blossom, and that it surpasses Druschki in dimensions." [JR37/151]

Capitaine Jouen (Boutigny, 1901) trans., "Captain Jouen"
From 'Eugène Fürst' (HP) × 'Triomphe de l'Exposition' (HP).
"Bright vivid crimson, very large and full; growth very vigorous." [P1]
"Sown in 1887, the original plant, preserved by its breeder Monsieur Boutigny…is trained in a palmate form, ten feet in height and six in width, and each year the show is of a rare beauty. The plant makes a very vigorous bush, perhaps even climbing…it blooms freely." [JR27/7]

Capitaine Louis Frère
Listed as 'Monsieur le Capitaine Louis Frère'.

Capitaine Peillon (Liabaud, 1893) trans. "Captain Peillon"
"Vigorous bush with upright canes; beautiful dark green foliage; flower large, full, perfect form spherical; color, beautiful crimson purple red." [JR17/164] "Tall." [Sn]

Captain Hayward (Bennett, 1893)
Seedling of 'Triomphe de l'Exposition' (HP).
"Brilliant carmine-crimson; flowers very full, cupped, fragrant; very, very floriferous; very vigorous." [Cx] "Not very full…fine petals of great

substance." [J] "Of perfect form; very sweet and opening well. An early bloomer." [P1] "Flowers long, pointed, beautiful form, scarlet-crimson, fragrant; likes partially shaded places." [Hn] "Well-formed long petals; needs to be well done [*i.e., given liberal treatment with water and fertilizer*] if to give of its best. Very free-flowering, somewhat inclined to be thin." [DO] "The flowers, which are none too full, are of scarlet-crimson shade...An easy rose to grow, and one that gives a few blooms in autumn." [DO] "At its very best, grown as strongly as possible, in a cool season, it is with its pointed form and long smooth petals...as magnificent an example of the bright red H.P.'s as we have...petals are rather thin and few in number...opens very quickly." [F-M2] "Fragrant, light crimson, high-centred, double...excellent orange hips...6×4 [ft; ca. 1.75×1.25 m]." [B] "Nearly all the flowers come out at the same time...twice in the year...ablaze with its bright coloured, well formed blossoms, which are carried on stiff stalks, bolt upright. In between times and after the autumn flowering we get a few blooms, but not enough to be of much value." [NRS/13] "Perfect form when grown in cool, moist conditions; fragrant...Poor in hot weather." [Th2] "Extra vigorous growth with very fine foliage...not much liable to fungoid pests or to come malformed." [F-M2] "An admirable Rose in all ways and very sweetly scented." [K1]

Cardinal Patrizzi (Trouillard/E. Verdier, 1857)
Seedling of 'Géant des Batailles' (HP).
"Crimson, with a tinge of purple." [EL] "Growth vigorous." [S] "A superb Rose in a temperate climate, but which, in the North, and in England in particular, doesn't bloom well except under glass." [R-H63] "A seedling of Monsieur Trouillard's, of 1855, released to commerce in 1857 by Monsieur Eugène Verdier. Of moderate vigor...flower medium-sized, well formed, very full, velvety purplish red tending towards black; edges a bright flame...more sensitive to frost than other HPs...Monseigneur Constantin Patrizzi is, it seems, an Italian prelate born in Siena in 1798...and was bishop of Portugal and Ste.-Rufine." [JR10/77] Sometimes said to be synonymous with 'Vainqueur de Solferino'.

Hybrid Perpetuals • 429

Caroline d'Arden (A. Dickson, 1888)
From 'Alfred K. Williams' (HP) × 'Marie Baumann' (HP).
"Very delicate pure pink. Its blossoms are very large, sumptuous, and perfect as to form. The scent is delicious, the petals firm, large, rounded, and very smooth. Particularly good for exhibition. It blooms profusely; the leaves are very large; the plant is robust." [JR12/105-106]

Caroline de Sansal (Desprez/Jamain & Paillet, 1849)
Seedling of 'Baronne Prévost' (HP).
"Flesh color, deepening towards the centre; large, full flowers, flat form, often indented; subject to mildew; very hardy. An unreliable sort, but beautiful when in perfection; generally it is of better quality in September than in June." [EL] "Clear flesh colour with blush edges...a fair-weather rose only." [P2] "Very free, strong grower. The foliage is large and luxuriant. The flowers are very large, double, and cupped like the old Centifolias. The color is a pale silvery blush, with a fleshy tinge in the center, resembling very much...'Souvenir de la Malmaison'." [HstIX:492] "Nearly as large and fine as 'La Reine'...decidedly the best light colored one we have yet seen." [WHoII] "A blush 'Baronne Prévost'...This is a very desirable variety from its hardiness, size, and fine habit." [C] "A robust growing and most excellent rose, though in cold damp conditions it does not open freely." [JC] "Very vigorous, with red-tinged branches lightly bethorned; foliage dark green sometimes touched with yellow; flower large, full, well-formed, imbricated, well-held...[I]t bears the name of ...the daughter of Monsieur Desprez, married to Monsieur Arthur de Sansal." [JR10/77] "Monsieur Hippolyte Jamain has, among a crowd of the most precious introductions, two roses bred by Monsieur Desprez, whose death threatened to deny to Horticulture...'Berthe de Sansal' [*HP, 1849, bright pink*] and 'Caroline de Sansal'...Very vigorous, with slightly reddish bark which has brown, upright, and unequal thorns; leaves, 5-7 large leaflets of a dark green above, oval-oblong, sharply toothed, the upper leaflets larger and rounded; the blooming and blossom form resemble

those of 'Baronne Prévost'...[T]he flower stems are erect, to 1½ inches long [ca. 3.75 cm], covered with rust-colored glandular bristles; the blossoms are solitary, or in a cluster of 3-5 at the tip of the cane; the calyx tube is funnel-shaped, not contracted at the mouth, bristly-glandular like the flower-stem; the blossom is 4-4½ inches across [ca. 1+ dm], with rounded, imbricated petals." [R-H49] "Does very well grafted as well as own-root." [l'H53/172] "Hard to beat." [HstXXVI:331] "Always bonnie, always bountiful." [R1/203]

Catherine Soupert (Lacharme, 1879)
Seedling of 'Jules Margottin' (HP).
"Rosy-peach; distinct." [EL] "White, shaded with rose, large and full; form and habit perfect. A beautiful Rose." [P1] "Reblooms very freely, is vigorous and hardy, and is beginning to be appreciated for the garden...flower large, full, imbricated, well formed, white washed pink, held on a long stem. It is dedicated to the daughter of Monsieur Soupert, the able rosarian of Luxembourg." [JR10/92]

Centifolia Rosea (Touvais, 1863) trans., "Pink Centifolia"
Seedling of 'La Reine' (HP).
"Rich rosy-pink, flowers large and cupped; petals smooth and even; a very distinct and beautiful rose, with abundant foliage, habit vigorous." [JC] "Bright rose, circular, shell form; light green wood, with numerous red thorns; foliage crimpled." [EL]

Charles Bonnet (Bonnet, 1884)
"Pearly pink." [LS] "Large, full, medium height." [Sn] "Much liked in Switzerland and in Haute-Savoie, next to Lake Léman...It's a rose with very tenacious foliage, hardy, vigorous, floriferous, and extremely remontant; its pretty and graceful blossoms are semi-double and delicate pink; the numerous buds open quite late into the Fall. This variety is so vigorous that it can be used to advantage to make shrubberies...'Charles Bonnet' should be better known, and deserved to be propagated in all countries. It

originated in Switzerland where it was bred a long time ago by an arbori-culturist of Renens-sous-Lausanne, who gave it his own name." [JR22/50] "It was in 1873, in a garden belonging to Monsieur Bonnet, a horticultur-alist then at Vanves (Seine), that Monsieur F. Jamin first saw it [*"it" being the Boursault 'Mme. de Sancy de Parabère', which is examined in our book* The Old Rose Adventurer]; and, upon the request of Mme. Bonnet, he provisionally named it 'Mme. de Sancy de Parabère'." [JR9/124]

[**Charles Darwin**] (Laxton/G. Paul, 1879)
From 'Pierre Notting' (HP) × 'Mme. Julia Daran' (HP).
"Crimson brown, very floriferous, with well-rounded blossoms." [JR3/12] "Good growth and foliage, the blooms having a color described univer-sally as brownish-crimson. I have been unable to detect the brown shade, but must, as I have said, leave these delicate distinctions of tints to experts. Rather late, and a good autumnal. The shape is open, and the variety does not prove very satisfactory with me, though often well shown by others." [F-M3] Charles Robert Darwin, English naturalist; lived 1809-1882.

Charles Dickens (W. Paul, 1886)
"Vigorous, very hardy and blooming abundantly; blossoms large, full, beautiful pink; a splendid variety for gardens and beds." [JR10/19] Charles Dickens, English author; lived 1812-1870.

Charles Gater (G. Paul, 1893)
"Brownish crimson." [LS] "Carmine brown." [JR20/6] "Deep crimson brown. Flower globular. Exhibition rose." [JR19/36] "Deep crimson; vig-orous; good, late." [TW] "Brownish red; vigorous and hardy." [P1] "Clear red, globular blooms…good foliage…4×3 [ft; ca. 1.25×1 m]." [B] "A grand rose; extra large size, fine full form, dark rich crimson, exquisitely shaded; very fragrant and handsome. A good healthy grower and free bloomer." [C&Js99] "My [*George Paul's*] old friend and foreman, the late Mr. Charles Gater." [NRS17/103] "Charles Gater, of Cheshunt, and his brother William, of Slough,…were probably the best growers of pot Roses the world has seen." [NRS20/26]

Charles Lamb (W. Paul, 1883)

"Bright cerise." [Ÿ] "Carmine-red. Good foliage." [H] "Flower large, full, perfectly held; color light glossy red; abundant bloom in Summer and Fall; magnificent garden rose and much to be recommended for cutting." [S] "Bright red, lovely clear colour, very beautiful in the bud; foliage handsome, habit hardy. This variety flowers continuously." [P1] Charles Lamb, English author; lived 1775-1834.

Charles Lefebvre (Lacharme, 1861) syn., 'Paul Jamain'

From 'Général Jacqueminot' (HP) × 'Victor Verdier' (HP).

"Bright crimson, with purplish centres, large, very double, and of fine form." [P1] "Velvety scarlet, smooth and thick petals, flowers evenly and beautifully formed, a very fragrant and most superb rose, habit moderate." [JC] "Flower about 3½ inches across [ca. 8 cm], cupped, full, well-formed, very fragrant, bright red with touches of maroon. Magnificent flowering...Monsieur Charles Lefebvre is the son of a great lover of roses from Autun." [JR10/139] "A superb dark crimson, indescribably rich...This stands almost alone for its vigorous strong wood and large leathery foliage, that possesses almost the substance of the leaves of a camellia. It is excellent for all purposes." [WD] "Fine in petals, centre and size, lovely in colour, very fragrant and beautifully round and smooth...open and semi-imbricated...not a good form to last...free in bloom and a good autumnal...the G.O.M. ['*Grand Old Man*'] of the dark crimson roses." [F-M2] "Has the form of a Ranunculus, expanded." [HstXXIV:253] "Fades quickly and blues under heat." [Th2] "Few roses are as beautiful when it is at its best." [J] "One of the sweetest in scent." [E] "Beautiful in both flower and leaf." [ElC] "A few thorns of light red; the wood and foliage are of light reddish-green. A splendid rose." [EL] "Of strong growth, with stout stiff smooth wood and fine foliage, requiring strong soil...more liable to orange fungus than to mildew...can stand rain." [F-M2] "Very floriferous." [JR3/26] "Flower stalks pretty long, slender, strong, supporting the blossom well; petals of the circumference large, those of the center smaller. Calyx pear-shaped, nearly globular. A very pretty variety of the Jacqueminot sort." [JF] "Vigorous; branches of medium size, divergent; bark smooth, light green, bearing thorns here and there which are reddish, clinging, and hooked; leaves light green, 3-5 leaflets, oval-acuminate, dentate; leafstalks thin, light green, armed with 3-4 little prickles; flower is about three inches across [ca. 7.5 cm], full, strongly cupped, either solitary or in twos or threes." [S] "4×4 [ft; ca. 1.25×1.25 m]." [B] "Vigorous upright growth to 5 [ft; ca. 1.5 m]." [HRG] "In good soil makes shoots eight to ten feet [ca. 2.25-3 m] in a season." [WD] "A marvelous production by a well-known breeder." [VH62/102] "A magnificent rose." [DO]

Charles Margottin (Margottin, 1863)
Seedling of 'Jules Margottin' (HP).
"Brilliant carmine...centres fiery red, very large, full, and sweet; growth vigorous." [P1] "Rich in nuance and size." [l'H67/54] "Form fine; outer petals large and round." [FP] "Retains the color well; smooth, reddish wood armed with occasional red spines; foliage slightly crimpled. An excellent, distinct rose, quite unlike the parent in habit. It doubtless comes from a natural cross of some dark sort like 'Charles Lefebvre' on 'Jules Margottin'." [EL] "This notable variety was developed...in 1859...[V]ery vigorous, with large well-formed flowers of a beautiful sparkling carmine red, intense flame in the center. Grafted, this variety boasts luxuriant growth, while on its own roots it is feeble." [JR3/29] "Branches dark green, slightly reddish, with small upright red thorns; leaves of five leaflets, oval-lanceolate; flower stem bristling with hairs; sepals long, two or three of them leaf-like; blossom about three inches across [ca. 7.5 cm], full, fragrant, charming, slightly cupped, very bright carmine red, center scarlet red...bears the name of...the son of its raiser." [JR10/140]

Charles Martel (Oger, 1876)
"Flower very large, nearly full, well formed, very remontant, blooms late, good rose to force; color, purple red, which sometimes takes on a violet

tinge." [S] "Tall." [Sn] Charles Martel, ruler of the Franks; lived 689-741; defeated the Moslems at Tours in 732, stopping the spread of Islam in Europe.

Charles Turner (Margottin, 1869)
"Very large flower opening into a cup; beautiful sparkling intense red." [l'H70/125] "Flower large, full, cupped, well held; color, bright grenadine." [S] "Crimson-vermilion, large, full flowers, flat form, resembling 'Général Washington'; wood armed with numerous dark red thorns. A shy bloomer." [EL] "Tall." [Sn]

[Charles Wagner] (Van Fleet/Conard & Jones, 1907)
From 'Jean Liabaud' (HP) × 'Victor Hugo' (HP).
"A vigorous growing rose with large double flowers of clear bright red (approaching scarlet). Blossoms appear in clusters of 3 to 5, of great substance and exceedingly fragrant. It has luxuriant foliage, usually composed of seven leaflets, of dark rich green and not liable to mildew. It is one of the best bloomers." [C&Js07] "Rev. Charles Wagner, Mission Chapel, Paris, France. Author of *Simple Life* in whose honor by special permission this Rose is named." [C&Js07]

Charles Wood (Portemer, 1864)
"Red, reverse white." [Ÿ] "Beautiful exhibition rose." [S] "Flowers deep red, shaded with blackish-crimson, very large, full, and of fine form; growth vigorous." [FP]

Chot Pĕstitele (Böhm, 1932)
Sport of 'Frau Karl Druschki' (HP).
"Pink, large, full, light scent, tall." [Sn]

Christina Nilsson
Listed as 'Mme. Boutin'.

Clara Cochet (Lacharme, 1885)
Seedling of 'Jules Margottin' (HP).
"Very vigorous; flowers very large, rather globular, full; petals very large; color, beautiful light pink, center brighter pink; petal edges have the sparkle of diamonds." [JR8/165] It tells us something about the warm personality of Lacharme to note how many of his roses are named after family members of his colleagues and friendly rivals in the rose business!

Claude Jacquet (Liabaud, 1892)
"Bush very vigorous with smooth upright canes, small and rare thorns, beautiful close-set foliage of a glaucous green; flower very large, full, plump; color, scarlet purple, shaded light. The beginning of a new race!" [JR16/152] "Medium scent, tall." [Sn]

Claude Million (E. Verdier, 1863) syn., 'Claude Millon'
"Flower large, full, cupped, slightly flaring; color, scarlet bordered deep violet and dark grenadine." [S] "Scarlet-crimson, dashed with rose and violet, velvety, large, full, and of excellent form, habit good." [FP] "Flowers cupped, beautiful velvety carmine scarlet, highlighted with pink and violet, growing in 4s-5s in a terminal cluster." [l'H63/224] "Rich velvety crimson, beautifully shaded with violet, petals smooth and even, flowers large, cupped and well formed; habit vigorous." [JC]

Clémence Joigneaux (Liabaud, 1861)
"Carmine." [Ÿ] "Flower very large, full; color, bright sparkling red." [S] "Red and lilac color, and grows with great vigor." [FP] "At the top level of the schools may be placed the National School of Horticulture at Versailles, created in 1873 on the initiative of Joigneaux, replacing the former kitchen-garden of the King." [Pd]

Clémence Raoux (Granger/Lee, 1869)
"Vigorous bush; canes robust, glossy deep green, thorns straight, flat; flower large, full, well formed; color, bright pink shaded silvery pink." [S] "A washed-out pink; large, fragrant flowers, quartered shape; worthless." [EL]

Clio (W. Paul, 1894)

"Flesh colour, shaded in centre with rosy pink, very large; fine globular form, and freely produced…splendid…unsurpassed in the beauty of its flowers and their effect in the garden." [P1] "A beautiful color of pink-tinted cream; it is very vigorous with long stems." [JR32/34] "Almost globular shape…very pale pink…practically white on the outside…by no means first-class in form or colour…rain soon spoils it." [F-M2] "They open well outside in the open air." [JR18/66] "The numerous blossoms are of pretty form, the bud is very large, and when the flower has opened the color is a beautiful rose-pink." [JR32/13] "Slight fragrance; needs thinning…Balls badly in damp weather." [Th2] "Imbricated." [Cx] "A very vigorous variety; the shoots are so strong that they should be pegged down instead of being cut back at pruning time. The flowers…come in thick clusters, but they are not very attractive." [OM] "Hardy, strong, almost rank grower, with large foliage and thorns…not much liable to mildew." [F-M2] "Healthy plant…4×3 [ft; ca. 1.25×1 m]." [B] Clio, the Greek Muse of History.

Colonel de Sansal (Jamain, 1875)

"Flower large, full, well-formed; velvety carmine shaded very deep carmine." [S] "Pink." [Ÿ]

Colonel Félix Breton (Schwartz, 1883)

"Vigorous, having the look of 'Charles Lefebvre', foliage ample, cheerful green; flower large, full, with regularly imbricated petals, velvety grenadine red, exterior petals aniline violet, brilliantly velvety, with a matte amaranth reverse, a totally novel coloration." [JR7/121] "Canes of medium size, branching; bark smooth, with occasional much-compressed red thorns which are slightly hooked; foliage…of 3-5 oval-acuminate dentate leaflets; leafstalk slender, light green, armed with 4-5 prickles; flower…well formed, solitary or in twos or threes." [S]

Colonel Foissy (Margottin, 1849)

"Flower large, full, well formed, very remontant; blooms till Winter; color, light cerise." [S] "Flower…6-8 cm [ca. 3 inches]…very abundant bloom." [M-V50/229] "Vigorous plant; blooms in clusters; medium size, full, bright cerise." [l'H53/171] "Bush having a great resemblance to [*those of*] the Bourbon group. Vigorous canes, flower-clusters at the tips, dark green, bearing large, very numerous reddish thorns as well as leaves composed of 3-5 medium-sized, slightly long, dark green, irregularly dentate leaflets; flowers a beautiful bright cherry red, full, from 6-8 cm in diameter [ca. 3 inches], in clusters of 5-10 in a terminal panicle; peduncles long, upright; calyx-tube inflated in the middle, slightly glandular, with sepals often foliaceous." [VH439/534-534d]

Commandeur Jules Gravereaux (Croibier, 1908)

From 'Frau Karl Druschki' (HP) × 'Liberty' (HT).

"Vermilion-red. Vigorous. Garden. Semi-double. Distinct in colour." [NRS10/99] "Growth vigorous, with strong, upright canes; medium-sized thorns; foliage ample and beautiful dark green; blossoms borne on a strong, rigid stem; buds generally solitary, well-formed, long, and pointed; blossoms large and full; petals very large and thick, scalloped at the edge, giving the opening flower a particular elegance; color, beautiful fiery red, velvety, lightly shaded maroon within; does not blue; very fragrant…has the growth and bloom of Druschki, but is a little less vigorous; very remontant." [JR32/152] "Lovely pointed buds and rather single, peony-like, velvety red, fragrant flowers…the large blooms, with ragged petals, are often 6 inches across [ca. 1.5 dm], and make a very striking picture in a bud-vase. The bush is low and blooms all summer." [ARA29/55]

Comte Adrien de Germiny (Lévêque, 1881)

Seedling of 'Jules Margottin' (HP).

"Bright rose." [EL] "Very vigorous, beautiful ample dark green foliage, flower large, full, very well formed, imbricated, handsome bright pink, very brilliant and sparkling, very remontant and beautiful." [JR5/149]

Comte Bobrinsky (Marest, 1849)

"Velvety deep crimson." [LS] "Medium-sized, very full, bright carmine." [Pq] "Deep maroon." [JR2/59] "Brilliant scarlet-crimson, a most attractive colour, though the flowers are not well formed." [JC] "Full or nearly full...blooms continuously...It does well grafted, less well own-root." [l'H53/171] "This is a Bourbon hybrid, with very vigorous branches, smooth, with long, narrow, and slightly hooked thorns which are brownish green; leaves glossy green, smooth, with 5-7 oval-oblong leaflets which are sharp at the tip, and bordered with slightly reddish teeth; flowers solitary or in twos, 3½ to 4 inches across [to ca. 1 dm], resembling in form 'Sidonie', outer petals flat, somewhat erect, poppy-red above, pink beneath; center petals muddled, but the same color; flower stem about 3 inches [ca. 7.5 cm], quite upright, covered with glandular bristles; calyx funnel-shaped, glabrous, in five linear segments, of which three are lacy, foliaceous at the tip. The rich color of this rose, more brilliant than that of 'Géant des Batailles', gives a very pretty effect; unfortunately, not all the blossoms open up easily; but its earliness makes up for this—its blossoms are among the first to open, and among the last to fade." [R-H49]

Comte Charles d'Harcourt (Lévêque, 1897)

"Very vigorous, foliage dark green, large flowers, full, very well formed, beautiful bright carmine red, abundant bloom." [JR21/164]

Comte de Falloux (Trouillard/Standish & Noble, 1863)

"Crimson-pink." [Ÿ] "Not very vigorous, the canes being quite weak." [S]

Comte de Flandres (Lévêque, 1881)

Seedling of 'Mme. Victor Verdier' (HP).

"Very vigorous, foliage brownish green, flower very large, full, very well formed, plump, handsome velvety blackish purple red shaded carmine." [JR5/150]

Comte de Mortemart (Margottin fils, 1879) syn., 'Comtesse de Mortemart'
"Flesh pink." [Ÿ] "Light lavender rose; very large, with fine petals. A splendid early rose." [CA90] "Flower large, full, well formed; color, beautiful light pink. Very fragrant; of much merit." [S] "Rose color, very fragrant; smooth, pale-green wood." [EL]

Comte de Nanteuil (Quétier, 1852)
"Large, full, bright pink." [R&M62] "Flower plump, bright pink at the center, exterior petals lightly veined violet pink." [l'H52/172] "Growth vigorous; flowers medium-sized or large, very full, perfect 'plump' form, deep pink nuanced lilac; superb." [l'H56/199] "Vigorous growth; blossom large, full, globular; color, bright pink, petal edges deep crimson." [S] "Pale flesh, a most beautiful formed, cup-shaped rose, distinct, and of good free habit of growth." [JC] Has been seen misclassified as a Gallica.

[Comte de Paris] (Laffay, 1839) syn., 'Général Hudelet'
"Purplish pink, full, very large, cupped, superb." [LF] "Dark crimson." [HoBoIV] "Light crimson, lilac tinge." [JWa] "Large, full, violet-red, often striped." [R-H42] "Very large." [Pq] "Growth moderate; prune long; flower very large, full, cupped; color, delicate pink." [S] "Rosy lilac, glossy, sometimes purplish, very large and very double. Habit, erect; growth, moderate. A noble Rose, and very sweet." [P] "Very remontant." [JR6/43] "Much esteemed." [M'I]

Comte de Paris (Lévêque, 1886)
"Very vigorous; flowers large, full, very well formed, poppy red nuanced and illuminated bright purple, brown, and intense crimson. Magnificent color and form." [JR10/149] "A large full red Rose, of ordinary growth and habits, with flowers of 'reflexed' shape." [F-M3]

Comte Florimund de Bergeyk (Soupert & Notting, 1879)
"Very vigorous, flower large, very full, Centifolia form; color pink-brick distinctly nuanced orange red, very fragrant and effective." [JR3/168]

Comte Frédéric de Thun-Hohenstein (Lévêque, 1880)
"Blackish." [JR20/5] "Reddish crimson." [EL] "Very vigorous, foliage large, dark green; flower large, full, very well formed, beautiful deep crimson nuanced brown and carmine, very distinct coloration." [JR4/164] "Canes with green bark, armed with thick, small, white thorns...flower to 3½ inches across [ca. 8.75 cm], fairly well formed, but showing the stamens; color, crimson red shaded brown. This variety bears the name of an enthusiastic Austrian rose fancier." [JR10/141]

Comte Horace de Choiseul (Lévêque, 1879)
"Flower large, full, well imbricated, fiery vermilion brightened with scarlet, velvety, brown nuances; color much brighter than that of 'Duc de Montpensier'." [JR3/166-167] "Deep orange-red, large, full, medium scent, tall." [Sn]

Comte Odart (Dupuy-Jamain, 1850)
"Very vigorous, but with short brown-green canes having numerous, nearly straight, deep maroon thorns; leaves ample, of 5-7 nearly round leaflets which are a beautiful dark green; flowers large, 8-9 cm [to ca. 4 inches], full, well formed, beautiful bright red passing to violet; the center petals are quartered. This variety is close to 'Géant des Batailles'." [l'H51/8]

[Comte Raimbaud] (Rolland/E. Verdier, 1867)
"Flowers large, full, deep carminy cerise." [l'H68/49] "Flower large, semi-full; color, deep cerise." [S]

Comte Raoul Chandon (Lévêque, 1896)
"Very vigorous bush, foliage comber green; flower large, full, very well formed, vermilion nuanced with brown; color and flower both superb." [JR20/162]

Comtesse Bertrand de Blacas (E. Verdier, 1888)
"Soft bright rose colour; large, full, and globular. Very sweet; an excellent and effective variety." [P1] "Vigorous, with strong, erect, delicate green

canes; thorns remote, straight, pink; leaves composed of 3-5 very large light green leaflets, elliptical with irregular, fairly deep serrations; flowers large, full, of an admirable globular form, cupped; color, the most beautiful, very fresh, most seductive bright pink; fragrance elegant and penetrating." [JR12/162]

Comtesse Branicka (Lévêque, 1888)
""Very vigorous; leaves ample, handsome glossy green. Flower large, full, very delicate pink…Very pretty." [JR12/181]

Comtesse Cahen d'Anvers (Widow Lédéchaux, 1884)
Seedling of 'La Reine' (HP).
"Deep pink." [Ÿ] "Vigorous, canes upright, leaves of 5-7 leaflets of a handsome dark green, flowers large, full, globular, beautiful bright pink." [JR8/165] "This variety sprang from 'La Reine', to which it is superior; it grows well in a pot, and is popular among florists." [S]

Comtesse Cécile de Chabrillant (Marest, 1858)
Seedling of 'Jules Margottin' (HP).
"Pink with a paler reverse." [JR2/59] "Medium size, very good habit and very full, silky flesh-coloured. Vigorous growth, erect. Very fragrant." [Hn] "Satiny-pink, never above medium size, full, fragrant; of perfect, globular form; numerous dark thorns of small size; foliage dark and tough. A lovely rose." [EL] "When in its best state, it is of matchless beauty." [P2] "A perfect model of symmetry, though scarcely large enough to satisfy the craving for monstrosity, which is the failing of the public taste among rosarians at the present day; in all other respects it is perfect." [WD] "Shell-like petals, so beautifully set in cup-like form, and so sweetly tinted with shaded pinks…each rose is so perfect, not crowded in a cluster so close that none can get room to unfold in perfection, but singly, borne on the point of each strong shoot." [HstXXVIII:167] "Bright rose colour, surface of petals like satin, reverse having a silvery tinge, large and full flower; grows vigorously; foliage very much polished; good and valuable

variety. Very fragrant; altogether a lovely rose." [B&V] "Very vigorous bush with stocky, fat canes growing no longer than 40 cm [ca. 16 inches], and forming a well-rounded head; the thorns, which are rather plentiful, are small, thin, slightly hooked, very unequal, and intermixed with glandular bristles. The foliage is ample, and composed of leaves with 5 or 7 oval-elliptic leaflets which are slightly stalked, nearly obtuse, unequally dentate—lower dentation glandulose—bright green above, paler beneath. The blossoms, a fetching bright icy pink with silvery reflections, are globular, very full, perfectly formed, and regularly imbricated in the outer rows of petals, which are mostly obovate, pure pink above, and silvery beneath. The peduncle is strong, very glandulose, and flaring at the tip into a glabrous calyx tube which is funnel-shaped, and not contracted at the throat; the sepals are slightly glandular, the two outer ones being somewhat foliaceous, while the three inner ones are simple and very pointed. This new rose was developed by Monsieur Marest, rue d'Enfer, Paris. It is very remontant and blooms very abundantly. We have been watching it bloom since Spring, and have satisfied ourselves that the last blossoms are quite as beautiful as the first." [l'H58/97-98] "Vigorous, forming a bushy, somewhat tall, shrub; branches with green bark, fairly upright, armed with small unequal red prickles intermingled with bristles; leaves of 3-5 leaflets, oval-elliptical, of a soft green; petiole glandular; flower 2 to 2.5 inches in diameter [ca. 5-6 cm], full, globular, well-held, beautifully symmetrical; silvery pink fading to lilac; fragrant; strong stems covered with bristles." [JR10/184-185] "Good perfume. Good, strong foliage…4×3 [ft; ca. 1.25×1 m]." [B] "What a name!…[A] superb rose, without a doubt." [HstXV:426]

Comtesse d'Oxford (Guillot père, 1869)
Seedling of 'Victor Verdier' (HP).
"Carmine with soft violet shades; velvety, flowers large, full, and cupped; petals smooth and well formed." [JC] "Vermilion red." [Cx] "Of the largest size…good in petal and centre…shape…open…fairly

lasting...colour soon gets dull." [F-M2] "Fades quickly...subject to mildew." [EL] "Good foliage which is most lovely in the early spring...does not suffer much from mildew...especially liable to...rust." [F-M2] "Very vigorous with upright branches. Its foliage is very handsome. As for the blossom, it is very large and supported on a firm stem, very double and of good form. Its rich color is a bright, dazzling carmine-red." [JR4/101] "Branches large, with green bark; foliage of 2 to 5 leaflets of a dark green on top, more pale beneath; thick; much serrated; leafstalk thick; flower stalk upright and strong; the blossom is of a rare elegance, being 4-4½ inches across [ca. 1 dm], somewhat flat, somewhat fragrant...very vigorous and remontant...It bears the name of the English countess Eliza Nugent, daughter of the Marquess of Westmeath, Countess of Oxford; it was found desirable to frenchify the name of the rose." [JR10/185] "A reliable Rose when well treated." [DO] "A fine showy Rose, the best type of its style." [WD]

Comtesse de Bresson (Guinoisseau-Flon, 1873)
Seedling of 'Jules Margottin' (HP).
"Very vigorous bush; flower large, full within, folded into a rosette; color, bright pink, petal edges white." [S]

Comtesse de Falloux (Trouillard/E. Verdier, 1867)
"Flowers very large, very full, pink nuanced mauve." [l'H68/49] "Delicate pink shaded crimson." [S]

Comtesse de Flandre (E. Verdier, 1877)
"Vigorous bush; flower large, full, very globular, beautiful light silvery pink, very delicate, very fresh, center bright pink, beautiful cupped form, well held; large petals; canes strong, upright, delicate green; thorns very rare; leaves of 3-5 very delicate green leaflets, teeth large and deep." [S] "Tall." [Sn]

Comtesse de Fressinet de Bellanger (Lévêque, 1885)
"Very vigorous, foliage light green, flower very large, full, well formed, beautiful flesh pink. Very beautiful." [JR9/148] "Tall." [Sn]

Comtesse de Mortemart
Listed as 'Comte de Mortemart'.

Comtesse de Paris (E. Verdier, 1864)
"Crimson, edges of petals tipped with silvery shade, a perfect deep reflexed flower, large and full. Very fine." [B&V] "Vigorous, flowers full, 10-12 cm [ca. 4 inches], beautiful intense currant pink, lined whitish." [l'H64/327] "Vigorous bush; ample beautiful dark green foliage; flower large, full, globular, perfect form, magnificent bright pink, petal edges nuanced white; considering color, form, and its abundant bloom, it will be ranked as a top of the line variety." [S]

Comtesse de Polignac (Granger/Lévêque, 1862)
"Vigorous bush; blossom medium-sized, full; color, bright crimson nuanced deep purple." [S] "Growth very vigorous; foliage glaucous green; flower medium or full, very brilliant poppy red, velvety, nuanced flame-red." [l'H62/278] "Tall." [Sn]

Comtesse de Roquette-Buisson (Lévêque, 1888)
"Very vigorous, leaves handsome light green and very large. Flower very large, beautiful light pink nuanced or tinted both a darker and a lighter pink; form most attractive." [JR12/181]

[**Comtesse de Serenyi**] (Lacharme, 1874) syn., 'Comtesse de Serenye'
Seedling of 'La Reine' (HP).
"Rosy flesh, with silvery reflexed petals; full and finely shaped." [CA90] "Very vigorous bush; canes strong, dark green, bearing flattened, hooked thorns; foliage dark green, regularly dentate; flower very large, full, character of the Centifolia; color, delicate pink shaded carmine. Much to be recommended for forcing." [S] "Of fair growth and foliage, rather liable to

mildew, and easily spoiled by rain. A very free bloomer and good autumnal. This is a Rose with awkward manners, for it has great possibilities and can be very fine when it chooses, but it is one of the 'coarse' varieties, too full in petal, in regard to which the stronger you grow them the worse they are. On a maiden growth, especially if the buds be thinned, the survivor will often be a most unsightly object, and indeed it is very seldom that a large bloom will come without distorted shape; but on the side-shoots of a cut-back in a dry autumn, flowers of a beautiful 'globular imbricated' shape may be got, of good lasting qualities." [F-M3] "Very good variety from 'La Reine', which it is much like. Max Singer calls it good for forcing; its breeder, *au contraire*, says in a note which he was so kind as to send us that it forces poorly. It can be propagated just as well by cuttings as by budding; it needs to be pruned long, and bears 15°-20° of frost. It is dedicated to the wife of the Count Serenyi, a great Hungarian rose fancier." [JR10/186]

Comtesse de Turenne (E. Verdier, 1867)
"Flesh pink." [Ÿ] "Growth vigorous; canes robust; very handsome dark green foliage; flower large, full." [S]

[Comtesse Duchatel] (Laffay, 1842)
"Blossom large, very full, cupped; color, purple pink." [S] "Medium-sized or large, bright carminy pink, cupped." [R&M62] "Flower large, double and cupped; petals finely imbricated, of a bright rose color. This superb variety remains a much longer time expanded than the 'Mme. Laffay'." [MH45/28] "Colour brilliant rose, shape cupped and perfect; her flowers are also large, very double and fragrant." [R9]

Comtesse Hélène Mier (Soupert & Notting, 1876)
"Vigorous, flower large, full, light satiny pink, nuanced darker." [JR1/6/10] "A superb variety; indispensable." [S]

Comtesse Henrietta Combes (Schwartz, 1881)

"Vigorous, having the look of 'Marie Baumann', flower large, full, centifolia form; color, bright satiny pink with silvery reflections, reverse of petals lighter, very fragrant, and quite remontant." [JR5/149]

Comtesse O'Gorman (Lévêque, 1888)

"Violet red, large, full, medium height." [Sn] "Growth vigorous, leaves ample, glaucous green; flower large, full, very well formed, bright red nuanced poppy and violet." [JR12/181]

Comtesse Renée de Béarn (Lévêque, 1896)

"Vigorous, leaves glaucous green, flower large, full, magnificent form, beautiful nuanced carmine, brightened with blackish purple nuanced flame. Superb." [JR20/163]

Coquette Bordelaise (Duprat, 1896) syn., 'Panachée de Bordeaux', 'Paul Neyron Panachée'; trans., "Bordeaux Flirt"

Sport of 'Mme. Georges Desse' (HP, Desse/Duprat, 1897; pink and red; parentage unknown).

"Clear, bright rose, richly shaded with dark velvety red and broadly striped with pure white." [C&Js02] "Deep pink striped white, very large, full, medium scent, tall." [Sn] "Buds large and flat; blossom bright pink with a large white central blotch on each petal, which, though having the form of a rose, gives it the look of a Camellia…As for growth, foliage, wood, etc., it is just like 'Paul Neyron'." [JR21/88]

Cornet (Lacharme, 1845) syn., 'Rose Cornet'

"Of a delicate roseate color, with imbricate petals." [WRP] "Flower large with rounded petals, of a fresh delicate pink color." [An47/209] "Its flowers are of a light rose, very double, and very fragrant." [R9] "Vigorous bush; canes very flexile, supporting the flower with difficulty; flower very large, full, cupped. Very beautiful form. Good exhibition rose, not only because of its form, but also because of its color, grenadine nuanced pink." [S] "Flowers rose, tinted with purple, very large and double; form, cupped. Habit, branching; growth, vigorous. A very showy rose, partaking somewhat of the nature of the Provence, whose scent it bears." [P] Benoit Cornet was one of Lacharme's fellow *rosiéristes* in Lyon.

[**Coronation**] (H. Dickson, 1913)
"The flowers are of immense size and great substance; color shading from flesh to bright shrimp-pink." [C&Js14] "Vigorously growing bush. Canes upright, smooth, with magnificent foliage, quite refined; [*the flower*] is enormous…The largest rose known." [JR37/58] "A magnificent Rose." [C&Js16]

[**Countess of Rosebery**] (Postans/W. Paul, 1879)
Seedling of 'Victor Verdier' (HP).
"Fine carmine red, large and full, finely cupped form, makes a handsome bush with few thorns." [C&Js99] "Flower large, full; color, bright pink-carmine; beautifully cupped; foliage dark green; wood smooth." [S] "Of long strong growth, with distinct smooth wood and fair foliage. A little liable to mildew but not much injured by rain. The blooms do not come very well, only a small percentage being quite regular in shape, which is somewhat open. The petals are good and very smooth, and a capital specimen may be had occasionally, though not of the largest size. Only fair in freedom of bloom, and not first-class as an autumnal." [F-M3]

Crimson Bedder (Cranston, 1874) syn., 'Souvenir de Louis Van Houtte'
"Vigorous bush; flower large, full, well formed; color, bright grenadine." [S] Belongs to Giant of Battles type. Crimson." [EL] "As a crimson bedding rose this variety surpasses every other rose for brilliancy of colour and continuous blooming; its habit of growth is moderate, and shoots short-jointed, producing a mass of flowers the whole season; colour scarlet and crimson, very effective and lasting, clean glossy foliage, and free from mildew." [JC]

Crimson Queen (W. Paul, 1890)
"Velvety crimson, shaded with fiery red and maroon; very large; globular and handsome; fine foliage." [P1] "Center nuanced flame, interior petals maroon." [JR19/36]

Crown Prince (W. Paul, 1880)
Seedling of 'Duke of Edinburgh' (HP).
"Bright purple, centres shaded with lurid crimson, very large and double, petals fine, very floriferous, and of excellent growth and habit; a most effective garden Rose, yielding large quantities of fine flowers." [P1] "Globular in form, deep crimson; early and free." [W/Hn] "Charmingly scented." [S] Crown Prince at the time of introduction would have been Prince Albert, the King Edward VII to be; lived 1841-1910.

Dames Patronesses d'Orléans (Vigneron, 1877) trans., "Patron-Ladies of Orléans"
"Vigorous, flowers large, full, deep crimson red, very floriferous." [JR1/12/12]

Denis Hélye (Gautreau/Portemer fils, 1864)
"Brilliant rosy-carmine; lovely color; very large and full; very effective; growth vigorous." [FP] "In clusters, purplish violet red, red on the reverse." [S] "Quite floriferous." [l'H67/54] "Intense carmine; flower very large, cupped, fragrant; pretty vigorous." [Cx] "Our much esteemed comrade Denis Hélye was born on the Rue de la Clef in Paris on June 7, 1827. He signed on with the Jardin des Plantes at the age of ten after the death of his father, having thus become the only means of support for his aged and infirm mother, receiving as an apprentice there only sixty centîmes a day, a sum too small to meet his needs. This, however, did not defeat him. After work, he went to his night job as a stevedore. His taste for gardens and horticulture grew as he grew; the layouts he designed showed much intelligence; and his merit was noted by both amateurs and his superiors. At length, he was named Chief Horticulturist at the Natural History Museum at the age of 20. Whenever offered more lucrative positions elsewhere, he would refuse them in order to retain his old post, which indeed he kept until his death last March 29 [1884] at the age of 57." [JR8/67]

Desgaches (Lacharme, 1850)
"Growth vigorous; canes upright, having many irregular thorns; leaves delicate green; the young growth, reddish green; flower medium-sized, full, well formed; color, bright red; exterior petals bordered crimson." [S]

Desirée Fontaine {Fontaine, 1884)
"Vigorous, flower large, full, well formed, well held, cupped, 4-5 blossoms per branch; color, deep rich grenadine, illuminated with bluish violet." [JR8/164]

Deuil de Dunois (Lévêque, 1873) trans., "Mourning for Dunois"
"Blackish-red." [Ÿ]

Deuil de Colonel Denfert (Margottin père, 1878)
"Vigorous, flower large, full. Color, velvety purplish black—one of the darkest." [JR3/10]

Devienne-Lamy (Lévêque, 1868)
"Deep carmine, a large full flower of imbricated form." [JC] "Flower medium-sized, full, very well formed; color, bright carmine; center cupped; globular; of moderate growth, blooms in the Fall." [S] "A good sort." [EL]

Directeur Alphand (Lévêque, 1883) trans., "Director Alphand"
"Growth very vigorous; ample dark green foliage; flower large, full, perfect form; deep blackish purple, highlighted by velvety brown and bright fiery red." [JR7/158] "Tall." [Sn] Sometimes equated with 'Alsace-Lorraine'.

Directeur N. Jensen (E. Verdier, 1883) trans., "Director N. Jensen"
"Vigorous, look of 'Charles Lefebvre', with strong branches; thorns remote, short, hooked; leaves composed of 5 beautiful rounded leaflets with slightly deep and irregular serration; flowers large, full, well formed; color, carmine red strongly nuanced and marbled velvety purplish amaranth red; very beautiful variety dedicated to the director of an impressive establishment in Sweden." [JR7/171]

Dr. Andry (E. Verdier, 1864)

From 'Charles Lefebvre' (HP) × 'Victor Verdier' (HP).

"Flowers dark bright-red; very large, full, and perfectly imbricated." [FP] "Rosy-crimson, large, semi-cupped flowers, double; sometimes full, fades badly; foliage large and glossy; wood moderately smooth; thorns large and red. A better rose in England than in this country [*U.S.A.*]." [EL] "Blooms…apt to be divided…sometimes irregular…fair in size, good in petal and centre, and very bright at first in colour…very free flowering…not good in autumn." [F-M2] "Very vigorous, flowers full, 12 cm across [ca. 4¼ inches], very intense dark carmine red." [l'H64/327] "Vigorous; wood smooth; flower large, full, cupped; color, bright crimson shaded grenadine. In the style of 'Charles Lefebvre'; good autumnal." [S] "Double, crimson flowers flushed deep pink, opening cupped, upright vigorous growth…43 [ft; ca. 1.25×1 m]." [B] "Of perfect form…Very fragrant." [DO] "Fine smooth petals…robust." [JC] "Excellent for pillars; pegs down well." [WD] "Capital growth and foliage, hardy and of strong constitution…early…not much subject to mildew or orange fungus…standing rain…A useful and thoroughly reliable Rose." [F-M2]

Dr. Antonin Joly (Besson, 1886)

Seedling of 'Baronne Adolphe de Rothschild' (HP).

"Vigorous plant of the 'Baronne A. de Rothschild' sort from which it came and of which it retains the characteristics and growth. Blossom about 12-15 cm across [ca. 6 inches], very full, well formed, cupped; color, bright pink on a brighter ground, illumined with salmon." [JR10/149]

Dr. Auguste Krell (E. Verdier, 1877)

"Vigorous with upright canes, slightly reddish green; thorns numerous, unequal, straight, pink; leaves composed of 3-5 leaflets, rounded, dark green, finely dentate; flowers large, full, well-formed, with petals rounded and curled under; color, carmine cerise red shaded purple, whitish on the reverse." [JR2/29]

Dr. Baillon (Margottin père, 1878)
"Vigorous, flower large, full, well-formed. Color, bright crimson red, shaded purple." [JR3/10]

Dr. Brada's Rosa Druschki (Brada, 1934) trans., "Dr. Brada's Pink Druschki"
"Pink, very large, full, tall." [Sn]

Dr. Bretonneau (Trouillard, 1858)
Seedling of 'Géant des Batailles' (HP).
"Large; red passing to pink and to violet." [l'H58/198] "Vigorous bush; flower large, full; color, reddish violet." [S] "Tall." [Sn] "This variety [*Prune 'Dunmore*] was also announced in the catalog of Monsieur André Leroy of Angers; but it is to Dr. Bretonneau, of Tours—a very distinguished amateur—that we owe its introduction into France." [l'H52/195]

Dr. Georges Martin (Widow Vilin & fils, 1907)
From 'Mme. Prosper Laugier' (HP) × 'L'Ami E. Daumont' (HP).
"Red, pink middle, very large, very full, tall." [Sn] "Very vigorous, reblooming until frost; wood smooth, tinted antique bronze; foliage dark green; thorns recurved and fairly numerous; bud well held on strong, upright stem; flower large, very full, opening well; its very fine pink is enclosed by very intense dark madder petals, brightened by pretty Peruvian yellow reflections, which give it a superb appearance; and, oddly enough, the rose keeps its pretty coloration even when fully open." [JR31/137]

Dr. Hogg (Laxton/G. Paul, 1880)
Seedling of either 'Pierre Notting' (HP) or 'Duke of Edinburgh' (HP).
"Deep violet-red, medium size." [EL] "Deep violet, the nearest approach to blue, pretty bell-shaped petals; growth vigorous." [P1] "Not very floriferous." [S] "A splendid variety, a good strong grower and free bloomer; color bright violet red; good size and substance, very sweet." [C&Js99] "Not delicate." [JR4/39] "Of good habit. The flowers are not large but of good shape." [B&V]

Dr. Hurta (Geschwind, 1867)
Sport 'Panachée d'Orléans' (HP).
"Lilac-pink." [Ÿ] "Flower large, full, flat; color, glossy purplish pink." [S]
"Rose passing to rosy-purple, a flower very similar in form and colour to
'Baronne Prévost'...robust." [JC]

Dr. Ingomar H. Blohm (Lambert, 1919)
"Deep red, large, full, very fragrant, tall." [Sn]

Dr. Jamain (Jamain, 1851)
"From a variety derived from 'Gloire des Rosomanes'." [l'H56/248]
"Vigorous shrub, with glaucous canes, glabrous, armed with some thorns
which are much enlarged at the base, very sharp, and slightly hooked.
Leaves fairly ample, brownish red nuanced green when young, aging to
beautiful green, paler beneath, glabrous on both sides; 3-7 smooth, fairly
long, finely dentate, and not very thick leaflets; flower large, well formed,
beautiful bright crimson fading to pink." [S] "Moderately vigorous; flowers medium-sized, full, ruffled, deep intense red, often pink;...it much
resembles ['Gloire des Rosomanes'], but it is not worth as much as 'Comte
de Bobrinsky', 'La Bedoyère', etc., etc. Best own-root." [l'H56/248] "This
variety, which Monsieur Verdier compares to 'Comte de Bobrinsky' and
'Labedoyère', has much in common with 'Comte d'Eu', going by its
growth and inflorescence." [JDR56/47] "The leaves are pretty lush,
brown-red nuanced red when young, then beautiful green in age; paler
beneath; glabrous on both sides; composed of 3-7 leaflets which grade
smaller from summit to base, and are smooth, not stiff, and fairly longly
and finely dentate; the terminal one is larger, and oval-acute; the lateral
ones are lanceolate and nearly sessile; the lower part of the rachis is bristly,
and has long, slightly hooked, very sharp prickles beneath; the upper part
is nearly glabrous, or only slightly glandular; the ciliate stipules are pretty
large in the adherent portion, and subulate in the divergent part...The
peduncle is thick, long, very stiff, and glandular-bristly, as is the calyx-
tube, which gradually enlarges into a funnel which is slightly enlarged at

the mouth. The sepals are long, green, glandular on the back, white-downy within; three are lacily acuminate towards the tip, and two are more or less completely foliaceous. The outer petals are concave, nearly round, obtuse or terminating in a tiny point smaller than is the case with the petals of 'Comte de Bobrinsky'; those of the center are longitudinally folded and slightly ragged as well as intermixed with the long, feeble styles and a few perfect stamens." [l'H51/171] "Branches slender, divergent, reddish; when young, bark light green, with reddish-brown thorns which are nearly straight, elongate, flattened at the base, and very sharp. Beautiful dark green foliage, glossy, divided into three or five oval, much rounded, and regularly dentate leaflets; petiole slender, nodding, with three or four little prickles which are hooked and pointed. Flowers about three inches across [ca. 7.5 cm], full, plump, solitary on the branchlets, in groups of four or five on the most vigorous branches; color, deep red nuanced crimson, sometimes bright pink; outer petals pretty large, muddled and interfolded towards the center. Calyx rounded; sepals leaf-like. Very remontant and vigorous when grown on its own roots; contrariwise, it grows very little when grafted onto the Briar; hardy." [JF]

Dr. Marx (Laffay, 1842)
"Carmine, very large." [HoBoIV] "Red, tinged with violet; a bad shade." [EL] "Rich rosy crimson, glowing, very large and full; form, cupped. Habit, erect; growth, moderate. A superb Rose, and very sweet." [P] "Lacking in form." [VH62/92] "Growth very vigorous; branches very short, with cylindrical thorns; leaves rough, dark green, regularly dentate; flower large, full, cupped; color, very bright crimson shaded satiny white." [S] "*Rivers*—Rosy carmine—perfect—superb—large, *Lane*—Crimson—large and fine, *Wood*—Very deep red, shaded with lilac, *Curtis*—Rich carmine—perfect—superb—and highly fragrant...Of a brilliant shaded carmine and crimson color, and remarkably fragrant perfume, of vigorous growth—though in this respect not quite equal to 'Louis Bonaparte', which fine rose it closely resembles—and of a hardy nature; it makes a fine

tree, either as a standard or dwarf, and is a good autumnal bloomer." [C] "It blooms freely both in summer and autumn, is very fragrant, and opens well." [R9]

Dr. Müllers Rote (Müller, 1920) trans., "Dr. Müller's Red" "Purplish red." [Ÿ]

Dr. William Gordon (W. Paul, 1905) "Brilliant satiny carnation pink." [Ÿ] "Large satiny pink flowers." [JR29/53]

Druschka (Kordes, 1932) From 'Frau Karl Druschki' (HP) × 'Hawlmark Scarlet' (HT). "Pink, large, full, light scent, tall." [Sn]

Druschki Listed as 'Frau Karl Druschki'.

Druschki Rubra (Lambert, 1929) trans., "Red Druschki" From 'Frau Karl Druschki' (HP) × 'Luise Lilia' (HT); but see below. "Crimson red." [Ÿ] "A hybrid of 'Frau Karl Druschki' and 'American Beauty'. The bud and bloom have the same form and size as 'Frau Karl Druschki', and the color is a dull—the furniture man would say 'egg shell finish'—crimson lightening to scarlet around the edges of the petals. 'American Beauty' has also transmitted its delightful perfume. The habit of the plant is very similar to 'Frau Karl Druschki', although perhaps not quite as vigorous, but its foliage is better and less subject to mildew, and it has the same recurrence of bloom." [C-Ps29]

Duc d'Anjou (Boyau/Lévêque, 1862) "Crimson, shaded with dark red, very large, full, and well formed." [FP] "Growth very vigorous; foliage dark green; flower very large, full, crimson red nuanced somber red." [l'H62/278] "Tall." [Sn]

Duc d'Audiffret-Pasquier (E. Verdier, 1887)

"Vigorous, canes upright, delicate green; thorns very numerous, unequal, straight, thin, yellowish; leaves of 3-5 leaflets, oblong, rounded, somber green, with fine, irregular, fairly deep serration; flowers large, full, well formed; color, carmine red with bright purplish hue, center brighter, sometimes bordered white." [JR11/167]

Duc d'Harcourt (Robert & Moreau, 1863)

"Bright reddish-carmine, blooming freely and in clusters, large and full." [FP] "Very vigorous, making a bush with strong, straight thorns; foliage, somber green and very abundant; flower large, full, globular; color, carmine red; outer petals, light carmine." [S]

Duc de Bragance (E. Verdier, 1886)

"Very vigorous bush, having a habit all its own, with out-thrust canes which are strong and very erect and brown; thorns strong, straight, blackish; leaves composed of three to five elliptical leaflets which are reddish green, and irregularly and deeply toothed; flowers in corymbs, large, full, globular and very well formed, of very good hold; coloration new—poppy red strongly illuminated with violet. Very beautiful variety." [JR10/170]

[Duc de Cazes] (Touvais, 1861)

Seedling of 'Général Jacqueminot' (HP).

"Purplish crimson, so deep as almost to appear black." [FP] "A very distinct variety, with purplish crimson flowers, velvety, very effective in the garden; it is a vigorous plant, and only needs moderate pruning." [R-H63] "Petals cupped...habit moderate." [JC] "Growth vigorous; flower large, full, recurved; color, very dark purple mixed with deep violet; reverse of petals brown. Magnificent exhibition flower." [S] "Monsieur le Duc Decazes [*sic*], who died suddenly in Paris October 24th [*1860*]. He was over 80 years old...[*He was*] the founder and keeper of the rich nurseries of the Luxembourg, and was the person who put together the greatest collection of grape-vines in the entire world." [R-H60]

Duc de Chartres (E. Verdier, 1876)
"Growth very vigorous; branches amply covered with recurved thorns; leaves rough and dark green; flower large, full, very well formed, majestically held; found almost inevitably solitary high on the cane; color, violet purple red nuanced crimson and plumed flame and carmine." [S]

Duc de Constantine (Soupert & Notting/Schmitt, 1857)
"Bright lilac-y pink.—Flower very large, full, cupped, fairly vigorous." [Cx] "Very vigorous growth; blossom satiny pink, large, *puriforme*, full." [S] "Large, full, bright pink, center lighter, vigorous." [R&M62] Evidently has some Multiflora or Arvensis heritage.

Duc de Marlborough (Lévêque, 1884)
"Very vigorous, ample dark green foliage, flowers large, full, very well formed, bright crimson red, sparkling, very remontant and very beautiful." [JR8/150]

Duc de Montpensier (Chédane-Guinoisseau/Lévêque, 1875)
"Very vigorous; branches green, somewhat blackish; thorns hooked; very subject to mildew; blossom very large, full, of notable form, taking First in nearly all the votes; color, beautiful red, nuanced with crimson and enhanced with brown." [S] "Medium scent, tall." [Sn] "A good sort." [EL]

Duc de Wellington (Granger/C. Verdier, 1864) syn., 'Duke of Wellington'
Seedling of 'Lord Macaulay' (HP)
"Bright crimson, full, of fine form and free." [DO] "Flower large, 10-12 cm across [ca. 4 inches], intense velvety red shaded blackish and brightened with intense flame towards the center." [l'H64/327] "The pointed form...capital in petals and fullness, grand in dark crimson colour and lasting qualities...of fair average size." [F-M2] "Bright velvety red, shaded with blackish maroon; large and very effective; growth moderate." [P1] "Centre fiery-red; large and full; growth vigorous." [FP] "Good size, cupped and well up in the centre." [JC] "Shapely flowers...Scented...4×3 [ft; ca. 1.25×1 m]." [B] "Fair in vigour and foliage...not very liable to

mildew or much injured by rain, a free bloomer and quite a good autumnal." [F-M2] Arthur Wellesley, 1st Duke of Wellington; lived 1769-1852.

Duchess of Bedford (Postans/W. Paul, 1879)
Seedling of 'Charles Lefebvre' (HP).
"Very vigorous, beautiful foliage, very floriferous; flower large, full, perfectly formed; color, a crimson red surpassing all other similarly colored roses in its sparkling scarlet color...globular." [S] "Belongs to the 'Victor Verdier' type. Cherry red; not very promising." [EL] "Of rather weakly growth and best as a maiden. A lovely and striking flower, beautiful in its semi-imbricated form, and bright with glorious colour, a mixture of scarlet and crimson. Not strong in constitution, free-flowering, or good as an autumnal, and often fails to come good, either in colour or shape. An exhibitor's Rose, and never very large, it seems to like a cool season, and is said to be best in the North and Midlands." [F-M2]

Duchess of Connaught (Standish & Noble, 1882)
"Flower large, full, globular; color, sparkling crimson red shaded velvety purple-black sometimes with metal-blue reflections." [S] "Medium scent, medium to tall." [Sn] Not to be confused with the similarly-named 1879 HT from Bennett, which was pink.

[Duchess of Edinburgh] (Schwartz/Bennett, 1874)
Seedling of 'Jules Margottin' (HP).
"Vigorous growth; of the 'Jules Margottin' sort; flower large, full; color, delicate shaded silvery pink, center brighter." [S] Not to be confused with the red Tea of the same name.

Duchess of Fife (Cocker, 1892)
Sport of 'Countess of Rosebery' (HP).
"Delicate silvery pink, a thoroughly new color; the flower is large and full, and beautifully cupped; beautiful foliage and satisfactory habit; very elegant scent." [JR16/19] "A lighter and beautifully coloured sport from 'Countess of Rosebery', similar in all other respects." [F-M3] "Very fragrant, tall." [Sn]

"Occurred in our Morningfield nursery during Autumn, 1888, and has since maintained its reputation." [JR16/19]

Duchesse d'Aoste (Margottin, 1867)

"Rich vivid rose, flowers large, full, and well up in the centre, beautifully formed, habit free." [JC] "Flowers very large, full, flat, beautiful frosty bright pink." [l'H68/48] "Tall." [Sn] "Vigorous, with canes which are light maroon nuanced olive green, and covered with a fine bloom like that on a plum; the thorns are carmine, laterally flattened, recurved like a corbel, unequal in size, the smaller ones being straight and grading into glandular bristles which cover the upper part of the cane; the leaves, light green above and pale whitish green beneath, are of 3-5 leaflets borne on a petiole which is angled at the point where the upper leaflet is attached, creased into furrows, reddish, clothed with glandular hairs above, and armed with some rudimentary prickles beneath. The stipules are green, ciliate along the edges, enlarged in the attached section, very lacy, linear-lanceolate, and pointed in the free portion, forming a right angle to the petiole. The leaflets are of a consistency between that of the Bourbons and that of the Hybrids: the two lower leaflets, much smaller, are oblong-lanceolate and pointed; the upper two are oval-oblong, growing thinner towards the tip; all are unequally and finely dentate, glabrous above, and having glandular hairs on the mid-vein beneath. The peduncle, which is very large and stiff, is light maroon red, and bristles with numerous short glandular hairs. The blossom, held strongly on its peduncle, is large, very full, a pretty carmine currant pink, nuanced paler, exhaling a fine Centifolia perfume. The outer petals are obovate, first upright, then more or less spreading, forming a collar; [they are] pale pink veined bright pink above, and silvery pink beneath; the center petals, a beautiful bright carmine pink, are smaller or more or less folded, like the center of the rosette of an officer of the Legion of Honor. The calyx-tube or ovary is oblong, slightly contracted at the tip, and olive green nuanced light brown in color; the sepals or calyx-leaflets are very unequal: two are edged to their bases with appendages on both sides, thoroughly foliaceous and more or less deeply toothed to the tip; two others are entire, and terminating in a point or in a small foliate extension; the fifth is intermediate, which is to say that it only has appendages on one side. It is indeed this last sepal which allows us to pose the Latin enigma of the botanical poet:

> *Quinque sumus fratres, duo sunt sine barba*
> *Barbatique duo, sum semi-barbis ego*

which is to say: we are five brothers; two are beardless, two are bearded around the edges, and me—I am bearded on only one side...Margottin...was permitted to dedicate it to Mme. la Princesse Dalpozzo della Cisterna, just married to one of the sons of the king of Italy, his royal highness of Duke of Aoste." [l'H68/205]

Duchesse d'Orléans (Quétier, 1851)

"Fine lavender-blush, large, full, and good." [FP] "Beautiful soft rosy-peach, back of petals glaucous white, a flower of great substance, very full, and of extra large size...vigorous." [JC] "A good exhibition rose, with carmine-lilac, full, large, well-formed blossoms." [R-H63] "Often opens badly, and is subject to mildew." [EL] "[*This rose*] is not the first [*nor the last*] to bear the name of her ladyship the Duchess of Orléans; the rosarium has possessed, in fact, since 1836, another very pretty rose dedicated to that princess who is one of the most generous and devoted protectresses of French Horticulture. The *first* plant so dedicated is a Tea, and *this* one is relegated to that section of Roses called *remontant hybrids*. This new obtention is evidently a seedling of 'La Reine'; it has that variety's deportment, foliage, and floral form. Its very vigorous canes generally lack large thorns in the upper reaches; they are tipped by 3, 4, or indeed 5 buds. The flowers, perfectly formed with large, well imbricated, petals, measure perhaps 9 cm across [ca. 4 inches]; they are a very noticeable hydrangea pink, giving them a certain cachet of sweetness and distinction not to be found in any other of the 'La Reine' sort." [l'H53/29-30]

Duchesse d'Ossuna (Jamain, 1876)
"Fine vermilion rose, large, full, well formed, blooming in clusters; growth vigorous." [JC] "Very vigorous, flower large, full, handsome and very bright vermilion pink." [JR1/6/10] "Very floriferous, and a person may gather blossoms from it up until the latter part of the season; good to force for March." [S]

Duchesse de Bragance (E. Verdier, 1886)
"Vigorous, canes upright, delicate green; thorns unequal, short, straight, brown; leaves of 3-5 oval-elongate leaflets, dark green, irregularly and not very deeply toothed; flowers extra large, full, well formed; color a beautiful and delicate satiny pink nuanced brighter pink." [JR10/170]

Duchesse de Cambacérès (Fontaine, 1854) syn., 'Mme. de Cambacérès'
"Blossom large, globular, pink." [JDR55/19] "Lilac rose, impure color; double." [EL] "Large flowers, full, cupped, carmine pink with distinct purplish tones; also a good autumnal, and to be recommended above all for its very beautiful foliage." [R-H63] "A most vigorous growing rose, blooming in immense clusters, giving flowers with a powerful fragrance." [R8] "This rose, according to Monsieur Fontaine's way of thinking, is the product of a cross involving the Centifolia 'Des Peintres', or the Quatre-Saisons 'De Puteaux'. In any case, it is a vigorous plant, blooming abundantly...has large flowers, full, well formed, globular, and a beautiful bright pink." [JR5/118] "Growth very vigorous; canes pretty big, upright or branching; bark smooth, glaucous green, slightly yellowish; thorns numerous, gray-brown, unequal, slightly hooked, and enlarged at the base. Foliage thick, large, glaucous green, slightly rugose, divided into 5 or 7 oval-rounded, strongly toothed leaflets; leafstalk pretty strong, slightly reddish at the base, armed all along its length with small, sharp, hooked prickles. Flowers about four inches across [ca. 1 dm], well formed, full, globular, solitary on the branchlets, in clusters of 3-5 on the stronger branches; color, beautiful bright pink; petals large and concave, those of the center muddled and folded; flower stalk pretty long, glandular-hirsute.

Ovary very long; sepals very leaf-like. This variety is very vigorous...in form and color it resembles the old Centifolia." [JF]

Duchesse de Caylus (C. Verdier, 1864)
Seedling of 'Alfred Colomb' (HP).
"Brilliant carmine red, beautiful blossom of perfect form...very vigorous and truly remontant." [JR3/11] "Glowing rosy-crimson, flowers large, full, and beautifully cupped, fine outline with high centre...habit free." [JC] "Of moderate growth; beautiful form, though small; of the 'Alfred Colomb' type; flower large, full, globular; color, brilliant carmine pink." [S] "Foliage very rich and fine." [FP] "Vigorous, with light green canes; flower large, full, of the most perfect form, bright light carmine." [l'H64/327] "Only fair in growth with rather weak foliage, the wood and habit being very distinct in appearance. Not liable to mildew or any injury from rain. The blooms come wonderfully well, every one being alike...Sweet-scented, perfect in form, good in centre and bright in colour, but decidedly below par in size. Not free-flowering or a good autumnal." [F-M3]

Duchesse de Dino (Lévêque, 1889)
"Very vigorous bush; beautiful ample dark green foliage; flower very large, full, perfectly imbricated and held; beautifully colored blackish crimson nuanced carmine and velvety purple." [JR13/164] "Tall." [Sn]

Duchesse de Galliera (Portemer, 1847)
"Bright rose, shaded with flesh colour, large and full; form, cupped. Habit, erect; growth, moderate." [P] "Flower...delicate pink shaded lilac." [S] "Freely remontant Hybrid Perpetual. Canes strong and upright; thorns strong and numerous, nearly straight, very sharp, brownish-red. Leaves of three to five oval-obtuse leaflets, mostly serrated, a pretty fresh green. Peduncle and ovary like the preceding, the ovary not so big; calyx with foliaceous sepals. Flower 7-8 cm [ca. 3 inches], pretty full, center petals forming several bundles, beautiful bright pink nuanced flesh; outer petals

large, well imbricated, reticulated. Scent very strong and quite pleasant. The blossoms are sometimes solitary, but more often in threes or fours. The buds are round and take on, when opening, a fresh bright purple color. Bearing and hold perfect." [An47/204-205]

Duchesse de Morny
Listed as 'La Duchesse de Morny'.

Duchesse de Sutherland (Laffay, 1839) syn., 'Duchess of Sutherland'
"Bright glossy pink, changing to pale rose; an old and very beautiful rose." [JC] "Medium-sized, full enough, expanded, flesh pink of an incomparable shade." [JR3/26] "Double, bright crimson-pink blooms...4 [ft; ca. 1.25 m]." [HRG] "Large, full, cupped, fragrant." [S] "'*Lane*—Glossy blush—very beautiful.' '*Wood*—bright rose—mottled—very splendid.'...'*Curtis*—Deep pink—most beautiful form and very sweet.'...In some situations and in particular seasons it may not be so constant an autumnal bloomer as some of its family, but this defect has rarely come under our notice. To cause it to bloom freely in the autumn recourse must be had to summer pruning, shortening some of the shoots to half their length; but by making it a general rule to cut long stems to all blooms, a similar result will be produced...vigorous habit...It appears from [*one*] of the above descriptions that its petals are sometimes 'mottled,' but this we have never yet observed." [C] "Fresh rosy pink, very large and very double; form, cupped. Habit, erect; growth, vigorous...One of the finest of autumnal Roses, although not the freest bloomer. A good seed-bearer." [P] "Luxuriant habits and fine foliage, with flowers of the most perfect shape, and of a delicate roseate hue...it will not give autumnal flowers constantly in a moist climate, or during a wet period." [WRP] "Pale green leaves." [Hd] "This rose, known for about three years, is very interesting; its foliage is a beautiful fresh green, composed of leaves with 5 or 7 leaflets which are finely dentate and bordered purple when young; canes big, thorny, topped by 2 or 3 flowers, which are large, quite double, and with large, notched petals of a very fresh flesh pink, paler at the nub, stamens

showing at the center. It is the clearest [*or possibly "lightest"*] color in this class; very fragrant." [An42/332-333] "One defect this rose has which ought not to be concealed—it will not give autumnal flowers constantly, but often makes shoots without a termnal flower-bud." [R9] "Branches vigorous, stocky, green, bristling with numerous prickles of varying size, not compressed, enlarged at the base, slender...Foliage fairly ample, more or less reddish in youth, pale green beneath, dark green above, composed of three to five unequal leaflets, ciliate, finely dentate, glandular along the edges...Leafstalks flexuose, of a light green, caniculate above...Stipules long, often very large where adjoining the leafstalk...[F]lowers flesh pink, lightly shaded pale violet, very full, large to 3 or 3½ inches [ca. 7.5-8.75 cm], ordinarily in threes at the summit of the cane. Flower stem very short, fat, upright, very glandular-pilose...Calyx an oblong tube, contracted at the mouth, very glandular in the lower part...Sepals longly narrowed, then enlarged at the tip, light green and glandular without, white-lanate within...Buds rounded. Petals of the circumference large, slightly concave, upright, regularly imbricated, those of the center narrow, more or less ruffled, mixed with the stamens...Hips oblong, red...[A] worthy counterpart to 'La Reine'...its canes, short but vigorous, upright, and pretty nearly all of the same size, form a large rounded head, entirely covered during the first bloom with large and plenteous open blossoms, perfectly full, of a very fresh color, and opening regularly. Aside from these wonderful qualities, however, it does have a little peccadillo which cannot be hidden. Around the end of each season, the flowers are no longer very full—indeed, they don't have more than two or three rows of petals...The rose 'Duchesse de Sutherland' has many similarities to 'Baronne Prévost': the same deportment, the same growth. But in this latter, the foliage is larger and less shiny...It is the product of an unknown cross between a Hybrid China and a Portland." [PlB]

Duchesse de Vallombrosa (Dunand/Schwartz, 1875)
Seedling of 'Jules Margottin' (HP).
"Blush, centre delicate flesh, flowers large, full, and cupped; an exquisitely formed and beautiful rose." [JC] "Flesh, changing to white. Good and free-flowering; impatient of wet." [H] "Pink, generally opens badly; not valuable." [EL] "Very vigorous, with upright dark green canes; the foliage is perfect and ample by all reports. As for the blooms, they are large, full, and well formed, the deep pink of the central petals grading nicely through delicate pink to the blush of the outer petals. This rose reblooms freely." [JR1/8/9] "Requires good soil and generous treatment; with these it will grow strongly with distinct habit and foliage, but it will not thrive everywhere. It is not very liable to mildew, but the blooms cannot stand rain at all, and being of a light colour are subject to injury from thrips in a dry season. They have a decided tendency to come badly shaped, often with me having a gap or chasm in the outline, as though a piece had been cut out. The shape is rather too open and flat at the best, but it is of large size, free-flowering, fair in lasting qualities, and pretty good in a dry autumn." [F-M2]

Duhamel-Dumonceau (H. Vilin/C. Verdier, 1872)
"Fiery-red, splendid colour, like the old 'Tuscany'; tolerably well shaped and full." [JC] "Large, full, bright red, very brilliant at the center, shaded and nuanced violet around the edges." [JR3/27] "Growth vigorous." [S] Often classified as a Bourbon.

Duke of Edinburgh (W. Paul, 1868)
Seedling of 'Général Jacqueminot' (HP).
"Rich velvety fiery crimson-shaded; flowers large and very attractive; the best of its line, and perhaps the finest colour." [WD] "Large, full, bright shining orange-scarlet, shaded with carmine, often shaded with maroon, large, full, and very effective...one of the best of my seedlings." [P1] "Vermilion crimson...not lasting in colour or shape." [F-M2] "Not constant in autumn...few [*HPs*] will do well under our hot [*American*] sun."

[ElC] "Of perfect form. A few blooms may be expected in autumn. Easy to grow." [OM] "Little fragrance; foliage large and attractive. Occasionally this is very fine early in the season, but the flowers lack substance and durability of color. It is more shy in the autumn than [*'Général Jacqueminot'*]; not to be commended for general culture." [EL] "Most beautiful and useful Rose, always to be found in exhibition stands, and one of those that flower freely in autumn; should be lightly pruned." [DO] "Fair growth; very few blooms; poor foliage." [ARA18/115] "Strong good growth and foliage...rather apt to run to wood...should therefore be lightly pruned...seems to stand the extreme...temperatures well." [F-M2] "An erect, robust plant...4×3 [ft; ca. 1.25×1 m]." [B] "A very bright red rose, certainly first-rate and grows well." [HmC] Prince Alfred, Duke of Edinburgh and Saxe-Coburg-Gotha; lived 1844-1900.

Duke of Fife (Cocker, 1892)
Sport of 'Étienne Levet' (HP).
"A deep crimson sport from [*'Étienne Levet'*], and a much worse grower. Noteworthy, as a sport generally comes of a lighter colour than the type." [F-M2] "The richest crimson-scarlet, with perfectly folded petals, large, full, and well formed." [JR16/19] "Very good in dull weather." [H]

Duke of Teck (G. Paul, 1880)
Seedling of 'Duke of Edinburgh' (HP).
"Brilliant crimson-scarlet, a color both clear and distinct, truly an advance towards a true scarlet rose. Flowers large, very double, quite globular; plant floriferous, upright, with handsome foliage." [JR4/39] "Clear and distinct in colour, but not large." [P1] "Globular form and rather pointed centre, comes true to shape. Good growth and foliage with characteristic wood without thorns; not very liable to mildew." [B&V] "Not well tested in the country [*U.S.A.*]; we were much pleased with it as seen at Cheshunt." [EL] "Strong and hardy...not so dark in crimson and not so brilliant in vermilion as [*'Duke of Edinburgh'*], but, like it, should be left long in pruning, and is of good repute in America. Best on old plants, and good under glass." [F-M2]

Duke of Wellington
Listed as 'Duc de Wellington'.

Dupuy-Jamain (Dupuy-Jamain, 1868)
"Cherry-red, with a shade of crimson; large, double, well-formed, fragrant; a good seed-bearer. Were this more full, it would be a rose of the first rank." [EL] "Brilliant carmine-crimson, colour very fine, petals large, broad, and smooth, flowers well formed, luxuriant foliage...vigorous." [JC] "Brilliant cerise, of fine form and substance." [P1] "Round fat smooth blooms...centre is weak in hot weather...large size but a bad one to last; very free in bloom." [F-M2] "Free-flowering and hardy; good in autumn, especially in cool seasons." [W/Hn] "Of nice fragrance...should be lightly pruned." [DO] "Very strong, stiff, stout growth and foliage." [F-M2] "Tidy, well foliage and healthy plant...4×3 [ft; ca. 1.25×1 m]." [B] "A good Rose." [WD] "French horticulture has lost one of its most trusty servants in the death of Monsieur Dupuy[-] Jamain, who died May 9 [1888] at the age of 72. He was the founder of one of the oldest horticultural establishments in Paris, and was above all distinguished in arboriculture, in which he stood in the first rank." [JR12/98]

E.Y. Teas
Listed as 'Monsieur E.Y. Teas'.

Earl of Dufferin (A. Dickson, 1887)
"Velvety-crimson, shaded with maroon, large, full, and finely formed; a continuous bloomer; of vigorous growth, and bushy habit." [P1] "Very large, erect, fine form, bright velvety carmine-red, shaded with deep chestnut-brown. Flowers a long time." [Hn] "Highly-coloured blooms of semi-globular shape, sweet-scented, lasting, sometimes very fine...not very free-flowering...I have never had a decent bloom." [F-M2] "Delicious perfume." [JR14/41] "Blossoms need to be tied; late flowering." [DO] "Long but pliable growth...must be staked...[F]or exhibitors, but not for garden culture." [F-M2]

Earl of Pembroke (Bennett, 1882)
From 'Marquise de Castellane' (HP) × 'Maurice Bernardin' (HP).
"Vigorous, good form, few thorns; color, velvety crimson with the petal edges bright red; very distinct, good for any sort of rose." [S] "Of fair thorny growth, late, and a distinct shade of colour; a free bloomer, rather thin in petal, and only worth classing for its value in autumn, when it is often at its best." [F-M3]

Éclair (Lacharme, 1883) trans., "Lightning"
Seedling of 'Général Jacqueminot' (HP).
"Handsome vermilion red; flower very large, cupped, fragrant." [Cx] "Of the 'Charles Lefebvre' sort; flower large, well formed, full, bright fiery red; of the greatest merit." [S] "Very dark…almost black. Fairly vigorous, free flowering and scented…4×2 [ft; ca. 1.25 m × 6 dm]." [B] "Vigorous, nice dark green foliage, and quite floriferous. The blossoms are medium-sized to large…their fragrance is delicious." [JR13/56] "Fine habit…Stems slender with many prickles." [Hn] "At its best one of the very brightest of the crimsons. The growth is good, the form the Cabbage type…very good autumnal…difficult to get form and colour really good…the beginner would do well to avoid it." [F-M2]

Éclaireur (Vigneron, 1895) trans., "Scout"
Seedling of 'Duhamel-Dumonceau' (HP).
"Very vigorous, beautiful very dark green foliage, flower large, well-formed, cupped, handsome dark bright red, exterior petals velvety, stem very strong, perfectly poised, flower usually solitary, very remontant, fragrant." [JR19/147]

Edelweiss (Dienemann, 1925)
Seedling of 'Frau Karl Druschki' (HP).
"White, medium size, full, medium height." Edelweiss, the far-famed but rather modest Alpine flower.

Édouard André le Botaniste (E. Verdier, 1879) trans., "The Botanist Édouard André"

"Red, tinged with purple." [EL] "Very vigorous, having the appearance of 'Mme. Victor Verdier', with delicate green, upright, firm canes; thorns somewhat numerous, irregular, pointed, pink; leaves composed of 5 light green, oblong, finely dentate leaflets; flowers large, full, well-formed, an even currant red, bright and very attractive." [JR3/181] "E. André, editor-in-chief of *Revue-Horticole*." [JR17/80]

Édouard Fontaine (Fontaine, 1878)

"Vigorous, flower large, very well formed, full. Color, frosty pink." [JR3/10] "In color, it resembles 'Baron [G.-B.] Gonella'." [S]

Édouard Hervé (E. Verdier, 1884)

"Vigorous, canes reflexing, pinkish green; thorns long, unequal, very sharp; leaves composed of 3-5 leaflets, oblong, dark green, deeply toothed; flowers large, full, very well formed, dark intense currant red, very fragrant." [JR8/165]

Egeria

Listed as 'Peach Blossom'. Not to be confused with Bennett's 1878 HT 'Ægeria', which was bright crimson.

Élisa Boëlle (Guillot père, 1869)

Seedling of 'Mme. Récamier' (HP).

"White, delicately tinged with pink, medium size, full, beautiful circular form...a lovely rose." [EL] "Light rose-red, becoming pure white; free." [Hn] "A vigorous rose with shapely, cupped flowers having incurved petals. Whitish-pink. Highly scented...3×3 [ft; ca. 9×9 dm]." [B] "Small." [TW] "Moderate vigor." [Cx] "Vigorous and branching, strong enough, smooth stems of a light green, bearing enormous straight reddish-brown prickles of varying small sizes, which are in rows. The flowers are numerous, large, full, well formed, usually solitary at the ends of the branchlets, sometimes in a cluster of two or three at the end of a particularly strong shoot. White, lightly tinted flesh-pink, passing quickly to pure white. The petals are concave, imbricated." [JR3/8] "Petals in a cup; those in the center, smaller, are crumpled and very numerous, and fill the center of the flower; flower stem fairly long, slender, and nodding. Calyx rounded. This rose, in which the wood is tender and pith-filled, doesn't live long grafted; it is necessary to renew it every two or three years." [JF] "Leaves of 5-7 leaflets, which are oval and finely toothed." [S] "Very pretty." [P1]

[Elisabeth Vigneron] (Vigneron/W. Paul, 1865)
From 'La Reine' (HP) × 'Duchesse de Sutherland' (HP).
"Growth very vigorous; very floriferous; branches upright, light green; thorns pretty numerous, chestnut; leaves light green, 5-6 leaflets; flower very large, very full; petals large; beautifully colored light pink, darker within; resembling in size, color, and scent, the Centifolia; buds very large, opening well; as beautiful in Fall as in Spring." [S] "Bright carmine, flowers very large and double; habit vigorous." [JC]

Elise Lemaire (Breeder unknown, 1885)
"Vigorous bush; canes glossy dark green, nearly thornless; leaves yellowish dark green; blossom medium sized, Centifolia form; color, delicate pink. Much to be recommended. It blooms up to Winter, and forces well in January." [S]

Eliska Krásnohorská (Böhm, 1932)
From 'Captain Hayward' (HP) × 'Una Wallace' (HT).
"Rose-red, large, full, very fragrant, tall." [Sn]

Emden (Schmidt, 1915)
From 'Frau Karl Druschki' (HP) × 'Veluwezoom' (Pern).
"Deep pink, large, full, medium height." [Sn]

Émile Bardiaux (Lévêque, 1889)
Seedling of 'Mme. Isaac Pereire' (B).
"Very vigorous, leaves dark green, very large; flower very large, full, well formed; bright carmine red nuanced poppy and deep violet. From 'Mme. Isaac Pereire', from which it takes its growth and flower size." [JR13/164]

Emily Laxton (Laxton/G. Paul, 1876)
Seedling of 'Jules Margottin' (HP).
"A large full flower with globular, pointed bud, opening into a large globular flower…rich cherry-rose…strong vigorous habit." [JC] "Light pink." [Ÿ] "Of the 'Jules Margottin' tribe; much like 'Monsieur Normand' [*sic*; *'Monsieur Nomann', HP, Laffay, 1866*], but the color is darker and the form prettier." [S]

Empereur du Maroc (Guinoisseau-Flon, 1858) trans., "Emperor of Morocco"
Seedling of 'Géant des Batailles' (HP).
"Intensely deep crimson and purple, changing to bluish-purple; petals thick, and the flowers of good form, but not large…free habit." [JC] "Flowers large, in a cluster of five to ten, bright red, velvety purple passing to blackish red." [JDR58/36] "Large, very full, intense red tinged dark purple." [JR1/2/8] "At a distance, the blossoms appear to be totally black globes." [VH62/98] "Not large, nor perfectly cupped…yet they are most beautiful, their colour is so remarkably rich." [R8] "The summits of the petals folding back with so much regularity and grace, are unique and lovely." [P2] "Flattish…Rather subject to mildew, and a poor autumnal." [Hn] "Fragrant; moderate vigor." [Cx] "Vigorous, flower large, full, imbricated, in clusters, very full [*again*], opening well, bright velvety red passing to blackish." [l'H58/128] "The most known of roses…To my way of thinking, it burns too much in the sun in our climate [*that of Tunisia*], capricious growth." [JR34/171] "43 [ft; ca. 1.25×1 m]." [B] "To 5 [ft; ca. 1.5 m]." [HRG] "Very distinct." [P1]

Emperor (W. Paul, 1883)
"Flower small, full, beautiful form; color, very dark, nearly blackish; good growth, beautiful foliage, and abundant bloom." [S] "Hardy." [JR7/173] "Tall." [Sn]

Empress of India (Laxton/G. Paul, 1876)
Seedling of 'Triomphe des Beaux-Arts' (HP).
"Brownish-crimson, medium size, globular, fragrant; dark green foliage, spines light colored. Many of the buds do not open well, and it is shy in the autumn; a splendid sort when perfect." [EL] "Rich velvety crimson and purple, somewhat in form and colour like 'Louis Van Houtte'." [JC] "Very well formed...very easily damaged by the sun." [S] "Vigorous, flower large, full, blackish-red, of the 'Louis XIV' sort." [JR1/6/10] "A strong grower and a very free autumnal." [Cr76]

Enfant de France (Lartay, 1860) trans., "Child of France"
"Flower large, full; color, violet red." [S] "Pink, edged white, big and full, well foliated, growth strong." [N] "Huge rose of silvery pink with a satin-like texture. Very full and scented. A beautiful rarity...4×3 [ft; ca. 1.25×1 m]." [B] Not to be confused with various Gallicas or an Alba, all of the same name. We look forward to finding something more nearly contemporary with the release of the variety to clarify its description.

Erinnerung an Brod (Geschwind, 1886) trans., "In Remembrance of Brod"
From *R. setigera* × 'Génie de Châteaubriand' (HP).
"Flower nearly purplish-or violet-blue, most often with a dark red center, large, very full, flat; it is the only rose that approaches true blue, and surpasses 'Reine des Violettes'...Very vigorous, with pendant branches." [JR10/26] "One of the prettiest 'Hungarian Climbers'...Though the canes don't grow as long as those of the Ayrshires, Multifloras, or Sempervirenses, it is nevertheless true that pillars of perhaps 8 feet in height [ca. 2.25 m] produce a superb effect during the flowering season when planted with this variety...It is a very vigorous bush covered with

handsome dark green foliage, giving many fragrant blossoms in clusters, the flowers being mid-sized or large, flat, blue-maroon or violet, especially in somewhat moist soil; center, darker…The name recalls a town which is in the Austrian province of Carniole." [JR31/156] Can be found classified as both a Hybrid Perpetual and as a Setigera hybrid.

Ernest Morel (P. Cochet, 1898)
Seedling of 'Général Jacqueminot' (HP).
"Flower large, full, well formed, light grenadine red, illumined with flame-color, reverse of petals somewhat velvety, with a bloom. Bush very vigorous and extremely floriferous." [JR22/166] "Very fragrant, tall." [Sn] "Entirely hardy and excellent for garden planting." [C&Js02]

Ernest Prince (Ducher Children & Successors, 1881)
Seedling of 'Antoine Ducher' (HP).
"Very vigorous, with strong and upright canes, rather numerous thorns, beautiful dark green foliage, flower very large, very well formed, globular, light red, darker at the center, reverse of petals silvery, abundant bloom." [JR5/185] "Without particular merit." [JR7/157]

Étienne Dubois (Damaizin, 1873)
"Vigorous bush; flower large, full; color, deep velvety crimson." [S] "Tall." [Sn]

Étienne Levet (Levet, 1871)
Seedling of 'Victor Verdier' (HP).
"Pinkish carmine." [Ÿ] "Carmine, large, full, and of fine form." [P1] "Carmine-red, one of the finest in the type." [EL] "Growth robust and upright, of the 'Victor Verdier' sort. Resembles 'Hippolyte Jamain' and 'Président Thiers'; flower very large, full, globular at first, then flat." [S] "Of robust and smooth but very uncertain growth; long, strong, and stout in rich soil where it has a good hold, but otherwise quite short and stumpy. The foliage is very fine, and the blooms come early and well, with large very smooth shell-like petals; there is, or should be, a good point, but

the general shape is open, the centre weak, and the form not lasting…of no use in hot weather. Not much injured by mildew or rain, but not good as a free bloomer or autumnal, and of no use in hot climates. It is of large size, and its grand petals and smooth even outline make it an effective show Rose in a cool season…For general cultivation or on weak soils it is not one of the best." [F-M2]

Eugène Appert (Trouillard/Standish & Noble, 1859)
Seedling of 'Géant des Batailles' (HP).
"Blossom medium-sized, full; color, velvety crimson scarlet. One of the best of the purple and crimson roses." [S] "Belongs to Giant of Battles type. Velvety maroon, shaded with deep crimson. A rose of superb color, but with all the family failings." [EL] "Brilliant scarlet-crimson, colour superb and lasting, petals of unusual substance though rather pointed, flowers tolerably well formed, robust habit and fine foliage; a most striking and beautiful rose." [JC] "Free bloomer." [FP] "Better than its elders through the vigor of its growth, the size of its foliage, the graceful disposition and amplitude of its petals, its most brilliant tintings, etc., etc. [*sic*]." [VH61/129]

Eugène de Luxembourg
Listed as 'Prince Eugène de Luxembourg'.

[Eugène Verdier] (Guillot fils, 1863)
Seedling of 'Victor Verdier' (HP).
"Rich dark violet, large, full, and of perfect form; one of the best." [FP] "Of moderate growth." [S] "Very vigorous; flowers very large, full, well formed, superb deep violet." [l'H64/62] Not to be confused with the 1872 Moss of the same name.

Eugène Fürst (Soupert & Notting, 1875)
Sport or seedling of 'Baron de Bonstetten' (HP).
"Crimson-purple…considerable size…upright plant…4×3 [ft; ca. 1.25×1 m]." [B] "Very vigorous, with handsome foliage; its large-petaled flowers

are large, full, and splendidly colored velvety crimson, shaded glowing purple, the reverse of the petals being dark violet mingled with silvery pink. The very fragrant blossoms are cupped." [JR7/57] "Of good shape." [P1] "A very strong grower with good foliage, liable to orange fungus, and to mildew which appears even on the petals, but not much injured by rain. This is a Rose whose manner it is to waste all its strength upon the wood, and have none to spare to swell the bud…This rose has small blooms on very long shoots…comes generally well, of a good dark velvety colour, and nice shape, lasting fairly." [F-M3]

Everest (Easlea, 1927)
From 'Candeur Lyonnaise' (HP) × 'Mme. Caristie Martel' (Pernetiana)
"Immense blooms of creamy white, sometimes with a decided lemon cast, and they remind me more of a peony than any rose I know…little bloom after June." [ARA34/76] "Only a once-bloomer, but…well worth growing…plants vary from climbinglike growth to dwarfs, producing an abundance of enormous blooms which last for many days…likely to ball in wet weather…*Middleton* divides the name in the middle and suggests that we let it Ever Rest." [ARA32/183] "Coarser than 'Frau Karl Druschki' and lacks remontant qualities…a little tender in winter…a bloom of very fine quality, especially in shape and substance." [ARA31/195]

Exposition de Brie-Comte-Robert
Listed as 'Maurice Bernardin'.

Felbergs Rosa Druschki (Felberg-Leclerc, 1925) trans., "Felberg's Pink Druschki"
From 'Frau Karl Druschki' (HP) × 'Farbenkönigen' (HT).
"Rich pink…The plants and flowers resemble 'Frau Karl Druschki' in everything but color, which is a rich shade of pink." [C-Pf33] "Flower large, clear bright rose-pink, borne on long, strong stem." [ARA29/225] "Full, light scent, tall." [Sn]

Félicien David (E. Verdier, 1872)

"Deep rose, tinged with purple." [EL] "Brilliant rose, purple shaded, flowers large and very full, partakes of the Bourbon habit; a well formed and good flower." [JC] "Moderate growth; flower very large, full, plump; color, dark red nuanced carmine, magenta pink, and light violet." [S]

Félix Mousset (E. Verdier, 1884)

"Vigorous with upright canes, delicate green; thorns unequal, short, straight, pink; leaves composed of 3-5 leaflets, rounded, dark green, regularly and somewhat deeply toothed; flowers large, full, very well formed, petals curling beneath, deep intense purplish pink, very fragrant." [JR8/165]

Ferdinand Chaffolte (Pernet fils, 1879)

"Reddish-crimson, not well formed, without fragrance; does not seem an addition of merit." [EL] "Very vigorous rose; big-wooded with upright canes, and beautiful close-set somber green leaves; flower very large, nearly full, cupped, very well formed, beautiful brilliant red, first two rows of petals nuanced superb violet; flower nearly always solitary. Good growth, top-of-the-line." [S] "Same hold as 'Baronne Adolphe de Rothschild', this magnificent variety leaves nothing to be desired; good growth, very well branched, reblooms with the greatest freedom...dedicated to a great fancier of roses." [JR3/165]

Ferdinand de Lesseps

Listed as 'Maurice Bernardin'.

Ferdinand Jamin (Levêque, 1888)

"Very vigorous, foliage ample, dark glaucous green. Flower large, full, extremely well formed, rich bright vermilion red; floriferous." [JR12/181] Not to be confused with the HP 'Mme. Ferdinand Jamin'.

Ferdinand Pichard (Tanne, 1921)
"Striped red and pale pink and white…fragrant…to 2 metres [ca. 6 ft]…recurrent." [G] "Double…crimson striped on pink background, free-flowering, 5 [ft; ca. 1.5 m]." [HRG] "Luscious foliage…5×4 [ft; ca. 1.5×1.25 m]." [B]

[**Firebrand**] (Labruyère/W. Paul, 1874)
"Flower very large, full; color, bright crimson, sometimes shaded maroon brown; robust; it is 'Baronne [Adolphe] de Rothschild' in crimson." [S] Not to be confused with A. Clark's HT of 1924 of the same name.

Fisher Holmes (E. Verdier, 1865)
Possibly a seedling of 'Maurice Bernardin' (HP).
"Rich purplish-crimson, flowers large, cupped, double, and of fine imbricated form." [JC] "Reddish scarlet shaded with deep velvety-crimson, very brilliant, medium size, full, and of good form; growth vigorous." [P1] "Large, full, camellia-like form, brilliant scarlet with deeper shades. A good autumnal. A splendid rose." [Hn] "The blooms come well, of…good pointed shape…and the shape is lasting, though the brightness soon fades." [F-M2] "High-centred." [S] "Perhaps the prettiest rose in the reds, a color so common in the HPs; the blossom is large, globular, full, and imbricated, with slender petals which are a very brilliant scarlet red. The bush is vigorous and abundantly floriferous." [JR17/102] "Requires careful disbudding." [DO] "Sheer beauty. Smaller than most of the Hybrid Perpetuals, it is the brightest." [ARA29/49] "An improved 'Général Jacqueminot'; the flowers are fuller and more freely produced…very valuable." [EL] "Quite one of the best of the Hybrid Perpetuals…This variety flowers again in autumn. Seems to thrive best as a standard. In bush form growth is often poor." [OM] "Good growth and foliage. Particularly liable to mildew." [F-M2] "Shapely bud…Healthy…4×3 [ft; ca. 1.25×1 m]." [B] "Excellent for pegging down." [WD] "Its beautifully shaped and exquisitely fragrant blooms of dark velvety reddish crimson are regally magnificent." [ARA34/78]

Florence Paul (W. Paul, 1886)
"Scarlet red." [JR25/13] "Scarlet-crimson, shaded with rose, large and full; form compact, petals recurved; habit good." [P1] "Very floriferous...good garden rose." [JR10/19]

Fontenelle (Moreau-Robert, 1877)
"Red, spotted." [Ÿ] "Vigorous, flowers large, full, carmine red." [JR1/12/12] "In clusters." [S]

Fortuné Besson
Listed as 'Georg Arends'.

François I (Trouillard, 1858)
Seedling of 'Géant des Batailles' (HP).
"Red, shaded with crimson." [EL] "Clusters, cerise-red; well-formed." [l'H58/198] "Flower large, full, well formed; color, cherry red nuanced deep red." [S]

François Arago (Trouillard, 1858)
Seedling of 'Géant des Batailles' (HP).
"Belongs to Giant of Battles type. Velvety-maroon, illumined with fiery red. Resembles 'Lord Raglan'." [EL] "Moderate growth; flower medium-sized, full; color, velvety amaranth, nuanced." [S] "Extremely abundant with very beautiful amaranth blossoms clouded with black." [VH62/100]

François Coppée (Widow Lédéchaux, 1895)
Seedling of 'Victor Verdier' (HP).
"Vigorous, with very erect dark green canes, numerous thorns which are short, straight, and brown; leaves of 3-5 medium, oblong, dark green leaflets, with fine, irregular dentations; flowers medium sized, full, good form, opening very well, crimson, brilliant, illuminated with velvety grenadine red, darker reverse; the bud is long and well formed...quite remontant." [JR19/130] "Very fragrant." [JR21/9] "One of the most beautiful roses, with a velvety crimson red hue; good vigorous plant with blossoms

burning little in the sun of our clime [*that of Tunisia*], a merit not shared by many of the red roses which find themselves cooking under the African sun. Beautiful long buds on long and rigid stems...dedicated to the great poet François Coppée, who died recently in Paris." [JR34/169]

François Gaulain (Schwartz, 1878)
"Violet." [Ÿ] "Deep purplish crimson." [EL] "Very vigorous with upright branches, dark green foliage, wood smooth, nearly thornless, flower large, full, well formed, intense wine-dregs red, one of the darkest known." [JR2/166]

François Levet (Levet, 1880)
Seedling of 'Anna de Diesbach' (HP).
"Cherry-rose, medium size; style of 'Paul Verdier'." [EL] "Vigorous and very remontant, branches firm, foliage light green, thorns short and straight, flower of medium size, beautiful China pink." [JR4/167]

François Michelon (Levet, 1871)
Seedling of 'La Reine' (HP).
"Fine deep rose, reverse of petals silvery-white, flowers large and full; habit vigorous." [JC] "Well-formed; color, very lively cerise-red with ashy shadings." [S] "Deep rose, tinged with lilac, very large, full, of fine, globular form; fragrant, free-blooming. The wood and foliage are light-green, erect habit, thorns not numerous, wood long-jointed, the foliage somewhat crimpled. A very distinct choice sort; excelling in June and July, when other kinds are past their prime, and also in the autumn." [EL] "Blooms come fairly well, but the centre though almost always well covered has seldom a defined point and is sometimes irregular. The outline is often rough and the colour is not lasting. It cannot be called a free bloomer." [F-M2] "One of the finest Roses for exhibition." [WD] "Green slender yet fairly stiff stems, and thin poor foliage...requires...a cool season, and generous treatment." [F-M2] "Little affected by mildew. Do not prune as much as the average." [Th2] "Exceedingly fine." [DO]

François Olin (Ducher Children & Successors, 1881)
"Vigorous bush with strong, upright canes; numerous thorns; beautiful dark green foliage; flower large, full, and very well formed; form of a camellia; blooms in clusters; large long buds; color, cerise red marbled with pure white, very floriferous; novel coloration." [JR5/186]

Frau Karl Druschki (Lambert, 1901) syn., 'Druschki', 'Mme. Charles Druschki', 'Reine des Neiges', 'Schneekönigen'; trans., "Mrs. Charles Druschki"
From 'Merveille de Lyon' (HP) × 'Mme. Caroline Testout' (HT).
A wish expressed in 1879: "A white HP with the form and size of 'Charles Lefebvre' or 'Marie Baumann' would be a true Koh-i-noor among Roses." [JR3/170]
The wish granted: "For a long time, rose growers have sought to develop a rose which was both remontant and completely white. Such a desirable variety has at last made its appearance…It is a vigorous variety, robust and very hardy, and covered with handsome foliage; the blossoms are solitary but numerous, and what is more they are borne on long, strong stems. They are snow white, and of a firm consistency which allows them to stay fresh for a long time, thus resisting bad weather better than any other white variety. This rose is very remontant; but the main bloom is in June-July." [JR25/20] "Snowy white, of large size, and beautiful form. Extra fine in bud; growth vigorous; thoroughly perpetual. An excellent addition to this group." [P1] "Pure white; flower large, full, cupped; very floriferous." [Cx] "Shell-shaped petals; flowers with a high pointed centre; large, free, and a good grower." [DO] "Now and then there is a flower with a faint violet perfume." [NRS12/93] "An abundant bloomer, and a good autumnal…will not hold their shape very long in hot weather." [F-M] "Most admired white in bloom [*of all whites in Houston, Texas*]." [ET] "Does well here [*in Mexico*] too!" [VD] "Gives freely of its symmetrical blooms." [E] "50 to 129 blooms per season." [ARA21/90] "Indispensable…a splendid June bloom…also a fine fall display."

[ARA34/76] "I do not like Frau Karl; she has very little scent or none; mere giganticness as such, makes no appeal to me; and her flowers are the colour of inferior type-writing paper, and make me feel chilly with the thin deadness of their white." [Fa] "Very vigorous growth, shoots running up to 5-ft. [ca. 1.5 m] and from maidens at times to 10-ft. [ca. 3.3 m]. Foliage dark green, but unfortunately liable to mildew…it is one of the most continuous bloomers among the HP's…this beautiful Rose is Queen of the white Roses." [NRS/10] "Foliage is large and dark…to 7 feet [ca. 2 m]." [W] "Beautiful light green foliage." [Th] "Upright bush…6×4 [ft; ca. 1.75×1.25 m]." [B] "Finest, least troublesome, and most vigorous." [PS] "Dedicated to the wife of the general superintendent of the great Spaeth nurseries in Berlin, herself a noted horticulturalist." [K] "Karl Druschki, businessman [*in*] Gorlitz." [JR12/109] "Still the best white rose." [OM] This rose appears to have been first released as a Hybrid Tea; but very quickly found itself placed pretty firmly into the Hybrid Perpetual class, of which it has a typical habit.

Frau Karl Druschki × Cristata (Jacobs, ca. 1938)
From 'Frau Karl Druschki' (HP) × 'Cristata' (Moss).
"White, large, full, medium to tall." [Sn]

Frederic Schneider II (Ludovic, 1885)
"Pink and red." [Ÿ] "Deep pink with red, large, full, tall." [Sn]

Frère Marie Pierre (Bernaix, 1891) trans., "Brother Marie Pierre"
"Cerise." [Ÿ] "Vigor, bearing, and ample foliage of 'Baronne Adolphe de Rothschild'. Flower usually solitary at the tip of the cane, borne horizontally on a strong, upright stem. Flower very large, about 11 cm across [ca. 4.5 inches], very double, large thick petals, symmetrically arranged in a perfect cup, very beautiful China pink, fading to blush…penetrating fragrance." [JR15/150]

Friedrich von Schiller (Mietzsch, 1881)
"Blossom medium sized, very full; outer petals imbricated; color, sparkling crimson shaded with violet; very floriferous and very fragrant." [S] Johann Christoph Friedrich von Schiller, 1759-1805; influential German poet and dramatist. We often quote his line from *The Maid of Orléans*: "In vain do the gods themselves fight against stupidity."

Fürst Leopold IV zu Schaumburg-Lippe (Kiese, 1918) trans., "Prince Leopold IV of Schaumburg-Lippe"
"Deep red, large, full, medium scent, tall." [Sn]

Gaëtano Gonsoli
Listed as 'Gonsoli Gaëtano'.

Gaspard Monge (Moreau-Robert, 1874)
"Flower large, full, globular; color, crimson and lilac." [S] Not to be confused with the light pink and lilac Centifolia of the same name.

Géant des Batailles (Nérard/Guillot père, 1846) trans., "Battle-Giant"
Seedling of 'Gloire des Rosomanes' (B).
"Sparkling red, changing to dark lilac." [BJ] "Crimson, shaded with purple; form expanded; growth vigorous." [P1] "Very good fragrance." [LR] "Still one of the best and most constant flowering roses grown; habit free and good." [JC] "Deep, fiery crimson, very brilliant and rich when first opening, but quickly fades, medium or small size, full, well formed, handsome, Bourbon-like foliage, very liable to mildew...of delicate constitution." [EL] "Perhaps no rose among the Hybrid Perpetuals has been so famous, and so much praised...but we cannot fully echo the commendations...requires more skill and precaution for successful culture...more or less liable to mildew...by no means of...vigorous growth...Its flowers, however, are very brilliant, and, in a favorable season, are produced in abundance. In color, they resemble those of 'Général Jacqueminot'." [FP] "Doubtless has Bourbon blood in its veins." [ElC] "Supposed to be nearly related to that very brilliant Rose, 'Gloire des Rosomanes'..." [Rivers in C]

[Général Appert] (Schwartz, 1884)
Seedling of 'Souvenir de William Wood' (HP).
"Very vigorous, quite remontant…flower large, full, well formed; velvety blackish purple red." [S]

[Général Baron Berge] (Pernet père, 1891)
"Large, finely formed flowers of exquisite shape. Color, brilliant currant red, shaded silvery maroon. Very fragrant and free flowering." [CA96] "Bush vigorous, shooting out upright, strong canes; foliage very closely set; flower large, nearly full, perfect hold, beautiful grenadine red, outer rows of petals nuanced violet, very fragrant, freely remontant, continuously covered with flowers during the height of the season." [JR15/163]

Général Barral (Damaizin, 1867)
"Violet red." [Ÿ] "Medium-sized, full, violet pink." [S]

Général Bedeau (Margottin, 1851)
"Rose red, large, full, tall." [Sn] "Flower large, full, very bright red, admirable form." [VH51/112] "Plant moderately vigorous; flowers medium-sized, full, bright red. Good variety grafted." [l'H53/225] "Very vigorous bush; canes dark green, sometimes touched violet; leaves olive green, irregularly serrated; flower large, full, form very beautiful; color, bright pink." [S]

Général Cavaignac (Margottin, 1849)
"Large, full, deep bright pink." [Gp&f] "Large flower of 7 to 8 cm in diameter [ca. 3 inches], full, in five to six bundles, outer petals imbricated, perfect form, intense cerise; very fragrant, superb plant." [M-V48/229] "*Rivers*—Light carmine—new and very beautiful both in shape and colour. *Paul*—Rosy pink—fine form—large and full cupped—of a moderate growth. *Wood*—Deep flesh—a very fine rose. *Curtis*—Brilliant light carmine, medium size—an abundant late bloomer—very fragrant and distinct. We here present our readers with a rose of great beauty, quite a gem amongst the bright carmine roses. It was raised by Monsieur

Margottin, and sent to this country [*England*] in the autumn of 1850. 'Général Cavaignac' is a brilliant light carmine, of beautiful shape, and although of rather medium size, it compensates by the abundance of its blooms and its great fragrance. It is a charming rose for the conservatory or for forcing, worked on the 'Céline' or 'Manettii' stock. As it is of some- what dwarf habit, it should never be grown on stocks exceeding two feet in height [ca. 6 dm]." [C]

Général de la Martinière (de Sansal/Jamain, 1869)
"Carmine pink." [Ÿ] "Not very vigorous; canes unequal and weak; flower very large and full; color, wine red, center glossy crimson pink; outer petals lilac pink; beautiful exhibition rose." [S]

Général Désaix (Moreau-Robert, 1867)
"Growth vigorous; flower large, full; color, sparkling fiery red, shaded poppy red." [S] Not to be confused with Boutigny's pink Gallica of the same name.

Général Duc d'Aumale (E. Verdier, 1875)
"Beautiful bright dark cerise red." [JR3/27] "Crimson; a good sort, not unlike 'Maurice Bernardin'." [EL] "Deep rose, good even petal, and a good second-class flower." [JC] "A superb flower, very effective; solitary at the ends of the canes; color, deep crimson shaded bright red." [S] "Large, full, finely shaped flowers; superb, growth vigorous." [Cr76]

Général Jacqueminot (Roussel/Rousselet, 1853)
Seedling of 'Gloire des Rosomanes' (B).
"Crimson." [E] "Large, full, dark purple shaded bright crimson." [JR9/163] "A dark red, and a model in shape." [WHoIII] "Loose, flimsy, and often washy in colour." [P2] "Large, globular, dazzling red, velvety, very abun- dant." [JR1/2/7] "Of a fine crimson, and, though not perfectly double, is, nevertheless, one of the most splendid of roses. Its size, under good cultures, is immense. It is a strong grower and abundant bloomer, and glows like a fire- brand among the paler hues around it. It is one of the hardier kinds, and is

easily managed. Its offspring are innumerable." [FP] "Luxuriant growth and magnificent clusters of flowers…its large crimson flowers are not so full and perfect in shape." [R8] "Large, well-formed blooms." [OM] "Exquisite in its dazzling brightness." [Ed] "Produces here [*on the Riviera*] flowers of great splendour, but they are very jealous of the sun, which quickly turns the lovely crimson into a false mauve, and gives the petals an appearance of being parboiled." [B&V] "Elegant fragrance." [LR] "Very fragrant buds of scarlet-crimson, opening into moderate-sized, clear red flowers of fine shape…of strong, bushy growth; often blooms the second time in fall." [ARA34/78] "One of our new Roses, and most striking, from the size of its flowers, which are of rich shaded crimson. It has, however, two faults—its flowers are not sufficiently double, and its habit of growth is rather slender and delicate." [HstX:84] "A strong grower, and when in bud, one of the most beautiful of roses. Its open flower, not being perfectly double, is surpassed by others. Its color is a scarlet crimson, with a soft velvety sheen, and a few thousand of them in full bloom is a sight to be remembered." [SBP] "Very free-flowering, fragrant, and a good autumnal, but decidedly thin…not lasting or of the largest size." [F-M2] "Gives single flowers [*in Havana*]." [JR6/44] "[*Very satisfactory in Brazil*]." [PS] "[*Does*] not get wide enough awake to give us a blossom even in the spring." [ET] "[*Reblooms*] some in fall *if* old flowers are removed…4 to 7 feet [ca. 1.25-2 m]." [W] "The flowers standing high and clear above the plant, rendering it very conspicuous." [HstXXVI:331] "Flower to four inches across [ca. 1 dm], nearly full, globular, solitary or in clusters of two or three on vigorous canes…[O]uter petals large and close-set, those of the center smaller and shorter; flower stem slender, slightly nodding. Calyx rounded; sepals leaf-like." [JF] "Good but rather slender growth and fine but thin foliage; liable to mildew." [F-M2] "Rich green foliage…4×3 [ft; ca. 1.25×1 m]." [B] "To 6 [ft; ca. 1.75 m]." [HRG] "For bush, pillar, or standard, it is scarcely surpassed." [WD]

"Vigorous growth, with large sparkling velvety flowers which are nearly full, globular, large (8-10 cm [to ca. 4 inches]). This plant, because of the abundance of its flowers and the richness of its coloration, will ornament the most beautiful collections; it was put into commerce by Monsieur Rousselet, gardener at Meudon, near Paris. The jury of the Versailles Exhibition gave it First Prize." [l'H53/242-243] "This magnificent flower, known to all rosarians, is found in the best collections. Much grown for selling the bud…Growth, vigorous; the branches are slender and divergent; the bark is green, bristling with numerous prickles, which are unequal, short, and pointed; leaves are a somber green, pointed and finely toothed. Profuse flowering in the Summer, with good repeat in the Fall." [S] "An amateur, Monsieur Roussel, of Meudon, having gotten nothing from the various sowings he had made, left their result at his death to his gardener Rousselet, who the following year discovered amongst them this rose of the first order…of the most elegant bearing and the most vivid shadings." [JF] "An old Rose, but one still able to carry off medals." [DO "A free and responsive garden rose, blooming in great splendour for six weeks in spring and early summer. No rose can altogether take its place." [Dr] "Named for a French general of the early Nineteenth Century and a founder of a famous brewery of Paris still in existence today [*1938*]." [K] Not to be confused with Laffay's 1846 Hybrid China of the same name and color.

General Stefánik (Böhm, 1933) syn., 'Krázná Azurea'
Seedling or sport of 'La Brillante' (HP).
"Violet blue." [Ÿ]

General von Bothnia-Andreæ (Verschuren, 1899)
From 'Victor Verdier' (HP) × an unnamed seedling.
"Reddish violet, very large, full, medium height." [Sn] "The blossom is large, and very beautifully shaped; the bud, very long; color, very bright red, sometimes dark. Freely remontant. This very vigorous variety takes well to culture under glass." [JR23/150]

Général Washington (Granger, 1860)

Sport of 'Triomphe de l'Exposition' (HP).

"Red, shaded with crimson, large, very full, flat form; the flowers are often malformed, greatly lessening its value. A profuse bloomer, and when in perfection, a very fine sort." [EL] "Bright rosy red flowers of large size and full...sometimes splendid, but uncertain." [P2] "An HP *par excellence*, covered—above all, in the Fall—with magnificent blossoms of a light red inclining towards amaranth; it is a model in form." [VH62/98] "Very full, brilliant red blooms...very free flowering...3 [ft; ca. 9 dm]." [HRG] "Loses something of its brilliant coloration before it is completely open." [JR25/103] "One of the finest of its class. It is a good grower, very full bloomer, and a general favorite." [SBP] "Fairly vigorous; branches weak; flower very large, strongly built, quite full, expanded form." [S] "It is a new rose; but there can be little doubt of its merit." [FP] George Washington, general and president, and Father of his Country; lived 1732-1799.

Générale Marie Raiewsky (Ketten Bros., 1911)

From 'Frau Karl Druschki' (HP) × 'Fisher Holmes' (HP).

"Blossom flesh pink passing to bright pink, center nuanced yellowish salmon; vigor, habit, and size that of Druschki, but the flowers are fuller." [JR36/74]

[Génie de Châteaubriand] (Oudin, 1852)

"Flower large, full, very well formed; color, bishop's violet; reverse of petals pink." [S] "Amaranth with blackish reflections." [S] "It is to be regretted that the blossoms of this variety are not better formed and, above all, that they vary in coloration, which both detract from their merit." [l'H53/172] "The growth is vigorous, the canes are upright, with smooth wood, thorns...which are down-hooked, reddish on the young branches and grayish on the old, sharp, easily detached, unequally distributed in the proportion of 25-30 per decimeter [ca. 4 inches], mixed with...other smaller, less hooked, very small thorns, which are paler and which disappear on mature branches. The leaves are flat, dark green above, silvery light green beneath; nearly always comprised of 7 leaflets, occasionally 5, nearly always perfectly oval, sometimes cordiform at the base, lightly serrated, veins not very deep, always hollow and as if folded at the center. The rachis is covered with reddish pubescence, much colored carmine around the stipules, which are also pubescent, ciliated with short, purplish, glandular bristles. Altogether, the foliage is cheerful and vigorous; it takes on a brighter tint around the blossoms, about which it arches and recurves with elegance. The blossoms grow at the tips of the canes, on a very strong stem of about 4-5 cm [ca. 2 inches], nearly always in groups of 2, 3, or 4; the stems of the secondary buds are about twice as long as that which bears the central flower…The ovary is smooth, long, slightly inflated, rugose at the base; the sepals are velvety or rough, often bristling with purple bristles, and having small foliaceous appendages along the edges. The buds are short and nearly spherical…Each blossom is never less than 9-10 cm across (about four inches), sometimes more; the petals are very ample, and like a rosette in form; they grade smaller towards the center, where may be found petals rolled into a crown. The main color is red, or, indeed, a most beautiful bishop's violet, with scarlet reflections, and nuanced black violet, enhancing the blossom's sparkle; the reverse of the petals is a pale silvery-lilac, which neither the burin of the engraver nor the talent of the colorist can reproduce…It is perfectly remontant and double." [M-V50/321]

Georg Arends (Hinner, 1910) syn., 'Fortuné Besson'
From 'Frau Karl Druschki' (HP) × 'La France' (B).
"A marshmallow pink shade hinting at the slight lilac shading found in 'La France'. A splendid grower flowering with me in the shade both early and late." [RP] "Produces its flowers singly on the branches, of a handsome pink color. What is more, it also has the advantage of possessing an exquisite perfume like that of a Centifolia." [JR34/104] "The same vigor as Druschki; flower, very large, pure pink, color unchanging; stem, upright…of the greatest merit." [JR34/182] "Perfect in shape, enormous

in size, and sweetly fragrant." [ARA29/49] "Considered by many the most beautiful unshaded pink rose in existence…It blooms quite steadily, but not freely, practically all season, on a strong-growing plant that is rather tender for this class." [ARA34/77] "[*For*] everywhere…Foliage mildews…periods of no bloom, but gives plenty in bursts through entire season. Used as a semi-climber it is much finer than as a bush." [Capt28] "Color and fragrance [*make*] up for ugly habit of growth." [PS] "Better than most as a fall bloomer." [Th2] "Vigorous, healthy plant…4×3 [ft; ca. 1.25×1 m]." [B] "Originated by a French hybridist [*Monsieur Besson, sans doute*], but renamed by a German nurseryman, Hinner. The true name of this rose is 'Fortuné Besson'." [K]

George Dickson (A. Dickson, 1912)
"Deep velvety crimson, heavily veined." [NRS/14] "Indeed a wonderful flower, very large, full, and perfect in shape…flowers freely, nearly every flower being perfect…it hangs its head owing to the size and weight of the flower." [NRS/14] "Great, double, fragrant blooms of rich, dark, gleaming red." [ARA29.96] "Heavy, fleshy petals." [ARA21/66] "The best rose we ever raised [*at Dickson & Sons*]…bears the name of the oldest member of our family, who is nearing 80…It has an exquisite Tea scent…its color is a dark velvety red; the underside of the petals is veined blackish-red…For the last show, we had flowers nearly five inches across [ca. 1.25 dm]!" [JR35/90] "[*For the*] interior with heat…Not advised in seacoast climates. Does best leaning on a fence." [Capt28] "Has characteristics of Hybrid Perpetual…Growth and color good; form not of best…lacking in number of blooms…mildews badly." [ARA18/116] "The plant grows well and bears fragrant, finely formed blooms of deep crimson colouring. It is apparently valuable alike for garden and exhibition." [OM] "It is acknowledged by the originators and everybody else that as a garden rose (decorative or bedding) 'George Dickson' is worthless." [K] "One perfect bloom would pay for a year's waiting." [ARA29/49]

George Paul (E. Verdier, 1863)
"Bright red, velvety, blooming in clusters, large and full." [FP] "Flower 8-10 cm across [ca. 4 inches], beautiful, sparkling, bright, velvety pink, 6-8 to a cluster." [l'H63/224] George Paul, eminent rosarian of Cheshunt, England. "The lamented death of his [*i.e., George Paul the younger's*] father, Mr. George Paul, at the early age of 57 [*in the early 1870s*], left him in the charge of the large nursery." [NRS20/26]

George Sand (Gravereaux, 1909)
"Flesh pink." [Ÿ] George Sand, *nom de plume* of Amandine Aurore Lucie Dupin, Baronne Dudevant, French novelist; lived 1803-1876.

Georges Moreau (Moreau-Robert, 1880)
Seedling of 'Paul Neyron' (HP).
"Of extraordinary vigor, very beautiful dark green wood, nearly thornless; very beautiful foliage as well, of the most attractive green possible, composed of 5-7 leaflets; flower extra large, opening very well, globular, beautiful very bright satiny red, nuanced vermilion." [JR14/165] "A useful addition to the red-flowered roses because the flowers are of good size, very full, well formed, and brightly colored." [JR7/157]

Georges Rousset (Rousset, 1893)
"Satiny red." [Ÿ]

Gerbe de Roses (Vibert/Laffay, 1847) trans., "Spray of Roses"
"Rosy lilac, double. An abundant bloomer." [P] "Growth very vigorous; branches short, with short thorns flattened at the base; leaves dark green, nuanced myrtle green; flowers medium-sized, full, in clusters; color, lilac-pink." [S]

Giuletta (Laurentius, 1858)
"Remontant, branches upright, vigorous, and nearly thornless; blooms in panicles; white with light flesh, effective; large leaves of a handsome somber green, blossoms of the 'Souvenir de la Malmaison' sort, smaller,

but opening better." [JDR58/48] "Nevertheless, far from being as pretty [*as 'Souvenir de la Malmaison'*]." [S]

Gloire de Bourg-la-Reine (Margottin, 1879) trans., "Bourg-la-Reine Glory"
"Vivid red, double." [EL] "Very vigorous, flowers large, full; color, beautiful very brilliant scarlet red." [JR3/181] Bourg-la-Reine was the Margottin headquarters: "Monsieur Jules Margottin fils is going to build up his nursery at Bourg-la-Reine (Seine), near the railway station. His nurseries, which escaped damage in the war [*Franco-Prussian War*], are composed of the very best existing varieties of Roses, the same as his father had. The name of Margottin is one which needs no recommendation: its good reputation, buttressed by the very beautiful roses sent out by Margottin père, is an established fact." [l'H70/327]

Gloire de Chédane-Guinoisseau (Chédane-Pajotin, 1907) trans., "Chédane-Guinoisseau's Glory"
Seedling of 'Gloire de Ducher' (HP).
"Beautiful bright crimson blooms of delicate fragrance, and fades less in heat than most roses…blooms over a long season on a healthy, vigorous plant." [ARA34/78] "Gave some fine large blooms early in July, but has not flowered since." [NRS14/159] "A deep crimson rose of real quality, has an unusually good plant." [ARA29/49] "Very vigorous, erect, thorny, ample foliage, leaves dark green; magnificent very long bud, nearly always solitary, strong flower-stem; superb flower, cupped, very large, very full, of perfect form, with large rounded petals; opens slowly and well in all conditions; color, very intense vermilion red, sometimes velvety and of very beautiful appearance. This variety in which the flowers easily attain six inches [ca. 1.5 dm] or more in width is expected to be much used for pot-culture." [JR31/150] "Growth is fairly vigorous, but the blooms are not freely produced." [OM] "Floriferous." [Cx] "Good foliage, growth, and stem." [Th2]

Gloire de Bruxelles
Listed as 'Gloire de l'Exposition de Bruxelles'.

Gloire de Ducher (Ducher, 1865) trans., "Ducher's Glory"
"Maroon at the center, shaded slate-violet around the edges; flower large, flat, somewhat imbricated." [Cx] "Crimson-purple, large, very full, subject to mildew. If the color were permanent, this would be a good kind." [EL] "Well formed, dull purple." [JR1/2/8] "Appeals through its handsome maroon-violet color." [JR32/34] "Red to maroon with paler reverse, double flowers on arching canes to 7 [ft; ca. 2.3 m]." [HRG] "Borne abundantly...vigorous...6×5 [ft; ca. 1.75×1.5 m]." [B] "Branches strong, divergent...foliage ample, dark green." [S] "Calyx pear-shaped." [JF] "Its branches are quite strong, with light reddish bark. The thorns, brownish red, are unequal and slightly hooked. The blossoms of this beautiful variety, which are four or so inches in diameter [ca. 1 dm +], are of the expanded form, solitary or sometimes clustered in twos or threes. The color is purplish red, 'bluing' at the edge. The petals are very large, while the stem is long and firm, holding the blossom well. It is a variety of much merit." [JR5/104]

[**Gloire de Guérin**] (Guérin, 1833) trans., "Guérin's Glory"
Seedling of 'Malton' (HCh).
"Purple." [V4] "Purplish red." [TCN] "Deep carmine, full, medium sized." [LF] "Flower large, full, widely cupped; flesh pink." [S] "Rich deep cherry, of medium size, full; form, cupped. Habit, branching; growth, dwarf." [P] "This is a dwarf rose, adapted for the front of the rose border; its habit is, however, too delicate for general culture." [R9] As we learn from *Les Amis des Roses*, no. 215 (p. 5), Guérin was a gardener-florist on the Paris road in Angers—and, as we find on studying his total *œuvre*, a very enterprising hybridist!

Gloire de l'Exposition de Bruxelles (Soupert & Notting, 1889) syn., 'Gloire de Bruxelles'; trans., "Glory of the Brussels Exposition"
From 'Souvenir de William Wood' (HP; or poss. the HP 'La Rosière') × 'Lord Macaulay' (HP)
"Deep velvety purplish amaranth, almost black, base of petals fiery red; large, full, and very sweet." [P1] "Very vigorous, handsome foliage; flower...of good form...reverse of the petals wine red; very fragrant." [JR13/147] "Very large flowers of 60 or more petals of velvety crimson to purple in colour. Highly scented and upright in growth...4×3 [ft; ca. 1.25×1 m]." [B]

Gloire d'un Enfant d'Hiram (Vilin, 1899) trans., "Glory of a Child of Hiram"
Seedling of 'Ulrich Brunner fils' (HP).
"Red, shaded." [LS] "Planted outside, in the garden, it will figure in the top rank of good roses due to its abundant bloom and resemblance to 'Ulrich Brunner fils' in all characteristics...One of its great advantages is that the cupped blossom is very sturdy; when the blossom opens out, it doesn't change color...The bush is vigorous, and very floriferous; the medium or large flowers, full and fragrant, are vermilion red lightly touched carmine, and shaded a velvety violet. It is dedicated to a Masonic society of Melun: *The Children of Hiram*, taking its name from the famous architect of Tyre, who constructed the first Temple of Jerusalem in 985 BC." [JR24/120]

Gloire Lyonnais (Guillot fils, 1884) trans., "Lyon-ish Glory"
Third generation from a cross between 'Baronne Adolphe de Rothschild' (HP) and 'Mme. Falcot' (T).
"Lightly creamy white; flower large, full, cupped; floriferous." [Cx] "Tea-scented, lemon-colored, with pretty buds." [HRH] "Medium-sized, tinted light yellow and largely bordered in white." [JR10/46] "White, tinted yellow-fawn; large, but somewhat flat; slight tea perfume; only one blooming period in the East. Never sets seed-hips, and generally has been considered sterile. Foliage remarkably fine and lasting." [Th2] "[*For*] seacoast districts;

very hardy…In California it blooms well and over a long season,, but comes in bursts; foliage immune to disease." [Capt28] "Much to be recommended for its great vigor, the beauty of its foliage, and the size of its flowers." [JR30/17] "Small to medium-sized flowers." [ARA17/29] "Practically white, the yellow shade being very faint. Of very strong growth, even in poor soil, not liking clay land…The buds are beautiful, but the petals are very thin, and it will not stand in hot weather. Not free-flowering if pruned hard, but capital in autumn, when fine well-shaped blooms may sometimes be gathered." [F-M3] "Very vigorous, strong and upright branches, purplish and smooth; thorns somewhat numerous, straight and strong; leaves composed of 5-7 leaflets, with prominent purplish serrations; flowers very large, full, very well formed, with large firm petals, well held, and a fragrance of Tea roses, which the blossom also resembles in shape; the color is a nice chrome yellow, with the edges of the petals pretty much gone towards icy white; the flowers are solitary." [JR8/133] "Often surpasses three feet [ca. 1 m]…In June, I have seen this variety to blossom exceptionally well while others were depleted by poor conditions. To be fully remontant, this plant needs to be cut long." [JR10/155] "The leaves have a distinct fragrance." [Ro] "A good grower, and evergreen; does not care for a too strong soil. Nothing in the rose world much finer than really good examples of this rose, an opinion shared alas! by the rose bugs who are greatly attracted by these beautiful flowers. Resembles a Tea Rose both in form and fragrance." [B&V] "Of queenly form and bearing." [Dr] "Good and distinct." [J]

Glory of Waltham
Listed in the chapter on Noisettes and Climbers.

Golfe-Juan (Nabonnand, 1872)
Seedling of 'Victor Verdier' (HP).
"Moderate growth; flower very large, full, imbricated; color, ruby red." [S] "Superb in form…of the greatest merit for the Winter [*florist's*] trade." [R-H75] Golfe-Juan was the headquarters of the Nabonnand firm.

Gonsoli Gaëtano (Pernet père, 1874)
"Delicate satiny white, in the way of 'Souvenir de [la] Malmaison', and very beautiful." [R7/417] "Bush vigorous, upright, blooms in clusters; flower large, nearly full, fragrant; color, satiny flesh." [S] "Pinkish white, very large, very full, very fragrant, tall." [Sn]

Graf Fritz Metternich (Soupert & Notting, 1895) trans., "Count Fritz Metternich"
From 'Sultan of Zanzibar' (HP) × 'Thomas Mills' (HP).
"Deep red, large, full, very fragrant, tall." [Sn] "Vigorous bush; flower large, full; color, velvety brownish red shaded black, the center bright cardinal red. Very fragrant." [JR19/148]

Grand-Duc Alexis (Lévêque, 1892)
"Very vigorous bush; large very green foliage; flowers large, full, extremely well formed, beautiful blood red nuanced purple and light vermilion and brightened with intense carmine." [JR16/167]

Grand Mogul
Listed as 'Jean Soupert'.

Grandeur of Cheshunt (G. Paul, 1883)
"Flower very large, full; color, bright carmine nuanced pink. Abundant autumn bloom. Very beautiful exhibition rose. Growth vigorous, quite remontant." [S]

Gruss an Weimar (Kiese, 1919) trans., "Greetings to Weimar"
From 'Frau Karl Druschki' (HP) × 'Lyon-Rose' (Pernetiana)
"Yellowish white, pink center, very large, full, medium to tall." [Sn] "Bud yellowish pink; flower very large, pink on yellowish ground." [ARA21/164]

Gruss aus Pallien (Welter, 1900) trans., "Greetings from Pallien"
From 'Baronne Adolphe de Rothschild' (HP) × 'Princesse de Béarn' (HP). "The wood and foliage of this variety as well as the growth are all nearly identical to those of 'Baronne Adolphe de Rothschild'. The bright fiery red with purple center coloration as well as the fragrance are much like those of 'Princesse de Béarn'. The long bud holds in a semi-open state quite a long time on the plant; in opening, the blossom takes on the cupped form of 'Baronne Adolphe de Rothschild'. Neither high temperature nor humidity affect the pretty color...According to the breeder, no other HP's bud can rival that of 'Gruss aus Pallien'." [JR24/18] Welter was located at Pallien in Prussia.

Guillaume Gillemot (Schwartz, 1880)
Seedling of 'Mme. Charles Wood' (HP).
"Rosy-carmine." [EL] "Vigorous, flower very large, full, globular, form and poise perfect; color, beautiful delicate carmine pink with pale silvery pink reflections...blooms freely." [JR4/165]

Gustave Piganeau (Pernet-Ducher, 1889)
From 'Charlotte Corday' (HP, Joubert, 1864, purple-red) × 'Baronne Adolphe de Rothschild' (HP).
"Bush vigorous; flowers extra large, full, cupped; color, beautiful bright carmine lake red." [JR13/167] "Very short in growth, which is nearly the only fault of this very fine Rose. The foliage is good, and the plump fat buds above it open into very large, brilliant, grandly shaped blooms, with broad stout petals, and beautiful centre. Very little liable to mildew, and not much injured by rain. It was a great disappointment when this splendid Rose proved to be a poor grower. Moreover the plant is not lasting in vigour, but often gets weaker...It is very free-flowering, which seems to be a cause of its weakness of growth; it will not make wood, but is constantly forming buds. A good autumnal, capital for forcing, and a large lasting reliable exhibition Rose of the first rank." [F-M2]

Gustave Thierry (Oger, 1881)
"Lilac pink." [Ÿ] "Growth vigorous; flower full, globular; color, bright cherry red fading to lilac pink." [S] Gustave Thierry, *rosiériste* of Caen, Normandy, France.

Haileybury (G. Paul, 1895)
"Crimson cerise." [Ÿ] "Red, large, very full, medium scent, tall." [Sn]

Hans Mackart (E. Verdier, 1884)
"Cinnabar scarlet." [JR20/5] "Vigorous with long branches, which are reddish green; numerous thorns, which are unequal, recurved, fine, and brown; leaves of 3-5 leaflets, quite rounded dark green with irregular dentations, which are fairly deep-set; flower stem very long; blossom of medium size, full, with fine petals; color, very bright scarlet red; very remontant." [JR8/165]

[Harmony] (Nicolas/Conard-Pyle, 1933)
"A new type of H.P. of strong growth which makes a splendid short pillar. Salmon-pink flowers with a golden center. Rare 'old rose' perfume. Beautiful Hybrid Tea flowers on Hybrid Perpetual plants. Blooms over a long period in early summer." [C-Pf33]

Heinrich Münch (Hinner/Münch & Haufe, 1911)
From 'Frau Karl Druschki' (HP) × a seedling (which resulted from crossing the HT 'Mme. Caroline Testout' with the HT 'Mrs. W.J. Grant')
"Monsieur Heinrich Münch, of Münch & Haufe, at Leuben near Dresden, has discovered a pink-flowered Druschki." [JR35/118] "The growth is quite as vigorous as that of Druschki, a little less thorny, and covered with soft green foliage. The buds are round though pointed, and are borne on long and upright stems; they come singly, and open slowly but nevertheless easily. The large full flowers are as pretty a silvery pink as one might imagine; they stay half open for a long time…One of their salient qualities is that the petals, expanded around the perimeter, nevertheless clothe the heart of the blossom much in the way of 'La France',

while having a softer color which is more elegant and more pleasing to the eye." [JR35/106] "The flowers are large and firm and the bud is magnificent; as it opens the petals curl over in the manner of a 'La France'. The flowers arc a deep pink, with a sheen not often found." [C&Js15] "Not a good bloomer." [ARA18/116]

Heinrich Schultheis (Bennett, 1882)
From 'Mabel Morrison' (HP) × 'Monsieur E.Y. Teas' (HP)
"Delicate pinkish rose, large, full, and sweet." [P1] "Well-formed, of a very clean pink." [JR11/50] "Pinkish-rose, bright in colour, but apt to go off when expanded. Very fragrant." [DO] "Early and free bloomer, and a good autumnal…large handsome petals…beautiful shape and color when young, but soon loses both." [F-M2] "Large but shapely. Fragrant. Soft pink…Vigorous…4×3 [ft; ca. 1.25×1 m]." [B] "Capital growth and fine foliage…Not liable to mildew or injury from rain and does well in America." [F-M2] "Much appreciated in England." [JR11/2] "Excellent exhibition variety." [S]

Helen Keller (A. Dickson, 1895)
"Beautiful cerise color. Superb." [JR19/67] "Of striking cherry colour inclined to red, large flower with well defined cup. A very effective variety." [B&V] "At its best this is a very beautiful Show Rose. In a favourable season it would often be among the three or four most noteworthy H.P.'s, in the large stands of the leading nurserymen. Not of very strong growth, 'moderately vigorous' representing it fairly. The blooms are of the ordinary 'semi-globular' shape, very regular and seldom malformed, of a very bright shade of pink catalogued as 'rosy cerise,' fragrant, full-sized, with stout petals and good lasting qualities. The buds form early, with frequent fatal results…It is only in exceptionally good seasons that any but the longer later shoots yield good blooms with me: but the variety is well worth growing if only a few fine specimens can be secured." [F-M2]

Henri IV (V. & C. Verdier, 1862)
"Violet maroon." [Ÿ] "Shaded vermilion, very good." [FP] "Flower large, full; color, bright purple red shaded violet." [S] Henri IV, king of France; lived 1553-1610.

Henri Coupé (Barbier, 1916)
From 'Frau Karl Druschki' (HP) × 'Gruss an Teplitz' (B).
"China pink." [Ÿ]

Henriette Petit (Margottin, 1879)
"Very vigorous, flowers large, full, well-formed; color, beautiful red and deep amaranth." [JR3/181]

Henry Bennett (Lacharme, 1875)
Seedling of 'Charles Lefebvre' (HP).
"Velvety fiery red." [JR25/13] "Crimson, medium size, mildews, and burns badly; shy in autumn, and of no value." [EL] "Intense violet-crimson, colour very rich, flowers cupped, good even petals, but not sufficiently full." [JC] "Flower large, full, well formed; color, red, flame, and blackish carmine; growth vigorous." [S] Not to be confused with Levet's 1872 Tea of the same name. Henry Bennett, proponent of cross-breeding; his interest in cross-breeding had taken him to Lyon, where Lacharme must have met him and perhaps discussed the matter with him, as Lacharme was also a judicious cross-breeder.

Henry Irving
Listed in the chapter on Noisettes and Climbers.

Henry Nevard (F. Cant, 1924)
"A deep red Rose with large, perfect blooms of old-fashioned form and exhilarating perfume, nesting in a tuft of verdant foliage. If pruned short in the spring and the blooms picked with long stems, it will be an almost continuous bloomer. Sometimes mildews in late autumn; is worth protecting." [C-Ps29] "Massive, intensely fragrant...gorgeous dark red, but

of only fair growth and once-blooming." [ARA30/170-171] "Very fine and [*blooms*] quite recurrently." [ARA31/118] "The finest production in the red Hybrid Perpetual class, to date...very healthy...finely-formed, very fragrant, crimson-scarlet blooms with a greater continuity than any other red Hybrid Perpetual, being almost as free as a Hybrid Tea in this respect." [ARA34/79] "Good-sized crimson-scarlet blooms of splendid fragrance on a moderately vigorous plant. Continuous...Slight mildew; bad black-spot...bore 36 blooms." [PP28] "Bud very large, ovoid; flower very large, very double, full, very lasting, strong fragrance...borne singly on a long stem. Foliage abundant, large, dark green, leathery. Many thorns. Vigorous, bushy, compact; continuous bloomer from May to December." [ARA25/184] "A good everblooming red rose on a Hybrid Perpetual plant." [ARA29/49]

Her Majesty (Bennett, 1885)
From 'Mabel Morrison' (HP) × 'Canari' (T).
"Light pink...very full, enormous (six inches [ca. 1.5 dm]), with thick, ponderous petals and a perfectly symmetrical form." [JR10/39] "Huge blooms of clear rose pink with deeper flecks towards the center. Not the most healthy...but very beautiful...3×3 [ft; ca. 9×9 dm]." [B] "Pale rose; vigorous upright habit. Flowers very large...late-flowering...scentless." [J] "Without contradiction, the biggest of roses." [JR30/18] "The largest rose next to 'Paul Neyron'." [Hn] "Clear and bright satiny rose, very large and full; petals most symmetrically arranged, foliage handsome...An extraordinary rose, but unfortunately very liable to mildew." [P1] "The leaves have the glossiness of those of the Teas." [S] "Very robust, having uniquely strong wood." [JR5/22] "It could be considered that this colossal flower is not only the best rose of its color, but that it is also the best introduction to this day." [JR10/148]

"Manners and customs are notoriously strict and exacting in royal circles, and in this remarkable Rose we certainly have some striking peculiarities. Of long, strong and yet robust growth if well fed, but by no means free: it makes extraordinary growth under favourable conditions, but a poor show if not treated regally and favoured with queen's weather [*Victorian weather had a knack of clearing up whenever Queen Victoria was to appear*]. Prune high or low you will get but few shoots to a plant, and if the single growth of a maiden shoot be stopped, instead of breaking [*i.e., branching out*] in several places like the vulgar herd, 'Her Majesty' generally shoots only from the top bud left, and continues one stem upwards as before. We may place the plants close together, for the stems of each are few in number and upright and stiff. It has fine foliage and large stems with tremendous thorns, the whole being extremely and notoriously subject to mildew, so that it is best planted by itself for among the Teas, where the infection will be less dangerous in the summer season. It is a very slow starter in growth if pruned hard, and as it is advisable to get the blooms as early as possible before the plant is crippled with the inevitable mildew, this Rose alone of all may, with possible advantage, be pruned in the Autumn, as it will still not start growth early enough to be injured by frost. Better still perhaps is to leave it so long in pruning as to get a plump and well developed bud for the coming shoot. If grown well, a large proportion of the blooms come good, and they can stand a little rain. They have fine stout petals, and are wonderfully full in the centre, so much so that the Rose has quite two shapes, and the best one was not known for the first year or two: for it has in the first stage a grand regular semi-globular shape, and when expanded and overblown it is yet so perfectly full, even when flat as a pancake, as to show no eye, and to be still presentable and wonderful, though not so beautiful as a Rose. The colour is best and purest in the first of these stages: in the second it is more mixed…When presented for the Gold Medal, which was granted by acclamation, it was shown by Mr. Bennett in great quantity, several large boxes of it being staged. Every bloom was fully expanded, and its true beauty remained unknown. It was then sold to America and we had to wait a year for it. When it was at last obtainable, there was a large demand for the half-guinea plants, with the result I believe that there was hardly a bloom seen in the country that year, the plants having no doubt been budded from non-flowering shoots. The following year the true form was seen, and it is not now quite so shy a bloomer as it was. In size and lasting qualities it is quite at the top of the tree: as a free bloomer and autumnal, absolutely at the bottom. A secondary or true autumnal bloom is rare: it does bloom as a maiden, otherwise its title to the term Perpetual might yet be in abeyance. It is decidedly a hot-season Rose with us, and is very highly esteemed in America, for a valued correspondent in Philadelphia calls it 'The Queen of all the Roses' and tells me that he has had eleven very fine blooms from one plant. It is, however, liable to be killed outright by the very severe winters of that latitude, unless protected, and is therefore even more highly valued in southern and warmer districts of U.S.A., as Florida. A remarkable point about this Rose is its reputed parentage; for it is said, though it is generally supposed there must have been some mistake or accident [*the vagaries of Mendelian genetics not being perfectly understood by most rosarians of the day*], to be a seedling from the old Tea 'Canary' [*sic*], a yellow flimsy thing according to modern notions, and 'Mabel Morrison', a white sport from 'Baroness Rothschild', which is particularly open and deficient in the centre. If this is so, it should strictly be called a Hybrid Tea. Mr. Bennett was one of the first to practice hybridizing in this country, and sent out his new issues as Pedigree Roses: but one would think that on beholding the illustrious progeny of this apparently assorted pair he must have been inclined to consider chance as likely to be successful as the careful choosing of seed-parent." [F-M2]

Hippolyte Jamain (Faudon, 1869)
Seedling of 'Victor Verdier' (HP).
"Large, full, well formed, beautiful bright pink." [JR3/27] "Growth vigorous, with smooth wood; very remontant…flower very large, full, semiglobular; color, bright carmine pink; resembling 'Étienne Levet' and 'Président Thiers'. The most hardy of the 'Victor Verdier' clan." [S] Not to be confused with the below.

Hippolyte Jamain (Lacharme, 1874)
Seedling of 'Victor Verdier' (HP).
"Intense red; flower very large, cupped." [Cx] "Full, expanded form, well held; one of the best seedlings of the breeder, who has given rosarians a great number of roses, always appreciated and much admired. Color, bright pink, shaded carmine." [S] "Carmine-rose...vigorous habit...good strong growth...with fine foliage." [HstXXX:236] "Carmine-red, well-built flowers; the foliage when young has a deeper shade of red than is seen in any other sort, and is also the handsomest." [EL] Not to be confused with the above, nor with the maroon Bourbon of 1856 by Pradel of the same name, nor with the light pink HP of 1871 by Garçon/Jamain called '*Mme.* Hippolyte Jamain'.

Hold Slunci (Blatná, 1956)
"Light yellow, medium size, full, light scent, medium to tall." [Sn]

Horace Vernet (Guillot fils, 1866)
Seedling of 'Général Jacqueminot' (HP).
"Rich brilliant velvety crimson, petals large and smooth, flowers large, full, and most perfectly imbricated; a truly superb rose." [JC] "Large, fairly well-filled, half cup-shaped, velvety carmine; strong-growing, free-flowering, fragrant." [Hn] "Beautiful velvety purplish red, shaded with dark crimson...growth moderate." [P1] "Crimson, illumined with scarlet...beautiful wavy outline; nearly smooth wood, of delicate constitution. Few roses have such a lovely form as this." [EL] "A typical show Rose; grand...on the exhibition table...but to be avoided...for ordinary garden purposes...Blooms are large...stoutest of petals...capital centre, perfect shape...good dark colour, and lasting...Not a free bloomer." [F-M2] "Very fragrant, high centred, rich crimson...Tidy, well-foliated...4×3 [ft; ca. 1.25×1 m]." [B] "Growth moderate...By no means an easy Rose to grow in many localities." [J] "Weak constitution...plant is almost sure to dwindle...not very liable to mildew." [F-M2] "A perfect exhibition variety, and indispensable to those who grow for show." [OM] "Hundreds of

gardeners and rosarians, who would otherwise never have heard of the great French artist, have had his name 'familiar in their mouths as household words' by the help of this most noble Rose." [F-M2]

Hugh Dickson (H. Dickson, 1905)

From 'Lord Bacon' (HP) × 'Gruss an Teplitz' (B)

"A good crimson shaded scarlet...very fragrant." [F-M] "Large, quite full, well held, of perfect form, dark red; very beautiful." [JR31/178] "High-pointed centre." [DO] "Thoroughly satisfactory in every respect, and keeps its colour in the sun better than most crimsons do." [NRS/14] "Gives bloom off and on during the summer in Southern California sea-coast. Best on a leaning fence. Fair growth and foliage, with cutting value." [Capt28] "Flowers borne quite continuously on a plant almost rivaling Druschki in growth." [ARA34/79] "Considered the finest autumn bloomer of all roses." [Dr] "Very vigorous, free from mildew...in the front rank." [F-M] "Strong, thick shoots, which are often six to eight feet long [ca. 1.75-2.25 m]." [OM] "More fitted for pillars than for growing as bushes." [NRS/17] "Young foliage is very beautiful, and carried well above the leaves. The perfume is delightful...It is not mildew proof, neither is it especially troublesome in this respect...The flowers stand wet well." [NRS/13] "Strong erect shoots four to five feet in height [ca. 1.25-1.5 m], which later in the season become rather straggling...The foliage is good, at first red, then green with a bronze tinge becoming green in autumn, indicating a connexion with the HT's...not specially free-flowering. The flowers are carried erect on long stems but full flowers are inclined to droop. It has large firm rounded petals of considerable substance of a fine crimson colour slightly tinged with scarlet which never turns purple. The flowers last well when cut and are very fragrant...one of the most reliable of the red exhibition Roses." [NRS/10] "The finest of all the Hybrid Perpetuals, and a rose that should be in every garden in the country." [OM]

Hugh Watson (A. Dickson, 1905)
"Fiery red, shaded carmine." [Ÿ] "Crimson but with a good deal of carmine in its flowers. This is a good exhibition variety—fairly vigorous in growth—the bloom of medium rather than of large size but excellent in shape. Should be more grown." [F-M]

Impératrice Maria Feodorowna (Lévêque, 1892)
"Vigorous, foliage ample, glaucous green, flowers large, globular, perfectly formed, magnificent bright delicate pink." [JR16/167] Not to be confused with Nabonnand's Tea of 1883.

Ingénieur Madèlé (Moreau-Robert, 1874)
"Currant red." [Ÿ] "Growth moderate; floriferous; flower very large, full, imbricated; color, currant pink." [S]

Inigo Jones (W. Paul, 1886)
"Vigorous, very floriferous; flowers large, full, globular, perfectly formed, beautiful pink tinted purple. Good for exhibitions, and a good autumnal." [JR10/19] Inigo Jones, English architect; lived 1573-1652.

Isabel Llorach (Dot, 1929)
From 'Frau Karl Druschki' (HP) × 'Bénédicte Seguin' (Pernetiana).
"Bud very large, long-pointed; flower very large, semi-double, open, lasting, moderately fragrant, nankeen-yellow, tinted red, borne singly on a long stem. Foliage abundant, large, dark green, glossy, disease-resistant. Few thorns. Growth very vigorous, semi-climbing; abundant, intermittent bloomer from May to July and again in October." [ARA29/229]

J.B. Clark (H. Dickson, 1905)
From 'Lord Bacon' (HP) × 'Gruss an Teplitz' (B).
"Dark scarlet shaded blackish crimson; flower very large, very full; very floriferous; very vigorous." [Cx] "Deep scarlet, shaded plum." [NRS/10] "In full sun the color bleaches. Averages 80 blooms." [ARA21/90] "Fragrant." [ARA17/29] "A wonderful pillar rose, growing twelve to fifteen

feet [ca. 3.5-4.5 m] and producing hundreds of handsome flowers. Its color is much better in partial shade." [ARA23/64] "More fitted for pillars than for growing as bushes." [NRS/17] "Does well when left to grow at will." [NRS/14] "A positive nuisance—there is no keeping it within bounds." [NRS/12] "Has fine bold foliage and makes huge growth of stiff upright very thorny stems, eight to twelve feet long [ca. 2.25-3.5 m] when growing well. It flowers very freely and for a long time at each flowering…The flowers are large and rather coarse, generally fairly well shaped and pointed, sometimes beautiful. The colour is very variable. At times it is a washed out crimson-scarlet, at others a fine shade of that colour, especially when young. Very rarely the flowers are covered with a plum coloured bloom like a bunch of grapes, and then they are a magnificent colour…It is not troubled with mildew." [NRS/12] "[*Among the only HPs*] that pay their board bills [*in Texas*]." [ET] "The best red rose I ever saw." [ARA25/113]

Jacques Laffitte (Vibert, 1846)
"Carmine pink." [R-H56] "Rosy-crimson." [EL] "Flower 7-8 cm [ca. 3 inches], full, carmine-pink, superb. Very vigorous bush." [M-L46/272] "Bright rose, large and full; form, expanded. Habit, erect; growth, vigorous; the flowers often produced singly for some distance along the stem. The colour stands the sun well, and is clear and decided." [P] "[*The blossom's width is*] 7-8 cm [ca. 3 inches], full, carmine pink, superb flower." [VPt48/153]

James Bougault (Renaud-Guépet/C. Verdier, 1887)
Sport of 'Auguste Mie' (HP).
"Vigorous…flowers medium, full, white lightly tinted pink when opening, fading to pure white." [JR11/168] "Blooms more easily than its progenitor, which, as we know, opens only with difficulty, particularly when the weather is somewhat damp. This sport of 'Auguste Mie' appeared 12-14 years ago in the nurseries of Monsieur Renaud-Guépet…who, after assuring himself that the sport would not revert, sold it to Monsieur Charles Verdier." [JR16/56]

Jan Böhm (Svoboda, 1934)
From 'Hugh Dickson' (HP) × 'King George V' (HP, H. Dickson, 1912, crimson, parentage unknown).
"Red, large, full, very fragrant, medium height." [Sn]

Janine Viaud-Bruant (Viaud-Bruant, 1910)
From 'Triomphe d'Orléans' (HP, Corbœuf, 1902, red/deep violet) × 'Princesse de Béarn' (HP).
"Growth more vigorous than that of either parent, flowers large, shaped like a champagne glass. This new rose is a lovely small one sparkling with a crimson purple ruby color. The very brilliant color shines and glows; it is a warmer color than has 'Princesse de Béarn'. Exquisite scent." [JR34/166]

Jean-Baptiste Casati (Widow Schwartz, 1886)
"Bush vigorous; flower large, well formed, cupped, very full, very delicate lilac pink, center whitish; very fragrant." [JR10/182]

Jean Cherpin (Liabaud, 1865)
"Plum color, double, often semi-double, inclined to burn; fragrant and a fine seed parent. One of the richest shades of color yet produced." [EL] "Flower very large, full; velvety purple red with a lighter center, brightened with flame." [l'H65/339] "Rich violet-plum, a superb colour, petals smooth and well formed, flowers cupped, a good and distinct rose; habit moderate." [JC] "Growth vigorous." [P1] Jean Cherpin, rosarian, horti-culturist, editor of various mid-century horticultural periodicals.

Jean Goujon (Margottin, 1862)
"Fresh pink." [Ÿ] "Bright red." [JR25/23] "Rich deep rose, flowers extra large and handsome, a robust growing fine rose." [JC] "Beautiful clear red, very large, full, and good." [FP] "Vigorous; color, deep pink; flower very large, full, cupped; much to be recommended for its late bloom, which lasts until Winter." [S] "Nearly smooth wood; of second quality." [EL]

Jean Lelièvre (Oger, 1879)

"Vigorous, flowers large, very full, well formed, blooms easily; color, bright deep crimson." [JR3/181] "Very floriferous; one of the best." [S]

Jean Liabaud (Liabaud, 1875)

Seedling of 'Baron de Bonstetten' (HP).

"Fiery crimson, centre rich velvety-crimson, flowers large, double, and well formed." [JC] "Crimson-maroon, illumined with scarlet, large, full; a lovely rose, but shy in the autumn." [EL] "Rich crimson, shaded violet and maroon." [WD] "Does not 'blue'. Flower large, full, cupped, fragrant." [Cx] "Of fair growth and foliage, not liable to mildew or injury from rain. A free bloomer, but a poor autumnal, and a Rose of shocking manners. Occasionally one gets a lovely bloom, of open imbricated shape, not strong in the centre, but shaded in the most beautiful way with all sorts of tints from vermilion to the deepest crimson or maroon. But if you get one such in the course of a year from a dozen plants, you will be pretty lucky, for most of the flowers come distorted in all sorts of ways." [F-M3] "Of good stature and growth." [JR3/120] "Growth not good; poor bloomer." [ARA18/116] "Vigorous and floriferous, but not continuous." [JR10/29] "French horticulture has lost one of its most estimable veterans in the person of Monsieur Jean Liabaud, senior horticulturist at La Croix-Rousse, near Lyon (Rhone), who died last January 14 [1904] at the age of 90. Monsieur Liabaud, officer of the Agricultural Order of Merit, vice-president of the Society of Applied Horticulture of the Rhône, member of the Pomological Society of France, and member as well of the Lyon Horticultural Association, was a self-made man. It is just tribute to his intelligence, energy, and work that he was able to attain a proper renown throughout French horticulture...'Our colleague was born April 18, 1814, at Volesures, Paray-le-Monial (Seine-et-Loire). Son of a laborer and orphaned at the age of 12, he found a place at that time with a great agriculturist, Monsieur Dujonchet...where he stayed until 1831. [*After learning his trade at various locations*], he began to work as chief gardener...for the Marquis de Tournon, with whom he remained until 1844...After this...he decided to go into business for himself, and it was Lyon...which saw him succeed Monsieur Mille, horticulturist, whose operation he transformed...' All know the handsome old man, tall, patriarchal, energetic, strong, gaunt and angular, hair and beard completely framing his face, from which shone bright and perceptive eyes. Loved by all, he would animate meetings with his verve and jollity." [JR28/24-26]

Jean Rosenkrantz (Portemer fils, 1864)
Seedling of 'Mme. Victor Verdier' (HP).
"Very brilliant coral-red; flower large, full." [S] "Rich rosy-crimson, flowers large and globular, a beautiful rose, with fine, handsome foliage." [JC] "Large flowers neatly formed of pinkish-red petals on an upright, vigorous plant...4×3 [ft; ca. 1.25×1 m]." [B]

Jean Soupert (Lacharme, 1875) syn., 'Grand Mogol'
From 'Charles Lefebvre' (HP) × 'Souvenir du Baron de Sémur' (HP).
"Plum purple, almost black, flowers good size and evenly formed; a superb dark rose." [JC] "Carmine crimson, shaded with fiery scarlet and black, large, full, expanded; very free and sweet." [P1] "Crimson-maroon, in the way of 'Jean Liabaud'; dark green foliage, with many thorns; not free in the autumn." [EL] "The foliage is fair and the growth good, but characteristic and peculiar. One or two shoots run away considerably above the others and give promise of good blooms, and when the bud forms it is of very good typical shape and seldom comes cracked or divided; but now, when you expect the plant to put all its strength into the bud, it does not do so; the stem thickens at the base, and tempting buds for budding form all up the stem, but the flower buds swell very little, although they open slowly. The bloom, though sometimes of fair average size, is smaller and weaker than one would expect from the size of the shoot, but the shape is quite first class, with a round smooth button in the centre, the petals perfectly imbricated, and the outline regular. It is quite one of the three or four best examples of the imbricated form among H.P.'s. The bloom is not

very lasting, the colour, though striking in its very deep shade, is sometimes rather dull, and it cannot be called a free bloomer or reckoned as a good autumnal. Decidedly liable to mildew, which sometimes affects the petals. A late bloomer, which is well worth growing if only for its thoroughly distinct appearance in many particulars." [F-M2] "One of the greatest rosarians in the world…Jean Soupert, died last July 16th [*1910*] at the age of 76. With him disappears one of the great figures of rosedom…Born February 19, 1834, in the environs of Luxembourg, Soupert, still quite young, began work at the horticultural establishment of Monsieur Wilhelm, a well-known firm there, where he was well able to study all branches of horticulture…It was at Wilhelm's that he got to know his future brother-in-law, later his business associate, Monsieur Pierre Notting…It was in 1855 that the firm Soupert & Notting was born…All his colleagues became his friends…The death of Notting hit Soupert hard, and…his robust health began to decline." [JR34/135-136]

Jeanne Masson (Liabaud, 1891)
"White, flesh reflections." [LS] "Whitish pink, medium size, full, medium scent, medium height." [Sn]

Jeanne Sury (Faudon, 1868)
"Moderately vigorous; flower large, full; light crimson." [S] "Bright claret and crimson, flowers very large and full, petals smooth and well formed; a large and handsome rose." [JC]

[Jeannie Dickson] (A. Dickson, 1890)
"Rosy pink, edged with silvery pink; very large, full, high-scented flowers, thick smooth petals." [CA93] "Apparently hybridized, though perhaps remotely, with the Teas, the shape of the foliage suggesting some such strain. A good grower, but requires generous treatment, not liable to mildew or much injured by rain, free-flowering and pretty good in the autumn. The blooms have capital long large smooth petals, with centres high and finely pointed. Not very lasting, and difficult to keep clean in trying weather, but a fine show flower if grown strong, cut young, and tied up if necessary." [F-M3]

Joachim du Bellay (Moreau-Robert, 1882)
"Very vigorous, handsome dark green foliage, flower very large, full, well formed, beautiful vermilion red nuanced flame, very floriferous." [JR6/163] Joachim du Bellay, French poet; lived 1522-1560.

John Bright (G. Paul, 1878)
"Bright crimson, medium size." [EL] "The blossom is a bright color—a sparkling and pure crimson; the form of the rose is round, globular, with large petals sometimes recurved; the interior petals are shorter." [S]

John Gould Veitch (Lévêque, 1864)
"Flower large, full; color, beautiful brilliant red." [S]

John Hopper (Ward, 1862)
From 'Jules Margottin' (HP) × 'Mme. Vidot' (HP).
"I open several catalogs, and find there the following descriptions: *Duval, rose-grower of Montmorency*, 'H.P., vig., lg., full, brilliant pink with a crimson center'; *Cochet, at Suisnes*, 'Bourbon, very lg., full, globular, brilliant pink'; *Dauvesse, in Orléans*, 'H.P., lg. Full, globular, brilliant pink'; *Schwartz, of Lyon*, 'H.P., lg., full, brilliant pink with a carmine center'; *Van Houtte, the Ghent rosarian*, 'H.P., extremely vigorous, giving canes a yard long, short stems, very stocky, fl. very lg., very full, cupped, very pretty carmine'." [JR1/3/4] "Centre brilliant rosy-crimson, the outer petals paler, flowers...well formed." [JC] "Bright rose, with carmine center...light red thorns, stout bushy growth. A free blooming, standard sort." [EL] "Lilac-rose, their centres rosy-crimson." [P1] "Took the Rose world by storm. A splendid grower, and equally grand as a flower—brilliant rosy-scarlet, with silvery back." [WD] "Reverse of petals purplish-lilac." [FP] "Blooms come early...and are fairly regular, but the shape is open...colour is beautifully fresh just at first, but is...fleeting...Of fair size, a free bloomer...a capital garden Rose." [F-M2] "Petals of the circumference large, center ones smaller; flower stem short and strong; bud pretty. Calyx pear-shaped." [JF] "Upright and healthy...Fragrant...4×3 [ft; ca. 1.25×1 m]." [B] "A very

strong grower, very hardy, with good constitution and foliage." [F-M2] "Extremely vigorous, it throws out canes a meter in length [ca. 1 yard], but the flower-peduncles are short, holding the blossoms quite upright; the blossoms are very large, very full, and superbly cupped." [VH62/99-100] "Much appreciated because of the prices the blossoms fetch on the market, and because of the luxuriant growth. Vigorous; very large branches, straight upright or divergent; smooth bark, green with a bloom, reddish in the sun; prickles very clinging, hooked, and pointed. Leaves large, light green, in 3-5 acuminate, dentate, rounded leaflets; leafstalk pretty strong, light green though somewhat reddish at the base, armed with a few prickles. Hardy." [S] "Mr. Ward named his glorious seedling after his friend." [R1/251]

John Keynes (Simon Louis/E. Verdier, 1864)
"Bright reddish-scarlet, shaded with maroon; large and full; growth vigorous." [FP] "Sparkling red." [JR8/27] "Rich dark cherry-red blooms; delightfully fragrant. Foliage sufficient to plentiful. Tall. Averages 64-148 blooms per season." [ARA21/89] "One of the most celebrated English rosarians has died—Mr. John Keynes, of Salisbury—at the age of 72. He began his horticultural work in growing carnations, and particularly, dahlias, with which he had great success...John Keynes was much esteemed in the horticultural world; the citizens of Salisbury had elected him mayor last year [*1876*]." [JR2/49]

John Laing (E. Verdier, 1872)
"Crimson-maroon, colour of the old 'Tuscany'; flowers moderate size, rather small." [JC] "Growth moderately vigorous, blooming in clusters; flower medium sized, full; color, deep bright crimson, velvety and sparkling." [S] "One of the principal English horticulturists, Mr. John Laing, has died at the age of 77 at Forest Hill, where he had an establishment both vast and very well known. He was a worker best known and appreciated in England for his numerous and interesting hybridizations." [JR24/145] Not to be confused with the pink HP 'Mrs. John Laing'.

John Stuart Mill (Turner, 1874)
Seedling of 'Beauty of Waltham' (HP).
"Bright clear red, large, full, and beautiful form; fine shell-like petal of good substance." [JC] "Rosy crimson, large, full, or double; does not bloom until late; shy in the autumn." [EL] "Growth vigorous; color, light red; flower large, full, imbricated, lasting; grows erect; wood smooth...of the 'Sénateur Vaïsse' sort." [S] "Of strong long growth, not liable to injury from mildew or rain. A late bloomer, uncertain as to quality and usefulness. In some seasons all the flowers come as mere red lumps but in others the majority come of fine imbricated shape and colour, and it is then a good show rose, of average size and fair lasting qualities, but it is not a free bloomer or a good autumnal. In my experience it comes best in a cool season." [F-M2] John Stuart Mill, British utilitarian philosopher; lived 1806-1873.

Joséphine de Beauharnais (Guillot fils, 1365)
"Growth vigorous, flower very large, full, well formed, cupped; beautiful delicate pink, reverse of petals silvery." [S] "Petal edges silvery." [l'H65/340] Joséphine de Beauharnais, the Empress Josephine, wife of Napoléon, superlatively important early patroness of horticulture and the Rose in particular; lived 1763-1814.

Jubilee (Walsh/F. Cant, 1897)
From either 'Victor Hugo' (HP) or 'Louis Van Houtte' (HP) × either 'Prince Camille de Rohan' (HP) or 'La Rosière' (HP).
"Rich pure red, shading to deep crimson and velvety maroon." [P1] "The darkest, sweetest rose of all, every bloom perfect and each petal like a piece of dark red velvety with a blackish sheen." [ARA29] "Large, well-shaped blooms of deep velvety crimson. Foliage sufficient and healthy...medium to tall...Averages 57 blooms per season." [ARA21/89] "Has done well in Massachusetts." [Th2] "It is a pleasure to offer this Grand New Hardy Perpetual Rose, knowing that it is one of the most beautiful and satisfactory roses for general planting ever introduced. It is a true hybrid perpetual, and blooms finely in the fall as well as in the early summer. Perfectly

hardy, and needs no protection; a healthy vigorous grower, with handsome dark green foliage, blooms abundantly, three flowers on each shoot. The flowers are very large, frequently 6 inches across [ca. 1.5 dm], outer petals partially reflexed, the center petals upright, giving grace and beauty without showing the center. The buds are long and rounded; the color is bright flashing red, shading to glowing velvety crimson, the fragrance is delightfully rich and lasting. It is a truly magnificent rose in every way, and cannot be recommended too highly." [C&Js99] The name commemorates Queen Victoria's Diamond Jubilee.

Jules Barigny (E. Verdier, 1886)
"Very vigorous, light green erect canes; thorns remote, straight, large, pink; leaves, 3-5 large oval-rounded somber green leaflets, irregularly and rather deeply toothed; flowers large, very full, beautiful plump form, firmly held; color, carmine red with a paler reverse, very fragrant." [JR10/170]

Jules Chrétien (Schwartz, 1878)
"Belongs to the 'Prince Camille [de Rohan]' type. Crimson, tinged with purple." [EL] "Upright canes with whitish thorns, having very large glossy green leaves...the form of the leaflets is oval-lanceolate acuminate, the upper leaflets most distinctly so; the stipules are linear, entire; the sepals are nothing more than little linear segments. The flower is large, well-formed, and perhaps the only one of its color...It is full, bright poppy red, showing up well, the backs of the petals having a light violet tint which brings out the bright red...This variety was announced under the name 'André Schwartz', but...I have dedicated it to my friend Jules Chrétien, the able chief floral horticulturist of the Tête d'Or park in Lyon." [JR2/167-168]

Jules Seurre (Liabaud, 1869)
Seedling of 'Victor Verdier' (HP).
"Growth vigorous; color, carmine red nuanced blue; flower large, full." [S]

Julius Finger
Listed as a Hybrid Tea.

Jules Margottin (Margottin, 1853)
Seedling of 'La Reine' (HP).
"Bright carmine." [JR1/7/7] "Bright cherry-colour, large and full; form cupped." [P1] "Imbricated, perfect, very bright cerise pink." [JR1/2/8] "Brilliant glossy pink; a glowing fresh colour, flowers large, beautifully smooth and cupped...robust." [JC] "Large, full, of beautiful centifolia form, deep pink; free-flowering, strong-growing, and good in autumn." [Hn] "Very free bloomer and good autumnal, but a poorly shaped rough bloom...Early, sweet scented." [F-M2] "Nearly without fragrance." [JR10/151] "Globular." [JR3/27] "Carmine rose, large, full, somewhat flat, slight fragrance; five to seven leaflets, foliage light green, and somewhat crimped; wood armed with dark red thorns; free flowering and hardy." [EL] "Has no superior in its way: it is of a clear, rosy-crimson color, and its half-opened buds are especially beautiful." [FP] "More often semi-double than full." [JDR56/48] "Very strong, thorny, hardy growth...good foliage and strong constitution." [F-M2] "Very liable to mildew." [B&V] "One of the most widely cultivated roses; very vigorous and remontant; branches olive green, somewhat glaucous, armed with numerous and very unequal thorns of a brownish red...the foliage is very ample, dark green above, whitish beneath...the flowers are large, full, rounded, regular; color, carmine-maroon with shades of pink." [S] "Vigorous; canes of moderate size, branching; bark light green, reddish where the sun strikes, with numerous thorns which are somewhat long, fairly upright, and very sharp. Leaves very ample, smooth, somber green, divided into 5-7 oval-pointed and finely toothed leaflets; leafstalk light green, reddish above and bearing beneath several small slightly hooked prickles. Flowers nearly four inches across [ca. 1 dm], full, well formed into a cup, solitary or in clusters of two or three on the strongest branches...outer petals concave; inner ones smaller; flower stem strong

and pretty long. Calyx long, slightly pear-shaped; sepals very leaf-like. A superb variety, very remontant, and of great merit; it has the elegance, the bearing, and the color of 'Brennus'." [JF] "Quite worthy of its descriptive English name, 'Perpetual Brennus'; its very vigorous habit, and large finely-shaped light vivid crimson flowers, remind us much of that very fine old Hybrid China." [HstX:84]

"Wood large, very strong and long, yellowish-green where shaded, reddish-green in the sun; long internodes…Flower-stem strong, pretty long, holding the flowers firmly, studded with little brownish bristles…Buds large, nearly globular, flat at the base, eight to a dozen at the end of the cane on young plants; on older, only two to three, sometimes but one…Flowers very large (more than 4½ inches [ca. 1.25 dm]), full, regular; petals very numerous, ample, substantial, swirled elegantly in the center; concave at first, making the blossom at that stage deeply goblet-shaped; next, the petals stand up, indeed becoming slightly convex, the flower, when expansion is complete, appearing to be somewhat reversed; sexual organs apparent…scent elegant though faint…This Rose came from the nurseries of Monsieur Margottin of Paris, and is perhaps his most notable introduction…It is a hybrid of Bourbon extraction, of energetic growth and easy remontancy." [PlB] "A most superb old Rose…good for beds and groups." [WD] "Of admirable quality, from which many fine seedlings have been procured." [WD] "4×3 [ft; ca. 1.25×1 m]." [B] "It is no longer necessary to sing the praises of this charming and magnificent rose." [JR4/184] "Monsieur Jules Margottin, whose father's nursery was just opposite the gateway of the horse market, depicted in Rosa Bonheur's famous picture, was my [*George Paul's*] boy chum, and we have been friends for sixty years." [NRS17/101] "Monsieur Margottin, Jacques-Julien, more commonly known as Margottin père, because of his sons, also horticulturists, died last May 13th [*1892*] at his home at Bourg-la-Reine in his 75th year. Born September 7, 1817, in the community of Val-St.-Germain, Margottin became an orphan at 14, without any means of support. It was then that he commenced his profession, as an apprentice gardener with Count Molé at Marais Castle, where he stayed three years. Then, in 1835, he went to Monsieur Boscary's, in Romaine, community of Lésigny, Brie-Comte-Robert (Seine-et-Marne), where he stayed up to 1838. Monsieur Boscary thought so much of Margottin, that he remained one of his faithful customers until he died, and even now his widow who lives at Pau, keeps up with the family of our late colleague. Having a decided taste for Horticulture, and wanting to complete his knowledge of the Art, around the end of February, 1838, Margottin entered Monsieur Soulange-Bodin's establishment at Fromont in Ris (Seine-et-Oise), at which the chief horticulturist was Monsieur Keteleer. He remained there six months, gaining the modest sum of 1 franc a day. Exempt from military service as the eldest of orphans, he left Ris to go to Châteauneuf-sur-Loire (Loiret), to Monsieur Josselin's, where he stayed only a short time, having contracted the fevers. He returned to Paris, to Monsieur Quentin's, florist, rue des Fossées-Saint-Michel; and finally, in 1839, he began work at the Jardin du Luxembourg as chief gardener at the rosarium, under the supervision of Monsieur Hardy père. In 1840, he left the Luxembourg to get married, and to establish his rose business on the Boulevard de la Gare, outside the wall, community of Ivry, then rue du Marché-aux-Chevaux, no. 33, which he left at the end of the lease, in 1859, to go to Bourg-la-Reine, where he became the owner of a property which was to be his firm. Founding member of the Société Nationale d'Horticulture de France, and member of the editorial board, he was as well a member of a great number of other societies, and municipal councilor or his community, Margottin was held in high estimation. He developed a great many good roses, 'Jules Margottin' among others...dedicated to his oldest son." [JR16/83]

Juliet (Easlea/W. Paul, 1910)
From 'Captain Hayward' (HP) × 'Soleil d'Or' (Pernetiana)
"Outside of petals old gold; interior rich rosy red changing to deep rose. Very remarkable color. Fragrant...Foliage, poor." [Th] "Vermilion-red,

reverse of petals old gold. Very vigorous." [NRS/11] "The color of the flower is somewhat variable. When it is warm and humid, weather often found in England during the summer, the predominating color is a crimson-rose...the petal exterior taking on a golden color, richly and noticeably contrasting with the red shades. When cold and dry, the crimson shades are replaced by a bright pink lit by scarlet, with the exteriors still yellow, though perhaps a little more brilliant. This rose blooms during the Summer and Fall...Of remarkable vigor, this is a good variety to choose for making shrubberies in the garden." [JR34/140-141] "Really a most incongruous mixture of colours, but at the same time nearly everyone admits that it is fascinating and very beautiful." [NRS/12] "Early bloom only." [M-P] "A very pretty novelty which blooms as well in Fall as it does in Summer...The very large flowers have an exquisite scent." [JR34/85] "A lovely variety, and as fragrant as beautiful." [OM] "Blend of Damask and Fruit-scented [*perfumes*]." [NRS/17] "Does not ball...does not do well in extremely hot climates...Prune very lightly." [Th2]

Kaiser Wilhelm I (Elze/Ruschpler, 1878)
"Light purple red, large, full, medium scent, medium height." [Sn] "Vigorous bush; canes short, nearly thornless; leaves dark green, much veined; undersides of leaves grayish-green; blossom very large, full, good form; color, golden grenadine nuanced reddish violet." [S] Kaiser Wilhelm I, king of Prussia; lived 1797-1888.

Katkoff (Moreau-Robert, 1887)
Seedling of 'Charles Lefebvre' (HP).
"Growth vigorous; very handsome glossy green foliage; flower large, full, perfectly formed, imbricated like a camellia; bright cerise red sparkling with carmine, nuanced currant red, very floriferous and very fragrant; very beautiful plant." [JR11/150]

King of Sweden
Listed as 'Oscar II, Roi de Suède'.

König Friedrich II von Dänemark (Breeder unknown, date uncertain) trans., "King Friedrich II of Denmark"
"Dark red, medium size, full, lightly scented, medium height." [Sn]

Krásná Azurea
Listed as 'General Stefánik'.

L'Ami E. Daumont (Vilin, 1903) trans., "Friend E. Daumont"
"Growth of great vigor with upright canes; few thorns; foliage delicate green; bud conical, very large; flower very full; well held; color, alizarine scarlet red tempered by old-rose red, the underside of the petals becoming silvery towards the base, the edges of the flower taking on purplish madder tones." [JR28/27]

L'Ami Maubray (Mercier, 1890) trans., "Friend Maubray"
Seedling of 'Xavier Olibo' (HP).
"Vigorous, making a beautiful bush. Flower solitary, sometimes in a cluster, very fragrant, very double, very remontant, light red shaded delicate violet." [JR15/164]

L'Esperance (Lartay/Fontaine, 1871) trans., "Hope"
"Sparkling pink." [Ÿ] "Rosy-cerise, colour clear and satiny, flowers large and double, highly scented...habit moderate." [JC] "Growth vigorous; flower large, full, flat; color, light cherry red." [S] The privations and difficulties of the Franco-Prussian War no doubt inspired the name.

L'Étincelante (Vigneron, 1891) trans., "The Sparkling One"
Seedling of 'Bijou de Couasnon' (HP)
"The most dazzling scarlet imaginable, flowers very large and nearly full, an abundant bloomer, and very effective, growth vigorous." [Cr76] "Vigorous, very floriferous, flower large, full, cupped, perfectly poised, extremely bright red, somewhat velvety within." [JR15/148]

La Brillante (V. & C. Verdier, 1861) trans., "The Brilliant One"
"Light clear carmine." [l'H61/264] "Bright crimson, a clear shade, large, double, fragrant; a free bloomer." [EL] "Transparent carmine, very bright and beautiful, large, and of fine form." [FP] "Growth vigorous; branches upright, very thorny; flower medium sized, full, very well formed, in clusters of 10-12 flowers." [S]

La Brunoyenne (Bourgeois, 1908) trans., "The Lady from Brunoy"
"Very vigorous, flower large, very full, well formed, cupped, deep velvety lake towards the outside, fading to golden lake red with flame reflections; center light but very intense madder red; reverse of petals bright madder pink with bluish reflections; very fragrant. Dedicated to Mme. Gutierrez de Estrada, the great philanthropist [*of the French town of Brunoy*]." [JR32/135]

La Duchesse de Morny (E. Verdier, 1863)
"Bright but delicate rose-color, the reverse of the petals silvery, large and full, form globular." [FP] "Bright rose; erect growth; mildew." [EL] "Brilliant pleasing rose, flowers large, full, and beautifully formed...robust." [JC] "Growth vigorous, very remontant, with robust canes armed with some unequal thorns on the lower part; ample foliage, dark above, pale green beneath; each leaf is comprised of 3-5 large, oval-cordate, pointed, finely dentate leaflets; the canes are all topped by a solitary blossom of the Centifolia form, perfect, globular at first, then opening into a cup, at that point not measuring less than four inches across [ca. 1 dm]; its color is one of the most delicate—very fresh, tender pink, reverse of petals pale pink nuanced matte silver; beneath this terminal blossom, 5 or 6 other flowers grow from the axils of the upper leaves, the opening of which blossoms prolongs the Spring bloom up until the appearance of the reblooming canes; in form, size, and color, these blossoms ceded nothing to the Spring bloom." [l'H63/223] "Of fair growth and foliage in strong rich soil, the wood and leaves being very distinct and characteristic. Decidedly liable to mildew, and cannot stand much rain.

The blooms come well shaped, with very smooth stout petals, beautifully full, of distinct and lovely colour, large size, and fair lasting qualities. This Rose is one of the very smoothest and most regular in semi-globular imbricated shape that we have; a free bloomer, but not so good in autumn, and rather dainty as to soil and treatment. The buds should be well thinned…the shoots often come wholly or partly fasciated." [F-M]

La Nantaise (Boisselot/Cochet, 1885) trans., "The Lady from Nantes"
Seedling of 'Général Jacqueminot' (HP).
"Vigorous, stocky, erect canes bearing medium sized, hooked thorns, and foliage of good size, dark green. The large flowers, regularly cupped, borne on a strong, upright stem, are quite full with large petals, intense red darkened by deeper reflections, especially at the end of the season, when it blooms nicely. The vigorous canes bear clusters of blossoms, while the branchlets bear solitary roses…[S]eems to belong to the Jacqueminot group." [JR8/169]

La Reine (Laffay, 1844) trans., "The Queen"
Possibly a seedling of 'William Jesse' (HB).
"Bright rose tinged with lilac." [HoBoIV/319] "One of the gems of the [*1844*] season…pink with a lilac hue, very glossy…globular in shape, large, and very sweet." [P2] "Its flowers open freely, of a pale rose colour, blooming freely all season, holding its place with '[Rose] du Roi' in every character." [Bu] "The largest and most magnificent of all the Perpetuals, often attaining the size of a double Pæony…a brilliant satin rose…very slightly tinged with lilac, of most regular and perfect cupped form, and delightfully fragrant; the growth of the plant is very strong and vigorous, and each new spring shoot is crowned with flowers." [WRP] "Often shaded with lilac, and sometimes with crimson." [P] "Has the appearance of a true perpetual Cabbage, but much larger; strong robust grower, and free bloomer." [HstVI:367] "Sometimes coarse, and its flowers are so very double that they frequently open badly." [HstX:30] "Sometimes fine, but very uncertain." [P2] "It varies very much in quality with the circumstances of soil

and cultivation, and in its color is surpassed by many other roses. Its very large size when well grown, its fine form and perfect hardiness, are its points of merit." [FP] "In dry seasons, most beautiful and fragrant." [R8] "Very large, full blooms of pink with silvery rose-pink reverse, robust...4×4 [ft; ca. 1.25×1.25 m]." [HRG] "Semi-globular form, somewhat fragrant; the foliage slightly crimpled, five to seven leaflets." [EL] "Suitable for dwarf groups." [Hn] "Vigorous, with branches of medium size, straight upright or branching; smooth bark, green with a bloom, with occasional thorns which are reddish, unequal, and enlarged at the base; foliage pale green, 5-7 leaflets, acuminate and irregularly dentate; leafstalk the same color, with no prickles; flower about four inches across [ca. 1 dm], full, well formed, cupped, solitary, or in twos or threes on strong branches...petals very large and concave; not very hardy." [S] "Calyx elongated, pear-shaped. 'La Reine' is worthy of the name it bears; it rivals the Centifolias in scent and color, but surpasses them in the size of the flower." [JF] "In some situations—particularly late in the autumn—delicately striped or veined with carmine; its form globular, very double and massive. The singularly stiff reflexed edges, contrasting with the glossy pale pink on the backs of the petals, give a distinct character to this rose, while the guard petals, being very stout and rigid—more so than any other rose we know—enable it to retain its perfect form to the last. In warm situations 'La Reine' blooms of an immense size, forming an almost solid mass of petals, frequently measuring fifteen inches in circumference [ca. 3.75 dm] by three inches in depth [ca. 7.5 cm]...To induce this rose to flower luxuriantly in the autumn, two or three of the central shoots should be shortened to three or four eyes as soon as the terminal flower buds appear, and the tree be kept well watered with liquid manure." [C] "Has stood for a long time at the head of the HPs." [JR4/40] "Grown so much formerly, today somewhat neglected." [JR31/124] "Others have now surpassed it. It is, however, still valuable for its glossy rose color, and its large, full, semi-globular form." [SBP]

"The appearance of this magnificent rose is an event. It always seems as if we could never develop roses more beautiful than those we have already; and yet, here is one which surpasses them all, because it equals the most beautiful Centifolias by its size, its form, the abundance of its petals, and the beauty of its coloration, as well as by its fragrance. But it surpasses them in merit because, from the beginning of the blooming season until frost, it is covered, continuously, with numerous blossoms, which always open perfectly. The bush is vigorous, the branches upright; the strong stems seem to have been made to bear the enormous flowers, which are always solitary...The foliage is that of the Bourbons, slightly glaucous beneath; the wood is glaucous as well. The only thing left to be desired would be Centifolia foliage. The flower, among the biggest of the class, seems full because many of the inner petals fold back, clothing the center and hiding the stamens. The inner surface of the petals is a pretty pink when the flower is completely open, after having been a brighter pink; the underside of the petals is a whitish lilac-pink...We owe this beautiful rose to the efforts of Monsieur Laffay, whose skills are well known; it is the product of planned breeding. The seeds were produced in 1835, and first bloomed in 1841." [R-H43] "The *Journal d'Horticulture Pratique*, which is always the first horticultural publication to note and call attention to wonderful newcomers, had the first word on the Rose de la Reine. Here is what we said in the issue of September 16, 1843: 'With two thousand and more varieties of Roses known, here we find the Rose de la Reine, which is to say the most beautiful of all Ross, the Rose of artists, the Rose which dethrones the Centifolias! It was on September 5, 1843, that Monsieur Laffay, amateur horticulturist of Bellevue, near Paris, presented to the general circle of horticulture four samples of a large Rose attaining a diameter of about four inches [ca. 1 dm], in which the exterior petals, very large and hollowed, form a cockade; the central petals are equally large, folded, sometimes gracefully recurved in such a way as to hide twenty-ish stamens, which a person only sees if an indiscreet hand uncovers them. This magnificent Rose, held on an iron-strong stem, is a whitish-pink on the

exterior and a beautiful light lilac-pink towards the center, shaded delicately, lightly, a quality intensified by the satiny nature of the petals. The
fragrance is that of the Centifolia, but the color of the foliage is a glaucous
green; the leaves are comprised of five, or—only at the branch-ends—
three leaflets which are extra long, flat, a little wavy, pretty large, and look
rather like those of the Bourbons. The branches are upright, armed with
some remote, feeble prickles insecurely held on the cane. The bark is a
glaucous green like the leaves, very smooth, and laden with the same sort
of powdery substance as raisins and plums have. The shrub is very vigorous, giving many flowers which open well all the time, except on those
rare occasions when three buds are found together in a cluster. What is
notable is that it was nearly the only flower in Paris that 13th of
September...' The following January, the *Journal* gave as lagniappe to its
subscribers a beautiful double plate representing 'La Reine', of which two
hundred slips were delivered into commerce, slips which had been [*hur-
riedly*] rooted in the hot-house such that they were starved and etiolated;
these were sold in February, March, and April at 2, 3, 4, or 5 francs apiece,
depending upon the conscience of the vendors as well as the strength of
the plants. It was in 1844 that 'La Reine' bloomed for the fanciers and
vendors. All agree that here we have a beautiful Rose...Monsieur Laffay,
who has bred many introductions, always dedicates them to English
princes. It is perhaps due to our intervention that the name 'Reine
Victoria' was not used...Might one hope for something better than 'La
Reine'? Yes! Though perhaps we have arrived at the apogee with Dahlias,
we are still far off with Roses...'La Reine' holds the middle ground
between hybrids properly-called, and the Bourbons. By the wood and
foliage, it is kin to the Hybrid Chinas; considering its ovary, it has something of the Portland or Centifolia...We will end this article by stating
that 'La Reine' perfectly justifies the name 'The Autumnal Centifolia'."
[PlB]

La Rosière (Damaizin, 1874)

"Maroon crimson, shaded with black, of medium size, cupped, double and effective." [P1] "Vigorous, flowers large, full, fiery amaranth red, petal edges crimson. The bud is long and borne on a strong stem." [JR18/56] "Belongs to the 'Prince Camille [de Rohan]' type. Crimson, the flowers are identical in color and form with Prince Camille, but seems a little fuller, and are more freely produced; the habit of growth, too, seems somewhat stronger; it may usurp the place of its rival." [EL] Ingrid Verdegem kindly passes on to us the information that "*la rosière*" was the name given to the purest and most virtuous girl in the village, who was chosen yearly among the village maids; her reward consisted of a rose wreath and a small dowry. Less specifically, it was also applied to any virtuous or guileless girl.

La Syrène (Touvais, 1874) trans., "The Siren"

"Cherry." [LS] "Light red, large, full, medium height." [Sn] Not to be confused with the China 'Sirene', a synonym for 'Charlotte Klemm'.

La Tendresse (Oger, 1864) trans., "Tenderness"

"Flower large, full; color beautiful, Hydrangea pink." [S]

La Vierzonnaise (André/Lévêque, 1893) trans., "The Lady from Vierzon"

Seedling of 'Jules Margottin' (HP).

"Delicate pink, or rather light lilac pink, nuanced darker pink, shaded and frosted a light carmine pink." [JR17/179] "This pretty rose, of which the salient qualities are the fresh color, the graceful form, the perfume, the great abundance of flowers, and continuity of bloom from June till October, was raised from seed at Vierzon by Monsieur Charles André, a longtime horticulturist...The growth is upright, the wood cheerful green, few thorns, which are red and hooked...The blossoms are borne in clusters; the buds, with foliaceous sepals, are very fresh looking." [JR16/52]

Lady Arthur Hill (A. Dickson, 1889)

Seedling of 'Beauty of Waltham' (HP).

"Lilac-pink, quite distinctive and charming, a shade unknown till now. The flowers are large, full, very symmetrical, and appear abundantly, each branch bearing a bud. The growth is vigorous, the foliage distinctive and very pretty…This rose is unique in form." [JR13/90] "Blooms abundantly and late; flower…of good form." [JR22/105] "Distinct in colour but small." [F-M3]

[Lady Helen Stewart] (A. Dickson, 1887)
"Bright scarlety crimson; flowers fully rounded out, petals large and thick; highly perfumed and very beautiful." [CA93] "Large round solid flowers, very fragrant; color bright crimson, flamed with scarlet, very beautiful." [C&Js99] "The same fault [*as has 'Lady Arthur Hill'*], want of size, is noticeable in this Rose, which is however very bright and free blooming and a good grower." [F-M3] "Vigorous growth having strong, upright wood, and pretty thick foliage. Flower carried well on a long, thick stem; it is full, of good form and exquisite scent. Color, bright crimson scarlet; petals large, uniform, of great substance, and a very beautiful lustre. Very distinct and beautiful, blooming in profusion the whole season until late, when it is especially pretty." [JR11/93]

Lady Overtoun (H. Dickson, 1907)
"Salmon flesh." [Ÿ] "Much like 'Ulster' in leaf and growth, and 'La France' in color, though perhaps lighter pink." [JR31/38]

Lady Stuart (Portemer, 1852)
"Pink, changing to blush; five to seven leaflets." [EL] "Very remontant hybrid resembling the non-remontant hybrid of the same name, which is to say: flower large, very full, regular, and prettily colored delicate flesh." [l'H52/187] "Very vigorous bush; flowers medium or large, very full, globular, very pale flesh, darker at the center; very beautiful variety, but not very remontant and doesn't always open perfectly." [l'H56/201]

Laforcade (Lévêque, 1889)
"Vigorous, very strong upright canes, foliage ample, dark green; flower very large, cupped, beautiful carmine red…dedicated to the very able Chief Gardener of Paris." [JR13/164]

Lamotte Sanguin (Vigneron, 1869)

"Growth vigorous; canes pretty big, branching; bark somber green, reddish where the sun strikes, with numerous thorns of a reddish brown, and straight, strong, unequal, and stout. Foliage thick, quite rugose or bullate, somber green, generally of 5 acuminate, dentate, oval-rounded leaflets; petiole pretty strong, armed with 3 or 4 little prickles of the same color as those on the canes. Flower about 4 inches across [ca. 1 dm], full, widely cupped, slightly plump, usually solitary, occasionally in twos or threes; color, a beautiful bright carmine red; very large petals, peduncle glandular, short, strong. Ovary pear-shaped; sepals leaf-like. Plant very vigorous and of good stature. It makes magnificent, hardy, bushes." [JF]

Laurent de Rillé (Lévêque, 1884)

"Vigorous bush...flower large, full, imbricated; color, very bright light cerise red; foliage glaucous green." [S] "Very abundant bloom; one of the breeder's best introductions." [JR8/150]

Le Havre (Eude, 1871)

"Brilliant vermilion, large, and very double; form expanded." [P1] "Beautifully formed." [EL] "Of good substance." [DO] "Beautiful show rose...imbricated form but...not...in bad weather...not often large." [F-M2] "Good foliage: not specially liable to mildew." [F-M2] "Vigorous...very floriferous." [S] "Bushy plant...leathery foliage...4×4 [ft; ca. 1.25×1.25 m]." [B] "Habit moderate." [JC] Le Havre is a seaport town in northern France.

Le Triomphe de Saintes (Derouet, 1885) trans., "Saintes' Triumph"

"Vigorous; flower large, very full, sparkling scarlet red, very floriferous. Remarkably beautiful." [JR9/166]

Lecoq-Dumesnil (E. Verdier, 1882)

"Very vigorous bush with upright reddish canes; thorns numerous, unequal, short, very pointed, pink; leaves comprised of five oblong leaflets with fairly deep irregular serration, dark green; flower extra large, quite full, and perfectly imbricated; unique coloration; sparkling red much marbled and shaded crimson brown and violet." [JR6/165]

Léna Turner (E. Verdier, 1869)
"Cerise, shaded with violet, flowers large, full, and imbricated; a good rose." [JC] "Cerise-red with slaty nuances; camellia form." [S] "The blossom is of perfect form, wonderfully imbricated except right in the center, where the petals are slightly ragged; ideally double; good size; excellently held. Its color is a rich deep carmine, brightened at the center with flame red, leaving nothing which could improve on its sparkling effect. The foliage is, above, a beautiful dark green, slightly reddish along the crenelated edges; delicate green veined darker beneath; the thorns are reddish. The bush is vigorous, very floriferous, and quite hardy." [VH80/283]

Léon Delaville (E. Verdier, 1885)
"Red, shaded." [Ÿ] "Very vigorous, with strong canes; foliage dark green; flowers large, full, well-formed, dark red strongly shaded carmine, illuminated with violet crimson." [JR8/178]

Léon Renault (Widow Lédéchaux, 1878)
Seedling of 'Général Jacqueminot' (HP).
"Cherry-red, very large, full; promises well." [EL] "Vigorous bush; flower large, well formed; color, beautiful light red with the reverse of the petals tinted carmine." [JR3/10]

Léon Robichon (Robichon, 1901)
"White, large, full, medium scent, tall." [Sn]

Léon Say (Lévêque, 1882)
"Vigorous, leaves large, thick, glaucous green; flower very large, bright red shaded brown, light pink, and lilac pink shaded white; the size of the foliage and the very curious and effective coloration make this variety head the list for bedding." [JR6/148] "Centifolia scent." [S]

Leonie Lambert (Lambert, 1913)

From 'Frau Karl Druschki' (HP) × 'Prince de Bulgarie' (HT).

"Vigorous bush, stiff, like 'Baronne Adolphe de Rothschild'; large leaves. Flower very large, 10-14 cm across [ca. 5 inches], solitary, erect on a long, stiff stem, silvery pink, with a glossy yellowish pink center; petal edges pink becoming violet. Fragrant. Height, 1.5-2 m [ca. 4.5-6 feet]; everblooming until October." [JR38/56].

Léonie Lartay (Lartay, 1860)

"Wine-lee." [Ÿ] "Flower large, full; color, bright scarlet." [S]

[Léopold I, Roi des Belges] (Van Asche, 1863) syn., 'Léopold Premier'; trans., "Léopold I, King of the Belgians"

Seedling of 'Général Jacqueminot' (HP).

"Velvety purple." [LS] "Bright dark-red, very large and full, fine form." [FP] "Flower very large, full; color, shining dark red; resembles 'Mme. Victor Verdier'." [S] "Crimson, with soft tint of violet, flowers large, full, and imbricated; a good rose; habit vigorous." [JC] "A magnificent Rose...very full and fragrant." [C&Js12] Has been called a Hybrid China.

Léopold Premier

Listed as 'Léopold I, Roi des Belges'.

[Lion des Combats] (Lartay, 1850) trans., "Combat-Lion"

"Reddish-violet, often shaded with scarlet, large and full." [FP] "Hardy." [S] "Very vigorous plant; flowers large, full, dark red nuanced flame. Superb grafted or own-root. We are fortunate to be able to save the reputation of this Rose, which some have discredited. Having received it in bloom, we thought well of it at once; we only regret that, along with this variety, the same year brought us ten other varieties which should have been scrapped." [l'H53/226] Parent of 'A.M. Ampère' (HP).

Lisette de Béranger (F. Moreau/Guillot fils, 1867)
"Vigorous, wood and foliage resembling those of 'Lord Raglan'; blossoms medium-sized, full, well formed, globular, well held, a pretty very fresh flesh pink, much like that of 'Reine des Île-Bourbons', fading later to a ground of white with petals much bordered pink, like the Tea 'Homère'; totally new coloration." [l'H67/287]

Lœlia
Listed as 'Louise Peyronny'.

Lord Bacon (W. Paul, 1883)
"Deep crimson, illumined with scarlet, and shaded with velvety black, large, full, and globular. A very fine and showy Rose, blooming abundantly, and till late in the season; growth vigorous." [P1]

Lord Beaconsfield (Schwartz/Bennett, 1878)
"Crimson, nuanced." [Ÿ] "Crimson, large, well formed." [EL] "Growth vigorous; flower very large, full, globular; color, blackish crimson." [S] Not to be confused with 'Earl of Beaconsfield'.

Lord Frederick Cavendish (Frettingham, 1884)
"Flower large, full, of unique form—globular and quite perfect; sparkling bright red; petals pointed…Growth vigorous." [S]

[Lord Macaulay] (W. Paul, 1863)
Seedling of 'Alfred Colomb' (HP).
"Bright crimson." [LS] "Flower large, full, perfectly held; form nearly globular; magnificent exhibition rose. Its scarlet red coloring changes depending upon the soil in which it grows; in clay soil, the blossom becomes maroon red, and may be burned by the sun." [S] A parent of 'Gloire de Bruxelles' (HP).

Lord Raglan (Guillot père, 1854)

Seedling of 'Géant des Batailles' (HP).

"Burgundy crimson, a lovely shade; tender and shy in autumn." [EL] "Deep crimson, changing to mottled crimson, flowers large, full, and well formed, habit vigorous; a very superb rose." [JC] "Vigorous, wood reddish, nearly thornless, blossoms fiery red, brighter at the center, and violet purple at the edge." [JDR55/9] "Growth very vigorous and remontant, with robust upright canes of a delicate green armed with some reddish thorns of medium size, nearly straight, perhaps a little hooked at the base of the cane. The young foliage has a strong tint of red, which disappears bit by bit, making way for a beautiful dark green. Each leaf is comprised of 7 or sometimes 5 leaflets of varying size. The blossom is of the greatest size, very full, well formed, opens perfectly." [S] "One of the very finest flowers of this section [*i.e., progeny of 'Géant des Batailles'*]; and the plant is more vigorous, and less liable to mildew, than the rest of the group." [FP]

Louis XIV (Guillot fils, 1859)

Seedling of 'Général Jacqueminot' (HP).

"Bright red shaded maroon." [BJ] "Rich blood-color, large and full, form globular; a distinct and beautiful variety." [FP] "Intense dark crimson, velvety, medium-sized, full, very beautiful, though unfortunately the blossoms nod somewhat, weak growth." [N] "Vigorous…intense red, nuanced poppy-red." [S] "Many varieties that are quite second-rate in respect of habit are grown for the sake of some peculiar quality, and a good example of this is 'Louis XIV', which is so exquisitely beautiful, 'when you can catch it,' that the amateur who loves high quality will be content and happy to have its half dozen flowers, while other varieties, not altogether wanting in quality, are producing their flowers by the hundred." [Hd] "Good fragrance…3×3 [ft; ca. 9×9 dm]." [B] King Louis XIV, the Sun King; lived 1643-1715.

Louis Calla (E. Verdier, 1885)

"Vigorous bush with erect canes; leaves very large, rounded, dark green; blossoms large, full, plump; color, scarlet purple red nuanced poppy and marbled whitish." [JR9/178]

Louis Donadine (Gonod, 1887)

Seedling of 'Duhamel-Domonceau' (HP).

"Very vigorous, canes upright, strong; leaves of five leaflets, dark green, the odd one very long, stem strong; flower large, full, well formed; color, deep velvety maroon red, nuanced flame red; very remontant, very fragrant." [JR11/163]

[Louis Gulino] (Guillot père, 1859)

Seedling of 'Général Jacqueminot' (HP).

"Velvety-maroon, fine." [FP] "Very fragrant...reblooms freely." [JDR59/28] "Vigorous bush, flower medium-sized, nearly full, red mixed with purple, new coloration." [l'H59/109]

Louis Lille (Dubreuil, 1887)

From 'Baronne Adolphe de Rothschild' (HP) × 'Firebrand' (HP).

"Bush vigorous but stocky with ample beautiful dark green foliage; flower very large, full, cupped, bright red with light flame reflections." [JR11/184]

Louis Noisette (Ducher, 1865)

"Flowers full, globular, beautiful carmine pink; like those of 'Baronne Prévost'." [l'H65/340] "Growth vigorous, flower large, full, in a cluster; carmine-pink." [S]

Louis Philippe Albert d'Orléans (E. Verdier, 1884)

"Vigorous with upright light green canes; thorns unequal, short and hooked, pink; leaves composed of 3-5 leaflets, large, rounded, somber green, with irregular slightly deep serrations; flowers large, full, very well formed, bright cerise red nuanced and illuminated purplish scarlet grenadine." [JR8/165]

Louis Rollet (Gonod, 1886)

"Extra vigorous, notable for its growth, with red wood, large thorns of the same color, leaves with five large leaflets; in Spring, the foliage is as red as that of a Coleus; flower large, full, purplish red, very remontant." [JR10/148]

Louis Van Houtte (Lacharme, 1869)

Seedling of 'Général Jacqueminot' (HP).

"A new rose...quite remontant...'vigorous, with very large flowers, full, beautiful Centifolia form, fiery red and amaranth, bordered with blackish crimson, shaded a blue resembling that in a rainbow'." [R-H69] "Velvety crimson; mottled and shaded with violet-purple, flowers very large, full, and cupped, a superb rose; habit vigorous." [JC] "Reddish scarlet and amaranth, the circumference blackish crimson, large, full, and of fine globular form; large foliage, fewer thorns than most other dark roses, highly perfumed. This is a tender sort, but it is very free blooming, and decidedly the finest crimson yet sent out." [EL] "Color at its most perfect in Summer." [JR28/11] "Of weak growth and small foliage: not much injured by mildew, but suffers from orange fungus and rain and 'burns' in hot weather. The blooms will only come fine if strong shoots are produced...a fine well-built bloom when you get it, with stout petals, high centre, fine globular outline, full size and dark, sometimes rather dull, colour. The flowers being heavy and the wood weak, flowering shoots...should be staked when the bud is formed. The lasting powers of the blooms are particularly good...a respectable bloom even on strong shoots is a rarity: but many others grow it well and esteem it highly." [F-M2] "Grown mainly for show purposes, very sweet." [Wr] "Vigorous; branches dark green; thorns somewhat numerous; flower large, full...one of the best in commerce." [S] "Medium-sized canes, which branch; bark smooth, light green, slightly reddish, with an occasional evenly-sized reddish thorns which are short and tapered. Leaves glossy, light green, 5-7 oval-acuminate finely dentate leaflets; leafstalk slender and slightly nodding. Flowers to four inches across [ca. 1 dm], full, well formed, globular, solitary on the branchlets, in clusters of two or three on vigorous canes; beautiful fiery red nuanced amaranth and bordered bluish crimson; outer petals large, center petals slightly smaller; flower stalk slender, longish. Calyx rounded. Beautiful variety, of magnificent coloration; hardy." [JF] "This variety sparked an act of rare probity which we are lucky to be able to report. Last September, at the Horticultural Exhibition, the jury have the top prize to one of Monsieur Guillot père's roses. That honorable breeder having heard that Monsieur Lacharme had one which was quite similar in color, which, upon comparison, he had recognized as the better rose, he withdrew his own rose [*from commerce*] even though it had taken first place, and instead advertised and sold his competitor's rose—'Louis Van Houtte'. Monsieur Guillot's conduct is above all praise." [l'H69/351] "Houtte (Louis Van).—Well-known Belgian horticulturist…his very large company propagated many plants. He published *Flore des Serres et Jardins de l'Europe*, a veritable plant museum including over 2,000 colored plates." [R-HC] Not to be confused with Granger's similarly-named carmine HP of 1863.

"Often it is said that great men have no homeland, that all countries have an equal share in them as all have profited by their efforts. Such is the case with Louis Van Houtte…Louis Van Houtte, who died at Ghent May 9, 1876, was born at Ypres on June 29, 1810 [*a footnote adds:* At that time, Ypres, as a consequence of the wars of the First Empire, was capital of the department of Lys. Thus, Louis Van Houtte was born in France, and, above all, was French in his heart. Further, he pursued part of his studies in France, where he lived for a great many years.] Very early in life, he showed a great aptitude for Science; and, after having spent two years at l'Institut Supérieur du Commerce, in Paris,…he went, while still young, to Brazil as a botanical explorer, where he spent nearly four years; later, he explored the western coast of Africa…Coming back to Belgium shortly thereafter, he was named director of the Brussels botanical garden. Meanwhile, a most distinguished Belgian naturalist, Alexandre Verschaffelt, determined the future of Louis Van Houtte by settling in

Ghent, where Van Houtte was. It was then that he took up decidedly the horticultural career which he followed so brilliantly…But Monsieur Van Houtte was not only a horticulturist and savant—he was also an artist in every sense of the word. All of his doings were marked by that special cachet which showed the grandeur of his concepts. The boldness of his enterprises astonished everyone; even his friends quailed. He founded at Ghent an establishment which today is unique, not only in extent, but also in concept and direction. At the side of the horticulturist was always found the artist, and the one sometimes got the better of the other…Such labors were still not enough for the powerful imagination of Monsieur Van Houtte, who added to an already considerable establishment a lithographic and chromolithographic print-shop, where aside from the numerous catalogs which, by their appearance and editing, were models of the sort, he printed the gigantic work, the *Flore des Serres et des Jardins de l'Europe*, which, alone, would be more than sufficient to establish his reputation and immortalize his name…In personal relationships, few men were as agreeable as Monsieur Van Houtte; his wide and varied knowledge, and his lively spirit, joined with his good will, made him one of the most charming storytellers. Always, with his upright nature, he detested lies, and was appalled at dissimulation and bad faith; if circumstances forced him to have anything to do with persons he could not respect, the relations were kept distant. But if he realized that he had made a mistake, he sometimes went to extremes in making it up to the person, a consequence of an extremely honest nature…'He was no more than ten years old when he lost his father. The considerable fortune of the family was shaken by the events of 1815. An energetic and courageous woman, the mother of Van Houtte tried nevertheless to continue the great enterprises of her husband; but—poorly helped and too trusting—she had the misfortune to see all her hopes dashed; her entire fortune was soon gone. The young Louis…was sent to Paris, to l'École Centrale du Commerce.' He would get up every day at 3 or 4 a.m., and would rarely leave his desk before ten at night…All in all, fatigue on the one hand, and the overstimulation native to his lively and impressionable nature on the other, joined to make the cruel illness which had long since undermined his health, and which put an end to his life...'Tuesday, the 9th of May, around 3, he felt a certain feeling of disquietude, and arose, speaking of the plants he loved so well, quite himself. Suddenly, he said with pain the name of one of his daughters—his hand clenched—his eyes closed. They thought it would pass, but, alas!, the great horticulturist was dead.' All the horticultural world feels the loss of one whom we can regard as the prince of 19th Century Horticulture." [R-H76]

Louise Cretté (Chambard, 1915)
From 'Frau Karl Druschki' (HP) × 'Climbing Kaiserin Auguste Viktoria' (Cl. HT).
"Snow-white, cream center; very large, full, fine form...Described...as being a grand exhibition rose of 'Frau Karl Druschki' type, with a slightly yellowish tint." [Th2] "Perfect form, opening well; some fragrance. Growth vigorous; almost thornless. One of the finest and largest white Roses and a decided improvement on 'Frau Karl Druschki'." [C-Ps29] "An almost continuous bloomer when once established." [C-Ps30]

[Louise d'Autriche] (Fontaine, 1857) trans., "Louise of Austria"
Sport of 'La Reine' (HP).
"Violet red." [JDR57/37] "Rose, large and full." [FP] "Very vigorous bush; flower large, full; color, bishop's violet." [S]

Louise Peyronny (Lacharme, 1844) syn., 'Lœlia'
Supposedly a seedling of 'La Reine' (unlikely due to the time factor).
"Silvery rose." [EL] "Bright pink; finer than 'La Reine'." [HstXI:224] "Very large, full; color, deep pink shaded carmine." [S] "Satin rose, globular, fine bold petal, a handsome rose; habit moderate." [JC] "Brilliant rose color—globular—a very handsome variety...a free opener, this extremely handsome new variety will be a great acquisition to the north of England...It is of a bright rose color with petals slightly incurved, of great

size and substance…remarkably hardy, very fragrant." [C] "[*Resembling*] a large gown in disorder." [VH62/92] "Charming…opens well in all seasons." [R8] "Or great beauty, though scarcely so vigorous as 'La Reine'." [FP] "Monsieur François Lacharme, the eminent *rosiériste* of Lyon, died last November 5th [*1887*]. Lacharme…was born at St.-Didier-sur-Chalaronne (Ain) the 23rd of January, 1817. His father was a local farmer, and wanted him to follow in that career; but, despite this, loving flowers and particularly roses in his childhood, and learning horticulture from his father, he was placed in 1836 in the nursery firm of Monsieur Poncet…He would often visit the gardens of Monsieur Plantier…In 1840, Monsieur Plantier offered to sell him his establishment in Lyon. He accepted, and, aided by Plantier's counsel, began to sow rose seed." [JR11/177] "Lacharme astonished the rosarians with the splendid and enormous 'Louise Peyronny'." [JR12/52] "We have only this to add, that, while being honest and loyal, he was at the same time modest to the extreme; indeed, he did not believe that it was his place to perpetuate his name by giving it to any of his varieties…Rosarians will not forget him, and are going to honor his memory by erecting on his grave a lasting token of their sympathy and friendship." [JR12/54]

Lucien Duranthon (Bonnaire, 1893)
"Extra vigorous bush with stiff, upright canes, thornless, beautiful foliage; flower large, full, form of 'Baronne Adolphe de Rothschild'; color, pure carmine red, very bright, a color unique in the sort; continuous bloom; very good for cutting and forcing." [JR17/147]

Lyonfarbige Druschki (Sangerhausen, 1928) trans., "Lyon[-Rose] Colored Druschki"
From 'Frau Karl Druschki' (HP) × 'Lyon-Rose' (Pernetiana).
"Pink on yellow, large, full, light scent, medium height." [Sn]

Lyonnais (Lacharme, 1871) trans., "Lyon-ish"
Seedling of 'Victor Verdier' (HP).
"Satin rose, colour clear and beautiful, flowers cupped, very large and full; a very distinct and superb rose, habit vigorous." [JC] "Pink, with deeper centre, fades quickly; a coarse, inferior sort." [EL] "Bush vigorous; flower very large, full, Centifolia-form; color, delicate pink, center brighter." [S]

M.H. Walsh (A. Dickson, 1905)
"Beautiful velvety crimson...especially notable during the autumn-tide." [JR29/153] "This Rose is apt to be rather too late in flowering to come in as a useful exhibition variety, but in a very early season it would be wanted. Velvety crimson in colour, it is a first-rate autumnal, fairly vigorous grower, and fragrant, needs shading as it is apt to burn." [F-M] M.H. Walsh, the rose-breeder, most of whose work was on Wichuraianas.

Mabel Morrison (Broughton, 1878)
Sport of 'Baronne Adolphe de Rothschild' (HP).
"Flesh white, changing to pure white, in the autumn it is sometimes tinged with pink; semi-double, cup-shaped flowers...not so full as we would like, it is yet a very useful garden rose, and occasionally it is good enough for exhibition." [EL] "In every way, an extra fine white rose. Blooms in full clusters. Buds handsome. Foliage elegant. Delicate perfume." [Dr] "Immaculate bloom and unsurpassed foliage." [L] "Large, loosely-filled, pure white to pale pink. Growths sturdy, very prickly, erect." [Hn] "Vigorous, hardy." [S] "4×3 [ft; ca. 1.25×1 m]." [B] "This new rose was obtained by Mr. Joseph Broughton, a Leicester florist." [JR2/65]

Madeleine Nonin
Listed as 'Mlle. Madeleine Nonin'.

Magna Charta (W. Paul, 1876)
"Bright pink, suffused with carmine, very large, full, of good form, habit erect, growth vigorous; magnificent foliage; flowers produced in more than usual abundance for so fine a variety." [P1] "Fresh rose-pink."

[ARA29/96] "Imbricated." [Cx] "Globular; foliage and wood light green; numerous, dark spines. A fragrant, excellent variety." [EL] "Very big, full, and cupped; held upright; the foliage is large and a handsome glossy dark green...very remontant." [S] "Very large flower...rough and irregular, very full and showy...a very bad autumnal." [F-M2] "A new English rose possessing all the necessary qualifications to make a rose of the first order; it is luxuriant, robust, and very floriferous." [JR1/6/9] "Probably the hardiest pink variety...exceptionally fine during its blooming period." [ARA34/77] "Very fragrant...tall...50 [*blossoms*] per season." [ARA21/90] "To 10 [ft; ca. 3 m]...some rebloom." [HRG] "This splendid variety...merits a place of honor in the most choice collection." [JR2/40]

Magnolija (Kosteckij, 1940) trans., "Magnolia"
"White, large, full, medium height." [Sn]

Maharajah (B.R. Cant, 1904)
"Rich crimson, bright golden anthers; bush." [NRS18/135] "Deep red, large, not very full, medium scent, tall." [Sn] "Deep velvety crimson.— Vigorous.—Pillar.—Semi-single." [Cat12]

Marchioness of Exeter (Laxton/G. Paul, 1877)
Seedling of 'Jules Margottin' (HP).
"Cherry-rose, fragrant." [EL] "Beautiful light bright pink." [JR1/12/13] "Beautiful rose with recurved petals; color, pale pink nuanced cherry pink; very well formed, semi-globular...of the 'Annie Laxton' [*HP, Laxton, 1869, pink*] sort." [S]

Marchioness of Londonderry (A. Dickson, 1893)
Possibly a seedling of 'Baronne Adolphe de Rothschild' (HP).
"Large, beautiful form, borne on erect stalks, ivory-white tinted with rose; strong, free, fragrant." [Hn] "Often a very unpleasant shade of white." [J] "Of great substance. Magnificent in form and size, but rather dull in colour when expanded." [P1] "Globular." [DO] "Full, cupped, fragrant; vigorous; stocky." [Cx] "Not free-flowering enough for general cultivation...very

large and smooth and of great substance, on very stout stems, but they do not open well, and the colour, which is a greyish-white, is not pleasing...of no use as an autumnal." [F-M2] "'This rose is superb' say Messieurs Dickson and Sons, 'and incontestably one of the most beautiful we have ever grown. It is quite certain that it takes a premier place in the world of Roses. The flowers are of an extraordinary size, of perfect form, and borne on firm and upright stems. The colour is a very pure ivory-white; the petals are large, thick, substantial, and reflexed. The vigorous bush is clothed in very thick and handsome foliage, and the flowers have their share of perfume'." [JR17/85] "The blossom is lightly perfumed." [JR23/105] "The foliage is fine and free from mildew." [F-M2] "The best white HP that we have." [JR22/106]

Marchioness of Lorne (W. Paul, 1889)
"Fulgent rose colour, full, finely cupped. The blossoms are freely produced throughout the season, and they are deliciously fragrant." [P1] "Crimson." [LS] "Vivid carmine...large, sweet." [TW] "Rich rose-colour, cup-shaped, double and deep." [Dr] "This beautiful rose, dedicated by special permission of Her Majesty Princesse Louise...produces extremely bright pink flowers, which are tinted at the center with bright carmine. The flowers are large, full, and well formed; petals, large; buds, pretty. Above all, the variety is notable for its continuous bloom; each branch bears a bud." [JR13/70] "1.5 metres [ca. 4.5 ft]." [G]

Margaret Dickson (A. Dickson, 1891)
From 'Lady Mary Fitzwilliam' (HT) × 'Merveille de Lyon' (HP).
"White, with pale flesh centres; large shell-like petals of good substance. Form good, foliage handsome." [P1] "Large, rather flat, blush-white flowers." [OM] "Long petals forming a good point...a poor autumnal." [F-M2] "It is full and magnificent in form; its growth is very vigorous; its stalk is replete with very strong thorns; its foliage is very large and of a handsome dark green. This rose is, without a doubt, the best introduction of the last six years." [JR15/84] "Vigorous in growth, with fine foliage

sadly liable…to mildew." [F-M2] "Should not be too closely pruned; very large, and strong grower." [DO]

Margaret Haywood (Haywood, 1890)
Sport of 'Mme. Clémence Joigneaux' (HP)
"Brilliant pink." [Ÿ] "Light pink, very large, full, tall." [Sn]

Marguerite Brassac (Brassac, 1874)
"Purplish crimson. One of the best Roses grown; very fragrant." [H] "Petals very large, well rounded, deep velvety carmine." [JR3/27] "Very smooth and even in form." [JC] "Growth very vigorous; flower large, full, well formed; petals large, color, deep velvety carmine; magnificent exhibition rose." [S] Considered by some to be synonymous with 'Charles Lefebvre'.

Marguerite de Roman (Schwartz, 1882)
"Vigorous bush, having the look of 'Mlle. Eugénie Verdier'; canes upright and strong; foliage light green; flower very large, well formed, flesh white with flesh pink center; plant effective; freely remontant." [JR6/148]

Marguerite Guillard (Chambard, 1915)
Sport of 'Frau Karl Druschki' (HP).
"A sport from 'Frau Karl Druschki' and similar except that it is absolutely thornless, has superior foliage, and a mild but distinct perfume…Flower lasts longer after being cut although perhaps a trifle smaller. Blooms almost the entire year in Southern California and is in full bloom in December." [Capt28] "5×4 [ft; ca. 1.5×1.25 m]." [B] "Fair…not so good as others." [ARA18/116] "I like it very much." [ARA34/77]

Marguerite Jamain (Jamain, 1873)
"Vigorous bush; flower large, very full; color, very fresh flesh pink." [S]

Marguerite Lecureaux (Cherpin, 1853)
Seemingly a sport of 'Géant des Batailles' (HP).
"Flowers medium sized, full, bright red plumed white." [l'H54/14]
"Sometimes, in the Spring, striped with a single white line down the middle of each petal. Of little merit due to its inconstancy." [l'H56/250] "A striped variety of 'Géant des Batailles'. Its canes are frailer, its foliage thinner and more dentate, and its blossoms slightly less full…We first saw it in a little garden in 1846 or 1847…We began to propagate it in 1849, as we wanted to be certain of the permanence of the stripe characteristic, which only occurs during the first bloom, up to July. We must add quickly that this variety has already given us two others…[A] very strong Provins perfume throughout the season." [JDR54/10] "Not very vigorous, and inconstant in its striping, as are all striped roses…It is nevertheless one of the best varieties for bedding, as, striped or not, its flowers come all year." [JDR56/48]

Marie Baumann (Baumann, 1863) syn., 'Mme. Alphonse Lavallée'
From 'Général Jacqueminot' (HP) × 'Victor Verdier' (HP).
"Delicate carmine." [LS] "Rich carmine-crimson, flowers large and of exquisite form, perfectly full, and very beautiful; habit vigorous." [JC] "A Rose of great reputation. The growth as a cutback cannot be called more than fair, and the foliage is not large. The wood is weak and pliable, and the flowering shoots of dwarfs must be staked, as the stem is not stiff enough to support a heavy bloom. This habit much detracts from the appearance of the flowers while on the plant, as they generally fall over with their faces to the ground. Fragrant, not much injured by rain, but decidedly liable to mildew. It is especially noted as one of the most reliable of Roses, for the blooms nearly always come good and well shaped, semi-globular, without high centre. Free blooming and a good autumnal, fair in petal, good in centre, of large size and fair lasting qualities, and particularly excellent in smoothness and regularity. More often good than 'Alfred Colomb', which is sometimes very like it in shape and colour, though the

habits of the plants are widely different. Does fairly as a standard, but not so well on the manetti[i], must be highly cultivated, and requires rich soil. Not a hardy sort of strong constitution, but it has been for many years, and appears likely to continue to be, one of the most popular of exhibition Roses, though it does not seem too succeed in the hot summers of America." [F-M2]

Marie Boissée (Oger, 1864)
"Blush-white in opening, passing to pure white when expanded; flowers double and cup-shaped; habit vigorous; very free-flowering." [FP] "Flower large, full, very beautiful form." [S]

Marie Louise Pernet (Pernet père, 1876)
Seedling of 'Baronne Adolphe de Rothschild' (HP).
"Deep rose." [EL] "Moderate growth...flower large, full, cupped; color, very bright pink." [S]

Marie Menudel (Barbier, 1927)
"Bud and flower very large, double, full, open, lasting, moderate fragrance, rose-pink tinted salmon, borne singly on long, strong stem. Foliage sufficient, large, rich green, leathery, disease-resistant. Few thorns. Growth very vigorous, upright; free and continuous bloomer." [ARA28/239]

Marie Pochin
Listed as 'Mary Pochin'.

Marie Rady
Listed as 'Mlle. Marie Rady'.

Marquise Boccella
Listed as a Damask Perpetual. See also 'Jacques Cartier' (DP).

Marquise de Castellane (Pernet père, 1869)
Seedling of 'Jules Margottin' (HP).
"Clear cherry-rose. Stout, bold, and free-flowering." [H] "Carmine-rose, a bright and permanent shade, very large, very full, not fragrant but effective, does not bloom until late—a valuable sort for exhibition purposes. Does not propagate from cuttings." [EL] "Beautiful bright rose, very large and full; form perfect; blooms freely; growth robust. One of the best." [P1] "Deep cerise, colour clear and good, flowers large, circular and full; a superb rose." [JC] "Growth vigorous, hardy, floriferous...flower very large, full, scentless, globular, pointed center; color, bright pink; very good to force." [S] "Of robust habit; sometimes a very strong grower with thick long thorny shoots and fine foliage, but capricious in this matter, and rather difficult to please. Sometimes it will grow well in light soil, but at any rate it will be of little use if it does not make strong growth. The blooms are frequently of uneven shape, occasionally rough and coarse, but they are large, and effective when they come good with a pointed centre. Not liable to mildew or much injured by rain, early, and free-flowering if it grows well. Not very good in lasting qualities, but quite noted as an autumnal, fine large blooms being frequently produced even till quite late in the season." [F-M2]

Marquise de Gibot (de Sansal, 1868)
"Pale rose, flowers large, full, and globular; a fine and distinct rose." [JC] "Growth very vigorous; foliage beautiful bright dark green, reddish beneath; flower large, full, plump, very floriferous; color, pale pink, bright pink rebloom." [S]

Marquise de Mortemart (Liabaud, 1868)
Seedling of 'Jules Margottin' (HP).
"Blush, well formed. A fine rose of delicate habit." [EL] "Blush-white, centre pale flesh, colour delicate and beautiful, petals smooth and even, flowers large and cupped; an exquisite rose, and one of the best light varieties...vigorous." [JC] "Growth vigorous; flower large, full, very well

formed, very pretty delicate pink; nice scent; reminiscent of 'Duchesse de Sutherland', and much resembles 'Souvenir de la Malmaison'." [S]

Marquise de Verdun (Oger, 1868)
"Growth vigorous; flower large, full, globular; color, bright carmine pink." [S]

Marshall P. Wilder (Ellwanger & Barry, 1885)
Seedling of 'Général Jacqueminot' (HP).
"Studied for three years [*before being released to commerce*]...very vigorous, handsome foliage, large flowers tending towards the globular, full, well-formed; cherry-carmine...this is a perfected 'Alfred Colomb'." [JR8/29] "A very handsome rose with extra-large, full flowers of deep dark red. Sufficient healthy foliage...most bloom in spring, a little in fall...about 71 [*blossoms per season*]." [ARA21/89] "Expanded form, well 'built'; color, cherry-red mixed with carmine...in wood, foliage, and flower-form much like 'Alfred Colomb', but superior; in flowering, it blooms much longer than do other remontant roses." [S] "Practically duplicates 'Alfred Colomb', but is a better grower generally." [ARA34/79] "Rich foliage; flowers, enormous and semi-globular, full, of a very handsome outline...exquisite scent. It is one of the best autumnals." [JR16/37] Marshall P. Wilder, quondam president of the Massachusetts Horticultural Society.

Martin Liebau (Kiese, 1930)
"Pink, large, full, medium scent, medium height." [Sn]

Mary Corelly (Prince, 1901)
"Deep salmon, medium size, full, tall." [Sn]

Mary Pochin (Pochin/Cranston, 1881)
"Of moderate vigor; color, bright red tinted velvety crimson; flower of medium size, well formed, with large smooth petals." [S]

Maurice Bernardin (Granger, 1861) syn., 'Ferdinand de Lesseps', 'Souvenir de l'Exposition de Brie-Comte-Robert'
Seedling of 'Général Jacqueminot' (HP).
"Bright crimson, large, moderately full; a good free-flowering sort, generally coming in clusters." [EL] "Blooms come pretty well, of good semi-globular shape and fair general qualities...a fair average crimson rose." [F-M2] "Bright cherry crimson colour." [SBP] "Globular with high centre...sweetly fragrant." [W/Hn] "Vermilion, large, full, and of fine form; growth vigorous." [P1] "Moderate [*in growth*], rich crimson shaded with violet; colour superb...a splendid Rose in suitable localities." [WD] "Good growth and foliage, rather liable to mildew." [F-M2] "Growth very vigorous; foliage dark green; flowers large, well imbricated, in clusters, beautiful light vermilion red; very effective plant." [l'H61/166] "One of the best of its color." [S] "Quite first-rate." [P2]

Maurice Lepelletier (Moreau-Robert, 1868)
"Bright pink." [Ÿ] "Growth vigorous; flower large, full; globular; color, vermilion red." [S]

Maxime de La Rocheterie (Vigneron, 1871)
Seedling of 'Victor Verdier' (HP).
"Growth vigorous; flower large, full; color, velvety blackish purple red." [S] "Monsieur Maxime de La Rocheterie, president of the *Société d'Horticulture d'Orléans et du Loiret*." [JR9/168]

Mère de St. Louis (Lacharme, 1851) trans., "Mother of St. Louis"
Seedling of 'La Reine' (HP).
"A waxy flesh-color, and, though not very full, is distinct and beautiful." [FP] "Pink, medium size." [EL] "A beautiful and important prize; its large, nearly full, flowers pass from white to very delicate pink." [l'H51/173] "A novel coloration." [VH51/112]

Merrie England (Harkness, 1897)
Sport of 'Heinrich Schultheis' (HP).
"Pink striped silvery." [LS] "Crimson, blush; vigorous...early, striped."
[TW]

Merveille de Lyon (Pernet père, 1882) trans., "Lyon Marvel"
From 'Baronne Adolphe de Rothschild' (HP) × 'Safrano' (T).
"Large, closely filled, cup-like form, white with a pink centre, becoming
pink with age. Growth erect, sturdy." [Hn] "Pure white, sometimes
washed with satin-rose, very large, full, and cupped." [P1] "White, center
slightly peach." [ARA17/29] "Generally of a lovely pure white colour, but
comes sometimes rather pink in the autumn...A grand rose of the largest
size...weak in the centre." [F-M2] "Uni-blossomed strong stems...a
handsome white, tinted flesh pink." [JR31/105] "Practically scentless."
[ARA34/76] "No scent." [JR9/41] "Monster size." [J] "Does not last. No
fall bloom...Prune long. Best pegged down." [Th2] "Of 'Baroness
Rothschild' race...this race has a splendid hardy robust constitution." [F-
M2] "Sadly given to mildew." [K2] "Vigorous; heavy growth; numerous
thorns, not hooked; handsome light green foliage, thick on the bush;
flowers very large, full, perfectly cupped, and opening very well; well held;
attaining a size of about 4.5 inches [ca. 1.2 dm]. The blossom is a beautiful pure white with large petals which are well rounded and very fine,
lightly washed satin pink at the center. The flowers are always solitary, and
the plant is quite remontant." [JR6/149] "It resembles 'Mabel Morrison'
too much to please me." [JR7/156]

Meyerbeer (E. Verdier, 1867)
"Flowers very large, full; petals wavy, purple red nuanced bright flame."
[l'H68/49] "Growth vigorous." [S] Giacomo Meyerbeer, German composer; lived 1791-1864.

Michel-Ange (Oger, 1863)
"Flower large, full; color, bright grenadine." [S] Michelangelo Buonarroti,
the great Italian artist; lived 1475-1564.

Michel Strogoff (Barault, 1882)

"Vigorous, branches upright, thorns remote, short, brown; leaves composed of 3-5 deeply toothed oval leaflets; flowers medium, full, well-formed, imbricated; unique color, slaty violet red, shaded crimson." [JR6/165]

Miller-Hayes (E. Verdier, 1873)

Seedling of 'Charles Lefebvre' (HP).

"Moderate growth; flower large, full; color, crimson red with brighter center, nuanced poppy." [S]

Miss Annie Crawford (Hall/Hammond, 1915)

"Light pink, very large, full, medium height." [Sn] "Vigorous-growing and an almost continuous bloomer in bright pink with deeper veins; sweetly perfumed. Blooms in clusters, but if disbudded, the remaining buds will attain a very large size. Has long stems, excellent for cutting. Specially adapted to form hedges, or as a mate to 'Gruss an Teplitz'." [C-Ps29] First developed circa 1907.

Miss Ethel Richardson (A. Dickson, 1897)

"Completely new and different from everything else we [*Dickson's*] have seen. Very vigorous and floriferous, with very large blossoms in a rather cone-like shape with the center extruding. Petals large, slightly folded back on themselves as if hemmed. Color, cream with a flesh center. Exhibition Rose." [JR21/68]

Miss Hassard (Turner, 1874)

Seedling of 'Marguerite de St.-Amand' (HP, de Sansal, 1864, pink).

"Rosy flesh, round, and full." [R7/534] "Delicate pinkish flesh, large, perhaps rather loose in shape; early to bloom and very sweet scented. Has quantities of strong thorns." [B&V] "Fine form, very sweet, free autumnal bloomer." [JC] "Many imperfect blooms." [EL] "Growth not very vigorous; canes feeble, with strong thorns; flower large, full, very beautiful form, well held; color, delicate flesh; fragrant; one of the hardiest; early

bloom...Resembles 'Elisabeth Vigneron' and 'Duchesse de Vallombrosa'."
[S] "Of strong thorny growth, hardy, free blooming and a pretty pink
colour, but weak and loose in shape. A garden Rose, worthy of note as
being one of the earliest to bloom." [F-M3]

Miss House (House, 1838?)
"Satiny white." [LS] Further efforts to find out more about this elusive
variety have been fruitless.

Mistress Elliot
Listed as 'Mrs. Elliot'.

Mlle. Annie Wood (C. Verdier and/or E. Verdier, 1866) syn., 'Annie Wood'
"Brilliant crimson-scarlet, flowers large and full, imbricated; a first-rate
rose; habit free." [JC] "Beautiful clear red, very large, full, and of excellent
form; growth vigorous." [P1] "Very vigorous, having reddish canes with
strong, straight thorns of the same color as the canes; foliage large and
dark green; the blossom is large and sometimes measures four inches
across [ca. 1 dm], very full, perfectly imbricated; color, a beautiful light
red." [S] "Flower very large, full, poppy-red with velvety reflections."
[JR1/2/7, as a rose having certain affinities with 'Général Jacqueminot']
"Bright crimson with a shade of vermilion; a good autumnal rose." [EL]
"Here we have a Rose with manners and customs (fortunately) peculiar to
itself. It is a fine strong grower, with fair foliage, liable to mildew and
orange fungus, but not much injured by rain. A great quantity of buds
form on each stem: the top bud of all, which one would naturally reserve,
is nearly always cracked, hollow, and distorted before it is much bigger
than a thimble, and sometimes has a great green pip in the centre. You
may search for the best-shaped bud, and do away with all others for its
sake. Even then, nine out of ten buds will show a great eye before they are
more than half expanded, and the tenth will do it soon after being cut.
You make up your mind to discard the sort altogether: but, just at the
close of the season, a beautiful bloom makes its appearance on a shoot you

had not noticed, with brilliant colour, full size, delightful fragrance, and good imbricated shape—a lovely Rose: and the plants are spared to serve you just the same trick another season...It seems impossible to avoid sooner or later bringing in the time-honoured anecdote of the traveller who, describing the 'manners and customs' of some native tribes he had been visiting, was constrained to dismiss one of them with the terse remark, 'manners none—customs disgusting.' If it be possible to say anything so bad of a Rose, I am doubtful whether a better example than 'Annie Wood' can be found." [F-M3]

Mlle. Berthe Lévêque (Céchet père/Lévêque, 1865)

"Vigorous, even very vigorous, with strong upright canes; leaves very large (I have measured them at up to 6.5 inches [ca. 1.65 dm]), rough to the touch, ordinarily having five leaflets, which are oval-elongate, slightly but regularly dentate; leafstalk prickly; stipules foliate and adnate-subulate; flowers about 2.5 inches across [ca. 6.5 cm], flesh white changing to pink. Messrs. Ketten [*the nurserymen*] find that this variety resembles 'Caroline de Sansal'...dedicated to the daughter of Monsieur Levêque, the well-known *rosiériste* of Ivry-sur-Seine." [JR10/36]

Mlle. Bonnaire (Pernet père, 1859)

"White, rosy-centre, large, full, and of exquisite form; one of the best." [FP] "Pure white, centre shaded palest flesh; flowers of medium size, full and well formed; a beautiful free blooming and distinct rose; habit free." [JC] "Closely resembles 'Mme. Noman', it is difficult to see any points of difference by which one may be distinguished from the other." [EL] "Vigorous bush, flowers 10-11 cm across [ca. 4 inches]." [l'H59/138] "Moderate growth; flower large, full; color, pure white, sometimes pink at the center. The first white HP." [S]

Mlle. Elisabeth de La Rocheterie (Vigneron, 1881)

"Flesh pink." [Ÿ] "Vigorous, canes large and upright, beautiful dark green foliage, thorns chestnut brown, somewhat numerous, flower very large, full, well-formed, beautiful delicate pink, outside of the petals silvery, well held, quite remontant." [JR5/185]

Mlle. Elise Chabrier (Gautreau/S. Cochet, 1867) syn., 'Mlle. Louise Chabrier'
"Growth vigorous; flower large, full, well formed; color, delicate pink; petal edged satiny blush white." [S]

Mlle. Eugénie Verdier (Guillot fils, 1859)
Seedling of 'Victor Verdier' (HP).
"Very intense flesh." [Ÿ] "Flower medium-sized, full; color, blush-pink." [S] "Large, globular, bright flesh pink, center darker." [JR3/27] "Pearly-white with the palest flesh centre, flowers of moderate size, cupped, and finely formed; distinct and very beautiful." [JC] "Silvery-pink, tinged with fawn; a lovely shade; fine in the bud. One of the best of the type." [EL] "Bright flesh-coloured rose, the reverse of the petals silvery white, very large and full, of fine form and habit; growth robust…One of the best." [P1] "Of 'Victor Verdier' race, with all the manners and customs of the family, and of moderate growth. Of large size, and beautiful and attractive colour, which might be called silvery pink, but not of very good lasting qualities, the centre being rather weak, and the form soon lost. Very free blooming, and an excellent autumnal. A great favorite in America." [F-M2] "Growth vigorous; canes pretty strong, erect; bark smooth, pale green, armed with occasional thorns, which are blackish, hooked, and sharp. Leaves light green, divided into 3 or 5 leaflets, which are oval, pointed, and dentate; petiole slender, bearing two to three little prickles. Flowers about four inches across [ca. 1 dm], quite full, widely cupped, usually solitary; color, light pink, brighter at the center, with silvery reflections; outer petals large, inner ones smaller; flower stem short, pretty thick, and glabrous. Ovary pear-shaped; sepals leaf-like. Hardy, but nevertheless suffers from frost in the coldest Winters." [JF]

Mlle. Gabrielle de Peyronny (Lacharme, 1863)
"Vigorous bush; flowers large, full, well formed, fiery red nuanced violet towards the center." [l'H64/63]

Mlle. Grévy
Listed as 'Mlle. Jules Grévy'.

Mlle. Hélène Croissandeau (Vigneron, 1882)
Seedling of 'Victor Verdier' (HP).
"Velvety pink." [Ÿ] "Vigorous, big-wooded, upright, few thorns, beautiful dark green foliage, very large elongated bud, flower enormous, a beautiful delicate color, center brighter, held perfectly, quite remontant." [JR6/164]
"From 'Victor Verdier', but more vigorous." [S]

Mlle. Hélène Michel (Vigneron, 1883)
"Pink." [Ÿ] "Very vigorous, upright, thorns chestnut brown, fairly numerous, foliage light green, flower large, full, well-formed, beautiful deep red, center brighter, exterior petals velvety, free bloomer." [JR7/170]

Mlle. Honorine Duboc (Duboc, 1894)
"Winy pink." [Ÿ] "Vigorous, handsome brownish green foliage; the flowers are solitary, very large, full, very well formed, beautiful bright pink, and very fragrant. Reblooms freely...dedicated to...the daughter of its raiser." [JR18/120]

Mlle. Jules Grévy (Gautreau, 1879) syn., 'Mlle. Grévy'
Seedling of 'Duhamel-Dumonceau' (HP).
"Flower large, full, well formed; color, intense dark red, with velvety reflections...quite remontant." [S]

Mlle. Léonie Giessen (Lacharme, 1876)
"Growth vigorous; canes bushy, with long recurved thorns; flower large, full, Centifolia form; pink washed white." [S]

Mlle. Léonie Persin (Fontaine, 1861)
"Flower large; color, a frosty intense silvery pink." [S]

Mlle. Louise Chabrier
Listed as 'Mlle. Elise Chabrier'.

Mlle. Madeleine Nonin (Ducher, 1866) syn., 'Madeleine Nonin'
"Moderate growth; flower medium-sized, full, globular; color, pink with some salmon." [S]

Mlle. Marie Achard (Liabaud, 1896)
"Very vigorous with upright canes, ample dark green foliage; flower very large, cupped, delicate frosty pink." [JR20/147]

Mlle. Marie Chauvet (Besson, 1881)
Seedling of 'Baronne Adolphe de Rothschild' (HP).
"Deep rose." [EL] "Remontant...very well held." [JR5/117] "Very vigorous, canes upright, flowers very large, very full, very well formed, very fresh deep pink fading to pink, center darker." [JR5/172] One sometimes wonders if "very" is the most used word on rosarians' lips.

Mlle. Marie Closon (E. Verdier, 1882) syn., 'Mme. Marie Closon'
"Vigorous; canes upright, delicate green; thorns very numerous, unequal, upright, brown; leaves composed of five elongated leaflets with fairly regular dentations, and dark green; flowers medium-sized or large; very full and very well formed; color, very delicate and fresh pink, edged perfectly in white; very fragrant; very floriferous and remontant, nearly as much as a China." [JR6/165]

Mlle. Marie Dauvesse (Vigneron, 1859)
"Bright light pink." [LS] "Medium size, full, medium height." [Sn] "Vigorous bush, flowers large, full, beautiful light intense pink." [l'H59/138]

Mlle. Marie de la Villeboisnet (Trouillard, 1864)
"Delicate pink." [Ÿ] "Growth vigorous; flower large, full, very well formed; color, bright pink." [S]

Mlle. Marie Magat (Liabaud, 1889)
"Vigorous with upright canes, handsome dark green foliage...thorns pretty strong, sparse, reddish. Flower large, full, well-formed, brilliant light red, very elegant." [JR13/163]

Mlle. Marie Rady (Fontaine, 1865) syn., 'Marie Rady'
"Rich rose, flowers large and beautifully imbricated...vigorous." [JC] "Flower large, full; color, bright red, bordered and touched pink." [S] "Fine brilliant red, very large, full, and of perfect form, blooms freely; growth vigorous." [P1] "Vermilion-red shaded with crimson, large or very large, very full, of splendid globular form, very fragrant; it has more vermilion than 'Alfred Colomb', making it somewhat lighter and more dull; the shoots are armed with numerous red thorns, the foliage shows considerable lustre. There is no finer exhibition sort among the red roses, and were it as constant, it would be quite as valuable as 'Alfred Colomb' and 'Marie Baumann', varieties which bear it some considerable resemblance." [EL]

Mlle. Renée Denis (Chédane-Guinoisseau & Pajotin/Chédane, 1906)
From 'Margaret Dickson' (HP) × 'Paul Neyron' (HP).
"Very vigorous, beautiful light green foliage; bud long, nearly always solitary and borne on a long, strong stem; flowers very large, quite full, perfect form, cupped; petals very large, founded; color, ground of white, edge of petals strongly washed delicate pink, center very salmony...[V]ery remontant, opens well under all circumstances, very distinct." [JR30/167]

Mlle. Suzanne-Marie Rodocanachi (Lévêque, 1883)
Seedling of 'Victor Verdier' (HP).
"Growth vigorous; handsome ample dark green foliage; flower very large, full, globular, beautifully colored very delicate pink, clear, shaded, washed and bordered silvery white." [JR7/158] "Of 'Victor Verdier' race, and requiring therefore no description here of manners and customs. A noble Rose, the best of this family, and much esteemed in America. The colour

is not only bright, glowing, and most attractive, but also lasting, a most desirable attribute for a show Rose; it also retains its shape when cut better than any other Rose of the globular form that I know. The growth is good, it does well as a standard, is free-flowering and a good autumnal, and the blooms are very large and well formed, but nearly scentless. A Rose held in high estimation by exhibitors, and worthy of a name more suitable to British tongues and pencils." [F-M2]

Mlle. Thérèse Levet (Levet, 1866)
Seedling of 'Jules Margottin' (HP).
"Light carmine-rose, flowers large and full, beautifully imbricated; a superb rose...vigorous." [JC] "Salmon-rose, medium size, free blooming." [EL] "Has all the vigor and hardiness of its mother. Quite remontant. The wonderful flower is large, rounded, of perfect form, and very full. Its very fine coloration is a superb and brilliant bright pink, with the reverse of the petals being silvery." [S]

Mme. A. Labbley (Breeder unknown,-1885)
"Pink or lilac-y." [LS] "Blossom medium-sized, full; color, pink, shaded lilac." [S] Most probably an error for the pre-1846 hybrid Centifolia 'Mme. l'Abbey' (listed in *The Old Rose Adventurer*); the time came in Rose History when everyone thought "hybrid" always meant "Hybrid Perpetual"!

Mme. Albert Barbier (Barbier, 1925)
From 'Frau Karl Druschki' (HP) × ? a Pernetiana?
"An almost indescribable combination of fawn-yellow, white, and pinkish tints, with colors varying in different blooms. It is of medium growth and practically as free blooming as a Hybrid Tea." [ARA34/79] "Full, double, yellow flowers, shaded soft pink." [ARA29/96] "Pearly white at the edge of the petals, blending through flesh-pink to orange-yellow at the center, fading to soft flesh-pink: of very good lasting quality and slightly fragrant...abundant, leathery, disease-resistant foliage. Compact habit (3 feet [ca. 9 dm]); blooms continuously...the thorns are vicious." [ARA27/138]

"Foliage mildews." [ARA27/138] "As good color and free-flowering as any HT; very desirable [*in Massachusetts*]...delicate salmon-buff, with yellow suffusion and strong yellow at base of petals when first opening...Not profuse [*Massachusetts, again*]...Should be in every garden [*Pennsylvania*]...Neat, healthy, free-blooming [*Iowa*]...Healthy, even under adverse conditions [*Missouri*]...Cream, pink, apricot—but wood and growth poor [*Idaho*]...Very vigorous, upright...Stands rain well [*state of Washington*]...Does well in interior valleys [*California*]...Only 40 blooms the first year, but each was a real event [*California*]...high quality and delicate color." [PP28] "Bud very large; flower large, double, slightly fragrant, very lasting, salmon, tinted nankeen-yellow, darker center of orange-yellow and light rose (does not fade in sunlight in France), borne singly. Foliage abundant, light green, glossy, leathery, large, resistant to disease. Very vigorous, upright, bush; profuse, continuous bloom. Claimed to be a truly everblooming H.P. of remarkable color." [ARA26/183] "Is a gem...the inside of a half-opened bloom has the iridescence of a pearl...practically an everbloomer, but I would want it if it were not." [ARA29/49]

Mme. Alexandre Jullien (Vigneron, 1882)
Seedling of 'Elisabeth Vigneron' (HP).
"Satiny pink." [Ÿ] "Very vigorous, upright, many thorns, beautiful light green foliage, flower large, full, beautiful very fresh light pink, bud elongated, accompanied by leaflets, quite remontant, well held, a superb plant." [JR6/164] "Big-wooded." [S]

Mme. Alfred Leveau
Listed as 'Monsieur Alfred Leveau'.

Mme. Alice Dureau (Vigneron, 1867)
"Lilac pink." [Ÿ] "Belongs to 'La Reine' type. Rose color; much like the parent, but more shy in the autumn." [EL] "Flower large, full; beautiful light pink; a variety of the greatest merit. A rose which will always cause a stir at exhibitions." [S]

Mme. Alphonse Lavallée
Listed as 'Marie Baumann'.

Mme. Alphonse Seux (Liabaud, 1887)
Seedling of 'Victor Verdier' (HP).
"Very vigorous, branches upright; foliage glaucous green, with two pairs of leaflets; flower very large, full, delicate pink, sometimes bright pink."
[JR11/165]

Mme. Amélie Baltet (E. Verdier, 1878)
"Vigorous, with strong and upright delicate green canes; thorns remote, short, slightly recurved, yellowish; leaves composed of 5-7 leaflets, rounded, light green, regularly and finely toothed; flowers large, full, beautifully cupped; color, handsome satiny delicate pink of the greatest freshness, nuanced, silvery, superb." [JR2/187] "Well formed." [EL]

Mme. Anatole Leroy (L.-A. Leroy, 1892)
"Delicate pink." [Ÿ]

Mme. André Saint (Barbier, 1926)
From 'Frau Karl Druschki' (HP) × 'Bénédicte Seguin' (Pernetiana).
"Bud large, long-pointed, cream-white; flower large, double, full, cupped, moderately fragrant, mild-white passing to pure white with creamy or clear chamois center, borne on strong stem. Foliage sufficient, beautiful. No thorns. Growth vigorous, stocky. Bushy; profuse bloomer." [ARA28/239]

Mme. Antoine Rivoire (Liabaud, 1894)
"Very vigorous, canes erect, growth compact, leaves light green, flower extra large, cupped, very delicate frosty pink with carmine reflections."
[JR18/146] Not to be confused with the Hybrid Tea 'Antoine Rivoire'.

Mme. Apolline Foulon (Vigneron, 1882)
"Growth very vigorous; wood upright; few thorns; flower large, full, beautifully colored light salmon; petal reflexes lilac-y; good hold; very remontant; superb plant; novel coloration." [JR6/164]

Mme. Auguste van Geert (P. Robichon, 1861)

"Rosy-pink, striped white, very beautiful." [FP] "Flower medium-sized, full; color, bright deep red, striped sometimes." [S]

Mme. Baulot (Lévêque, 1885)

"Vigorous bush; foliage glaucous green; flower large, full, beautifully imbricated; beautiful coloration: very bright pink nuanced carmine; bloom abundant and continuous." [JR9/148]

Mme. Bellon (Pernet père, 1871)

"Brilliant cerise, flowers very large, and well formed, full high centre; a very fine rose; habit vigorous." [JC] "Moderate growth; flower very large, full, well held; color, delicate pink." [S]

Mme. Bernutz (Jamain, 1873)

"Vigorous bush; flower very large, full, cupped; color, satiny pink." [S]

Mme. Bertha Mackart (E. Verdier, 1883)

"Very vigorous, with very long, reddish-green, upright canes; thorns long, straight, unequal, very sharp, pink; leaves composed of 5-7 leaflets, oblong, dark green, regularly and deeply toothed; flowers extra large, full, impressively formed, cupped, globular; color, the most beautiful bright carmine pink, the freshest imaginable, reverse of petals silvery...[N]ot perfectly remontant, though it depends; its name is that of the wife of the celebrated Viennese painter." [JR7/171] "One of the best large-flowered kinds." [S]

Mme. Boll (Boll/Boyau, 1859; but see below)

Two parentages have been given: (1) an unspecified HP × 'Belle Fabert' (DP); or (2), 'Baronne Prévost' (HP) × 'Portlandica' (DP); we suspect the truth might be 'Baronne Prévost' (HP) × 'Belle Fabert' (DP).

"Beautiful intense pink; flower very large...vigorous." [Cx] "Bright pink; well formed." [BJ] "Opens well." [TW] "Foliage very good and ample, large flowers, flat, carmine-pink, very hardy, and a late bloomer." [JR4/60]

"Carmine-rose…very stout shoots." [EL] "Flower about three inches [ca. 7.5 cm]…it is said that this rose is descended from 'Baronne Prévost'. Such is possible, but it would have to be that variety crossed with a Portland…Mme. Boll is a lady rosarian of New York, originally from Switzerland." [JR10/37] "Very vigorous bush, blossom 10 cm [ca. 4 inches], very full, perfect form, slightly plump, beautiful bright pink; very fragrant." [l'H59/138] "'Mme. Boll' was raised by Monsieur J. Boyau père, horticulturist of Angers (successor to Monsieur Guérin), who secured the seedlings in 1856 from a cross between an HP and a Portland ('Belle Favert' [*sic*]), which latter the flowers resemble. This beautiful variety, released to commerce in 1859, was dedicated to the wife of a Swiss horticulturist, Monsieur Boll, who resided for a long time in America, where he was well known. The rose 'Mme. Boll' is of extraordinary growth, with large leaves carried on long stems. The usually solitary flowers are very large, full, of perfect form, and of a lively pink. The fragrance is quite penetrating." [JR6/168] "Vigorous; canes large and upright; bark light green, with numerous dark gray prickles which are unequal, small, straight, and pointed. Leaves large, light green, strongly nerved, divided into 3 or 5 oval-rounded, finely dentate leaflets; leafstalk slender, nodding, same color as the leaves. Flowers large, approaching four inches across [ca. 1 dm], very full, flat, somewhat rounded, generally solitary; color, a handsome intense pink; outer petals large, those of the center very numerous, muddled, unequal, and folded; flower stem short, stout, bristly, glandular. Calyx flared-tubular; sepals leaf-like. A variety of the first order." [JF] "Most perfect in all that constitutes a fine rose." [R8]

Mme. Boutin (Jamain/Carré, 1861) syn., 'Christina Nilson'
Seedling of 'Général Jacqueminot' (HP).
"Cherry-crimson, large and full." [FP] "Well formed, opening easily, beautiful bright cerise red, very fragrant." [l'H61/263] "Cerise, a beautiful clear colour; flowers very large and full, petals broad, even, and well disposed; an excellent rose of robust habit." [JC] "Growth vigorous; flower large, very full, cupped." [S] "A good garden rose." [EL]

Mme. Bruel
Listed as 'Mme. François Bruel'.

[Mme. Campbell d'Islay] (Baudry, 1849)
Sport of 'La Reine' (HP).
"Flesh." [LS] "Variety of the rose 'La Reine', enfixed by means of the graft by Monsieur Baudry, horticulturist at Avranches (Manche). The ground-color is the same as that of our beautiful rose 'La Reine', but it is enriched by carminy lilac stripes which give it a curious look." [M-V49/325] "We have already written…our opinion on the subject of these two roses ['*Mme. Campbell d'Islay*' and '*Triomphe de Valenciennes*']. These names will not be slow to disappear from the catalogs once we establish the same striping on a great quantity of specimens of the old and magnificent 'La Reine'. This bizarrerie takes nothing away from the merit of that beautiful variety, while meantime indeed adding nothing to it, as those interested have declared. We advise our subscribers to be on guard against the innovations upon which we can't relay favorable opinions; it is known that our editorship only favors real improvements—such are the inclinations of his opinion—which he never hesitates to make known—about anything which has the cachet of charlatanism." [M-V50/215]

Mme. Cécile Morand (Corbœuf-Marsault, 1890)
"Moderately vigorous, flower large, very full, very well formed; color, deep carmine red, reverse of petals silvery; very floriferous." [JR14/178]

Mme. Céline Touvais (Touvais, 1859)
"Flower large, full, peony-shape; color, bright pink." [S] "Very vigorous bush, flowers 12 cm across [ca. 4¼ inches], full, sparkling intense pink." [l'H59/138]

Mme. César Brunier (Bernaix, 1887)
"Bush with strong, upright growth bristling with numerous unequal thorns all mixed together; leaves, five relatively short leaflets which are obtuse-acuminate and keel-shaped; blossom well-formed, very double,

with an elegant, strong scent; not hollow at the center; opening well; upright, borne on a strong stem; 1, 2, or 3 at the tip of the cane; outer petals reflexed, curled at the edge; center petals more muddled, unequal, all colored China pink, satiny and bright; bud oval, long at the moment of expansion. Very profuse, amply double, uncommon coloration, elegant Centifolia perfume." [JR11/152]

Mme. Charles Crapelet (Fontaine, 1859)
"Bright cerise frosted lilac and currant red." [JR3/27] "Flower large, full, very well formed; color, cerise shaded satiny pink." [S] "Rosy scarlet, often veined with lilac, large and full; form cupped; growth vigorous." [P1] "Rosy-carmine, large smooth petals, exquisitely formed and beautifully disposed…[H]abit free." [JC] "Very vigorous, branches upright, flower four or so inches across [ca. 1 dm], cherry red nuanced lilac." [JDR59/43] "Fragrant and good; wood armed with numerous thorns." [EL] "Canes with green bark; thorns numerous, small, unequal; leaves of three and five leaflets, large and rugose; petiole prickly; flower to three inches across [ca. 7.5 cm], solitary, well formed, often cupped and showing the stamens; color, cerise red. This variety is certainly not perfect, but is nevertheless much appreciated in the garden due to its vigor and hardiness; what is more, it is very fragrant and well held, things which hardly detract from a rose! Prune to 4 to 6 buds." [JR10/139] "Very good at its best, as a smooth refined show Rose of the popular imbricated shape. Best as a maiden, being rather a weak grower, and liable to mildew, but not soon spoiled by rain, and a sort which well repays high cultivation…[P]robably best in a cool season. Of capital form, very smooth, regular, and full, of good lasting quality and fair size. Not a free bloomer or a good autumnal, but though never of strong or hardy constitution…it cannot…be suspected of having deteriorated." [F-M2]

Mme. Charles Druschki
Listed as 'Frau Karl Druschki'.

Mme. Charles Meurice (Meurice de St.-Quentin/Lévêque, 1878)
"Maroon, nuanced." [Ÿ] "Growth very vigorous; foliage glossy light green; flower large, full, well formed; color, purple red, very dark, velvety, blackish; very beautiful. This is one of the darkest roses we have seen to date." [JR2/166]

Mme. Charles Montigny (Corbœuf-Marsault, 1900)
From 'Prince Camille de Rohan' (HP) × 'Éclair' (HP).
"Red, large, full, tall." [Sn] "Vigorous bush, well-branched; flower large, full, very well formed; bud conical; color, blackish red, nuanced velvet and flame; very fragrant and very floriferous." [JR24/165]

Mme. Charles Truffaut (E. Verdier, 1878)
"Vigorous, with short, upright canes of a delicate green; thorns straight, pointed, pink; leaves composed of five oblong, light green leaflets, regularly dentate; flowers large, full, very well formed, imbricated; color, very delicate pale satiny pink, distinctly bordered silvery, superb; a charming variety." [JR2/187]

Mme. Charles Verdier (Lacharme, 1863)
"Belongs to the 'Baronne Prévost' type. Rosy vermilion, very large, a free bloomer." [EL] "Very well proportioned in form and color." [l'H67/54] "Vigorous, with a flower which is full, large, well formed, globular, fragrant, and rosy pink...It is dedicated to the wife of Monsieur Charles Verdier, horticulturist of Ivry-sur-Seine." [JR10/140] "Charles-Félix Verdier, who died, at his home at Ivry-sur-Seine, August 18 [1893], at the age of 64." [JR17/129]

Mme. Charles Wood (E. Verdier, 1861)
"Vinous-crimson, very large, full, and effective." [FP] "Flower very large, very full, with large petals; well held; beautiful sparkling intense red fading to bright deep pink; reverse of petals whitish; superb." [l'H61/264] "Beautiful clear rosy-crimson, petals large and of good substance, expanded, full, and beautifully formed, a distinct and magnificent rose;

habit moderate." [JC] "Vigorous; flower large, very full, cupped, then flat; color, dazzling bright red." [S] "Dwarf…Reddish crimson, large or very large, nearly full; one of the freest flowering kinds, but not of first quality. Occasionally, as with 'Général Washington', some first-rate blooms are produced." [EL] "A bad grower, divided, and rain will spoil them. Sometimes a strong fine Rose, with large petals, rather flat in shape, and tightly incurved in the centre. A good lasting flower, of full size, but a 'bad doer' and not to be recommended." [F-M3] "Beautiful foliage…the flower expands rather quickly and is soon overblown." [P2] "One of the best of its own, or of any, class of roses. Large, full, flat roses of crimson, without a dull or purplish shade throughout the hottest summer. Begins to bloom on quite young bushes and continues to bloom better as growth advances. Dwarf bush, but luxuriant, rich, dark green foliage. Very long-lived and hardy." [Dr]

Mme. Chirard (Pernet père, 1867)
"Velvety pink." [Ÿ] "Rose, tinged with vermilion, full, peculiar rich scent; bushy habit, shy in autumn, many malformed flowers." [EL] "Growth very vigorous; flower large, full, globular; very well formed; color, bright pink." [S]

Mme. Clémence Joigneaux (Liabaud, 1861)
"Lilac-rose. Bold and distinct in growth and foliage." [H] "Very vigorous; canes upright, heavily thorned; leaves large, beautiful dark green, regularly serrated; color, bright pink, shaded light violet. This rose should only be grown in the warmer areas; in Germany and the north of France, the blossoms opens only occasionally. Much to be recommended for forcing." [S]

Mme. Clert (Gonod, 1868)
"Salmon rose." [EL] "Growth vigorous; flower large, full; color, salmon pink." [S]

Mme. Constant David (Boutigny, 1909)
"Grenadine red illuminated with velvety vermilion, very large, about five inches across [ca. 1.25 dm], full, very well held, long bud, growth very vigorous with long canes of the 'Ulrich Brunner' sort; thorns long; very handsome ample foliage, dark green, very remontant." [JR33/169]

Mme. Cordier (L.-A. Leroy, 1903)
"Violet-and lilac-pink." [Ÿ]

Mme. Crespin (Damaizin, 1862)
"Rose, shaded with dark violet, medium size, full, form good." [FP]

Mme. Crozy (Levet, 1881)
Seedling of 'Souvenir de la Reine d'Angleterre' (HP).
"Rose color, very large." [EL] "Growth with very strong wood; foliage dark green; thorns very pointed; color, China pink; flower large, plump, with large petals; well formed." [S]

Mme. de Ridder (Margottin, 1871)
"Beautiful bright amaranth red." [S] "Rich dark shaded crimson, large, handsome, well formed flowers; habit vigorous; a most excellent rose." [JC] "Free or vigorous...Red, shaded with violet-crimson, large, full, fine globular form; green wood and thorns. A distinct sort, fragrant and beautiful, but fades easily." [EL]

Mme. de Selve (Bernède, 1886)
Seedling of 'Monsieur Fillion' (HP).
"Very vigorous; flowers very large, well formed, beautiful bright red with lilac reflections." [JR10/171]

Mme. de Trotter (Granger, 1854)
"Vigorous plant, flower medium-sized, bright red, reblooms with difficulty." [JDR55/9] "A free bloomer in the spring." [EL] "Very vigorous bush with canes armed with very unequal thorns; the large ones are laterally flattened, straight, or slightly back-hooked; the small ones grade down

to glandular bristles. The stipules are long and lacy in the free part. The flowers are full, carmine pink, 'Duchesse de Sutherland' form, 7-8 cm in size [ca. 3½ inches], clustered in 2-4s at the tip of the cane; occasionally solitary. This variety is pretty and very interesting in its origin. Born of a non-remontant variety, it is very floriferous in Spring, and grows, after first bloom, vigorous canes which, for the most part, give flowers which are as pretty as the early ones. It is not freely remontant; but with age seems to become so." [l'H55/29]

Mme. Desirée Giraud (Giraud-d'Haussy/Van Houtte, 1854; but see below)
Sport of 'Baronne Prévost' (HP).
"Flower very large, full, ground white and pink, consistently plumed crimson, slate, amaranth, etc." [l'H54/15] "An HP with consistently variegated blossoms is something breeders of roses have sought for a long time…This Rose was not raised from seed, but is rather a sport from the HP 'Baronne Prévost'…Monsieur Van Houtte bought out the entire stock of this variety from Mme. L. Giraud d'Haussy of Marly, at whose establishment this sport occurred…[A] white and pink g round, plumed with crimson, violet, and amaranth." [R-H53] "Vigorous…Blush-white, striped with deep rose." [EL] "Moderate growth…flower large, full; color, white striped pink and crimson." [S] "Branches so meager that we are unable to appreciate it; and whenever the branches are frail, they don't always give striped flowers." [JDR57/28] "Its blossoms are often deformed and small. This variety is much inferior to 'Panachée d'Orléans'." [JR12/172] "It will be released to commerce on April 1, 1854, as Winter grafts, at the price of five francs." [VH52/281] "We do not count 'Mme. Desirée Giraud, [*the picture of which*] appears to such good effect in *Flore des Serres* [*a publication of Van Houtte's*], as Monsieur Van Houtte has not yet released it to commerce—because the picture is too good and the rose too bad." [l'H55/54]

[**Mme. Domage**] (Margottin, 1853)

"Bright rose, very large and double." [FP] "Flower large, Centifolia form; very fragrant; color, bright crimson." [S] "Very vigorous plant; flower very large, full, well-formed, Centifolia form, beautiful intense pink, very fragrant. This rose has the habit and foliage of the rose 'Baronne Prévost'." [l'H53/243]

Mme. Edmond Fabre (E. Verdier, 1884)

"Pink, large, full, medium scent, medium height." [Sn]

Mme. Édouard Michel (E. Verdier, 1886)

"A clear deep pink, flowers of beautiful shape when perfect, but in the early part of the season they are not unfrequently divided. Very smooth, good petals and a capital pointed centre, attractive colour, one of the best shades of pink among the Hybrid Perpetuals, and sweet scented. Hardy and good constitution." [B&V] "Vigorous, canes light green, upright, strong; thorns unequal, straight, pink; leaves delicate green, 3-5 leaflets, fairly deeply but irregularly toothed; flowers extra large, full, with large petals, beautiful form, very well held; color, very beautiful and fresh bright pink; Tea-scent." [JR10/170]

Mme. Elisa Tasson (Lévêque, 1879)

"Scarlet cerise." [Ÿ] "Very vigorous, handsome ample foliage of a glossy green, flowers very large, full, beautiful globular form; petals well imbricated, handsome light cerise, intense…gives quantities of very large blossoms." [JR3/166]

Mme. Ernest Levavasseur (Vigneron, 1900)

From 'Mme. Isaac Pereire' (B) × 'Ulrich Brunner fils' (HP).

"Soft carmine-red, in the way of 'Ulrich Brunner [fils]', but brighter in colour; very large and full, growth vigorous." [P1] "Very vigorous, beautiful very dark green foliage, flower very large, to four inches in diameter [ca. 1 dm], globular, very full, opens admirably well, borne on a very rigid stem; color, bright vermilion red shaded fiery carmine; extremely floriferous, fragrant. Enormous very long bud, well formed...Surpasses 'Ulrich Brunner [fils]' in form and beauty." [JR24/146]

Mme. Eugène Verdier (E. Verdier, 1878)

"Delicate pink." [Ÿ] "Belongs to 'La Reine' type. Mottled rose, very large, full, globular; a promising kind." [EL] "Silvery rose, large and full; form, globular; growth vigorous. One of the best." [P1] "A fine large-petaled Rose." [H] "Vigorous with strong, upright, and short light green canes; thorns numerous, unequal, slightly recurved, pink; leaves composed of 2-5 oval-elongate leaflets, deeply toothed with large teeth; flowers extra large, full, satiny pink, strongly nuanced and shaded silver; a splendid vigorous variety, quite remontant." [JR2/187] "Grows well as a maiden, but the first growths of cutbacks are sometimes very short: still the blooms come just as well, as the foliage is fine. The constitution is delicate in some localities and the plants often gradually die...It is not very liable to mildew, but a slight shower will stain the colour, and much rain will cause the petals to...stick together, and rot. The blooms are likely to be coarse and are not often of refined shape or appearance; but they are very large with wonderfully fine petals and well-filled centres. Fairly free in bloom and a pretty good autumnal; the shape is globular, but delicacy and regularity of outline are often wanting, and really it is sometimes almost like a prize cabbage, for it is quite one of the largest Roses." [F-M2] "One of the most able breeders of roses has left us—Monsieur Louis-Eugène-Jules Verdier, who died March 11, 1902, at his home, 37 rue Clisson, Paris, at the age of 75. He was the last survivor of the Verdier family which played a very great role in French rosiculture in the last century...For many years, Monsieur hadn't left his home; having been struck down by blindness, and it being a struggle to go out, he was reduced to complete inaction." [JR26/82-83] "Madame Eugène Verdier...has died at the age of 64 after a long illness. The obsequies will take place the 17th of October [*1893*]." [JR17/163]

Mme. Eugénie Frémy (E. Verdier, 1884)

"Very vigorous bush; canes strong and upright, delicate green; thorns unequal, straight, brown; leaves composed of 5 rounded leaflets, thick and glossy, dark green, with fine and irregular serration; flower very large, very full, uniquely convex form; color, very bright fresh pink with silvery reverse." [JR8/166]

[Mme. Ferdinand Jamin] (Lédéchaux, 1875)

"Rosy-claret, deep petals, and large bold flower, distinct and good." [JC] "Deep carmine-rose, colour of old 'William Jesse', a large globular flower with deep broad petals, highly scented, a good rose." [Cr76] *Jamin*, not *Jamain. Cf.* 'American Beauty'.

Mme. Fillion (Gonod, 1865)

Seedling of 'Mme. Domage' (HP).

"Fresh rosy pink, flowers large, full, and of good form, a very distinct and beautiful rose, very fragrant; habit moderate." [JC] "Growth vigorous; canes strong, covered with thick blackish green foliage; flower large, full; color, bright salmon pink, center deep salmon; magnificent exhibition rose." [S]

Mme. Fortuné Besson (Besson/Liabaud, 1881)

Seedling of 'Jules Margottin' (HP)

"Very vigorous, abundantly floriferous up to frost; flowers very fragrant, very large, very full, very delicate flesh." [JR5/117] "Branches upright, perfect deportment, flowers fragrant, very large, very full, very delicate flesh, blooming abundantly until frost...should be considered as being in the first rank." [JR5/172]

Mme. Francis Buchner (Lévêque, 1884)

"Very vigorous, foliage shiny green, flowers large, full, beautiful very light pink nuanced darker pink towards the center, beautiful shading, a plant of the first order, quite remontant." [JR8/150]

Mme. François Bruel (Levet, 1882) syn., 'Mme. Bruel'
From 'Victor Verdier' (HP) × 'Comtesse d'Oxford' (HP).
"Carmine-rose." [EL] "Vigorous, foliage light green; flower large, carmine pink, few thorns, very remontant; a quite beautiful variety." [S]

Mme. Gabriel Luizet (Liabaud, 1877)
Seedling of 'Jules Margottin' (HP).
"Light silvery pink; one of the most beautiful pink Roses that we have; early flowering, very free, and fragrant; should be lightly pruned." [DO] "Pale pink, a delicate and beautiful tint of colour, large and full, cupped, very sweet…quite first-rate." [P1] "Large, full, purple cherry red." [JR1/12/12] "The blooms are occasionally divided, but generally good…not…lasting…but of fair size, very smooth, with good petals and a capital pointed centre…delightful fragrance…the most attractive shade of pink among HP's. A very free bloomer, but a shocking autumnal." [F-M2] "An early bloomer; does not last; no fall bloom. Prune long." [Th2] "Long foliage; a promising kind, worthy of attention." [EL] "Strong, vigorous growth…The foliage is very fine, but liable to mildew…quite a big bush…in good soil." [F-M2] "5×3 [ft; ca. 1.5×1 m]." [B] "Certainly a rose of the first merit, much surpassing 'Mrs. John Laing' in growth, rigidity of branch, and size of flower." [JR32/30] "Luizet (Gabriel).—Born in 1794, died at Écully (Rhône) in 1872. Meritorious arboriculturist. Developed many valuable varieties of fruits. It is to him that we owe the practice of budding fruit trees, something he popularized. Author of *Classification du Genre Pêcher*." [R-HC] Not to be confused with the Bourbon of the same name.

Mme. Georges Schwartz (Schwartz/Guillot père, 1871)
"Glossy rose with soft lavender shade, flowers large, full, and cupped, a very deep well formed flower, and a fine rose; habit vigorous." [JC] "Very large, very well-formed, full, beautiful Hydrangea-pink fading to frosty pink." [JR3/27] "Belongs to the 'Victor Verdier' type. Silvery-rose, fades badly and is coarse." [EL] "Growth very vigorous; magnificent first-rate flower." [S]

Mme. Georges Vibert (Moreau-Robert, 1879)
"Veined bright pink, attractive on its ground color of fresh pink."
[JR12/172] "Very vigorous, flower very large, full, opens well, very delicate pink, center carmine, blooms a great deal, and in clusters, handsome dark green foliage." [JR3/167]

Mme. Grandin-Monville (E. Verdier, 1875)
"Flower large, full, well formed, growing in a cluster; color, bright sparkling crimson, edged bright pink; vigorous." [S]

Mme. Henri Pereire (Vilin, 1886)
"Bright red with flame reflections." [Ÿ] "A crimson rose of pretty good growth that is generally well spoken of, but it is very liable to mildew and proves of little value with me." [F-M3]

Mme. Henri Perrin (Widow Schwartz, 1892)
"Lilac carmine." [Ÿ] "Vigorous, foliage abundant, bullate. Flower large, perfect form, bright carmine lilac pink, exterior petals large and concave, inner petals ragged, sometimes striped pure white; always bordered and brightened with delicate pink, with silvery reflections; nubs yellowish." [JR16/154]

Mme. Hersilie Ortgies (Soupert & Notting, 1868)
"Growth vigorous; flower medium-sized, full, very well formed; color, delicate pink and pinkish lilac." [S] Not to be confused with Moreau-Robert's salmon-white 1868 Bourbon of the same name.

Mme. Hippolyte Jamain (Garçon/Jamain, 1871)
"Blush, flowers globular, large, and full; habit moderate." [JC] "White, tinged with rose, very large, full." [EL] "Of good growth and foliage, not very liable to mildew, but rain will injure the blooms. A coarse Rose, generally rough and irregular if grown strong, but occasionally of even globular shape in hot dry weather and then valuable for exhibition as it is very large, full, and lasting. A free bloomer in the season, but not much of an

autumnal." [F-M3] "Growth vigorous; canes of medium size, branching; bark a glaucescent green with numerous slender reddish thorns. Leaves light green, slightly glaucous, 5-9 oval-acuminate, finely dentate leaflets; leafstalk slim, light green. Flowers about 4½ [ca. 1.25 dm], very full, cupped, often solitary, sometimes in clusters of three or four on the strongest branches; color, lightly blushing white; outer petals large and thick, central petals smaller, numerous, muddled; very pretty bud, shaded carmine; flower stalk pretty long, and has glandular bristles. Calyx tubular; sepals leaf-like. A plant of the first order; hardy." [JF]

Mme. Jean Everaerts (Geduldig, 1907)

From 'Eugène Fürst' (HP) × a seedling (which resulted from crossing the HP 'Mme. Eugène Verdier' with the HT 'Johannes Wesselhöft').
"Dark flame red." [Ÿ] "Deep red, large, full, medium scent, tall." [Sn] Called—though as a "subtitle" rather than as a synonym—the "Improved Princesse de Béarn."

[Mme. Julia Daran] (Touvais, 1861)

"Purplish-vermilion, glossy, very large and full; one of the best." [FP] "Flower large, full, globular, very fragrant; color, bright scarlet." [S] "Violet-crimson, flowers cupped and beautifully formed, having large smooth petals of good quality; a rose of vigorous habit." [JC] Ancestor of the HT 'Balduin'.

Mme. Knorr (V. & C. Verdier, 1855)

"Pink, reverse white." [LS] "Soft rose…fragrant." [TW] "Medium size, full, flat form, very sweet." [EL] "100 mm across [ca. 4 inches]…rather loose." [G] "Darker in the center." [S] "HP with large, full flower which is bright pink at the center, lighter at the edge." [l'H55/246] "Semi-double…4×3 [ft; ca. 1.25m × 9 dm]." [B] "Flowers freely." [P2] "Very vigorous." [Cx]

[Mme. la Comtesse de St.-Andréol] (Renaud-Guépet/Mercier, 1889)
Seedling of 'Boïldieu' (HP).
"Very large flower borne on an upright cane, of a beautiful Carthamus pink tinted bright carmine, very fragrant, plant compact and always in bloom." [JR13/166]

Mme. la Générale Decaen (Gautreau, 1869)
"Flower large, full, very well formed; color, bright pink with a flesh pink center." [S]

Mme. Lacharme
Listed as a Hybrid Tea.

[Mme. Laffay] (Laffay, 1839)
Seedling of 'Général Allard' (HCh).
"Carmine pink, full, large, cupped, superb." [LF] "Rich purplish rose, large and very double; form cupped. Habit, erect, fine; growth, vigorous. Too well known to need recommending. An excellent seed-bearer, and very sweet." [P] "Light red." [R-H56] "Rosy-crimson." [FP] "Rose color, large, double, cupped form, red spines; surpassed by many others of the same shade." [EL] "Growth very vigorous; flower medium-sized, full, widely cupped; very fragrant; good seed-bearer; bright crimson." [S] "At present unrivalled; words cannot give the effect of this rose; with its fine large foliage and rosy crimson flowers, it is perfectly beautiful, highly fragrant, and ought to be in every garden." [R9]

Mme. Lefebvre (Moreau-Robert, 1885)
"Vigorous; handsome glossy green foliage; flower large, full, cupped, very delicate satiny pink, center brighter; blooms in clusters; very floriferous; very beautiful." [JR8/149]

Mme. Lemesle (Moreau-Robert, 1890)
"Very vigorous, big-wooded and robust, with recurved thorns, beautiful dark green foliage, large flowers, full, globular, velvety purplish red nuanced violet." [JR14/148]

Mme. Léon Halkin (Lévêque, 1886)
"Vigorous, flowers large, full, perfect form, globular, beautiful bright crimson red nuanced sparkling purple." [JR10/149-150]

Mme. Lierval (Fontaine, 1868)
"Flower large, full; very well formed, and distinctive in form; color, delicate pink mixed with bright crimson." [S]

[Mme. Loeben de Sels] (Soupert & Notting, 1878)
"Vigorous, flowers medium-sized, full, flat, beautifully rosette-formed; color, deep red nuanced velvety crimson passing to bishop's violet." [JR3/12] Not to be confused with Soupert & Notting's 1879 HT 'Mme. de Loeben-Sels', which was silvery white.

Mme. Louis Lévêque (Lévêque, 1873)
Seedling of 'Jules Margottin' (HP).
"Cerise, colour brilliant and distinct, flowers very large, full, and expanded; a good rose." [JC] "Moderate growth; flower very large, full, globular; color, flesh pink, brighter center." [S] "Belongs to the 'Jules Margottin' type, large, very full, somewhat flat form, slightly fragrant; blooms late in the season, but is shy in the autumn." [EL]

Mme. Louis Ricard (Duboc, 1892) syn., 'Mme. Louis Ricart'
Possibly a seedling of 'Monsieur le Baron G.-B. Gonella' (B).
"Dedicated to the wife of our simpatico deputé…freely remontant…vigorous, with somewhat lengthy canes, few thorns, which are nearly straight, and pink; leaves of 5 oval leaflets, somewhat contracted at the tip, pale green, no stipule; large bud, solitary; stem strong and short; ovary medium-sized. Flower large and quite full; petals large, thick, and reflexed,

pale pink, brighter around the center; adequately fragrant…easy to propagate." [JR16/34]

Mme. Louise Piron (Piron-Medard, 1903)
From 'La Reine' (HP) × 'Ulrich Brunner fils' (HP).
"This plant bears strong blossoms of beautiful light pink." [JR27/100]
"Light pink, large, full, medium height." [Sn]

Mme. Louise Vigneron (Vigneron, 1882)
Seedling of 'Elisabeth Vigneron' (HP).
"Very vigorous, upright, thorns fairly numerous, brown, foliage light green, flower large, full, well-formed, beautiful light pink, center darker, beautiful elongated bud, well held, quite remontant, a magnificent plant." [JR6/164]

Mme. Lucien Chauré (Vigneron, 1884)
Seedling of 'Souvenir de la Reine d'Angleterre' (HP).
"Very vigorous, upright, thorns chestnut, slightly numerous, foliage dark green, beautiful very large bud which always opens well, flower very large, about five inches across [ca. 1.25 dm], very full, globular, well formed, handsome bright cerise red, flower generally solitary; quite remontant." [JR8/134]

Mme. Lureau-Escalaïs (Maindion/E. Verdier, 1886)
Seedling of 'Victor Verdier' (HP).
"Vigorous…flowers large, full, well formed, very beautifully held; color, beautiful smooth delicate pink." [JR10/183]

Mme. Marcel Fauneau (Vigneron, 1886)
Seedling of 'Alexis Lepère' (HP).
"Vigorous bush, heavy wood, upright, few thorns, foliage light green; bud very large, conical; flower very large, full, globular form, beautifully colored lilac pink, darker within, perfect hold, very floriferous." [JR10/147]

Mme. Marguerite Marsault (Corbœuf-Marsault, 1894)
"Bush of moderate vigor, well branched; flowers large, full, well formed, plump; color, bright red with violet reflections, petal exteriors bluish at full expansion. Extremely floriferous." [JR18/162]

Mme. Marie Closon
Listed as 'Mlle. Marie Closon'.

Mme. Marie Legrange (Liabaud, 1882)
Seedling of 'Sénateur Vaïsse' (HP).
"Very vigorous, flower large or very large, nearly full, well-formed, handsome brilliant carmine lake, stalk firm, hold perfect. Blooms freely. Very beautiful." [JR6/150]

Mme. Marie Van Houtte (Margottin, 1857)
"Delicate pink." [JDR57/37] "Flower large, full; satiny pink." [S] Not to be confused with the yellow/pink Tea 'Marie Van Houtte'.

Mme. Marthe d'Halloy (Lévêque, 1881)
Seedling of 'Mme. Boutin' (HP).
"Cherry-red." [EL] "Vigorous, foliage glaucous green, flower large, full, very well formed, beautiful carmine cerise pink, very remontant, constantly in bloom, very beautiful." [JR5/150]

[Mme. Masson] (Masson/Marest, 1854)
"Fine dark crimson, large well filled flowers; a most constant and profuse bloomer, highly prized for bedding." [C&Js98] "Very vigorous variety, giving blossoms of an immense size—12-15 cm [to ca. 6 inches]—color, purple crimson brightened with intense red, passing to violet." [l'H55/30] "Foliage ample and a beautiful green, the perfect accompaniment to the very large and quite full magnificent blossoms." [S] "For some reason we cannot explain, this splendid constant blooming hybrid perpetual rose has never had the attention it deserves; it blooms the first season and all the time, the flowers are large, full and delightfully perfumed, the color is

bright rich crimson, it is a robust sturdy grower, continues loaded with flowers almost the whole season. Entirely different from the ever-blooming roses, and a real floral treasure." [C&Js00]

Mme. Maurice Rivoire (Gonod, 1876)
"Fine deep flesh colour, moderate size, compact and full." [JC] "Vigorous, flower large, full, well-formed...exterior petals white." [JR1/6/10] "Branches strong, dark green, sometimes touched violet on the sunny side." [S]

Mme. Montel (Liabaud, 1880)
Seedling of 'La Reine' (HP).
"Light pink, large petals." [EL] "Delicate rose colour, large petals, almost full." [P1] "Very vigorous, branches strong, erect, ample foliage of a cheerful green; flower very large, nearly full, beautiful delicate pink, with large petals, beautiful form, well held, a superb variety." [JR4/167] "Disappoints us; the flowers are a pretty pink, with a beautiful petal; but they are thin and lack refinement." [JR7/157]

Mme. Noman (Guillot père, 1867)
Seedling of 'Mlle. Bonnaire' (HP).
"Moderate growth; floriferous; flower medium-sized, full; color, pure white." [S] "Another pure white H.P., but a weak bad grower with small foliage. The blooms also are quite small but of exquisite form and the purest colour. This Rose and 'Boule de Neige' are much better shaped than 'Mme. Lacharme' or 'Merveille de Lyon', but are so very small in comparison as to be completely out of it." [F-M3] "White, sometimes with shaded centre, medium size, full, globular; foliage somewhat crimpled, wood armed with quite numerous, small spines. A rose of exquisite beauty." [EL]

Mme. Petit (Corbœuf-Marsault, 1900)
From 'Charles Lefebvre' (HP) × 'Pride of Reigate' (HP).
"Vigorous, big-wooded, well branched, very floriferous; cluster-flowered; color, velvety carmine shaded purple; petals striped with one pure white line…[V]ery fragrant." [JR24/164]

Mme. Pierre Margery (Liabaud, 1881)
Seedling of 'Jules Margottin' (HP).
"Vigorous, freely remontant, flower large, full, very fresh pink with a luminous center; very beautiful." [JR5/171] "Very beautiful rose of a charming cerise color." [JR7/157]

Mme. Prosper Laugier (E. Verdier, 1875)
Seedling of 'John Hopper' (HP).
"Velvety pink." [Ÿ] "Rich clear rose, flowers extra large size, flowers some-what expended, petals even and well formed." [JC] "Red, quartered shape, not fragrant, numerous red thorns; of second quality." [EL] "Of good strong stiff growth with characteristic appearance and habit. Distinct also in colour, but unreliable and not to be recommended, of irreproachable form, very full, distinctly fringed; color, bright clear pink; growth very vigorous; canes strong and upright, handsome reddish green; thorns numerous, compressed, brown; leaves of 3-5 leaflets which are somber green and oblong with unequal, deep, dentations; bud very well formed, and very beautiful." [S]

Mme. Rambaux (Widow Rambaux & Dubreuil, 1881)
"Very vigorous, with leaves which are dark green above and glaucescent beneath. Flowers very large, very full, the same in the Fall; petals concave and imbricated in the outer rows, beautiful nuanced carmine pink, paler amaranth on the reverse. Perfectly shaped conical buds." [JR5/186] "Very good rose to force." [S]

[**Mme. Récamier**] (Lacharme, 1853)
"Plant forming a cute small bush of the 'Aimée Vibert' sort; flower medium-sized, well-formed, a pretty flesh-white while opening, passing to pure white." [l'H53/244-245] "Bush pretty vigorous; flowers medium-sized, full or nearly full, in clusters, light flesh white fading to pure white. Rather pretty Noisette cross; very floriferous." [l'H56/250] Possibly of similar parentage to the 'Mme. Alfred de Rougemont' etc. group of Bourbons. Jane Frances Julia Adélaïde Récamier, French beauty; lived 1777-1849; see her portrait by David.

Mme. Renahy (Guillot & fils/E. Verdier, 1889)
"Vigorous, flowers large, full, well formed, globular; color, carmine pink with a brighter center, reverse of petals delicate pink." [JR13/181]

Mme. Renard (Moreau-Robert, 1871)
Seedling of 'Jules Margottin' (HP).
"Moderate growth; blooms in clusters; flower large, full, globular; color, icy salmon pink." [S]

Mme. Roger (Moreau-Robert, 1877)
"Bluish purple pink." [Ÿ] "Vigorous, flower large, full, very delicate pink, nearly white." [JR1/12/12]

Mme. Rosa Monnet (Monnet, 1885)
"Very vigorous; flower large, full, of perfect form, superbly colored bright fresh amaranth with bluish shadings after the blossom has expanded; a delightful perfume; it opens well no matter what the weather, and is very remontant." [JR9/179]

Mme. Rose Caron (Lévêque, 1898)
"Vigorous, foliage light green, flower large, well imbricated, even pink, nuanced carmine pink at the center; very beautiful." [JR22/147]

Mme. Roudillon (Vigneron, 1903)

From 'Mme. Isaac Pereire' (B) × 'Mme. Ernest Levavasseur' (HP).

"Very vigorous bush, very beautiful dark green foliage; enormous flower, very full, beautiful form, beautiful slightly carmine bright red; very fragrant, extremely floriferous. The blossom is borne on a very stiff stem. A magnificent plant." [JR27/131]

Mme. Schmitt (Schmitt, 1854)

"Shaded rosy-pink, large and beautiful." [FP] "Flowers full, 12-15 cm in size [ca. 4-4½ inches], in a cluster, beautiful pink, shaded carmine, reverse silvery white." [l'H55/34] "Of Bourbon ancestry, with upright branches, vigorous, occasional thorns; leaves somber; blossoms big and globular or large and with petals slightly ruffled at the center." [JDR56/32]

Mme. Scipion Cochet (Desmazures/S. Cochet, 1872)

"Purplish pink bordered delicate light pink; flower full, cupped; center petals ruffled a bit." [Cx] "Cherry-rose." [EL] "Vigorous, floriferous, particularly in Summer; flower large, full, well-formed, forming a rosette in the center; color, cerise-pink bordered fresh white; a very pretty variety, recommended by all." [S] "Flowers wrinkled when fully open...4×3 [ft; ca. 1.25×1 m]." [B] "Its large and strong branches...are complemented by husky leaves of a very pretty green. The flowers are very large and full; the numerous petals, which are imbricated and slightly ruffled, give a sort of lightness to the flower which, though bold, is nevertheless graceful. What is more, the form is perfect; the bright cerise-pink petals are silvery on the back, producing reflections which contrast prettily with the darker color of the rest of the petals. All in all, it is a top-of-the-line variety." [JR1/4/8] Not to be confused with Bernaix' Tea of the same name.

Mme. Sophie Stern (Lévêque, 1887)

"Very vigorous bush; very ample blackish green foliage; flowers very large, very well formed, globular, with large petals, magnificently colored very brilliant light bright rose, lit by metallic reflections, whitish at the center. A plant which is very effective. Superb." [JR11/162]

Mme. Sophie Tropot (Levet, 1876)
Seedling of 'Victor Verdier' (HP).
"Pale satin rose, broad, smooth, even petals, flowers cupped; a beautiful rose." [JC] "Bright rose, nearly smooth wood; a shy autumnal and not of first quality." [EL] "Very vigorous, nearly thornless, flower large, full, well-formed, centifolia-form; color, handsome bright pink to good effect." [JR1/1/7-8]

Mme. Soubeyran (Gonod, 1872)
"Growth vigorous; flower small, full, very well formed, very fragrant; bright pink." [S]

Mme. Théobald Sernin (Brassac, 1876)
"Vigorous, having a flower which is large, full, and well-formed, with a currant-red color nuanced carmine." [JR1/2/14]

Mme. Théodore Vernes (Lévêque, 1891)
"Vigorous, foliage ample, dark green; flower large, full, very well formed, bright pink with lighter edges, very beautiful." [JR15/167]

Mme. Thévenot (Jamain, 1877)
"Moderate growth; very floriferous; flower large, very full; color, bright red, nuanced." [S]

Mme. Thibaut (Lévêque, 1889)
"Vigorous bush, foliage bright green, flower large, full, imbricated in the camellia fashion; beautiful satiny pink nuanced carmine pink; very pretty variety dedicated to the wife of our simpatico colleague Monsieur Thibaut of Thibaut & Keteleer." [JR13/164]

Mme. Verlot (E. Verdier, 1876)
"Bright velvety pink." [Ÿ] "Flower extra large, slightly cupped, very full, very fragrant." [S] "Vigorous; flower very large, sufficiently full, cupped, well-formed, beautiful very fresh bright pink." [JR1/6/10]

Mme. Verrier Cachet (Chédane-Guinoisseau, 1895)
"Very vigorous, canes green, very large light green foliage of five leaflets, thorns red, flower very large, very full, globular; color very fresh, pink nuanced vermilion with slaty reflections, very fragrant." [JR19/131] "Very pronounced and pleasing fragrance." [JR25/104] *Cachet* not *Cochet*.

Mme. Veuve Alexandre Pommery (Lévêque, 1882)
"Very vigorous; leaves large, dark green; flower very large, well formed, delicate pink nuanced bright pink within; petal edges very light pink." [JR6/148]

Mme. Victor Verdier (E. Verdier, 1863)
From (either 'Général Jacqueminot' (HP) or 'Sénateur Vaïsse' (HP)) × 'Victor Verdier' (HP).
"Rich, bright rosy-cherry color, large, full, and fine formed, cupped; blooms in clusters." [FP] "Carmine-crimson, large, full, globular form, very fragrant; a superb rose." [EL] "Carmine-rose...though not new, excellent." [SBP] "Brilliant rosy-crimson, colour very beautiful, flower...very lasting; a distinct and very superb rose." [JC] "Crimson...later blooms on the longest and strongest shoots are the best, and occasionally these are very fine, full, lasting, and bright. Fairly free-flowering." [F-M2] "Somewhat resembles 'Sénateur Vaïsse'; excellent for every purpose; one of the finest rich-coloured Roses." [WD] "An excellent old rose, strong growing, and bearing its light crimson flowers freely in summer." [OM] "Very free flowering, and constant." [DO] "A strong grower with fine foliage beautifully coloured in the early spring...large clusters of buds which should be carefully thinned...high cultivation is necessary for...really good blooms." [F-M2] "5×4 [ft; ca. 1.5×1.25 m]." [B] "Vigorous, of medium size, branching; bark smooth, light green, bearing the occasional reddish thorn, which is slightly hooked; leaves large, somber green, in 3-5 crowded leaflets which are oval and rounded, terminating in a point; leafstalks pretty strong, with some prickles; flower about three inches across [ca. 7.5 cm], full, cupped, solitary, or sometimes in

clusters of two or three on the most vigorous branches; color, brilliant cerise-pink; outer petals large; center petals smaller; flower stalk short and slender; magnificent flower for exhibition, very remarkable in every respect…good autumnal." [S] "Calyx pear-shaped, nearly round." [JF] "A rose of the first merit." [JR25/180] "Flowers cupped, beautiful bright cherry pink, 10-12 in a terminal cluster…the name it bears will always be attached to the history of rose-culture in France; Monsieur Eugène Verdier could not have chosen a worthier name to call attention to the merit of this magnificent variety than that of his mother." [l'H63/224]

Mme. Vidot (Couturier fils/E. Verdier, 1854)

"A model in form; its blossom is large and full…clear flesh shaded pink." [R-H63] "This rose…is very vigorous and produces charming flowers of a delicate satiny pink, most perfectly formed." [l'H55/30] "Much to be recommended; hardy." [S] "Canes stocky, light green, covered with a fine layer of bloom; armed with very unequal thorns, not laterally flattened, nearly straight or slightly back-hooked, the larger ones no longer than 5 mm in length and 2 mm in diameter [ca. .25 × .125 inch] at their thickened base, very sharp at the tip; the smaller ones grade down into glandular-stipitation, and are more numerous than the thorns in the upper reaches of the canes. Leaves ordinarily composed of 5 slightly stiff leaflets, which are fairly smooth, beautiful light green above, paler beneath, oval-elliptical, pointed, and cordate at the base; the lateral leaflets are nearly sessile and gradually smaller; the mid-vein bristles with rudimentary prickles; the rachis is completely glandulose and is furrowed into a groove above, and armed with several small hooked prickles beneath; the stipules are very lacy and short, divergent, ciliate along the edges, adherent for a third of their length to the petiole, at the base of which they form two very lacy flanges hardly larger than a millimeter. The flowers are above the median in size, perfect in form, and admirable in color, which is delicate clear flesh-pink-white, nuanced brighter pink. The peduncle is larger, short, very glandular, widening gradually into the funnel-shaped calyx-tube, which is not contracted at the mouth; the sepals are five in number, long, acuminate for the most part, glandulose on the back, downy within and at the edges; in three of the segments, the tip is more or less enlarged and foliaceous, and the edges have one or two small linear ciliate processes. The petals are very numerous, obovate straightened out, a little spoon-shaped, admirably and very regularly imbricated in the outer rows, the central petals being more or less folded and a little muddled, making a veritable Legion of Honor officer's medal. No stamens. Styles salient, free, numerous, topping off the ovaries enclosed in the calyx." [l'H55/101-102]

Mme. Yorke (Moreau-Robert, 1881)
"Vigorous bush; beautiful dark green foliage; flower large, full; color, vermilion red shaded carmine and nuanced blackish purple; extraordinary coloration." [JR5/172]

Monseigneur Fournier (Lalande/Lévêque, 1876) syn., 'Monsieur Fournier'
"Flower very large, full, very well formed; color, beautiful very brilliant light red." [S]

Monsieur Albert La Blotais (Moreau-Robert, 1881) syn., 'Albert La Blotais'
"Vigorous, beautiful light green foliage, flower medium, full, globular, perfect form, color velvety blackish nuanced flame, very floriferous." [JR5/172] "Monsieur Albert La Blotais, quondam cavalry officer, died May 22 [1895] after a sad and cruel illness…He was a passionate fancier of roses, a man who conquered all by the affability, his modesty, his loyalty, his good heart, and by the esteem and consideration he showed to all." [JR19/98] Not to be confused with Pernet's climbing red HP of 1887, 'Albert La Blotais'.

Monsieur Alfred Leveau (Vigneron, 1880) syn., 'Alfred Leveau', 'Mme. Alfred Leveau'
"Carmine-rose." [EL] "Flower large, bright carmine pink." [JR5/42] "Growth vigorous, canes upright, stocky; flower large, full, well formed, solitary; bright carmine pink; later, delicate pink; handsome dark green foliage; thorns chestnut brown, not very numerous." [S]

Monsieur Bonçenne (Liabaud, 1864)

From 'Général Jacqueminot' (HP) × ? 'Géant des Batailles' (HP)?

"Velvety maroon which does not 'blue'; flower very large, full, cupped, fragrant." [Cx] "Fine form, velvety deep dark carmine-red. Growth strong, erect. A beautiful rose of the first order, but only fairly good in autumn." [Hn] "Very deep crimson, double, medium size; a good rose, but now displaced by 'Baron de Bonstetten'." [EL] "Intensely dark crimson, colour very superb…one of the best dark flowers; habit vigorous." [JC] "Nearly scentless; it can be grown own-root as well as budded; does well in a pot, forced. Good bloom in Summer. It is hardy and needs to be pruned long. 'Baron de Bonstetten' and 'Baron Chaurand' are two varieties coming from 'Monsieur Bonçenne' which are very much like it. *Monsieur Bonçenne* is a judge in the Fontenay-le-Comte court, and is president of the horticultural society of that town." [JR10/58] "A strong grower with fair foliage, but liable to mildew and orange fungus, and not liking rain. Very early; one of the first to show flower buds. A poorly shaped flat bloom at the best, only a small proportion of them coming good, but a beautiful dark colour, particularly 'velvety'. Requires a hot season, and yet is likely to be 'burnt'. Fairly free blooming and of average size, but not lasting or a good autumnal and of no use as an exhibition Rose." [F-M3] "Vigorous; branches of medium size, divergent; bark dark green, with fairly numerous blackish-brown thorns which are unequal, slightly hooked, and sharp. Leaves somber green, composed of 3-5 leaflets which are oval-rounded, slightly acuminate, and finely dentate; leafstalks slender, dark green, somewhat reddish. Flowers around three inches across [ca. 7.5 cm], full, cupped, solitary or in clusters of two or three on the stronger branches; color, dark velvety maroon, petals large; flower stem short, glabrous, slightly nodding. Calyx rounded. This is a variety of the first order, and one of the darkest." [JF] "Monsieur Ernest Bonçenne, president of the Société d'Horticulture de Fontenay-le-Comte." [JR26/31]

Monsieur Cordier

Listed as 'Monsieur Jean Cordier'.

Monsieur de Montigny (Paillet, 1855)

"Lilac pink." [Ÿ] "Rosy-carmine, large and full." [FP] "Brilliant rose colour, fresh and beautiful, flowers very large and well formed; a handsome robust growing rose." [JC] "Growth vigorous; flower large; color intense pink." [S] "Strong canes armed with large dark slightly hooked purple-red thorns; leaves lush, light green above, whitish beneath; leaflets deeply toothed; flowers fairly large, to 8-10 cm [ca. 4 inches], purplish pink passing to slaty violet, solitary or in twos at the tip of the cane." [l'H56/49]

Monsieur de Morand (Widow Schwartz, 1891)

Seedling of 'Général Jacqueminot' (HP).

"Vigorous bush; graceful foliage, quite denticulate; flower large, of good hold, full, opening easily; color, bright crimson cerise nuanced bluish lilac purple; center petals imbricated in such a way as to give the blossom the form of a camellia; margined pinkish white." [JR15/149]

[Monsieur E.Y. Teas] (E. Verdier, 1874) syn., 'E.Y. Teas'

Seedling of 'Alfred Colomb' (HP).

"Flower very large, full, globular, fragrant; color, bright sparkling deep cerise red. From 'Alfred Colomb', and resembles 'Sénateur Vaïsse' [*q.v.*] and 'François Fontaine' [*HP, Fontaine, 1867, vermilion*]." [S] "Only moderate in growth and foliage. Not much liable to mildew, and stands rain fairly. The blooms come well, very full and fragrant, of compact regular smooth globular shape, a very bright colour, and good lasting qualities, but below the average in size. Fairly free in bloom, but of little use as an autumnal, and not to be recommended for any but exhibitors." [F-M2]

Monsieur Édouard Detaille (Gouchault, 1893)
"Flower very full, opens well, deep purple red shaded black, center vermilion red, very fragrant and very floriferous. The habit of this plant makes it good for pot culture." [JR17/165-166]

Monsieur Ernest Dupré (Boutigny, 1904)
"Flower large, full, very bright carmine red nuanced deep carmine, velvety; beautiful camellia form; well held, long bud, very vigorous. Dedicated to the former vice-president of the Horticultural Society of Seine-Inférieure." [JR28/89]

Monsieur Étienne Dupuy (Levet, 1873)
From 'Victor Verdier' (HP) × 'Anna de Diesbach' (HP).
"Pale satin and rosy pink, colour beautifully clear and fresh, cupped, large, and full; a distinct and very fine rose; habit vigorous." [JC] "Flower large, full; color, delicate pink; reverse of petals silvery pink." [S]

Monsieur Eugène Delaire (Vigneron, 1879)
"Very vigorous bush, with upright canes; beautiful green foliage, thorns chestnut brown; flower large, full, in a cluster or solitary; color, velvety red illuminated with bright flame-color; freely remontant, very floriferous." [JR3/167]

Monsieur Fillion (Gonod/Lévêque, 1876)
"Vigorous, flower large, carmine pink, center brighter." [JR1/6/11] "Belongs to the 'Victor Verdier' type. Carmine-rose, not of first quality." [EL] "Flower very large, full, imbricated; color, magenta pink, brighter at the center." [S] "Fine rose, striking in the centre, very large, full and well formed, good bloomer, a first-class variety; growth vigorous." [JC]

Monsieur Fournier
Listed as 'Monseigneur Fournier'.

Monsieur Francisque Rive (Schwartz, 1883)
"Poppy." [Ÿ] "Very vigorous, having the look of 'Marie Baumann', foliage light, flower very large, full, well formed, bright cerise red nuanced carmine, petals concave, reverse glaucescent, producing a charming contrast, very fragrant, quite remontant." [JR7/122]

Monsieur Hoste (Liabaud, 1884)
Seedling of 'Baron de Bonstetten' (HP).

"Bush very vigorous; flower large, full, beautiful velvety crimson red. Magnificent thick, dark green foliage." [S]

Monsieur Jean Cordier (Gonod, 1871)
Seedling of 'Géant des Batailles' (HP).
"Flower very large, full, flat, camellia-form; scarlet." [S]

Monsieur Joseph Chappaz (Schmitt, 1882)
Seedling of 'Jules Margottin' (HP).
"Very vigorous bush; flower very large, full, perfectly globular, beautiful lilac pink. Has the look of 'Jules Margottin'." [JR6/164]

Monsieur Journaix (Marest, 1868)
"Vigorous...brilliant red." [EL] "Weak growth; flower large, full; very remontant; scarlet, nuanced dark red." [S]

Monsieur Jules Deroudilhe (Liabaud, 1886)
"Very vigorous bush with stocky, upright canes; beautiful light green foliage with two pairs of leaflets; flower medium sized or large, crimson purple red, perfectly cupped. Blooms constantly." [JR10/171]

Monsieur Jules Lemaître (Vigneron, 1890)
Seedling of 'Mme. Isaac Pereire' (B).
"Very vigorous with stiff, upright canes; dark green foliage; flower very large, full, globular, very beautifully colored bright carmine red. Perfect hold; very remontant and floriferous; the blossoms have the most charming

scent...dedicated to Monsieur Jules Lemaître, well-known writer." [JR14/148-149]

Monsieur Jules Maquinant (Vigneron, 1882)
Seedling of 'Jules Margottin' (HP).
"Very vigorous, flower large, full, well formed, beautiful light red, center brighter, perfectly held." [JR6/164]

Monsieur Jules Monges (Guillot fils, 1881)
Seedling of 'Souvenir de la Reine d'Angleterre' (HP).
"Cerise pink." [Ÿ] "Carmine-rose, cupped." [EL] "Superbly poised." [JR5/147] "Very vigorous; canes upright, light green; leaves light green, composed of 5-7 leaflets; flowers very large, full, well formed, cupped; superbly colored a very sparkling carmine pink; stalk firm, holding the flower well." [JR5/116]

Monsieur Lauriol de Barney (Trouillard, 1866)
"Purple, nuanced." [Ÿ] "Growth vigorous; flower large, full, imbricated; color, currant red." [S]

Monsieur le Capitaine Louis Frère (Vigneron, 1883)
"Velvety crimson." [Ÿ] "Very vigorous, upright, thorns small, chestnut brown, fairly numerous, foliage beautiful green, flower very large, full, well formed, handsome bright light red, freely remontant." [JR7/170]

Monsieur le Préfet Limbourg (Garçon/Margottin fils, 1878)
Seedling of 'Pierre Notting' (HP).
"Crimson, tinged with violet, double, or full; a rose of fine color." [EL] "Vigorous bush; flower large, full, well formed; color, beautiful nuanced light red; very beautiful, very floriferous." [S]

Monsieur Louis Ricard (Boutigny, 1901) syn., 'Monsieur Louis Ricart'
From 'Simon de St.-Jean' (HP) × 'Abel Carrière' (HP).
"A large and showy Pæony-like flower; deep velvety crimson shaded with vermilion and black; does not burn; growth very vigorous and good

habit." [P1] "Vigorous growth, with more or less somber green canes, thorns sharp and recurved, leaves of five oblong leaflets, light green beneath, darker above. Bloom is continuous, producing enormous rounded buds, borne on long, strong stems, beautiful blackish purple, very velvety, brightened by brilliant vermilion. The flowers, sometimes solitary, are very large, to five inches [ca. 1.25 dm], full, globular, Peony-shaped, excellently held, with very long petals, large and thick, bullate, lighter at the nub, sometimes striped white on the reverse, fragrant." [JR16/119] Originally bred in 1894.

Monsieur Louis Ricart
Listed as 'Monsieur Louis Ricard'.

Monsieur Mathieu Baron (Widow Schwartz, 1886)
"Vigorous bush; flower large, full, red with deep violet; fragrant." [JR10/182]

Monsieur Victor Verdier
Listed as 'Victor Verdier'.

Montebello (Fontaine, 1859)
"Red, medium size, full, tall." [Sn] "—Not big enough." [VH62/92]

Mrs. Baker (Turner/Laxton, 1876)
Seedling of 'Victor Verdier' (HP).
"Red lake." [JR20/5] "A smooth-petaled rosy crimson flower of good substance, the older flowers being tinted with purple." [R7/534] "Of moderate size." [JC] "Of 'Victor Verdier' race, with the usual habits of the family. The brightest of them all in colour, with a beautiful pointed shape, one of the earliest of H.P.'s, of large size, but not very lasting in colour or form." [F-M3] "Vigorous, flower large, pretty form, handsome delicate pink." [JR1/6/11] "Moderate growth, with smooth wood; has the look of 'Comtesse d'Oxford'; flower very large, full, globular, pointed center; color, bright carmine shaded crimson." [S]

Mrs. Cocker (Cocker, 1899)
From 'Mrs. John Laing' (HP) × 'Mabel Morrison' (HP).
"A seedling, I believe, from 'Mme. Gabriel Luizet', this Rose is like it in wood, foliage, and habit, often not blooming as a maiden, and of not much use in autumn. The blooms are a lovely shade of pink, large and very full but not pointed, with fine petals and good lasting qualities. It is a fine Exhibition Rose, but, as a new Rose of which we have had but short experience, it would hardly seem to be among the best for general cultivation." [F-M2]

[Mrs. Cripps] (Laffay,-1845)
"Flower large and double; petals undulated and numerous, of a fine rose, the centre of a brighter shade." [MH45/28] "Blossom large, full; color, delicate pink, with a deep pink center." [S]"A pretty vareity, blooming in large clusters: colour, bright rose." [R9] Mrs. Cripps, probably wife of Thomas Cripps, English nurseryman of the time located in Tunbridge Wells, Kent.

[Mrs. Elliot] (Laffay, 1841) syn., 'Mistress Elliot'
"Variable lilac, full, large, cupped." [LF] "Foliage glaucous." [R-H42] "Flower large, full, flaring; color, bright crimson; growth vigorous." [S] "Purplish rose, very large and very double; form, cupped, fine. Habit, erect; growth, vigorous. A beautiful Rose, with fine large petals, and handsome foliage." [P] "A beautiful free-flowering and free-opening rose, with flowers of light crimson, tinged with lilac. Like some others in this clas, barren shoots are often produced in the autumn." [R9] "The bush reblooms pretty freely; blossom medium-sized, cupped, showing the stamens, quite double; petals deeply notched, large, round, well arranged, a pretty purplish pink which is fresh and silky, sometimes having a tint of violet; elegant foliage; canes bearing short, pointed, reddish thorns; very fragrant; blooms in threes and fours; growth from seed by Monsieur Laffay, and entered into commerce in November, 1841." [An42/333]

Mrs. F.W. Sanford (Curtis, Sanford, and Co., 1898) syn., 'Pride of the Valley'
Sport of 'Mrs. John Laing' (HP).
"Pale blush pink shading to white…possesses all the good points of the parent." [P1] "The form is perfect; full. This rose is an excellent exhibition variety." [JR21/164] F.W. Sanford was the business partner of Henry Curtis (who wrote *Beauties of the Rose*) in their nursery at Torquay, England.

Mrs. George Dickson (Bennett, 1884)
Seedling of 'Mme. Clémence Joigneaux' (HP).
"Very vigorous and…robust…blooming early, persistently, and late…the flowers are large, not very full, opening well. A new color, brilliant satiny pink." [JR8/54] "Vigorous, rather like '[Mme.] Clémence Joigneaux'; flower large, full, double, opens well; brilliant satiny pink. Blooms early and abundantly to the end of the season. No fungal problems." [S]

Mrs. Harkness (Harkness, 1894)
Sport of 'Heinrich Schultheis' (HP).
"White striped pink." [JR20/6] "Lighter than ['Heinrich Schultheis']." [F-M2]

Mrs. J.F. Redly (Breeder unknown, date uncertain)
Flesh pink. No further information!

Mrs. John Laing (Bennett, 1887)
Seedling of 'François Michelon' (HP).
"Silvery lilac pink…superbly fragrant." [RP] "Rosy pink." [J] "Clear, bright rose, a continuous bloomer, fragrant, and always to be relied on. The best of the late Mr. Bennett's seedlings." [DO] "Lovely shell pink. Elegant in form, texture and habit of growth. Large, full and double roses. Large well-shaped buds. Tea-scented. Blooms as continuously as the best of Tea roses. No finer rose exists for the out-of-door garden, park, or cemetery. Fine for cut-roses." [Dr] "First-rate in petal, fulness, semi-globular

pointed shape, lasting qualities, size, and freedom of bloom...the pink colour is not very decided or bright." [F-M2] "Bright pink, richly fragrant blooms of splendid shape." [ARA29/100] "Very large, well-filled, cupped, bright glossy pink colour. Free flowering, good in autumn. Stems erect, slightly prickled." [Hn] "Long buds...Strong grower; free bloomer, averaging 50 blooms [*per season*]." [ARA21/90] "Almost always some flowers, and no thorns to bother." [ARA29/49] "An excellent rose, with characteristic upright shoots, and beautiful big, clear pink blooms which are produced more or less in autumn as well as in July. A rose that all should grow." [OM] "Longer flowering period than most of the class." [Th2] "One of the best half-dozen...Not liable to mildew or injured by rain, and retaining its foliage well in the autumn." [F-M2] "Holds its leaves, but capriciously." [JR37/170] "Extremely free from mildew. It commences to flower very early, is remarkably profuse, and continues to bloom till late in Autumn; quite first-rate." [P1] "The growth is hardy and vigorous, and the habit erect, the foliage is good, light green, and retained well into autumn, but decidedly subject to mildew as far as my experience goes...It flowers well again in the autumn, giving a few stray blooms in between, but it is not continuous...The flowers are grand exhibition blooms, full, pointed, and globular, with a good depth of petal, soft pale pink in colour. They stand sun and rain well, but are apt to be dull when much shaded...It is very sweet scented." [JR10] "4×3 [ft; ca. 1.25×1 m]." [B] "Although introduced as far back as 1887, 'Mrs. John Laing' has never been superseded, and looks like holding its own indefinitely." [Wr] "One of the principal English horticulturists, Mr. John Laing, has died at the age of 77 at Forest Hill, where he had a vast and well-known establishment. He was one of the most esteemed and distinguished hybridists in England because of his numerous and interesting crosses." [JR24/145]

[**Mrs. John McLaren**] (California Nursery Company?, by 1905)
"Deep pink." [CA05] "Silvery pink." [CA10]

Mrs. Laing (E. Verdier, 1872)
"Growth vigorous; flower medium-sized, full, very fragrant; color, bright carmine pink." [S] Not to be confused with 'Mrs. John Laing'.

Mrs. R.G. Sharman-Crawford (A. Dickson, 1894)
"Rosy-pink." [H] "Beautiful deep pink, magnificent in bud." [JR19/38] "A very valuable introduction, and has gained much popularity both here and in America, where it is one of the few H.P.'s which bloom in the autumn. It is of fair growth and not much liable to mildew, very free-flowering, and a capital autumnal: in fact it is almost a continuous bloomer. The flowers are a lovely shade of pink, and quite large enough; they seldom come malformed, though the shape is not of the highest class. It has a high reputation as being easy to grow, and not exacting in its requirements." [F-M2]

Mrs. Rumsey (Rumsey, 1899)
Sport of either 'Mrs. George Dickson' (HP) or 'Margaret Dickson' (HP). "Rosy pink, very freely produced, and the growth is quite proof against mildew." [P1]

Napoléon III (E. Verdier, 1866)
"Two distinct colors: very bright scarlet and deep slaty violet." [l'H66/370] "Bush vigorous; flower large, full, imbricated." [S] Not to be confused with Granger's deep crimson HP of 1855, 'Empereur Napoléon III'.

[Nardy Frères] (Ducher, 1865) trans., "Nardy Bros."
Seedling of 'Mme. Boll' (HP).
"Rose, shaded with soft lavender, flowers very large, full, and well formed; a very distinct and first-rate rose...habit vigorous." [JC] "Medium-sized bush; flower very large, full, globular; color, violety pink with slaty reflections." [S]

Notaire Bonnefond (Liabaud, 1868)
"Flower very large, full; color, velvety purple; vigorous." [S]

Nuria de Recolons (Dot, 1933)
From 'Canigó' (HT) × 'Frau Karl Druschki' (HP).
"[*Has the*] greatest thrips resistance of any white rose…good form but no fragrance." [ARA39/215]

Oakmont (May, 1893)
"Deep pink." [Hÿ] "Clear light pink. Profuse and constant bloomer." [Dr] "Peach-pink, fragrant…of good size. Sufficient healthy foliage. Growth tall. Blooms mostly in spring…about 132 [*blooms per season*]." [ARA21/90] "Large and sweet, good bloomer, hardy and productive; always gives satisfaction." [C&Js06]

Olivier Belhomme (V. & C. Verdier, 1861) syn., 'Olivier Delhomme'
"Flower medium-sized, full, bright intense red." [l'H61/264] "Brilliant purplish-red, large, and perfect shape, foliage handsome." [FP] "Brilliant rosy-carmine, flowers well formed, of good depth and high centre, fine petal and good outline; a superb rose." [JC] "Vigorous bush; flower medium-sized, full, very well formed; color, fiery red." [S]

Olivier Delhomme
Listed as 'Olivier Belhomme'.

Olivier Métra (E. Verdier, 1884)
"Vigorous with upright delicate green canes; thorns pink, somewhat numerous, very long and recurved; leaves composed of five large, elliptical, dark green leaflets with irregular very deep dentations; flowers large, quite full, of a very beautiful globular form, brilliant bright cerise red." [JR8/166]

Orderic Vital (Oger, 1858)
Sport of 'Baronne Prévost' (HP).
"Large, full, delicate pink." [JR3/27] "Silvery-rose, large and full, good form." [FP] "Vigorous…A little lighter in color than the parent, the habit is the same." [EL] "Very distinct and very constant. The bush is quite

vigorous; flower large, very full, rosette in the center, delicate pink nuanced and shaded." [JDR58/36] Orderic Vital, 12th Century French historian born in Attingham, England, in 1075, but living near Lisieux, Normandy, France, when writing the thirteen books of his ecclesiastical history.

Orgeuil de Lyon (Besson, 1886) trans., "Pride of Lyon"
"Plant vigorous; flower medium-sized, well-formed, pretty full; color, velvety poppy crimson brightened with vermilion and flame reflections; petals waffled at expansion; abundant bloom; wood upright and pretty thornless." [JR10/149]

Oriflamme de St. Louis (Baudry & Hamel, 1858) trans., "St. Louis' Banner"
Seedling of 'Général Jacqueminot' (HP).
"A very brilliant rose." [FP] "Brilliant crimson; resembles the parent, but is inferior to it." [EL] "Very vigorous and very remontant; from 'Général Jacqueminot'; flower fuller, brighter; very large, sparkling carmine red." [l'H58/98]

Ornement du Luxembourg (Hardy, 1840) trans., "Ornament of the Luxembourg [Palace]"
"Violet red, small, full, very fragrant, medium height." [Sn]

Oscar II, Roi de Suède (Soupert & Notting, 1889) syn., 'King of Sweden'
From 'Dupuy-Jamain' (HP) × 'Mme. Victor Verdier' (HP).
"Vigorous bush; flower large, full, well formed; buds long and beautifully formed; color, carmine-vermilion with silvery reflections. Very fragrant." [JR12/147] "Very dark, rich and handsome, a splendid rose." [C&Js99]

Oskar Cordel (Lambert, 1897)
From 'Merveille de Lyon' (HP) × 'André Schwartz' (T).
"Bright rich carmine, large and full; sweetly scented. Very free and distinct." [P1] "Cup-like. Bright deep rosy-red. Flowers always solitary. Growth

strong." [Hn] "Very fragrant; fairly vigorous." [Cx] "Very vigorous, bushy, stems upright, with slender and large thorns. In appearance and growth, it resembles 'Merveille de Lyon'. Each branch bears only one blossom, which is very large, rounded, cupped, and has rather large petals. Color, light bright carmine, very floriferous and remontant. Good as a garden plant...Dedicated to the Editor-in-Chief of the *Voss Gazette*." [JR21/51]

Pæonia (Lacharme, 1855) syn., 'Plonia'; trans., "Peony"
"Growth vigorous; flower large, full, crimson red." [l'H56/2] "Moderate vigor, hardy, floriferous, of the 'Jules Margottin' tribe;...much to be recommended." [S] "Grows strong and erect, flowers very large, regular, full form, perfectly double, deep flashing crimson, very fragrant, a grand rose in every way." [C&Js02] Not to be confused with the following.

Pæonia (Geduldig, 1914) trans., "Peony"
From 'Frau Karl Druschki' (HP) × seedling (resulting from crossing the HP 'Ulrich Brunner fils' and the HP 'Mrs. John Laing')
"Pink, large, full, medium height." [Sn] Not to be confused with the preceding.

Panachée d'Angers (Moreau-Robert, 1879) syn., 'Commandant Beaurepaire'; trans., "The Plumed One from Angers"
"Intense pink variegated purple and violet, and spotted white; flower large, full, cupped; moderate vigor." [Cx] "Strong bush with fresh green leaves. Large double crimson flowers striped pink and purple and marbled white...occasionally repeating...4×4 [ft; ca. 1.25×1.25 m]." [B] "The late Monsieur Vibert had raised a single-flowered, striped HP seed-bearer around 1845, which later, in 1856, produced the HP 'Belle Angevine', a rose with full, striped blossoms, but not very vigorous. The rose 'Commandant Beaurepaire' arose from the same seed-bearer. Sown in 1864, the plant...grew with extraordinary vigor the first year. The second year, its luxuriant growth made it look like a Banksiana; its canes measured as long as nine to twelve feet [ca. 3-3.75 m]. I cut back these enormous

branches the *third* year, branches which gave me some blossoms, and made sure to use only these for the budding…At length, the growth having slowed down, my hope in 1872 was to coax this variety into reblooming. After three years of effort, despairing of success, and being importuned by many fanciers to bring the variety into commerce, I decided to do so. The difficulty was in classifying the thing. Doubtless, its place was among the 'unknown hybrids,' but this class having nearly disappeared from cultivation, I chose the Gallica class, having lost all hope of seeing this variety rebloom. But—voila!—in 1876, after the Spring pruning, forty or fifty specimens gave me blossoms over the course of the Summer, and the same thing happened again in 1877 and 1878. And so it was that I recognized the necessity of reclassifying the variety among the HPs under the name 'Panachée d'Angers', noting that it was the same as 'Commandant Beaurepaire', only remontant. I earnestly wish that its HP name, 'Panachée d'Angers', be retained, as it is a name it most assuredly merits. It is very vigorous, with medium-sized flowers which are double and of a soft pink striped and marbled with purple and violet." [JR6/72]

Panachée d'Orléans (Dauvesse/Wilhelm, 1854) trans., "The Plumed One from Orléans"
Sport of 'Duchesse d'Orléans' (HP).
"A white and rose color striped." [HstXV:252] "A freely remontant perpetual, with a pink blossom striped lilac." [JDR55/10] "Flesh striped lilac-red; constant." [l'H57/62] "Vigorous bush; canes strong, olive green, nearly thornless; flower large, full, in a cluster of 5 or 7 blossoms at the end of the branch; color, delicate pink striped purple…[O]ne of the more striped." [S] "Identical with the parent sort, except that the flowers are striped with rosy-white. It is not constant, soon running back to the original." [EL] "This variety comes from 'Duchesse d'Orléans' and not 'Baronne Prévost' as we sometimes see mentioned." [JR12/172]

Panachée de Bordeaux
Listed as 'Coquette Bordelaise'.

Panachée Langroise (Rimancourt, 1873)
Sport of 'Jules Margottin' (HP).
"Reticulated carmine pink." [JR12/172] "Growth vigorous; flower large, full; color, bright cherry red, plumed deep carmine." [S]

Paul de la Meilleraye (Guillot fils, 1863)
"Very vigorous; flowers very large, full, well formed, with large petals, beautiful purple cerise." [l'H64/62]

Paul Jamain
Listed as 'Charles Lefebvre'.

Paul Neyron (Levet, 1869)
From 'Victor Verdier' (HP) × 'Anna de Diesbach' (HP).
"Dark lilac-rose, of extra size, fine form and habit." [P1] "Pale soft rose, violet shade, flowers immensely large and full; habit robust." [JC] "Huge crimson flowers." [HRH] "Giant blooms, stout in petal and very full...wanting in delicacy and symmetry...colour of the peony type." [F-M2] "Outstanding...in size and shape...rich, warm pink...4×3 [ft; ca. 1.25×1 m]." [B] "Deep rose, very large, very full, somewhat fragrant, free blooming; the wood is nearly smooth, the foliage tough and enduring, somewhat tender, the growth is very upright. The largest variety known, and a very desirable sort for the garden." [EL] "Liable to ball in wet." [Th2] "Unusually strong growth and foliage, almost entirely untouched by mildew and little injured by rain." [F-M2] "Very vigorous; large branches; bark with a bloom; thorns somewhat numerous, blackish, unequal, a few of them big and strong. Handsome, large foliage of a light green; leaves divided into 3-4 acuminate and finely toothed leaflets; leaf-stalks strong, with some small prickles; flower about five inches across [ca. 1.25 dm], quite full, cupped, solitary or in a cluster of 2-4 on the more vigorous branches; beautifully colored bright rose; outer petals very large, those in the center smaller and folded. This variety is notable for the size of the enormous blossoms. Hardy, and a good autumnal." [S] "Occasional

bloom after spring." [ARA18/114] "Bud pretty; flower stem short and firm. Calyx pear-shaped; sepals leaf-like." [JF] [*Among the only HPs*] that pay their board bills [*in Texas*]." [ET] "The favorite rose amongst Brazilians." [PS] "Dedicated to a medical student...who died in 1872 after having borne the fatigues of the 1870-1871 war [*siege of Paris by the Prussians*]." [JR34/14]

Paul Neyron Panachée
Listed as 'Coquette Bordelaise'.

Paul Ricault
Listed in the Hybrid Bourbon chapter.

Paul Verdier (C. Verdier, 1866)
"Magnificent bright pink." [l'H66/370] "Carmine-red, large, globular flowers, well built; a splendid sort." [EL] "Bright pink double...medium to large...fragrant." [G] "Rich pink to light red. Perfumed. Good foliage...4×3 [ft; ca. 1.25×1 m]." [B] "Rich rosy-crimson, flowers large, double, and of fine imbricated form; a beautiful rose, habit very vigorous, forming a good pillar rose." [JC]

Paul's Early Blush (G. Paul, 1893)
Sport of 'Heinrich Schultheis' (HP).
"Light silvery blush." [P1] "Flesh-pink with silvery reflections; flower large; vigorous." [Cx] "Has the singular habit of bearing flowers of two different colors in the same cluster; sometimes two colors are found in the same blossom." [JR21/40] "Flowers large, full, purple-red becoming whitish; habit of 'Heinrich Schultheis'." [JR17/178] "Huge, very double, scented flowers of pale pink on a sturdy plant...3×3 [ft; ca. 9×9 dm]." [B]

Paula Clegg (Kiese, 1912)
From 'Kaiserin Auguste Viktoria' (HT) × *R. fœtida* 'Bicolor'
"This introduction is very hardy. The blossom has the same form and color as that of 'Richmond'—which is to say bright scarlet red—but is

fuller, and has a very pleasant scent. It always opens very well. It is one of the most fragrant roses." [JR37/57]

Pauline Lansezeur (Lansezeur/E. Verdier, 1855)
"Red, shaded with violet-crimson, medium size, free blooming." [EL] "Bright crimson when opening, passing later to violet-pink." [l'H55/246] "Growth very vigorous, very remontant, giving flowers until the end of Fall; flower medium-sized, full; color, brilliant violet, and pink." [S]

Peach Blossom (W. Paul, 1874) syn., 'Egeria'
Seedling of 'Jules Margottin' (HP).
"Flesh." [Ÿ] "Bush vigorous; its large, full flowers are a delicate pink nuanced carmine and washed with white." [VH75/81] "Salmon-pink, a very lovely shade; medium size, full, semi-globular; not of good constitution. For experienced cultivators this is a superb sort." [EL] "Fairly hardy; profuse summer bloom." [S]

[Perpétuelle de Neuilly] (V. Verdier, 1834) trans., "Perpetual from Neuilly" Seedling of 'Athalin' (HB).
"Lilac-pink, full, cupped, medium-sized, superb." [LF] "Flowers rose-colour, large and full; form, globular. Habit erect, fine; growth moderate. A superb forcing Rose, and very sweet. Rarely flowers well out of doors." [P] "[*Such roses, of which 'Perpétuelle de Neuilly' is one,*] form dwarf bushes of great beauty: De Neuilly is also of this race, and, as a rose for forcing, is really beautiful, as it gives large thick petalled and very fragrant flowers of a clear rose-colour. Owing to their substance, these bear strong heat, and retain their colour a long time: for the open air, this variety cannot be recommended." [R9] "A variety of great excellence, having all the peculiar beauty of the Bourbon Rose, one of its parents [*say, rather, "grandparents"*], with the fragrance of the Damask. It is a most abundant autumnal bloomer, and ought to be extensively cultivated." [WRP]

Peter Lawson (Thomas, 1862)
"Brilliant red, shaded with carmine, large and double." [FP] "Vigorous; flower very large, full, poppy red, very intense, shaded with carmine." [l'H62/278]

Pfaffstädt (Herzogin Elsa von Württemberg, 1929)
From 'Frau Karl Druschki' (HP) × 'Lyon-Rose' (Pernetiana)
"Yellowish white, large, full, medium scent, tall." [Sn]

Philipp Paulig (Lambert, 1908)
From 'Captain Hayward' (HP) × 'Baronne Adolphe de Rothschild' (HP).
"Deep red, large, full, medium scent, tall." [Sn]

Philippe Bardet (Moreau-Robert, 1874)
"Growth vigorous; blooms in clusters; flower very large, full; color, bright sparkling red nuanced carmine." [S]

[Pie IX] (Vibert, 1848) syn., 'Pius IX'
"Large, full, crimson." [Pq] "Deep rose, tinged with crimson." [FP, who places it in the 'La Reine' tribe] "9-10 cm [ca. 4 inches], full, incarnate pink going to crimson, flat, nearly thornless, very vigorous. This rose is among the most beautiful." [M-L48/427-428] "Branches vigorous; brown at first, bristling with numerous little stickers and some fairly large, though remote, thorns which are hooked and brownish red; foliage ample, a handsome light green, shiny above, pale and slightly glaucous beneath; composed of 3-7 unequal, nearly smooth, leaflets, upturned at the edge, irregularly dentate; the flowers are fragrant, large, full, a handsome bright crimson red, usually in threes at the end of the cane." [S] "Does as well grafted as own-root." [l'H53/172] "Large, double, full and of deep red colour. The bush is tree-like in habit. Unless cut regularly, it will preempt more space than an ordinary garden allows for one rose-bush...bold, dark green foliage, free from diseases, the constitutional strength and healthful growth overbalancing any harm to foliage or flowers done by insects. The immense red roses and large buds are in evidence from early spring to late

autumn. The only 'Pius IX' I can recall stands in an old garden where it was planted fifty years ago. It is as vigorous and prolific now as it was when planted." [Dr]

"Horticulturists place the rose 'Pie IX' in the category of those hybrids which resemble *Hybrid Chinas* in wood and foliage, but *Portlands* in the ovary. All of such hybrids have wood of a delicate green, sometimes more or less brown in youth, clothed with numerous very unequal prickles, sharp and slightly hooked; some are small, like a large bristle enlarged at the base; others are longer and look quite completely like thorns. The leaves are perfectly glabrous, smooth in youth; in age, however, they become slightly thicker, stiff, and somewhat rugose; it is this which distinguishes these hybrids from the *true* Portlands, which have soft leaves which are slender and downy. The ovary is oblong or elongate, or funnel-shaped. The rose 'Pie IX' is a charming introduction of Monsieur Vibert's…The canes…are vigorous, brown when young, bristling with numerous small sharp points as well as with some pretty big hooked reddish-brown thorns. The leaves are lush, beautiful light green, glossy above, paler and slightly glaucous beneath; they are composed of 3-7 unequal leaflets which are nearly smooth, rolled at the edges, irregularly dentate and ciliate; the odd leaflet is shortly acuminate, with a mid-vein bristling with small prickles; the side-leaflets grade smaller, are nearly sessile, and are, in form, quite variable—oval, elliptical, oblong—with a slightly bristly midvein. The petiole is flexuose, glandulose, bearing several prickles beneath, and marked with a shallow furrow; red-brown above. The stipules are very lacy, ciliate, longly adherent to the petiole, with the free part linear and subulate. The flowers are fragrant, large, full, beautiful bright crimson red, usually in threes, at the tip of the cane, and borne on fairly strong, upright peduncles which are 2-3 cm long [ca. 1 inch] and covered with glandular hairs. The calyx-tube (ovary), an extension of the peduncle, gradually enlarges into funnel-form, and is not constricted at the summit; it is a very delicate green, glabrous, or only glandular at the base. The calyx-leaflets (sepals) are long, gradually and lacily narrowing towards the tip, glandular and green on the back, slightly cottony within; two are quite entire; two others have, on both sides, small, lacy, glandular processes; the fifth has these processes only on one edge. The many petals which constitute the corolla are all a beautiful bright crimson above, paler and somewhat violet beneath, and white at the base; the outer petals are large, mostly obovate—somewhat spoon-like—rather spreading out than upright; the central petals are unequal, slightly ragged, quite serrate, sometimes reflexed on the interior, and covering some occasional stamens which one finds within the bundle that clothes the much-dilated, glabrous, mouth of the ovary. Inside the tube, which is bristling with silky white bristles in the lower part, one finds many ovules which are usually sterile, each one tipped with a silky style, fleshed out and tipped with enlarged, greenish stigmata." [l'H51/121-122]

Pierre Caro (Levet, 1878) syn., 'Pierre Carot'
Seedling of 'Victor Verdier' (HP).
"Bush vigorous; canes upright; foliage dark green; blossom medium-sized or large, full, perfect form; color, dark red, fading to a beautiful, superb light red." [JR2/166]

Pierre Notting (Portemer, 1863)
Seedling of 'Alfred Colomb' (HP).
"Blackish red, shaded with violet, very large and full; form globular; habit good." [P1] "Deep velvety shaded crimson, a fine deep globular flower, very large; a superb rose." [JC] "A muddy maroon." [JR10/29] "Cluster-flowering...very fragrant." [S] "Egg-shaped bud." [WD] "Strong-growing...good in autumn." [Hn] "Of vigorous strong growth, good on all stocks, with extra large fine foliage rather liable to mildew. A fine-weather Rose that will rot without opening in a wet season. It comes badly as a rule, slow in opening, and often showing a great hollow in the centre down to the eye before it expands. The plants are passed by as hopeless again and again; then, with some mysterious climatic change, for fine weather alone will not do it, toward the end of the season the blooms

sometimes begin to open properly when all the strongest are over, and we see what a grand flower it can be when it chooses. Though still inclined to be weak in centre and endurance, it is then excellent in shape, colour, size, fragrance, and substance…It is free-flowering but late, and not a good autumnal, as the second crop is rarely of any value. The violet shade on the outer petals is one of the nearest approaches to blue that we have." [F-M3] "Upright, vigorous plant…4×3 [ft; ca. 1.25×1 m]." [B] "Most beautiful." [EL] "One of the best." [FP] "Born February 11, 1835, at Bollendorf, a hamlet near La Sare on the border of Luxembourg, Monsieur Notting passed his youth in very modest circumstances. From his most tender years, he evinced a passion for flowers…In 1845, he settled in Luxembourg, and labored as friend and worker at Monsieur Wilhelm's establishment, where he worked until 1855. It was then that he got to know Monsieur Jean Soupert, ten years younger than himself; and the two of them founded the company so well known since that time." [JR19/177]

Piron-Médard (Piron-Médard, 1906)
"Very vigorous, canes upright, nearly thornless, handsome foliage. Bud well formed and long, flower full. Color, beautiful satin pink." [JR31/7]

Pius IX
Listed as 'Pie IX'.

Plonia
Listed as 'Pæonia'.

Polar Bear (Nicolas, 1934)
From 'Schoener's Nutkana' (HNut) × 'New Century' (Rugosa).
"Bud large, ovoid, white with blush; flower large, very double, full, globular, extremely lasting, intensely fragrant (wild rose), white with a faint blush, becoming pure white, on long, strong stem. Foliage abundant, large, leathery, wrinkled. Vigorous, upright, bushy, like 'Radiance'; abundant, continuous bloomer." [ARA34/220] "Fragrant blooms reminiscent

of the old Bourbons." [ARA37/242] "A fine, vigorous, everblooming Hybrid Tea with Hybrid Perpetual vigor and hardiness. Flowers are intensely fragrant…freely produced its very double, fragrant, white flowers in rather drooping clusters." [ARA35/197] "Quantities of flowers off and on all season…makes a good background rose." [ARA36/206] "Flowers are not outstanding but the plant is vigorous, blooms freely and requires little care, so why complain." [ARA39/217] The placement of 'Polar Bear' seems odd, given its parentage; but it is an example of placement by use in the garden rather than by genetic background.

[**Ponctué**] (Laffay,-1845) trans., "Spotted"
"Flower medium size, double, flat, of a bright rose color, spotted with lilac and pure white." [MH45/28]

Préfet Limbourg
Listed as 'Monsieur le Préfet Limbourg'.

Président Briand (M. Guillot/Mallerin, 1929)
From a cross of two unnamed seedlings: Seedling A (from another unnamed seedling which came from 'Frau Karl Druschki' (HP) and which was crossed with 'Lyon-Rose' (Pernetiana)) × Seedling B (from 'Frau Karl Druschki' × 'Willowmere' (Pernetiana)).
"Light pink, tinted mauve." [Ÿ] "Bud and bloom very large, double, high-centered, globular, very lasting, moderately fragrant, pink with salmon suffusion, borne singly on strong stem. Foliage abundant, large, rich green, wrinkled, mildews. Growth vigorous (about 3 feet), upright, compact; profuse, intermittent bloomer. Very hardy." [ARA30/224] "Named for Aristide Briand, President of the French Republic, to commemorate the Kellogg Peace Pact, of which Briand was the instigator. 'President Briand' is 'Perpetual' in the full meaning of the word, sending out in quick succession crop after crop of mammoth 'peony' Ross. The bud is globular and for a long while the open flower retains the globular form of a peony of the bomb type and bears a delicious fragrance. In color it is a bright

clear pink with a salmon suffusion, and the bloom is long-lasting, either on the plant or cut. The plant is vigorous, extremely hardy, and, when once established, will make a large bush seldom out of bloom throughout the season. Its wood is very thorny and the foliage interestingly goffered. A splendid example of the new strain of Hybrid Perpetuals." [C-Ps29]

Président Carnot (Degressy, 1891)
"Bright red nuanced carmine." [Ÿ] "Vigorous, nearly thornless, bullate beautiful dark green foliage; flower large, full, well formed, well held, bright pink nuanced carmine with flame reflections. Very remontant." [JR15/164]

Président Lincoln (Granger/Lévêque, 1862)
Seedling of 'Lord Raglan' (HP).
"Wine-red." [Ÿ] "Vigorous…flower large, full; cerise-red." [S] "Vermilion-red, tinged with crimson, the flowers are much like 'Général Washington', but inferior in quality to that variety, the habit of growth is stronger." [EL] "Very vigorous; foliage dark green; flower very large, full, imbricated, beautiful cerise pink nuanced superb brown; from 'Lord Raglan'." [l'H62/278]

Président Schlachter (E. Verdier, 1877)
"Reddish crimson, tinged with violet." [EL] "Vigorous bush; flower large, full, well formed, velvety crimson red shaded purple, flame, and violet; canes strong and upright, reddish green; thorns rare, thick, short and straight, pink; leaves composed of 5 close-set oblong leaflets, dark green with irregular, shallow serration." [S]

Président Sénélar (Schwartz, 1883)
"Very vigorous and with a look all its own, foliage brownish green, flower large, full, petals rounded, imbricated, mucronate, deep cerise red, brilliantly velvety, illuminated by some flame-color, fading to purple nuanced cinnabar. A magnificent variety." [JR7/122]

Président Willermoz (Ducher, 1867)
"Flower very large, full; bright pink." [S] "Rich brilliant carmine, with a very soft and pleasing violet tint, color new and distinct, fine petal and very beautiful; habit vigorous." [JC]

Pride of Reigate (J. Brown/G. Paul, 1884)
Sport of 'Comtesse d'Oxford' (HP).
"Light crimson plumed and splotched white and pink." [JR25/24] "All the manners and customs of the 'Victor Verdier' race. This Rose has at least the merit of being the most distinct in colour of all H.P.'s, so that the merest tyro could pick it out anywhere, for it has the dark ground shade of the original striped and splashed with white." [F-M3]

Pride of the Valley
Listed as 'Mrs. F.W. Sanford'.

Pride of Waltham (W. Paul, 1881)
Sport of 'Comtesse d'Oxford' (HP).
"Light salmon-pink, shaded violet. Similar in growth and foliage to 'Comtesse d'Oxford'." [H] "Delicate flesh-colour richly shaded with bright rose, very clear and distinct. The flowers are very large and full, with petals of great substance. Habit and constitution good. One of the best." [P1] "A sport from ['Comtesse d'Oxford'], with all the manners and customs of the family…as good a grower as any of them, with large blooms opening well to good shape with stout petals and fine colour…popular in Australia." [F-M2] "Vigorous; foliage and wood perfect." [S]

[Prince Albert] (Laffay/Rivers, 1837)
From 'Gloire des Rosomanes' (B) × a Damask Perpetual.
"Color changing from pink to pansy purple and crimson, superb." [LF] "Medium or large, very full, color varying from pink to dark violet." [R-H42] "Large, carmined rose, changing to dark velvety crimson." [JWa] "Rich crimson purple, large and full; form, compact. Habit, branching; growth, moderate. Uncertain out of doors, but a good forcing Rose, and

very sweet." [P] "Very vigorous; flower large, full, very dense, unique scent; color, deep purple shaded carmine; cold changes color to a shade of carmine which is rather towards violet." [S] "In full bloom in December [*in Havana*], its best season; it is much like because it has four bloom-periods during the year." [JR8/41] "Vigorous bush; leaves of three or five glaucous green leaflets. Thorns rare, but long; flowers cupped, very full, 5-6 cm across [ca. 2-2.5 inches]. Their color is variable; while some are fresh pink, others are a more or less dark purple, sometimes with a crimson tint, or indeed an intense, velvety violet, more so than that of a Pansy. Each blossom is uniform in coloration, but these differing shades can be found on different flowers from the same specimen. What is more, they have the advantage of wafting a fairly strong, pleasant scent, more pronounced than that of the Quatre-Saison [*i.e., Damask Perpetual*]." [An40/89] Not to be confused with A. Paul's 1852 Bourbon of the same name, which is crimson. Prince Albert of Saxe-Coburg-Gotha, beloved husband of Queen Victoria of Great Britain; lived 1819-1861.

Prince Arthur (B.R. Cant, 1875)
"Shaded crimson; vigorous. A good exhibition and garden Rose." [J] "Belongs to the 'Général Jacqueminot' type. Deep crimson, smaller but better formed than Jacqueminot." [EL] "Vigorous; flower medium-sized, full; intense crimson." [S] "Of good vigorous growth, but the wood is not quite stiff enough to support the blooms…[L]iable to mildew and orange-fungus, but not much injured by rain. The blooms come generally well, in a capital characteristic form, and though the petals are thin and the flowers look fragile, they last well. I gathered from the last Mr. B.R. Cant that the origin of this fine rose is rather obscure, but the general appearance points to 'Général Jacqueminot' as an ancestor. It is however much darker in colour, larger, and does better with me in every way. It is very free blooming and fairly good in autumn, but requires good treatment to be seen in perfection, though it is hardy and healthy in most soils and appreciated in America." [F-M2] "The best dark red rose. A hybrid, and therefore, of

course, it gets red rust and loses its leaves." [HmC] Prince Arthur, one of Queen Victoria's children.

Prince Camille de Rohan (E. Verdier, 1861)
Either a seedling of 'Maurice Bernardin' (HP); or possibly from 'Général Jacqueminot' (HP) × 'Géant des Batailles' (HP).
"Flower medium-sized or large, full, maroon crimson, very dark, velvety, nuanced blood red." [l'H61/264] "Large, well-filled, deep velvety chestnut brown with blood red; flowers freely in clusters. An old and proved rose—one of the best dark HP's." [Hn] "Intensely dark crimson colour, and deliciously sweet." [E] "Crimson and maroon highlighted with bright red." [JR1/2/7] "Intense maroon red which does not blue." [Cx] "The blooms are apt to 'burn,' but are not much injured by rain, thin and apt to show the eye, below the average size, but remarkable for colour...velvety in the highest degree...free blooming and a good autumnal...requires a cool season." [F-M2] "Its maroon blooms, with black shading, are fine in June, but seldom appear afterward. The plant is moderate and divergent in growth." [ARA34/78] "Moderately full, habit somewhat spreading, shy in autumn." [EL] "Hardy...flower of moderate size, full, cupped, imbricated...beautiful exhibition rose." [S] "Opens well in dampness." [Th2] "Weak neck...a fascinating rose...almost colossal...vigorous...3×3 [ft; ca. 9×9 dm]." [B] "A poor grower." [HmC] "Growth vigorous." [P1] "Of good growth and foliage...very liable to mildew and orange fungus." [F-M2] "Of weak growth, and useless for garden display." [OM] "Does not care for too much sun. Blooms freely, but here [*on the Riviera*] is not vigorous or a good doer, dirty and a prey to many insect pests." [B&V] "This very pretty plant makes a vigorous bush, stocky, floriferous, providing round buds and large flowers...still among the most notable of its sort." [JR30/169] "Still prince of its hue." [WD]

Prince de Joinville (W. Paul, 1867)
"Flowers light crimson; a fine, large, showy rose, of vigorous and hardy habit." [FP] "Flower medium sized, quite full, very robust; color, very bright carmine red." [S]

Prince de Portia (E. Verdier, 1865)
"Flowers about 10 cm [ca. 4 inches], full, a most beautiful deep vermilion." [l'H65/340] "Vermilion, large, full, well formed, one of the most fragrant, somewhat subject to mildew. A splendid variety." [EL] "Bush vigorous; flower large, full; color, deep scarlet." [S]

Prince Eugène de Beauharnais (Moreau-Robert, 1864)
"Brilliant reddish-scarlet, shaded with purple." [FP] "Bush vigorous; flower large, full, plump; color, sparkling fiery red; beautiful exhibition rose." [S]

Prince Henri d'Orléans (E. Verdier, 1886)
"Brilliant pink." [Ÿ] "Vigorous, big erect light green canes; thorns very numerous, unequal, usually thin and sharp, slightly hooked, greenish pink; leaves of five elliptical dark green leaflets, deeply serrated with large teeth; flowers large, full, very well formed, cupped, charming when half open; color, light carmine cerise red." [JR10/170]

Prince Noir (Boyau, 1854) trans., "Black Prince"
"Deep crimson shaded with almost black. Large and globular, with high centre. Nice rose of good shape." [B&V] "Bush of moderate vigor; flower medium-sized, nearly full; color, blackish-purple; exterior petals deep velvety carmine." [S] "Very dark maroon, good climber." [FP] Not to be confused with the HP 'Black Prince'.

Prince Stirbey (Schwartz/Guillot père/ 1871)
"Bush of moderate vigor; flower large, full; color, flesh pink." [S]

Prince Waldemar (E. Verdier, 1885)
"Very vigorous, canes strong, look of 'Dr. Andry'; leaves large, delicate green; flowers large, full, very well formed, cupped, a most beautiful bright carmine cerise red bordered whitish." [JR8/179]

Princesse Louise (Laxton/W. Paul, 1869)
From 'Mme. Vidot' (HP) × 'Virginale' (HP).
"White, sometimes bluish [*sic; 'blush,' perhaps?*]-white, pretty, but wanting in substance." [JC] "Flower medium-sized, full, well-formed, white, sometimes flesh." [S]

Princess of Wales (W. Paul, 1864)
"Bright crimson, with thick and firm petals." [FP] "Double." [EL] "Carmine, colour bright and beautiful, flowers good size, cupped, and well formed; a fine rose, habit vigorous." [JC] Not to be confused with Laxton's pink HP of 1871, or with Bennett's Tea of 1882, both of the same name.

Princesse Amedée de Broglie (Lévêque, 1885)
"Very vigorous, beautiful large dark green foliage; flower very large, full, globular, perfectly imbricated, beautiful bright light pink, silvery towards the center, reverse of the petals blush, very remontant." [JR8/148]

Princesse Charles d'Aremberg (Soupert & Notting, 1876)
From 'Dupuy-Jamain' (HP) × 'Mme. de Sevigné' (HP).
"Flower large, full; petals large; Centifolia form; outer petals very delicate silvery lilac; center, bright carmine; much to be recommended; quite remontant; blooms until the end of the season." [S] "Vigorous." [JR1/6/11]

Princesse de Béarn (Lévêque, 1885)
Seedling of 'Duc de Cazes' (HP).
"Very vigorous, dark green leaves, flowers very large, globular, full, extremely well formed, rich blackish poppy red, nuanced and brightened

with brilliant vermilion...abundant bloom." [JR8/150] "Strong stems, excellently held...very pretty foliage...dedicated to Mme. la Princesse de Béarn, a great fancier of roses, who died, alas, in the bloom of life." [JR16/152]

Princesse de Joinville (Poncet/V. Verdier, 1840)

"Medium-sized, full, bright pink [*and listed as a 'remontant hybrid'*]." [Pq] Not to be confused with the 1840 Tea of the same name.

Princesse de Naples

Listed as 'Principessa di Napoli'.

[Princesse Hélène] (Laffay, 1837)

"Pink and crimson, nuanced, large, full, superb." [LF] "Lilac-rose." [HoBoIV] "Rosy purple, of medium size, very double; form globular. Habit, erect; growth, moderate. A most abundant bloomer, when in full vigour." [P] "It was in 1837 that Monsieur Laffay...sent to Mr. William Paul, his friend, the first cross-bred hybrid from the old Damasks, then so much in fashion...a superb purple Rose...This hybrid was, fortunately, fertile, and gave seed abundantly. Not four years had passed before Mr. William Paul and other rosarians had grown more than twenty varieties." [R-H63]

Princesse Hélène d'Orléans (E. Verdier, 1886)

"Brilliant pink." [Ÿ] "Vigorous, canes unbranched and erect, light green; thorns somewhat numerous, strong, fairly straight, yellowish pink; leaves composed of five oval undulate dark green leaflets, with irregular shallow dentations; flowers large, full, of very beautiful rounded form, cupped, firmly held; color, beautiful very fresh brilliant pink, very fragrant." [JR10/170]

Princesse Lise Troubetzkoï (Lévêque, 1877)

"Vigorous, flower medium-sized or large, full, very well formed, imbricated, handsome delicate pink, petals bordered white; very fetching, most attractive." [JR1/12/11]

Princesse Marie d'Orléans (E. Verdier, 1885)
"Very vigorous, with upright canes; foliage large, rounded, and very glossy, light green; flowers large, full, well-formed, a most beautiful bright cerise pink shaded silvery." [JR8/179]

Princesse Marie Dolgorouky (Gonod, 1878)
Seedling of 'Anna de Diesbach' (HP).
"Bush very vigorous, with stiff, upright canes; foliage of five leaflets, very dark green; peduncle strong; flower very large, cupped, very well formed, magnificent coloration—satiny bright pink, very frequently striped with carmine to good effect." [JR2/167]

Princesse Radziwill (Lévêque, 1883)
"China pink." [Ÿ] "Very vigorous, foliage bright light green, flower large, full, perfect form, perfectly imbricated, beautiful light pink or bright carmine pink shaded bright crimson; superb." [JR7/158] "The Radziwill grounds would also present a specimen of a taste more than genteel: To cross a twenty-foot water course, it would be necessary to board a boat moored at the side of a sphinx, the emblem of the perils of navigation, with an altar to Hope on the other side. Debarking would take place in a sacred grove filled with other altars, where a shady footpath led to a Gothic shelter, sanctuary of Melancholy. The visitor would then pass a Greek temple where vestal figures were grouped around statues of Love and Silence, and then a knight's tent, an Oriental salon with mahogany doors, a museum of ersatz antiquities, and, as the crowning touch, the funeral monument erected, before need, by the Princess Radziwill. no doubt to cheer up the visitor." [Pd]

Principessa di Napoli (Gaëtano, Bonfiglioli & figlio, 1897) syn., 'Princesse de Naples'
"Silvery pink on a ground of cream." [Ÿ] "In the deportment of the plant and the form of the flower, very much like 'Captain Christy'. The fragrance would seem to be superior to that of 'La France'. The growth is vigorous,

compact, and regular; the foliage ample and beautiful brilliant light green. Flower, very large, imbricated, silvery flesh pink, very fresh, reverse of petals bright lilac pink; very fragrant. The plant blooms abundantly, and is quite remontant." [JR21/82]

Prinz Max zu Shaumburg-Lippe (Herzogin Elsa von Württemberg, 1934) trans., "Prince Max of Schaumburg-Lippe"
From 'Frau Karl Druschki' (HP) × 'Lyon-Rose' (Pernetiana).
"Salmon pink, large, full, medium scent, tall." [Sn]

Prinzessin Elsa zu Schaumburg-Lippe (Herzogin Elsa von Württemberg, 1929) trans., "Princess Elsa of Schaumburg-Lippe"
"Yellowish-white, very large, full, medium scent, tall." [Sn]

Professeur Charguereaud (Lévêque, 1890)
"Vigorous, foliage ample, dark green, flower large, full, well formed, deep red marbled brown and poppy, very distinct and effective." [JR14/179]

Professeur Maxime Cornu (Lévêque, 1885)
"Very vigorous; foliage ample, lanceolate, glaucous green; flower very large, full, well formed, beautiful bright cerise red; color very scintillating...blooms abundantly." [JR8/148]

Prosper Laugier (E. Verdier, 1883)
"Flower large, full, bright crimson-red." [JR9/146] "Cupped, fragrant." [Cx] "Very vigorous; branches strong and upright, reddish; numerous unequal, pointed, recurved, pink thorns; leaves comprised of five leaflets, oblong, dark green, irregularly but deeply toothed; flower large, full, of a form most perfect and regular; color very brilliant—scarlet red with very bright carmine. A superb variety." [S]

Prudence Besson (Lacharme, 1865)
"Cerise pink." [Ÿ] "Growth vigorous; flower very large, semi-full, flat, very effective; color, carmine red." [S] "Much like 'Souvenir de la Reine d'Angleterre'." [l'H65/340]

[**Queen of Edgely**] (Florist's Exchange, 1901)
Sport of 'American Beauty' (HP).
"Color a bright pink; flowers large and deep cup shaped; very fragrant, like its parent." [CA02] "This famous New Rose originated near Philadelphia, and is a sport from the well-known 'American Beauty', of which it is an exact counterpart in every particular except color. It has the same vigorous growth and beautiful foliage, and the same exquisite fragrance. The color is a lovely shade of bright, clear pink, very beautiful. The flowers are large and very deep, averaging over five inches across, and are borne on long stiff stems." [C&Js02] Called, as a sort of subtitle, the "Pink American Beauty."

Queen of Queens (W. Paul, 1882) syn., 'Reine des Reines'
From 'Victor Verdier' (HP) × a seedling (which was the result of crossing the HP 'La Reine' with the Alba 'Great Maiden's Blush').
"Pink, with blush edges, large and full; growth vigorous." [P1] "Of perfect form; grows and flowers freely." [EL] "Of 'Victor Verdier' race with the usual habit, but not quite so strong in growth as most of them. Hardly full-sized, but of nice globular form." [F-M3] "Good both as a garden rose and as an exhibition variety; one of the best modern introductions." [S]

Red Druschki
Listed as 'Ruhm von Steinfurth'.

Reine d'Espagne (Fontaine, 1861) trans., "Queen of Spain"
"Blossom medium-sized, full; color, flame red." [S] Has been mis-classified by modernity as a Gallica.

Reine de Castille (Lartay, 1852) trans., "Queen of Castile"
"Flower large, full, globular, deep carmine red." [l'H56/199] "Whitish-rose, large and full, of good habit, and blooms freely." [FP] "Bush very vigorous; flower large, very full, imbricated, very well formed; color, velvety flame red." [S]

Reine de Danemark (Granger, 1857)
"Flesh-lilac flowers, large, full, admirably clear, fairly often a rose of the first merit, but not a dependable bloomer." [R-H63] "Growth vigorous; canes short, nearly thornless; leaves small, pointed, very serrate; flower large, full, well formed, opening with difficulty; color, pinkish lilac tending towards flesh pink." [S]

Reine des Neiges
Listed as 'Frau Karl Druschki'.

Reine des Reines
Listed as 'Queen of Queens'

Reine des Violettes (Mille-Malet, 1860) trans., "Queen of Violets"
Seedling of 'Pie IX' (HP).
"Light violet." [BJ] "Violet-red, a muddy color." [EL] "Vigorous, hardy; flower large, full, flat; dark violet; one of the best of its color." [S] "Foliage...having a greyish sheen...incurved petals forming a wide, flat, quartered flower with button eye." [T1] "Abundant leaves...velvety, violet flowers in early Summer...some later. Fragrant...6×6 [ft; ca. 1.75×1.75 m]." [B] "Healthy, robust, long and upright canes; the flower's perfume is of the sweet-yeasty variety, not unlike that of 'Souvenir de la Malmaison'." [BCD] "Lavender-rose with a velvety violet center...ages to a rich purple. Large and very double, with cupped petals, it flowers freely in early summer and intermittently thereafter...7-8 feet [ca. 2-2.25 m]...dull, smooth, green leaves...practically thornless." [W] This cultivar is very close to the Trianon series of Damask Perpetuals, such as 'Joasine Hanet'.

[Rembrandt] (Van Rossem, 1914)
From 'Frau Karl Druschki' (HP) × 'Lyon-Rose' (Pernetiana)
"A fair representative of the new type of Hybrid Perpetual, the product of a renaissance of this once-neglected class. The blooms are creamy pink, with a tawny center, and are enormous, with leathery, long-lasting petals, full to the center. Growth and habit of 'Frau Karl Druschki', but with

better foliage, and almost thornless. Can be used as a pillar or trained on a fence." [C-Ps29] Not to be confused with the Damask Perpetual of the same name.

Réveil du Printemps (Oger, 1883) trans., "Spring's Awakening"
"Growth very vigorous; flower large, very full, well formed; very delicate flesh white; of the 'Mme. Vidot' sort." [S]

Reverend Alan Cheales (G. Paul, 1897)
"This variety is very different from previously known roses; the flower is very big, in a very original peony form; color, pale lake pink, petal reverse shaded darker. The very floriferous plant is extremely decorative; its foliage appears very early in the Spring, and does not fall until the heavy frosts. It is dedicated to the secretary of the Brockham Rose Society." [JR21/66] "A pretty good grower which does not require close pruning. It flowers freely and is a 'good doer'. The blooms are of a nice fresh colour—'pure lake with reverse of petals silvery white'—but not very lasting. The shape is rather loose, and the raiser calls it a 'peony-like Rose' but I do not think it is quite as bad as that, and I have seen it with a good point, and shown well. Still, it should not be relied on as an Exhibition Rose, and would be better for garden purposes if its growth was stronger." [F-M2]

Riccordo di Fernando Scarlatti (Italy?, ca. 1925) trans., "In Memory of Fernando Scarlatti"
"Dark red, large, full, very fragrant, tall." [Sn]

Robert de Brie (Granger, 1860)
"Salmon pink." [LS] "Flower large, full; color, lilac-pink marbled white." [S] "Outer petals of a gray leaden pink, inner petals lighter pink, where they form a belt around the reproductive organs…And, when it rains, all the blossoms become little reservoirs of water of a very picturesque metallic appearance." [VH62/93]

Robert Duncan (A. Dickson, 1897)
"Plant very vigorous and floriferous; flowers large, well-formed, with large and markedly concave petals. Color, light pinkish lake. Garden and exhibition variety." [JR21/68]

Roger Lambelin (Widow Schwartz, 1890)
Sport of either 'Prince Camille de Rohan' (HP) or 'Fisher Holmes' (HP).
"Deep velvety red, spotted with white; distinct and curious." [P1] "Frilled petals...crimson maroon with unusual white and pink stripes. Needs extra care. 4×3 [ft; ca. 1.25×1 m]." [B] "Quite a free bloomer and unique in color but not of exceptionally good form." [ARA34/79] "Abundant light green foliage. Flower medium-sized, well formed; the petals are a magnificent velvety currant-red, abundantly touched and margined with white and pink. The numerous stamens are very evident." [JR14/149] "A 6-to 8-foot pillar [ca. 1.75-2.25 m]...beautiful and also full of scent." [W] "Wine-scented." [JR33/101] "This variety makes a bush which is vigorous and very floriferous, and having growth somewhat like its parent [*referring to 'Prince Camille de Rohan'*]. The numerous blossoms are full...sometimes touched but always edged with pure white and light pink. We have often seen striped blossoms as well, like our very pretty striped Gallicas." [JR19/72] "The royalist, Roger Lambelin." [JR34/8]

Rosa Verschuren (Verschuren, 1905)
Seedling of 'Souvenir de la Reine d'Angleterre' (HP).
"Very fresh pink." [Ÿ] "Pink, large, full, medium scent, medium height." [Sn]

Rose Cornet
Listed as 'Cornet'.

Rose de France (E. Verdier, 1893) trans., "Rose of France"
"Vigorous with erect canes; flowers medium or large, full, of admirable form and exquisite freshness; color, beautiful bright carmine pink with reverse of petals silvery; fragrance notably Centifolia-like. Superb." [JR17/178]

Rosiériste Harms (E. Verdier, 1879)
"Bush vigorous, having the look of 'Mme. Victor Verdier'; canes stiff and upright, light green; thorns fairly numerous, very fine and pointed, yellowish; leaves composed of 3-5 delicate green leaflets; deep serration; flower large, full, extremely well formed; color, beautiful velvety scarlet red." [JR3/181]

[Rosslyn] (A. Dickson, 1900)
Sport of 'Mlle. Suzanne-Marie Rodocanachi' (HP).
"Large full flowers and very sweet, color exquisite rosy flesh, very fragrant and attractive, free bloomer and entirely hardy." [C&Js02]

Rosy Morn (W. Paul, 1878)
Seedling of 'Victor Verdier' (HP).
"Delicate peach color, richly shaded salmon pink; they are very large with thin petals; the fragrance is delicate, and for form perfect. Its foliage is abundant and pretty, while the growth is very vigorous, the wood strong and lightly spiny." [JR2/7] "Belongs to the 'Victor Verdier' type. Salmon-pink, a deeper shade than '[Mlle.] Eugénie Verdier'; peculiar wood and foliage more like 'Captain Christy' than any other variety. A good rose, but with too many imperfect blooms." [EL]

Rouge Angevine (Chédane-Guinoisseau & Pajotin-Chédane, 1907) trans., "Angers Red"
"Vigorous, canes upright, wood light green, very smooth, nearly thornless, foliage very beautiful green; bud long, with spiraled petals; flower opens very well; nearly full, large, with very large rounded petals; color, the most beautiful madder red, resembling the color of the prettiest red geraniums, never bluing, early, continuous till frost." [JR31/149]

Royal Mondain (Veysset, 1901)
"Crimson red nuanced light red, petals pointed, some edges lined white to a sixteenth of an inch. The blossom is large, full, fragrant, and held on a strong stem. The growth is vigorous and very floriferous." [JR25/147] "Distinct." [P1]

Rubens (Laffay, 1852)
"Amaranth." [LS] "Bright red, a fine color, flowers loose." [EL] Not to be confused with Robert's Tea of 1859.

Ruhm von Steinfurth (Weigand, 1920) syn., 'Red Druschki'; trans., 'Steinfurth Glory'
From 'Frau Karl Druschki' (HP) × either 'Ulrich Brunner fils' (HP) or 'General MacArthur' (HT).
"Double, high centred flowers of ruby red. Very fragrant with dark green leathery foliage...4×3 [ft; ca. 1.25×1 m]." [B] "Bud very large, long-pointed; flower very large, full, double, cupped, lasting; pure red, does not 'blue'; borne, singly and several together, on long, strong stems; strong fragrance. Foliage abundant, large...glossy...Few thorns. Very vigorous, upright; blooms profusely in June and July and in September and October." [ARA22/154-155] "Profuse all-season bloom...tall, sturdy bush with good foliage...cutting value." [Capt28] "Bright red...very healthy...produces fine, fragrant blooms profusely and to a less extent in fall." [ARA34/79]

Rushton-Radclyffe (E. Verdier, 1864)
"Flowers beautiful clear bright red; large, full, and of perfect form; growth vigorous." [FP] "Vigorous, flowers full, from 10-12 cm [ca. 4 inches], beautiful light bright cherry red." [l'H64/327] "Mr. Radclyffe, a clergyman, a horticulturalist, an excellent amateur of the rose, and a very amusing contributor to the *Florist*." [FP]

[Sa Majesté Gustave V] (Nabonnand, 1922)
From 'Frau Karl Druschki' (HP) × 'Avoca' (HT).
"His Majesty, Gustave, King of Sweden by birth but rosarian by choice, offered a cash premium for an everblooming Rose that would resist the bleak winters of the land of the midnight sun. Such an offer caused a flurry among European hybridizers and started a Renaissance of the Hybrid Perpetual. The winner was Nabonnand, the French Master of the

Tea Rose (irony of fate!) from the Riviera that knows not the meaning of the word 'winter'. The bud is ovoid, the bloom large size and double, beautifully imbricated, solid 'Paul Neyron' pink and sweetly perfumed. One of the most finished Roses of the Hybrid Perpetual class. Blooms recurrently at brief intervals until fall when it makes a wonderful display. Plant extra vigorous with beautiful, healthy foliage." [C-Pf29]

Salamander (W. Paul, 1891)
"Bright scarlet-crimson, magnificent colour. Very free and effective." [P1] "Very bright in the Summer, and a shade more brilliant and more somber in the Fall...blooms very freely, notable foliage and bearing, vigorous growth and good constitution." [JR15/87] "Notable for the beautiful color of bright, dark red, and for the form recalling that of 'Charles Lefebvre'. The petals are large, recurved, and substantial.—Certainly a pretty exhibition flower considering its symmetry and form." [JR14/174] "The blossom is curious in form, the outer petals being reflexed, and those of the center drawn up [*similar characteristics are noted in 'Jules Margottin*']." [JR17/101] "The growth and foliage seem to be good, and I have had no mildew on it. The blooms are bright and almost always try to come of good pointed shape, and in a cool season on good soil they may possibly be excellent, but it seems to be rather a small and thin Rose and hardly likely to be a good laster in a general way. It is free blooming and a fair autumnal." [F-M3] There was a legend that salamanders were able to live in fire (see, for instance, the autobiography of Benvenuto Cellini), making this a curious but appropriate name for a rose which the introducer perhaps hoped would be considered flame-colored.

Schneekönigen
Listed as 'Frau Karl Druschki'.

Schön Ingeborg (Kiese, 1921) trans., "Beautiful Ingeborg"
From 'Frau Karl Druschki' (HP) × 'Natalie Böttner' (HT).
"Light pink, large, full, medium height." [Sn] Not to be confused with 'St. Ingebert' (HP).

Secrétaire J. Nicolas (Schwartz, 1883)

"Very vigorous bush; canes upright with thin thorns; foliage light green; flower fragrant, large, full, well formed, cupped, globular; petals concave, exterior ones imbricated, gracefully reflexed; color, beautiful somber red with intense velvety purple, matte reflections; reverse of petals amaranth, pale, pruinose; plant of good deportment and very effective; the blossom is solitary on strong canes and in a cluster of two or three on the even more vigorous ones; freely remontant; well held and effective." [S]

[Sénateur Vaïsse] (Guillot père, 1859)
Seedling of 'Général Jacqueminot' (HP).

"Vigorous, flower large, full, some stamens in the center, bright red." [JDR59/28] "Intense glowing scarlet, fine petal, flower full, with high centre, large and perfectly formed, free growing, handsome foliage, and one of the very best roses in cultivation." [JC] "A very effective variety; deep velvety crimson; wood smooth; hardy...continuous bloom; good rose to force; excellent exhibition flower." [S] "Bright flashing crimson, flamed with scarlet; very large, full and double. 15 cts. Each." [C&Js01] "Senator Vaïsse, in charge of the administration of the Département du Rhône." [R-H63]

Silver Queen (W. Paul, 1887)
Sport of 'Queen of Queens' (HP).

"Silvery pink." [Ÿ] "Silvery red." [JR20/5] "Flowers extra large, full and deep, with broad thick petals and delightful fragrance; color exquisite silvery rose, passing to delicate rosy pink; beautiful cupped form, very handsome and an abundant bloomer." [C&Js02] "Silvery blush, shaded in the centre with very delicate rosy pink, distinct and lovely, large and full, of beautifully cupped form, and produced in great abundance, every shoot being crowned with a flower bud, the latter characteristic rendering it a fine autumnal bloomer." [P1] "Of 'Victor Verdier' race, of the same class as 'Queen of Queens', from which it appears to be a lighter coloured sport. Very free flowering, a good autumnal, fragrant, of fine form and attractive colour." [F-M3] "Medium height." [Sn] "A Hybrid Perpetual with smooth wood, whose flowers are a pure silvery pink of great beauty and perfect form." [JR12/107]

Simon de St.-Jean (Liabaud, 1861)
"Velvety purple." [LS] "Flower large, nearly full; purple nuanced velvety deep grenadine." [S]

Sir Garnet Wolseley (Cranston, 1875)
Seedling of either 'Prince Camille de Rohan' (HP) or 'La Rosière' (HP).
"Rich vermilion shaded with bright carmine, and the colour well maintained throughout, flowers very large, full, and perfectly formed, standing out bold and erect; habit strong and vigorous, producing flowers most freely." [JC] "Branches with coppery brown thorns; each branch bears a rose at the tip; flower large, very well formed, plump; color, vermilion red nuanced brilliant carmine." [S]

Sir Rowland Hill (Mack, 1887)
Sport of 'Charles Lefebvre' (HP).
"Violet red." [JR25/13] "Very large and full, with petals of great substance; sweet." [P1] "Vigorous, covered with beautiful foliage; flower large, full, and of good form, delicate perfume. Port-wine color, nuanced blackish maroon when opening, changing to brilliant Bordeaux-wine color. Very floriferous." [JR11/166] "'Deep velvety plum' is the general description, and, when seen at its best, it certainly has a very deep, almost dark blue, shade. But it must be grown very strong to show its colour to perfection, and more often comes of a dark claret or maroon, or even simply crimson...It seems decidedly less hardy and strong, and not so good a grower as the type from which it sprang: in other respects it has the same habit. A Rose of unique colour, but tender, liable to orange fungus and requiring high cultivation: not to be recommended for general culture." [F-M2]

[**Sisley**] (Sisley, 1835)

"Light carmine, full, flat, medium size." [LF, where listed among the Damask Perpetuals] "Rosy crimson, of medium size, full. A shy grower." [P] "Growth vigorous; flower large, full; color, violet amaranth." [S] "Medium or large, full, bright cherry-violet." [R-H42] "French horticulture has lost one of its oldest and most intelligent adepts in the person of Jean Sisley, who died last January 12 [1891] at Montplaisir-Lyon, at the age of 87...Born at Flessingue, Holland, in 1804, Jean Sisley later became a naturalized Frenchman; he was the nephew of the famous painter Jean Van Dael...Monsieur Sisley was one of the creators of the Lyon Horticultural Circle, of which he was General Secretary, and which has since become the Lyon Horticultural Association." [JR15/17] "Sisley, who developed at Lyon the first double white zonale pelargonium." [JR22/160] Jean Sisley, also notable as an early (if largely unheeded) advocate of systematic cross-breeding, at length reaffirming Henry Bennett's own determinations on the subject.

Souvenir d'Adolphe Thiers (Moreau-Robert, 1877) trans., "In Memory of Adolphe Thiers"

Seedling of 'Comtesse d'Oxford' (HP).

"Red, tinged with vermilion, very large." [EL] "Bush vigorous; flower very large, full; color, vermilion red...Very floriferous. This rose gets as big as those of 'Paul Neyron'." [S]

Souvenir d'Alexandre Hardy (Lévêque, 1898) trans., "In Memory of Alexandre Hardy"

"Very vigorous bush; ample foliage, bright dark green; flower large, full, very well formed; richly colored maroon red lit with carmine and bright vermilion, superb shades." [JR22/147]

Souvenir d'Aline Fontaine (Fontaine, 1879) trans., "In Memory of Aline Fontaine"

"Beautiful, well-formed flowers, opening from tight buds, cupped, reflexed, quartered, well filled with crinkled petals of flesh pink, becoming paler with age. The pale colour of the foliage makes a pleasing complement. Perhaps 4 feet [ca. 1.25 m]." [T3] "Bush very vigorous; flower large, very full; color, light salmon pink within, purplish carmine red towards the edge. Beautiful form; blooms in panicles." [S]

Souvenir d'Alphonse Lavallée (C. Verdier, 1884) trans., "In Memory of Alphonse Lavallée"

"Large, full, imbricated, dark grenadine maroon." [JR8/164] "Lovely double...many shades of crimson to purple maroon. Scented. Inclined to wander if not tethered...8×7 [ft; ca. 2.25×2 m]." [B] "The growth is vigorous enough, with branches which are nearly thornless, and somewhat red at the tip; the leaves are dark green, and the bloom abundant...Among the dark roses, 'Souvenir d'Alphonse Lavallée' is one of the best; its one fault, which it shares with others of the color, is that it burns under the rays of the Summer sun." [JR25/21] "Rather sparse, small foliage of mid-green." [T3] "Lavallé [*sic*] (Alphonse).—Amateur, well-known dendrologist, who died in 1884 at Segrez (Seine-et-Oise) at the age of 51. Created the 'Arboretum Segrezianum', now gone, where he brought together 4,500 species. Member of the Academy of Agriculture and President of the National Horticultural Society of France." [R-HC]

Souvenir d'André Raffy (Vigneron, 1899) trans., "In Memory of André Raffy"

"Vigorous, erect bush; foliage dark; flower large, full, globular, borne on strong stem; beautifully colored vermilion red, with light velvety touches. Blossom doesn't burn in the sun. Extremely floriferous." [JR23/149]

Souvenir d'Arthur de Sansal (Guénoux/Jamain, 1875) trans., "In Memory of Arthur de Sansal"
Seedling of 'Jules Margottin' (HP).
"Beautiful clear rose, colour of 'Jules Margottin', but brighter; flowers large and well formed; a fine exhibition rose." [JC] "Flower large, full, perfect Centifolia form; color, bright pink, sometimes silvery; very fragrant. Growth vigorous." [S]

Souvenir d'Auguste Rivière (E. Verdier, 1877) trans., "In Memory of Auguste Rivière"
"Belongs to the 'Prince Camille [de Rohan]' type. Velvety crimson." [EL] "Vigorous, flower very well formed, rich crimson red, purple and scarlet reflections." [JR1/12/13] "Very vigorous with strong reddish brown canes; thorns numerous, unequal, very sharp, reddish; leaves composed of five elongate leaflets, delicate green, irregularly and deeply toothed; flowers large, full, well formed; color, crimson red, bright, velvety, and sparkling, brilliant poppy-scarlet reflections, strongly shaded deep maroon." [JR2/30]

Souvenir de Béranger (François-René Bruant, 1857) trans., "In Memory of Béranger"
"Light rose, very large and double." [FP] "Pink, medium size, full, tall." [Sn]

Souvenir de Bertrand Guinoisseau (Chédane-Guinoisseau, 1895) trans., "In Memory of Bertrand Guinoisseau"
"Bush vigorous; foliage dark green; thorns yellowish, numerous; flower large, very full, purple red nuanced crimson; very fragrant and very floriferous." [JR19/130-131]

Souvenir de Caillat (E. Verdier, 1867) trans., "In Memory of Caillat"
"Flowers large, full, in clusters, purple and flame." [l'H68/50] "Moderate growth." [S]

Souvenir de Charles Montault (Robert & Moreau, 1862) trans., "In Memory of Charles Montault"
"Brilliant red, cupped." [FP] "Velvety purple, suffused with crimson, large and double; free blooming and pretty; habit free." [JC] "Growth vigorous; flower large, full, cupped; color, sparkling fiery red." [S]

Souvenir de Grégoire Bordillon (Moreau-Robert, 1889) trans., "In Memory of Grégoire Bordillon"
"Very vigorous, wood big and strong, with sharp and dense thorns; handsome dark green foliage; flower very large and full, globular, perfect form, beautiful sparkling bright red nuanced vermilion, very floriferous. This variety is dedicated to the late Grégoire Bordillon, former prefect of Maine-et-Loire." [JR13/146]

Souvenir de Henri Lévêque de Vilmorin (Lévêque, 1899) trans., "In Memory of Henri Lévêque de Vilmorin"
"Very vigorous, beautiful dark green foliage, flower large, full, extremely well formed, handsome deep velvety crimson red with brown." [JR23/178]

Souvenir de John Gould Veitch (E. Verdier, 1872) trans., "In Memory of John Gould Veitch"
"Deep crimson, shaded with violet-purple, flowers imbricated." [JC] "Growth vigorous; flower large, full; color, deep velvety carmine." [S]

Souvenir de l'Ami Labruyère (Gonod, 1884) trans., "In Memory of Friend Labruyère"
"Growth very vigorous, upright; buds with bracts; outer petals China pink; central petals darker." [S]

Souvenir de l'Exposition de Brie-Comte-Robert
Listed as 'Maurice Bernardin'.

Souvenir de la Princesse Amélie des Pays-Bas (Liabaud, 1873) trans., "In Memory of Princess Amélie of The Netherlands"
"Moderate growth; flower large, full, globular; color, grenadine red shaded purple. Good forcing variety; very good exhibition rose." [S]

Souvenir de la Reine d'Angleterre (Cochet Bros., 1855) trans., "Remembrance of the Queen of England"
Seedling of 'La Reine' (HP).
"Bright silvery pink." [Ÿ] "Bright rose, very large, double, shy in autumn." [EL] "This charming variety is extra hardy and extremely vigorous; it makes, in three or four years, a bush which is three to four feet high [ca. 1-1.25 m] and six to ten feet around [ca. 2-3 m]. Reblooms freely; until the end of good weather it is covered with its foliage of a beautiful green and bears beautiful large bright pink blossoms...doesn't blue." [JR3/60] "Foliage large, beautiful green; flowers measure up to 15 cm across [ca. 6 inches], full, cupped, bright pink, held upright on its stem." [l'H55/246] "Vigorous, perhaps even climbing, excellent for covering walls or trellises, recommended for its very large, full flowers of beautiful crimson pink." [R-H63] Commemorates a visit to Paris undertaken by Queen Victoria in 1855: "'*Souvenir de Sa Majesté la reine d'Angleterre*' is large, colored centifolia pink; corolla effective, petals free, sexual organs visible—much like 'Mme. Domage'. Its name seems to us to be rather on the laconic side; we would rather call it '*Souvenir de voyage en France de Sa Majesté la Reine du Royaume-Uni: Angleterre, Écosse et Irlande; accompagnée de son Altesse royale la princesse Adélaïde Victoria sa fille*', etc., etc. This name would perhaps take a little more room in the catalogs, but what sacrifice of paper should *not* be made for horticulturists in order to thus simplify and render more harmonious the nomenclature of plants!" [l'H55/207]

Souvenir de Laffay (E. Verdier, 1878) trans., "In Memory of Laffay"
"Violet-crimson." [EL] "Very vigorous, with short, upright, delicate green canes; thorns large, short, and upright, pink; leaves composed of 5-7 leaflets which are oblong and dark green, also being regularly and fairly

deeply toothed; flowers medium or large, very full, admirably shaped, in clusters; color, crimson red, bright, center fiery red, nuanced and shaded poppy, purple, and violet; superb." [JR2/187]

Souvenir de Léon Gambetta (Gonod, 1883) trans., "In Memory of Léon Gambetta"
Seedling of 'Victor Verdier' (HP).
"Flesh." [Ÿ] "Very vigorous, canes upright, flower stem very strong, thorns large, recurved, foliage of 3-5 bright green leaflets, flower very large, about five inches across [ca. 1.25 dm], very well formed, beautiful nuanced carmine red, very floriferous." [JR7/160]

Souvenir de Léon Roudillon (Vigneron, 1908) trans., "In Memory of Léon Roudillon"
From 'Général Appert' (HP) × 'Louis Van Houtte' (HP).
"Vigorous, beautiful dark green foliage; flower large, full, very beautiful deep velvety red with a fiery red nub. Borne on a strong, rigid stem." [JR32/134]

Souvenir de Leveson-Gower (Guillot père, 1852) trans., "In Memory of Leveson-Gower"
"Fiery red." [Ÿ] "Effective plant; blossoms deep ruby red fading to light ruby." [l'H52/148] "Fine dark red, changing to ruby, very large and full." [FP] "Deep-rose, very large, double, or full, fine flowers; quite tender, and subject to mildew." [EL] "Very vigorous bush; flowers very large, full, very intense deep ruby red; brilliant, magnificent color." [l'H56/200]

Souvenir de Louis Van Houtte
Listed as 'Crimson Bedder'.

Souvenir de Maman Corbœuf (Bénard/Corbœuf-Marsault, 1899) trans., "In Memory of Mother Corbœuf"
Seedling of 'Her Majesty' (HP).
"Pink, medium size, full, medium height." [Sn]

Souvenir de McKinley (Godard, 1902) trans., "In Memory of McKinley"
From 'Magna Charta' (HP) × 'Captain Christy' (HT).
"Delicate pink." [Ÿ] Has been called a Portland, reflecting its appearance.

Souvenir de Mme. Alfred Vy (Jamain, 1880) trans., "In Memory of Mme. Alfred Vy"
"Growth vigorous; very floriferous; flower large, full; color, deep currant red, intense; well formed; well held. A variety of the first merit." [S]

Souvenir de Mme. Berthier (Berthier/Liabaud, 1881) trans., "In Memory of Mme. Berthier"
From 'Victor Verdier' (HP) × 'Jules Margottin' (HP).
"Velvety red." [Ÿ] "Very vigorous, very profuse, and above all very remontant…well-held, with large imbricated petals of a bright red sometimes streaked white; lit from behind, the blossom has violet reflections. Sown in 1872, this plant bloomed for the first time in 1876, In Spring, when the leaves begin to develop, they are a handsome nuanced purple, changing thereafter to dark green." [JR5/171]

Souvenir de Mme. Chédane-Guinoisseau (Chédane-Guinoisseau, 1900) trans., "In Memory of Mme. Chédane-Guinoisseau"
"Bush vigorous; canes upright; foliage ample, deep green; bud long; flower very large, very full, well formed, flat, with very large petals, very bright red, sparkling; very floriferous; novel coloration; of the greatest merit for pot culture." [JR24/147]

Souvenir de Mme. de Corval (Gonod, 1867) trans., "In Memory of Mme. de Corval"
"Flower medium-sized, semi-full, dawn-color." [S]

Souvenir de Mme. H. Thuret (Texier, 1922) trans., "In Memory of Mme. H. Thuret"
From 'Frau Karl Druschki' (HP) × 'Lyon-Rose' (Pernetiana).
"A new and very interesting tint in Hybrid Perpetuals. The bud is long-pointed, coppery when the sepals divide, and the bloom is semi-double

and fairly recurrent. Throughout the day the color is a blend of shiny salmon, copper and pink, drawing to each one according to time of day and angle of the sun's rays. Quite perfumed. Plant vigorous and could be used as a low pillar." [C-Ps29, mysteriously attributing it to "Nabonnand, 1926"] "A semi-pillar Hybrid Perpetual well worth trial. Foliage a little small, but the large, fairly remontant bloom is exquisite, of deep salmon-rose with yellow at base...fragrant...a 'Frau Karl Druschki' in habit and blooming and shape...superb." [PP28]

Souvenir de Mme. Hennecart (Carré/S. Cochet, 1869) syn., 'Souvenir de Mme. Hennecourt'; trans., "In Memory of Mme. Hennecart"
"Bush vigorous; flower large, full; color, glossy pink fading to icy pink." [S]

Souvenir de Mme. Hennecourt
Listed as 'Souvenir de Mme. Hennecart'.

Souvenir de Mme. Jeanne Balandreau (Vilin/Robichon, 1899) trans., "In Memory of Mme. Jeanne Balandreau"
Sport of 'Ulrich Brunner fils' (HP).
"Madder-red, shaded with vermilion; growth moderate." [P1] "Deep pink with vermilion highlights. Shapely, large flowers on strong necks. Scented...4×3 [ft; ca. 1.25×1 m]." [B]

Souvenir de Mme. Robert (Moreau-Robert, 1878) trans., "In Memory of Mme. Robert"
Seedling of 'Jules Margottin' (HP).
"Very vigorous bush; flower large, full, opens well, cupped; color, delicate icy salmon-pink, center brighter; very floriferous." [S]

Souvenir de Mme. Sadi Carnot (Lévêque, 1898) trans., "In Memory of Mme. Sadi Carnot"
Seedling of 'Mme. Victor Verdier' (HP).
"Very vigorous, very ample beautiful glaucous green foliage, flowers very large, perfect form...vigor, continuous bloom...beautiful deep carmine red nuanced purple and velvety brown." [JR22/147]

Souvenir de Monsieur Boll (Boyau, 1866) trans., "In Memory of Monsieur Boll"

"Cerise tinted saffron." [Ÿ] "Cherry-red, large, very full." [EL] "Bright shaded red, very large, full, and well formed, habit very robust." [JC] "A strong hardy grower, with very large full red blooms, very sweet, and occasionally good enough to show, making a useful garden Rose." [F-M3]

Souvenir de Monsieur Droche (Pernet père, 1881) trans., "In Memory of Monsieur Droche"

"Carmine-rose, double." [EL] "Growth vigorous; flower large, nearly full; globular while opening, later a flat cup; color, carmine pink." [S]

Souvenir de Monsieur Faivre (Levet, 1879) trans., "In Memory of Monsieur Faivre"

"Very vigorous, with branches strong and upright; handsome brilliant green foliage; flower very large, full, well formed; color, beautiful poppy red with slate reflections; very pretty." [JR3/165]

Souvenir de Monsieur Rousseau d'Angers (Fargeton/Lévêque, 1861) trans., "In Memory of Monsieur Rousseau of Angers"

"Scarlet, changing to crimson, shaded with maroon, very rich and velvety, large and very double." [FP] "Bloom medium-sized, full; color, bright red, nuanced carmine." [S] "Bush vigorous; foliage light green; flowers large, full, imbricated; form and hold perfect; bright red nuanced carmine, center sometimes brightened with white; beautiful plant." [l'H61/166] In naming the variety, Monsieur Fargeton specifies that the name refers to Monsieur Rousseau *of Angers*, evidently lest we think he have any affection for *Jean-Jacques Rousseau* of Geneva, Ermenonville, etc.

Souvenir de Paul Dupuy (Levet, 1876) syn., 'Souvenir de Pierre Dupuy'; trans., "In Memory of Paul Dupuy"

Seedling of 'Général Jacqueminot' (HP).

"Red, large, globular flowers, well formed, fragrant." [EL] "Fine deep velvety red, enormous size, growth very vigorous, extra fine." [JC] "Growth vigorous; branches olive green armed with irregular thorns of a dark yellow red; flower very large, full, beautifully held...it should be considered non-remontant." [S] Being non-remontant, it could also be considered a Hybrid China.

Souvenir de Pierre Dupuy
Listed as 'Souvenir de Paul Dupuy'.

Souvenir de Pierre Sionville (J.-P. Boutigny, 1906) trans., "In Memory of Pierre Sionville"
"Bright red." [Ÿ] "Blossom large, very full, cupped, beautiful bright pink; very vigorous growth, covered with beautiful green foliage like the Centifolia, from which it arose. The bloom is continuous. Very meritorious variety." [JR30/153] Sometimes seen listed as a Hybrid Tea.

Souvenir de Spa (Gautreau, 1873) trans., "Remembrance of Spa"
Seedling of 'Mme. Victor Verdier' (HP).
"Very beautiful dark red pink with flame reflections." [JR22/23] "Bright red, shaded with crimson, well formed." [EL] "Deep red with scarlet reflex, large, full, and globular, and very well formed...vigorous habit." [JC]

Souvenir de Victor Hugo (Pernet père, 1885) "In Memory of Victor Hugo"
Seedling of 'Ambrogio Maggi' (HP).
"Vigorous bush with canes upright, thick; beautiful thick light green foliage; flower very large, nearly full, globular, beautiful and very bright satiny pink; very well held; freely remontant." [JR9/148] Not to be confused with Bonnaire's pink Tea of 1885 of the same name.

Souvenir de Victor Verdier (E. Verdier, 1878) "In Memory of Victor Verdier"
"Red, shaded with violet crimson, a well-formed, good rose." [EL] "Vigorous with upright branches, which are reddish green; thorns fairly numerous, recurved, sharp, pink; leaves composed of 5-7 leaflets which are oval, delicate green, and regularly and deeply toothed; flowers large,

full, well formed; color, brilliant scarlet poppy-red nuanced purple crimson, flame, and violet; splendid, very remontant, and most effective." [JR2/187] "Much to be recommended for exhibitions." [S]

Souvenir de William Wood (E. Verdier, 1864) trans., "In Memory of William Wood"
Seedling of 'Général Jacqueminot' (HP).
"Flowers dark blackish-purple, shaded with scarlet; darker than 'Prince Camille de Rohan'; large, full, and very effective; growth vigorous." [FP] "A bright flower and sweet." [B&V] "Vigorous, floriferous; flower large, full, cupped; color, very deep black-purple nuanced flame." [S] "Belongs to the 'Prince Camille [de Rohan] type. A fine, very dark crimson, not equalling Prince Camille." [EL] "Centre deep violet-purple, outer petals rich velvety crimson, colour superb, though somewhat inclined to burn, flowers good size, compact and full, habit free." [JC] "Vigorous, flowers full, 9-10 cm [ca. 4 inches], very dark purplish black nuanced flame, much like 'Prince Camille de Rohan', but darker." [l'H64/327]

[Souvenir du Baron de Sémur] (Lacharme, 1874) trans., "In Memory of Baron de Sémur"
Seedling of 'Charles Lefebvre' (HP).
"Growth vigorous; flower large, full; color, very dark purplish red nuanced flame red and shaded black; beautiful exhibition variety." [S] A parent of 'Jean Soupert' (HP).

Souvenir du Comte de Cavour (Margottin, 1861) trans., "In Memory of Comte de Cavour"
Seedling of 'Génie de Châteaubriand' (HP).
"Growth very vigorous; flower large, full, very well formed; of much merit; color, bright velvety crimson shaded darker crimson." [S]

Souvenir du Dr. Jamain (Lacharme, 1865) trans., "In Memory of Dr. Jamain"
From 'Général Jacqueminot' (HP) × 'Charles Lefebvre' (HP).
"Flowers full, large, bluish violet." [l'H65/340] "Deep rich plum colour, velvety and superb, petals thick and smooth, flowers moderate size; distinct and beautiful." [JC] "Shaded with deep crimson." [EL] "Of moderate vigor…flower large, full, ruffled; color, dark velvety black violet." [S] "Requires shade to prevent the flowers from burning…deep port-wine colour…a rich fragrance." [G] "A sumptuous rare beauty of shape, texture and bouquet…9×7 [ft; ca. 2.75×2 m]." [B]

Souvenir du Président Porcher (T. Granger/Vigneron, 1880) trans., "In Memory of President Porcher"
Seedling of 'Victor Verdier' (HP).
"Deep rose." [EL] "Vigorous, with upright canes, big-wooded, few thorns, handsome light green foliage, flower large, full, beautiful dark pink, outside of the petals lighter, blooms freely, beautiful plant." [JR4/166]

Souvenir du Rosiériste Gonod (Ducher fils, 1889) trans., "In Memory of Rose-Man Gonod"
"Very vigorous; flowers very large, full, well formed; color, cerise red veined bright pink." [JR13/167] This cultivar was found by Ducher the younger on the late Gonod's grounds.

Spencer (W. Paul, 1892) syn., 'Spenser'
Sport of 'Merveille de Lyon' (HP).
"Beautiful satin pink, outer petals reflexed with white. A magnificent and effective Rose." [P1] "Shimmering pink." [JR20/6] "Cupped; vigorous." [Cx] "Flat, fully double…Good foliage…4×3 [ft; ca. 1.25×1 m]." [B] "Very large, quite full, and of a compact form; of robust growth…opens freely; and, due to its fulness, it keep for a long time. As a garden flower, it is without rival for its color." [JR16/6] "Apparently a stouter and fuller 'Baroness Rothschild', with similar growth and habit. Likely to be very

valuable, if this estimate should be maintained; but, as seen up to the present, its additional fulness makes it a bad opener in wet weather." [F-M3]

St. Ingebert (Lambert, 1926)
From 'Frau Karl Druschki' (HP) × 'Mme. Mélanie Soupert' (HT).
"One of Lambert's steps towards a yellow Druschki...a very interesting combination of colors—white outer petals as a collarette, toning to yellowish toward the center which is reddish. Well-formed bloom with a sweet fragrance. The plant is erect, the branches slender for the class and almost thornless. Foliage olive-green and glossy." [C-Ps29] "Bud long-pointed, creamy yellow; flower large, double, moderately fragrant, lasting, white with yellowish and reddish center, borne singly. Vigorous, upright growth." [ARA26/186]

Stämmler (Tantau/Conard-Pyle, 1933) From 'Victor Verdier' (HP) × 'Arabella' (HT).
"Strong pink." [Ÿ] "A new, pink, everblooming Hybrid Perpetual with slightly cupped, fully double pink flowers. Pleasing perfume. Plants make about 4-foot canes [ca. 1.25 m], literally hidden behind the first mass of bloom in June." [C-Ps33]

Star of Waltham (W. Paul, 1875)
"Deep crimson, colour very rich and effective, very large, double, and of fine form, smooth petals and fine substance, said to be a very fine rose." [JC] "A full, globular-shaped, rosy-lilac, Hybrid Perpetual kind, suffused with crimson, the petals wax-like in substance and smooth." [R8/17] "Carmine-crimson, medium size, semi-globular, full, fragrant; very large foliage, smooth green wood, with occasional red thorns. A good rose but not reliable." [EL] "Vigorous bush; branches very thorny; leaves dark and velvety, with irregular serration; flower large, full, well formed, very effective. The color changes, depending upon the soil, from carmine pink to deep crimson. Rain makes the color violet red." [S] "Of strong growth with fine foliage; not very liable to mildew but requiring fine weather.

This Rose cannot be depended upon to come good, but it is a splendid bloom when seen at its best, in petal, shape, colour, smoothness, size, and lasting qualities. Not one of the best as a free bloomer or autumnal; it requires the best of weather to show its qualities to perfection, and should be left long in pruning and the buds not thinned too much, as it is extra full and often fails to open properly." [F-M2]

Sultan of Zanzibar (G. Paul, 1876)
Seedling of 'Duke of Edinburgh' (HP).
"Blackish-maroon, shaded with crimson, flowers globular." [JC]
"Crimson-maroon, in the style of S. Reynolds Hole' [*Hybrid Perpetual, G. Paul, 1874, maroon red*], but a weaker grower with a very bad constitution. This is one of the very few Roses I cannot keep alive at all, and I do not think I have once succeeded in getting even a decent bloom. A magnificent dark colour, and a splendid flower as sometimes shown, but a Rose to be avoided as more than likely to give absolutely no return." [F-M3]

Suzanne Carrol of Carrolton (P. Nabonnand, 1924)
From 'Frau Karl Druschki' (HP) × 'Mme. Gabriel Luizet' (HP).
"Light salmon pink, large, semidouble, moderate scent, tall." [Sn]

Suzanne-Marie Rodocanachi
Listed as 'Mlle. Suzanne-Marie Rodocanachi'.

Suzanne Wood (E. Verdier, 1869)
"Flower large, full; very floriferous; color, beautiful pink." [S]

Symmetry (G. Paul, 1910)
Seedling of 'Mrs. John Laing' (HP).
"Crimson red." [Ÿ]

Symphony (Weigand, 1935)

From 'Frau Karl Druschki' (HP) × 'Souvenir de Claudius Pernet' (Pernetiana).

"Continuously blooming…a shell-pink Druschki…good throughout the season…very much taken with the dainty color of the splendidly formed flowers." [ARA37/252] "Poor color in extreme heat, but superb blooms in the fall…moderate vigor." [ARA39/233] "A poor grower and bloomer." [ARA36/217] "Bud very large, long-pointed; flower unusually large, double, high-centred, extremely lasting; flesh-pink to Venetian pink, on long, strong stem. Foliage large, leathery, dark green. Vigorous (as tall as 'Frau Karl Druschki'), upright; free, intermittent bloomer all season." [ARA35/218]

Tancrède (Oger, 1876)

"Flower medium-sized, full, globular; color, very bright red. Moderate vigor." [S] Tancrède, alias Tancred, Norman leader of the First Crusade; lived 1078-1112.

Tartarus (Geschwind, 1887)

From 'Erinnerung an Brod' (HP) × 'Souvenir du Dr. Jamain' (HP).

"Violet purple." [Ỵ] Tartarus, a.k.a. Hades.

Tatik Brada (Brada, 1933)

From 'Frau Karl Druschki' (HP) × 'Louise Catherine Breslau' (Pernetiana)

"Orange-pink, large, full, tall." [Sn]

Tendresse

Listed as 'La Tendresse'.

Théodore Liberton (Soupert & Notting, 1886)

"Vigorous bush; flower large, full, Centifolia form; color, sparkling carmine red nuanced madder pink fading to deep pink; reverse of petals light purple. Scent one of the best." [JR10/148]

Thomas Mills (E. Verdier, 1872)

"Bright crimson, large and double." [P1] "Flowers extra large, full, and of fine cup shape, colour dazzling bright rosy-carmine, with whitish stripes; a very free bloomer." [JC] "Very vigorous, erect, pretty hardy; flower…imbricated; color, bright carmine cherry pink, bordered lighter." [S] "A good garden variety." [EL]

Thorin (Lacharme, 1866)

"Growth very vigorous; flower large, nearly full, widely cupped; color, brilliant carmine pink." [S]

Thyra Hammerich (H. Vilin/C. Verdier, 1868)
Seedling of 'Duchesse de Sutherland' (HP).

"Rosy-flesh, large, well formed; distinct and good." [EL] "Delicate clear flesh changing to paler flesh, colour beautiful and even throughout, flowers erect, very large, full and cupped; a superb rose, and one of the best of its colour." [JC] "Growth very vigorous, with heavy wood armed with some small hooked thorns; its very ample and light violet leaves are usually of 3-5 leaflets; its very large and full blossoms, cupped at first, then outspread, are white slightly tinted flesh pink, more intense at the base of the petals. This variety sprang from 'Duchesse de Sutherland', the growth and floriferousness of which it inherited; good rose to force." [S]

Tom Wood (A. Dickson, 1896)

"Cerise red." [Ÿ] "Deep red, very large, full, tall." [Sn] "Large, cherry-red flowers; shell shaped petals." [C&Js06] "A very useful Rose, of vigorous hardy growth, with good foliage, not much liable to mildew. The blooms are well-shaped and seldom deformed, of average size and with stout petals, but the colour is rather a dull shade of red. It is a good autumnal, and the plants seem to have a good constitution, growing and doing well where others fail." [F-M2]

Triomphe d'Alençon (Chauvel/Touvais, 1859) trans., "Alençon's Triumph"
"Vigorous bush; flower very large, very full, form of 'Baronne Prévost'; sparkling intense red." [l'H59/138] "Much to be recommended because of its good habit and perfume." [S]

Triomphe de Caen (Oger, 1861) trans., "Caen's Triumph"
"Purplish currant-red." [Ÿ] "Crimson, tinged with purple, a non-permanent shade, not desirable." [EL] "Deep velvety-purple, shaded with scarlet-crimson, large and full." [FP] "Flower large, full, globular; deep velvety grenadine nuanced flame red." [S] "Brilliant scarlet, shaded with purple; large and full; growth vigorous." [P1]

Triomphe de France (Garçon, 1875) trans., "France's Triumph"
"Bright carmine rose, colour beautiful, a very large full expanded flower, but too coarse for exhibition." [JC] "Flower very large, full, of very beautiful form; blooms abundantly from June to October; color, beautiful bright carmine pink; very beautiful exhibition rose." [S]

Triomphe de l'Exposition (Margottin, 1855) trans., "Triumph of the Exposition"
"Large, crimson-purple." [JR3/28] "Dark red; flower large, full, flat." [Cx] "Reddish crimson...rather coarse flowers, fragrant, numerous red thorns, hardy; occasionally comes very fine, but generally the quality is inferior." [EL] "This rose makes a large bush with many long, strong, and upright branches...The foliage is very ample...The stems are long and strong...The flowers, which open well in all seasons, come at the tips of the branches in twos, threes, or fours, or sometimes solitary...large (four to five inches [ca. 1-1.25 dm]), sumptuous, regular, full, the upright petals holding out well against the sun; open; bright velvety red, tinted and spotted dark purple towards the tips of the petals; the perfume is pleasant though faint." [JR8/71-72] "Very vigorous, giving big, long canes, green with a bloom, also having very unequal thorns, flattened at the edges, straight or nearly so, of a brownish red. The foliage is very ample and of a

beautiful green; each leaf is composed of 5-7 oblong or oval-lanceolate leaflets, pointed, toothed, sometimes finely toothed; the flower...varies according to the weather or exposure: bright crimson red in the sun, darker in the shade." [S] "The upper face [*of the leaf*] is glabrous, and beautiful green; the lower face is pale green, and slightly downy as with the Centifolia; some rudimentary prickles may be seen on the mid-vein; the terminal leaflet is much larger than the lateral ones...[T]he rachis is big, firm, and pretty straight, glandular, particularly above where it is slightly furrowed; 8-10 very unequal small prickles may be found beneath. Two very lacy stipules, adherent at the base to the petiole...are edged with numerous glandular hairs; the free part is linear, narrowing into an awl, very divergent, making a right angle to the petiole. At first bloom, the canes are tipped with 4 or 5 blossoms; the reblooming canes [*i.e., those which grow to bloom later in the season*] usually only have one blossom." [l'H55/217] "Canes pretty strong and branching; bark smooth, a slightly reddish dark green, thorns the same color, and big, thick, hooked, and sharp. Leaves somber green, divided into 3 or 5 leaflets which are acuminate and dentate; leafstalk pretty strong, armed with 3 or 4 little prickles. Flowers 3.5-4 inches across [ca. 8 cm-1 dm], full, cupped, concave, well formed; solitary or in clusters of 3 or 4 on the strongest canes; color, crimson red, dark as well as intense; outer petals large and concave, those of the center smaller; bud very pretty; flower stalk firm and long. Calyx rounded and pear-shaped; sepals leaf-like...This rose...took first prize at the Universal Exposition of 1855 at Paris." [JF]

Triomphe de la Terre des Roses (Guillot père, 1864) trans., "Triumph of *la Terre des Roses*" (see below)
"Flower 14-15 cm [ca. 5½ inches], full, beautiful violet pink, very fragrant, freely remontant." [l'H64/328] "Moderate vigor; flower very large, full, violet pink." [S] *La Terre des Roses* was the name of Guillot père's establishment. "Monsieur Guillot père has decided, after so many years of fatigue and stubborn work during which he has given us such good and

beautiful roses, to take some rest, which is both well merited and honorably achieved. He has sold his firm [*in 1870*] to Monsieur Joseph Schwartz, who has indeed run the nursery for six years." [l'H70/327]

Triomphe de Saintes
Listed as 'Le Triomphe de Saintes'.

[Triomphe de Valenciennes] (Schneider, 1849) trans., "Valenciennes' Triumph"
Sport (or, possibly, seedling) of 'La Reine'.
"Now I am going to bring to your attention an unfortunate outcast, the merit and unique beauty of which ceded nothing at all to the more or less shining glories of the favorites *du jour*. It is a rose. It was raised, in 1848, by Monsieur Schneider, of Marly-les-Valenciennes, who released it to commerce in 1849 under the name 'Triomphe de Valenciennes'. I believe it to be the daughter of close relative of the rose 'La Reine', of which it has the stature, the form, and basic coloration. But further, it is shaded on the outer edge of the petals with irregular waves of a very bright pink or a beautiful violet purple. I saw it at a fancier's, in 1851; I was struck with its sparkle, its vigor, and its good hold. Since that time, I have asked our country's nurserymen for it twenty times!—and twenty times have received the invariable response, 'It's an old rose, we don't do it any more.' And why not? Is it because it is insignificant, or lacking scent, or color, or is of bad form? 'No.' Is it because it dates from eight or ten years ago, and that today we have sixty or eighty ones that, while, less beautiful, are younger than it? '*Oui.*' This system results in gardeners and fanciers who started growing or collecting only in the last few years never knowing anything about a series of roses which were admired by their predecessors...Seek out 'Triomphe de Valenciennes', and if you find it, you'll be doing well!" [RJC60/126-127]
"The roses 'Triomphe de Valenciennes' (Schneider) and 'Mme. Campbell d'Islay' (Baudry) are only fixed striped sports of the rose 'La Reine'." [l'H51/8] "This Rose...was sent to us last August by Monsieur Schneider,

horticulturist at Marly-lez-Valenciennes (Nord), who raised it, he says, in his 1847 seedling crop. Its wood, thorns, leaves, and flower-form show precisely the characteristics of 'La Reine'; only, the petals, of a pale pink— as far as we can judge, at least, from the slightly wilted cutting we were sent—are more or less largely plumed deep red, and nuanced with violet. This striping gives the flower a certain cachet of original beauty, which is all its merit. But did this Rose really come from seed, or is it not a striped sport from a 'La Reine', mixed up, in the operations of repotting, with the seedlings, and that Monsieur Schneider was able to enfix? Such great affinities existing between 'Triomphe de Valenciennes' and 'La Reine', we would like to float this opinion, which, besides, is confirmed by the appearance of another rose that Monsieur Baudry, horticulturist at Avranches (Manche) delivered to commerce as a straight sport of 'La Reine', and which he named 'Mme. Campbell d'Islay'. We indeed would like to add that, judging by the debris of this latter rose which we saw last Fall, and the description by Monsieur Baudry which we found—'color, lilac-y pink, lined, striped, or marbled with carmine red'—we consider 'Triomphe de Valenciennes' and 'Mme. Campbell d'Islay' as one and the same variety, coming from a sport of the rose 'La Reine'. However, not to be too reckless in our judgment on these two roses, we await the next bloom of 'Mme. Campbell d'Islay' in order to decide the question of identity. As to origin, it would seem to be the same for both. Now, an enfixed rose does not have the merit of a rose from seed; and we believe that Mssrs. Baudry and Schneider have exaggerated the price of subscribing the varieties, which they raise to 25 francs for specimens from half a meter to a full meter in height. The rose of Monsieur Baudry is for sale this Fall; that of Monsieur Schneider will not be until next Fall; but we encourage him to sell it sooner to get some benefit from it." [V-H50/21]

"I've read in the *Revue-Horticole* the description of a Rose grown, they say, from seed in the environs of Valenciennes. For those who have long experience in growing roses, it is easy to recognize, from the illustration given in the *Revue*, one of those fairly numerous sports which one sees among the HPs, and to which 'La Reine', 'Comte de Paris', 'Lady Alice Peel', etc., are particularly prone. Thus it is that I believe Monsieur Schneider to have erred in regarding the rose 'Triomphe de Valenciennes' as the result of seed. What is more, these sorts of errors are very frequent. To speak only of reblooming roses, the Quatre-Saisons 'Blanc' and 'Presqu'Inerme', 'Monstrueux', 'Bernard', 'Mogador', etc., were originally announced as coming from seed, when in reality they were only fortuitous sports enfixed by technique. Nature does not always take into consideration our self-esteem or our interests; often she protests against the errors which are not always involuntary on our part in endowing several canes with characteristics which are natural and more fixed than the varieties she gave us in the first place. The sports which occur as far as flowers of the Rose go are, in effect, of several sorts—stripes, flamings, variations of form, of color, of size, of doubleness can be enfixed with the petals maintaining their normal form; we have as examples 'Camaïeu' [*sic*], purple striped with white, 'Bernard', striped 'Rose du Roi', 'Mogador', etc.; but when, following particular degenerations, the striped or flamed petals lose the primitive form of the variety from which they sprang, and they crisp, or twist, or scallop, or are cut more deeply or less so along the edge, it becomes much more difficult to enfix these sorts of sports. The color changes, the flowers lose the regularity of their form—in a word, they seem to suffer, and the sported characteristic disappears. Also, the degenerations, fairly common among HPs, are still not presented in commerce with their characteristic in a state of fixity. I must say that I have indeed often tried—with little success—to keep or enfix such degenerations. Nevertheless, I am far from saying that it is not possible to enfix these bizarre sports in many cases; but I believe that I can state that this will never be anything other than a pretty rare case. Perhaps the sport obtained by Monsieur Baudry will give us the first exception, seeing as he has maintained it for two years on a certain number of specimens. We should be grateful to that horticulturist for honestly declaring its origin. [*signed:*] Vibert." [V-H50/21-22]

"We have received from Monsieur Prévost the following letter: '…You have good reason, Monsieur, to believe exaggerated the price of 25 fr. asked for the roses called 'Mme. Campbell d'Islay' and 'Triomphe de Valenciennes' (which I believe you have reason to consider as being identical), because the figure which accompanies your description is very exactly that of a sport of the rose 'La Reine' which I noticed on my premises and enfixed in 1845, sold in 1846 at the price of 3 fr., and since at only 2, which seemed to me to be sufficient for a now-enfixed accidental striping, constant and very remarkable without a doubt, but which, as you give to understand in your description, adds nothing to the merit of the magnificent rose 'La Reine' from Monsieur Laffay.' [*signed:*] Prévost." [V-H50/22]

"Parisian horticulture, generally not very kind to anything that doesn't come from itself, has already sought to denigrate the rose 'Triomphe de Valenciennes' in insinuating that it indeed might not have arisen from seed, as Monsieur Schneider of Marly-lez-Valenciennes has affirmed in releasing it to commerce. It is only—in the belief of *Revue-Horticole*—a mere fortuitous sport, coming from enfixing it by graft; the rose 'Triomphe de Valenciennes' would be a sportive striping of the rose 'La Reine'. They have the same supposition about another new rose from seed, raised by Monsieur Baudry of Avranches, to which he has given the name 'Mme. Campbell d'Islay'. About this latter rose, we have nothing to say, as it is not known to us. As to the rose 'Triomphe de Valenciennes', it doubtless has some resemblance in its foliage, form, and main color, to the rose 'La Reine'; it pertains, certainly, to the same series. But there isn't in that resemblance—less complete than its detractors say—sufficient motive, in our opinion, to accuse an honorable grower like Monsieur Schneider not of bad faith—no one would dare to—but of negligence in arranging the products of his operations. A grower of roses who is at the same time a fancier of the highest distinction does not err in that way; bring up against him suspicion of negligence and error, it shows that a person is unable to charge him with anything worse. Good novelties coming from Roses are not common; when he produces one with such clear-cut, truly remarkable characteristics, it should not be denigrated with a lightness which it would not be unjust to term *severe*." [JHP50/1-2]

Turenne (V. & C. Verdier, 1861)
"Brilliant red, large, handsome petals, very effective." [FP] "Vigorous bush; flower medium-sized, full, with large petals; color, sparkling red; blossom often imperfect." [S]

Turnvater Jahn (Müller-Almrich, 1927)
From 'Frau Karl Druschki' (HP) × a seedling (resulting from crossing the HT 'Mme. Abel Chatenay' and the HT 'General MacArthur').
"White, pink center, very large, full, tall." [Sn]

Ulrich Brunner fils (Levet, 1881) trans., "Ulrich Brunner, the son"
Seedling of 'Paul Neyron' (HP) or possibly 'Anna de Diesbach' (HP); but see also below.
"Bright cerise red, very large and full...of magnificent petal, and in all respects one of the best." [P1] "Large flowers, with splendid petals, well-formed, brilliant rosy crimson with light purple tints." [JR7/157] "Rather loose blooms of rosy-carmine fading quickly. Sweetly scented and vigorous...5×4 [ft; ca. 1.5×1.25 m]." [B] "Extra-large flowers of light red, bordering on scarlet or crimson. Foliage plentiful...very vigorous...about 30 blooms per season." [ARA21/90] "Shell-petaled Rose of sweet fragrance, and a great favorite." [DO] "Blooms come well, of extra large size, with stout petals generally tightly incurved in the centre, fine regular smooth shape...capital lasting qualities, not much injured by rain, though the colour soon fades...free-blooming and capital in the autumn." [F-M2] "Beautiful in spring." [ARA18/114] "June-blooming only." [ARA34/78] "Another Hybrid Perpetual which is not very perpetual." [JR37/171] "Of moderate vigor, coming, say some rosarians, from 'Paul Neyron', or by open pollination, writes the breeder—we incline towards the latter opinion. The branches are upright and strong, with few thorns, and bear large, cupped flowers which are fragrant and of a nice cherry-red when well

open." [JR12/105] "Good leathery foliage, free from mildew...A great Rose in many ways...of strong constitution and does well almost anywhere." [F-M2] "Plant is symmetrical." [ARA29/49] "A variety of the first order." [S] "Ulrich Brunner, rose-grower at Lausanne." [JR30/53]

Ulster (A. Dickson, 1900)

"Salmon pink, deep petaled, large and full." [H] "Large, salmon-pink in colour, full, and of great substance. A poor grower." [P1] "The flower, as seen in a show stand, is magnificent, very large, and very finely and regularly formed, with beautiful bright colour and good fragrance. But as to its growth I can say nothing, simply because I have not succeeded in getting it to grow...more than a very few inches. What little growth it does make is robust, and it is plainly a Rose for exhibitors only, and for those only of them who can give it the most 'liberal treatment'." [F-M2]

Urdh (Tantau/Conard-Pyle, 1933)

From 'Victor Verdier' (HP) × 'Papa Lambert' (HT).
"Strong pink." [Ÿ] "Pink, very large, very full, very fragrant, tall." [Sn] "Very double, medium-sized blooms of lovely old-rose are freely produced throughout the season. The rich, old-time perfume is unforgettable." [C-Pf33]

Vainqueur de Goliath (F. Moreau/Pernet père, 1862) trans., "Goliath's Conqueror"

"Brilliant crimson-scarlet, very large and double." [FP] "Growth vigorous; flower large, full; color, bright sparkling red; very fragrant. Magnificent exhibition rose." [S]

Velours Pourpre (E. Verdier, 1866) trans., "Purple Velvet"

"Velvety bright crimson illuminated with deep brown, scarlet, and violet." [l'H66/370] "Bush very vigorous; flower large, full; color, bright velvety carmine with violet reflections." [S]

Venus (Kiese/Schmidt, 1895)
From 'Général Jacqueminot' (HP) × 'Princesse de Béarn' (HP).
"Purple-red, large, full, very fragrant, tall." [Sn]

Vick's Caprice (Vick, 1889)
Sport of 'Archiduchesse Elisabeth d'Autriche' (HP).
"Imperial pink, distinctly variegated with deep rose, unique and lovely."
[Dr] "Very much like 'Hermosa' in form; the color is dark scarlet with
touches of white." [JR13/91] "Large, double, cupped flowers with high
centres...pale pink and lilac with white and deep pink stripes. Attractive
foliage...4×3 [ft; ca. 1.25×1 m]." [B] "Flowers large with a ground color
of soft satiny pink, distinctly striped and dashed with carmine. It is beautiful in bud form, being quite long and pointed also plainly showing the
stripes and markings." [CA93] "Elegant buds. Constant." [Dr] "Without
rival in its type; it is quite remontant and all the flowers are always distinct
in their characteristic; they are light pink, a satiny carnation, bizarrely
plumed and striped white and carmine. The blossoms are solitary, and
develop at the end of the erect and vigorous branches. This variety is very
hardy, has plain green foliage, and is good for forcing...of a finesse and
incontestable elegance, it is the striped rose *par excellence*." [JR22/42]

Vicomte de Lauzières (Liabaud, 1889)
"Purple." [Ÿ] "Very vigorous with erect canes, beautiful dark green
foliage...Flower very large, well formed, full, plump, handsome purplish
red without other tints." [JR13/163]

Vicomte Maison (Fontaine, 1868)
"Cherry-red, double, fades quickly, straggling habit." [EL] "Growth very
vigorous; flower large, full; color, cerise red nuanced white." [S]

Vicomtesse de Vezins (Gautreau, 1867)
"Velvety pink." [Ÿ] "Growth vigorous; flower very large, full, center in a
rosette formation; color, fresh bright pink." [S]

Vicomtesse Laure de Gironde (Pradel, 1852)
"Moderately vigorous bush; flowers medium-sized, full, imbricated, clear delicate pink." [l'H56/200]

Victor-Emmanuel (Guillot père, 1859)
"Purple and purplish-maroon, large and double, good and distinct." [FP] "Medium or large, full, red, varies to purple, very beautiful." [JDR59/28] "Richly-coloured and finely-shaped flowers." [R8] "Admirable in color and form, velvety black carmine." [JR3/29] "Moderate vigor." [S] Victor Emmanuel II, 1st king of Italy 92nd of that name of Sardinia); lived 1820-1878.

Victor Hugo (Schwartz, 1884)
Possibly a seedling of 'Charles Lefebvre' (HP).
"Brilliant crimson, shaded with purple, very striking, of medium size, almost full." [P1] "Sparkling crimson red; flower large, imbricated, fragrant; vigorous." [Cx] "When 'well done by,' the blooms are very handsome, of fine shape, fair petal and centre, glorious colour, and good size...fairly free blooming...but the petals are rather thin, and the blooms not very lasting." [F-M2] "A bright 'Xavier Olibo'; will be, without a doubt, a valuable newcomer." [JR12/21] "A great favorite with many rosarians on account of its brilliant crimson-scarlet blooms of perfect form, which always compel admiration. Growth is rather weak, and a fine display is not to be expected." [OM] "Of good growth in rich soil with very distinct foliage and habit, liable to mildew, and requiring high cultivation." [F-M2] "One of the best of its colour." [DO] Not to be confused with the rosy-lilac Hybrid Bourbon of the same name. Victor Marie Hugo, French *littérateur*; lived 1802-1885.

Victor le Bihan (Guillot père, 1868)
"Beautiful bright carmine pink." [JR3/28] "Flower very large, full; well-formed." [S]

Victor Lemoine (Lévêque, 1888)

"Very vigorous bush; large dark green leaves. Blossom large, very well formed, dark red nuanced purple, brown, and violet. Very beautiful." [JR12/181]

Victor Verdier (Lacharme, 1859) syn., 'Monsieur Victor Verdier'
From 'Jules Margottin' (HP) × 'Safrano' (T).

"Bright rose, with carmine centre, a very fresh shade, but not permanent, semi-globular form, of good size, not fragrant; very free, the wood is all but smooth, the foliage lustrous. This variety is doubtless of Bourbon origin; it is a beautiful rose, but with its entire progeny is more tender than any other types in the class." {EL} "Very bright pink, with violet." [JR2/60] "Rosy carmine, purplish edges, very large and full; form cupped; growth robust." [P1] "Pink shaded with carmine, of an admirable shade." [JR3/28] "Intense red; flower large, full, globular, high-centered; very floriferous; vigorous." [Cx] "Very vigorous bush; flower very large, full, pink nuanced very intense carmine." [l'H59/138] "Deep rose, centre brilliant rose, a beautiful colour...an exquisite rose, free-flowering, and of good habit." [JC] "Large flowers and wondrously beautiful large petals so shell-like." [R8] "Rather small, bright crimson." [HRH] "Bounteous summer flowering, good autumnal." [S] "Beautiful foliage." [P2] "Much like ['John Hopper']; a first-rate hardy kind." [WD] "Still in favour [*in 1908*]." [K2] "Verdier (Philippe-Victor).—Horticulturist of Ivry (Seine); died in 1878 at the age of 75. Was vice-president of the National Horticultural Society. Important breeder of Roses, Peonies, Irises, and Gladioli." [R-HC] "Born August 5, 1803, at Yerres (Seine-et-Oise), died in February, 1878...He was still under-manager of cultures at Neuilly when he undertook growing roses from seed. He developed at that time, in collaboration with his uncle [*Antoine Jacques*], the Sempervirens line: 'Adélaïde d'Orléans', 'Félicité-Perpétue', 'Léopoldine d'Orléans', 'Mélanie de Montjoie', 'Princesse Louise', 'Princesse Marie', and, finally, 'Général Athalin [*i.e.,* 'Athalin']', a non-remontant variety, but one which at length stood at the head of the new race to which we have given the name of Hybrid Perpetuals—despite the fact that Monsieur Verdier never in the least practices cross-breeding between the genres which he perfected! It's from 'Général Athalin' that his 'Perpétuelle de Neuilly' came in 1834, as well as so many others bred by his contemporaries Hardy, Vibert, Prévost, and Laffay, whose [*recent*] death we mourn. In 1838, the remontant roses began to take the place of the non-remontants, and Victor Verdier, who had the most complete collection of the latter, disposed of them, rebuilding a new collection with the new roses—it indeed became one of the largest and most admired…The roses of Victor Verdier remain in collections as being among the most perfect in form and color…The first white-striped-pink variety [*of Gladiolus*], 'Mme. Hérincq', was a charming obtention of Monsieur Verdier's. Entered into commerce by him in 1851, it was at the same time bought and vended in England by Mr. Cole, who announced it as the product of a cross between *Gladiolus gandevensis* and *G. floribundus*." [SNH78/279] "*Catalog of Species and Varieties of the genus* Rosa, *cultivated by Monsieur Verdier at Neuilly-sur-Seine, near Paris, available Autumn 1833 and Spring 1834*. It is particularly in the China, Tea, and Noisette sorts of Roses, remontant or perpetual, that Monsieur Verdier is rich in novelties and meritorious sorts, not however neglecting the best of the other sections. The moderate prices, sizes, forms, and flower-colors are indicated for each variety. The order and intelligence with which his establishment is run inspire confidence." [R-H34] "An attempt to cultivate the friendship of a rosarian, whose name is borne by my last selection, 'Victor Verdier'. I called upon him in the year 1861, and supposing that he knew a little English, and that I knew a little French, I anticipated a rush of fraternal sympathy and sweet communion of kindred spirits. The gush did not take place. We could not understand each other in the least; and I do not suppose that two large men ever looked, or felt themselves to be, so small. I fled to my wife (I was on my wedding tour)…It is one of the grandest and most constant of roses." [R1/251]

Victory Rose (Dingee-Conard, 1901)
"Pink." [Ÿ]

Ville de Lyon (Ducher, 1866) trans., "City of Lyon"
"Metallic rose and silvery-white, flowers large, full and of fine form; habit vigorous." [JC] "Very vigorous hybrid; flowers upright, very large, globular, full, and very well formed; deep pink. Good for forcing." [RJC66/209]

Ville de St.-Denis (Thomas, 1853) trans., "City of St.-Denis"
Sport or seedling of 'La Reine' (HP).
"Bright crimson." [S] "Flowers large, full, beautiful pink nuanced brighter." [l'H54/15] "Carmine pink…inferior, however, to ['Louise Peyronny']." [R-H63] "Rosy-carmine, flowers large and globular, exquisitely formed; a free growing, constant, and excellent rose." [JC] "Vigorous bush from 'La Reine', the characteristics of which are retained in this variety; flowers large, very full, beautiful red. Good variety." [l'H56/251]

Vincent-Hippolyte Duval (H. Duval, 1879)
"Dedicated to Monsieur Duval père…[V]ery vigorous, with very large, full, and well-formed flowers; color, beautiful bright carmine pink." [JR3/182]

Vincente Peluffo (Lévêque, 1902)
"Very vigorous bush, beautiful glaucous green foliage; flowers very large, full, well formed, light cerise pink nuanced darker. Very remontant." [JR26/149]

Violet Queen (G. Paul, 1892)
"Violet red, medium size, full, tall." [Sn]

Violette Bouyer (Lacharme, 1881)
From 'Jules Margottin' (HP) × 'Mlle. de Sombreuil' (T).
"Very vigorous, large flowers, well formed, white nuanced very delicate flesh. Of the 'Jules Margottin' sort." [JR5/172] "Globular form, later a flaring cup, fragrant." [S] "A good grower, very distinct in habit. This is

perhaps the earliest to bloom of all the H.P.'s mentioned here, and one of the few which at its best is of true globular shape. It is practically white, though tinted sometimes on the outer petals, and is only good in dry weather, being easily spoiled by rain. A free bloomer, but not of much use as an autumnal." [F-M2] "Lacharme had announced some new roses, and I [*Monsieur Bouyer*] asked him to give one of his new-borns the name of my second granddaughter Violette Bouyer." [JR26/123]

Virginale (Lacharme, 1858) trans., "Virginal"
"Pearly white, with the palest flesh centre, flowers of moderate size and well formed, though not full; an exquisite rose, but a delicate and unsatisfactory grower." [JC] "Moderate vigor; flower medium-sized, full, well formed, pure white." [l'H58/127] "A pure white rose raised from seed at Lyons, with petals rather too thin and unequal...[S]till a very interesting variety, and quite worthy of culture." [R8]

Vulcain (V. & C. Verdier, 1861)
"Bright purplish-violet, shaded with black, good and distinct." [FP] "Rich crimson, double, well formed; a rose of splendid color." [EL] "Flower large, nearly full, deep intense violet purple, nuanced blackish, in clusters of 8-15." [l'H61/264] "Dwarf habit...small flowers of a deep purplish maroon colour." [R8] "Moderate vigor." [S] Vulcain, alias Vulcan, Roman god of fire.

Vyslanec Kalina (Böhm, 1935)
"Red, large, full, very fragrant, tall." [Sn]

Waldfee (Kordes, 1960) trans., "Woodsprite"
From 'Independence' (Floribunda, red) × 'Mrs. John Laing' (HP).
"Very bright...large, fragrant, blood-red...glossy foliage, strong growth...recurrent." [G]

Waltham Standard (W. Paul, 1897)

"Violet crimson." [Ÿ] "Rich carmine color, shaded scarlet and violet; the slightly opened bud has a very bright color, with the very firm petals holding well to the end; flower and petals like those of 'A.K. Williams'...Handsome foliage." [JR21/50] "Vigorous." [JR21/66] "Of fair growth and foliage, this variety produces moderately sized flowers of good shape and of beautiful colour with capital fragrance; but I am doubtful if it will survive many seasons among choice selections." [F-M2]

White Baroness (G. Paul, 1883)

Sport of 'Baronne Adolphe de Rothschild' (HP).

"More double than 'Mabel Morrison'; color, pure white; vigorous." [S] "Flowers large and full." [P1] "Was studied for three years in the Cheshunt nurseries [*prior to release to commerce*]." [JR8/130]

William Griffith (Portemer, 1850)

"Glossy pink changing to light satin-rose, petals curiously curved; a very beautiful and free growing rose." [JC] "An old and excellent rose, of a peculiar light satin rose-color." [FP] "Remarkable for the elegance and profusion of its flowers." [R8] "Pink, much resembling 'Comtesse Cécile de Chabrillant', but the flowers are somewhat smaller, the wood smoother, and in habit it is more vigorous, but also much more liable to injury from the cold." [EL] "A fine distinct variety, of robust and upright growth; the flowers are of a rosy lilac, with petals very stout and leathery, and with foliage luxuriant and Bourbon-like." [C] "Very remontant hybrid...large, slightly hooked, reddish thorns. The leaves are composed of 5-7 lush leaflets, reddish in youth, then dark green above, pale beneath, oval-cordate, slightly rugose; petiole glandular-bristly, with some prickles beneath. Flowers fragrant, deep pink with frosty reflections, very full, cupped, rather like those of the Centifolia, opening perfectly, solitary or in twos or threes at the tip of the cane." [l'H51/8] "This rose is, without a doubt, one of the best introductions of this decade; its habit is vigorous, its canes strong and light green, clothed in a fine coating of bloom or glaucous dust, often tinted brown; thorns reddish, very large at the base; foliage dark green, glaucescent beneath. The blossoms have the form of our old well-beloved Centifolia, and are a very fresh carmine pink. This beautiful rose is for sale for 15 francs at the breeder's, Monsieur Portemer's, nursery-man at Gentilly." [M-V50/192] "In this plate [*picturing William Griffith*] in which the calm and reflective expression is animated by an elegant and melancholy frown, we have the whole story of a strong intelligence paus-ing in its wonderful dreams of the future. William Griffith is one of that phalanx of botanists who, having chosen to devote themselves to Science…work on the yoked disciplines of organic anatomy and physiol-ogy, the morphological ramifications of their structure, and the study of plants considered as members of floras and natural groups. Born March 4, 1810, at Ham Common, near Kingston-on-the-Thames in Surrey, he undertook, when it came time to choose a career, to study medicine. His taste for Botany brought him to the attention of Lindley. In 1832, we find him debuting as an author, and becoming an assistant surgeon in the serv-ice of the East India Company. Due to this position…W. Griffith was able to explore, as a naturalist, the most wide-ranging possessions of the Company." [VH49/535b]

William Jesse
Listed as a Hybrid Bourbon.

William Warden (Mitchell, 1878)
Sport of 'Mme. Clémence Joigneaux' (HP).
"Light pink." [Ÿ] "Salmon-pink." [H] "Fine shape." [P1] "Vigorous growth…flower very large, full; carmine red nuanced pink." [S] "The habit, etc., is the same as that of the parent." [EL]

Xavier Olibo (Lacharme, 1865)
Sport of 'Général Jacqueminot' (HP).
"Velvety black, shaded with amaranth…'cockscomb colour'…blooms come divided sometimes, but it is often a fine Rose…centre sometimes

incurved...sometimes with a fine point; a good lasting bloom, of full size...not a free bloomer." [F-M2] "Rich, velvety crimson, often blackish-crimson, the colour of this rose is most superb, petals large and smooth, flowers finely cupped and very beautiful." [JC] "Pleasing in colour when it does not burn, but irregular in shape; pretty, but much over-praised." [P2] "Large and full; very showy...a moderate grower." [P1] "Very fragrant, a beautiful rose, but not full." [JR10/29] "A shy bloomer." [ARA17/29] "Has the merit of flowering well at the end of summer." [Wr] "A weak grower with poor constitution...liable to mildew...must be 'liberally treated'...not...suitable for general cultivation." [F-M2] "4×3 [ft; ca. 1.25×1 m]." [B] "Such blooms...magnificent in size and beautifully full; of a deep, yet brilliant velvety scarlet when first open, and gradually changing to darkest crimson. It is an exceedingly showy rose...beautiful when only its thick, deep green glossy leaves are to be seen, but gorgeous when mingling with its shining foliage, the darkly glowing roses are seen in the height of their beauty." [HstXXVIII:166] "A superb rose." [EL]

End of Volume I.
Chapters on Noisettes and Climbers, Polyanthas, and Hybrid Teas,
As well as the Appendices and Bibliography,
Will be found in Volume II.

About the Author

Brent C. Dickerson is the internationally-known author of the most influential modern works on old roses. This is the enlarged second edition of his acclaimed first book *The Old Rose Advisor*; also in print are his definitive works *The Old Rose Adventurer, Roll Call: The Old Rose Breeder*, and *The Old Rose Informant*, the latter two books also being available from iuniverse.